Current perspectives in social psychology

Readings with commentary

Current perspectives

Third edition

Readings with commentary

New York

OXFORD

in social psychology

Edited by

EDWIN P. HOLLANDER and RAYMOND G. HUNT

STATE UNIVERSITY OF NEW YORK AT BUFFALO

UNIVERSITY PRESS

London   Toronto   1971

Second printing, 1972
Copyright © 1963, 1967, 1971 by Oxford University Press, Inc.
Library of Congress Catalogue Card Number: 79–129639
Printed in the United States of America

Preface to the third edition

It is nearly a decade now since we initially began planning the first edition of this book. The guiding principles and goals with which we started have served us well and have been maintained in this third edition. They are worth re-statement: to provide a current view and understanding of the various empirical problems studied under the banner of social psychology; to give a place and to pay due attention to the broadest range of prominent and productive viewpoints which characterize the field today; and to show the interrelationships as well as the divergencies which exist in these areas of social psychology.

The structure of this edition is the same as that for the previous one. This time we have sixty-seven selections under essentially the same ten headings; of these, forty-one are carried over from the second edition, and twenty-six are new.

As before, we have sought newer papers and chapters from books that would reveal current developments in the field, in keeping with our title and goals. It is noteworthy, in this regard, that two dozen of the new selections have appeared from 1966 onward, the year of the second edition's completion. But we have also attempted to achieve a balance that would not favor newness for its own sake, since many of the "older" selections continue to be reflective of important trends in the contemporary field.

In the new material are selections dealing with lively contemporary concerns including ecological factors in social behavior, bystander intervention, psychological reactance, social protest, deviancy, technology, social control, game theory, cognitive dissonance, interaction process analysis, stereotypes and prejudice, and life in cities.

Once again we have prefaced each section with a succinct chapter to provide a perspective on that area of social psychology and indicate the contribution the selections there make to its present character. We have also tried to emphasize the fundamental coherence of social psychology, even within the organization by sections. To compensate for unrealistic separations, we have as before cross-referenced extensively in the introduction to each of the ten sections. Ideally these introductions should be read in advance of the papers in a section so as to provide a needed backdrop to the ideas presented there. We also feel that using the book in sequence has some merit in building progressively toward a working acquaintance with the field. Furthermore, the cross-referencing of materials, together with the comprehensive bibliography and indexes at the end of the book, should provide the student with ready access to many related sources here and elsewhere.

In the selection and editing of papers our primary interest once again has been to include those which go beyond the presentation of a single study to a fuller representation of a point of view and range of research within the wider spectrum of the field. Thus we have sought out papers which reflect the major ideas and orientations of a whole line of investigation. Our selections are those which we feel achieve our goals, within our limitations of structure and scope, and with no judgment on our part as to the absolute merit of the many worthy contributions which could not be accommodated.

We have been fortunate again to have the wholehearted co-operation of our contributors and we are grateful especially for their willingness to have some abbreviations made to their papers, many of which were chapters of books, to bring them within manageable proportions for inclusion here. Our editing has not affected the internal content of material; we have not altered the sequence or flow of content whether we have "abridged" or "excerpted." Where these terms are used in the acknowledgment at the beginning of a paper, they signify in our usage distinct differences. *Abridgment* means the use of an entire paper with moderate deletions here and there of paragraphs, footnotes, and illustrative matter not affecting its total sense. *Excerption* means that one or more portions of a work have been republished to represent a particular point made there. Editing has therefore primarily involved moderate deletions with the sense of the selection still retained though usually in briefer form. Ellipses have *not* been employed to signify breaks in the material thus permitting each paper to be printed as an uninterrupted whole.

It is a pleasure to take this occasion again to publicly record our thanks to the contributors and to the publishers whose names appear in the acknowledgment at the beginning of each selection. Once again, in the name of all the contributors, the American Psychological Foundation shares in the royalties from this edition.

Paul Whitfield, who graciously saw us through the first two editions of this book, has since retired from his editorship at Oxford University Press, New York. A stalwart friend, we would like to take this occasion to record our great indebtedness to him, and to extend to him our warmest good wishes.

We also wish to express our appreciation to Elizabeth Murray for her secretarial assistance with many of the details involved in preparing this edition.

For the third time, which by now could become burdensome, our wives have provided a continuing source of aid in the not inconsiderable editorial tasks of referencing and proofreading, among others. For these efforts as well as for their steadfast support, we are pleased to express our deep gratitude.

Buffalo, New York   E. P. H. & R. G. H.
September 1970

Special note to the reader

The procedures adhered to in editing the selections in this volume are set out in the Preface. It should be emphasized again that, while some papers are republished virtually in their entirety, the specific omission of sentences, paragraphs, footnotes, illustrations, or tables is usually *not* indicated. Especially in those cases where excerption rather than abridgment of a paper is stated in the acknowledgment, readers would do well to consult the primary sources to find related information or the expansion of certain points.

Contents

IV LANGUAGE AND COMMUNICATION

V SOCIAL INTERACTION AND ROLE

VI ATTITUDES AND COGNITION

VII   NORMATIVE BEHAVIOR, CONFORMITY, AND INTRA-GROUP PROCESSES

VIII   LEADERSHIP, POWER, AND CHANGE

IX   ORGANIZATIONAL PROCESSES

Current perspectives in social psychology

I BASIC ORIENTATIONS AND PROCESSES

Social psychology is a field of study which takes as its problem the understanding of social behavior. It seeks in particular to understand the nature of influence relationships between individuals, either in the person-to-person sense or with respect to larger groups, institutions, and society. The distinctiveness of social psychology arises from two features: first, its essential focus upon the *individual* as a participant in social processes; and second, its concern with the *analysis* of these processes, through appropriate research methods, to provide explanations rather than mere descriptions.

Whichever research methods of many in the field are employed, their appropriateness and usefulness depend upon the particular questions and concepts which guide the inquiry in the first place. The importance of the findings of research therefore rests quite relevantly on their theoretical sources and contributions to theory. This book emphasizes the conceptual side of social psychology, not to the exclusion of research findings, but as a way of better understanding them.

The most comprehensive source for a detailing of the field is the latest edition of *The Handbook of Social Psychology* (Lindzey & Aronson, 1968). Its five volumes afford the widest coverage of topics in social psychology, with the second volume devoted entirely to research methods. While the methodology of the field has grown increasingly experimental, a variety of research techniques may be employed, often in combination. These include observation, interviews, attitude scales, projective tests, sample surveys, content analysis, and sociometric ratings. Among other works which present the methodological side of social psychology are those by Blalock and Blalock (1968), Festinger & Katz (1953), Selltiz *et al.* (1959), Lazarsfeld & Rosenberg (1955), Webb *et al.* (1966), Hyman (1955), and Kish (1965).

In this section we hope to provide an orientation to the kinds of issues and processes with which social psychology is concerned. Our coverage will include historical guideposts as well as indications of significant contemporary trends, among which is the continuing attention to the interrelationship of motivation and perception in determining social behavior.

Though it is quite true to say that social psychology derives historically from psychology and sociology, this fact by itself may convey a mistaken view of the field, in the sense of a literal melding. Many of the concepts in social psychology are clearly derivative of concerns which persist in these older disciplines, as are some of the problems. However, this does not mean that bits and pieces of each have been simply mixed together in a potpourri. The integrity of social psychology today comes from its steady movement toward a distinctive understanding of the psychology of the individual as an active agent in social situations.

Although it is a comparatively new field of study, one sees in current social psychology lines of emphasis that have origins in philosophical antiquity. In that sense, its heritage is dotted with problems that are centuries old. These include controversies surrounding "mind-body," "heredity-environment," "group mind," "mental elements," and the differences characterized by "phenomenological vs. behavioristic" approaches (see G. W. Allport, 1968; Hitt, 1969). Because these concerns were often not resolvable as stated, they have ceased being major issues of current interest. Their residues, however, are discernible in the ways in which the nature, source, and course of social behavior are construed; illustrative of these emphases are rationalistic vs. nonrationalistic models of behavior, and attention to conscious vs. unconscious processes and to personalistic vs. situational determinants of action. Surveys of these and related issues are contained in the recent books by Lana (1969) and by Shaw & Costanzo (1970).

The distinction between individual and situational sources of social behavior, while not nearly as sharply drawn as it once was, continues to bear upon approaches in the field, as one witnesses here, notably in Sections III, VII, and IX. Indeed, two early and highly influential textbooks of social psychology, published in 1908, dramatized this divergence. In the text by William McDougall, a major figure in psychology identified with the "instinct" theory of behavior, though his position was far richer in its ramifications, the stress was on dispositional tendencies which individuals bring to the situation. E. A. Ross, the noted sociologist, stressed situational determinants of behavior in his text, and furthered especially the concepts of imitation and suggestion as explanations for social behavior.

In the more than half a century since these initial works laid out a difference in orientation to social behavior, social psychology has moved increasingly to a fusing of social and psychological variables. A vestige of this distinction remains, however, in connection with an emphasis on the individual's dispositions, including his past history and his intra-psychic processes, as against an emphasis on social forces in his immediate situations, such as social structure. The common ground for this development, as we shall be noting further, rests in the recognition that individuals perceive and thus define situations based upon their past experiences and present motivations. Since other people are among the most interesting elements in a situation, the study of their effects on action was an early focus of attention.

In the first paper in this section, Zajonc provides an instructive view of some of this early research on social facilitation. This work commonly dealt with concepts like imitation or suggestion which have a much diminished popularity today, though their function exists in new constructs such as social influence and reference group processes. The effect of the presence of one individual upon the behavior of another was basic to this research but, as Zajonc notes, a distinction was required between two kinds of situations: the effect of an audience of onlookers, and the effect of other persons who were working side by side in a co-acting arrangement. He also indicates that performance and learning were differentially influenced by each of these situations. Thus, performance of something already well learned is facilitated by the presence of an audience, while initial learning is inhibited by having spectators present. As Zajonc notes: "The generalization which organizes these results is that the presence of others as spectators or as co-actors enhances the emission of dominant responses." The significant common feature which helps to explain these effects of social interaction is the hypothesis that the presence of other members of the same species tends to increase arousal. While the relevant physiological mechanisms are not completely understood, there is reason to believe that social interaction plays a vital preservative function for the individual.

In his treatment of social interaction, Zajonc draws on early human research, and on studies with animals (see Zajonc, 1969). The findings of such studies do not provide a view of how the individual perceives and is motivated to act in this situation, since only effects are observed. Greater attention is being given now to how the individual construes his world as a major determinant of his behavior, and increasingly social psychology is inclining toward a study of the nature and content of experience. This approach, which is associated with phenomenology (see MacLeod, 1951), emphasizes the necessity to get beneath the level of observable actions to an understanding of their psychological bases. This point is the essence of Asch's paper which follows here.

Asch considers that social psychology cannot develop without reference to individual experience. Furthermore, he contends that the distinction between behavior and experience is misleading, since the significance of actions can only be appreciated with reference to their meaning to the individual. This viewpoint is basic to many of the "cognitive" approaches in social psychology today (see Sections V and VI, especially). In this respect, Asch argues for a focus on the individual as the primary actor whose perception of the world about him requires attention.

In the paper which follows, taken from his recent book, *Ecological Psychology* (1968), Barker treats a related issue, the representation of the ecological environment in the individual's actions and associated psychological states. Thus, his focus is on "behavior settings" that hold meanings and make demands for variations in behavior. While drawing upon Lewin's seminal work on the "life space" (1936), Barker builds a case for going beyond, to a detailing of the characteristics which go to make up the *structure* of the ecological environment.

This structure, he says, is essentially the pattern which produces certain common understandings and recurring behavior among individuals.

6

Thus, Barker's contribution lies in establishing a bridge between ecology, in the sense of the environment for action, and psychology, in the sense of the individual's premises for action in and on the environment. It is also noteworthy that Barker's concern with the psychological effects of behavior settings is well exemplified by Zajonc's report of the psycho-physiological stresses associated with crowding. The paper by Jackson in Section II, on the classroom as a setting for interaction, is an illustration of the Barker approach; and, in a broadened sense, so are the studies of the effects on interpersonal relations of the city as an environment, reported by Milgram in Section X. Some parallel ecological interests are represented in the work of Sommer (see Section V, and 1967, 1969), and Hall (1959, 1966), both of whom are concerned with the socio-cultural practices and social psychological processes linked to the use of space in the physical environment.

Related to the emphasis on perception, and the cognitive approach in general, is the contemporary view of motivation as a state of arousal rather than as a pushing or pulling force (see Berlyne, 1960; Cofer and Appley, 1964). In addition to arousal, the effect of motivation is also to direct behavior (see Hebb, 1966). The older view of motivation persisted in an Aristotelian tradition, conceiving motives as inherent and sovereign forces. The newer look is represented here by White's paper which presents a reconception of motivation in terms of "effectance," a movement toward efficacy or competence. Man, says White, is distinguished by his competence in handling the environment, and this cannot be accounted for fully in terms of energy supplied by drives or instincts, but can be understood rather as the way humans relate to the environment through perception and action. His formulation is part of the growing and widely based discontent with the deficiencies in traditional conceptions of "drive states" as the major source of human action (see Miller, Galanter, and Pribram, 1960). White emphasizes exploratory and playful activities, as well as behaviors instigated by drives, as bases for the acquisition of competence. Among other implications, these ideas have considerable relevance for understanding the nature of work and the human side of organizational life (see Section IX). A related approach to social motivation is represented in McClelland's extensive study of achievement motivation (see McClelland *et al.*, 1953, and his *The Achieving Society*,

1961). A selection from the latter book in Section III considers achievement motivation as a characteristic of personality which has wide ramifications for society's cycle of development.

Among the newest formulations about social motivation is Brehm's concept of "reactance." In his paper here, taken from the first chapter of his definitive book, A *Theory of Psychological Reactance* (1966), Brehm focuses on the "free behaviors" about which persons expect to have a choice. His major point is that when such a freedom is threatened or eliminated, reactance is aroused to restore it. This has a similarity to the cognitive dissonance formulation of Festinger, with whom Brehm had worked. Thus, while Festinger in effect postulates a motive to restore consonance, Brehm says that under threat to a free behavior a motive to restore freedom acts to enhance the attractiveness of the choice alternative which is threatened. Without drawing the direct tie, Brehm's theory also extends from the concept of effectance motivation to take account of the consequences ensuing when such motivation is thwarted by the elimination of expected freedoms. The source of the threat and the importance of the freedom at stake are among the other components of the Brehm theory which enlarge it and provide it with richer social psychological significance.

In addition to the implications afforded by these papers for the perceptual and motivational dynamics of behavior, there is a counterpart development occurring in the study of physiological effects of the social environment upon the individual. A representation of this is seen in the work of Bovard (1959) to which Zajonc refers here. Drawing upon Selye's concept of stress (1950), Bovard considers that social stimuli may be stressors insofar as considerable symbolic content is conveyed by them as a function of past experience mediated through perception. Most relevant to social psychology is his contention that the presence of another member of the same species has a protective effect on the vertebrate organism under stress. Schachter's work (1959) on birth order also bears on this in that he finds, for first-borns especially, affiliation needs serve a protective function in reducing anxiety under threat. Such findings add a new dimension to usual statements of the bases for group affiliation, considered in Section VII.

A larger view of human motivation is represented by Cantril's paper here which considers the universals of "human nature." It reveals a growing interest in motivations for competence, mastery, and understanding that direct Man's actions. In this vein, Cantril's thinking is consistent with that of Goldstein (1940), Maslow (1970), Rogers (1959), and G. W. Allport (1955), all of whom stress human motivations toward "self-actualization," "self-realization," or "becoming" (see Section III). A parallel set of concepts is introduced by Gardner in his emphasis on commitment and meaning in Section II. Thus, Cantril's theme captures the broadening trend toward a conception of the individual's interaction with the social environment and its meaning to him as central elements in social existence.

The final paper in this section is drawn from Homans's recent book, *The Nature of Social Science* (1967). In this selection, he ranges widely over some major features and central issues involved in the social science enterprise. In discussing the distinction between discovery and explanation, he draws comparisons with the physical and biological sciences, and makes a special point of noting that merely labeling phenomena serves neither function, though it is made to give the appearance of doing so. Two elements of special importance in Homans's contribution are his emphasis on psychological propositions as a basis for individual actions, and the place of past history in determining human behavior, which he calls "historicity." While it may not be a problem for other sciences, he says, it cannot be disregarded in the social sciences.

In concluding, Homans urges his view that the central problem of social science remains the question of how the behavior of individuals creates the characteristics of groups. He points to the utility of "small group research" in observing the behavior of individuals and obtaining the information necessary for the explanation of such phenomena as conformity and status. These matters are treated more fully in Section VII. Homans's paper in that section provides a further expansion of his position, especially regarding social exchange as a fundamental process in social interaction.

1 Social facilitation

ROBERT B. ZAJONC

Most textbook definitions of social psychology involve considerations about the influence of man upon man, or, more generally, of individual upon individual. And most of them, explicitly or implicitly, commit the main efforts of social psychology to the problem of how and why the *behavior* of one individual affects the behavior of another. The influences of individuals on each others' behavior which are of interest to social psychologists today take on very complex forms. Often they involve vast networks of interindividual effects, such as one finds in studying the process of group decision-making, competition, or conformity to a group norm. But the fundamental forms of interindividual influence are represented by the oldest experimental paradigm of social psychology: social facilitation. This paradigm, dating back to Triplett's original experiments on pacing and competition (1897), examines the consequences upon behavior which derive from the sheer presence of other individuals.

Research in the area of social facilitation may be classified in terms of two experimental paradigms: audience effects and co-action effects. The first experimental paradigm involves the observation of behavior when it occurs in the presence of passive spectators. The second examines behavior when it occurs in the presence of other individuals also engaged in the same activity. We shall consider past literature in these two areas separately.

Audience effects

Simple motor responses are particularly sensitive to social facilitation effects. Travis (1925) obtained such effects in a study in which he used the pursuit-rotor task. In this task the subject is required to follow a small revolving target by means of a stylus which he holds in his hand. If the stylus is even momentarily off target during a revolution, the revolution counts as an error. First each subject was trained for several consecutive days until his performance reached a stable level. One day after the conclusion of the training the subject was called to the laboratory, given five trials alone, and then ten trials in the presence of from four to eight upperclassmen and graduate students. They had been asked by the experimenter to watch the subject quietly and attentively. Travis found a clear improvement in performance when his subjects were confronted with an audience. Their accuracy on the ten trials before an audience was greater than on any ten previous trials, including those on which they had scored highest.

Dashiell, who, in the early 1930's, carried out an extensive program of research on social facilitation, also found considerable improvement in perform-

Abridged from **Science**, 1965, 149, No. 3681, 269–74, with permission of the author and the publisher. Copyright © 1965 by the American Association for the Advancement of Science.

ance due to audience effects on such tasks as simple multiplication or word association (1930). But, as is the case in many other areas, negative audience effects were also found. Pessin asked college students to learn lists of nonsense syllables under two conditions, alone and in the presence of several spectators (1933). When confronted with an audience, his subjects required an average of 11.27 trials to learn a seven-item list. When working alone they needed only 9.85 trials. The average number of errors made in the "audience" condition was considerably higher than the number in the "alone" condition. Husband found that the presence of spectators interferes with the learning of a finger maze (1931), and Pessin and Husband (1933) confirmed Husband's results. The number of trials which the isolated subjects required for learning the finger maze was 17.1. Subjects confronted with spectators, however, required 19.1 trials. The average number of errors for the isolated subjects was 33.7; the number for those working in the presence of an audience was 40.5.

The results thus far reviewed seem to contradict one another. On a pursuit-rotor task Travis found that the presence of an audience improves performance. The learning of nonsense syllables and maze learning, however, seem to be inhibited by the presence of an audience, as shown by Pessin's experiment. The picture is further complicated by the fact that when Pessin's subjects were asked, several days later, to recall the nonsense syllables they had learned, a reversal was found. The subjects who tried to recall the lists in the presence of spectators did considerably better than those who tried to recall them alone. Why are the learning of non-sense syllables and maze learning inhibited by the presence of spectators? And why, on the other hand, does performance on a pursuit-rotor, word-association, multiplication, or a vigilance task improve in the presence of others?

There is just one, rather subtle, consistency in the above results. It would appear that the emission of well-learned responses is facilitated by the presence of spectators, while the acquisition of new responses is impaired. To put the statement in conventional psychological language, performance is facilitated and learning is impaired by the presence of spectators.

This tentative generalization can be reformulated so that different features of the problem are placed into focus. During the early stages of learning, especially of the type involved in social facilitation studies, the subject's responses are mostly the wrong ones. A person learning a finger maze, or a person learning a list of nonsense syllables, emits more wrong responses than right ones in the early stages of training. Most learning experiments continue until he ceases to make mistakes —until his performance is perfect. It may be said, therefore, that during training it is primarily the wrong responses which are dominant and strong; they are the ones which have the highest probability of occurrence. But after the individual has mastered the task, correct responses necessarily gain ascendency in his task-relevant behavioral repertoire. Now they are the ones which are more probable—in other words, dominant. Our tentative generalization may now be simplified: audience enhances the emission of dominant responses. If the dominant responses are the correct ones, as is the case upon achieving mastery, the presence of an audience will be of benefit to the individual. But if they are mostly wrong, as is the case in the early stages of learning, then these wrong responses will be enhanced in the presence of an audience, and the emission of correct responses will be postponed or prevented.

There is a class of psychological processes which are known to enhance the emission of dominant responses. They are subsumed under the concepts of drive, arousal, and activation (e.g., see Dufy, 1962; Spence, 1956; Zajonc & Nieuwenhuyse, 1964). If we could show that the presence of an audience has arousal consequences for the subject, we would be a step further along in trying to arrange the results of social-facilitation experiments into a neater package. But let us first consider another set of experimental findings.

Co-action effects

The experimental paradigm of co-action is somewhat more complex than the paradigm involved in the study of audience effects. Here we observe individuals all simultaneously engaged in the same activity and in full view of each other. One of the clearest effects of such simultaneous action, or co-action, is found in eating behavior. It is well known that animals simply eat more in the presence of others. For instance, Bayer had chickens eat from a pile of wheat to their full satisfaction (1929). He waited some time to be absolutely sure that his subject would eat no more, and then brought in a companion chicken who had not eaten for 24 hours. Upon the introduction of the hungry co-actor, the apparently sated chicken ate two-thirds again as much grain as it had already eaten. Recent work by Tolman and Wilson fully substantiates these results

(1965). In an extensive study of social-facilitation effects among albino rats, Harlow found dramatic increases in eating (1932). In one of his experiments, for instance, the rats, shortly after weaning, were matched in pairs for weight. They were then fed alone and in pairs on alternate days. It is clear that considerably more food was consumed by the animals when they were in pairs than when they were fed alone. James (1953, 1960; and James & Cannon, 1956), too, found very clear evidence of increased eating among puppies fed in groups.

Perhaps the most dramatic effect of co-action is reported by Chen (1937). Chen observed groups of ants working alone, in groups of two, and in groups of three. Each ant was observed under various conditions. In the first experimental session each ant was placed in a bottle half filled with sandy soil. The ant was observed for 6 hours. The time at which nest-building began was noted, and the earth excavated by the insect was carefully weighed. Two days afterward the same ants were placed in freshly filled bottles in pairs, and the same observations were made. A few days later the ants were placed in the bottles in groups of three, again for 6 hours. Finally, a few days after the test in groups of three, nest-building of the ants in isolation was observed.

There is absolutely no question that the amount of work an ant accomplishes increases markedly in the presence of another ant. In all pairs except one, the presence of a companion increased output by a factor of at least 2. The effect of co-action on the latency of the nest-building behavior was equally dramatic. The solitary ants of session 1 and the final session began working on the nest in 192 minutes, on the average. The latency period for ants in groups of two was only 28 minutes. The effects observed by Chen were limited to the immediate situation and seemed to have no lasting consequences for the ants. There were no differences in the results of session 1, during which the ants worked in isolation, and of the last experimental session, where they again worked in solitude.

If one assumes that under the conditions of Chen's experiment nest-building *is* the dominant response, then there is no reason why his findings could not be embraced by the generalization just proposed. Nest-building is a response which Chen's ants have fully mastered. Certainly, it is something that a mature ant need not learn. And this is simply an instance where the generalization that the presence of others enhances the emission of dominant and well-developed responses holds.

The experiments on social facilitation performed by Floyd Allport (1920) and continued by Dashiell (1930), both of whom used human subjects, are the ones best known. Allport's subjects worked either in separate cubicles or sitting around a common table. When working in isolation they did the various tasks at the same time and were monitored by common time signals. Allport did everything possible to reduce the tendency to compete. The subjects were told that the results of their tests would not be compared and would not be shown to other staff members, and that they themselves should refrain from making any such comparisons.

Among the tasks used were the following: chain word association, vowel cancellation, reversible perspective, multiplication, problem solving, and judgments of odors and weights. The results of Allport's experiments are well known:

in all but the problem-solving and judgments test, performance was better in groups than in the "alone" condition. How do these results fit our generalization? Word association, multiplication, the cancellation of vowels, and the reversal of the perceived orientation of an ambiguous figure all involve responses which are well established. They are responses which are either very well learned or under a very strong influence of the stimulus, as in the word-association task or the reversible-perspective test. The problem-solving test consists of disproving arguments of ancient philosophers. In contrast to the other tests, it does not involve well-learned responses. On the contrary, the probability of wrong (that is, logically incorrect) responses on tasks of this sort is rather high; in other words, wrong responses are dominant. Of interest, however, is the finding that while intellectual work suffered in the group situation, sheer output of words was increased. When working together, Allport's subjects tended consistently to write more. Therefore, the generalization proposed in the previous section can again be applied: if the presence of others raises the probability of dominant responses, and if strong (and many) incorrect response tendencies prevail, then the presence of others can only be detrimental to performance. The results of the judgment tests have little bearing on the present argument, since Allport gives no accuracy figures for evaluating performance. The data reported only show that the presence of others was associated with the avoidance of extreme judgments.

There are experiments which show that learning is enhanced by the presence of other learners (Gurnee, 1939; Welty, 1934), but in all these experiments, as far as I can tell, it was possible for the subject to *observe* the critical responses of other subjects, and to determine when he was correct and when incorrect. In none, therefore, has the co-action paradigm been employed in its pure form. That paradigm involves the presence of others, and nothing else. It requires that these others not be able to provide the subject with cues or information as to appropriate behavior. If other learners can supply the critical individual with such cues, we are dealing not with the problem of co-action but with the problem of imitation or vicarious learning.

The presence of others as a source of arousal

The generalization which organizes these results is that the presence of others, as spectators or as co-actors, enhances the emission of dominant responses. We also know from extensive research literature that arousal, activation, or drive all have as a consequence the enhancement of dominant responses (see Spence, 1956). We now need to examine the hypothesis that the presence of others increases the individual's general arousal or drive level.

The evidence which bears on the relationship between the presence of others and arousal is, unfortunately, only indirect. But there is some very suggestive evidence in one area of research. One of the more reliable indicators of arousal and drive is the activity of the endocrine systems in general, and of the adrenal cortex in particular. Adrenocortical functions are extremely sensitive to changes in emotional arousal, and it has been known for some time that organisms subjected to prolonged stress are likely to manifest substantial adreno-

cortical hypertrophy (Selye, 1946). Recent work (Nelson & Samuels, 1952) has shown that the main biochemical component of the adrenocortical output is hydrocortisone (17-hydroxycorticosterone). Psychiatric patients characterized by anxiety states, for instance, show elevated plasma levels of hydrocortisone (Bliss, *et al.*, 1953; Board, *et al.*, 1956).

While there is a fair amount of evidence that adrenocortical activity is a reliable symptom of arousal, similar endocrine manifestations were found to be associated with increased population density. Crowded mice, for instance, show increased amphetamine toxicity—that is, susceptibility to the excitatory effects of amphetamine—against which they can be protected by the administration of phenobarbital, chlorpromazine, or reserpine (Lasagna & McCann, 1957). Mason and Brady (1964) have recently reported that monkeys caged together had considerably higher plasma levels of hydrocortisone than monkeys housed in individual cages. Thiessen (1964) found increases in adrenal weights in mice housed in groups of 10 and 20 as compared with mice housed alone. The mere presence of other animals in the same room, but in separate cages, was also found to produce elevated levels of hydrocortisone.

Needless to say, the presence of others may have effects considerably more complex than that of increasing the individual's arousal level. The presence of others may provide cues as to appropriate or inappropriate responses, as in the case of imitation or vicarious learning. Or it may supply the individual with cues as to the measure of danger in an ambiguous or stressful situation. Davitz and Mason (1955), for instance, have shown that the presence of an unafraid rat reduces the fear of another rat in stress. Bovard (1959) believes that the calming of the rat in stress which is in the presence of an unafraid companion is mediated by inhibition of activity of the posterior hypothalamus. But in their experimental situations (that is, the open field test) the possibility that cues for appropriate escape or avoidance responses are provided by the co-actor is not ruled out. We might therefore be dealing not with the effects of the mere presence of others but with the considerably more complex case of imitation. The animal may not be calming *because* of his companion's presence. He may be calming *after* having copied his companion's attempted escape responses. The paradigm which I have examined in this article pertains only to the effects of the mere presence of others, and to the consequences for the arousal level. The exact parameters involved in social facilitation still must be specified.

2   The data of social psychology

SOLOMON E. ASCH

The place of experience in human social psychology has been settled in a purely practical way. It is not possible, as a rule, to conduct investigation in social psychology without including a reference to the experiences of persons. The investigator must, for example, take into account what the person under observation is saying; and such utterances have to be treated in terms of their meaning, not as auditory waves, or sounds, or "verbal behavior." One can hardly take a step in this region without involving the subject's ideas, feelings, and intentions. We do this when we observe people exchanging gifts, engaging in an economic transaction, being hurt by criticism, or taking part in a ritual. The sense of these actions would disappear the moment we subtracted from our description the presumed mental operations that they imply. This requirement to include mental happenings in an account of human activities, one which the social disciplines generally must observe, should have spurred an examination of the systematic properties of experience and their relations to action. Instead we find that the situation has been accepted half-heartedly, and that its implications have not been explored with care.

To see how the problem of experience arises in this area, let us consider how we follow the actions of persons. The first observation we make is that persons

Excerpted from "A Perspective on Social Psychology" in Vol. 3 of S. Koch (Ed.) **Psychology: A Study of a Science** (Copyright © 1959 by McGraw-Hill Book Company) New York: McGraw-Hill Book Company, 1959, pp. 374–9, with permission of the author and the publisher.

invariably describe the doings of others (and their own doings) in *psychological* terms. We say that a person sees, hears, prefers, demands. This is also the way we describe happenings between persons; thus we say that one person helped another, or distrusted him. These are the ways in which we order the actions of persons whom we observe to be living and conscious.

An organism that relates itself to the environment in this manner is observed to act in it in a special way. Heider (1944) has pointed out that we observe persons to produce effects intentionally. They relate themselves to the environment by wanting, by being interested, by liking, by understanding. In the case of persons, a cause is not merely a preceding state of affairs; it is a state of affairs as known or understood by the actor. An effect is not merely a later state of affairs; persons make things happen, or intend them. The movements of persons thus gain the status of actions.

With these is connected the most significant property of persons: that we experience them as capable of responding to *us*. They alone can understand our thoughts and feel our needs. Therefore they become the adequate objects of praise and blame. It is only to beings having these properties that we can relate ourselves by cooperation and competition, by affection and hatred, by admiration and envy. It is in these terms that we follow the actions of a friend, the happening in a play of Sophocles or in the life of a primitive society. Events of this kind form much of the content of the mutually relevant fields of persons.

From the standpoint of a powerful tradition there is something suspect about these everyday observations. The main charge is that they do not speak the language of science. They refer, of course, to what the other person does, but they are not simply descriptions of the movements he carries out; they are not simply statements of the geometrical displacements of persons and things. At this point the temper of one theory in general psychology recommends the wholesale dismissal of the layman's concepts and language when we turn to investigation. His accounts are, it is said, contaminated by the inclusion of subjective conditions that are not observable because they are not describable in terms of physical operations. This formulation, although it has not originated in social psychology and would, if taken seriously, drastically curb further inquiry in this field, has nevertheless left a strong impress upon it.

The following illustration may clarify the point at issue and the difficulties it raises. Among his prescriptions for a psychological utopia, Skinner includes the training of children to tolerate frustration, and proposes an ingenious procedure (Skinner, 1953). He would occasionally have the children in his utopia come to their meals, but delay their eating for a few minutes while they watch some delicious specialties that had been prepared for them. Gradually he would extend the period of deprivation, the intention being to instill self-control without injurious consequences. As Skinner describes the procedure, it is exclusively an affair of timing responses to given physical conditions. One may be permitted to wonder whether the children, however carefully reared, might not take a different view of the proceedings. Are they not likely to wonder what their caretakers are up to? And will not the outcome depend on the answers the caretakers give? If it should come into the children's heads that the caretakers are malicious, it might go ill with the effects of the scheduling. On the other hand, if the children trusted their mentors, and particularly, if they credited the caretakers with the meritorious motive of instilling self-control without injurious consequences, the discipline might prove more successful. The elimination of any reference to these internal events amounts to a failure to describe the relevant conditions with any adequacy.

The problem arises whenever we refer to action between persons. A determined effort to treat the relation of frustration to aggression in nonexperiential terms could not avoid defining frustration as damage attributed to a particular instigator (Dollard, et al., 1939). In a recent discussion, while again insisting that we give priority in psychological investigation to action, on the ground that it alone is public, Sears uses the following example: ". . . if a child wants to be kissed good-night, his mother must lean toward him affectionately and kiss him. He, in turn, must slip his arms around her neck and lift his face to her receptively" (Sears, 1951, p. 480). This sentence is surely not an unadulterated description of geometrical displacements; it does not supply the kinematics of affection, or even of slipping, lifting, or leaning.

The sources of disagreement about the place of experience in psychological investigation are too deep-seated to be dealt with summarily. We will consider only a few points most relevant to this discussion. In the first place, there are certain misconceptions to be noted. It is often asserted that actions are public but experiences are private, and that therefore the latter have no place in science. Surely there is an error here. The observation of actions is part of the observer's experience. Indeed, the same writers who make the first assertion as a rule subscribe to the second. There is thus no ground for calling actions objective and experience in general subjective. This confusion has been discussed by Köhler (1929); it is not necessary to repeat it in full.

There is another, seemingly more substantial reason for the difference in status accorded to behavior and experience. We can, it is asserted, arrive at a high degree of consensus about behavior, but not about our respective experiences. (In the light of the preceding point, this assertion claims that some kinds of experience produce consensus superior to others.) In particular, the conclusion is drawn that the positions and displacements of objects in space provide the only dependable consensus.

This conclusion will not withstand scrutiny. There is often, indeed, excellent consensus about events which, according to the preceding view, are unobservable or incommunicable. The size of an afterimage, or the experience of a causal connection, can be described with a lawfulness that permits the study of their dependence on inner and outer conditions. This suffices to qualify the data of experience as data of science. Instead of pursuing this fruitful direction, the physicalistic doctrine has attempted to demonstrate that the data of experience can be treated as verbal behavior. It can be shown, though, that the occurrence of an experience is not the occurrence of a verbal response.

It is not probable that the preceding formal arguments are actually responsible for the efforts to eliminate all reference to experience from human investigation. To locate the sources of difficulty we must look elsewhere. Perhaps the most decisive assumption is that the data of experience are not functionally connected with, and provide no help toward understanding, other concurrent events in the individual. This belief is contrary to what we know about the relations of mental and physical events. The physicalistic program also derives from the elementaristic assumption that the properties of action can be exhaustively described in terms of component movements. Were this the case, it might indeed follow that the data of experience have a limited place. But human actions are extended spatio-temporal events having a definite form, and we cannot describe them without reference to goals, and to means related to goals. These characteristics of actions are lost from view when we concentrate on their most minute components one at a time, just as we lose the quality of a form or a melody when we attend only to its smallest components. It has been convincingly shown that the most consistently behavioristic procedures do not actually deal with stimulus and response in these elementaristic terms (Koch, 1954). Behaviorism must and does include action; it grants in practice all that is needed when it speaks of "running toward a goal," or of "pushing" and "pulling."

What is the relation of the distinction we have tried to draw between movement and extended action to the data of experience? First, the data of experience point to, and thus help identify, the conditions in the environment to which we are responsive. Second, the data of experience provide hints concerning the internal events that steer action.

Those who dream of an objectivistic social psychology fail to realize that such a program can be pursued only if the data of experience are taken into account openly. We are today far from able to describe the most obvious and the most significant social acts except in the language of direct experience. What are the event-sequences corresponding to such data as "the mother praised the child," or "the boy refused to heed the teacher"? And how much more difficult is it to describe the actions of "keeping a promise" or "telling the truth"? Not only are we at a loss to report adequately the actual sequences of such events; there is often no fixed set of actions corresponding to them from occasion to occasion. How, then, could we go about locating and identifying the relevant action patterns unless we were guided to them by the distinctions of direct experience? Even if we succeeded in such a description, it would remain a foreign language until it was translated back into the terms we ordinarily employ. At this point the categories of the layman are actually in advance of those that formal psychology today has at its command. He has, without the benefit of a psychological education, identified some of the conditions and consequences of action. To be sure, these categories are descriptive, not explanatory. Also, everyday thinking identifies them in a shorthand, summary manner, which must be replaced with far more detailed description. But to counsel their abandonment is to give up the prospect of social understanding, and to bar the very advance toward which we aim.

Throughout this discussion we have noted the prevalence of the assumption that one can move directly from a few selected notions, derived mainly from the study of lower organisms, to an account of human actions, and that the latter require no concepts appropriate to them. Actually, concepts such as conditioning, stimulus generalization, extinction, response strength, secondary reinforcement, and reinforcement itself have as a rule been extrapolated to social settings without a serious effort to demonstrate their relevance under the new conditions. In this passage the terms lose the relatively clear sense they initially have. The extrapolations become largely verbal; we are not the wiser when the translation has been accomplished. This procedure, instead of increasing objectivity, often conceals distinctions long familiar to ordinary observation. It discourages the exploration of those differences between persons and things, between living and dead, that are at the center of the subject. It creates the curious presumption that hardly anything new remains to be discovered in a field that has barely been studied.

The conclusion we have reached could have been arrived at more simply. Every field of inquiry must begin with the phenomena that everyday experience reveals, and with the distinctions it contains. Further inquiry may modify our understanding of them, but the phenomena themselves will never be displaced. In social psychology the phenomena with which we begin are qualitatively diverse and the description of them prior to formal investigation is consequently of particular importance. Let us, for the purpose of this discussion, assume that concepts such as "role," or "internalizing of values," have a place in social psychology. They must then be shown to apply to the ways in which the actors, who are often innocent of these notions, see their situation. The latter act in terms of conceptions and emotions peculiar to them—in terms of envy and trust, hope and suspicion. The concepts must be relevant to this world of appearances, which are among the indispensable data of the field. Those who avoid this initial phase of investigation run the danger of placing themselves in the position of the hero in Greek mythology who was shorn of his power the moment he lost contact with mother earth.

Having said this, it is necessary to add that a psychology based on phenomenal data alone must remain incomplete. The latter are always part of a wider field of events within the individual; any order they may reveal will be partial unless completed by a more comprehensive knowledge of psychological functioning. We need, therefore, an objective psychology that will account for the structure of experience. It also follows that the examination of experience should not become either an aimless or an endless occupation. It should strive to issue in inductive inquiry and, where possible, experimentation.

These conclusions should not hide the difficulties that face investigation in social psychology. In one area of psychology, that of perception, the reliance on phenomenal data has proceeded fruitfully. Such investigation possesses one indisputable advantage: phenomenal events are studied in their dependence on stimulus conditions which are describable in terms of well-understood physical operations, and in relation to internal processes that are also described in terms of natural science categories. This advantage deserts us in most parts of social psychology. Here we must abandon, at least for the foreseeable future, the yardsticks of physics, and describe both the stimulus conditions and the effects they produce in psychological terms. Since the dimensions of these events are frequently complex and only vaguely known, the prospect of discovering clear functional relations may arouse skepticism. It would be misleading to minimize the difficulties, but it would also be premature to prejudge the outcome. This is a challenge social psychology must accept.

3 The ecological environment

ROGER G. BARKER

One of the obvious characteristics of human behavior is its variation. Every day of a person's life is marked by wide fluctuations in almost every discriminable attribute of his behavior: in the intelligence he exhibits, in the speed with which he moves, in the emotion he expresses, in the loudness with which he speaks, in the goals he pursues, in his friendliness, his humor, his energy, his anxiety. Even geniuses think ordinary thoughts much of the time; they, too, have to count their change and choose their neckties. Continuous records of the behavior of children show that the ever-changing aspect of the child's stream of behavior is one of its most striking features: trouble and well-being, quietude and activity, success and failure, dominance and submission, correct answers and wrong answers, interest and boredom occur in bewildering complexity (Barker & Wright, 1955). Laymen know of this dimension of human variation from their own experiences and observations; novelists, dramatists, and biographers have described it. But it is not prominent in scientific psychology.

Scientific psychology has been more concerned with another dimension of behavior variability, namely, with differences between individuals. It is one of the great achievements of psychology that in spite of the variation of every individual's behavior, methods have been devised for identifying and measuring individual behavior constants. An important part of scientific psychology is concerned with the great number of behavior constants that have been measured and with the relations between them.

It is unfortunate that these accomplishments have not been accompanied by equal progress in studying naturally occurring, individual behavior variation. But there is an incompatibility here: to achieve stable behavior measurements, stable conditions must be imposed upon the person, and the same conditions must be reimposed each time the measurement is repeated. This method provides measures of individual constancies (under the designated conditions), but it eliminates individual variations (under different conditions), and it destroys the naturally occurring contexts of behavior.

The general sources of intra-individual behavior variation are clear. A person's behavior is connected in complicated ways with both his inside parts (with his neurons, his muscles, his hormones, for example) and with his outside context (with the school class where he is a pupil, the game in which he is a player, the street on which he is a pedestrian). The *psychological person* who writes essays, scores points, and crosses streets stands as an identifiable

Reprinted from Chapter 1 of **Ecological Psychology: Concepts and Methods for Studying the Environment of Human Behavior** by Roger G. Barker, with the permission of the author and the publisher, Stanford University Press. © 1968 by the Board of Trustees of the Leland Stanford Junior University.

entity between unstable interior parts and exterior contexts, with both of which he is linked, yet from both of which he is profoundly separated. The separation comes from the fact that the inside parts and the outside contexts of a person involve phenomena that function according to laws that are different from those that govern his behavior. Brain lesions, muscle contraction, and hormone concentration are not psychological phenomena. In the present state of our understanding, they involve laws that are utterly incommensurate with those of psychology. The same is true of the environment with which a person is coupled. The school class where he is a pupil, the game in which he plays, and the street where he walks all function according to laws that are alien to those that govern his behavior as a person. This is the inside-outside problem which Allport (1955) has discussed. The outside context constitutes the *molar ecological environment*. It consists of those naturally occurring phenomena (1) outside a person's skin, (2) with which his molar actions are coupled, but (3) which function according to laws that are incommensurate with the laws that govern his molar behavior (Barker, 1960a). The ecological environment differs from the psychological environment (or life space) and from the stimulus, as the following discussion will make clear. The fact that behavior varies under the influence of the alien, incommensurate outside contexts of the psychological person places psychology in a serious dilemma. How is a unified science to encompass such diverse phenomena? Neither physics, nor astronomy, nor botany has to cope with psychological inputs to the systems with which it deals. How can psychology hope to cope with nonpsychological

inputs? This is the core problem of ecological psychology.

In order to study environment-behavior relations on any level, the environment and the behavior must be described and measured independently; otherwise one becomes entangled in a tautological circle from which there is no escape. Thus, for example, three children who were each observed an entire day were found to interact with 571, 671, and 749 different objects; the total number of interactions with these objects were 1,882, 2,282, and 2,490, and each of these interactions had a number of attributes (Schoggen, 1951; Barker & Wright, 1955). But these objects did not constitute the ecological environments of the children, for the behavior of the children provided the sole criteria for identifying and describing the objects. When one uses a person's behavior as the only evidence of what constitutes his environment, one deals with psychological variables, i.e., with life-space phenomena. The naturally occurring life-space deserves investigation, but it is not the ecological environment, and the latter cannot be discovered by using the person's behavior as sole reference point. This is true not because it is impossible to see all the behavior that occurs, but because the ecological environment comprises a different class of phenomenon and can only be identified and understood independently of the behavior with which it is linked.

This confronts us with the essence of the ecological environment in its relation to people. One can easily conceive of the problems of students of light perception if they had no physical description of light, or only a physical description of light at the precise point of contact with the receptor. To understand this point of intersection, it is essential to know the structure of light, for the point of intersection takes part of its characteristics from the total matrix of which it is a part, and this cannot be known from the point of contact, i.e., the stimulus, alone.

This is a general problem in science. When we are concerned with the outside context of any entity, whether a behaving person, a supporting beam, or a word in a sentence (a product of behavior), this context cannot be described in terms of the points of contact with the entity alone. The properties of the points depend upon the structure of which they are parts. Take the word "brought" in the succeedingly more inclusive contexts in which it occurs.

brought
were brought under
provisions were brought under cover
fresh provisions were brought under cover
of darkness

The immediate points of contact between the word "brought" and its context are clearly insufficient to define this context; the properties of the contact points "were" and "under" depend upon the total sentence. That is, "were" and "under" are not the context of the word "brought"; the whole sentence is the context. The contexts of all words in Stevenson's writings, and in all meaningful writings, occur in organized units that are larger than the preceding and succeeding connecting words.

This is true of the ecological environment of persons too. A person's momentary behavior is completely determined by his life-space, but if we wish to understand more than the immediate cross section of the behavior stream, knowledge of the ecological environment is essential. For example, giving and receiving love between mother and child is an important variable in some theories of psychological development. From the developmental viewpoint, such an exchange takes part of its significance from the total context of the mother's and the child's life. It is important to know the larger ecological situation within which this type of contact occurs, because this is often, technically, the only way to understand what actually happens at the momentary intersection between the person and the ecological environment. But, more important, knowledge of the ecological context is essential because development is not a momentary phenomenon (in fact, most behavior in which we are interested is not momentary), and the *course* of the life-space can only be known within the ecological environment in which it is embedded.

Problem of structure

The most primitive and simple thing we know about the ecological environment is that it has structure; it has parts with stable relations between them. One task is to describe this structure. It is clear that structure cannot be discovered by observing a single part, such as the point of intersection of the environment with a particular person, or by considering the parts separately, one by one. For example, a complete description of a player's behavior in a ball game, or the complete statistics of all the plays occurring in the game does not reveal the game of baseball. It is the rules of the game, and the arrangement of things and people according to the rules, which constitute the essential, unitary ecological environment of the players; it is these that shape the life-space of each player. By dealing with such contexts in terms of their discriminable parts, and processing them by probability statistics, we destroy what we are searching to discover. This approach has the value of a filing system, or of a concordance; but we cannot understand a book from its concordance. By these methods, the structure of the context is dismantled and rearranged; the structure is destroyed.

This does not mean, of course, that such investigations are without value. Important information about one level of a functioning system can be obtained when the system is dismantled. All sciences have structure-destroying methods and make valuable use of them. Essential components of the brain can be determined by excising and macerating brain tissue and analyzing it by physical and chemical techniques, even though this ignores or destroys the brain's macrostructure. But most sciences have, also, special nondestructive techniques for studying the structure of their phenomena. X-ray analysis and electrical, magnetic, and resonance techniques are instances. A primary concern of geologists, oceanographers, cytologists, mineralogists, geneticists, and astronomers is precisely with the naturally occurring, unrearranged structure of things: from chromosomes to the solar system and beyond. So it is important for psychology to discover tender-minded, nondestructive techniques for preserving intact naturally occurring behavior and its ecological environment. Here are some guides for this discovery from general ecological methodologies translated into terms of behavior phenomena.

The behavior with which one is concerned must be identified. There are many levels of behavior, each of which has a special environmental context. In the present case we are interested in molar behavior, in the behavior of persons as undivided entities; we are not interested in the behavior of eyelids or glands.

The problem of identifying and describing the ecological environment of behavior is an empirical one. It is necessary to observe and describe the environment in order to develop theories that later can guide further empirical investigation.

The identification of the ecological environment is aided by the fact that, unlike the life-space, it has an objective reality "out there"; it has temporal and physical attributes.

Since the physical-temporal world is not homogeneous but exists in natural parts with definite boundaries, the ecological environment occurs in bounded units. Arbitrarily defined physical-temporal units will not, except by chance, comprise an environmental unit. Furthermore, the boundaries and characteristics of the ecological environment cannot be determined by observing the persons within it.

The individual persons within a bounded unit of the ecological environment differ in psychological attributes; their behavior in the same environment will, therefore, differ. However, since people en masse can be expected to have common attributes, the inhabitants of identical ecological units will exhibit a characteristic overall extra-individual pattern of behavior; and the inhabitants of different ecological units will exhibit different overall extra-individual patterns of behavior.

Ecological units

An initial practical problem of ecological research is to identify the natural units of the phenomenon studied. The essential nature of the units with which ecology deals is the same whether they are physical, social, biological, or behavioral units: (a) they occur without feedback from the investigator, they are self-generated; (b) each unit has a time-space locus; (c) an unbroken boundary separates an internal pattern from a differing external pattern. By these criteria, an electron, a person, and a waterfall are ecological units. This is true also of most towns and cities; and within a city it is true of a particular school, of the geometry lesson within the school, and of student Joe Doakes raising his hand to ask to recite. On the other hand, a square mile in the center of a city is not an ecological unit; its boundary is not self-generated. Neither are the Republican voters of the city or the school system ecological units; they have no continuously bounded time-space locus.

Many ecological units occur in circumjacent-interjacent series, or assemblies. A chick embryo, for example, is a nesting set of organs, cells, nuclei, molecules, atoms, and subatomic particles. In these assemblies the number of included levels is sharply restricted (in the 14-day chick embryo, for example, there are nine or ten levels of units); at each level there are a limited number of discriminable varieties of units (at the level of organs in the chick embryo there are about 40 varieties of units); and within each variety there are differing numbers of individual units (within the organ variety *heart* there is a single unit). Within this arrangement, each circumjacent assembly is reciprocally linked with the interjacent units it is composed of. This is clearly exemplified by the relation between words, punctuation marks, and sentences: words and punctuation marks form sentences from which, in turn, the words and punctuation marks derive their precise meanings.

This raises the theoretical problem, mentioned above, of accounting within a univocal explanatory theory for the reciprocal relations between different levels of phenomena. How, for example, can we account for the fact that a gas molecule behaves according to the laws of molecular motion, and at the same time according to the entirely different laws of the jet of gas of which it is a part? How can the explanations of the movement of a train of wheat across the Kansas plains by an economist (a scientist of circumjacent assemblies) and by an engineer (a scientist of interjacent units) ever be incorporated into a single theory? Both the laws of economics and the laws of engineering are true; both operate in predictable ways upon the train, but they are as utterly incommensurate as the price of wheat in Chicago and the horsepower of the engine. How can we ever subsume the laws of individual motivation and the principles of institutional operation within one system of concepts?

The difficulty in all of these cases resides in the fact that the "laws" that govern individual units are different from those applicable to the compound, circumjacent series or assemblies of units; yet units and unit assemblies are closely coupled. Behavioral ecology is concerned with molar behavior and the ecological contexts in which it occurs. The problem can be illustrated by an example.

Anne Matson was 10 years and 11 months of age and in the sixth grade of the Midwest public school. It was 2:09 p.m. and time for the daily music lesson with Miss Madison. The first three minutes of the record, made at the time (March 8, 1951), reported Anne's behavior as follows (Barker *et al.*, 1961):

Mrs. Nelson said in a businesslike manner, "All right, the class will pass."

Anne picked up her music book from her desk.

She stood.

Anne motioned urgently to her row, indicating that they should follow her around the front of the room.

The class filed out, carrying their music books.

Anne walked quickly to the music room; she was near the end of the single-file line.

2:10. The children seated themselves in a semicircle across the front of the music room.

Anne sat with Opal Bennet directly on her

right and Rex Graw on her left. Alvin Stone was one seat over from Rex.

Miss Madison said briskly, "All right, let's open our books to page 27."

Anne watched Miss Madison solemnly.

Anne licked her finger.

She turned to the correct page.

Miss Madison asked the class, "How would you conduct this song?"

Immediately Anne raised her hand urgently, eager to be called on.

2:11. Miss Madison called on Ellen Thomas to show how she would conduct this song.

Ellen waved her right arm in three-four rhythm.

Miss Madison watched Ellen critically.

With her hand still partway in the air, Anne watched earnestly.

Someone in the class objected that Ellen's beat wasn't quite right.

Persistently, Anne put her hand up higher wishing to be called on.

Miss Madison called on Stella Townsend.

Anne put her hand down with disappointment showing in her facial expression.

Intently she watched Stella demonstrate the pattern for conducting the song.

Miss Madison called on Opal Bennet.

Anne didn't raise her hand.

(*There was really no opportunity for hand-raising.*)

She turned toward her right.

With interest she watched Opal demonstrate the way to lead the song.

Miss Madison demonstrated how three-four time should be led.

Anne watched with an interested expression.

2:12. She started to practice, moving her arms in the demonstrated pattern.

Some of the other children also started practicing.

Miss Madison said pedagogically, "All right, let's all do it together."

She stood sideways in a businesslike way so that the children could see her hands.

She led the children as they all practiced conducting three-four time.

Anne let her fingers hang loosely in a consciously graceful manner.

With restraint and enjoyment she moved her arm up, down, and across in the correct pattern.

2:13. Miss Madison said, "Now we want one person to get up in front of the class and conduct."

Anne immediately raised her hand very eagerly straight up into the air.

On her face was a look of expectancy.

She held her hand in the air until Miss Madison called on Ellen Thomas.

This is an example of the dependent variable with which we are concerned, namely, a child's molar actions, e.g., watching teacher demonstrate three-four time, practicing three-four time, raising hand to be called on, looking at Opal. We have raised the question: What are the ecological contexts of such behavior?

There are an infinite number of discriminable phenomena external to any individual's behavior. In the case of Anne Matson during the music class there were, for example, her neighbors Opal and Rex, the music book, the song on page 27, the piano, the fifth and sixth grade classroom across the hall, the cool overcast day, the town of Midwest, the country of U.S.A.; there were Anne's hand, the windows of the room, Andrea French sitting five seats away, Ellen's smile, and so on without limit. With which of these innumerable exterior phenomena was Anne's behavior linked? And were these phenomena related only via their links with Anne, or did they have a stable independent structure; were they an ecological assembly of units independent of Anne and her behavior?

How does one identify and describe the environment of behavior? Students of perception have been centrally concerned with this problem, and they have had some success in dealing with it. When perception psychologists have turned from the nature of perception to the preperceptual nature of light and sound, they have discovered something very important about the ecological environment of vision and hearing: it is not random; it involves bounded manifolds of individual elements with varied and unusual patterns. The environment of vision and hearing has a structure that is independent of its connections with perceptual mechanisms. All science reveals that nature is not uniform; the environments of atoms and molecules, of cells and organs, of trees and forests are patterned and structured, and this greatly facilitates their identification.

It would appear that students of molar behavior might profitably emulate students of perception, and consider the ecological environment of the behavior with which they are concerned entirely aside from its connection with behavior. This requires, in fact, a new science which stands with respect to molar behavior as the physics of light and sound stand with respect to vision and hearing. An analogy may help to make the problem clear.

If a novice, an Englishman, for example, wished to understand the environment of a first baseman in a ball game, he might set about to observe the interactions of the player with his surroundings. To do this with utmost precision he might view the first baseman through field glasses, so focused that the player would be centered in the field of the glasses with just enough of the environment included to encompass all the player's contacts with the environment, all inputs and outputs: all balls caught, balls thrown, players tagged, etc. Despite the commendable observational care, however, this method would never provide a novice with an understanding of "the game" which gives meaning to a first baseman's transactions with his surroundings and which, in fact, constitutes the environment of his baseball-playing behavior. By observing a player in this way, the novice would, in fact, fragment the game and

destroy what he was seeking. So, also, he might by observations and interviews construct the player's life-space during the game: his achievements, aspirations, successes, failures, and conflicts; his judgments of the speed of the ball, of the fairness of the umpire, of the errors of his teammates. But this would only substitute for the former fragmented picture of "the game" the psychological consequences of the fragments, and thus remove the novice even further from the ecological environment he sought. Finally, the novice might perform innumerable correlations between the first baseman's achievements (balls caught, players tagged, strikes and hits made, bases stolen, errors, etc.) and particular attributes of the ecological environment involved (speed of balls thrown to him, distance of throw, weight of bat, curve of balls, etc.). But he could never arrive at the phenomenon known as a baseball game by this means.

It would seem clear that a novice would learn more about the ecological environment of a first baseman by blotting out the player and observing the game around him. This is what the student of light and sound does with elaborate instrumentation, and it is the approach we have taken in the present studies.

It is not easy, at first, to leave the person out of observations of the environment of molar behavior. Our perceptual apparatus is adjusted by our long training with the idiocentric viewing glasses of individual observations, interviews, and questionnaires to see *persons* whenever we see behavior. But with some effort and experience the extra-individual assemblies of behavior episodes, behavior objects, and space that surround persons can be observed and described. Their nonrandom distribution and bounded character are a crucial aid. If the reader will recall school class meetings, some of the characteristics of environmental units will be clearly apparent:

It is a natural phenomenon; it is not created by an experimenter for scientific purposes.

It has a space-time locus.

A boundary surrounds a school class meeting.

The boundary is self-generated; it changes as the class changes in size and in the nature of its activity.

The class meeting is objective in the sense that it exists independent of anyone's perception of it, *qua* class; it is a preperceptual ecological entity.

It has two sets of components: (*a*) behavior (reciting, discussion, sitting) and (*b*) nonpsychological objects with which behavior is transacted, e.g., chairs, walls, a blackboard, paper, etc.

The unit, the class meeting, is circumjacent to its components; the pupils and equipment are *in* the class.

The behavior and physical objects that constitute the unit school class meeting are internally organized and arranged to form a pattern that is by no means random.

The pattern within the boundary of a class meeting is easily discriminated from that outside the boundary.

There is a synomorphic relation between the pattern of the behavior occurring within the class and the pattern of its nonbehavioral components, the behavior objects. The seats face the teacher's desk, and the children face the teacher, for example.

The unity of the class is not due to the similarity of its parts at any moment; for example, speaking occurs in one part and listening in another. The unity is based, rather, upon the interdependence of the parts; events in different parts of a class meeting have a greater effect upon each other than equivalent events beyond its boundary.

The people who inhabit a class are to a considerable degree interchangeable and replaceable. Pupils come and go; even the teacher may be replaced. But the same entity continues as serenely as an old car with new rings and the right front wheel now carried as the spare.

The behavior of this entity cannot, however, be greatly changed without destroying it: there must be teaching, there must be study, there must be recitation.

A pupil has two positions in a class; first, he is a component of the supra-individual unit, and second, he is an individual whose life-space is partly formed within the constraints imposed by the very entity of which he is a part.

Such entities stand out with great clarity; they are common phenomena of everyday life. We have called them K-21 *behavior settings* (frequently shortened to *behavior settings* and *settings*). Studies of K-21 behavior settings provide evidence that they are stable, extra-individual units with great coercive power over the behavior that occurs within them (Barker & Wright, 1955; Gump & Sutton-Smith, 1955; Gump, Schoggen & Redl, 1957; Raush, Dittmann & Taylor, 1959 & 1960; Barker, 1960a; Jordan, 1963; Gump, Schoggen & Redl, 1963; Soskin & John, 1963; Ashton, 1964; Barker & Gump, 1964; Wicker, 1967).

4 Motivation reconsidered: the concept of competence

ROBERT W. WHITE

When parallel trends can be observed in realms as far apart as animal behavior and psychoanalytic ego psychology, there is reason to suppose that we are witnessing a significant evolution of ideas. In these two realms, as in psychology as a whole, there is evidence of deepening discontent with theories of motivation based upon drives. Despite great differences in the language and concepts used to express this discontent, the theme is everywhere the same: Something important is left out when we make drives the operating forces in animal and human behavior.

The chief theories against which the discontent is directed are those of Hull and of Freud. In their respective realms, drive-reduction theory and psychoanalytic instinct theory, which are basically very much alike, have acquired a considerable air of orthodoxy. Both views have an appealing simplicity, and both have been argued long enough so that their main outlines are generally known. In decided contrast is the position of those who are not satisfied with drives and instincts. They are numerous, and they have developed many pointed criticisms, but what they have to say has not thus far lent itself to a clear and inclusive conceptualization. Apparently there is an enduring difficulty in making these contributions fall into shape.

In this paper I shall attempt a conceptualization which gathers up some of the important things left out by drive theory. To give the concept a name I have chosen the word *competence*, which is intended in a broad biological sense rather than in its narrow everyday meaning. As used here, competence will refer to an organism's capacity to interact effectively with its environment. In organisms capable of but little learning, this capacity might be considered an innate attribute, but in the mammals and especially man, with their highly plastic nervous systems, fitness to interact with the environment is slowly attained through prolonged feats of learning. In view of the directedness and persistence of the behavior that leads to these feats of learning, I consider it necessary to treat competence as having a motivational aspect, and my central argument will be that the motivation needed to attain competence cannot be wholly derived from sources of energy currently conceptualized as drives or instincts. We need a different kind of motivational idea to account fully for the fact that man and the higher mammals develop a competence in dealing with the environment which they certainly do not have at birth and certainly do not arrive at simply through maturation. Such an idea, I believe, is

Excerpted from the **Psychological Review**, 1959, 66, 297–334 (Copyright © 1959 by the American Psychological Association), with permission of the author and the publisher.

essential for any biologically sound view of human nature.[1]

Effectance

The new freedom produced by two decades of research on animal drives is of great help in this undertaking. We are no longer obliged to look for a source of energy external to the nervous system, for a consummatory climax, or for a fixed connection between reinforcement and tension-reduction. Effectance motivation cannot, of course, be conceived as having a source in tissues external to the nervous system. It is in no sense a deficit motive. We must assume it to be neurogenic, its "energies" being simply those of the living cells that make up the nervous system. External stimuli play an important part, but in terms of "energy" this part is secondary, as one can see most clearly when environmental stimulation is actively sought. Putting it picturesquely, we might say that the effectance urge represents what the neuromuscular system wants to do when it is otherwise unoccupied or is gently stimulated by the environment. Obviously there are no consummatory acts; satisfaction would appear to lie in the arousal and maintaining of activity rather than in its slow decline toward bored passivity. The motive need not be conceived as intense and powerful in the sense that hunger, pain, or fear can be powerful when aroused to high pitch. There are plenty of instances in which children refuse to leave their absorbed play in order to eat or to visit the toilet. Strongly aroused drives, pain, and anxiety, however, can be conceived as overriding the effectance urge and

[1] For an elaboration of these points, omitted here, the reader is referred to pp. 297–321 of the original.—Eds.

capturing the energies of the neuromuscular system. But effectance motivation is persistent in the sense that it regularly occupies the spare waking time between episodes of homeostatic crisis.

In speculating upon this subject we must bear in mind the continuous nature of behavior. This is easier said than done; habitually we break things down in order to understand them, and such units as the reflex arc, the stimulus-response sequence, and the single transaction with the environment seem like inevitable steps toward clarity. Yet when we apply such an analysis to playful exploration we lose the most essential aspect of the behavior. It is constantly circling from stimulus to perception to action to effect to stimulus to perception, and so on around; or, more properly, these processes are all in continuous action and continuous change. Dealing with the environment means carrying on a continuing transaction which gradually changes one's relation to the environment. Because there is no consummatory climax, satisfaction has to be seen as lying in a considerable series of transactions, in a trend of behavior rather than a goal that is achieved. It is difficult to make the word "satisfaction" have this connotation, and we shall do well to replace it by "feeling of efficacy" when attempting to indicate the subjective and affective side of effectance.

It is useful to recall the findings about novelty: the singular effectiveness of novelty in engaging interest and for a time supporting persistent behavior. We also need to consider the selective continuance of transactions in which the animal or child has a more or less pronounced effect upon the environment—in which something happens as a consequence of his activity. Interest is not aroused and sustained when the stimulus field is so familiar that it gives rise at most to reflex acts or automatized habits. It is not sustained when actions produce no effects or changes in the stimulus field. Our conception must therefore be that effectance motivation is aroused by stimulus conditions which offer, as Hebb (1949) puts it, difference-in-sameness. This leads to variability and novelty of response, and interest is best sustained when the resulting action affects the stimulus so as to produce further difference-in-sameness. Interest wanes when action begins to have less effect; effectance motivation subsides when a situation has been explored to the point that it no longer presents new possibilities.

We have to conceive further that the arousal of playful and exploratory interest means the appearance of organization involving both the cognitive and active aspects of behavior. Change in the stimulus field is not an end in itself, so to speak; it happens when one is passively moved about, and it may happen as a consequence of random movements without becoming focalized and instigating exploration. Similarly, action which has effects is not an end in itself, for if one unintentionally kicks away a branch while walking, or knocks something off a table, these effects by no means necessarily become involved in playful investigation. Schachtel's (1954) emphasis on focal attention becomes helpful at this point. The playful and exploratory behavior shown by Laurent is not random or casual. It involves focal *attention* to some object —the fixing of some aspect of the stimulus field so that it stays relatively constant—and it also involves the focalizing of *action* upon this object. As Diamond (1939) has expressed it, re-

sponse under these conditions is "relevant to the stimulus," and it is change in the *focalized* stimulus that so strongly affects the level of interest. Dealing with the environment means directing focal attention to some part of it and organizing actions to have some effect on this part.

In our present state of relative ignorance about the workings of the nervous system it is impossible to form a satisfactory idea of the neural basis of effectance motivation, but it should at least be clear that the concept does not refer to any and every kind of neural action. It refers to a particular kind of activity, as inferred from particular kinds of behavior. We can say that it does not include reflexes and other kinds of automatic response. It does not include well-learned, automatized patterns, even those that are complex and highly organized. It does not include behavior in the service of effectively aroused drives. It does not even include activity that is highly random and discontinuous, though such behavior may be its most direct forerunner. The urge toward competence is inferred specifically from behavior that shows a lasting focalization and that has the characteristics of exploration and experimentation, a kind of variation within the focus. When this particular sort of activity is aroused in the nervous system, effectance motivation is being aroused, for it is characteristic of this particular sort of activity that it is selective, directed, and persistent, and that instrumental acts will be learned for the sole reward of engaging in it.

Some objection may be felt to my introducing the word *competence* in connection with behavior that is so often playful. Certainly the playing child is doing things for fun, not because of a desire to improve his competence in dealing with the stern hard world. In order to forestall misunderstanding, it should be pointed out that the usage here is parallel to what we do when we connect sex with its biological goal of reproduction. The sex drive aims for pleasure and gratification, and reproduction is a consequence that is presumably unforeseen by animals and by man at primitive levels of understanding. Effectance motivation similarly aims for the feeling of efficacy, not for the vitally important learnings that come as its consequence. If we consider the part played by competence motivation in adult human life we can observe the same parallel. Sex may now be completely and purposefully divorced from reproduction but nevertheless pursued for the pleasure it can yield. Similarly, effectance motivation may lead to continuing exploratory interests or active adventures when in fact there is no longer any gain in actual competence or any need for it in terms of survival. In both cases the motive is capable of yielding surplus satisfaction well beyond what is necessary to get the biological work done.

In infants and young children it seems to me sensible to conceive of effectance motivation as undifferentiated. Later in life it becomes profitable to distinguish various motives such as cognizance, construction, mastery, and achievement. It is my view that all such motives have a root in effectance motivation. They are differentiated from it through life experiences which emphasize one or another aspect of the cycle of transaction with environment. Of course, the motives of later childhood and of adult life are no longer simple and can almost never be referred to a single root. They can acquire loadings

of anxiety, defense, and compensation, they can become fused with unconscious fantasies of a sexual, aggressive, or omnipotent character, and they can gain force because of their service in producing realistic results in the way of income and career. It is not my intention to cast effectance in the star part in adult motivation. The acquisition of motives is a complicated affair in which simple and sovereign theories grow daily more obsolete. Yet it may be that the satisfaction of effectance contributes significantly to those feelings of interest which often sustain us so well in day-to-day actions, particularly when the things we are doing have continuing elements of novelty.

The biological significance of competence

The conviction was expressed at the beginning of this paper that some such concept as competence, interpreted motivationally, was essential for any biologically sound view of human nature. This necessity emerges when we consider the nature of living systems, particularly when we take a longitudinal view. What an organism does at a given moment does not always give the right clue as to what it does over a period of time. Discussing this problem, Angyal (1941) has proposed that we should look for the general pattern followed by the total organismic process over the course of time. Obviously this makes it necessary to take account of growth. Angyal defines life as "a process of self-expansion"; the living system "expands at the expense of its surroundings," assimilating parts of the environment and transforming them into functioning parts of itself. Organisms differ from other things in nature in that they are "self-governing entities" which are to some extent "autonomous." Internal processes govern them as well as external "heteronomous" forces. In the course of life there is a relative increase in the preponderance of internal over external forces. The living system expands, assimilates more of the environment, transforms its surroundings so as to bring them under greater control. "We may say," Angyal writes, "that the general dynamic trend of the organism is toward an increase of autonomy. . . . The human being has a characteristic tendency toward self-determination, that is, a tendency to resist external influences and to subordinate the heteronomous forces of the physical and social environment to its own sphere of influence." The trend toward increased autonomy is characteristic so long as growth of any kind is going on, though in the end the living system is bound to succumb to the pressure of heteronomous forces.

Of all living creatures, it is man who takes the longest strides toward autonomy. This is not because of any unusual tendency toward bodily expansion at the expense of the environment. It is rather that man, with his mobile hands and abundantly developed brain, attains an extremely high level of competence in his transactions with his surroundings. The building of houses, roads and bridges, the making of tools and instruments, the domestication of plants and animals, all qualify as planful changes made in the environment so that it comes more or less under control and serves our purposes rather than intruding upon them. We meet the fluctuations of outdoor temperature, for example, not only with our bodily homeostatic mechanisms, which alone would be painfully unequal to the task, but also with clothing, buildings, controlled fires, and such complicated devices as self-regulating central heating and air conditioning. Man as a species has developed a tremendous power of bringing the environment into his service, and each individual member of the species must attain what is really quite an impressive level of competence if he is to take part in the life around him.

We are so accustomed to these human accomplishments that it is hard to realize how long an apprenticeship they require. At the outset the human infant is a slow learner in comparison with other animal forms. Hebb (1949) speaks of "the astonishing inefficiency of man's first learning, as far as immediate results are concerned," an inefficiency which he attributes to the large size of the association areas in the brain and the long time needed to bring them under sensory control. The human lack of precocity in learning shows itself even in comparison with one of the next of kin: as Hebb points out, "the human baby takes six months, the chimpanzee four months, before making a clear distinction between friend and enemy." Later in life the slow start will pay dividends. Once the fundamental perceptual elements, simple associations, and conceptual sequences have been established, later learning can proceed with ever increasing swiftness and complexity. In Hebb's words, "learning at maturity concerns patterns and events whose parts at least are familiar and which already have a number of other associations."

This general principle of cumulative learning, starting from slowly acquired rudiments and proceeding thence with increasing efficiency, can be illustrated by such processes as manipulation and locomotion, which may culminate in the acrobat devising new stunts or the dancer working out a new ballet. It is especially vivid in the case of language, where the early mastery of words and pronunciation seems such a far cry from spontaneous adult speech. A strong argument has been made by Hebb (1949) that the learning of visual forms proceeds over a similar course from slowly learned elements to rapidly combined patterns. Circles and squares, for example, cannot be discriminated at a glance without a slow apprenticeship involving eye movements, successive fixations, and recognition of angles. Hebb proposes that the recognition of visual patterns without eye movement "is possible only as the result of an intensive and prolonged visual training that goes on from the moment of birth, during every moment that the eyes are open, with an increase in skill evident over a period of 12 to 16 years at least."

On the motor side there is likewise a lot to be cumulatively learned. The playing, investigating child slowly finds out the relationships between what he does and what he experiences. He finds out, for instance, how hard he must push what in order to produce what effect. Here the S-R formula is particularly misleading. It would come nearer the truth to say that the child is busy learning R-S connections—the effects that are likely to follow upon his own behavior. But even in this reversed form the notion of bonds or connections would still misrepresent the situation, for it is only a rare specimen of behavior that can properly be conceived as determined by fixed neural channels and a fixed motor response. As Hebb has pointed out, discussing the phenomenon of "motor equivalence" named by Lashley (1942), a rat which has been trained

to press a lever will press it with the left forepaw, the right forepaw, by climbing upon it, or by biting it; a monkey will open the lid of a food box with either hand, with a foot, or even with a stick; and we might add that a good baseball player can catch a fly ball while running in almost any direction and while in almost any posture, including leaping in the air and plunging forward to the ground. All of these feats are possible because of a history of learnings in which the main lesson has been the effects of actions upon the stimulus fields that represent the environment. What has been learned is not a fixed connection but a flexible relationship between stimulus fields and the effects that can be produced in them by various kinds of action.

One additional example, drawn this time from Piaget (1952), is particularly worth mentioning because of its importance in theories of development. Piaget points out that a great deal of mental development depends upon the idea that the world is made up of objects having substance and permanence. Without such an "object concept" it would be impossible to build up the ideas of space and causality and to arrive at the fundamental distinction between self and external world. Observation shows that the object concept, "far from being innate or readymade in experience, is constructed little by little." Up to 7 and 8 months the Piaget children searched for vanished objects only in the sense of trying to continue the actions, such as sucking or grasping, in which the objects had played a part. When an object was really out of sight or touch, even if only because it was covered by a cloth, the infants under took no further exploration. Only gradually, after some study of the displacement of objects by moving, swinging, and dropping them, does the child begin to make an active search for a vanished object, and only still more gradually does he learn, at 12 months or more, to make allowance for the object's sequential displacements and thus to seek it where it has gone rather than where it was last in sight. Thus it is only through cumulative learning that the child arrives at the idea of permanent substantial objects.

The infant's play is indeed serious business. If he did not while away his time pulling strings, shaking rattles, examining wooden parrots, dropping pieces of bread and celluloid swans, when would he learn to discriminate visual patterns, to catch and throw, and to build up his concept of the object? When would he acquire the many other foundation stones necessary for cumulative learning? The more closely we analyze the behavior of the human infant, the more clearly do we realize that infancy is not simply a time when the nervous system matures and the muscles grow stronger. It is a time of active and continuous learning, during which the basis is laid for all those processes, cognitive and motor, whereby the child becomes able to establish effective transactions with his environment and move toward a greater degree of autonomy. Helpless as he may seem until he begins to toddle, he has by that time already made substantial gains in the achievement of competence.

Under primitive conditions survival must depend quite heavily upon achieved competence. We should expect to find things so arranged as to favor and maximize this achievement. Particularly in the case of man, where so little is provided innately and so much has to be learned through experience, we should expect to find highly advantageous arrangements for securing a steady cumulative learning about the properties of the environment and the extent of possible transactions. Under these circumstances we might expect to find a very powerful drive operating to insure progress toward competence, just as the vital goals of nutrition and reproduction are secured by powerful drives, and it might therefore seem paradoxical that the interests of competence should be so much entrusted to times of play and leisurely exploration. There is good reason to suppose, however, that a strong drive would be precisely the wrong arrangement to secure a flexible, knowledgeable power of transaction with the environment. Strong drives cause us to learn certain lessons well, but they do not create maximum familiarity with our surroundings.

This point was demonstrated half a century ago in some experiments by Yerkes and Dodson (1908). They showed that maximum motivation did not lead to the most rapid solving of problems, especially if the problems were complex. For each problem there was an optimum level of motivation, neither the highest nor the lowest, and the optimum was lower for more complex tasks. The same problem has been discussed more recently by Tolman (1948) in his paper on cognitive maps. A cognitive map can be narrow or broad, depending upon the range of cues picked up in the course of learning. Tolman suggests that one of the conditions which tend to narrow the range of cues is a high level of motivation. In everyday terms, a man hurrying to an important business conference is likely to perceive only the cues that help him to get there faster, whereas a man taking a stroll after lunch is likely to pick up a substantial amount of casual information about his environment. The latent learning experiments with animals, and experiments such as those of Johnson (1953) in which drive level has been systematically varied in a situation permitting incidental learning, give strong support to this general idea. In a recent contribution, Bruner, Matter, and Papanek (1955) make a strong case for the concept of breadth of learning and provide additional evidence that it is favored by moderate and hampered by strong motivation. The latter "has the effect of speeding up learning at the cost of narrowing it." Attention is concentrated upon the task at hand and little that is extraneous to this task is learned for future use.

These facts enable us to see the biological appropriateness of an arrangement which uses periods of less intense motivation for the development of competence. This is not to say that the narrower but efficient learnings that go with the reduction of strong drives make no contribution to general effectiveness. They are certainly an important element in capacity to deal with the environment, but a much greater effectiveness results from having this capacity fed also from learnings that take place in quieter times. It is then that the infant can attend to matters of lesser urgency, exploring the properties of things he does not fear and does not need to eat, learning to gauge the force of his string-pulling when the only penalty for failure is silence on the part of the attached rattles, and generally accumulating for himself a broad knowledge and a broad skill in dealing with his surroundings.

5   A theory of psychological reactance

JACK W. BREHM

Freedom of behavior is a pervasive and important aspect of human life. People are continually surveying their internal and external states of affairs and making decisions about what they will do, how they will do it, and when they will do it. They consider their wants and needs, the dangers and benefits available in their surroundings, and the ways in which they can accomplish various ends. This is not to say that behavior is always freely selected. It will frequently be true that individuals perform given acts without quite knowing why, and it will

Abridged from Chapter 1 of **A Theory of Psychological Reactance** by J. W. Brehm, New York: Academic Press, 1966, with permission of the author and the publisher.

also be true that they perform acts because they knew they were not free to do otherwise. Nevertheless, most of the time people will feel that they are relatively free to engage in a variety of different behaviors and that they can select among these as they please.

There is good reason for the belief that one has freedom of action. Objectively there frequently are multiple possibilities, and subjectively there are frequently multiple needs, none of which demands immediate gratification. Thus, subjectively at least, it seems that one scans the possibilities and their effects, and then decides which of the several possibilities to take. Whether or not a person "really" has freedom, he can and almost certainly will believe that he has.

The freedom to choose when and how to behave is potentially beneficial. To the extent a person is aware of his needs and the behaviors necessary to satisfy those needs, and providing he has the appropriate freedom, he can choose behaviors so as to maximize need satisfaction. An individual, for example, who felt more thirsty than hungry and who, at the moment, was free to go either to a soda fountain or a restaurant, could satisfy his dominant need by choosing to go to the soda fountain. Without the freedom to select behaviors appropriate to various needs, the satisfaction of needs would be a more haphazard affair which would not only fail to maximize need satisfaction but could frequently result in extreme deprivation, pain, and even death. Given some minimal level of valid knowledge about oneself and the environment, freedom to choose among different behavioral possibilities will generally help one to survive and thrive.

It is reasonable to assume, then, that if a person's behavioral freedom is re-

duced or threatened with reduction, he will become motivationally aroused. This arousal would presumably be directed against any further loss of freedom and it would also be directed toward the re-establishment of whatever freedom had already been lost or threatened. Since this hypothetical motivational state is in response to the reduction (or threatened reduction) of one's potential for acting, and conceptually may be considered a counterforce, it will be called "psychological reactance."

The theory

It is assumed that for a given person at a given time, there is a set of behaviors any one of which he could engage in either at the moment or at some time in the future. This set may be called the individual's "free behaviors." Free behaviors include only acts that are realistically possible: smoking a cigarette could be a free behavior, while walking to the moon could not. Behaviors may become free in a variety of ways. A person may become free to spend company money for lunches by formal agreement between himself and the company; a person may acquire the freedom to read a book by learning how to read; one may feel free to spit on the walk because one always has done so; and one may feel free to vote because the right is guaranteed by law. In general, we may say that for specified behaviors to be free, the individual must have the relevant physical and psychological abilities to engage in them, and he must know, by experience, by general custom, or by formal agreement, that he may engage in them.

Given that a person has a set of free behaviors, he will experience reactance whenever any of those behaviors is elim-

inated or threatened with elimination. That is, if a person felt free to engage in behaviors A, B, and C, and then learned that he could not engage in, for example, A, he would experience reactance.

The magnitude of reactance is a direct function of (1) the importance of the free behaviors which are eliminated or threatened, (2) the proportion of free behaviors eliminated or threatened, and (3) where there is only a threat of elimination of free behaviors, the magnitude of that threat. Let us consider each of these determinants in somewhat greater detail.

1. Given that a certain free behavior has been threatened or eliminated, *the more important is that free behavior to the individual, the greater will be the magnitude of reactance*. The importance of a given behavior is a direct function of the unique instrumental value which that behavior has for the satisfaction of needs, multiplied by the actual or potential maximum magnitude of those needs. By unique is meant that no other behavior in the individual's repertoire of behaviors would satisfy the same need or set of needs. In other words, the importance of a free behavior derives from its necessity for the reduction of potentially important needs. However, it is *not* necessary for the relevant needs to be of great magnitude at all times for the free behavior to have high importance at all times. It is only necessary that the individual believe he *might* have the needs in question. This may become more clear if we consider the example of Mr. Smith, who is told by his wife to go play golf, and who according to the present view should therefore experience increased motivation to watch television or putter in his workshop. Smith may actually have preferred to

play golf prior to his wife's pronouncement and, further, he may not, on this particular Sunday, have an active interest in watching television or puttering. But to the extent that he believes he *might* want to do either of these things, the freedom to engage in them is important and the loss of that freedom should arouse reactance.

1a. The magnitude of reactance is also a direct function of the relative importance of the eliminated or threatened behavioral freedom compared to the importances of other freedoms of the moment. Considering all of a person's free behaviors at a given time, and holding constant the absolute importance of the one which is eliminated or threatened, its relative importance increases as the absolute importance of the other freedoms decreases. When one's choice alternatives are an orange, an apple, and a pear, he should experience a noticeable degree of reactance when someone swipes the apple; but when the choice alternatives are an orange, an apple and an automobile, one will not care much about the loss of the apple.

2. Given the individual's set of free behaviors, *the greater is the proportion eliminated or threatened with elimination, the greater will be the magnitude of reactance*. If a person believed himself free to engage in behaviors A, B, C, and D, all of which have some importance, then the elimination of both A and B would create more reactance than would the elimination of either A or B alone. Or, given that behavior A is eliminated, if the original set of free behaviors consisted of A and B there will be more reactance than if the original set consisted of A, B, C, and D.

3. Given that an important free behavior has been threatened with elimination, *the greater is the threat, the*

greater will be the magnitude of react-ance. A threat becomes greater as the likelihood increases that it could and would be carried out. A threat of the elimination of a free behavior will frequently be located in a social source, i.e., another person. When the threat is social, the question of how great the threat is will center on the formal and informal relationships between the threatener and the person threatened. Those who have equal or greater amounts of social power than oneself can issue threats of relatively great magnitude to one's own free behaviors, while those with less power would be relatively unable to muster serious threats.

3a. When a person's free behavior, A, is eliminated or threatened with elimination, there may also be the implication to him that other free behaviors, say B and C, or the same behavior on future occasions, A_2 and A_3, will also be eliminated. That is, by the loss of a single free behavior there may be by implication a threat of elimination of other free behaviors either in the present or in the future. This proposition assumes, of course, that the free behaviors in question are ordered such that the loss of one implies the loss of others. The ordering may be as simple as membership in a class. For example, if a secretary were informed she was not to chew gum while at work, she might easily imagine that other similar behaviors, such as smoking and sucking on candies would also be eliminated.

3b. Just as a free behavior may be threatened by virtue of elimination of or threat to another free behavior, so a free behavior may be threatened by the elimination of or threat to another person's free behavior. The implication in this case relates the observed person to oneself; if the loss of a free behavior to

an observed person could just as well happen to oneself, then one's own free behavior is threatened. When an observed person loses a free behavior similar to a free behavior for oneself, the greater is the implication that the loss could as easily have happened to oneself, the greater will be the magnitude of the reactance. If, for example, co-equal secretaries worked together in an office and normally felt free to go to the water cooler for a drink whenever they felt like it, the elimination of this freedom for one should threaten the same freedom for others, leading to their experiencing reactance.

JUSTIFICATION AND LEGITIMACY

If Mr. Smith says to Mr. Brown "You cannot have Betty for baby-sitting this evening," when Mr. Brown might have wanted Betty, then Brown should experience reactance. It will be obvious, however, that Brown's reaction will be affected by the justification and/or legitimacy of Smith's interference. If Smith adds that Betty's mother has gone to the hospital for an emergency operation, thus justifying the restriction, Brown will not show a strong negative reaction. If Betty is a young teenager and Smith happens to be her father, then Smith can legitimately control Betty's activities and again, Brown is not likely to show a strong negative reaction.

Justification and legitimacy, however, are complicated variables from the point of view of reactance theory. They tend, on the one hand, to affect the magnitude or reactance aroused by the loss of a freedom, and they tend on the other hand, to affect restraints against the effects of reactance. Let us consider these in turn.

When person A tells person B what to do, and thereby threatens a specific freedom of the latter, there may or may not be further freedoms threatened by implication, as we have already seen. One possible effect of justification is to limit the threat to a specific behavior or set of behaviors. So if Smith says that he is interfering with Brown's expectations because of a personal emergency, this keeps Brown from imagining that Smith will likely interfere on future occasions as well. Fewer of Brown's behavioral freedoms have been threatened. In a similar way, legitimacy may indicate the set of behaviors threatened since there will be a general presumption that illegitimate interference with one's freedoms is less likely to occur. There is an additional implication in the notion of legitimacy of behavioral restriction that one's freedom was equivocal anyway. In the above example, if Betty is a young teenager, then Brown could never have been sure of his freedom to have her babysit since she is normally subject to restrictions from her parents. Conversely, an illegitimate attempt to restrict one's freedom may be capable of arousing a great deal of reactance since it may imply a threat to a large number of free behaviors. If Smith is *not* the father of Betty and has no more legitimate control over her than does Brown, then Smith's attempted interference (without justification) also carries the implication that Smith may well attempt similar interferences on future occasions. From Brown's point of view, if Smith gets away with this, what can't he get away with?

Although justification and legitimacy may be seen as affecting the magnitude of reactance aroused by a given elimination or threat, lack of justification and legitimacy are not necessary conditions for the occurrence of reactance. A loss of freedom no matter how well justified, should still create reactance. And if we bear in mind that legitimacy (formal rules, agreement, etc.) is only one of several sources of freedom, we can also say that a loss of freedom, no matter how legitimate, can also result in reactance.

How a person responds to reactance will doubtless be affected by both justification and legitimacy. In general, these conditions will create restraints against direct attempts at restoration of freedom. For this reason, these conditions will tend to give rise to attempts at indirect restoration of freedom, such as through behavioral or social implication, when that kind of restoration is possible.

The effects of reactance

Psychological reactance is conceived as a motivational state directed toward the re-establishment of the free behaviors which have been eliminated or threatened with elimination. Generally, then, a person who experiences reactance will be motivated to attempt to regain the lost or threatened freedoms by whatever methods are available and appropriate. It should be helpful, of course, to be somewhat more specific about the effects of reactance, and in the following paragraphs we shall indicate several distinguishable possibilities.

THE PHENOMENOLOGY OF REACTANCE
While there is no assumption that a person will necessarily be aware of reactance, it should be true that when he is, he will feel an increased amount of self-direction in regard to his own behavior. That is, he will feel that he can do what he wants, that he does not have to do what he doesn't want, and that at least in regard to the freedom in question, he

is the sole director of his own behavior. If the magnitude of reactance is relatively great, the individual may be aware of hostile and aggressive feelings as well. In this connection it may be noted that reactance can be an "uncivilized" motivational state since it frequently is directed against the social acts of others. For this reason it would not be surprising to find that a person in whom reactance has been aroused would tend to deny that he was either motivated to restore freedom or upset, and he might even convince himself of this. This tendency to defend against reactance can be expected to extend to nonverbal behavior as well. As will be seen, the studies in support of reactance theory have tended to use measures which do not require people to be uncivilized, or they have measured relatively subtle uncivilized responses.

When reactance does not lead to "uncivilized" or antisocial behavior, it should tend to result in some awareness of one's increased motivation to have what was lost or threatened. That is, a person's desire for a given behavior, A, should increase as a consequence of its being eliminated, or threatened with elimination, from his set of free behaviors. Correspondingly, behavior A should appear to increase in attractiveness.

DIRECT RE-ESTABLISHMENT OF FREEDOM
The greater is the magnitude of reactance, the more will the individual attempt to re-establish the freedom which has been lost or threatened. However, attempts at re-establishment can be expected to occur only to the extent that there is a realistic possibility of succeeding. In general, reactance will result in attempts at restoration of freedom when there is some equivocality about the

elimination of the free behavior in question, or, in other words, where there has only been a threat of elimination. When the loss of a free behavior is irreversible, as when one's left arm has been amputated or one has been told to do something by a person with immense power over oneself, there will not normally be attempts at direct restoration.

Direct re-establishment of freedom means engaging in that behavior which one has learned one cannot or should not engage in. If behavior A has been free and one is then told not to engage in A, the resultant reactance will lead the individual to engage in A. If one's set of free behaviors consisted of A and B and one were then told to do A, the direct restoration of freedom would consist in doing B.

Where freedom is threatened by social pressure, reactance will lead one to resist that pressure. If an habitual smoker, for example, were told by a friend that he should stop smoking, the resultant reactance would operate against the otherwise persuasive effects of the friend's advice. Continuing to smoke at the same rate or at a greater rate would re-establish the freedom to smoke. Quite obviously, however, the direct social influence might be greater than the magnitude of reactance, in which case a compromise response of reduced smoking would occur.

RE-ESTABLISHMENT OF
FREEDOM BY IMPLICATION
When there are restraints against the direct re-establishment of freedom, attempts at re-establishment by implication will occur where possible. Consider again, for example, the secretary who has learned she can no longer chew gum on the job. She can re-establish her

freedom by engaging in other behaviors of the same class, e.g., sucking on candy or smoking, or better yet, she can engage in what she would assume to be even less acceptable behaviors such as putting on lipstick, combing her hair, or eating candy bars.

Freedom can also be re-established by social implication. If a person has lost a free behavior through social threat, then the engagement in a similar free behavior by another person like himself and "in the same boat" will tend to re-establish his own freedom. In terms of our earlier example of the co-equal secretaries who felt free to go for a drink of water whenever they wanted, if secretary A has been told she can no longer do this and secretary B's freedom has thereby been threatened by implication, the freedom of A will be re-established by implication if secretary B proceeds to have a drink as she pleases. We might plausibly expect that when possible, one of the effects of reactance will be for a person to try to get someone else to engage in a threatened or eliminated behavior.

THE ROLE OF IMPORTANCE

As has been stated, the magnitude of reactance aroused by the loss of a given freedom is directly proportional to the importance of that freedom to the individual. But though importance therefore helps to determine the amount of reactance aroused, it does not serve in the reduction of reactance. This is because reactance is defined *not* simply as an unpleasant tension which the individual will reduce in any way that he can, such as reducing the importance of any freedom which he happens to lose, but rather as a motivational state with a specific direction, namely, the recovery of freedom. Indeed, the only reasonable

expectation about the effect of reactance on the importance of a lost free behavior is that importance may increase.

VOLUNTARY VERSUS
INVOLUNTARY ELIMINATION

Although the hypothetical examples used to illustrate the theory all concern eliminations of freedom or threats which are involuntary, this is not meant to imply that threats and eliminations must be involuntary in order to arouse reactance. The reason that voluntary eliminations or threats have not been used in examples and research is that they involve a decision process, that is, a giving up of one or more alternatives in order to select something, which in turn would involve various conflict type and postdecisional psychological processes.

Related concepts

The notion that people will be motivated to re-establish freedom which is threatened or eliminated is probably not new but it has not been utilized in current experimental research in psychology. For this reason we have tried to show in our examples that this theoretical formulation deals with a special set of problems and is not to be identified with various theories which deal with somewhat similar problems such as frustration, social power, etc. Nevertheless, there are theoretical concepts which are related to reactance and it may help the reader to locate the present theory if these related concepts are indicated.

While theories concerning frustration and aggression (e.g., Dollard, Doob, Miller, Mowrer, and Sears, 1939) are peripherally relevant since they deal with the blocking of goal attainment, which will sometimes also involve elimination of freedom, the most relevant concepts are those which have to do with social power. French and Raven (1959), for example, distinguish between "resisting forces" and "opposing forces" as factors which operate against positive social influence. Their definition of resisting forces as motivation instigated by the inducing force but opposite in direction is conceptually similar to the reactance formulation. However, the bases they suggest for the instigation of resisting forces are coercive measures to obtain compliance, and especially illegitimate coercion. It is only with regard to coercive inducing forces, then, that there is a close parallel between the approach of French and Raven and that of reactance theory.

Other views of social power, of course, would also tend to be relevant. For example, the analysis of power and counterpower by Thibaut and Kelly (1959) could in part be translated into terms of freedom, freedom reduction, and ways of re-establishing freedom. At the same time, one fundamental difference between their approach and reactance theory is that they do not posit a motivation to gain or recover power but rather concern themselves with the reward-cost outcomes of various kinds of power relationships.

The concepts of "personal weight" and "weight reduction" (Horwitz, 1958) seem particularly relevant and close to reactance theory. Personal weight is defined as the expected power which a person has in a given social relationship. When two people disagree, the legitimate outcome of the disagreement is a function of their weighted desires. When the actual outcome deviates from the legitimate outcome there is the implication that the disfavored member's weight has been reduced. Horwitz explicitly assumes that if the disfavored person does not redefine what is legitimate, he will generate a tension system for restoring his power to its expected level. As may be seen, this formulation is quite similar to reactance theory where personal eliminations of or threats to freedom are concerned. It is obvious, of course, that the concept of personal weight was not formulated to handle impersonal events. A second point worth noting is that while enhancement of personal weight is assumed by Horwitz to be satisfying, there is no assumption in reactance theory about reactions to increases in freedom where there has been no prior reduction.

The intention of this brief discussion of related concepts is to indicate the kinds of theoretical conceptions to which it is related, not to explore these conceptions and relationships exhaustively. While there is other relevant literature, such as Heider's (1958) discussion of "retribution," this review should suffice to locate reactance theory among previous theoretical ideas.

6 The human design

HADLEY CANTRIL

With the mounting discussion of "existentialist" and "humanistic" psychology on both sides of the Atlantic, together with the search of political scientists for a psychological interpretation useful for their level of analysis, it seems appropriate to try to spell out what seem to be the demands human beings impose on any society or political culture because of their genetically built-in design. Furthermore, in bringing together recently in summary form the conclusions of a cross-national study of 13 different countries (Cantril, 1965), I kept realizing anew that in describing differences found among people, it is all too easy to neglect basic functional uniformities which take diverse forms and to leave the accounting or explanation at that level. Differences are often dramatic and easier to detect than the similarities they may obscure. Here I shall try to orchestrate the diversities of mankind found in different societies into some systematic unity.

The aspects of "human nature" differentiated here are those that seem to me to be pointed to by the data of psychology and by the observations sensitive observers have made of the way people live their lives in a variety of circumstances. I shall try to use a level of accounting appropriate both to an understanding of people and to an understanding of social and political systems. In doing this some of the absurdities may be avoided that result when a single man-made abstraction, usually devised to account for some single aspect of behavior, is the sole theme song. As the different characteristics of the human design are reviewed here, it must be recognized and emphasized that they all overlap, intertwine and are interdependent. One must differentiate artificially in order to focus and describe.

1. *Man requires the satisfaction of his survival needs.* Any listing of the characteristics of any living organism must begin here. Neurophysiologists have located and described in a most general way two built-in appetitive systems found in higher animals: one system propelling them to seek satisfying and pleasurable experiences, the other protecting them from threatening or unpleasant experiences (Cantril & Livingston, 1963). These two systems together can be thought of as the basic forces contained within all human beings which not only keep them and the species alive as their simple survival needs for food, shelter and sex are gratified, but that are involved in the desire for life itself.

These appetitive systems of course become enormously developed, refined and conditioned, especially in man, as new ways are learned to achieve satisfactions and avoid dangers and discomforts. It has often been noted that unless the survival needs are satisfied, a person devotes himself almost exclusively to a continued attempt to fulfill them, a preoccupation which pre-empts his energies and

Reprinted from the **Journal of Individual Psychology**, 1964, 20, 129–36, with permission of the author and the publisher.

repels any concern for other activities. Most people in the world today are still concerned with living a type of life that constitutes well-being on a relatively simple level with what amenities their cultures can provide.

2. *Man wants security both in its physical and its psychological meaning to protect gains already made and to assure a beachhead from which further advances may be staged.* Man wants some surety that one action can lead to another, some definite prehension which provides an orientation and integration through time. People invariably become embittered if they nurse a dream for what they regard as a long time with no signs of it becoming a reality.

In this connection it should be recalled that the story of evolution seems to tell us that members of every species stake out some territory for themselves within which they can provide for their needs and carry on their living, the extent of this territory being dependent on what is required for the survival of the species and being extended if it will contribute to such survival. In the present era the territories human beings stake out for themselves are largely bounded by the nation-state, a territorial unit rapidly replacing narrower geographical and psychological identifications but doing so just at the time when it is becoming more and more apparent that the concept of nation itself limits and threatens man's development in an age of increasing interdependence and highly developed weaponry.

3. *Man craves sufficient order and certainty in his life to enable him to judge with fair accuracy what will or will not occur if he does or does not act in certain ways.* People want sufficient form and pattern in life to be sure that certain satisfactions already enjoyed will be repeatable and will provide a secure springboard for take-offs in new directions.

The conflict of old loyalties with emerging new loyalties in the case of developing people is bound to create uncertainties, doubts and hesitations. If people become frustrated and anxious enough, they will do almost anything in a desperate attempt to put some order into apparent chaos or rally around new symbols and abstractions that enable them to identify with a new order that promises to alleviate the uncertainties experienced in the here and now.

In stressing process and change, the desire of people to preserve the status quo when it has proved satisfying and rewarding and to protect existing forms against alteration must never be overlooked. And the craving for certainty would include the satisfactions that come from the sense of stability provided by our habitual behavior—including much of our social and political behavior.

4. *Human beings continuously seek to enlarge the range and to enrich the quality of their satisfactions.* There is a ceaseless quest impelling man to extend the range and quality of his satisfactions through the exercise of his creative and inventive capacities. This is, of course, a basic reason why order of any kind is constantly being upset. Whitehead expressed the point eloquently and repeatedly, for example, in his statements that "The essence of life is to be found in the frustrations of established order" (1938, p. 119) and that "The art of progress is to preserve order amid change, and to preserve change amid order" (1929, p. 515).

The distinguished British philosopher John Macmurray has used the phrase *The Self as Agent* as the title of his book

(1957) analyzing the role of action in man's constant search for value-satisfactions. And in a companion volume he has noted that "Human behavior cannot be understood, but only caricatured, if it is represented as an adaptation to environment" (1961, p. 46). The search for an enlargement of satisfactions in the transactions of living can also be phrased as the *desire for development in a direction*, the desire to do something which will bring a sense of accomplishment as we experience the consequences of successfully carrying out some intention, and thereby have an occasional feeling that our lives are continuous creations in which we can take an active part. During a conversation in Beirut, a wise man once remarked to me that "people are hungry for new and good experiences."

It seems worthwhile to differentiate this search for value-satisfactions into two varieties: (a) value-satisfactions that are essentially new, different, more efficient, more reliable, more pleasurable or more status-producing results of activity along familiar and tried dimensions, and (b) value-satisfactions that are new in the sense of being emergent, a new quality a person discovers or creates himself for the first time as does the child who tries out and relishes new experiences as his own developmental pattern unfolds. The former variety, like the growth on the limb of a tree, builds people out and extends their range, while the latter, like the new growth at the top of the tree, lets them attain new heights and see new vistas. The satisfactions sought by a newly developing people are at first most likely to be of the former type.

The particular value-satisfactions man acquires are the result of learning. Some of the values learned will serve as the operative ideals of a people, others will be chiefly instrumental. People in rich countries have learned to want and to expect many aspects of a good life that less favored people have not yet learned are possibilities. From this point of view one might say that the competition between social and political systems is a competition in teaching people what to want, what is potentially available to them and then proving to them in their own private experience that these wants are best attainable under the system described.

5. *Human beings are creatures of hope and are not genetically designed to resign themselves*. This characteristic of man stems from the characteristic just described: that man is always likely to be dissatisfied and never fully "adapts" to his environment.

Man seems continually to hope that the world he encounters will correspond more and more to his vision of it as he acts within it to carry out his purposes, while the vision itself continuously unfolds in an irreversible direction. The whole process is a never-ending one. It is characteristic of man in his on-going experience to ask himself "Where do I go from here?" Only in his more reflective moods does a person ask "Where did I come from?" or "How did I get this way?" Most of the time, most people who are plugged into the changing world around them are future-oriented in their concerns.

6. *Human beings have the capacity to make choices and the desire to exercise this capacity*. Any mechanical model of man constructed by a psychologist or by anyone else is bound to leave out the crucially important characteristic of man as an "appetitive-perceptive agency." Perceptions are learned and utilized by people to provide prognoses or bets of a variety of kinds to weigh alternative

courses of action to achieve purposes. Consciously or without conscious awareness, people are trying to perceive the probable relation between their potential acts and the consequences of these acts to the intentions that constitute their goals.

The human nervous system, including the brain, has the capacity to police its input, to determine what is and what is not significant for it and to pay attention to and to reinforce or otherwise modify its behavior as it transacts in the occasions of living (Cantril & Livingston, 1963). In this sense, the human being is a participant in and producer of his own value-satisfactions: people perceive only what is relevant to their purposes and make their choices accordingly.

7. *Human beings require freedom to exercise the choices they are capable of making.* This characteristic of man related to freedom is deliberately worded as it is, rather than as a blanket statement that "Human beings require freedom," since the freedom people want is so relative to their desires and the stage of development they have attained. Human beings, incidentally, apparently require more freedom than other species of animals because of their much greater capacity to move about and to engage in a much wider variety of behavior.

While it seems true that maximum freedom is a necessary condition if a highly developed individual is to obtain maximum value-satisfaction, it is equally true, as many people have pointed out, that too much freedom too soon can be an unbearable burden and a source of bondage if people, like children, are insufficiently developed to know what to do with it. For freedom clearly involves a learning of responsibility and an ability to take advantage of it wisely.

The concept of freedom is essentially a psychological and not a political concept. It describes the opportunity of an individual to make his own choices and act accordingly. Psychologically, freedom refers to the freedom to experience more of what is potentially available, the freedom to move about and ahead, to be and to become. Freedom is thus less and less determined and more of a reality as man evolves and develops; it emerges and flowers as people learn what it can mean to them in terms of resolving some frustrations under which they are living.

The authoritarian leadership sometimes required to bring about man's awakening and to start him on the road to his definition of progress appears to go against the grain of the human design once man is transformed into a self-conscious citizen who has the desire to exercise the capacity latent within him. The definition of freedom in the Soviet dictionary, *Ushakov*, as "the recognition of necessity" is limited to those periods in the life of an individual or a people when they are willing to let others define what is necessary and to submerge their own individuality.

8. *Human beings want to experience their own identity and integrity,* more popularly referred to as the need for *personal dignity.* Every human being craves a sense of his own self-constancy, an assurance of the repeatability of experience in which he is a determining participant. He obtains this from the transactions he has with other individuals.

People develop significances they share with others in their membership and reference groups. If the satisfaction and significance of participation with others ceases to confirm assumptions or to enrich values, then a person's sense of self-constancy becomes shaken or insecure, his loyalties become formalized and empty or are given up altogether. He becomes alienated or seeks new significances, new loyalties that are more operationally real.

9. *People want to experience a sense of their own worthwhileness.* This differentiation is made from the desire for personal identity and integrity to bring out the important relationship between this search for identity and the behavior and attitudes of others toward us. A human being wants to know he is valued by others and that others will somehow show through their behavior that his own behavior and its consequences make some sort of difference to them in ways that give him a sense of satisfaction. When this occurs, not only is a person's sense of identity confirmed, but he also experiences a sense of personal worth and self-respect. The process of extending the sense of Self both in space and in time appears also to involve the desire that one's "presence" shall not be limited merely to the here and now of existence but will extend into larger dimensions.

People acquire, maintain, and enrich their sense of worthwhileness only if they at least vaguely recognize the sources of what personal identity they have: from their family, their friends and neighbors, their associates or fellow workers, their group ties or their nations. The social, religious, intellectual, regional, or national loyalties formed play the important role of making it possible for individuals to extend themselves backward into the past, forward into the future and to identify themselves with others who live at more or less remote distances from them. This means the compounding of shared experiences into a bundle that can be conceptualized, felt, or somehow referred to in the here and now of daily living, thus making a person feel a functional part of a more enduring alliance. Man accomplishes such feats of self-extension largely through his capacity to create symbols, images, and myths which provide focal points for identification and self-expansion. After reviewing the lessons from history, Herbert Muller noted as one of the "forgotten simplicities" the fact that "Men have always been willing to sacrifice themselves for some larger cause, fighting and dying for their family, tribe, or community, with or without hope of eternal reward" (1954, p. 392).

10. *Human beings seek some value or system of beliefs to which they can commit themselves.* In the midst of the probabilities and uncertainties that surround them, people want some anchoring points, some certainties, some faith that will serve either as a beacon light to guide them or a balm to assuage them during the inevitable frustrations and anxieties living engenders.

People who have long been frustrated and who have searched for means to alleviate their situations are, of course, particularly susceptible to a commitment to a new system of beliefs or an ideology that they feel holds promise of effective action.

Beliefs are confirmed in so far as action based on them brings satisfying consequences and they are denied with growing skepticism if disastrous results consistently occur because they are followed.

Commitment to a value or belief system becomes more difficult among well-informed and sophisticated people who self-consciously try to reconcile what they believe with what they know and what they know with what they believe. In such circumstances, beliefs become more and more secular and less important as personal identifications.

11. *Human beings want a sense of surety and confidence that the society of which they are a part holds out a fair degree of hope that their aspirations will be fulfilled.* If people cannot experience the effectivity of social mechanisms to accomplish some of the potential goals they aspire to, then obviously their frustrations and anxieties mount, they search for new means to accomplish aims. On the other hand, they make any sacrifice required to protect a society they feel is fulfilling their needs but appears seriously threatened.

It cannot be stressed too strongly that any people will become apathetic toward or anxious about ultimate goals they would like to achieve through social organizations if they continually sense a lack of reliability in the means provided to accomplish these goals. Obviously any society that is to be viable must satisfy basic survival needs, must provide security, must insure the repeatability of value-satisfactions already attained and provide for new and emerging satisfactions. The effective society is one that enables the individual to develop personal loyalties and aspirations which overlap with and are congenial to social values and loyalties, and which at the same time take full account of the wide range of individual differences that exist.

Such a social organization must, too, become the repository of values, must provide symbols for people's aspirations, must comprise and contain customs, institutions, laws, economic arrangements and political forms which enable an individual in various ways to give concrete reference to his values in his day-to-day behavior. If the gap between what his society actually provides in terms of effective mechanisms for living and what it purports to provide becomes too great, the vacuum created will sooner or later engender the frustrations that urge people on to seek new social patterns and new symbols. Whitehead wrote:

The major advances in civilization are processes which all but wreck the societies in which they occur—like unto an arrow in the hand of a child. The art of free society consists first in the maintenance of the symbolic code; and secondly in fearlessness of revision, to secure that the code serves those purposes which satisfy an enlightened reason. Those societies which cannot combine reverence to their symbols with freedom of revision, must ultimately decay either from anarchy, or from the slow atrophy of a life stifled by useless shadows (1927, p. 88).

Every social and political system can be regarded as an experiment in the broad perspective of time. Whatever the experiment, the human design will in the long run force any experiment to accommodate it. This has been the case throughout human history. And few would deny that the varied patterns of experiments going on today hold out more promise of satisfying the human condition for a greater number of people than ever before.

7 Discovery and explanation in social science

GEORGE C. HOMANS

I

Any science has two main jobs to do: discovery and explanation. By the first we judge whether it is a science, by the second, how successful a science it is. Discovery is the job of stating and testing more or less general relationships between properties of nature. I call this discovery only because in many sciences the relationships were unknown before research revealed them: for instance, the discovery that bats navigate on the sonar principle. As we shall see, discovery in this sense, particularly discovery of the more general relationships, is much less characteristic of the social sciences than of the others, making one of the most striking differences between them.

A discovery takes the form of a statement of a relationship between properties of nature. Let us be sure we understand what this means. Take Boyle's familiar law: The volume of a gas in an enclosed space is inversely proportional to the pressure on it. A statement, a sentence like this, consists of two parts: first, a reference to what the relationship applies to—gas in an enclosed space—and second, a specification of the relationship between the properties, which must, of course, be at least two in number. Here the two properties are volume and pressure, and the relationship is inverse proportionality: if pressure goes up, volume will go down. Volume and pressure are continuous variables. In another variety of this kind of sentence, the properties, to speak loosely, can take only two values, as in the sentence: A man who loses his kidneys is dead. Here the variables are really classes: first, having kidneys or not having kidneys, and second, being alive or dead. And the relationship between the two is association: not having kidneys is definitely associated with being dead. Sentences of these two varieties I shall call "propositions." Propositions are the one essential product of any science.

In the words of Percy Bridgman (1936), all propositions are accompanied, implicitly or explicitly, by a "text." In the case of Boyle's Law, the text would include answers to such questions as: What is a gas? What are pressure and temperature? How are they defined and measured? The text might also include a statement of the conditions within which the relationship held good. Boyle's Law holds good under the condition that the temperature of the gas is constant.

I have said that propositions, statements of relationships between properties of nature, were "more or less general." When I assert that the battle of Hastings was fought on October 14, 1066, I am certainly stating a relationship, but it is a relationship of association between a single event and a single time. If I asserted that all decisive bat-

Abridged from **The Nature of Social Science**, (copyright © 1967, by George C. Homans), by permission of the author and the publisher, Harcourt Brace Jovanovich, Inc.

tles were fought in October, the statement would, if true, begin to have some generality. And if I asserted that all battles whatsoever were fought in October, the generalization would be, in the terms used here, more general still. In the same way, Boyle's Law, which applies to all gases in an enclosed space and at constant temperature, is less general than a law applying to all gases at any temperature. But let us not worry much at the moment about the degree of generality of propositions. To have stated and tested a proposition of any degree of generality is no mean achievement.

Nonoperating definitions

I suppose every professor has horrid moments of feeling that he is teaching his students everything but what they really need to know, everything but the fundamentals. One reason why I have made the, after all, rather obvious points of the last few paragraphs is that I seldom teach my students how to recognize the different kinds of sentence that appear in the literature of social science, and I take the opportunity, belatedly and vicariously, of doing so now. Especially they need to be able to recognize a real proposition, or rather how to tell a real proposition from other kinds of sentence, for these nuggets are often few and far between. If, as Bridgman says, every proposition is accompanied by a text, the text in much of social science seems to take more room than it does in physical science. Indeed in some sociological writings no room is left for anything else.

Yet real propositions do appear in the literature of social science, and so do definitions of the terms that occur in them, the equivalents of the definition of pressure that accompanies Boyle's Law. These I call "operating definitions," because we actually work with them. An example might be a definition of the term "frequency" to accompany the proposition: The more valuable a man perceives the result of his action to be, the more frequently he will perform the action. I want my students to be able to distinguish operating definitions and real propositions from two other kinds of sentence, similar in form to definitions and propositions respectively, which appear very often in the literature of social science, particularly in introductory texts and in "general theory." These I call "nonoperating definitions" and "orienting statements."

Examples of nonoperating definitions include the definitions of some so-called central concepts in sociology and anthropology, concepts the workers in these fields take to be the glories of their sciences. Thus a "role" is the behavior expected of a man occupying a particular social position. And a "culture" is the inherited pattern of living of the members of a society. These are nonoperating definitions because they do not define variables that appear in the testable propositions of social science. Though "roles" and "cultures" could each perhaps be analyzed into clusters of variables, they certainly are not such themselves. It would be absurd to say: "The more the role, the more the something else." We might indeed say: "The more specific the role, the lower the social position in which the behavior is expected." But here the variable would be specificity and not role itself.

This example suggests that "role" may have the status in sociological propositions that "gas" has in Boyle's Law: we might speak of the specificity *of* the role as we speak of the pressure *on* the gas. But I am not sure that the parallel holds. Certainly the status of the two is not exactly alike. For some propositions, like Boyle's Law, that hold good of gases do not always hold good of non-gases—liquids and solids—but it is far from clear that there are propositions that hold good of roles but not of non-roles (whatever they may be). That is, the word "gas" makes a difference in meaning, and "role" may not.

I think the same sort of thing is true of "culture." But here I add a comment that gets me a little ahead of my argument. An anthropologist friend once said to me, in pointing out the usefulness of this concept: "If someone asks me, for instance, why the Chinese do not like milk, I can only say, 'Because of the culture.' "[1] All I could say in turn was that, if that was all *he* could say, he was not saying much. All that the use of the word "culture" implied was that disliking milk had been characteristic of the behavior of some Chinese for some generations. But we knew that already; "culture" did not add anything. What we should have liked to know was why milk, specifically, rather than, say, tea was disliked. Talking about culture did not answer this question at all—not at all. More generally, "explanation by concept" is not explanation.

Yet I am loath to argue that the concepts "role" and "culture" are useless. What I want to be sure of is that we recognize the sort of usefulness they possess. They tell us roughly the kinds of thing we are going to talk about. They and their definitions tell us that we are going to talk about expected behavior and inherited patterns of behavior, and

[1] For the notion that the concept of culture explains something, see, especially, Kluckhohn (1949), pp. 17–44.

it may indeed be well for a new student to be forewarned. But sooner or later we must stop "being about to" talk about something and actually say something— that is, state propositions. Lingering over nonoperating definitions may actually get in the way of this primary job of science.

Orienting statements

Just as "role" and "culture" are famous concepts, so what I call "orienting statements" include some of the most famous statements of social science. One is Marx's statement that the organization of the means of production determines the other features of a society. This is more than a definition and resembles a proposition in that it relates two phenomena to one another. But these phenomena—the means of production and the other features of a society— are not single variables. At best they are whole clusters of undefined variables. And the relationship between the phenomena is unspecified, except that the main direction of causation—determination—is from the former to the latter. Whereas Boyle's Law says that, if pressure goes up, volume will assuredly go down, what Marx's Law says is that, if there is some, any, change in the means of production, there will be some unspecified change or changes in the other features of society. Put the matter another way: Boyle will allow one to predict *what* will happen; Marx will only allow one to predict that *something* will happen. Accordingly I cannot grant his law the status of a real proposition.

In taking Marx's statement thus out of context, I do not in the least mean to imply that this is all he had to say about the relations between the infrastructure and the superstructure of society, or that his writings do not include other statements that are real propositions, or that this particular statement is unimportant. That is far from my view.

Another example of an orienting statement is the assertion by Parsons and Shils (1951, pp. 14–16) that, in social interaction between any two persons, the actions of each are sanctioned by the actions of the other. This is an important statement in that, in my view, the beginning of wisdom in the study of social behavior is to look at it as an exchange between at least two persons, in which the action of each rewards or punishes—that is, sanctions—the action of the other. But the statement in itself does not say what effect a change in the behavior of one will have on the behavior of another. Like Marx's Law, it implies that there will be *some* effect, but does not begin to say what. Only if Parsons and Shils had gone on to say, for instance, that the more rewarding (valuable) to one man is the action of the other, the more often will the first perform the action that gets him the reward—only then would they have stated a real proposition. Much of what they say suggests that they believe this proposition to be true, but they manage to avoid coming right out with it.

Much writing in social science consists of orienting statements when it does not consist of nonoperating definitions. Orienting statements do not qualify as real propositions: they are of little use in prediction and of none at all, as we shall see, in explanation. Yet I should be slow to argue that they did no good in other ways. I must testify, perhaps complacently, that I personally have been greatly helped both by Marx and by Parsons and Shils. I claim that statements of this sort are really imperatives,

telling us what we ought to look into further or how we ought to look at it. This is the reason why I call them orienting statements. Look at the relations between the means of production and the other features of society, for if you look, you will surely find! Look on social behavior as an exchange, for then you will begin to make progress! And, God knows, with the help of Marx at least, scholars have made progress. Looking where he pointed, they have discovered and tested statements that, if of smaller scope than Marx's, still have more of the character of real propositions.

The effects of familiarity

So far I have not stressed the most obvious difference between the social sciences and the other sciences. It is, of course, that they deal with the behavior of men. In no other science do the scientists study the behavior of things like themselves. The chief consequence of this condition, we often hear, is that social science can never become scientific, because the scientists, being men and thus holding strong feelings about human behavior, will let their emotions get in the way of their objectivity. I do not believe the danger to be as great as asserted. No doubt their emotions will lead them to study certain phenomena and not others. There are social scientists who prefer to study the things in society they like, and others who are positively compelled to study things they don't. But no great harm is done: the evidence is that either group gets great pleasure from pointing out to the other what it has deliberately left out, so that no trifle remains forever unconsidered. Nor is there any doubt that different social scientists will evaluate differently the conditions they do investigate, but with the present degree of acceptance of scientific standards, they will have less difficulty in agreeing on what the conditions *are*. We can all agree that American military officers on retirement often take important jobs in private industry, without all agreeing that this kind of link between government and industry constitutes—and here comes the evaluation—a conspiracy against democracy.

Much less often mentioned and at least as important is another kind of consequence of the unique position of social science. In studying human behavior social scientists are studying phenomena that human beings are uniquely familiar with. As social animals, nothing has been more important to them, and there is nothing that they have learned more about. Since they are also talking animals and can pass on their knowledge, the knowledge has been accumulating for hundreds of thousands of years. They even know the fundamentals in the form of the principles of behavioral psychology. Though we surely cannot rule out the possibility that principles still more fundamental will be discovered in the future, these are fundamental enough. The ordinary man knows them in the sense that he is hardly astounded—on the contrary—when they are stated to him, even though he himself would not state them in the language of behavioral psychology, and though he has been known to be astounded by some of their ulterior implications in psychopathology. Above all he acts on them, not always successfully, in planning his own behavior.

All this familiarity has bred contempt, a contempt that has got in the way of the development of social science. Its fundamental propositions seem so obvious as to be boring, and an intellectual, by definition a wit and a man of the world, will go to any mad lengths to avoid the obvious. Add to this the dilemma created by the assumption that making fundamental discoveries is the mark of a science. Then either, if its fundamental propositions are already well known and so need not be discovered, social science cannot be a science, or, if it is a science, its principles must remain to be discovered and so must be other than these. Both views make trouble. In order to avoid mentioning the principles, social science may abandon the standards of science in explanation, or it may look for its fundamental principles in the wrong places and hence without success. The most significant difference between social science and other science is that its principles do not have to be discovered but, what is much more difficult, simply recognized for what they are.

Yet I think that accepting the view that the fundamental propositions of all the social sciences are the same, and that the propositions are psychological, would be a great advantage to all of these sciences. To speak more practically, the acceptance of the view might mean that the solutions each of the social sciences has reached in dealing with its particular problems could be seen as relevant to, and contributing to the solution of, the problems of the others. This mutual support has already proceeded far, as for instance in economic and social history, but it has proceeded piecemeal, neither as far nor as fast as it might. A recognition that they all share the same principles might speed up the process. In short, what the social sciences have to gain is nothing less than intellectual unity.[2] We might

[2] For an interesting and important treatment of the social sciences as a single science see Kuhn (1963).

even teach our different subjects with less waste of the student's time, since we should not have to ask him to make a fresh start with each one.

II

The difficulties of social science lie in explanation rather than discovery. Explanation is the process of showing how empirical findings follow from, can be deduced from, general propositions under particular given conditions. The general propositions of all the social sciences are psychological, propositions about the behavior of men rather than about societies or other social groups as such. Although a time may come when these propositions will be shown in turn to follow from still more general propositions—physiological ones, for instance —this certainly cannot be done now.

These propositions are not only very general but also, in the sense I have already described, very well known. This fact supports the contention that the emphasis of social science must be rather different from that of many other sciences. If the fundamental propositions are already known, social science will put less energy into discovery, at least of fundamentals, and more into showing how the myriads of empirical findings follow from the fundamentals. I may have given the impression that this is easy—but then I chose easy, though important, examples. In fact it may in general be more difficult for the social sciences than for the others. Even if the propositions of behavioral psychology were accepted as the most general in the social sciences—and their very obviousness gets in the way of their acceptance at present—the difficulties with explanation that these sciences encounter would still be far from over. There may be propositions so general that they are of no use.

The organic analogy

At this point some persons will ask: You have tried the analogy with physical science and it has failed, but why not try the one with biological science? Perhaps a society is more like a living body than a gas? This is, in effect, the position of the functionalists in anthropology and sociology.

Organic bodies are highly integrated, their parts linked intricately together; the forces making for equilibrium are accordingly strong; and when equilibrium breaks down it is apt to do so with a bang: life and death are easy to tell apart, and provide a clear criterion of the viability of the organism as a whole. Physiology can make very general statements about the aggregates making up organic systems. It is able to tell us, for instance, what the kidney contributes to the functioning of the body without worrying very much about the individual cells of which the kidney is composed. (Of course there are other physiologists that do concern themselves with the nature of the cells.) Unlike those of physics, and like those of social science, the propositions of physiology are not always quantitatively very precise, but they have the alternative advantage that many of them come close to being of the all-or-nothing type, with sharp breaks in the values of the variables. If one loses one's kidneys, it makes, so to speak, not just a quantitative but a qualitative difference. Propositions like this are relatively, though only relatively, easy to establish, and with their help it is often possible to explain some clear and final result like death by spelling out the chain of relationships that leads, for instance, from the stab in the heart to the end of breathing.

All our dearest dreams to the contrary, we are not, when we deal with a group or society, dealing with a system like this. The social system is not as tightly integrated: a change in the other features of a society does not necessarily, for instance, mean a change in the family organization. The equilibrium forces are not as strong, and it is usually not at all clear when equilibrium breaks down. Beyond certain narrow limits of internal change a mouse body will simply die: it certainly cannot change into a hippopotamus. It is surprisingly hard to specify what constitutes the death of a society: the Assyrian empire is gone, but there are people, I hear, that still call themselves Assyrians. The organic analogy fails all along the line.

Social science gets the worst of both worlds. Its subject matter is remarkable neither for the relative simplicity of pre-atomic physics nor for the organic integration of physiology; its propositions are remarkable neither for quantitative precision nor for marked discontinuities. It is not easy to work out what contribution some social part makes to the integrity of a social whole, since the whole is so fluid. For purposes of discovery and explanation, these are all in their different ways great disadvantages.

Historicity

The question now is why, in social science, there should be such a gap between our general propositions, which are psychological and refer to individuals, and our propositions about aggregates, which are either of limited scope or of low explanatory power. One reason is obvious. Implied in the psychological propositions themselves is a strong element of historicity: past history combined with present circumstances determines behavior. Many of our propositions are limited by the variety of special historical circumstances in which they hold good.

The historicity, moreover, is double, lying both in the individual and in the group. For the individual the psychological propositions imply, for instance, that his past history of success in his activities under given circumstances determines whether he will try them again, or others like them, in similar circumstances. The reason why people with similar backgrounds behave in similar ways here and now—so far as they do behave in similar ways—is that they are likely to have had similar past experiences. But it is also history that makes our findings even at the level closest to individual behavior only statistically true. Many subjects with roughly similar backgrounds—say, American college freshmen—may respond in much the same ways to the experimental manipulations of small-group research, but a man differing even slightly from the rest in his past history may respond differently and upset the perfection of our correlations.

This historicity also, of course, holds good of groups and societies, large and small. The older generation of any group teaches the younger how it ought to behave. Though the elders may have lost confidence in some of their doctrines, they cannot go so far as to leave the young alone. True, the argument that "the socialization process" automatically prepares the young to take just those roles society is ready to offer them is a facile solution to the problem of social continuity (see Wrong, 1961). A society may teach its young men values subversive to its own stability. Let a boy learn at his mother's knee such impeccable social values as independence and achievement, and he may, when he grows up and if he finds the opportunity, take action that will change the society radically, not maintain it. Still, some initial tendency for the young to learn, and thus perpetuate, the customs of the past will undoubtedly be there. This tendency for the past history of societies to influence their present character is strengthened by the fact that, even in their most violent revolutions, the members of a society either cannot change, or have no interest in changing, all their institutions at once. Some they wittingly or unwittingly preserve, so that the way change takes place is modified by the adherence of individuals and groups to other rules, which have not changed. The past affects the very way in which the future comes into being.

There are, of course, physical and biological sciences, such as cosmology, historical geology, and paleontology, in which historicity makes as much trouble as it does in the social sciences. But for many of these sciences, including the most fundamental, it is not a problem. When it is one, the scientists may still be able to disregard it for practical purposes, since they are in a position to neutralize its effects. In most of the social sciences, on the other hand, historicity either in individuals or in groups is a problem right from the beginning, and the scientists are rarely able to neutralize it. I sometimes think that the social sciences are criticized as sciences for failing to do what a respectable physical science would not have even tried to do.

Epilogue

Years ago Chester Barnard (1938) wrote: "It seems to me quite in order to cease encouraging the expectation that human behavior in society can be anything less than the most complex study to which our minds may be applied" (p. xii). I hope I have done nothing to encourage the expectation. I have tried to point out the nature of the complexity and some of the reasons for it. If our results are limited, we should not excuse the fact with the argument that our science is young. It is not all that young, and it has been very energetic. Its difficulty is a better excuse than its youth, and one that does us more credit.

Our difficulty in explanation lies in the nature of the general propositions. They are propositions about individual behavior, yet what the social sciences often want to explain are the characteristics of social aggregates. The central problem of social science remains the one posed, in his own language and in his own era, by Hobbes: How does the behavior of individuals create the characteristics of groups? That is, the central problem is not analysis but synthesis, not the discovery of fundamental principles, for they are already known, but the demonstration of how the general principles, exemplified in the behavior of many men and groups, combine over time to generate, maintain, and eventually change the more enduring social phenomena.[3]

If the central problem of the social sciences is to show how the behavior of individuals creates the characteristics of groups, we should pay particular attention to the situations in which social phenomena can be most convincingly

[3] For an argument similar to the one advanced in this book, see Barth (1966).

explained by psychological propositions —convincingly, because in these situations we can directly observe the behavior of the individuals concerned and thus get the information necessary for explanation. This is the strategic justification of what is called small-group research. In the small group we can really observe and explain how conformity occurs, how power is exercised, and how status systems arise. These are surely among the most convergent of social phenomena, and ones we must begin by understanding intimately if we are ever to grasp the nature of larger societies.

II CULTURE, LEARNING, AND GROUP IDENTIFICATION

Most human behavior occurs through contact with an ever-present environment. The fact that people populate this environment insures that much behavior will emerge from processes generally labeled social learning (see Bandura & Walters, 1963). As a person behaves and develops in a social world, his performances become increasingly tied to the social-cultural milieu of which he is a part. The cultural agents with whom he interacts, the symbols he encounters, and the particular groups with which he comes to be identified, all work, however subtly and unconsciously, to mold and even control his actions.

As Cooley (1922) and Mead (1934), among others, have shown, the controlling features of the social-cultural environment are gradually internalized by people in the form of habits, beliefs, values, and other dispositions. Even in the absence of direct influence by others, therefore, human conduct is directed by symbolic representations of the social world (see Strauss, 1964). The varied processes by which these normative controls become internalized are generally summarized by the term "socialization." The groups with which a person is associated and the individuals with whom he interacts in the course of a lifetime are the "agents" of socialization.

All this is well known and various discussions of the features of socialization may be found in Faris (1964), Clausen (1968), Lindzey and Aronson (1968, Vol. 3), and in *Handbooks* edited by Mussen (1960, 1970), and Goslin (1969). The importance of group identifications has long been recognized, and psychologists, anthropologists, and sociologists have extensively documented interpersonal diversities linked with different group affiliations (see Kluckhohn, 1954; and Lindzey and Aronson, 1968, Vol. 4).

What a person is and does can be seen as proceeding, very largely, from the features of groups, real or imagined, to which he belongs, refers himself, or aspires. While not always used so broadly, the concept of the reference group is a useful tool for comprehending these matters and Hyman and Singer trace the development of this concept in their survey beginning this section. They make clear the difference between reference groups and membership groups taking notice of the existence of reference individuals. Significantly, they observe that the attitudes a person holds reflect the groups or persons to which he refers himself, while those attitudes he expresses reflect the groups of which he is a member and which hold the power to induce conformity to their standards. Showing some of the applications of the reference group idea, Hyman and Singer thereby illuminate its utility as a vehicle for understanding phenomena of social influence in a pluralistic society.

In such a society, a variety of reference groups, as well as membership groups, are available to people for reference, sometimes separately, other times in varied combinations. Kemper (1968), for one, has reviewed the many varieties of reference groups that can be discerned in a complex society and has explored the implications for socialization of the differential availability to given individuals of particular types of reference groups or reference group combinations. And here, Hyman and Singer show how the potentiality for making choices from among alternative reference sources contributes to enhancement of the individual's sense of control over his own fate—something Gardner also suggests in this section.

Thus, because in complex social systems many groups exist at the same time, an individual's behavior is unlikely to come under the exclusive sway of any single one of them. Which perspectives a person chooses and which, of those chosen, have greater significance, vary with the individual's attraction and sentiments relative to given groups and their members. As Shibutani (1955, 1961, 1962) has pointed out, shifts in preference are likely as the conditions for attraction and sentiment toward groups and people change; however, certain early and enduring identifications doubtless play major parts in a person's life.

Nevertheless, with regard to socialization, it follows that no single agent will be totally responsible for the whole process, even if some, such as parents, will be more important than others. One may also expect changes in the salience of agents in the face of changing circumstances, as, for instance, when the adolescent turns from his parents to his peer group as a normative reference. Whatever may be its specific attributes and membership, the reference group is a primary source of a person's "premises for action" and these premises or perspectives, as Shibutani (1955) has called them, regulate his behavior. Whether the group be a family, a neighborhood gang, a social class, or a society, the individual's behavior is organized with reference to the group's perspectives and these perspectives, in turn, are based in the group's "culture."

The special significance of the school and the classroom as an agent of socialization is the subject of Jackson's presentation in this section. Treating the classroom, after the fashion of Barker, as a behavior setting, Jackson pictures its role as a stable, socially intimate framework wherein children learn many modes of relationship to other people and to the larger social system. He identifies critical processes by which these accomplishments are effected and differentiates the contributions to their achievement made by the teacher, the peer group, and the institution. Portrayed is the ongoing operation of the "anticipatory socialization," alluded to by Hyman and Singer, and also the way the classroom, as a miniature replica of society, provides a forum for at least partial expression of the dispositions learned there.

Formed in the complex life-long socialization process, an individual's answer to the fundamental question "who am I" can be seen to derive from the patterns of his group participation and reference. The processes of identity formation and the development of self-esteem are both to be discerned in Jackson's observations, particularly in relation to the normative-evaluative processes that take place among teachers and students in the classroom (e.g. see Erikson, 1967).

Care must be taken, however, to avoid the error of many social theorists, among whom Freud was not the least, who have pictured the relation between the person and these cultural influences as wholly, or even as basically, negative. According to such views, culture operates mainly as a barrier to expressions of Man's egocentric predilections. By contrast, Gardner offers a different conception here of Man's nature that permits description of the interrelation of society and the individual in terms of the positive contributions of culture to human life.

For Gardner, Man in his nature is a rationalizing, if not a rational, being. The theme of human existence, in his eyes, is a continuing quest for meaning, a search for identity, growing from a fundamental personal need for a serviceable definition of reality and an understanding of relations between self and world. Culture, then, with its perspectives, is an indispensable guide to, and source of, the meanings essential to sentient Man.

From a distinctively humanistic posture, Gardner emphasizes the central value of the unique individual. Yet, Man at the same time is a social being possessed of responsibilities extending beyond himself, though still aware of and sometimes troubled by his individuality. In contrast with traditional Man, embedded in his culture and indistinguishable from it, Gardner perceives modern Man caught in the perplexing cross-currents of self and non-self. Often the resolution of Man's need for a stable identity takes the form of an alienation from society. But Gardner can discern a basis for a mature conception of self as a component of society leading to a creative appreciation of culture as a means to human ends. Some of these points will be treated further in Section III, especially by Yinger, and it might be said that, in its essentials, many of the thinkers represented in this volume share Gardner's view of the human condition and predicament: Cantril and White in Section I, and Allport in Section III, are a few of them.

With the evident dependence of individual behavior upon group characteristics, it is hardly surprising that social psychologists may refer to culture in their attempts to account for social behavior. Despite the concept's widespread use, however, it has not been clear exactly what culture is, as Homans observes in Section I. The paper here by Murdock addresses itself to this issue in the form of a characterization of the nature of culture and how it changes in time. First of all, Murdock asserts, cultures are learned. They constitute "systems of collective habits" and are dynamic in form, changing in response to both internal and external functional requirements. Moreover, with time and circumstance, cultures tend to differentiate themselves into variant- or sub-cultures reflecting different conditions of life within the compass of the larger system.

Whether culture is to be thought of as "real" or only as an abstraction is not at issue in Murdock's paper, although it is a subject for lively debate among anthropologists, as a reading of White's article on the concept of culture (1959) or of his book *The Science of Culture* (1949) will reveal. However, Murdock does treat as problematic the "social sharing of habits" and to account for it he invokes the socialization process dealt with at length in the two remaining papers of this section. In doing so, he draws an important distinction between culture and social behavior. Culture, he points out, is found not in behavior itself, but in the "collective habits" underlying it.

Actual behavior, however, is critical to cultural change for change arises from persistent deviations of behavior from existing norms. Murdock provides a discussion of several processes of cultural change, emphasizing the phenomenon of cultural borrowing through contact, and indicates the various conditions under which it proceeds. After a discussion of "cultural lag"—the disjunction between the acceptance of an innovation and its integration into the cultural pattern—he ends by underscoring the adaptive functions of culture and its linkage with "conditions of existence."

In this view, cultures do not exist in isolation; rather, they represent, partly anyway, techniques by which people accommodate themselves to the demands of their environments, including technological, economic, and other facets of them. The "present-time orientation" of the American lower class, as one example, may be a cultural characteristic directly tied to emphases upon immediate gratification fostered by comparative economic insecurity.

These ideas have significant implications for social learning and socialization which are frequently overlooked. Among other things, it has been suggested (Hunt, 1961) that specific socialization practices may be a function of particular conditions of life that are not "chosen," but are required by situational demands. Whether this is the case or not, it is true that most analyses of social learning and socialization rarely attempt to connect these processes with environmental factors. As anthropologist David Aberle (1961) has observed, studies of socialization commonly stop with efforts to show the impact of child-rearing on personality. Child-rearing practices are usually taken as causes and personality as an effect (cf. Whiting & Child, 1953; Sears, Maccoby, & Levin, 1957). However, it is equally useful, he suggests, to examine the causes of socialization practices themselves. The query he poses is, "Why do members of a particular system show uniformities in socialization rather than randomness?" The answer obviously must reside in controlling conditions common to many learning situations—a community or culture. Socialization and psychological representations of culture thus may be conceptualized as *dependent* variables changing in response to variations in cultural independent variables. Though psychologists may choose simply to take the latter as "givens," this progression remains unaltered.

In either case, socialization practices may be studied in relation to themselves and other cultural-environmental circumstances or in relation to personality and behavior. By the same token, processes of learning may be considered as independent variables controlling behavior, or as dependent variables contingent upon other antecedent cultural and extra-cultural factors.

Gordon is mainly concerned in the next paper with cultural responses to "environmental" events, in the form of extensive immigration by culturally alien groups, such as took place in nineteenth- and early twentieth-century America. In the selection here from his book *Assimilation in American Life* (1964) he views socialization as a process by which such migrant persons and groups achieve assimilation of and to an existing social-cultural pattern. It becomes clear from Gordon's treatment that the details of such processes depend upon the nature of the prevailing pattern and the relations between it and the properties of the immigrant culture.

Seven variables are identified by Gordon as involved in the assimilation process, and he uses them to identify types or stages of assimilation. Applying his seven-variable model to the analysis of four American "minority" ethnic groups, he shows that the American experience has been primarily one of their gradual, if uneven and incomplete, adaptation to a prevailing Anglo-Saxon core society. The fabled American melting pot apparently did little melting and produced no real blending of "old" and "new" cultural forms; instead it worked effectively to "transmute" the latter into the former.

The fact that America today displays a variety of sub-societies, Gordon attributes, for one thing, to a slower and more difficult absorption of and by immigrants of existing Anglo-Saxon structural patterns as compared with cultural ones. A major consequence of this is the pluralism to which Shibutani has given prominence in his writing (cf. 1955, 1961).

Along with the ethnic, religious, and similar sub-societies featured in Gordon's writing are others, some of which are associated with the so-called vertical organization of society. It is with these considerations that broad-gauge studies of socialization—e.g., Bronfenbrenner (1958, 1961a,b), Miller and Swanson (1958), and Sears, Maccoby, and Levin (1957)—have been concerned.

The social classes that figure so prominently in these works can be thought of as cultures or reference groups at least partly different from other groups with which they may be socially and/or geographically contiguous. Their agents will tend to employ socialization practices consistent with the sub-group's culture and will convey similarly consistent behavioral standards. Bronfenbrenner, in particular, has shown how different practices by given agents of socialization can be analyzed in relation to a matrix of such social-biological factors as age, sex, and social class (1958, 1961a,b).

The final selection in this section, by Brim, highlights the fact, often given little more than lip-service, that socialization is a process extending over a lifetime and is, moreover, ubiquitous (see Cain, 1964). Each time an individual, whatever his age, enters a new group, or a new job, or other social settings, a process of socialization ensues. Social patterns and expectations must be learned or tested and, in recognition of this, social relations have increasingly received analysis from perspectives of socialization. The acquisition of new social roles (see Section V) is a particularly transparent example of such socializing transactions, e.g., the socialization of the student-nurse (Olesen & Whittaker, 1968), the socialization of the psychiatric patient (Goffman, 1969; Ortgier and Hunt, 1965), and even such a seemingly unlikely phenomenon as the adaptation to dying (Glaser & Strauss, 1965).

Brim's work has been in the forefront of these developments in the understanding of adult socialization. In his selection here, he discusses his research along with prominent efforts by other investigators. He provides substantial consideration of relations between childhood and adult socialization, commenting on some of the limitations by the former on the latter and highlighting some of the basic differences between earlier and later socialization both as regards content and modality. He suggests that to perform in a role a person must have knowledge, ability, and motivation. Using a simple cross-classification of these factors, with behavior and values, Brim constructs a six-cell grid in terms of which he depicts changes in the content of socialization over the life span. He shows that socialization after childhood deals mainly with overt behavioral aspects of role performances in contrast with the earlier emphases on motivation and basic values, which are harder to alter in later life.

In sum, this section presents some prominent thought apropos the effects upon the person of his social-cultural surroundings. What is talked about is commonly represented under the rubric of personality and culture or, more recently, personality-in-culture. It is probably a fair statement that the guiding perspective of this rubric sees behavior under the rule of personality which, in turn, represents features of culture (cf. Kluckhohn & Mowrer, 1944; Kluckhohn & Murray, 1953; Child, 1954; Whiting, 1961; Hsu, 1961). This section and the next one, dealing more directly with approaches to personality as a "variable" in psychological theory, are therefore interlocking. Whatever personality may be thought to be, it has an inescapable social-cultural basis.

8 An introduction to reference group theory and research

HERBERT H. HYMAN and ELEANOR SINGER

Sociologists, social psychologists, and cultural anthropologists have always operated on the fundamental principles that an individual's attitudes and conduct are shaped by the group in which he has membership and that self-appraisal and the correlative feelings and behavior flow from the individual's location in a particular group within a social hierarchy. "That men act in a social frame of reference yielded by the groups of which they are a part is a notion undoubtedly ancient . . ." (Merton & Rossi, 1957). The evidence in support of such principles is, indeed, abundant, but, at times, faith in the principles becomes shaky in the face of contradictory examples: upper-class individuals with radical ideologies and revolutionary allegiances, those who feel deprived despite relatively advantaged positions, the products of an orthodox milieu who end up nonconformist. Ordinary language is rich in terms that describe such individuals who do not show the stamp of their group: the renegade Catholic, shabby gentility, the Tory worker.

Via the concept *reference group*, our confidence in the fundamental principles has been restored and theory and research on group influences has been invigorated. In the process of self-appraisal, from many possible groups available as a framework for social comparison, individuals make their own particular selection, thus reflecting the true complexities of their social location but not necessarily the arbitrary social position to which the scientist may have assigned them. In shaping their attitudes "men frequently orient themselves to groups other than their own . . ." (Merton & Rossi, 1957), thus reflecting the influences of the group to which they refer themselves, if not their membership group.

The fact that men may shape their attitudes by reference to groups other than their own and their self-evaluations by the choice of unusual points of social comparison is perhaps the most distinctive contribution of reference group theory. To be sure, anomalous patterns of behavior may be understood without recourse to the concept. Some members of a group may depart from the modal pattern of behavior simply because of their simultaneous membership in other groups. Some individuals in a particular status may have an incongruent self-image because they occupy other statuses as well and the status-set, rather than the discrete status, governs the process. But even here the concept of reference group makes a distinctive contribution to what otherwise would remain problematic. Which of the

Slightly abridged from the Introduction to Herbert H. Hyman and Eleanor Singer (Eds.) **Readings in Reference Group Theory and Research**, pp. 3–21 (Copyright © 1968 by The Free Press, a Division of the Macmillan Company), with permission of the authors and the Macmillan Company.

multiple memberships and multiple statuses is governant over the individual; what weights best represent their respective contributions?

The term was first used by Hyman, who elaborated the concept and explored some of its properties in an inquiry in 1942 into *The Psychology of Status* (Hyman, 1942). Seeking to understand the way individuals ranked themselves in terms of their choice of a social framework for comparison, he first explored by interview the reference groups and reference individuals that subjects employed and some of the dynamics underlying such selection, and then determined the effects of particular reference groups on self-appraisal by experimental manipulations. At about the some time, Newcomb, searching to understand processes of attitude change, or lack of change, among individuals all of whom had prolonged membership in Bennington College, explored systematically by interview and repeated testing the various ways in which they related themselves to the Bennington community—in other words, chose it as a reference group (Newcomb, 1943). These first systematic studies by social psychologists in *comparative* and *normative* reference group processes respectively (to use the distinction later developed by Kelley) stimulated no one but a few other social psychologists, notably, the Hartleys and Sherif, to continue research on reference groups. Sherif emphasized reference groups in his 1948 *Outline of Social Psychology*, which included a summary by Newcomb of his Bennington study, rephrased in terms of the explicit concept *reference group* (Sherif, 1948).

The concept had clarified for Newcomb various paradoxical findings. Similarly, Stouffer and his associates were led in their studies of *The American Soldier* to the concept of *relative deprivation*, a close cousin to the concept of comparative reference group, as they confronted the apparent contradictions between feelings of satisfaction or deprivation and the objective situation among groups of soldiers (Stouffer *et al.*, 1949). They then invoked the interpretive principle that the soldier's sense of deprivation was not dependent on an absolute level, but was relative to the perceived level in the groups with which he compared himself.

These ideas and concepts, however, had little prominence until 1950, when Merton and Kitt synthesized and presented in systematic form their "Contributions to the Theory of Reference Group Behavior" (1950). Since 1950 the concept has achieved, in Turner's phrase, "meteoric prominence" and has figured in so many writings that the more recent history defies brief review. The concept appears in Australia, Israel and India; in studies of farmers, scientists, drunkards, and newspapermen; it has been applied to problems of mental illness, formal organization, marketing and public relations, mass communication, acculturation, political behavior, consumer behavior, labor relations, and juvenile delinquency, as well as to opinion formation.[1] This sketchy sampling conveys the wild growth, but it should also be noted that despite the general flowering, some branches have not flourished. If we take as a comprehensive outline Merton's formulation: "Reference group theory aims to system-

[1] For some of these examples, see Emery & Katz (1951), Taft (1952), Varma (1965), Rogers & Beal (1958), Rogers (1958), Pool & Shulman (1959), Bennis **et al.** (1958), Foundation for Research on Human Behavior (1956), Duesenberry (1949), Wilensky (1963), and Haskell (1960–61). Other examples are scattered through Hyman & Singer (1968).

atize the determinants and consequences of those processes of evaluation and self-appraisal in which the individual takes the values or standards of other individuals and groups as a . . . frame of reference," the deficiencies as well as the accomplishments will become apparent.

Kelley's distinction between *comparative* and *normative* reference groups, corresponding to the two functions of reference groups as standards of comparison for self-appraisal or as the source of the individual's norms, attitudes, and values, is basic (Kelley, 1952). These two types of reference groups are sometimes regarded as separate but equal in importance for study, having only the common property that the individual's choice of a point of reference is the key to understanding either the process of self-appraisal or the formation of attitudes. The two types, however, may not always be empirically distinct. Contained within the structure of norms in a group may be the directive that one should not compare himself with his betters, or look down on his inferiors, or even be aware of their existence. Indeed, in Hyman's interviews, some subjects claimed that they did not employ any comparative reference group whatsoever, because of ideological distaste, and the comparative groups that other subjects employed were clearly shaped by their political attitudes. Given the possible interdependence of the two types of processes, it is all the more strange that although the study of the normative reference group has been cultivated, that of the comparative reference group has been neglected. The paths that Hyman, the Hartleys, Stouffer, and Merton took are now only byways, trodden by occasional investigators (see Hartley & Hartley, 1952; Kuhn & Mc-

Partland, 1954; Turner, 1955; Davis, 1959).

The equally basic distinction between reference *individuals* and reference *groups* has been neglected despite the emphasis on the reference individual as a point of social comparison in the early work and the obvious connection to such a prestigious concept as role-model. The parenthetical remark by Newcomb that a membership group may be a potent normative reference group "(particularly as symbolized by leaders . . .)" strongly suggests the role of the reference individual as the carrier of the reference group's norms, but it appears to have been lost inside the parenthesis. It would be greatly to our advantage to reinstate the concept. Merton incorporated into his original formulation both concepts, and in his subsequent essay gave greater prominence to the "reference individual" (Merton, 1957). Sherif described that glorified variety of reference individual to which he gave the apt title, the "reference idol."

The reference group concept reminds us that individuals may orient themselves to groups other than their own, not merely to their membership groups, and thereby explains why the attitudes and behavior of individuals may deviate from what would be predicted on the basis of their group membership. Thus a theory of the group determination of attitude has been properly enlarged by the concept of reference group. Parallel to a theory of group influences on attitude, a recent fruitful development of theory and research has dealt with social influences of an interpersonal sort mediated through direct interaction and communication, and has become known to us under the headings of "opinion leadership," "the influential," and "personal influence." But this latter theory would take on enlarged significance by some stress on "reference individuals" as sources of influence. Just as reference group reminds us of the influence of nonmembership groups, the concept of reference individual would remind us that there are influentials, or opinion leaders, with whom we are not in direct social relations. We model ourselves not only on those who are near but on those who are far away. Certainly the emphasis in recent research on intimates as sources of influence is an understandable and wholesome reaction to the earlier emphasis on hierarchical and feudal types of influence from superiors, but perhaps the balance has swung too far. The point to be stressed is that the links in the interpersonal chain do not have to be forged exclusively via direct social relations.

For the study of normative reference groups, Newcomb's distinction between the *positive* and *negative* type reminds us that individuals may form their attitudes in opposition to the norms of a group as well as in accordance with them. The concept of negative reference groups helps us understand not only the affective tone and content of an individual's attitude, but also such *formal* features as the congruence and organization of his attitudes. Clearly there are some instances in social life where to oppose the norms of a particular group—for example, the Republican Party in the United States—is to be thrown into the arms of its opposite, the Democratic Party. But there are many other instances where social relations between groups are not patterned in terms of polar opposites. Thus to regard one's parents or community as a *negative* reference group may provide

no other directive to the individual than to choose from among the norms of the myriad groups available. Individuals who form a constellation of attitudes under such conditions may well show the consequences in terms of diffuseness, lack of crystallization, inconsistency, and so on. But this remains a hypothesis to be tested when investigators pursue Newcomb's fruitful distinction.

The concept *referent power*, employed by French and Raven (1959) suggests many fundamentals of normative reference group processes. The power of a nonmembership reference group inheres essentially in the fact that the individual by his sheer identification with the group willingly accepts what he perceives to be its norms. By contrast, membership groups often have the power, even when the individual does not take them as reference groups, to exact conformity in behavior through brutish means or rewards and to induce attitudes through prolonged doses of socialization. Certainly, when there is no bond of identification, their influence may be attenuated, and the concept of reference group reminds us that the psychological equipment of an individual can provide some escape from victimization by a membership group. Of course, when referent power is joined to real power, that is an unbeatable combination.

From these distinctions flows the hypothesis that the attitude *held* tends to reflect the reference group, whereas the attitude *expressed* tends to reflect the membership group (Smith *et al.*, 1956). It is only when the individual reveals his nonconformity that he is in danger of sanctions from his membership group. Thus the membership group and the reference group normally divide the realm, the former holding sway over the sphere of expression and the latter over the sphere of private thoughts. More refined hypotheses follow. As a membership group develops apparatus and institutions that threaten privacy, even the attitudes that are formed and then held in mind may come under its sway, since the truly private sphere shrinks. Conformity to the membership group then becomes more comprehensive. But when nonconformity is expressed, it, no doubt, requires that the person have some reference group or individual strongly in mind to steel his resolve. William James put it very well: "When for motives of honor and conscience I brave the condemnation of my own family, club, and 'set'. . . . I am always inwardly strengthened in my course and steeled against the loss of my actual social self by the thought of other and better *possible* social judges than those whose verdict goes against me now. The ideal social self which I thus seek in appealing to their decision may be very remote. . . . Yet still the emotion that beckons me on is indubitably the pursuit of an ideal social self, or a self that is at least *worthy* of approving recognition by the highest possible judging companion, if such companion there be. . . . All progress in the social self is the substitution of higher tribunals for lower" (James, 1890, pp. 315–316). On a miniature scale, the support of reference groups for nonconformity is revealed in the selection from the studies of the Encampment for Citizenship, where observations were made of youth as they moved back and forth between the larger society and a special community whose norms were in conflict (Hyman *et al.*, 1962). And on a more extended time

scale, these processes are examined in Newcomb's follow-up study of Bennington graduates twenty-five years removed from its influence (Newcomb, 1963).

Merton's concept of *anticipatory socialization* is essential to this discussion (see Merton & Rossi, 1957). Individuals may take as a reference group a nonmembership group to which they aspire to belong, and begin to socialize themselves to what they perceive to be its norms before they are ever exposed to its influence. The power of some reference groups thus inheres in the fact that they will ultimately be membership groups—at least such is the belief of the aspirant—and therefore can exact some conformity as the price of admission or of more comfortable passage into their ranks. Eulau advanced and then tested twice an ingenious hypothesis bearing upon this discussion. He reasoned that anticipatory socialization may be an effective means for learning *attitudes*, but not *conduct*, since the aspirant will have had little real opportunity to practice the skills required and to be taught the correct performance of the role.

Basic to reference group theory is the fact that individuals often have *multiple* reference groups. Certainly, there are some individuals who have limited capacity to use many reference groups, who lack, in Cooley's phrase, rich "imaginative sociability." Others, however, in appraising the many facets of the self, employ various reference groups, each specialized as a point of comparison for one particular dimension (Turner, 1955). In forming their total constellation of attitudes, several reference groups may be employed, each accorded a limited jurisdiction over some specialized attitude sphere. Studies of normative reference groups have found differences in the legitimacy that individuals accord to groups promulgating norms in various spheres (Campbell *et al.*, 1960). There are also instances where multiple reference groups impinge simultaneously on the same sphere of comparison or the same realm of attitude, and then they may either reinforce the same outcome or produce conflicting consequences for the individual.

Over the life span of any person there will have been a multiplicity of reference groups, specialized less by sphere than by the life-segment to which they were keyed. Some are long departed, but since reference groups are represented by the symbolic processes of the individual, old reference groups may be carried over in memory. Recent groups may also be cast out of mind in the zealous adoption of a still newer reference group. The relations of multiple reference groups within a sequence suggest many fascinating problems that tie into the processes of social mobility (Merton & Rossi, 1957). Discussions of social mobility often assume that the past and future reference groups conflict, since the individual presumably wishes to break his ties to the old, inferior group. Litwak, however, presents an interesting reformulation, using the concept of the *stepping-stone reference orientation*. In a situation characterized by ordered change, "where integration into one group is considered to be a prerequisite for integration into a second group . . . it is possible for the individual to view both his current membership group and his future membership group as reference groups, without endangering his integration into his current group and without preventing his joining a different future group" (Litwak, 1960). Each group is valued by the individual as a stepping stone to help him in his advance.

The concepts reviewed in no way exhaust the literature, but are those basic to any clarification of the field. Merton's 1957 essay describes many other conceptual refinements and the extended network of connections to other branches of theory (see also Turner, 1955; Shibutani, 1955; Kuhn, 1964).

Research and theory on the selection of reference groups

The concept *reference group* has always implied that one cannot make arbitrary assumptions about the groups to which an individual refers himself. Given the multiplicity of groups and the variability among individuals and situations, must we then, as a symposium put it in 1956, "determine which kinds of groups are likely to be referred to by which kinds of individuals under which kinds of circumstances in the process of making which decisions . . ."—over and over again? (Foundation for Research on Human Behavior, 1956). There will always be a large amount of empiricism needed, and the development of simple instruments to measure a person's reference groups is of great importance. But, fortunately, research has already established certain regularities in the choices individuals make and some major factors governing selection.

Theorizing about the choice of reference groups and reference individuals is often based on simple assumptions about motivation. The individual chooses a normative reference group so that in fantasy, or ultimately in fact, he can feel himself part of a more favored group. Or, facing rapid social change, the individual latches onto a reference group. Thus anchored, he has a ready-made perspective to order the distressing complexities of the environment (Shibutani, 1955; Eisenstadt, 1954). For social comparisons, he chooses a group so as to enhance his self-regard or protect his ego. Certainly in the search for reference groups, such fundamental strivings play an important part. The pleasure principle is at work, but so too is the reality principle.

Recall Stouffer's reference that the *more* advantaged soldiers felt deprived because they chose to compare themselves with others who were even better off. It seems plausible that the institutional arrangements gave such sharp definition and prominence to certain groups that the soldier's attention was drawn to them as points of comparison. Perhaps when reality is less highly structured, there is more freedom for the pleasure principle to guide the selection of reference groups.

Turner (1955) hypothesized that only those groups will be taken as points of comparison which are *relevant* to a particular aspect of self-appraisal— when a group's standing is so high or so low that it is not meaningful to the individual, it will not be used as a comparative reference group. The similarity principle Festinger (1954) derived in his "theory of social comparison processes," that an individual chooses others who are close to his level of ability, is congruent with Turner's relevance principle, as is Merton's hypothesis, based on findings in *The American Soldier*, that "some similarity in status attributes between the individual and the reference group must be perceived or imagined, in order for the comparison to occur at all" (Merton & Kitt, 1950). The

Amba of East Africa dramatically illustrate that principle. They worked for Europeans for a much lower price than for employers from another tribe, and "are quite willing to explain this state of affairs. They say that a European is on a much higher social plane, and therefore comparisons are out of the question. Europeans are so wealthy that an increase in their wealth makes no difference in the . . . standing" of the Amba relative to Europeans. Qualitative evidence in Hyman's interviews also suggested the operation of the similarity principle, or what he called "affinity" in the choice of reference groups, but he observed instances where contrast in status made a reference group salient and likely to be chosen.

The principle of relevance or similarity still leaves much room for the play of psychological factors. As Merton remarks, *perceived* similarity is what counts, and there are many dimensions of similarity, only some of which are noted by the individual. And inside the range of similarity, in which direction will the individual turn then—toward relevant groups that are superior or inferior to him? Turner's college students seemed to compare themselves with higher reference groups, perhaps to their present discomfort, but because they were "future-oriented," desiring to surpass such groups in their future lives.

Patchen's study of industrial workers (1958) provides systematic evidence on the variables affecting the choice of a reference individual or reference group for economic comparisons and fundamentally clarifies the motivational assumptions of reference group theory. Men often choose reference groups which increase their *present* sense of relative deprivation, not only because formal institutional arrangements force such groups into attention, but, as Patchen (1958) demonstrates, when informal social influences make such groups salient. Men may choose groups above them at the price of present dissatisfaction because they are laying a claim to a future when their status will be higher and their relative deprivation diminished.

Research on the selection of *normative* reference groups is meager. That individuals identify with advantaged groups and thereby gain gratification must be qualified in terms of the societal context. Such modes of selection may be characteristic of societies with high rates of upward mobility (Merton & Rossi, 1957), or where upward mobility is a strong value or is perceived, correctly or not, to be frequent. Comparative research is clearly required.

Experimental research demonstrates that situational factors may heighten the salience of a membership group and increase the likelihood of its being used as a reference group whose perceived norms then affect some specific sphere (Charters & Newcomb, 1958; Kelley, 1955; Festinger, 1947). Whether such situational influences have enduring effects on the choice of normative reference groups remains unknown.

That normative reference groups are chosen in the spirit of identification perhaps also needs qualification. It may be true for many individuals seeking a source of norms, values, and attitudes, although the existence of *negative* reference groups obviously qualifies the proposition. Certainly the reference individual who is an idol or hero may be chosen with a sense of his distance and little feeling of identification. And what about the individual seeking a system of beliefs and *knowledge?* He may then choose his reference group in terms of its authority or expertness, and with the full awareness that he has no bond of identification. Systematic research on such determinants of choice does not exist, since the effects of reference groups on cognition have been neglected, to the detriment of an improved sociology of knowledge. Carlson, who demonstrated differences in the effectiveness with which rural Southern Negroes dealt with syphilitic infections, depending on their reference groups, and Beal and Rogers, who demonstrated that farmers who adopted better practices chose particular reference groups, illustrate the prospect for future research (Rogers & Beal, 1958; Carlson, 1952; Deutsch & Gerard, 1955; Newcomb, 1956).

Ruth Hartley's work represents a unique program of systematic research on psychological factors that influence the selection of a membership group as a normative reference group (Hartley, 1960 a, b, etc.). Using a large college community, she measured the degree to which students adopted their new community as a reference group, and correlated such individual differences with other characteristics. Taking on a new reference group is dependent on an acceptant personality pattern. A particular reference group is then likely to be chosen if it is seen as fulfilling personal needs, and if there is congruity between the individual's personal values and norms and the norms and values he perceives as characteristic of the group. Thus some of the apparent effect of reference groups on the values of individuals may be spurious, since their values were prior in time and determined the choice of the reference group.

PERCEPTION OF THE NORMS AND
STANDING OF A REFERENCE GROUP

For an individual to guide himself by a reference group requires some perception or cognition of its norms. Otherwise he may refer himself to the group all he wants, but no direction is indicated. Since reference groups may often be distant, nonmembership groups, perception of the true norms may be hazy and incorrect and not subject to any correction from the group. But even membership groups functioning as reference groups pose problems of perception, since the visibility of group norms is not always high and varies depending on one's position in the group (Merton & Rossi, 1957; Chowdhry & Newcomb, 1952). Comparative reference group processes also require some perception or knowledge of the standing of others on the dimensions selected for comparison.

Deviation from the objective position of a group thus may be inspired by conformity to a false norm that the individual has taken to be the true norm of the reference group, and conformity to the objective norms may be the perverse fate of a deviant who thinks he is flouting the norms, but who has misperceived them. Attempts to understand the *motivation* of conformists and deviants must for sure distinguish among these varieties, and therefore measure the norms imputed to groups.

The environmental conditions and psychological processes that aid or obstruct perception vary greatly depending on the nature of the reference group or reference individual. Organized groups announce their views to members and to outsiders; diffusion is aided by the mass media and spread by word of mouth. But self-appointed communicators and the diffusion process may also distort the norms that finally reach the individual. More fundamental problems must be considered. Even organized groups do not announce all of their views all of the time. A norm may not yet have been promulgated; a fundamental value may remain implicit and taken for granted. On other issues, the norms may be confused, not shared throughout the organization, exceedingly complex in nature, or not distinctive from other groups. There are even occasional groups whose fundamental value is that the individual shall be autonomous in regulating his conduct, thereby creating difficulty for those individuals seeking cues. Such are the burdens on the perceiver, but what comes to his aid is *time*. He has abiding loyalties to some reference groups or individuals, and what at first is dimly perceived finally takes on clarity.

Not all reference groups are organized entities. They may be vague collectivities, or sprawling social categories, or groups out of the dead past or not yet born. Some reference individuals may also be long departed. They are living structures only in the mind of the perceiver and do not communicate or transact behavior. Here there is relatively free rein for autistic perception of norms.

With respect to conditions governing knowledge of norms, surveys of political behavior provide some relevant evidence. Members of a given social category have greater awareness than nonmembers that a voting norm characterizes the group. Among nonmembers, awareness of the norm of another group is greater for those whose environment contains many representatives of the group (Campbell *et al.*, 1954; Hyman,

1960). One may speculate that the choice of reference groups from the immediate environment, or from membership groups, or the choice of *reference individuals* rather than groups, may be motivated by the individual's need to simplify his perceptual tasks.

Consequences of reference group selection

The recent popularity of reference group theory brings the danger, in Sherif's words, that the concept "is becoming a *magic* term to explain anything and everything concerning group relations" (1953). The concept is often invoked and the influence of a particular reference group alleged without benefit of direct evidence. Operating under the protection of such reckless practices, the claims of reference group theory can easily be exaggerated and the consequences overstated. Under such a semi-scientific regime, the true extent of the consequences can also be underestimated, since investigators may neglect to observe the influence of a particular reference group.

Certainly in the long past, before the short history of the concept, the reference group must have been missed many times. And although investigators, in the current period, often assert the influence of a *normative* reference group whose presence has not been measured, this excess is counterbalanced by the state of neglect into which the concept of the *comparative* reference group has fallen. that notion only seems to come back to life when we study categories of people whose self-regard is so obviously vulnerable to social arrangements, or who respond in paradoxical ways to being elevated or degraded. Is it not significant that two out of three studies included on the consequences of selecting a par-

ticular comparative reference group deal with Negroes, who, despite improvements in their status, still remain deprived *relative* to what they deserve and others get? Is it not a commentary on the general state of neglect of the comparative reference group that a dozen years after so prestigious a theorist as Festinger presented his theory of social comparison processes, there remains a "virtual absence of any experimental tests of its key assumptions"? (see Latane, 1966).

As one ponders the consequences of selecting a particular comparative reference group, one sees once again the convergence of comparative and normative reference group processes. Self-appraisal rests on the framework of social comparison, and the choice of a comparative reference group maintains, enhances, or injures self-regard. Certainly this is enough of a consequence in itself to make the comparative reference group worthy of study. The concept of the self has always been central to social psychology. McDougall (1921) long ago described the central importance in social life of the self-regarding sentiment, and traced the ebb and flow of negative and positive self-feeling as the child grows and takes as his point of comparison various social circles through which he moves. His English illustration is old-fashioned, but the point is up-to-date. He remarks about the student: " . . . [a]fter a successful career in the schools and the playing fields, how changed again is his attitude towards his college society! The dons he regards with kindly tolerance, the freshmen with hardly disguised disdain; and very few remain capable of evoking his negative self-feeling—perhaps a 'blue,' or a 'rugger-international,' or a don of worldwide reputation; for the rest—he has comprehended them, grasped their limits, labelled them, and dismissed them to the class that ministers to his positive self-feeling. And so he goes out into the world to repeat the process and to carry it as far as his capacities will enable him to do." [2]

But the process does not end there. From the deprived self, the fattened ego, flow corresponding attitudes and behavior. Thus although comparative and normative reference group processes may follow different courses, they arrive at the same end point: the comparative reference group working through the intervening variable of the self, and the normative more directly through the internalization of what is perceived as appropriate behavior. Both processes start with the same raw materials: society provides the rich assortment and

[2] For recent treatments of the concept of the self in the context of reference group theory, see Sherif (1962) and Sherwood (1965).

complex arrangement of groups from which the choices may be made. Some are pressed upon the individual but he is creative and his symbolic equipment is highly developed and can present to the mind's eye a much larger assortment than is given in immediate experience. Thus he maintains some control over his own self-regard by his choice of comparative reference groups and guides his own fate accordingly. Similarly, by his choice of normative reference groups, he can escape from the confines of a narrow social world. Otherwise provincialism would be the law of life, conformity to the parochial the rule. We would all be like those "portions of the sovereign people" whom Lippmann describes in his *Public Opinion* as moving "as if on a leash, within a fixed radius of acquaintances, according to the law and gospel of their social set" (Lippmann, 1946, p. 37).

9　Life in classrooms

PHILIP W. JACKSON

I

School is a place where tests are failed and passed, where amusing things happen, where new insights are stumbled upon, and skills acquired. But it is also a place in which people sit, and listen, and wait, and raise their hands, and pass

out paper, and stand in line, and sharpen pencils. School is where we encounter both friends and foes, where imagination is unleashed and misunderstanding brought to ground. But it is also a place in which yawns are stifled and initials scratched on desktops, where milk money is collected and recess lines are formed. Both aspects of school life, the celebrated and the unnoticed, are familiar to all of us, but the latter, if only because of its characteristic neglect, seems to deserve more attention than it has received to date from those who are interested in education.

In order to appreciate the significance of trivial classroom events it is necessary to consider the frequency of their occurrence, the standardization of the school environment, and the compulsory quality of daily attendance. We must recognize, in other words, that children are in school for a long time, that the settings in which they perform are highly uniform, and that they are there whether they want to be or not. Each of these three facts, although seemingly obvious, deserves some elaboration, for each contributes to our understanding of how students feel about and cope with their school experience.

The magnitude of 7000 hours spread over six or seven years of a child's life is difficult to comprehend. On the one hand, when placed beside the total number of hours the child has lived during those years it is not very great—slightly more than one-tenth of his life during the time in question, about one-third of his hours of sleep during that period. On the other hand, aside from sleeping, and perhaps playing, there is no other activity that occupies as much of the child's time as that involved in attending school. Apart from the bedroom (where he has his eyes closed most of the time) there is no single enclosure in which he spends a longer time than he does in the classroom. From the age of six onward he is a more familiar sight to his teacher than to his father, and possibly even to his mother.

Another way of estimating what all those hours in the classroom mean is to ask how long it would take to accumulate them while engaged in some other familiar and recurring activity. Church attendance provides an interesting comparison. In order to have had as much time in church as a sixth grader has had in classrooms we would have to spend all day at a religious gathering every Sunday for more than 24 years. Or, if we prefer our devotion in smaller doses, we would have to attend a one-hour service every Sunday for 150 years before the inside of a church became as familiar to us as the inside of a school is to a twelve-year-old.

The comparison with church attendance is dramatic, and perhaps overly so. But it does make us stop and think about the possible significance of an otherwise meaningless number. Also, aside from the home and the school there is no physical setting in which people of all ages congregate with as great a regularity as they do in church.

The translation of the child's tenure in class into terms of weekly church attendance serves a further purpose. It sets the stage for considering an important similarity between the two institutions: school and church. The inhabitants of both are surrounded by a stable and highly stylized environment. The fact of prolonged exposure in either setting increases in its meaning as we begin to consider the elements of repetition, redundancy, and ritualistic action that are experienced there.

A classroom, like a church auditorium, is rarely seen as being anything other than that which it is. No one entering either place is likely to think that he is in a living room, or a grocery store, or a train station. Even if he entered at midnight or at some other time when the activities of the people would not give the function away, he would have no difficulty understanding what was *supposed* to go on there. Even devoid of people, a church is a church and a classroom, a classroom.

Not only is the classroom a relatively stable physical environment, it also provides a fairly constant social context. Behind the same old desks sit the same old students, in front of the familiar blackboard stands the familiar teacher. There are changes, to be sure—some students come and go during the year and on a few mornings the children are greeted at the door by a strange adult. But in most cases these events are sufficiently uncommon to create a flurry of excitement in the room. Moreover, in most elementary classrooms the social composition is not only stable, it is also physically arranged with considerable regularity. Each student has an assigned seat and, under normal circumstances, that is where he is to be found. The practice of assigning seats makes it possible for the teacher or a student to take attendance at a glance. A quick visual sweep is usually sufficient to determine who is there and who is not. The ease with which this procedure is accomplished reveals more eloquently than do words how accustomed each member of the class is to the presence of every other member.

An additional feature of the social atmosphere of elementary classrooms deserves at least passing comment. There is a social intimacy in schools that is unmatched elsewhere in our society. Buses and movie theaters may be more crowded than classrooms, but people rarely stay in such densely populated settings for extended periods of time and while there, they usually are not expected to concentrate on work or to interact with each other. Even factory

workers are not clustered as close together as students in a standard classroom. Indeed, imagine what would happen if a factory the size of a typical elementary school contained three or four hundred adult workers. In all likelihood the unions would not allow it. Only in schools do thirty or more people spend several hours each day literally side by side. Once we leave the classroom we seldom again are required to have contact with so many people for so long a time. This fact will become particularly relevant in a later chapter in which we treat the social demands of life in school.

A final aspect of the constancy experienced by young students involves the ritualistic and cyclic quality of the activities carried on in the classroom. The daily schedule, as an instance, is commonly divided into definite periods during which specific subjects are to be studied or specific activities engaged in. The content of the work surely changes from day to day and from week to week, and in this sense there is considerable variety amid the constancy. But spelling still comes after arithmetic on Tuesday morning, and when the teacher says, "All right class, now take out your spellers," his announcement comes as no surprise to the students. Further, as they search in their desks for their spelling textbooks, the children may not know what new words will be included in the day's assignment, but they have a fairly clear idea of what the next twenty minutes of class time will entail.

In sum, classrooms are special places. The things that happen there and the ways in which they happen combine to make these settings different from all others. This is not to say, of course, that there is no similarity between what goes on in school and the students' experiences elsewhere. Classrooms are indeed like homes and churches and hospital wards in many important respects. But not in all.

The things that make schools different from other places are not only the paraphernalia of learning and teaching and the educational content of the dialogues that take place there, although these are the features that are usually singled out when we try to portray what life in school is really like. It is true that nowhere else do we find blackboards and teachers and textbooks in such abundance and nowhere else is so much time spent on reading, writing, and arithmetic. But these obvious characteristics do not constitute all that is unique about this environment. There are other features, much less obvious though equally omnipresent, that help to make up "the facts of life," as it were, to which students must adapt. From the standpoint of understanding the impact of school life on the student some features of the classroom that are not immediately visible are fully as important as those that are.

The characteristics of school life to which we now turn our attention are not commonly mentioned by students, at least not directly, nor are they apparent to the casual observer. Yet they are as real, in a sense, as the unfinished portrait of Washington that hangs above the cloakroom door. They comprise three facts of life with which even the youngest student must learn to deal and may be introduced by the key words: *crowds, praise,* and *power.*

Learning to live in a classroom involves, among other things, learning to live in a crowd. This simple truth has already been mentioned, but it requires greater elaboration. Most of the things that are done in school are done with others, or at least in the presence of others, and this fact has profound implications for determining the quality of a student's life.

Of equal importance is the fact that schools are basically evaluative settings. The very young student may be temporarily fooled by tests that are presented as games, but it doesn't take long before he begins to see through the subterfuge and comes to realize that school, after all, is a serious business. It is not only what you do there but what others think of what you do that is important. Adaptation to school life requires the student to become used to living under the constant condition of having his words and deeds evaluated by others.

School is also a place in which the division between the weak and the powerful is clearly drawn. This may sound like a harsh way to describe the separation between teachers and students, but it serves to emphasize a fact that is often overlooked, or touched upon gingerly at best. Teachers are indeed more powerful than students, in the sense of having greater responsibility for giving shape to classroom events, and this sharp difference in authority is another feature of school life with which students must learn how to deal.

In three major ways then—as members of crowds, as potential recipients of praise or reproof, and as pawns of institutional authorities—students are confronted with aspects of reality that at least during their childhood years are relatively confined to the hours spent in classrooms. Admittedly, similar conditions are encountered in other environments. Students, when they are not performing as such, must often find themselves lodged within larger groups, serving as targets of praise or reproof, and being bossed around or guided by persons in positions of higher authority. But these kinds of experiences are particularly frequent while school is in session and it is likely during this time that adaptive strategies having relevance for other contexts and other life periods are developed.

II

In crowded situations where people are forced to take turns in using limited resources, some must stand by until others have finished. When people are required to move as a group toward a goal, the speed of the group is, necessarily, the speed of its slowest member. Almost inevitably, therefore, in such situations some group members are waiting for the others to catch up. Moreover, whenever the future is thought to be more attractive than the present—a common perception among school children—slow movement can sometimes seem like no movement at all.

All of these different kinds of delay are commonplace in the classrooms. Indeed, when we begin to examine the details of classroom life carefully, it is surprising to see how much of the students' time is spent in waiting. The most obvious examples are to be found in the practice of lining up that has already been mentioned. In most elementary schools students stand in line several times a day. The entire class typically lines up during recess, lunch, and dismissal, and then there are the smaller lines that form sporadically in front of drinking fountains, pencil sharpeners, and the like. Furthermore, it is not uncommon for teachers to hold these lines motionless until talking has ceased and some semblance of uniformity and order has been achieved.

Thus, in several different ways students in elementary classrooms are required to wait their turn and to delay their actions. No one knows for certain how much of the average student's time is spent in neutral, as it were, but for many students in many classrooms it must be a memorable portion. Furthermore, delay is only one of the consequences of living in a crowd and perhaps not even the most important one from the standpoint of constraining the individual. Waiting is not so bad, and may even be beneficial, when the things we are waiting for come to pass. But waiting, as we all know, can sometimes be in vain.

The denial of desire is the ultimate outcome of many of the delays occurring in the classroom. The raised hand is sometimes ignored, the question to the teacher is sometimes brushed aside, the permission that is sought is sometimes refused. No doubt things often have to be this way. Not everyone who wants to speak can be heard, not all of the student's queries can be answered to his satisfaction, not all of their requests can be granted. Also, it is probably true that most of these denials are psychologically trivial when considered individually. But when considered cumulatively their significance increases. And regardless of whether or not they are justified, they make it clear that part of learning how to live in school involves learning how to give up desire as well as how to wait for its fulfillment.

Interruptions of many sorts create a third feature of classroom life that results, at least in part, from the crowded social conditions. During group sessions irrelevant comments, misbehavior, and outside visitors bearing messages often disrupt the continuity of the lesson. When the teacher is working individually with a student—a common arrangement in elementary classrooms—petty interruptions, usually in the form of other students coming to the teacher for advice, are the rule rather than the exception. Thus, the bubble of reality created during the teaching session is punctured by countless trivial incidents and the teacher must spend time patching up the holes. Students are expected to ignore these distractions or at least to turn quickly back to their studies after their attention has been momentarily drawn elsewhere.

Another aspect of school life, related to the general phenomena of distractions and interruptions, is the recurring demand that the student ignore those who are around him. In elementary classrooms students are frequently assigned seatwork on which they are expected to focus their individual energies. During these seatwork periods talking and other forms of communication between students are discouraged, if not openly forbidden. The general admonition in such situations is to do your own work and leave others alone.

In a sense, then, students must try to behave as if they were in solitude, when in point of fact they are not. They must keep their eyes on their paper when human faces beckon. Indeed, in the early grades it is not uncommon to find students facing each other around a table while at the same time being required not to communicate with each other. These young people, if they are to become successful students, must learn how to be alone in a crowd.

Adults encounter conditions of social solitude so often that they are likely to overlook its special significance in the elementary classroom. We have learned to mind our own business in factories and offices, to remain silent in libraries, and to keep our thoughts to ourselves while riding public conveyances. But

there are two major differences between classrooms and most of these other settings. First, except for the first few days of school, a classroom is not an *ad hoc* gathering of strangers. It is a group whose members have come to know each other quite well, to the point of friendship in many cases. Second, attendance in the room is not voluntary, as it is in many other social situations. Students are there whether they want to be or not and the work on which they are expected to concentrate also is often not of their own choosing. Thus, the pull to communicate with others is likely somewhat stronger in the classroom than in other crowded situations.

Here then are four unpublicized features of school life: delay, denial, interruption, and social distraction. Each is produced, in part, by the crowded conditions of the classroom. When twenty or thirty people must live and work together within a limited space for five or six hours a day most of the things that have been discussed are inevitable. Therefore, to decry the existence of these conditions is probably futile, yet their pervasiveness and frequency make them too important to be ignored. One alternative is to study the ways in which teachers and students cope with these facts of life and to seek to discover how that coping might leave its mark on their reactions to the world in general.

III

Every child experiences the pain of failure and the joy of success long before he reaches school age, but his achievements, or lack of them, do not really become official until he enters the classroom. From then on, however, a semi-public record of his progress gradually accumulates, and as a student he must learn to adapt to the continued and pervasive spirit of evaluation that will dominate his school years. Evaluation, then, is another important fact of life in the elementary classroom.

The chief *source* of evaluation in the classroom is obviously the teacher. He is called upon continuously to make judgments of students' work and behavior and to communicate that judgment to the students in question and to others. No one who has observed an elementary classroom for any length of time can have failed to be impressed by the vast number of times the teacher performs this function. Typically, in most classrooms students come to know when things are right or wrong, good or bad, pretty or ugly, largely as a result of what the teacher tells them.

But the teacher is not the only one who passes judgment. Classmates frequently join in the act. Sometimes the class as a whole is invited to participate in the evaluation of a student's work, as when the teacher asks, "Who can correct Billy?" or "How many believe that Shirley read that poem with a lot of expression?" [1] At other times the evaluation occurs without any urging from the teacher, as when an egregious error elicits laughter or an outstanding performance wins spontaneous applause.

Logically, evaluation in the classroom might be expected to be limited chiefly to the student's attainment of educational objectives. And, clearly these limits seem to hold insofar as most of the official evaluations go—the ones that are communicated to parents and en-

tered on school records. But there are at least two other *referents* of evaluation quite common in elementary classrooms. One has to do with the student's adjustment to institutional expectations; the other with his possession of specific character traits. Indeed, the smiles and frowns of teachers and classmates often provide more information about these seemingly peripheral aspects of the student's behavior than they do about his academic progress. Moreover, even when the student's mastery of certain knowledge or skills is allegedly the object of evaluation, other aspects of his behavior commonly are being judged at the same time.

As every school child knows, teachers can become quite angry on occasion. Moreover, every school child quickly learns what makes teachers angry. He learns that in most classrooms the behavior that triggers the teacher's ire has little to do with wrong answers or other indicators of scholastic failure. Rather, it is violations of institutional expectations that really get under the teacher's skin. Typically, when a student is scolded by the teacher it is not because he has failed to spell a word correctly or to grasp the intricacies of long division. He is scolded, more than likely, for coming into the room late, or for making too much noise, or for not listening to directions, or for pushing while in line. Occasionally, teachers do become publicly vexed by their students' academic shortcomings, but to really send them off on a tirade of invective, the young student soon discovers, nothing works better than a partially suppressed giggle during arithmetic period.

Because both the teacher and his fellow classmates may evaluate a student's behavior, contradictory judgments are possible. A given act may be praised by

[1] Jules Henry, an anthropologist, has witnessed signs of what he terms "a witch-hunt syndrome" in several elementary classrooms. A chief component of this syndrome is the destructive criticism of each other by the students, egged on, as it were, by the teacher (see Henry, 1957).

the teacher and criticized by peers, or vice versa. This may not be the normal state of affairs, to be sure, but it does happen frequently enough to bear comment. A classic example of this kind of a contradiction was observed in one second grade classroom in which a boy was complimented by his teacher for his gracefulness during a period of "creative" dancing while, at the same time, his male classmates teased him for acting like a sissy. This example calls attention to the fact that students are often concerned with the approval of two audiences whose taste may differ. It also hints at the possibility that the conflict between teacher and peer approval might be greater for boys than for girls. Many of the behaviors that the teacher smiles upon, especially those that have to do with compliance to institutional expectations (e.g., neatness, passivity, cleanliness), are more closely linked in our society with feminine than with masculine ideals.

From all that has been said it is evident that learning how to live in a classroom involves not only learning how to handle situations in which one's own work or behavior are evaluated, but also learning how to witness, and occasionally participate in, the evaluation of others. In addition to getting used to a life in which their strengths and weaknesses are often exposed to public scrutiny, students also have to accustom themselves to viewing the strengths and weaknesses of their fellow students. This shared exposure makes comparisons between students inevitable and adds another degree of complexity to the evaluation picture.

At the heart of the teacher's authority is his command over the student's attention. Students are expected to attend to certain matters while they are in the classroom, and much of the teacher's energies are spent in making sure that this happens. At home the child must learn how to stop; at school he must learn how to look and listen.

The distinction between work and play has far-reaching consequences for human affairs, and the classroom is the setting in which most people encounter this distinction in a personally meaningful way. According to one of its many definitions, work entails becoming engaged in a purposeful activity that has been prescribed for us by someone else; an activity in which we would not at that moment be engaged if it were not for some system of authority relationships. As pre-schoolers the students may have played with the concept of work, but their fanciful enactments of adult work situations usually lack one essential ingredient, namely: the use of some kind of an external authority system to tell them what to do and to keep them at their job. The teacher, with his prescriptive dicta and his surveillance over the students' attention, provides the missing ingredient that makes work real. The teacher, although he may disclaim the title, is the student's first "Boss."

The concepts of obedience and of independence are often thought to be antithetical and, in our society, the latter concept is more often the declared objective of our schools than is the former. Therefore, we typically play down or fail to recognize the extent to which students are expected to conform to the expectations of others and when this state of affairs is called to our attention the natural response is one of alarm.

Yet the habits of obedience and docility engendered in the classroom have a high pay-off value in other settings. So far as their power structure is concerned classrooms are not too dissimilar from factories or offices, those ubiquitous organizations in which so much of our adult life is spent. Thus, school might really be called a preparation for life, but not in the usual sense in which educators employ that slogan. Power may be abused in school as elsewhere, but its existence is a fact of life to which we must adapt. The process of adaptation begins during the first few years of life but it is significantly accelerated, for most of us, on the day we enter kindergarten.

10   Individuality, commitment, and meaning

JOHN W. GARDNER

Estrangement for all

If one had to select a single conception that is central to the consensus in our own society, it would be the idea of the dignity and worth of the individual. The individual is not just so many pounds of assorted chemicals plus a bucket of water. He is not just a link in a genetic chain or an element in a biological-social system. He is not just a "resource" (as in the phrase "human resources") that may be used to strengthen the social group. There is not only something important about him, there is something inviolable. At the most basic level this involves a right to life and to security of person; but it involves much more. There are limits beyond which his privacy should not be invaded, his individuality not threatened, his dignity not impaired.

Yet man is a social being, and to talk about individuality without talking about the social system that makes it possible is to talk nonsense. It will be useful for us to examine more closely the relationship of the individual to the group.

Most human beings who have trod the earth have been rather completely embedded in the culture of their tribe or community. The testimony of historians on earlier periods and of anthropologists on contemporary primitive societies agrees on this point. The man embedded in a traditional society hardly thinks of himself as separate or separable from his group. He is engulfed by his culture. He accepts the traditions, beliefs and way of life of his group so completely that he is not even aware that he is accepting them. He is a culturally defined man.

For such a man, his community is for all practical purposes "the world." Daniel Lerner (1958) found that when

Turkish villagers were asked, "If you could not live in Turkey, where would you want to live?" they could not answer the question because they could not imagine living anywhere else. They could more easily imagine destroying the self ("I would rather die") than separating that self from its familiar context (p. 148).

Although such embeddedness places severe limits on individuality and freedom as we think of them, the men and women involved are not conscious of these limits. It is said that the last thing a fish would be conscious of would be water. Embedded man swims just as innocently in the culture of his community.

Such embeddedness cannot exist unless the community enjoys some degree of insulation from other cultures. Even in the ancient world there were relatively cosmopolitan centers in which a good many individuals were by no means embedded in their culture. One need only call to mind Plato, who viewed his society with the cool eye of a physician studying a difficult patient.

In the light of these facts it is not strictly accurate to say—as some writers do—that "the emergence of the individual" came with the Renaissance. What does date from the Renaissance is the appearance of men who made a considerable point about their individuality—who were even, one might say, rather theatrical about it. The men of the Renaissance found that it was exciting not only to be an individual but to talk about it, to preen one's self on it and to build a life around it.

The premonitions of modern individualism in the Renaissance were amply confirmed in the course of the next three centuries. The Reformation, the rise of science, the Enlightenment, the Indus-

trial Revolution—each in its way contributed powerfully to the dissolution of embeddedness as a social norm. Only as this process gained ground did it become possible to think of the free society as we conceive it today—a society in which every man is encouraged and expected to become a free and morally responsible individual.

By the nineteenth century the stage was set for some of the more extreme manifestations of the modern cult of the individual. We encounter on a wide scale the individual who is intensely conscious of—even preoccupied with—his individuality. Kierkegaard said, ". . . if I were to desire an inscription for my tombstone, I should desire none other than 'That individual'" (1859). We encounter the individual who harbors an intense and explicit hostility toward his own society, the individual who is capable of the deepest feelings of alienation with respect to his community.

The rebellious individualists of the nineteenth century paved the way for an army of followers. The circumstances of modern life are highly favorable to the achievement of certain kinds of individual detachment and autonomy. Mobility is one such circumstance; traditions are apt to be strongly linked to family and locality, and cannot maintain their strength among a transient population. Urbanization and modern communications produce a confrontation of differing traditions. In the resulting confusion of voices, the hold of all traditions is weakened. Under such conditions the authority of the church diminishes, as does the authority of parents. In addition, a powerful literature of rebellion and dissent has accumulated and is available to all young people.

By the time the nineteenth century

was finished, any young man intelligent enough and literate enough to know his own tradition could rebel in the grand manner. Today it doesn't even require intelligence or education. The opportunity for estrangement has been fully democratized.

Escape from what?

Against this background, any observer at the beginning of the twentieth century might easily have believed that the path was leading on to ever loftier heights of individual autonomy. But he would have been wrong. Two major developments of the twentieth century forced us to re-examine that view. First, it became apparent that modern mass society was placing new restraints on the individual, a subject we have already discussed. Second, new totalitarian forms emerged and enjoyed devastating success. Most contemporary discussions of the individual and the group are attempts to cope with one or the other of these developments.

It is not easy for young people today to comprehend the shocking impact on free men everywhere of the rise of modern totalitarianism. During the eighteenth, nineteenth and early twentieth centuries, the notion had become more and more widespread that man was indeed progressing toward freedom. It was believed that slowly but surely he was liberating himself from benighted traditions, tyrannical social institutions and power-hungry rulers. Then in the face of twentieth-century totalitarianism the ideology of freedom that had grown into such a sturdy plant over the centuries appeared to wither. The depressing thought occurred to many observers that there might be something in human nature that was not, after all,

antagonistic to tyranny; perhaps even something that welcomed it.

That this is not strictly a modern phenomenon is emphasized by E. R. Dodds (1957) in describing the rising vogue of astrology in Greece in the second century B.C.:

> . . . For a century or more the individual had been face to face with his own intellectual freedom, and now he turned tail and bolted from the horrid prospect—better the rigid determinism of the astrological Fate than that terrifying burden of daily responsibility (p. 246).

In short, it is necessary to examine the capacity of the individual to accept the responsibility of freedom and the conditions under which he will sacrifice his freedom to gain other objectives. These were the questions, among others, that concerned Erich Fromm in *Escape from Freedom* (1941). In that memorable book, Fromm was particularly interested in discovering why the Nazi and Fascist movements of the 1930's found it so easy to win adherents. He explained it by pointing out that the man who submits willingly to an authoritarian regime relieves himself of the anxieties and responsibilities of individual autonomy. Eric Hoffer, in *The True Believer* (1951), explored the same thesis.

Before we comment further on that view, it might be well to pause for some common-sense reflections on individual autonomy. One frequently encounters the romantic notion that the individual can be master of himself and his fate, divested of all hampering ties, a free-soaring bird. Such notions create grave confusion. Complete individual autonomy is unthinkable. The dictum of Theocritus, "Man will ever stand in need of man," is borne out by all of modern psychology and anthropology. Man's social character is fixed in his biological nature. For at least the first half dozen years of his life the human infant is utterly dependent on his elders. By the time those years have passed he possesses deeply rooted social habits. And beyond that, all that makes us most human—communication, self-awareness, sympathy, conscience—is dependent on interaction with other beings of our own kind. So, although we cannot accept the totalitarian notion that man's highest fulfillment is to become a faceless member of the group, neither can we accept romantic notions of complete individual autonomy.

For two generations now we have seen (but have not always understood) that when modern civilization loosens the ties that bind the individual to his tradition and family, it may result in greater freedom or it may result in alienation and loss of a sense of community. Similarly, when the individual seeks autonomy he may achieve freedom and moral responsibility or he may achieve only aggrandizement of the self, with all the accompanying disorders of self-regard: cancerous pride, uncontrolled inflation of his self-evaluations, unfulfillable self-expectations.

Most human beings *are* capable of achieving the measure of autonomy and mature individuality required by our conceptions of individual dignity and worth. But certain kinds of separation of *the self* from *all that is beyond the self* are inherently destructive and intolerable to human beings.

It is important to keep these facts in mind when we use the phrase "escape from freedom." Unless we specify what the individual is running away from and what form the running away takes, we may conceal under one label a wide range of distinctive behavior patterns.

It makes a great deal of difference whether the individual is really running away from freedom—i.e., from the moral responsibility of individual choice —or from the meaningless isolation that modern life so often thrusts on us and the arid egocentrism into which we are so often driven by romantic notions of individualism. If it is the latter, then the flight is justifiable, and the only question is what the individual chooses to run *to*. He may make the catastrophic mistake of submerging his individuality in mindless conformity to a cause or group. Or he may be wise enough to relate himself —as a free and morally responsible individual—to the larger social enterprise and to values that transcend the self. This will be difficult, of course, if the larger social enterprise is so fragmented or decayed that he cannot in fact relate himself to it.

The mature person must achieve a considerable measure of independence if he is to meet the standards implicit in our ideals of individual freedom and dignity; but at the same time he must acknowledge the limitations of the self, come to terms with his membership in the society at large and give his allegiance to values more comprehensive than his own needs.

Some modern intellectuals have not been at all helpful in clarifying these paradoxical facts. Oppressed by the threats to individuality inherent in our modern highly organized society and frightened by the specter of the organization man, they have tended to resent any hint that the individual is not sufficient to himself.

A meaningful relationship between the self and values that lie beyond the self is not incompatible with individual freedom. On the contrary, it is an essential ingredient of the inner strength that must characterize the free man. The man who has established emotional, moral and spiritual ties beyond the self gains the strength needed to endure the rigors of freedom. Let us not doubt that those rigors exist and that the strength is needed. Learned Hand was correct when he said that freedom is a burden to all but the rare individual (1952).

Paul Tillich, who has explored these relationships more profoundly than any other contemporary thinker, points out that the seemingly contradictory requirements of self-affirmation and commitments beyond the self are most nearly resolved when man sees himself as reflecting a larger harmony, as a bearer of the creative process of the universe, as a microcosmic participant in the creative process of the macrocosm (1958).

Individual commitment

The mature individual, then, makes commitments to something larger than the service of his "convulsive little ego," to use William James' memorable phrase—religious commitments, commitments to loved ones, to the social enterprise and to the moral order.

One can accept this fact without at the same time under-rating the pleasant things in life. One is rightly suspicious of those who tell poor people that they should be content with poverty, or hungry people that hunger is ennobling. Every human being should have the chance to enjoy the comforts and pleasures of good living. All we are saying here is that they are not enough. If they were, the large number of Americans who have been able to indulge their whims on a scale unprecedented in history would be deliriously happy. They would be telling one another of their unparalleled serenity and bliss instead of trading tranquilizer prescriptions.

It is widely believed that man in his natural state will do only what is required to achieve strictly physical satisfactions; but, as every anthropologist can testify, this is not true. Primitive man is intensely committed to his social group and to the moral order as he conceives it. Man has to be fairly well steeped in the artificialities of civilization before he is able to imagine that indulgence of physical satisfactions might be a complete way of life.

Anyone with eyes in his head can see that most men and women are prepared to (and do) undergo hardship and suffering in behalf of a meaningful goal. Indeed, they often actually court hardship in behalf of something they believe in. "Virtue will have naught to do with ease," wrote Montaigne. "It seeks a rough and thorny path."

This is not to say that the aims that man conceives beyond the needs of the self are necessarily ones that would win our admiration. They may be characterized by the highest idealism or they may be crude, even vicious. That is a salient feature of the problem. If we make the mistake of imagining that only man's material wants need be satisfied and offer him no significant meanings, he is likely to seize upon the first "meanings" which present themselves to him, however shallow and foolish, committing himself to false gods, to irrational political movements, to cults and to fads. It is essential that man's hunger for dedication be directed to worthy objects.

It would be wrong to leave the implication that man is a selfless creature who only wishes to place himself at the service of some higher ideal. Having rejected the oversimplified view of man's nature as wholly materialistic and selfish, we must not fall into the opposite error. Man is a complex and contradictory being, egocentric but inescapably involved with his fellow man, selfish but capable of superb selflessness. He is preoccupied with his own needs, yet finds no meaning in his life unless he relates himself to something more comprehensive than those needs. It is the tension between his egocentrism and his social and moral leanings that has produced much of the drama in human history.

Hunger for meaning

Man is in his very nature a seeker of meanings. He cannot help being so any more than he can help breathing or maintaining a certain body temperature. It is the way his central nervous system works.

In most societies and most ages, however primitive they may have been technologically, man's hunger for meaning was amply served. Though some of the religions, mythologies, and tribal superstitions with which the hunger for meaning was fed were crude and impoverished, they did purport to describe a larger framework in terms of which events might be interpreted.

With the arrival of the modern age many misguided souls conceived the notion that man could do without such nourishment. And for a breath-taking moment it did seem possible in view of the glittering promises which modern life offered. Under the banner of a beneficial modernity, the individual was to have security, money, power, sensual gratification and status as high as any man. He would be a solvent and eupeptic Walter Mitty in a rich and meaningless world.

But even (or especially) those who came close to achieving the dream never got over the nagging hunger for meaning.

At one level, man's search for meanings is objectively intellectual. He strives to organize what he knows into coherent patterns. Studies of perception have demonstrated that this tendency to organize experience is not an afterthought or the result of conscious impulse but an integral feature of the perceptual process. At the level of ideas, his tendency to organize meaningful wholes out of his experience is equally demonstrable. He tries to reduce the stream of experience to orderly sequences and patterns. He produces legends, theories, philosophies.

To an impressive degree, the theories of nature and the universe which man has developed are impersonal in the sense that they take no special account of man's own aspirations and status (though they are strictly dependent on his conceptualizing power and rarely wholly divorced from his values). Out of this impersonal search for meaning has come modern science.

But man has never been satisfied to let it go at that. He has throughout history shown a compelling need to arrive at conceptions of the universe *in terms of which he could regard his own life as meaningful*. He wants to know where *he* fits into the scheme of things. He wants to understand how the great facts of the objective world relate to *him* and what they imply for his behavior. He wants to know what significance may be found in his own existence, the succeeding generations of his kind and the vivid events of his inner life. He seeks some kind of meaningful framework in which to understand (or at least to reconcile himself to) the indignities of chance and circumstance and the fact of death. A number of philosophers and scientists have told him sternly that he must not expect answers to that sort of question, but he pays little heed. He wants, in the words of Kierkegaard, "a truth which is true for me" (1835). He seeks conceptions of the universe that give dignity, purpose and sense to his own existence.

When he fails in this effort he exhibits what Tillich describes as the anxiety of meaninglessness—"anxiety about the loss of an ultimate concern, of a meaning which gives meaning to all meanings" (1952). As Erikson has pointed out, the young person's search for identity is in some respects this sort of search for meaning (1956). It is a search for a framework in terms of which the young person may understand his own aims, his relation to his fellow man and his relation to larger purposes. In our society every individual is free to conduct this search on his own terms and to find, if he is lucky, the answer that is right for him.

Meaning, purpose and commitment

There are those who think of the meaning of life as resembling the answer to a riddle. One searches for years, and then some bright day one finds it, like the prize at the end of a treasure hunt. It is a profoundly misleading notion. The meanings in any life are multiple and varied. Some are grasped very early, some late; some have a heavy emotional component, some are strictly intellectual; some merit the label *religious*, some are better described as *social*. But each kind of meaning implies a relationship between the person and some larger system of ideas or values, a relationship involving obligations as well as rewards. In the individual life, meaning, purpose and commitment are inseparable. When a man succeeds in the search for identity he has found the answer not only to the question "Who am I?" but to a lot of other questions too: "What must I live up to? What are

my obligations? To what must I commit myself?"

So we are back to the subject of commitment. As we said earlier, a free society will not specify too closely the kinds of meaning different individuals will find or the things about which they should generate conviction. People differ in their goals and convictions and in the whole style of their commitment. We must ask that their goals fall within the moral framework to which we all pay allegiance, but we cannot prescribe the things that will unlock their deepest motivations. Those earnest spirits who believe that a man cannot be counted worthy unless he burns with zeal for civic affairs could not be more misguided. And we are wrong when we follow the current fashion of identifying moral strength too exclusively with fighting for a cause. Nothing could be more admirable nor more appealing to a performance-minded people such as ourselves. But such an emphasis hardly does justice to the rich variety of moral excellences that man has sought and occasionally achieved in the course of history.

A good many of the most valuable people in any society will never burn with zeal for anything except the integrity and health and well-being of their own families—and if they achieve those goals, we need ask little more of them. There are other valuable members of a society who will never generate conviction about anything beyond the productive output of their hands or minds—and a sensible society will be grateful for their contributions. Nor will it be too quick to define some callings as noble and some as ordinary. One may not quite accept Oliver Wendell Holmes' dictum—"Every calling is great when greatly pursued"—but the grain of truth is there.

11 How culture changes

GEORGE PETER MURDOCK

It is a fundamental characteristic of culture that, despite its essentially conservative nature, it does change over time and from place to place. Herein it differs strikingly from the social behavior of animals other than man. Among ants, for example, colonies of the same species differ little in behavior from one another and even, so far as we can judge from specimens embedded in amber, from their ancestors of fifty million years ago. In less than one million years man, by contrast, has advanced from the rawest savagery to civilization and has proliferated at least three thousand distinctive cultures.

The processes by which culture changes are by now reasonably well known to science. They cannot be understood, however, without a clear comprehension of the nature of culture.

Culture is the product of learning, rather than of heredity. The cultures of the world are systems of collective habits. The differences observable among them are the cumulative product of mass learning under diverse geographic and social conditions. Race and other biological factors influence culture only in so far as they affect the conditions under which learning occurs, as when the presence of people of markedly different physique operates as a factor in the development of race prejudice.

Culture is learned through precisely the same mechanism as that involved in all habit formation. Hunger, sex, fear, and other basic drives, as well as acquired motivations, impel human beings to act. Actions encounter either success or failure. With failure, especially when accompanied by pain or punishment, an action tends to be replaced by other behavior, and its probability of recurring under similar conditions is diminished. Success, on the other hand, increases the tendency of responses to occur when the same drive is again aroused in a like situation. With repeated success, responses are established as habits, and are progressively adapted to the situations in which they are appropriate.

A culture consists of habits that are shared by members of a society, whether this be a primitive tribe or a civilized nation. The sharing may be general throughout the society, as is normally the case with language habits. Often, however, it is limited to particular categories of people within the society. Thus persons of the same sex or age group, members of the same social class, association, or occupational group, and persons interacting with others in similar relationships commonly resemble one another in their social habits, though diverging behaviorally from persons in other categories.

The social sharing of habits has several causes. The fact that the situations under which behavior is acquired are similar for many individuals conduces in itself to parallel learning. Even more im-

Reprinted from Chapter 11 of H. L. Shapiro (Ed.), **Man, Culture, and Society** (Copyright © 1956 by Oxford University Press, New York), pp. 247–60, with permission of the author and the publisher.

portant is the fact that each generation inculcates on the next, through education, the cultural habits which it has found satisfying and adaptive. Finally, the members of any society exercise pressure upon one another, through formal and informal means of social control, to conform to standards of behavior which are considered right and appropriate. This is particularly true of behavior in interpersonal relationships, where the success or failure of an action depends upon the reaction of another person to it, rather than, for example, upon its adaptiveness to the innate qualities of natural objects. Once one has acquired a limited number of stereotyped patterns of social behavior one is equipped to cope successfully with widely diversified social situations, and one is also provided with a body of reliable expectations regarding the probable responses of others to one's own behavior. This gives confidence and spares the individual an immense amount of individualized learning, which is ever a painful process. It is with good reason, therefore, that every society lays great stress on social conformity.

The habits that are variously shared within a society, and which constitute its culture, fall into two major classes, namely, habits of action and habits of thought. These may be termed, respectively, "customs" and "collective ideas." Customs include such readily observable modes of behavior as etiquette, ceremonial, and the techniques of manipulating material objects. Collective ideas are not directly observable but must be inferred from their expression in language and other overt behavior. They include such things as practical knowledge, religious beliefs, and social values. Moreover, they embrace a mass of rules

or definitions, which specify for each custom the persons who may and may not observe it, the circumstances in which it is and is not appropriate, and the limits and permissible variations of the behavior itself. Collective ideas also include a body of social expectations— anticipations of how others will respond to one's own behavior, especially of the sanctions, i.e., social rewards and punishments that can be expected from conformity and deviation. With every custom and with every organized cluster of customs, such as a "culture complex" or "institution," there is ordinarily associated a mass of collective ideas.

Actual social behavior, as it is observed in real life, must be carefully distinguished from culture, which consists of habits or tendencies to act and not of actions themselves. Though largely determined by habits, actual behavior is also affected by the physiological and emotional state of the individual, the intensity of his drives, and the particular external circumstances. Since no two situations are ever exactly alike, actual behavior fluctuates considerably, even when springing from the same habit. A description of a culture is consequently never an account of actual social behavior but is rather a reconstruction of the collective habits which underlie it.

From the point of view of cultural change, however, actual or observable behavior is of primary importance. Whenever social behavior persistently deviates from established cultural habits in any direction, it results in modifications first in social expectations, and then in customs, beliefs, and rules. Gradually, in this way, collective habits are altered and the culture comes to accord better with the new norms of actual behavior.

Changes in social behavior, and hence in culture, normally have their origin in some significant alteration in the life conditions of a society. Any event which changes the situations under which collective behavior occurs, so that habitual actions are discouraged and new responses are favored, may lead to cultural innovations. Among the classes of events that are known to be especially influential in producing cultural change are increases or decreases in population, changes in the geographical environment, migrations into new environments, contacts with peoples of differing culture, natural and social catastrophes such as floods, crop failures, epidemics, wars, and economic depressions, accidental discoveries, and even such biographical events as the death or rise to power of a strong political leader.

The events which produce cultural change by altering the conditions under which social behavior proves adaptive, i.e., is or is not rewarded, are invariably historical, i.e., specific with respect to time and place. Events occurring at different places and times may resemble one another, however, and exert parallel influences upon different cultures. It is thus possible to view changes in culture either in relation to their spatial and temporal setting or in relation to comparable events wherever and whenever they have occurred. The former or "historical" approach answers such questions as what? when? and where? The latter or "scientific" approach, by illuminating the processes by which change occurs, answers the question how? Both approaches are valid and completely complementary.

Historical anthropologists commonly discuss particular traits of culture, such as the use of tobacco, the wheel, the domesticated horse, the alphabet, or money, treating of their "invention" at specific times and places and of their "diffusion" from the points of origin to other parts of the world. Since our problem is to describe *how* culture changes, we must abandon the bird's-eye view of the historian and examine the processes within societies by which all changes, and not merely particular ones, take place. These processes may be conveniently grouped under the terms "innovation," "social acceptance," "selective elimination," and "integration."

Cultural change begins with the process of *innovation*, the formation of a new habit by a single individual which is subsequently accepted or learned by other members of his society. An innovation originates through the ordinary psychological mechanism of learning, and differs from purely individual habits only in the fact that it comes to be socially shared. It is nevertheless useful to distinguish several important variants of the process.

An innovation may be called a *variation* when it represents a slight modification of pre-existing habitual behavior under the pressure of gradually changing circumstances. The slow evolution in the forms of manufactured objects over time usually represents an accumulation of variations. In the same manner, tattooing can be extended over a wider area of the body, additional barbs may be added to a harpoon, skirts may be lengthened or shortened, folk tales may grow by accretion, or ceremonial may become increasingly elaborate and formalized. Variation occurs in all cultures at all times. The individual increments of change are often so slight as to be almost imperceptible, but their cumulative effect over long periods may be immense.

When innovation involves the transfer of elements of habitual behavior from one situational context to another, or their combination into new syntheses, it is called *invention*. At least some degree of creativeness is always present. Most of the important technological innovations are of this type. Thus the invention of the airplane involved the synthesis of such elements as the wings of a glider, an internal-combustion engine from an automobile, and an adaptation of a ship's propeller. Though less well known, inventions are equally common in the non-material aspects of culture. The city-manager plan, for example, represents an obvious transfer of techniques of business management to the sphere of local government, and most forms of religious worship are modeled on behavior toward persons of high social status, e.g., sacrifice upon bribery, prayer upon petitions, laudation upon flattery, ritual upon etiquette.

Since invention always involves a new synthesis of old habits, it is dependent upon the existing content of the culture. A synthesis cannot occur if the elements which it combines are not present in the culture. It is for this reason that parallel inventions so rarely occur among unconnected peoples of differing culture. With the exception of such simple and obvious combinations as the hafting of tools, anthropologists know of only a handful of genuine inventions that have been arrived at independently by historically unrelated peoples. Among them perhaps the most famous are the fire piston, invented by the Malays and a French physicist, and the dome, developed by the ancient Romans from the arch and independently invented by the Eskimos for their snow igloos.

Among peoples of the same or related cultures, on the other hand, parallel inventions are extraordinarily common.

The culture provides the same constituent elements to many people, and if one person does not achieve the synthesis others are likely to do so. The Patent Office furnishes thousands of examples. In one famous instance, the telephone, applications for a patent were received on the same day from two independent inventors, Bell and Gray. Another noted case is the independent formulation of the theory of natural selection by Darwin and Wallace. So common is this phenomenon that scientists often live in dread of the anticipation of their discoveries by rivals. Parallel invention thus appears to be frequent and almost inevitable among peoples of similar culture, though so rare as to be almost non-existent among peoples of different culture.

A third type of innovation may be called *tentation*. Unlike the previous types, which merely modify or recombine elements of habit already in existence, tentation may give rise to elements that show little or no continuity with the past. The mechanism by which these are acquired is that which psychologists call "trial-and-error learning." Tentation may occur in any situation in which established habits prove ineffective and individuals are so strongly motivated that they try out other modes of behavior in a search for an adequate solution to their problems. They will ordinarily try out first a number of variations and recombinations of existing habitual responses, but if all of these fail they will resort to "random behavior," in the course of which they may accidentally hit upon some novel response which solves the problem and thereby becomes established as a new cultural element.

Crises are particularly conducive to tentation. In a famine, for instance, people try out all sorts of things that they have never eaten before, and if some of them prove nutritious and tasty they may be added to the normal diet. An epidemic similarly leads to a search for new medicines, and both primitive and civilized peoples have discovered useful remedies in this way. War also leads to improvisation, as do economic crises. The New Deal in the recent history of the United States, for example, reveals numerous instances of tentation. Scientific experimentation, it should be pointed out, is often a form of controlled tentation, as when a new series of chemical compounds are systematically put to test. The saying that "necessity is the mother of invention" applies more forcefully to tentation than to invention proper.

When accidental discoveries lead to cultural innovations, the process is commonly that of tentation. The origin of the boomerang in aboriginal Australia will serve as an example. Over much of that continent the natives used curved throwing sticks to kill or stun small animals, and in a limited part of the area the true boomerang was used for this purpose. Almost certainly the first boomerang was produced by sheer accident in the attempt to fashion an ordinary throwing stick. Observing the unique behavior of the particular stick in flight, the maker and his fellows doubtless attempted to duplicate it. They must have resorted to tentation, or trial-and-error behavior, until they eventually succeeded, and thereby established boomerang manufacture as a habit. The history of modern "inventions" is full of such instances, the discovery of the photographic plate by Daguerre being one of the most familiar examples.

Tentation also accounts for a type of cultural parallel which is distinct from genuine independent invention. There are certain universal problems which every people must solve and for which there are a limited number of easy and obvious solutions, so that peoples in different parts of the world have often hit upon the same solution quite independently. Rules of descent provide a good illustration. In all societies, each individual must be affiliated with a group of relatives to whom he regards himself as most closely akin and to whom he can turn for aid in time of need. There are only three possibilities: patrilineal descent, which relates an individual to kinsmen in the male line; matrilineal descent, which affiliates him with relatives through females; and bilateral descent, which associates him with a group of his closest relatives irrespective of their line of descent. Every society must choose one of these alternatives or some combination thereof, and, since the possibilities are limited to three, many peoples have, of necessity, arrived independently at the same cultural solution. Funeral customs present another example, since there are only a limited number of feasible ways of disposing of a dead body. In all such instances, if a society is compelled for any reason to abandon its previous custom it will inevitably, through tentation, arrive at an alternative solution which other peoples have independently adopted.

The fourth and last type of innovation is *cultural borrowing*, which is what the historical anthropologist, with his bird's-eye view, calls "diffusion." In this case the innovator is not the originator of a new habit, but its introducer. The habit has previously been part of the culture of another society; the innovator is merely the first member of his social group to adopt it. From the point of view of psychology, cultural borrowing is merely a special case of the learning process known as "imitation." The innovator, faced with a situation in which the shared habits of his own society are not fully satisfactory, copies behavior which he has observed in members of another society, instead of resorting to variation, invention, or tentation to solve his problem.

Of all forms of innovation, cultural borrowing is by far the most common and important. The overwhelming majority of the elements in any culture are the result of borrowing. Modern American culture provides a good illustration, as can be shown by a few random examples. Our language comes from England, our alphabet from the Phoenicians, our numerical system from India, and paper and printing from China. Our family organization and system of real property derive from medieval Europe. Our religion is a composite of elements largely assembled from the ancient Hebrews, Egyptians, Babylonians, and Persians. Metal coinage comes from Lydia, paper money from China, checks from Persia. Our system of banking, credit, loans, discounts, mortgages, et cetera, is derived in its essentials from ancient Babylonia, with modern elaborations from Italy and England. Our architecture is still largely Greek, Gothic, Georgian, et cetera. Our favorite flavors in ice creams, vanilla and chocolate, are both borrowed from the Aztecs of Mexico and were unknown to Europeans before the conquest by Cortez. Tea comes from China, coffee from Ethiopia, tobacco from the American Indians. Our domesticated animals and plants, virtually without exception, are borrowed. If the reader were to make a list of absolutely everything he eats during the next week, analysis would probably show that one third are products that were already

cultivated in Neolithic times and that at least two thirds were being raised at the time of Christ, and it would be surprising if the list contained any item that was not cultivated for food somewhere in the world when Columbus sailed for America.

Our own culture is not unique in this respect, for it is doubtful whether there is a single culture known to history or anthropology that has not owed at least ninety per cent of its constituent elements to cultural borrowing. The reason is not far to seek. Any habit that has become established in a culture has been tried out by many people and found satisfactory. When a society finds itself in a dilemma, therefore, the chances that an element already present in the culture of another people will turn out to be an adequate solution to its own problem are vastly greater than those of any random and untested innovation of another type. Cultural borrowing is thus highly economical, and most peoples tend to ransack the cultural resources of their neighbors for adaptive practices before they resort to invention or tentation.

Cultural borrowing depends upon contact. Obviously the opportunity for borrowing is lacking in the case of a completely isolated society. Other factors being equal, the extent to which one culture will borrow from another is proportionate to the intensity and duration of the social intercourse between their bearers. Contact need not always be face-to-face, however, for there are numerous instances of cultural borrowing at a distance through the medium of written language or through copying of articles received by trade. By and large, however, societies borrow mainly from their immediate neighbors, with the result that the products of diffusion are ordinarily clustered in geographically contiguous areas.

Trade, missionary enterprise, and political conquest create conditions conducive to cultural borrowing. Peculiarly important, however, is intermarriage, for this brings individuals of differing culture together within the family, where children can learn from both parents. Diffusion then proceeds through the socialization process, which produces far more perfect copying than does cultural borrowing on the adult level. The American "melting pot" operates largely through this mechanism. Primitive peoples practicing local exogamy, i.e., requiring individuals to obtain spouses from another village or band, commonly reveal considerable cultural uniformity over wide areas, as in aboriginal Australia and among the Indians of the Northwest Coast. By contrast, in areas like Melanesia and Central California where marriage normally takes place within the community, even villages a few miles apart may differ strikingly in dialect and customs. In the one case culture is diffused through the same process by which it is transmitted; in the other, even adult contacts tend to be restricted to a minimum.

Incentive—a need or drive—is as essential in cultural borrowing as in other types of innovation. A people rarely borrows an alien cultural element when they already possess a trait which satisfactorily fills the same need. Thus the blubber lamp of the Eskimos was not borrowed by the Indians to the south, who had plenty of wood for fires to heat and light their dwellings. On the other hand, the extraordinarily rapid diffusion of tobacco over the earth after the discovery of America reflected the general absence of competing traits. It has been observed that the first individuals in a

society to borrow alien customs are likely to be the discontented, underprivileged, and maladjusted. Thus in India Christian missionaries have made many more converts among the "untouchables" than in the higher strata of society, and in our own country fascism and communism attract an unduly high proportion of unsuccessful and neurotic people.

The presence in a receiving society of some of the habit elements involved in a new trait greatly facilitates borrowing. It is for this reason that diffusion occurs most readily among peoples of similar culture, who already share many elements of habit. Thus Englishmen and Americans borrow more frequently and easily from each other than from Russians, Chinese, or Hottentots. Conversely, aboriginal peoples are greatly handicapped in taking over the complex technology of modern civilization. They cannot, for example, begin to manufacture the steel products which they want without also taking over such things as blast furnaces and rolling mills.

Cultural borrowing will occur only if the new habit is demonstrably rewarding. The native quickly adopts steel knives and axes from the white man because their superiority to his former stone implements becomes immediately apparent. On the other hand, Europeans were slow to borrow paper manufacture from the Chinese because the advantages of paper over parchment appeared very slight at first. The Chinese and Japanese have not yet adopted the alphabet from western civilization because, however great its ultimate advantages, it would impose heavy burdens and discomforts upon all literate persons during the necessary period of readjustment. Geographic and climatic factors may prevent diffusion by withholding or reducing the possibilities of reward, and social prejudices such as ingrained conservatism may counterbalance potential advantages by inflicting disapprobation upon innovators.

Borrowing need not be exact. Oftentimes, indeed, all that is borrowed is the external "form" of a custom and not its "meaning," i.e., the collective ideas associated with it. The familiar caricature of the cannibal chief wearing a silk hat provides a good illustration. Frequently an imperfect copy is quite adequate. Thus when the Plains Indians took over horses and riding equipment from the Spaniards they omitted the horseshoe, which was quite unnecessary on the prairie. Sometimes changes are imposed by the conditions of the geographical environment. When the Iroquois Indians adopted the birchbark canoe from their Algonkian neighbors, for example, they altered the material to elm bark because of the scarcity of birch trees in their habitat. Frequently cultural factors favor a modification. The original Phoenician alphabet lacked characters for vowels, the nature of their language being such that consonant signs sufficed for the identification of words. Since this was not true of the Greek language, when the Greeks borrowed the Phoenician alphabet they converted characters for which they had no need into symbols for vowels.

Modifications are so common in cultural borrowing that authorities like Malinowski have regarded the process as scarcely less creative than other forms of innovation. Often, indeed, it is inextricably blended with invention or tentation. This is well illustrated in instances of "stimulus diffusion," in which only the general idea of an alien cultural trait is borrowed, the specific form being supplied by improvisation. Thus a famous Cherokee chief named Sequoyah, though an illiterate man, had noticed that white men could somehow understand messages from pieces of paper on which peculiar marks were inscribed, and he came to the conclusion that this would be a useful skill for his own people to acquire. He therefore set himself the task of devising a system of marks by which the Cherokee language could be written. Inventing some signs of his own and copying some from pieces of printed matter —numbers and punctuation marks as well as letters, upside down or on their sides as often as upright—he produced a novel form of writing, a syllabary rather than an alphabet, which his tribesmen learned and still use to this day.

The second major process in cultural change is *social acceptance*. So long as an innovation, whether original or borrowed, is practiced by the innovator alone in his society, it is an individual habit and not an element of culture. To become the latter it must be accepted by others; it must be socially shared. Social acceptance begins with the adoption of a new habit by a small number of individuals. From this point it may spread until it becomes part of the subculture of a family, clan, local community, or other sub-group, or until it becomes a "specialty" characteristic of persons belonging to a particular occupational, kinship, age-graded, or other status category, or until it becomes an "alternative" widely but optionally practiced. Eventually it may.even become a "universal," shared by all members of the society. The term "degrees of cultural saturation" has been proposed for the various steps in social acceptance.

The learning mechanism involved in social acceptance is imitation, as in the case of cultural borrowing, but the model whose behavior is copied is a member of one's own rather than another society.

So similar are the two processes that the term "diffusion" is often applied to both; social acceptance is called "internal" or "vertical" diffusion to differentiate it from cultural borrowing, which is termed "external" or "horizontal" diffusion. With minor exceptions, most of what has previously been stated about the latter process applies equally to the former. Since close contact and similarity of culture can be taken for granted, however, copying is usually far more exact, and this is accentuated by social control.

A factor of considerable importance in social acceptance is the prestige of the innovator and of the group who are first to imitate him. Changes advocated by an admired political or religious leader are readily adopted, whereas few will follow an unpopular or despised innovator. Clothing styles accepted by "the four hundred" quickly diffuse throughout the masses, but the "zoot suit" does not spread from the taxi dance hall to the ballroom. Women imitate men more readily than *vice versa*. In our own society, for example, many women have adopted masculine garments, smoking and drinking habits, and occupations, but there appears to be no concerted movement among men to wear skirts, use cosmetics, or apply for positions as nurses, governesses, or baby-sitters.

Selective elimination constitutes a third major process of cultural change. Every innovation that has been socially accepted enters, as it were, into a competition for survival. So long as it proves more rewarding than its alternatives a cultural habit will endure, but when it ceases to bring comparable satisfactions it dwindles and eventually disappears. The process superficially resembles that of natural selection in organic evolution. It should be noted, however, that cul-

tural traits do not compete directly with one another but are competitively tested in the experience of those who practice them. Oftentimes the competition is carried on between organized groups of people with contrasting customs and beliefs, as between nations, political parties, religious sects, or social and economic classes, and the issue is decided indirectly by the victory of one group over the other. By and large, the cultural elements that are eliminated through trial and error or social competition are the less adaptive ones, so that the process is as definitely one of the survival of the fittest as is that of natural selection.

Few of the genuine gains of culture history—the achievements of technology, of science, of man's control over nature—have ever been lost. The so-called "lost arts of antiquity" are largely mythical. To be sure, particular peoples have declined in civilization, but not until they have passed on their contributions to others. What man has lost, in the main, is a mass of maladaptive and barbarous practices, inefficient techniques, and outworn superstitions. New errors arise, of course, in each generation, but it is comforting to realize that the mortality of error is vastly greater than that of truth.

It is the genuine achievements of man that anthropologists have in mind when they say that culture is cumulative, comparing culture history to the growth of a snowball as it is rolled down a hill. Even achievements that are superseded rarely disappear. Today the electric light has proved superior to earlier methods of lighting, but the gas mantle, the kerosene lamp, and the tallow candle still survive in out-of-the-way places or under special conditions. Survival is often assured through a change in function. The use of outmoded weapons has been preserved, for example, in athletic sports like fencing and archery and in boyhood toys such as the sling and the peashooter. Other ancient usages survive in legal, religious, and academic ceremonial. Written records, of course, preserve much of the culture of the past from oblivion. Our libraries bulge with the puerilities as well as the achievements of history.

The fourth and last important process of cultural change is that of *integration*. The shared habits that constitute a culture not only fluctuate in their degree of social acceptance, and compete for survival, but they also become progressively adapted to one another so that they tend to form an integrated whole. They exhibit what Sumner has called "a strain toward consistency." Every innovation alters in some respect the situations under which certain other forms of habitual behavior occur, and leads to adaptive changes in the latter. Similarly it must, in its turn, be adjusted to modifications elsewhere in the culture. While each such change is in itself, of course, an innovation, their reciprocal interaction and cumulative effect deserve special recognition as an integrative process.

The history of the automobile during the present century in our own culture provides an excellent example. The changes brought about by this technological invention are described by Professor Leslie Spier (1956). A similar story could be told for other modern innovations such as the telephone, the airplane, the radio, and electrical household gadgets, and all of them pale before the potentialities of atomic energy.

Certain anthropologists have erroneously assumed that the elements of any culture are in a state of nearly perfect integration, or equilibrium, at all times. Actually, however, perfect equilibrium is never achieved or even approached. The adjustment of other elements of culture to an innovation, and of it to them, requires time—often years or even generations. In the meantime other innovations have appeared and set in motion new processes of integration. At any given time, therefore, a culture exhibits numerous instances of uncompleted integrative processes as well as examples of others which have been carried through to relatively satisfactory completion. What we always encounter is a strain toward internal adaptation, never its full realization.

The period of time which must elapse between the acceptance of an innovation and the completion of the integrative readjustments which follow in its train Ogburn has aptly called "cultural lag." During such a period of lag people attempt, through variation, invention, tentation, and cultural borrowing, to modify old customs and ideas to accord with the new, and to adjust the new to the old, so as to eliminate inconsistencies and sources of friction and irritation. In a modern democratic society, politics is a major scene of such efforts.

The net effect of the various processes of cultural change is to adapt the collective habits of human societies progressively over time to the changing conditions of existence. Change is always uncomfortable and often painful, and people frequently become discouraged with its slowness or even despair of achieving any genuine improvement. Neither history nor anthropology, however, gives grounds for pessimism. However halting or harsh it may appear to participants, cultural change is always adaptive and usually progressive. It is also inevitable, and will endure as long as the earth can support human life. Nothing—not even an atomic war—can destroy civilization.

12 The nature of assimilation and the theory of the melting pot

MILTON M. GORDON

Let us, first of all, imagine a hypothetical situation in which a host country, to which we shall give the fictitious name of "Sylvania," is made up of a population all members of which are of the same race, religion, and previous national extraction. Cultural behavior is relatively uniform except for social class divisions. Similarly, the groups and institutions, i.e., the "social structure," of Sylvanian society are divided and differentiated only on a social class basis. Into this country, through immigration, comes a group of people who differ in previous national background and in religion and who thus have different cultural patterns from those of the host society. We shall call them the Mundovians. Let us further imagine that within the span of another generation, this population group of Mundovian national origin (now composed largely of the second generation, born in Sylvania) has taken on completely the cultural patterns of the Sylvanians, has thrown off any sense of peoplehood based on Mundovian nationality, has changed its religion to that of the Sylvanians, has eschewed the formation of any communal organizations made up principally or exclusively of Mundovians, has entered and been hospitably accepted into the social cliques, clubs, and institutions of the Sylvanians at various class levels, has intermarried freely and frequently with the Sylvanians, encounters no prejudice or discrimination (one reason being that they are no longer distinguishable culturally or structurally from the rest of the Sylvanian population), and raises no value conflict issues in Sylvanian public life. Such a situation would represent the ultimate form of assimilation—complete assimilation to the culture and society of the host country. Note that we are making no judgment here of either the sociological desirability, feasibility, or moral rightness of such a goal. We are simply setting it up as a convenient abstraction—an "ideal type"— ideal not in the value sense of being most desirable but in the sense of representing the various elements of the concept and their interrelationships in "pure," or unqualified, fashion (the methodological device of the "ideal type" was developed and named by the German sociologist, Max Weber).

Looking at this example, we may discern that seven major variables are involved in the process discussed—in other words, seven basic subprocesses have taken place in the assimilation of the Mundovians to Sylvanian society. These may be listed in the following manner. We may say that the Mundovians have

1. changed their cultural patterns (including religious belief and observance) to those of the Sylvanians;
2. taken on large-scale primary group

Excerpted from Chapters 3 and 5 of **Assimilation in American Life** (Copyright © 1964 by Oxford University Press, New York), with permission of the author and the publisher.

relationships with the Sylvanians, i.e., have entered fully into the societal network of groups and institutions, or societal structure, of the Sylvanians;

3. have intermarried and interbred fully with the Sylvanians;
4. have developed a Sylvanian, in place of a Mundovian, sense of peoplehood, or ethnicity;
5. have reached a point where they encounter no discriminatory behavior;
6. have reached a point where they encounter no prejudiced attitudes;
7. do not raise by their demands concerning the nature of Sylvanian public or civic life any issues involving value and power conflict with the original Sylvanians (for example, the issue of birth control).

Each of these steps or subprocesses may be thought of as constituting a particular stage or aspect of the assimilation process. Thus we may, in shorthand fashion, consider them as types of assimilation and characterize them accordingly. We may, then, speak, for instance, of "structural assimilation" to refer to the entrance of Mundovians into primary group relationships with the Sylvanians, or "identificational assimilation" to describe the taking on of a sense of Sylvanian peoplehood. For some of the particular assimilation subprocesses there are existing special terms, already reviewed. For instance, cultural or behavioral assimilation is what has already been defined as "acculturation." The full list of assimilation subprocesses or variables with their general names, and special names, if any, is given in Table 1.

Not only is the assimilation process mainly a matter of degree, but, obviously, each of the stages or subprocesses

distinguished above may take place in varying degrees.

In the example just used there has been assimilation in all respects to the society and culture which had exclusively occupied the nation up to the time of the immigrants' arrival. In other instances there may be other subsocieties and subcultures already on the scene when the new group arrives but one of these subsocieties and its way of life is dominant by virtue of original settlement, the preemption of power, or overwhelming predominance in numbers. In both cases we need a term to stand for the dominant subsociety which provides the standard to which other groups adjust or measure their relative degree of adjustment. We have tentatively used the term "host society"; however, a more neutral designation would be desirable. A. B. Hollingshead, in describing the class structure of New Haven, has used the term "core group" to refer to the Old Yankee families of colonial, largely Anglo-Saxon ancestry who have traditionally dominated the power and status system of the community, and who provide the "master cultural mould" for the class system of the other groups in the city (1952; 1958). Joshua Fishman has referred to the "core society" and the "core culture" in American life, this core being "made up essentially of White Protestant, middle-class clay, to which all other particles are attracted" (1961). If there is anything in American life which can be described as an over-all American culture which serves as a reference point for immigrants and their children, it can best be described, it seems to us, as the middle-class cultural patterns of, largely, white Protestant, Anglo-Saxon origins, leaving aside for the moment the question of minor reciprocal influences on this culture exercised by the cultures of later entry into the United States, and ignoring also, for this purpose, the distinction between the upper-middle class and the lower-middle class cultural worlds.

There is a point on which I particularly do not wish to be misunderstood. I am not for one moment implying that the contribution of the non-Anglo-Saxon stock to the nature of American civilization has been minimal or slight. Quite the contrary. The qualitative record of achievement in industry, business, the professions, and the arts by Americans whose ancestors came from countries and traditions which are not British, or in many cases not even closely similar to British, is an overwhelmingly favorable one, and with reference to many individuals, a thoroughly brilliant one. Taken together with the substantial quantitative impact of these non-Anglo-Saxon groups on American industrial and agricultural development and on the demographic dimensions of the society, this record reveals an America in mid-twentieth century whose greatness rests on the contributions of many races, religions, and national backgrounds (see Handlin & Handlin, 1955). My point, however, is that, with some exceptions, as the immigrants and their children

TABLE 1
THE ASSIMILATION VARIABLES

Subprocess or condition	Type or stage of assimilation	Special Term
Change of cultural patterns to those of host society	Cultural or behavioral assimilation	Acculturation [1]
Large-scale entrance into cliques, clubs, and institutions of host society, on primary group level	Structural assimilation	None
Large-scale intermarriage	Marital assimilation	Amalgamation [2]
Development of sense of peoplehood based exclusively on host society	Identificational assimilation	None
Absence of prejudice	Attitude receptional assimilation	None
Absence of discrimination	Behavior receptional assimilation	None
Absence of value and power conflict	Civic assimilation	None

[1] The question of reciprocal cultural influence will be considered later.
[2] My use of the term here is not predicated on the diversity in race of the two population groups which are intermarrying and interbreeding. With increasing understanding of the meaning of "race" and its thoroughly relative and arbitrary nature as a scientific term, this criterion becomes progressively less important. We may speak of the "amalgamation" or intermixture of the two "gene pools" which the two populations represent, regardless of how similar or divergent these two gene pools may be.

have become Americans, their contributions, as laborers, farmers, doctors, lawyers, scientists, artists, etc., have been made *by way* of cultural patterns that have taken their major impress from the mould of the overwhelmingly English character of the dominant Anglo-Saxon culture or subculture in America, whose dominion dates from colonial times and whose *cultural* domination in the United States has never been seriously threatened. One must make a distinction between influencing the cultural patterns themselves and contributing to the progress and development of the society. It is in the latter area that the influence of the immigrants and their children in the United States has been decisive.

Accordingly, I shall follow Fishman's usage in referring to middle-class white Protestant Americans as constituting the "core society," or in my terms, the "core subsociety," and the cultural patterns of this group as the "core culture" or "core subculture." I shall use Hollingshead's term "core group" to refer to the white Protestant element at any social class level.

Let us now, for a moment, return to our fictitious land of Sylvania and imagine an immigration of Mundovians with a decidedly different outcome. In this case the Sylvanians accept many new behavior patterns and values from the Mundovians, just as the Mundovians change many of their ways in conformance with Sylvanian customs, this interchange taking place with appropriate modifications and compromises, and in this process a new cultural system evolves which is neither exclusively Sylvanian nor Mundovian but a mixture of both. This is a cultural blend, the result of the "melting pot," which has melted down the cultures of the two groups in the same societal container, as it were,

and formed a new cultural product with standard consistency. This process has, of course, also involved thorough social mixing in primary as well as secondary groups and a large-scale process of intermarriage. The melting pot has melted the two groups into one, societally and culturally.

Whether such a process as just described is feasible or likely of occurrence is beside the point here. It, too, is an "ideal type," an abstraction against which we can measure the realities of what actually happens. Our point is that the seven variables of the assimilation process which we have isolated can be measured against the "melting pot" goal as well as against the "adaptation to the core society and culture" goal. That is, assuming the "melting pot" goal, we can then inquire how much acculturation of both groups has taken place to form such a blended culture, how much social structural mixture has taken place, and so on.[3] We now have a model of assimilation with seven variables which can be used to analyze the assimilation process with reference to either of two variant goal-systems: (1) "adaptation to the core society and culture," and (2) the "melting pot." Theoretically, it would be possible to apply the analysis model of variables with reference to carrying out the goal-system of "cultural pluralism" as well. However, this would be rather premature at this point since the concept of cultural pluralism is itself so meagerly understood.

Let us now apply this model of assim-

[3] I am indebted to Professor Richard D. Lambert of the University of Pennsylvania for pointing out to me that my array of assimilation variables must be applied with reference to the basic assimilation goal. In my original scheme of presentation I had implicitly applied it only to the goal-system of "adaptation to the core society and culture."

ilation analysis in tentative fashion to selected "minority" ethnic groups on the American scene. The applied paradigm presented in Table 2 allows us to record and summarize a great deal of information compactly and comparatively. We shall deal here, for illustrative purposes, with four groups: Negroes, Jews, Catholics (excluding Negro and Spanish-speaking Catholics), and Puerto Ricans. The basic goal-referent will be "adaptation to core society and culture." The entries in the table cells may be regarded, at this point, as hypotheses. Qualifying comments will be made in the footnotes to the table. The reader may wish to refer back to Table 1 for definitions of each column heading.

One of the tasks of sociological theory is not only to identify the factors or variables present in any given social process or situation, but also to hypothesize how these variables may be related to each other. Let us look at the seven assimilation variables from this point of view. We note that in Table 2, of the four ethnic groups listed, only one, the Puerto Ricans, are designated as being substantially unassimilated culturally. The Puerto Ricans are the United States' newest immigrant group of major size. If we now examine the entries for the Negro, one of America's oldest minorities, we find that assimilation has not taken place in most of the other variables, but with allowance for social class factors, *has* taken place culturally. These two facts in juxtaposition should give us a clue to the relation of the cultural assimilation variable to all the others. This relationship may be stated as follows: (1) *cultural assimilation, or acculturation, is likely to be the first of the types of assimilation to occur when a minority group arrives on the scene; and (2) cultural assimilation, or acculturation, of* *the minority group may take place even when none of the other types of assimilation occurs simultaneously or later, and this condition of "acculturation only" may continue indefinitely.*

If we examine the history of immigration into the United States, both of these propositions are seen to be borne out. After the birth of the republic, as each succeeding wave of immigration, first from Northern and Western Europe, later from Southern and Eastern Europe and the Orient, has spread over America, the first process that has occurred has been the taking on of the English language and American behavior patterns, even while the creation of the immigrant colonies sealed off their members from extensive primary contacts with "core society" Americans and even when prejudice and discrimination against the minority have been at a high point. While this process is only partially completed in the immigrant generation itself, with the second and succeeding generations, exposed to the American public school system and speaking English as their native tongue, the impact of the American acculturation process has been overwhelming; the rest becomes a matter of social class mobility and the kind of acculturation that such mobility demands. On the other hand, the success of the acculturation process has by no means guaranteed entry of each minority into the primary groups and institutions—that is, the subsociety—of the white Protestant group. With the exception of white Protestant immigrant stock from Northern and Western Europe—I am thinking here particularly of the Scandinavians, Dutch, and Germans—by and large such structural mixture on the primary level has not taken place. Nor has such acculturation success eliminated prejudice and discrimination or in many cases led to large-scale intermarriage with the core society.

The only qualifications of my generalizations about the rapidity and success of the acculturation process that the American experience suggests are these: (1) If a minority group is spatially isolated and segregated (whether voluntarily or not) in a rural area, as is the case with the American Indians still on reservations, even the acculturation process will be very slow; and (2) Unusually marked discrimination, such as that which has been faced by the American Negro, if it succeeds in keeping vast numbers of the minority group deprived of educational and occupational opportunities and thus predestined to remain in a lower-class setting, may indefinitely retard the acculturation process for the group. Even in the case of the American Negro, however, from the long view or perspective of American history, this ef-

TABLE 2

PARADIGM OF ASSIMILATION

APPLIED TO SELECTED GROUPS IN THE UNITED STATES—

BASIC GOAL REFERENT: ADAPTATION TO CORE SOCIETY AND CULTURE

Group	Type of assimilation						
	Cultural [4]	Structural	Marital	Identificational	Attitude Receptional	Behavior Receptional	Civic
Negroes	Variation by class [5]	No	No	No	No	No	Yes
Jews	Substantially Yes	No	Substantially No	No	No	Partly	Mostly
Catholics (excluding Negro and Spanish-speaking)	Substantially Yes	Partly (variation by area)	Partly	No	Partly	Mostly	Partly
Puerto Ricans	Mostly No	No	No	No	No	No	Partly

[4] Some reciprocal cultural influences have, of course, taken place. American language, diet, recreational patterns, art forms, and economic techniques have been modestly influenced by the cultures of non-Anglo-Saxon resident groups since the first contacts with the American Indians, and the American culture is definitely the richer for these influences. However, the reciprocal influences have not been great. See George R. Stewart (1954) and our subsequent discussion (Gordon, 1964, Ch. 4). Furthermore, the minority ethnic groups have not given up all their pre-immigration cultural patterns. Particularly, they have preserved their non-Protestant religions. I have thus used the phrase "Substantially Yes" to indicate this degree of adaptation.

[5] Although few, if any, African cultural survivals are to be found among American Negroes, lower-class Negro life with its derivations from slavery, post-Civil War discrimination, both rural and urban poverty, and enforced isolation from the middle-class white world, is still at a considerable distance from the American cultural norm. Middle- and upper-class Negroes, on the other hand, are acculturated to American core culture.

fect of discrimination will be seen to have been a delaying action only; the quantitatively significant emergence of the middle-class Negro is already well on its way.

Before we leave specific examination of the acculturation variable and its relationships, it would be well to distinguish between two types of cultural patterns and traits which may characterize any ethnic group. Some, like its religious beliefs and practices, its ethical values, its musical tastes, folk recreational patterns, literature, historical language, and sense of a common past, are essential and vital ingredients of the group's cultural heritage, and derive exactly from that heritage. We shall refer to these as *intrinsic* cultural traits or patterns. Others, such as dress, manner, patterns of emotional expression, and minor oddities in pronouncing and inflecting English, tend to be products of the historical vicissitudes of a group's adjustment to its local environment, including the present one (and also reflect social class experiences and values), and are in a real sense, external to the core of the group's ethnic cultural heritage. These may conveniently be referred to as *extrinsic* cultural traits or patterns (cf. Vickery & Cole, 1943, pp. 43–4). To illustrate, the Catholicism or Judaism of the immigrant from Southern or Eastern Europe represent a difference in *intrinsic culture* from the American core society and its Protestant religious affiliation. However, the greater volatility of emotional expression of the Southern and Eastern European peasant or villager in comparison with the characteristically greater reserve of the upper-middle class American of the core society constitutes a difference in *extrinsic culture*. To take another example, the variant speech pattern, or argot, of the lower-class Negro

of recent southern background, which is so widespread both in the South and in northern cities, is a product of external circumstances and is not something vital to Negro culture. It is thus an *extrinsic* cultural trait. Were this argot, which constitutes such a powerful handicap to social mobility and adjustment to the core culture, to disappear, nothing significant for Negro self-regard as a group or the Negro's sense of ethnic history and identity would be violated. While this distinction between intrinsic and extrinsic culture is a tentative one, and cannot be uniformly applied to all cultural traits, it is still a useful one and may help cast further light on the acculturation process, particularly in its relationship to prejudice and discrimination.

As we examine the array of assimilation variables again, several other relationships suggest themselves. One is the indissoluble connection, in the time order indicated, between structural assimilation and marital assimilation. That is, entrance of the minority group into the social cliques, clubs, and institutions of the core society at the primary group level inevitably will lead to a substantial amount of intermarriage. If children of different ethnic backgrounds belong to the same play-group, later the same adolescent cliques, and at college the same fraternities and sororities; if the parents belong to the same country club and invite each other to their homes for dinner; it is completely unrealistic not to expect these children, now grown, to love and to marry each other, blithely oblivious to previous ethnic extraction. Communal leaders of religious and nationality groups that desire to maintain their ethnic identity are aware of this connection, which is one reason for the proliferation of youth groups, adult clubs, and communal institutions which tend to confine their members in their primary relationships safely within the ethnic fold.

If marital assimilation, an inevitable by-product of structural assimilation, takes place fully, the minority group loses its ethnic identity in the larger host or core society, and identificational assimilation takes place. Prejudice and discrimination are no longer a problem, since eventually the descendants of the original minority group become indistinguishable, and since primary group relationships tend to build up an "in-group" feeling which encloses all the members of the group. If assimilation has been complete in all intrinsic as well as extrinsic cultural traits, then no value conflicts on civic issues are likely to arise between the now dispersed descendants of the ethnic minority and members of the core society. Thus the remaining types of assimilation have all taken place like a row of tenpins bowled over in rapid succession by a well placed strike. We may state the emergent generalization, then, as follows: *Once structural assimilation has occurred, either simultaneously with or subsequent to acculturation, all of the other types of assimilation will naturally follow.* It need hardly be pointed out that while acculturation, as we have emphasized above, does not necessarily lead to structural assimilation, structural assimilation inevitably produces acculturation. Structural assimilation, then, rather than acculturation, is seen to be the keystone of the arch of assimilation. The price of such assimilation, however, is the disappearance of the ethnic group as a separate entity and the evaporation of its distinctive values.

There are a number of other crucial hypotheses and questions which can be phrased by the manipulation of these variables. One of the most important, of course, is whether "attitude receptional" and "behavior receptional" assimilation—that is, elimination of prejudice and discrimination—may take place when acculturation, *but not structural assimilation,* occurs. This can be shown to be one of the key questions in the application of our analytical model to "cultural pluralism." Another interesting question is whether prejudice and discrimination are more closely related to differences between the core group and the ethnic minority in intrinsic culture traits or extrinsic culture traits. I would hypothesize that, at least in our era, differences in extrinsic culture are more crucial in the development of prejudice than those of an intrinsic nature (cf. Vickery & Cole, 1943, p. 45). Differences in religious belief, *per se,* are not the occasion for bitter acrimony in twentieth-century America,[6] particularly when these differences occur in middle-class Americans of native birth whose external appearance, speech patterns, and manner are notably uniform. On the other hand, the gap in extrinsic cultural traits between the zoot-suited side-burned slum juvenile and the conservatively clothed and behaving middle-class American distinctly gives the signal for mutual suspicion and hostility. This is not to say that differences in intrinsic values among ethnic groups in America, particularly as these differences spill over into demands on the shaping of American public life, may not result in power conflict. But one must make a distinction between irrational ethnic prejudice,

[6] Cf. R. M. McIver's statement: "But we do not find sufficient reason to regard religion by itself as of crucial importance in provoking the tensions and cleavages manifested in the everyday relationships of American society." (1948, p. 12; italics in original.)

in what might be called the old-fashioned sense, and the conflict of groups in the civic arena over issues based on opposing value-premises, sincerely held in each case.

We shall forgo additional manipulation of the variables in the analytical model at this point [7] since the preceding discussion should have clarified its potential use. We now have an analytical scheme—a set of conceptual categories—which allows us to appreciate the true complexity of the assimilation process, to note the varying directions it may take, and to discern the probable relationships of some of its parts. This set of analytical tools should serve us well as we consider the theories of assimilation and minority group life which have arisen historically in America.

Partisans of the idea of America as one huge melting pot, like adherents of Anglo-conformity, have provided no systematic delineation of their views. Indeed, the concept is one which singularly lends itself to expression in vague rhetoric which, however, noble its aims, gives minimal clues as to the exact implications of the term for the manifold spheres of societal organization and be-

havior. Nevertheless, certain logical inferences can be made, and one feature appears to be envisaged in all the statements of the idea: a complete mixture of the various stocks through intermarriage—in other words, marital assimilation, or amalgamation.

With regard to cultural behavior, the most characteristic implication is that the cultures of the various groups will mix and form a blend somewhat different from the cultures of any one of the groups separately. However, a neglected aspect of this model of cultural intermixture is whether all groups will make an equally influential contribution to the boiling pot, or whether there is to be a *proportionate* influence depending upon the size, power, and strategic location of the various groups. If, to illustrate hypothetically and simply, there are 100,000 Sylvanians occupying their own country, and 2000 Mundovians enter as immigrants, under the melting pot model of cultural interpenetration will the resulting blend—assuming some rough measurement were possible—consist of equal parts of Sylvanian and Mundovian culture, or will the Sylvania cultural contribution be fifty times as important and pervasive as the Mundovian contribution? The answer to this question obviously has significant consequences for the contributing societies, in relation to the questions of both objective cultural survival and group psychology.

Indeed, at one extreme of interpretation—a loose and illogical one, to be sure—the melting pot concept may envisage the culture of the immigrants as "melting" completely into the culture of the host society without leaving any cultural trace at all. It would appear that some exponents of the idea came close to feeling that this was the proper role for Southern and Eastern European im-

[7] The question, of great contemporary interest to social scientists and others concerned with problems of intergroup relations, of whether the objective behavioral phenomenon of discrimination can be reduced or eliminated prior to the reduction or elimination of the subjective attitudinal phenomenon of prejudice may be considered within this framework; thus, can "behavior receptional" assimilation take place prior to "attitude receptional" assimilation? The Supreme Court ban on racial segregation in the public schools, and state and municipal anti-discrimination legislation constitute, of course, a test of the hypothesis that legal curbs on discrimination may be successful even though prejudice still exists, and that such legal curbs may actually result in the reduction of prejudice. See Robert K. Merton (1949), David W. Petegorsky (1951), Arnold M. Rose (1951), John P. Roche and Milton M. Gordon (1957).

migrants to play in the American melting process. In this form, of course, the melting pot concept embraces a view of acculturation which is hardly distinguishable in nature from that of Anglo-conformity, except that the conformity is to be exacted toward a cultural blend to which the cultures of immigrant groups from Northern and Western Europe have been conceded an earlier contribution.

With regard to the remaining assimilation variables, the analysis may proceed as follows: If large-scale intermarriage is to have taken place, then obviously the immigrants must have entered the cliques, clubs, other primary groups, and institutions of the host society and, in addition, placed their own impress upon these social structures to some extent. Thus the process of structural assimilation must somehow reflect a blending effect, also. Identificational assimilation takes place in the form of all groups merging their previous sense of peoplehood into a new and larger ethnic identity which, in some fashion, honors its multiple origins at the same time that it constitutes an entity distinct from them all. Prejudice and discrimination must be absent since there are not even any identifiably separate groups to be their target, and "civic assimilation" will have taken place since disparate cultural values are assumed to have merged and power conflict between groups would be neither necessary nor possible. This, then, is the "ideal-typical" model of the melting pot process. With this analysis and the previous discussion in mind, let us take a quick look at the American experience to see how well the model applies.

While no exact figures on the subject are attainable, it is safe to say that a substantial proportion of the descendants of the non-English immigrants of colonial times and the first three-quarters of the nineteenth century (with the exception of the Irish Catholics and the German Jews) have by now been absorbed into the general white "sociological Protestant" sector of American life. That is to say, they do not live in communal subsocieties which are lineal descendants of those which their immigrant ancestors created, and so far as they understand it, are simply "Americans" who may be vaguely conscious of an immigrant forebear here and there from a non-English source but for whom this has little current meaning. This would include many descendants of the Scotch-Irish, German Protestants, Swedes, and Norwegians, among other groups from Northern and Western Europe, as well as, in all probability, a few with colonial Jewish ancestry whose early American progenitors converted to Christianity (not to mention occasional individuals who have a mulatto ancestor who, at some time, "passed" into the white group).[8] This does not mean that communal societies with appropriate institutions representing most of these ancestral groups do not still exist, but that, in relation to the total number of ethnic descendants, they become increasingly thinly manned as the third and fourth generation leave their rural or small town (occasionally urban) enclaves and venture forth into the broader social world.

The burden of our point should now be clear. Entrance by the descendants of these immigrants into the social struc-

[8] Estimates of the number of very light Negroes who "pass" permanently into the white group range from 2000 to 30,000 annually, although the practice is obviously so shrouded in secrecy that even these limits may not include the true figure. (See Maurice R. Davie, 1949; also Gunnar Myrdal, 1944.)

tures of the existing white Protestant society, and the culmination of this process in intermarriage, has not led to the creation of new structures, new institutional forms, and a new sense of identity which draws impartially from all sources, but rather to immersion in a subsocietal network of groups and institutions which was already fixed in essential outline with an Anglo-Saxon, general Protestant stamp. The prior existence of Anglo-Saxon institutional forms as the norm, the pervasiveness of the English language, and the numerical dominance of the Anglo-Saxon population made this outcome inevitable.

If we turn to the cultural realm, we find much the same result. The tremendous contributions of non-English immigrants—of both the "Old" and "New" varieties—to American civilization collectively in the form of agricultural and industrial manpower, as sources of population growth, as bearers of strategic new crafts and skills, and as patrons of the developing fine arts is not here in question. Nor is the brilliant record achieved by countless individual immigrants and their descendants in the business, professional, scientific, and artistic life of the nation. All this has been mentioned before. The question at issue is rather the alteration of cultural forms. Here we would argue that, in great part, rather than an impartial melting of the divergent cultural patterns from all immigrant sources, what has actually taken place has been more of a transforming of the later immigrant's specific cultural contributions into the Anglo-Saxon mould. As George Stewart has put it, a more accurate figure of speech to describe the American experience would be that of a "transmuting pot" in which "as the foreign elements, a little at a time, were added to the pot, they were

not merely melted but were largely transmuted, and so did not affect the original material as strikingly as might be expected" (1954, p. 23). Will Herberg echoes this view. "The enthusiasts of the 'melting pot' . . . ," he writes, "were wrong . . . in regard to the cultural aspect of the assimilative process. They looked forward to a genuine blending of cultures, to which every ethnic strain would make its own contribution and out of which would emerge a new cultural synthesis, no more English than German or Italian and yet in some sense transcending and embracing them all. In certain respects this has indeed become the case: our American cuisine includes antipasto and spaghetti, frankfurters and pumpernickel, filet mignon and french fried potatoes, borsch, sour cream, and gefüllte fish, on a perfect equality with fried chicken, ham and eggs, and pork and beans. But it would be a mistake to infer from this that the American's image of himself—and that means the ethnic group member's image of himself as he becomes American—is a composite or synthesis of the ethnic elements that have gone into the making of the American. It is nothing of the kind: the American's image of himself is still the Anglo-American ideal it was at the beginning of our independent existence. The 'national type' as ideal has always been, and remains, pretty well fixed. It is the *Mayflower*, John Smith, Davy Crockett, George Washington, and Abraham Lincoln that define the American's self-image, and this is true whether the American in question is a descendant of the Pilgrims or the grandson of an immigrant from southeastern Europe. . . . Our cultural assimilation has taken place not in a 'melting pot,' but rather in a [citing Stewart] 'transmuting pot' in which all ingredients have been transformed and assimilated to an idealized 'Anglo-Saxon' model" (Herberg, 1955, pp. 33–4).

Both structurally and culturally, then, the "single melting pot" vision of America has been something of an illusion— a generous and idealistic one, in one sense, since it held out the promise of a kind of psychological equality under the banner of an impartial symbol of America larger than the symbols of any of the constituent groups—but one which exhibited a considerable degree of sociological naïveté. Given the prior arrival time of the English colonists, the numerical dominance of the English stock, and the cultural dominance of Anglo-Saxon institutions, the invitation extended to non-English immigrants to "melt" could only result, if thoroughly accepted, in the latter's loss of group identity, the transformation of their cultural survivals into Anglo-Saxon patterns, and the development of their descendants in the image of the Anglo-Saxon American.

Culturally, this process of absorbing Anglo-Saxon patterns has moved massively and inexorably, with greater or lesser speed, among all ethnic groups. Structurally, however, the outcome has, so far, been somewhat different, depending on whether we are considering white Protestant descendants of the "Old" immigration, white Catholics and Jews of both periods of immigration, or the racial and quasi-racial minorities. Here, then, is where the "triple melting pot" hypothesis of Kennedy and others becomes applicable. While Protestant descendants of Germans and Scandinavians can, if they wish, merge structurally into the general white Protestant subsociety with relative ease, Jews, Irish Catholics, Italian Catholics, and Polish Catholics cannot do so without either

formal religious conversion or a kind of sociological "passing"—neither process being likely to attract overwhelmingly large numbers. Negroes, Orientals, Mexican-Americans, and some Puerto Ricans are prevented by racial discrimination from participating meaningfully in either the white Protestant or the white Catholic communities. Nationality background differences within the white population, however, appear to be more amenable to dissolving influences. The passing of the "nationality" communities may be slower than Kennedy and Herberg intimate and the rate of Catholic-Protestant intermarriage has been shown to be substantially higher in the country as a whole than in New Haven. However, a vastly important and largely neglected sociological point about mixed marriages, racial, religious, or national, apart from the rate, is *in what social structures the intermarried couples and their children incorporate themselves*. If Catholic-Protestant intermarried couples live more or less completely within either the Catholic social community or the Protestant social community, the sociological fact of the existence of the particular religious community and its separation from other religious communities remains.

The result of these processes, structurally speaking, is that American society has come to be composed of a number of "pots," or subsocieties, three of which are the religious containers marked Protestant, Catholic, and Jew, which are in the process of melting down the white nationality background communities contained within them; others are racial groups which are not allowed to melt structurally; and still others are substantial remnants of the nationality background communities manned by those members who are either of the first generation, or who, while native born, choose to remain within the ethnic enclosure. All of these constitute the ethnic subsocieties which we have described earlier, with their network of primary groups, organizations, and institutions within which a member's life may be comfortably enclosed except for secondary contacts with "outsiders" in the process of making a living and carrying out the minimal duties of political citizenship, if he so desires. Another pot besides the religious containers which is actually doing some structural melting is

labeled "intellectuals." All these containers, as they bubble along in the fires of American life and experience are tending to produce, with somewhat differing speeds, products which are culturally very similar, while at the same time they remain structurally separate. The entire picture is one which, with the cultural qualifications already noted, may be called a "multiple melting pot." And so we arrive at the "pluralism" which characterizes the contemporary American scene.

13   Socialization in later life
ORVILLE G. BRIM, JR.

Need for socialization after childhood

The socialization that an individual receives in childhood cannot be fully adequate as preparation for the tasks demanded of him in later years. As individuals mature, they move through a sequence of statuses corresponding to different stages in the life cycle (Glick, 1957). Even though some of the expectations of society are relatively stable through the life cycle, many others change from one age to the next. We know that society demands that the individual meet these changed expectations, and demands that he alter his personality and behavior to make room

in his life for newly significant persons such as his family members, his teachers, his employers, and his colleagues at work.

The effectiveness of childhood socialization certainly is greater in relatively unchanging societies. Cultural prescriptions of a powerful nature define the usual sequence of statuses and roles that individuals are to assume during their life span. The process of development and differentiation goes along in step with physical maturation—increases in stature, strength, capacity—that permits the individual to meet the enlarged demands upon him associated with new

Reprinted from Orville G. Brim, Jr., and Stanton Wheeler, **Socialization After Childhood,** New York: John Wiley & Sons, 1966, pp. 18–33, with permission of the author and the publisher.

statuses. The increased demands are timed according to age or growth and may be thought of as developmental tasks. Further advances of the individual to greater differentiation of his relationships with others occur according to certain schedules which integrate his capabilities with age-graded requirements of the society. For example, enrollment in school may occur at the age when the child's physical, linguistic, and social skills enable him to deal with the formal educational system.

Also, in such quiet societies, stability comes from the continuity over time of the significant others with whom one is involved. The earliest groups of significant persons remain on the scene through much of one's life. Parents may live on through one's middle years; friendships may persist through much of the life span; one marries into a homogamous group whose expectations are similar to those of prior reference figures. All of this enables socialization to be developmental in nature, that is, to occur in a regular progression from infancy through old age, and for anticipatory socialization for later-life roles to be more effective.

However, even in such relatively unchanging societies one cannot be socialized in childhood to handle successfully all of the roles he will confront in the future. Socialization in later years builds on attitudes and skills acquired earlier, using them as a foundation for later, more demanding learning. It is also true that for reasons fundamental to social organization individuals at certain age periods cannot be socialized completely for roles they may occupy in the future; socialization into the marital role is a case in point. There will be, also, some cultural discontinuities, as Benedict (1949) has pointed out, so that succes-

sive roles to be learned do not build upon each other and even may conflict with what was learned earlier.

The situation for most men is much more difficult, because they live in complex and changing societies. The inadequacies of early socialization for the role the person will play during his lifetime are much greater. The geographical mobility associated with the modern age and the social mobility characteristic of the achievement-oriented open-class society both contribute to the characteristically unforeseeable career pattern of modern man. The heterogeneity of subcultures in complex modern societies compounds the effects of mobility by the novel and unpredictable role demands placed on the individual. So, also, do the rapid social changes occurring during a lifetime render inadequate much childhood learning: technological obsolescence in one's occupation, shifts in sexual folkways, opportunities for equality in employment for minority group members, are but a few of a myriad of examples that might be set forth. Discontinuities between what is expected in successive roles are greater; the inabilities of the socializing agents to do an effective job rise as the rate of change increases; subgroups with deviant values emerge which do not prepare the child for performance of the roles expected of him by the larger society. Agents may be missing, as in broken homes, or key institutions or agencies lacking, as in the absence of an educational system in counties in Virginia when the public schools were closed; the parent himself may be inadequate to the task because he no longer cares or understands.

Faced with these challenges, complex and changing societies might try to lay the groundwork for the necessary learning in later life, when the child will be confronted with adult roles as yet only dimly seen, by providing the individual with initiative, creativity, the power of self-determination, insight, flexibility, and intelligent response to new conditions; to move, that is, away from indoctrination and habit formation toward development of broadly useful traits and skills enabling him to meet a variety of social demands. This, of course, is a familiar educational theory, deriving from changes introduced by John Dewey and others in the past fifty years. From the sociological viewpoint these changes are seen as an attempt by American society to provide for effective socialization of its members through life without being dependent on societal stability.

This is desirable but not sufficient; modern societies must provide for resocialization into roles for which the person has not been developmentally prepared. Societal institutions evolve that are specifically devoted to resocialization of the child or adult, much as the school and family are devoted to developmental socialization. Newly visible deficiencies in training are met by new resocialization efforts, good illustrations being the marital and parental roles. Poor developmental socialization is caused by inattention on the part of the child's parents, the absence of many siblings in the home, general decreased responsibility of children for helping parents in their duties, and so on. As a consequence, programs and institutions are emerging which are devoted to parent and family life education.

Limits of later-life socialization

Given the need for adult socialization,

what are the potentialities for new learning, and for change in personality, of the individual after his formative childhood years? The limits of socialization in later life are set by the biological capacities of an individual and by the effects of earlier learning or the lack of it. The effectiveness of later-life socialization is a consequence of the interaction of these two restrictions with the level of technology achieved by the society in its socialization methods. The latter depend primarily on the knowledge available about human behavior and to a lesser extent on mechanical developments; the remarks that follow assume a given level of socialization technology.

A substantial portion of the human raw material of society that is biologically inadequate in one respect or another is removed from natural progression through the life cycle by one of several methods and hence does not appear in the usual later-life socialization situations. By and large, the demands of a society upon adults are tailored to the capacities of the average man, and socialization proceeds without interference from biological limitations.

There are, nevertheless, two ways in which biological restrictions lead to limitations on later-life socialization. The first of these occurs primarily in an open-class society with a high level of achievement motivation. Here upward mobility into ever more demanding roles may lead an individual to positions in which he is unable to meet the challenges because of limited intelligence, strength, or other biological attributes. The second occurs when war or another disaster destroys the protection given to individuals by society from the direct impact of nature, and persons biologically adequate for the roles they will meet in the course of their normal civilized life cycle may suddenly find themselves unable to live under new and primitive conditions.

The effects of earlier learning, or the lack of them, are the other limits on later-life socialization. First we must recognize the durable qualities of early childhood learning. Socialization occurring during childhood correctly receives primary emphasis in research and theory. The potency and durability of the learning that occurs during this period are assumed on the basis of the frequency of learning situations, their primacy in the career of the organism, and the intensity of the rewards and punishments administered. Moreover, what is learned in childhood is difficult to change because much of it was learned under conditions of partial reinforcement.

In addition, it is held by many (and believed to be of utmost importance) that during early socialization the bulk of the unconscious material of the personality is accumulated, and the inertia established in the individual personality by its unconscious components, relatively inaccessible as they are to change through simple socialization procedures, is the cause of its manifest continuity. One might add that probably the characteristic modes of defense also are established early, thus painting the basic colors of personality for the life span.

Granted that there are enduring qualities to childhood learning, the effects of such learning on later-life socialization are more complicated than they may seem to be on quick consideration. It is not only that early learning interferes with and limits later learning. This is just one of several effects. Rather, it is the relationship of earlier learning, or its absence, to later learning which determines whether it will limit or facilitate adult socialization.

In some cases there is discontinuity and conflict between earlier and later learning. Later-life socialization requires replacement of the earlier with the later, of the old with the new, rather than building upon the existing personality base; the contrast in the premarital and postmarital roles of the American middle-class female is an outstanding example of this discontinuity.

In other instances, the childhood learning may facilitate later learning, if the elements learned first are compatible with what is to be learned in later life. As is pointed out later, adult socialization frequently consists of creating new combinations of old response elements; if these elements have been well learned, they may facilitate learning the adult role.

Sometimes it is the absence of certain childhood learning that affects later-life socialization. Here, at first glance, we would think that the absence of childhood learning would provide a clean slate for the later-life socialization effort, and that the absence of possibly competing responses would make the adult's learning tasks much easier. Training the new bride how to cook, or teaching a manual trade to the previously untutored adolescent, seems easier than changing skills that may already exist. This is true in many cases, but we should be cautious. It is doubtful that one comes on a role in later life without any fragments at all of relevant socialization; the inexperienced mother may seem to know little, but she knows something, and, even more, she has response elements for the role performance that are not manifest at the conscious level.

The absence of early learning clearly will hinder later-life socialization when something that should have been acquired as a basis for learning in later years in fact was not. It has been suggested (Caldwell, 1962) that the occurrence of critical periods in the life cycle, now demonstrated in subhuman species, may also characterize human development. If there are certain things that must be learned by human beings at specific stages in their development, then failure to learn this material at the appropriate period makes subsequent learning impossible. Such early deficiencies may even affect the learning ability itself. Although we know little as yet about possible critical periods in learning, we can speculate about adulthood; for example, learning certain attitudes during the formative middle years may lay the necessary basis for satisfactory socialization into the old-age role.

What data do we have on the effects of early-life experience? The main evidence comes from case histories obtained in clinical practice (Brim, 1959), and it has a *post hoc* and speculative quality. Recently more attention has been given to empirical studies of continuity in personality and to the durability of early childhood learning. LeVine (1963) cites many of these studies with reference to the acquisition of language and enduring political attitudes. Neugarten, in her review (1963) of research on the continuity of personality through time, reports that the studies present inconsistent conclusions which vary from study to study and from sample to sample. She states that while the evidence shows "continuity of personality" the larger proportion of the variance in personality at later times remains unaccounted for; that is, it is not predictable from earlier measurements of personality. She concludes that

"the nature of personality changes in adulthood may be relatively obscure; but the conviction is a reasonable one that changes do occur" (p. 55).

Many of the existing studies are unsatisfactory in another way. They report on specific personality traits, such as an attitude or some type of response, and the data often are the unintended output of a concern with some other topic. In comparison to the amount of information available about personality development in earlier age periods, we have little knowledge about older age groups. Sewell (1963) points out that there are relatively few sharply defined or clearly focused studies of adult socialization concerned with the process by which society, through its subgroups, socializes a person in later life into a specific role or set of roles, with attention given to the changes which may result in measurable personality characteristics. The few prototypical studies which can be cited are primarily in the area of job training or, more broadly, occupational socialization, especially the work of Becker and his colleagues (1961).

A study outside of the occupational role that is of special interest is Vincent's work on marital socialization (1964). His study demonstrates changes in scores on scales of the California Personality Inventory (such as dominance and self-acceptance) as a consequence of marriage. A control group of unmarried persons shows almost no change compared to the married group. Vincent also reports that the amount of change depends in part on the age of the couple at marriage, with those who marry early showing the greatest subsequent change. Other work on adults which may prove valuable comes from family life education. Most of the studies of family life education are highly valuable analyses of how one carries on adult socialization; the observations made in these studies about methods and the causes of change in adult personality are applicable to other adult socialization processes (Brim, 1959).

To summarize, both biological and early-learning limitations on later-life socialization exist, but their exact nature is not understood. Discussion of the problem, and the arguments pro and con, would be clarified by specifying the levels or types of behavior or personality characteristics which one has in mind, for example, political attitudes, feelings about one's father, reactions to authority, or beliefs about God. Much remains to be done, and too little attention has been given to the study of the possibly sizable changes which occur after childhood as a result of deliberate socialization processes by society. The powerful arguments for the potent effects of early-life experiences should not deter the study of large and important changes that may take place in later life.

Changes in content of socialization

The substantive content of socialization differs, of course, in important ways at different stages of the life cycle and in different major social institutions. People learn different things at different times and places in their lives.

It is uncertain, however, whether the types as opposed to the substance of the content differ throughout the life cycle. Still the needs for socialization and the effects of learning and biological characteristics in any given case would seem to dictate the nature of the socialization process; and since these vary by life-cycle stages, with the needs and limits of adult socialization being different from those of childhood, it is probable that the types of content vary accordingly. Six such probable changes in content will be discussed.

The most important change, perhaps, is the shift in content from a concern with values and motives to a concern with overt behavior.[1] Some other changes are described in other aspects of socialization content. These are as follows: from acquisition of new material to a synthesis of the old; from a concern with idealism to a concern with realism; from teaching expectations to teaching how to mediate conflict among expectations; from a concern with general demands of society to a concern with role-specific expectations; and finally, a change from "I-me" components of personality to other components.

VALUES AND MOTIVES VERSUS OVERT BEHAVIOR

There are three things a person requires before he is able to perform satisfactorily in a role. He must know what is expected of him (both in behavior and in values), must be able to meet the role requirements, and must desire to practice the behavior and pursue the appropriate ends. It can be said that the purposes of socialization are to give a person knowledge, ability, and motivation.

A simple cross-classification of these three concepts with values and behavior

[1] An analysis of adult socialization in terms of the relative emphasis on these two role components was introduced to the Social Science Research Council Conference by Irving Rosow in his paper, "Forms and Functions of Adult Socialization." See also Merton (1957).

establishes a paradigm which helps to analyze changes in the content of socialization through the life cycle. In this paradigm six cells are indicated by letters for simplicity of reference:

	behavior	values
knowledge	A	B
ability	C	D
motivation	E	F

Cells A and B indicate respectively that the individual knows what behavior is expected of him and what ends he should pursue; E and F indicate that the individual is motivated to behave in the appropriate ways and to pursue the designated values; C and D indicate that the individual is able to carry out the behavior and to hold appropriate values.[2]

With respect to changes during the life cycle, the emphasis in socialization moves from motivation to ability and knowledge, and from a concern with values to a concern with behavior.

The highest priority in childhood socialization is represented by Cell F, namely, to take the basic drives of the infant and transform them over time into desires for recognition and approval and finally to the pursuit of more specific cultural values. Early-life socialization thus emphasizes the control of primary drives, while socialization in later stages deals with secondary or learned motives generated by the expectations of significant others. Except in rare and extreme conditions, adult socialization does not need to teach the individual to control

and regulate the gratification of primary drive systems.[3]

The usual concern of adult socialization is represented by Cell A. Society assumes that the adult knows the values to be pursued in different roles, that he wants to pursue them with the socially appropriate means, and that all that may remain to be done is to teach him what to do. This is illustrated by the case of a military recruit. The training program starts at about the level of "This is a gun" and "This is how it is fired." If there are some things the individual is unable to do (Cell C), the training program seeks to upgrade his ability—for example, by instruction designed to reduce illiteracy. If he is unwilling to carry out his various tasks (Cell D), then motivational training occurs through administration of special rewards and punishments. If it appears that education about values is needed (Cell B), the individual is enrolled in a general orientation course on American values and the purpose of the wars; the "why we fight" training programs are instituted to provide an understanding of the appropriate ends to be sought. If the individual has serious conflicts within himself but does his best, therapeutic procedures are instituted to solve this problem, which lies in Cell D. Only in the last analysis, when other

[2] The question of being able or unable to hold values may at first seem somewhat peculiar, but the inability involved here arises from conflict within the personality. This instance of inability as a source of deviance in role performance is discussed in greater detail later on.

[3] The development of secondary motives oriented toward social approval (in a broad sense) and based on learning associated with the satisfaction of primary drives is a part of socialization but is not commensurate with it. It is true that sometimes one speaks of a person being unsocialized because of what appears to be a greater concern with the gratification of primary than of secondary motivation. But one also correctly calls unsocialized a person with deviant values and bizarre behavior, even when the primary drive system itself has been well socialized.

possible types of deficiencies in socialization have been ruled out, is it assumed that there is a problem in motivation toward the appropriate values, the case represented by Cell F. Such men are critical of the value system of their society; in our country they may be pacifists, Communists, or members of other groups which reject traditional American values. Sometimes resocialization efforts are launched in such cases, but more often retraining of these individuals is considered to be an impossible task, and they are jailed, ignored, or relegated to marginal, inconsequential positions.

In general, then, socialization after childhood deals primarily with overt behavior in the role and makes little attempt to influence motivation of a fundamental kind or to influence basic values. Society is willing to spend much less time in redirecting the motivation and values of adults than of children; for the latter it is understood that this is a necessary task of the institutions involved, such as the family, and they are organized to carry out this function.

Why should this difference exist? Probably it stems directly from the limitations on learning in later life, which makes impractical any attempt at thorough resocialization. Irving Rosow has asked if adult socialization can, in fact, generate suitable beliefs and attitudes, suitable motivation for certain types of performance, or whether the limitations on learning are such that the socializing agent must deal with overt performance only. It may be that the costs are too high and that it simply is not efficient from society's point of view to spend too much time on teaching an old dog new tricks. Perhaps an intensive and costly resocialization effort can be made for adults only when the need for a certain kind of manpower is unusually great and the question of efficiency becomes secondary to the demand for personnel.

Society has at least two major solutions to this possible problem. One is anticipatory: selection is made of candidates for an adult organization to screen out those who do not have appropriate motives and values for the anticipated roles. This procedure helps to assure that those who enter the organization will not present difficult problems for the socialization program. In this way adults probably get sorted out, more or less, and placed in social situations where they fit best in terms of the values and motives learned in their early-life socialization.

A second solution, which Rosow has pointed out, is that society may accept as evidence of satisfactory socialization conforming behavior alone, foregoing any concern with value systems. This entails risk, as he indicates, for if the social system undergoes stress, the conformity, since it is superficial, may break down rapidly.

As a last resort, the remaining instances of deviance in need of resocialization—the genuinely tough cases where the appropriate values have not been internalized—can be processed through the special correctional institutions (prisons, hospitals, etc.) of the society at large.

ACQUISITION OF NEW MATERIAL
VERSUS SYNTHESIS OF OLD MATERIAL

As a person moves through the life cycle he accumulates an extensive repertoire of responses, both affective and behavioral. These are organized according to roles and, at a more specific level, by episodes within a role. These responses can be detached from the contexts in which they have been learned and used, and joined with others in new combinations suitable as social behavior responsive to the complex demands of adulthood. We can say, therefore, that the content acquired in adult socialization is not so much new material as it is the aggregation and synthesis of elements from a storehouse of already-learned responses, with perhaps the addition of several fragments that are newly learned when necessary to fill out the required social acts. The usual objective of socialization in the later-life stages is to get one to practice a new combination of skills already acquired, to combine existing elements into new forms, to trim and polish existing material, rather than to learn wholly new complexes or responses, as in the case of the relatively untrained child, for whom the socialization effort starts with little more than initial intelligence and primary drives.

IDEALISM AND REALISM

The third change in content is the transformation of idealism into realism. As the individual matures, society demands that he become more realistic and lay aside his childish idealism. Early learning encompasses the formal status structure; later learning takes into account the actual and/or informal status structure. One designates as cynical a person who doubts that the actual and the formal are the same. However, we think of a person as naive if he does not make this distinction. In socialization the child is shielded from contact with the informal systems of society—or, at least, knowledge of these is not formally taught. This serves to maintain and legitimize the formal status differentiations and to protect them from change.

But at later stages in the life cycle, for the system to work effectively, the realistic aspects of status differentiation also must be taught.

Closely related is learning to distinguish between ideal role prescriptions and what is actually expected of one in a role. Here, as in the foregoing, the inculcation of ideal role prescriptions results in a desirable idealism which strengthens and perpetuates the ideal of the society. As the child matures he is taught to realize that there is a distinction between the ideal and the real, and learns to take his part in society according to the realistic expectations of others, rather than attempting conformity to ideal norms.

RESOLVING CONFLICTS;
META-PRESCRIPTIONS

The fourth type of change is to a greater concern with teaching the individual to mediate conflicting demands. As one moves through the life cycle, he is forced to develop methods of selecting among conflicting role prescriptions. The possible conflicts between the prescriptions of reference set members are classifiable into two basic types. First, there is intra-role conflict of two kinds: (a) the prescriptions of two or more individuals for the same aspect of a role may conflict: thus, the wife and the employer may differ in their prescriptions for the individual's job performance; (b) prescriptions of just one individual about different aspects of the role may be in conflict; the wife may expect her husband to be both companion with and taskmaster to his son.

Second, there is interrole conflict, again classifiable into two subtypes: (a) conflict between two or more individuals about two separate roles; for example, the employer's demands for job performance conflict with the wife's demands for familial performance; (b) conflict between the expectations of one individual for performance in two different roles, as in the case where the wife has conflicting expectations for her husband's behavior at home and on the job.

The need to learn how to handle such conflicts occurs to a greater extent in later life for at least two reasons. First, children tend to be shielded by society from the realities of life; and if the cultural norm is that children should be protected from seeing life's conflicts, then it follows that nothing will be taught about ways of mediating them. Second, in later life there are more roles and more complexity within roles, so that a much greater possibility exists of role conflict. To put it differently, the reference set of adults is considerably larger than that of children; their social systems are more extensive and more numerous. They have a past, for one thing; and they have occupational roles, as well as additional family roles gained through marriage. They are attuned more often to distant reference figures than they were as children, when their reference sets included mainly those near them.

Thus, as a person ages, he learns the ways of conflict resolution which Ralph Linton (1945) has described so well: avoiding the situation, withdrawing acceptably from conflict, and scheduling conflicting demands in temporal sequence, so that the conflict disappears. Also, as Howard Becker (1964) has pointed out, he learns another major method of conflict resolution, that is, to compromise between the opposing demands.

There is another important method of conflict resolution which may have been overlooked or at least has not been given formal conceptualization. In every society there are well-recognized prescriptions for solving certain kinds of conflicts that arise from the competing demands of reference set members. These prescriptions for mediating role conflict can be called *meta-prescriptions*. Such meta-prescriptions govern the resolution of conflict between demands on one's time and loyalties, and usually, although not always, pertain to inter-role rather than intrarole conflict.[4] Examples of meta-prescriptions are "Do what your employer asks of you, even if it means that you have little time for your children," and "Side with your wife when she disciplines the children, even if you think she is wrong." Meta-prescriptions, therefore, guide the process of compromise and dictate whether the solutions should be one-sided, as in the two examples given above, or more on a half-and-half basis, such as "Save at least three nights a week for your family, even if there is work you should be doing." It seems that a noticeable change in the content of socialization in later-life periods is the attention given to ways of resolving conflict through such meta-prescriptions.

INCREASE IN SPECIFICITY

The fifth characteristic of change in socialization content is along the dimen-

[4] A current study of executive personality and achievement carried out by the author and his colleagues [see Brim & Wheeler, 1966. Preface] has collected substantial data on the meta-prescriptions for resolving role conflict between the demands of parents and children, one's boss and his work colleagues, wife and employer, and so on. These meta-prescriptions may differ from one person to the next, and result in relatively more or fewer conflict resolutions being made in, say, the direction of favoring the prescriptions of one's work environment as contrasted with his home. These appear to be fairly powerful predictors of differential achievement.

sion of generality-specificity; that is, whether what is taught applies to many social situations or to just a few. This dimension can be applied to both components, values and means, of role prescriptions. There is no reason to maintain that values necessarily are general, and that methods of achieving them are specific. This is noted only because of the tendency to define values as something general; the concept is not being used in this sense.

A child is trained both deliberately and unwittingly by socializing agents in the goals and behavior appropriate for his sex. There are male and female styles of doing many different things, and these are learned early. These characteristics are general, in the sense that they are required in a variety of situations he will confront in society, either as major components or as necessary coloring to other aspects of his behavior.

The case is similar for cultural differences in basic values, such as those related to achievement, to nature, to the family, and indeed for all those general value orientations, to use Florence Kluckhohn's phrase (1953), which help to distinguish major cultural groups. They are acquired early (and, in contrast to sex roles, with perhaps less deliberate instruction), and they give shape and tone to the performance of many roles in society.

It also is true that a person is socialized for his socioeconomic position, a process that Charles E. Bidwell speaks of as socialization into a status level or a style of life.[5] Again, general skills and values are learned, appropriate to carrying out in a certain manner a number of specific role demands for behavior.

[5] Charles E. Bidwell, "Some Aspects of Pre-Adult Socialization," paper prepared for the Social Science Research Council Conference.

The values and behavior appropriate to a social class position, to a prestige level in life, usually are acquired in childhood; and, as was true with respect to sex roles and basic cultural values, some part of what is learned is gained outside of any deliberate formal training program.

One would have to say that these general values of one's culture are, on the whole, acquired in childhood. True, as Bidwell points out, there is some socialization into value systems of a given social class during the college age. He notes that one function of fraternities in certain colleges is to carry on this kind of socialization into a social class level higher than that of the individual's family of origin. The existence of formal socializing agencies with this recognized function is understood as a response to the "legitimate" need for resocialization resulting from the upward social mobility in American life in which the individual moves from one subculture to another, with corresponding differences in expectations.

Doubtless there are other occasions in which the general values are the content of socialization at later age periods, but these are not easy to identify. In most instances the content of later-life socialization tends to be role-specific, rather than general in nature.

FEWER "I-ME" RELATIONSHIPS

This final life-cycle comparison arises from the basic view presented earlier that part of personality consists of self-other systems. From what has been said, it follows that the content acquired in later stages of the life cycle would involve fewer of the "I-me" type of self-other relationships and more of the objective "they-me" and "I-them" components. Reviewing the reasons for the development of this kind of self-other system, one realizes that the causes for the lack of identification of the significant person or persons, and the resultant use of "I" in their place, exist to a much lesser degree in adulthood. At later ages the source of the material which is acquired is more readily identifiable; the "they" involved usually is quite clear. Moreover, with the growth of power in maturity, one increases the degree to which he is the instigator of the action and consequently is engaged more frequently in, and thus thinks about himself as, the "I-them" relationship.

If one equates the "I-me" component of personality with the core personality, with "identity," as indicated in the discussion earlier, then he could say that identity tends to be laid down in largest part in early stages of the life cycle. This is true to a degree, of course, but as was said in considering the limiting effects of childhood experiences, it is overemphasized. Not uncommonly, dramatic shifts in identity do occur at later stages of the life cycle, since significant persons may have an unusual impact on a person's appraisal of his own basic characteristics.

III   PERSONALITY AND SOCIETY

Because social behavior is a function of a person in an environment, a concept of personality has always been basic to social psychological thought. Much effort has gone into assessment of personality attributes and examinations of their relations with social processes. Some useful sources for general treatments of these subjects are books by Hall and Lindzey (1970), Lindzey and Hall (1965), Smelser and Smelser (1963), Sanford (1966), Mehrabian (1968), and especially the new *Handbook of Personality Theory and Research* (1968), edited by Borgatta and Lambert. Yet, personality theory and social psychological theory have developed essentially in parallel, as partly independent though mutually relevant, domains. Personality has commonly entered social psychology from the outside, so to speak, as a generalized representation of the "organismic" behavioral tendencies brought to the situation by the individual, acting with the properties of the setting to produce behavior.

Exactly how much relative weight to allocate to personality and how much to the situation has been a matter for much theoretical argument among social psychologists, reflecting their part in the long-standing dispositional-situational debate. Although more often than not personality has been conceived as something constant which people have inside them to govern their actions regardless of circumstances, it appears unduly arbitrary to consider the individual as categorically separate from his social surroundings. Indeed, the matters discussed in the preceding section, and later in Section V, indicate that personality must find a place within general theory in social psychology (see Sanford, 1963). Developments in the analysis of comparative cultures (see Kroeber, 1953), and direct investigation of social processes (see Hare, 1962), all emphasize the blending of the person and the social situation, as do the works of pioneering theorists like Emile Durkheim (1950), Max Weber (1946, 1947), Charles Cooley (1922), George Herbert Mead (1934), Abram Kardiner (1939), Erich Fromm (1941), and Ralph Linton (1945), to name a few.

Speaking in a general way to these same matters, but with more empirical evidence, J. McV. Hunt begins this section with a forceful challenge to traditional modes of thought about personality. He identifies five widespread and fundamental beliefs about personality which we take very much for granted. In the light of the evidence which he surveys, each of them proves dubious. He therefore presses for the adoption of a more cognitive point of view in contrast with the emotion-centered focus of the older post neo-Freudian theories. In Hunt's line of thought, meaning and information are key concepts. As touchstones of human conduct, they are significant determiners of the *relations* between persons and social situations. However, Hunt's viewpoint is an especially notable one for its stress on the idea that both meaning and information are components of these relations. They are not an exclusive feature of either one or the other. His thinking clearly leads in the direction of a closer scrutiny of the person and his environment, especially in its social aspects. Thus, Hunt questions the traditional intra-personal emphases in personality theory, preferring instead an emphatically interactional outlook.

Two papers here, one by Yinger and the other by the late Gordon Allport, confront directly and systematically the fundamental problem of interrelating the personal and the social in such a way as to afford separate justice to each while remaining faithful to interactionist premises. Allport, for his part, presents an incisive discussion of many of the same points just mentioned and some others as well. Contrasting the properties of "open" and "closed" social systems, in this paper he brings into focus the ideas and issues fundamental to an integration of personality and social concepts. He characterizes this task as "the knottiest problem in social science," and in addressing himself to it he provides a glimpse of modern systems theory in application (see Scott in Section IX).

Allport was well known as the foremost champion of an idiographic case history approach to personality theory. He long held the unique individual to be the only proper final unit of analysis (see Rosenzweig, 1958, and for a statement of the opposing "nomothetic" position, Eysenck, 1954). Few argued so effectively as he the difficulties associated with fixed-trait, psychometric, and past-oriented approaches to personality. Yet, traits, tests, and historical analysis all found places in his research and writing, but always interwoven with conceptions of potential, growth, and change (see Allport, 1937, 1954, 1960, 1961, 1966).

Allport's thinking pivoted on a view of personality as "becoming." The person is not simply transformed by his environment, he continuously deals creatively with it, and Allport, in his paper here, is openly critical of "integumented" constructions of personality as "closed system." The relation between personality and the social environment, he maintains, is open, even if not totally so. Openness, in Allport's usage, carries a sense of two systems (person and environment) that merge into one another through mutually permeable boundaries. But there are boundaries. He conceived Man as a social being through and through, yet also as an integral biological-psychological system, and social behavior was always thought by Allport to be patterned in and by the person as an active agent.

Many of these same thoughts recur in the selection from Yinger's book, *Toward a Field Theory of Behavior* (1965). In it he strives to write a field or interactionist theory of behavior that will demonstrate an integration of the person and the situation while reserving what he carefully calls the "analytic" distinction between the two. In the tradition of Kurt Lewin (see Cartwright, 1951; Marrow, 1969), Yinger views people and situations as interdependent; neither exists apart from the other, even if there are times in research when it is useful to treat them *as if* they did. All that is really essential is to keep in mind the "as if" character of such separatist operations, but it really is essential to do it.

Yinger's discussion here, in addition to making evident why so much confusion surrounds the idea of personality, focuses attention on the vital concept of self that looms so large in contemporary analyses of personal identity (cf., e.g., Erikson, 1963, 1967) as well as in many other discussions in this volume. Yinger draws serviceable distinctions between such notions as self, ideal self, and ego, while he makes evident the significance of self: first as a means for dealing with questions of individuality; second, as a focal point for understanding the coordination or integration of behavior through space and time; and third, as a crucial context for the interplay between the person and the situation.

The three papers comprising the rest of this section represent distinctive contributions to personality which have substantial ramifications to broader fields in social psychology. Each one also evidences a somewhat different handling of the concept of personality. It is these distinctive features on which we now focus.

The shaping of personality by social forces, especially the self-concept at its core, is vividly portrayed by Pettigrew in the excerpt here from his *Profile of the Negro American* (1964). He brings to sharp awareness the baneful effects of prejudice and discrimination upon the white as well as the Negro (see Allport, Section X). Both the blunt and the subtle interplay between social roles, social attitudes, and the individual's developing self-concept are revealed in Pettigrew's analysis. These are matters to which we shall turn again in Section V.

Taking the person's concept of self as a central feature of personality functioning, Pettigrew shows how the roles and social categories to which an individual is allocated cause him and the structure of his society to become inextricably entwined. Though in a different context, he develops themes also sounded by Erikson (1967), and describes the successive "identity crises" imposed upon the Negro by his position of subservience and by his immersion in a family which may be chronically disorganized. It is no wonder that these conditions may conspire to produce disfunctional social patterns including personal alienation, and with it crime, delinquency, and mental illness. In short, Pettigrew points up how being Black signifies relationships between the person and the society's norms which are lived out in direct social interaction.

By implication at least, the two remaining papers in this section—by McClelland on achievement motivation, and by Christie and Geis on "Machiavellianism"—treat personality in a trait-like manner, i.e., largely as a complex of enduring "integumented" tendencies of a person which make a difference in his behavior across widely varied situations. In this sense, personality is an *intra-personal* structure with behavior being "preprogrammed" in the form of relatively constant dimensions or dispositions that account for continuities in the person and his behavior in the face of environmental flux.

Social and general environmental factors enter into personality mainly in the course of development, i.e., via learning, especially during childhood. This view is manifest, for instance, in McClelland's discussion of the socializing influences likely to generate high or low levels of achievement motivation, presented in his book *The Achieving Society* (1961). McClelland postulates that the distribution of achievement motivation throughout the population serves as a principal personalistic basis for national economic development. The *development* of personality traits, tiated as a problem apart from their functioning. Suggested by this is like achievement needs (or Machiavellianism), is commonly differen- the assumption, explicit in the case of Freud (1920), that personality and its components become progressively less sensitive to immediate forces in the social environment and that personality and behavior are firmly tied to the person's past. Of course, it need not be assumed, and usually is not in modern views, that change is impossible or that present circumstances are totally irrelevant. McClelland, for example, mentions conditions that "engage" achievement needs and he has devised training programs for inducing achievement motivation (see McClelland and Winter, 1969). However, the inclination of most trait theorists is surely in the direction of stressing stability within a dispositional framework.

It is also noteworthy that the work of Christie and Geis and of McClelland bears on important contemporary approaches to the study of attitudes, covered more fully in Section VI. Furthermore, McClelland's work, growing out of a clinical tradition based in the theorizing of Henry Murray (1938), reveals the intimacy of connection between conceptions of personality and of motivation. Indeed, for many theorists the terms are virtual synonyms. The Christie and Geis paper, on the other hand, illustrates a popular approach to personality "structure" in terms of psychometrically derived dimensions; Cattell's (1957) and Eysenck's (1953) factor analysis approaches are other especially clear illustrations of this.

A discussion of various research methods in personality can be found in Shontz's recent book on the subject (1965).

Both as a trait model and because of its psychometric predilections, Christie and Geis's efforts are directly in the classic lines of thought regarding personality that proceed in essential continuity from McDougall's early (1908, 1923, 1937) personalistic formulations. Together with Rokeach's work on dogmatism (1960), their work further extends the seminal developments initiated by the earlier psychometric studies of the authoritarian personality (Adorno, et al., 1950). Their most recent work, of an experimental nature, is reported in *Studies in Machiavellianism* (Christie & Geis, 1970).

Whereas traditionally, personality theory, especially of the trait variety, tended to emphasize stability and historical determinants, Hunt, Allport, and Yinger all indicate that modern theory must deal as well with change and the influence of immediate situational forces. The nexus of this approach, as considered some years ago by Sears (1951), is to effect a closer coordination between personality theory and social psychological theory. In Sears's more situational view, no trait or disposition exists apart from its activating conditions (cf. Hollander, 1960b). Individual and group phenomena are too intermixed to be treated in total isolation.

The development of dynamic *inter*-personal models that consider the person in interaction with his surroundings is basic to Yinger's efforts as well as those of other modern writers (cf. Secord and Backman, 1961; Carson, 1969). Instead of conceptualizing personality in terms of dispositions that are distributed differentially *between* individuals, but that are essentially constant *within* persons and across situations, such viewpoints look upon personality characteristics as varying, in some degree, with the setting in which the person interacts.

Not only that, but viewpoints such as Yinger's accord no less emphasis to change than they do to stability. These interactionist theories consistently adopt a diadic instead of a monadic unit of analysis (cf. Sears, 1951) and commonly argue that particular *intra*-personal structures, as well as behavior, will be maintained only so long as such maintenance is consistent with an ongoing interaction process which is in a state of balance (cf. Aronson's and Osgood's papers in Section VI). Thus personal stability can be said to arise as much from situational constancies as it does from internal sources; or, more precisely, stability and change alike depend on patterns of relations between the person and his situation in the setting of a unitary interactional sysem. As Yinger notes, any rigid segregation of independent-dependent variable relations is inappropriate.

One conclusion remains inescapable from the contributions comprising this section; consensus relative to the *form* and *content* of any theory of personality and to relations between personality and larger social psychological systems is something less than complete. Effective integrating theories are needed, as Sears (1951) long ago pointed out, and toward that end some distinctive contributions have been presented here. In the light of the unsettled state of the art, Allport's injunction that we maintain open minds in the matter is quite obviously to the point. However, it has become increasingly evident that future developments in thinking about personality will need to go beyond mere allowance for societal influences. What is required is a more adequate set of propositions to conceptualize the essential interactional melding of the person and the situation.

14 Traditional personality theory in the light of recent evidence

J. McVICKER HUNT

Although science does ultimately yield a body of relatively definitive knowledge about a domain, it is in essence less this definitive knowledge that is science than the dynamic, self-corrective process of ongoing inquiry. This process of science, to quote Conant (1947, p. 37), consists in the "development of [I would prefer the phrase *creating of*] conceptual schemes" where the relative validity of competing concepts is tested against concept-directed observations so that "new concepts arise from . . . these observations [and experiments]." It has been common for many critics to contend that the failure of this dynamic yeast of science to get underway within our knowledge of persons result from the vagueness of the conceptual schemes which pass for personality theory. I wish to counter that any beliefs definite enough to make observed phenomena surprising or incredible constitute a suitable starting point. Moreover, a majority of personologists have been sharing a number of beliefs which are sufficiently definite to render a good many of the observations made since World War II, and some made earlier, very surprising and so incredible that they call for revision of these beliefs. My purpose in this paper is to state five of these beliefs and to synopsize some of the observations which they make surprising.

Are personality traits the major source of behavioral variance?

According to the first of these beliefs, the source of most of the variation in behavior resides within persons. Psychoanalysts, clinicians generally, personologists, and students of individual differences have shared this belief. Moreover, they have shared it in opposition to those social psychologists—their thought rooted in the work of C. H. Cooley (1902), George Herbert Mead (1934), and W. I. Thomas (see Volkart, 1951)—who have contended that the major source of the variation in behavior resides in the "situation."

In this context, individual differences have been conceived typically after the fashion of static dimensions and have been called traits. Those who have attempted to measure personality traits, however, have all too often found even the reliability and validity coefficients of their measures falling within a range of 0.2 and 0.5. If one takes the square of the coefficient of correlation as a rough, "rule-of-thumb" index of the proportion of the variance attributable to persons, it would appear to be limited to somewhere between 4 and 25% of the total. This is incredibly small for any source which is considered to be *the* basis of behavioral variation, but we personologists have blamed our instruments rather than

Abridged from **American Scientist**, 1965, 53, 80–96, with permission of the author and the publisher.

our belief in the importance of static dimensional traits. Such results, when coupled with the opposition of the social psychologists, suggest the desirability of a direct attempt to determine the relative amounts of common-trait variance attributable to persons, to the modes-of-response which serve as indicators of the traits, and to situations.

Norman Endler and Alvin Rosenstein, two of my former students, and I have attempted this for the trait of *anxiousness* (Endler, Hunt, & Rosenstein, 1962). We asked our subjects to report the degree (on a five-step scale) to which they had manifested a sample of 14 modes-of-response which are commonly considered indicative of anxiety. These included, for instance, "Heart beats faster," "Get an 'uneasy feeling,'" "Emotions disrupt action," "Feel exhilarated and thrilled," "Need to urinate frequently," "Mouth gets dry," "Seek experiences like this," "Experience nausea," and "Have loose bowels." We asked our subjects to report the degree to which they had manifested each of these modes-of-response in each of a sample of 11 specified situations. This sample of situations included, for instance, "Going to meet a [blind] date," "Crawling along a ledge high on a mountain side," "Getting up to give a speech before a large group," "Sailing a boat on a rough sea," "Being alone in the woods at night," "Going into an interview for a very important job," and "Entering a final examination in an important course."

When we made a three-way analysis of variance of these quantified reports of response, the largest main source came from the modes-of-response. This finding in itself is trivial, for one might expect an individual to "get an 'uneasy feeling'" to an extreme degree in many situations without ever having "loose bowels" in any. Far from trivial, however, is the fact that the second largest main source came from the situations. In one sample of Illinois sophomores, with the middle 70% on a measure of anxiousness removed, the mean square for situations (152) was 3.8 times that for persons (40); and in another sample of unselected Penn State freshmen, the mean square for situations (244) was somewhat more than 11 times that for persons (21).

When we have recited these facts to our colleagues, some of them have criticized our comparing of mean squares. Nevertheless, they have typically paid us the compliment of staring in disbelief. Such a reaction implies that personality theory has contained at least one proposition sufficiently definite to be the basis for incredibility of observational evidence. The compliment derives from the implication that we have apparently found evidence, the inappropriateness of comparing mean squares notwithstanding, which is sufficiently relevant to the belief in static trait-dimensions to be surprising. We admitted that the generality of our findings could not be inferred from comparing mean squares. Rather, the generality of our findings would have to derive from their reproducibility with other samples of modes-of-response, with other samples of situations, with other samples of subjects, and with other personality traits. If these results should prove to be reproducible in general, as I have defined general, they imply that our brethren from social psychology have had a conceptual slant which is more nearly congruent with reality than has been the slant of us personologists.

On the other hand, like many disputes in the history of science, this one is based on what is, in a sense, a pseudo-question. Behavioral variance is due primarily to neither persons nor situations. Although a comparison of mean squares for situations and for subjects may have surprise or shock value, actually the mean square for the situational source is a composite of the variances from situations *per se*, from the interaction of situations-by-subjects, from the interaction of situations-by-modes-of-response, from the triple interaction, and from the residual. Also, the mean square for subjects is a similar composite. If one employs the equations of Gleser, Cronbach, and Rajaratnam (1961) to partition these various sources properly, one finds that the modes-of-response do contribute about one-fourth of the variance, again a trivial point. But one also finds that neither situations nor subjects contribute substantially. Typically, neither contributes 5% of the total, and for subjects this is what would be expected from the reliability and validity coefficients for tests of personality traits. The simple interactions contribute nearly a third of the total variance (about 10% each), and the triple interaction with residual contributes about the final third. Thus, main sources, simple interactions, and triple interaction with residual each contribute about a third of the total variance (Endler & Hunt, 1964). Three-way analyses of variance for some 15 samples of subjects with three forms of the S-R Inventory have served to indicate that the percentages of total variance from these various main sources and interactive sources are quite stable. While increasing the variability of situations increases the percentage of variance from situations, the increase is only one from something of the order of 2 or 5% to something of the order of 7 or 8%. Thus, it is neither the individual differences among subjects, *per se*, nor the

variations among situations, *per se*, that produce the variations in behavior. It is, rather, the interactions among these which are important.

In the words of a Vermont farmer once quoted by Henry A. Murray, "people is mostly alike, but what difference they is can be powerful important." I am now guessing to be "powerful important" the variations in the meanings of situations to people and the variations in the modes-of-response they manifest. These results imply that, for either understanding variations of behavior or making clinical predictions, we should be looking toward instruments that will classify people in terms of the kinds of responses they make in various categories of situations. Osgood has provided us with the Semantic Differential, an important method of assessing the interaction between people and situations (Osgood, Suci, & Tannenbaum, 1957). Perhaps our own approach may also be helpful.

Is all behavior motivated?

The second belief which I wish to confront with evidence from recent investigation concerns personality dynamics or, particularly, motivation. It has most commonly taken the form of the assertion that "all behavior is motivated." In this form, which either originated with or was popularized by Freud, the assertion is indeed too vague to provide a basis for observational surprise, but Freud (1900, 1915), such physiologists as Cannon (1915), and such modern behavior theorists as Hull (1943), Miller and Dollard (1941), and Mowrer (1960), have all shared in filling out the statement so that it has come to say, "all behavior is motivated by painful stimulation, homeostatic need, sexual appetite, or by acquired drives, i.e., originally neutral stimuli which have been associated with painful stimuli, homeostatic need, or sex in the organism's past experience."

This is the well-known drive-reduction theory. According to this theory, the aim or function of every instinct, defense, action, habit, or phantasy is to reduce or to eliminate either stimulation or excitation within the nervous system. Once the assertion gets this form, it can readily provide the basis for observational surprise, for it implies that, in the absence of such motivation, organisms will become quiescent.

They do not become quiescent. I have reviewed these surprising observations elsewhere (1960, 1963a). It has been contended that I have reviewed them *ad nauseam*, so let me be brief here. These observations derive from the studies of play in children by Bühler (1928) and in animals by Beach (1945) and others, the studies of monkeys and chimpanzees manipulating puzzles by Harlow (1950) and by Harlow, Harlow, and Meyer (1950), the studies of spatial exploration in rats by Berlyne (1960) and by Nissen (1930), the studies of spontaneous alternation of rats in a T-maze by Montgomery (1953, 1955), the finding that monkeys will learn various things merely to get a peek at a new scene by Butler (1953), the studies of human beings under conditions of homogeneous input by Bexton, Heron, and Scott (1954), and the now classic studies by Hebb (1946) which found that fear in chimpanzees will occur with encountering something familiar in an unfamiliar guise.

Such evidence, however, has recently been given theoretical recognition in several unfortunate fashions. One of these is drive-naming. The literature is now full of drives (manipulative, exploratory, curiosity, etc.) and of needs (stimulus, change, etc.). This naming of new motives which merely describe the activities they are designed to explain, helps little. Moreover, in motive-naming, we are revisiting the instinct-naming which McDougall (1908) popularized early in this century but which was discredited just after World War I. We should know better.

A second unfortunate fashion of theoretical recognition is naming motives in terms of their telic significance. I refer to the "urge to mastery" promulgated by Ives Hendrick (1943) and to the concept of "competence motivation" proposed by Robert White (1959) in his excellent review of the evidence concerned. Unfortunately, concepts of telic significance seem to me to provide no means of developing hypotheses about antecedent-consequent relationships that can be tested against observations.

A third unfortunate fashion of theoretical recognition has consisted of postulating spontaneous activity. Some activity can be said to be spontaneous, from a descriptive standpoint, as Hebb has pointed out to me. But this does not make spontaneity a useful explanation, and I am indebted to my colleague, L. I. O'Kelly, for noting that postulating spontaneous activity as an explanation may be just as useless as postulating a list of instincts and drives, and for precisely the same reasons.

As I see it, these various lines of evidence combine to indicate that a system and a mechanism of motivation inheres within the organism's informational interaction with its environmental circumstances. I have described this mechanism elsewhere (Hunt, 1963a). The news of its existence was, I believe, one of the implicit messages of that now classic book entitled *The Organization of Behavior* (Hebb, 1949). This message has since been made explicit, and it has been confirmed by various lines of evidence.

Whatever the essential character of this informational organism-environment interaction and its relationship to arousal turns out to be, there appears to be an optimum amount of it for each organism at any given time. I suspect that this optimum is to a considerable degree a function of experience, and that it may obey Helson's (1959) notion of the adaptation level. When a situation offers too much, i.e., when the inputs from a situation are too incongruous with the information already coded and stored, the organism withdraws as illustrated by Hebb's (1946) fearful chimpanzees, and by some of the human beings whom Festinger (1957) has found to be avoiding or discrediting information dissonant with their commitments and plans. On the other hand, when a situation offers too little incongruity, i.e., when the inputs from a situation are too similar to the information already in storage, boredom results, and the organism withdraws from that situation to seek another one offering more incongruity, stimulus-change, novelty, dissonance, uncertainty, or what-have-you. It is this seeking of incongruity which is apparently illustrated by the college students in the McGill experiments of Bexton, Heron, and Scott (1954) who refused to remain under conditions of homogeneous input even though they were paid $20 a day. It is this seeking of incongruity which is also illustrated by the fact that Butler's (1953) monkeys will learn merely in order to get a peek at the world outside their monotonous cage-situations, and by that early study of Nissen's (1930) in which rats left their familiar nests and crossed an electrified grid (one

of Worden's obstructions) to get to a Dashiell maze filled with objects fresh and novel to them. This work of Nissen's never got into the textbooks, probably because it was too dissonant with the traditional propositions about motivation presented therein.

This line of conceptualizing has still largely unacknowledged implications for our traditional notions of both psychodynamics and psychological development. Both Sigmund Freud (1926) and Anna Freud (1936) conceived of the mechanisms of defense as serving to protect a person from anxiety. Sigmund Freud, at least in his later days when he came to see repression as a consequence of anxiety rather than as its source, saw anxiety originating from castration threats, Oedipal anxieties, and other overwhelmingly intense experiences of painful stimulation. The fact that Hebb (1946) has found chimpanzees withdrawing from sources of input which could never have been associated with painful stimulation (by virtue of the fact that the infants had been reared under observation in the Yerkes Laboratory), coupled with the fact that Festinger (1957) and his students have found human subjects utilizing various strategies to avoid dissonant information, and coupled again with the fact that evidence dissonant with prevailing theories—like that of Nissen's early study—seldom gets into the textbooks, suggest that the mechanism of defense may sometimes, or may even typically, function chiefly to protect individuals from information too incongruous with that which they already have coded in the storage or with that already involved in their commitments and plans. Probably the most important category of stored information for this theoretical context is that concerning the self, as the theorizing of Hilgard (1949) and as the clinical observations and theorizing of Rogers (1951) and George Kelly (1955) would indicate. I dare not take the time to elaborate; here it must be enough to point a direction.

Are emotional factors so much more important than cognitive factors in psychological development?

The third belief which I wish to discuss in the light of recently uncovered evidence is also motivational and dynamic, but it is developmental as well. Freud probably did more to emphasize the importance of infantile experience in psychological development than anyone else in the history of thought. Freud's (1905) theory of psychosexual development put the emphasis on the fate of the instinctive modes of infantile pleasure-striving, i.e., sucking, elimination, and genitality. Freud's influence has led to the very widespread belief among personologists that these extrinsic motivational or emotional factors are much more important in development than are cognitive factors. This minimization of the importance of cognitive and perceptual factors in early infantile, or preverbal, development has been abetted, moreover, by the beliefs in fixed intelligence and predetermined development so widely held among the earlier students of individual differences in intelligence.

Recent evidence indicates, perhaps, that just about the opposite should hold. Reviews of those relatively objective studies of the effects of the emotional factors pointed up in the theory of psychosexual development have generally tended to depreciate the importance of those factors (see Child, 1954; Hunt, 1946, 1956; Orlansky, 1949). Every study finding significant effects

can be matched with another which does not. Moreover, the better controlled the study, the less likely is it to have found significant effects. Similarly, while infantile feeding-frustration in rats appeared to increase eating speed and hoarding in adulthood (Hunt, 1941; Hunt, et al., 1947), thereby lending support to the importance of extrinsic motivational factors, these studies have not always been reproducible so far as the effect on hoarding is concerned (Marx, 1952; McKelvey & Marx, 1951). Moreover, having done the first of these studies, perhaps I should admit that I probably misinterpreted the facts anyway. Of course, it is still true that painful stimulation can inhibit eating and drinking and that prolonged failure to eat and drink can kill an organism. On the other hand, the studies of the effects of variations in the richness of early perceptual experience in animals have regularly shown (Forgays & Forgays, 1952; Forgus, 1954, 1955a, 1955b; Hymovitch, 1952) substantial effects on adult problem-solving. These studies have stemmed from Hebb's theorizing, and the first of the kind (Hebb, 1947) compared the performances of pet-reared rats with those of cage-reared rats in the Hebb-Williams (1946) test of animal intelligence. The pet-reared animals proved much superior to their cage-reared littermates. Thompson and Heron (1954) have made a similar experiment with dogs, and the evidence of the superiority of the pet-reared dogs over their cage-reared litter-mates is even more striking than that for rats. The fact that the evidence from dogs is stronger than that from rats suggests that the importance of early experience, and particularly the importance of early cognitive or perceptual experience, probably increases up the phylogenetic scale as that portion of the brain without direct connection to sensory input or motor outlet increases relative to the portion which does have direct sensory and/or motor connections (i.e., with the size of what Hebb [1949] has termed the A/S ratio). Moreover, there is direct evidence that such effects can be generalized from animal subjects to human beings in studies by Goldfarb (see 1955 for summary) which indicate that being reared in an orphanage, where the variety of circumstances encountered is highly restricted, results at adolescence in lower intelligence, less ability to sustain a task, less attentiveness, and more problems in interpersonal relations than being reared in a foster home. Moreover, those findings of Dennis (1960) that 60% of the two-year-olds in a Teheran orphanage, where changes in ongoing stimulation were minimal, were not yet sitting up alone and that 85% of the four-year-olds were not yet walking alone, serve to dramatize how very much the factor of variety of circumstances encountered in infancy can affect the rate of development— even the rate of development of posture and locomotion.

As I see it, these various lines of evidence combine to indicate that cognitive experience—or, more precisely, the organism's informational interaction with the environment—can be as important for psychological development as emotions based on the fate of instincts, and perhaps it is typically more important. In corollary fashion, these same bits of evidence would also appear to indicate that we have been wrong in our widespread belief that it is the intellectual characteristics of a person which are most nearly fixed by the genotype and that the emotional characteristics of a person are highly subject to substantial environmental influence. Although the life his-

tory is of considerable importance in the development of both types of characteristics, it appears that it may be the intellectual variety which is the more subject to substantial effects of environmental encounters, particularly those coming in early infancy.

Must emotional attachments derive from gratification of libidinal or homeostatic needs?

According to a fourth belief commonly held by personologists, the emotional attachments to objects, persons, and places —called cathexes in psychoanalytic terminology—derive from their association with the gratification of libidinal or homeostatic needs. In his *Three Contributions to the Theory of Sex*, Freud (1905) not only assumed a separation of libidinal from nutritional needs, but he also attributed all object-cathexes to libidinal energy (see p. 553, p. 611, and p. 743 footnote 2). These points, coupled with Freud's (1915) conception of instinct, appear to indicate that he attributed all emotional attachments to libidinal gratification, as he defined it. As I (Hunt, 1946) pointed out nearly 20 years ago, any such generalization is contradicted by the wide variety of studies in which preference for objects, persons, and places has been changed by association with food reward (see, e.g., Mowrer, 1960; Razran, 1938a, 1938b; Williams, 1929; Williams & Williams, 1943) or by association with success in goal-achievement (see Mierke, 1933; Nowlis, 1941; Rosenzweig, 1933).

More recently, it has been generally believed that such emotional attachment derives from the association of objects, persons, and places with homeostatic gratification. And so it is sometimes, but Harlow's (1958) work indicates that association with homeostatic gratification is far from the whole story. In his studies, you will recall, monkey babies, when frightened, went for solace to the soft surrogate-mothers covered with padded terry-cloth rather than to the wire surrogate-mothers on which they had sucked to gratify their need for food.

Nor can softness of contact be the whole story, for behavioral criteria defining emotional attachment appear to have another basis. Infants of various species appear to approach, to seek, and to take delight in objects which are becoming recognizably familiar in the course of repeated encounters (see Hunt, 1963b), and they show varying degrees of distress as these objects escape their perceptual ken. Piaget (1936) has described how his children came to make what is clearly an "intentional effort" to keep interesting spectacles within perceptual range. Anyone who has ever jounced an infant on his knee and stopped his motion only to find the infant starting a similar motion of his own, is familiar with this intentional effort of the infant to hold on to an interesting spectacle. One gathers from Piaget's (1936) observations that these interesting spectacles very commonly consist of objects or persons that are becoming familiar through repeated encounters. In an exploratory study of this phenomenon, Dr. Ina Uzgiris and I have got evidence consonant with this idea that the young human infant prefers a mobile which has been hanging over his crib to another mobile which he has never encountered before (Hunt & Uzgiris, 1966). Here, the term *prefers* is based on looking time. When the familiar mobile has been withdrawn for a time and is then returned with another unfamiliar one beside it, the infant looks more at the familiar than at the unfamil-

iar one. Similar phenomena of emotional attachment are to be found in animals. Since it is following an object and distress at its escape from perceptual ken that characterizes the one major component of what the ethnologists (Heinroth, 1910; Lorenz, 1935; Thorpe, 1944) call "imprinting," it intrigues me to consider that this effort to follow and to keep interesting spectacles within view and the distress at losing them in lower mammals and birds may be a special case of this more general principle of emotional attachment deriving from recognitive familiarity. If this be sensible, and I believe it is, one can then relate the marked variation in the number of encounters required to establish such recognitive emotional attachments to Hebb's A/S ratio. There appears to be a progression in the number of encounters or in the amount of exposure time required, from two or three hours in the grey-leg goose, through two or three days in the sheep or deer, some two weeks in the monkey infant, and some six or so weeks in the chimpanzee infant, to some six or so months in the human infant. Maternal attachment appears to be another special case of this same principle, but it is well contaminated also with skin contacts and with the gratification of homeostatic need. In all probability, fear of strangers is a direct derivative comparable to the fear of the familiar in an unfamiliar guise found in adult chimpanzees by Hebb (1946) and already mentioned.

But following is alone no indication of emotional delight. Evidence of the delight comes from the infant's smile and laugh of recognition. Spitz (1946) and others have considered smiling to be a social response, one based, presumably, on the fact that the human face is repeatedly associated with homeostatic gratification, but Piaget's (1936) observations and those of my colleague, Dr. Uzgiris, indicate that the infant will smile and show laughing delight at the appearance of various objects which are merely becoming familiar with repeated encounters (Hunt, 1963b; Hunt & Uzgiris, 1966).

Such observations and considerations strongly suggest that recognitive familiarity is in itself a source of emotional attachment, and this attachment is attested further by the fact that separation grief always concerns familiar objects and persons and by the fact that such grief is but transient in infants too young to have established object permanence. In a sense, this is a further elaboration of the importance of that intrinsic system of motivation which inheres in the organism's informational interaction with the environment.

Do encounters with painful stimulation in infancy result in sensitivity and proneness to anxiety?

According to a fifth belief, which we may call the "trauma theory of anxiety," encounters with painful stimulation or strong homeostatic need inevitably leave a young child or a young animal prone to be sensitive and anxious in most situations. This trauma theory assumes the conditioning conception of fear. Thus, it is presumed that the various sources of inputs present immediately before and during encounters with painful stimulation will acquire the capacity to evoke the autonomic and central emotional features incorporated within the total response to painful stimulation.

In spite of Hebb's (1946) strong evidence to the contrary, most clinicians of all professions act as if *the only source*

of anxious emotional disturbance were this association of originally neutral sources of input with pain. Recently, however, another source of evidence dissonant with this widely held belief has been the investigations of the effects of shocking infant animals before they are weaned. Although there may well be both species and strain differences in some of these effects, as indicated by reports—based on studies using mice as subjects—which deviate from those which I am about to mention (see Hall, 1934; Lindzey, *et al.*, 1960), rats shocked in infancy have been repeatedly found as adults to be less fearful than rats which have been left unmolested in the maternal nest. This is to say that they urinated less and defecated less in, were less hesitant to enter, and were more active in unfamiliar territory than were rats which had been left unmolested in the maternal nest (see Deneberg, 1962; Levine, 1959, 1961).

In two other investigations, moreover, rats shocked before weaning, with sufficient intensity to keep them squealing continually for three minutes each day, have been found as adults to require stronger shocks to instigate escape-activity than do rats left unmolested (Goldman, 1964; Griffiths, 1960). Finally, in a very recent study by Salama, one of my own students, rats shocked daily from their 11th through their 20th day were found to show much less "fixative effect" of shock after the choice-point in a T-maze than did rats left unmolested in the maternal nest or than did rats either gentled or handled for this same period (Salama & Hunt, 1964).

Let me explain this last experiment briefly. Some 16 years ago, Farber (1948) reported a study of "fixation" which showed that rats intermittently shocked just after the choice-point on their way to one of the goal-boxes in a T-maze, where they were fed, required substantially more unrewarded trials to give up going to that goal-box than did rats merely given food-reward in it. Salama (1962) has replicated this finding and found the mean number of unrewarded trials to be 20.7 for the shocked animals but only 2.8 for those merely given food-reward. He has gone further; he has compared the number of unrewarded trials required for rats shocked in infancy to give up the goal-box with the numbers required by rats gentled and handled. The means for those gentled (21.4) and for those handled (17.58) differed little from the mean for those left unmolested in the maternal nest (20.7), but the mean for those shocked (9) approximates only half the means for these other groups, and it differs significantly $(p < 0.001)$ from these and from the unmolested group not shocked after the choice-point.

It is very interesting in connection with these studies that Holmes (1935) has found the children of lower-class backgrounds from a day-care center to be less fearful than children of an upper-middle-class background from a nursery school. Holmes's study was conducted in 1935, right in the midst of the Great Depression, when children of lower-class parents could be expected to have encountered more painful stimulation and homeostatic need than children of the upper-middle class. This result suggests that the findings from these animal studies may well generalize to human beings.

It is clear from the evidence that all of these studies tend to disconfirm the present formulation of the trauma theory of anxiety based on the conditioning principle as the only experiential basis for anxiousness. They also suggest that encounters with painful stimulation may serve instead to raise what Helson (1959) calls the adaptation level for painful stimulation and thereby to reduce its aversiveness. The force of such evidence is hardly yet sufficient to warrant—and certainly not sufficient to call for—a change in child-rearing practices, for trauma is also a fact. There are varieties of early experience that leave infants prone to be sensitive and anxious, but we cannot yet clearly specify their nature. Perhaps it should be remembered in connection with this evidence, however, that the Spartan culture survived for several centuries while holding to a belief that infants should be exposed to cold and to painful stimulation to prepare them to bear the dire exigencies of later life.

15 The open system in personality theory

GORDON W. ALLPORT

The concept of system

Until a generation or so ago science, including psychology, was preoccupied with what might be called "disorganized complexity." Natural scientists explored this fragment and that fragment of nature; psychologists explored this fragment and that fragment of experience and behavior. The problem of interrelatedness, though recognized, was not made a topic for direct inquiry.

What is called system theory today—at least in psychology—is the outgrowth of the relatively new organismic conception reflected in the work of von Bertalanffy, Goldstein, and in certain aspects of gestalt psychology. It opposes simple reaction theories where a virtual automaton is seen to respond discretely to stimuli as though they were pennies-in-the-slot. Interest in system theory is increasing in psychology, though perhaps not so fast as in other sciences.

Now a system—any system—is defined merely as a complex of elements in mutual interaction. Bridgman (1959), as might be expected of an operationist, includes a hint of method in his definition. He writes, a system is "an isolated enclosure in which all measurements that can be made of what goes on in the system are in some way correlated" (p. 188).

Systems may be classified as closed or open. A closed system is defined as one that admits no matter from outside itself and is therefore subject to entropy according to the second law of thermodynamics. While some outside energies, such as change in temperature and wind may play upon a closed system, it has no restorative properties and no transactions with its environment, so that like a decaying bridge it sinks into thermodynamic equilibrium.

Now some authors, such as von Bertalanffy (1952b), Brunswik (1955), and Pumpian-Mindlin (1959), have said or implied that certain theories of psychology and of personality operate with the conception of closed systems. But in my opinion these critics press their point too far. We had better leave closed systems to the realm of physics where they belong (although even here it is a question whether Einstein's formula for the release of matter into energy does not finally demonstrate the futility of positing a closed cgs system even in physics). In any event it is best to admit that all living organisms partake of the character of open systems. I doubt that we shall find any advocate of a truly closed system in the whole range of personality theory. At the same time current theories do differ widely in the amount of openness they ascribe to the personality system.

If we comb definitions of open systems we can piece together four criteria: there is intake and output of both matter and energy; there is the achievement and maintenance of steady (homeostatic) states, so that the intrusion

Abridged from the **Journal of Abnormal and Social Psychology**, 61, 301–11 (Copyright © 1960 by the American Psychological Association), with permission of the author and the publisher.

of outer energy will not seriously disrupt internal form and order; there is generally an increase of order over time, owing to an increase in complexity and differentiation of parts; finally, at least at the human level, there is more than mere intake and output of matter and energy: there is extensive transactional commerce with the environment.[1]

While all of our theories view personality as an open system in some sense, still they can be fairly well classified according to the varying emphasis they place upon each of these criteria, and according to how many of the criteria they admit.

CRITERION 1

Consider the first criterion of material and energy exchange. Stimulus-response theory in its purest form concentrates on this criterion to the virtual exclusion of all the others. It says in effect that a stimulus enters and a response is emitted. There is, of course, machinery for summation, storage, and delay, but the output is broadly commensurate with the intake. We need study only the two poles of stimulus and response with a minimum of concern for intervening processes. Methodological positivism goes one step further, saying in effect, that we do not need the concept of personality at all. We focus attention on our own measurable manipulations of input and on the measurable manipulations of output. Personality thus evaporates in a mist of method.

CRITERION 2

The requirement of steady state for open systems is so widely admitted in personality theory that it needs little discussion. To satisfy needs, to reduce tension, to maintain equilibrium, comprise, in most theories, the basic formula of personality dynamics. Some authors, such as Stagner (1951) and Mowrer (1959), regard this formula as logically fitting in with Cannon's (1932) account of homeostasis.[2] Man's intricate adjustive behavior is simply an extension of the principle involved in temperature regulation, balance of blood volume, sugar content, and the like, in the face of environmental change. It is true that Toch and Hastorf (1955) warn against overextending the concept of homeostasis in personality theory. I myself doubt that Cannon would approve the extension, for to him the value of homeostasis lay in its capacity to free man for what he called "the priceless unessentials" of life (1932, p. 323). When biological equilibrium is attained the priceless unessentials take over and constitute the major part of human activity. Be that as it may, most current theories clearly regard personality as a *modus operandi* for restoring a steady state.

[1] von Bertalanffy's definition explicitly recognizes the first two of these criteria as present in all living organisms. A living organism, he says, is "an open system which continually gives up matter to the outer world and takes in matter from it, but which maintains itself in this continuous exchange in a steady state, or approaches such steady state in its variations in time" (1952a, p. 125). But elsewhere in this author's writing we find recognition of the additional criteria (1952a, p. 145; 1952b, p. 34).

[2] In a recent review Mowrer (1959) strongly defends the homeostatic theory. He is distressed that the dean of American psychologists, Robert Woodworth (1958) has taken a firm stand against the "need-primacy" theory in favor of what he calls the "behavior-primacy" theory. With the detailed merits of the argument we are not here concerned. What concerns us at the moment is that the issue has been sharply joined. Need-primacy which Mowrer calls a "homeostatic" theory does not go beyond our first two criteria for an open system. Woodworth by insisting that contact with, and mastery of, the environment constitute a pervasive principle of motivation, recognizes the additional criteria.

Psychoanalytic theories are of this order. According to Freud the ego strives to establish balance among the three "tyrants"—id, superego, and outer environment. Likewise the so-called mechanisms of ego defense are essentially maintainers of a steady state. Even a neurosis has the same basic adjustive function.[3]

To sum up: most current theories of personality take full account of two of the requirements of an open system. They allow interchange of matter and energy, and recognize the tendency of organisms to maintain an orderly arrangement of elements in a steady state. Thus they emphasize stability rather than growth, permanence rather than change, "uncertainty reduction" (information theory), and "coding" (cognitive theory) rather than creativity. In short, they emphasize being rather than becoming. Hence, most personality theories are biologistic in the sense that they ascribe to personality only the two features of an open system that are clearly present in all living organisms.

There are, however, two additional criteria, sometimes mentioned but seldom stressed by biologists themselves, and similarly neglected in much current personality theory.

TRANSATLANTIC PERSPECTIVE

Before examining Criterion 3 which calls attention to the tendency of open systems to enhance their degree of order,

[3] When we speak of the "function" of a neurosis we are reminded of the many theories of "functionalism" current in psychology and social science. Granted that the label, as Merton (1957) has shown, is a wide one, still we may safely say that the emphasis of functionalism is always on the usefulness of an activity in maintaining the "steady state" of a personality or social or cultural system. In short, "functional" theories stress maintenance of present direction allowing little room or none at all for departure and change.

let us glimpse our present theoretical situation in cross-cultural perspective.

Most men, the Hindus say, have four central desires. To some extent, though only roughly, they correspond to the developmental stages of life. The first desire is for pleasure—a condition fully and extensively recognized in our Western theories of tension reduction, reinforcement, libido, and needs. The second desire is for success—likewise fully recognized and studied in our investigations of power, status, leadership, masculinity, and need-achievement. Now the third desire is to do one's duty and discharge one's responsibility. (It was Bismarck, not a Hindu, who said: "We are not in this world for pleasure but to do our damned duty.") Finally, the Hindus tell us that in many people all these three motives pall, and they then seek intensely for a grade of understanding— for a philosophical or religious meaning —that will liberate them from pleasure, success, and duty (Smith, 1958).

Now we retrace our steps from India to modern Vienna and encounter the existentialist school of logotherapy. Its founder, Viktor Frankl, emphasizes above all the central place of duty and meaning, the same two motives that the Hindus place highest in their hierarchy of desire. Frankl reached his position after a long and agonizing incarceration in Nazi concentration camps. With other prisoners he found himself stripped to naked existence (1959a). In such extremity what does a person need and want? Pleasure and success are out of the question. One wants to know the meaning of his suffering and to learn how as a responsible being he should acquit himself. Should he commit suicide? If so, why; if not, why not? The search for meaning becomes supreme.

Neither Hindu psychology nor Frankl

underestimates the role of pleasure and success in personality. Nor would Frankl abandon the hard won gains reflected in psychoanalytic and need theory. He says merely that in studying or treating a person we often find these essentially homeostatic formulations inadequate. A man normally wants to know the whys and wherefores. No other biological system does so; hence, man stands alone in that he possesses a degree of openness surpassing that of any other living system.

CRITERION 3

Returning now to our main argument, we encounter a not inconsiderable array of theories that emphasize the tendency of human personality to go beyond steady states and to strive for an enhancement and elaboration of internal order even at the cost of considerable disequilibrium.

I cannot examine all of these nor name all the relevant authors. One could start with McDougall's proactive sentiment of self-regard which he viewed as organizing all behavior through a kind of "forward memory" (to use Gooddy's apt term—1959). Not too dissimilar is the stress that Combs and Snygg place on the enhancement of the phenomenal field. We may add Goldstein's conception of self-actualization as tending to enhance order in personality; also Maslow's theory of growth motives that supplement deficiency motives. One thinks of Jung's principle of individuation leading toward the achievement of a self (a goal never actually completed). Some theories, Bartlett and Cantril among them, put primary stress on the "pursuit of meaning." Certain developments in post-Freudian "ego psychology" belong here. So too does existentialism with its rec-ognition of the need for meaning and of the values of commitment. (The brain surgeon, Harvey Cushing, was speaking of open systems when he said: "The only way to endure life is to have a task to complete.")

No doubt we should add Woodworth's recent advocacy of the "behavior primacy" theory as opposed to the "need" theory, Robert White's emphasis on "competence," and Erikson's "search for identity."

Now these theories are by no means identical. The differences between them merit prolonged debate. I lump them here simply because all seem to me to recognize the third criterion of open systems, namely, the tendency of such systems to enhance their degree of order and become something more than at present they are.

We all know the objection to theories of this type. Methodologists with a taste for miniature and fractionated systems complain that they do not lead to "testable propositions" (cf. Roby, 1959). The challenge is valuable in so far as it calls for an expansion of research ingenuity. But the complaint is ill-advised if it demands that we return to quasiclosed systems simply because they are more "researchable" and elegant. Our task is to study what is, and not what is immediately convenient.

CRITERION 4

Now for our fourth and last criterion. Virtually all the theories I have mentioned up to now conceive of personality as something integumented, as residing within the skin. There are theorists (Kurt Lewin, Martin Buber, Gardner Murphy, and others) who challenge this view, considering it too closed. Murphy says that we overstress the separation of man from the context of his living. Experiments on sensory deprivation Hebb (1955) has interpreted as demonstrations of the constant dependence of inner stability on the flow of environmental stimulation. Why Western thought makes such a razor-sharp distinction between the person and all else is an interesting problem. Probably the personalistic emphasis in Judeo-Christian religion is an initial factor, and as Murphy (1958, p. 297) has pointed out the industrial and commercial revolutions further accentuated the role of individuality. Shinto philosophy, by contrast, regards the individual, society, and nature as forming the tripod of human existence. The individual as such does not stick out like a raw digit. He blends with nature and he blends with society. It is only the merger that can be profitably studied.

As Western theorists most of us, I dare say, hold the integumented view of the personality system. I myself do so. Others rebelling against the setting of self over against the world, have produced theories of personality written in terms of social interaction, role relations, situationism, or some variety of field theory. Still other writers, such as Talcott Parsons (1951) and F. H. Allport (1955), have admitted the validity of both the integumented personality system and systems of social interaction, and have spent much effort in harmonizing the two types of systems thus conceived.

This problem, without doubt, is the knottiest issue in contemporary social science. It is the issue which, up to now, has prevented us from agreeing on the proper way to reconcile psychological and sociocultural science.

In this matter my own position is on the conservative side. It is the duty of psychology, I think, to study the person-system, meaning thereby the attitudes, abilities, traits, trends, motives, and pathology of the individual—his cognitive styles, his sentiments, and individual moral nature and their interrelations. The justification is twofold: (a) there is a persistent though changing person-system in time, clearly delimited by birth and death; (b) we are immediately aware of the functioning of this system; our knowledge of it, though imperfect, is direct, whereas our knowledge of all other outside systems, including social systems, is deflected and often distorted by their necessary incorporation into our own apperceptions.

At the same time our work is incomplete unless we admit that each person possesses a *range* of abilities, attitudes, and motives that will be evoked by the different environments and situations he encounters. Hence, we need to understand cultural, class, and family constellations and traditions in order to know the schemata the person has probably interiorized in the course of his learning. But I hasten to warn that the study of cultural, class, family, or any other social system does not automatically illumine the person-system, for we have to know whether the individual has accepted, rejected, or remained uninfluenced by the social system in question. The fact that one plays the role of, say, teacher, salesman, or father is less important for the study of his personality than to know whether he likes or dislikes, and how he defines, the role. And yet at the same time unless we are students of sociocultural systems we shall never know what it is the person is accepting, rejecting, or redefining.

The provisional solution I would offer is the following: the personality theorist should be so well trained in social science that he can view the behavior of an individual as fitting any system of interaction; that is, he should be able to cast this behavior properly in the culture where it occurs, in its situational context, and in terms of role theory and field theory. At the same time he should not lose sight—as some theorists do—of the fact that there is an internal and subjective patterning of all these contextual acts. A traveler who moves from culture to culture, from situation to situation, is none the less a single person; and within him one will find the nexus, the patterning, of the diverse experiences and memberships that constitute his personality.

Thus, I myself would not go so far as to advocate that personality be defined in terms of interaction, culture, or roles. Attempts to do so seem to me to smudge the concept of personality, and to represent a surrender of the psychologist's special assignment as a scientist. Let him be acquainted with all systems of interaction, but let him return always to the point where such systems converge and intersect and are patterned—in the single individual.

Hence, we accept the fourth (transactional) criterion of the open system, but with the firm warning that it must not be applied with so much enthusiasm that we lose the personality system altogether.

Some examples

I suggest that we regard all sharp controversies in personality theory as probably arising from the two opposed points of view—the quasiclosed and the fully open.

The principle of reinforcement, to take one example, is commonly regarded as the cement that stamps in a response, as the glue that fixes personality at the level of past deeds. Now an open-system interpretation is very different. Feigl (1959, p. 117), for instance, has pointed out that reinforcement works primarily in a prospective sense. It is only from a *recognition* of consequences (not from the consequences themselves) that the human individual binds the past to the future and resolves to avoid punishment and to seek rewards in similar circumstances, provided, of course, that it is consonant with his interests and values to do so. Here we no longer assume that reinforcement stamps in, but that it is one factor among many to be considered in the programing of future action (Allport, 1946). In this example we see what a wide difference it makes whether we regard personality as a quasiclosed or open system.

The issue has its parallels in neurophysiology. How open is the nervous system? We know it is of a complexity so formidable that we have only an inkling as to how complex it may be. Yet one thing is certain, namely, that high level gating often controls and steers lower level processes. While we cannot tell exactly what we mean by "higher levels" they surely involve ideational schemata, intentions, and generic personality trends. They are instruments for programing, not merely for reacting. In the future we may confidently expect that the neurophysiology of programing and the psychology of proaction will draw together. Until they do so it is wise to hold lightly our self-closing metaphors of sowbug, switchboard, giant computer, and hydraulic pump.

Finally, an example from motivation theory. Some years ago I argued that motives may become functionally autonomous of their origins. (And one lives to regret one's brashness.)

Whatever its shortcomings the concept of functional autonomy succeeds in viewing personality as an open and changing system. As might be expected, criticism has come chiefly from those who prefer to view the personality system as quasiclosed. Some critics say that I am dealing only with occasional cases where the extinction of a habit system has failed to occur. This criticism, of course, begs the question, for the point at issue is why do some habit systems fail to extinguish when no longer reinforced? And why do some habit systems that were once instrumental get refashioned into interests and values having a motivational push?

The common counterargument holds that "secondary reinforcement" somehow miraculously sustains all the proactive goal-seeking of a mature person. The scientific ardor of Pasteur, the religio-political zeal of Gandhi, or for that matter, Aunt Sally's devotion to her needlework, are explained by hypothetical cross-conditioning that somehow substitutes for the primary reinforcement of primary drives. What is significant for our purposes is that these critics prefer the concept of secondary reinforcement, not because it is clearer, but because it holds our thinking within the frame of a quasiclosed (reactive) system.

Now is not the time to re-argue the matter, but I have been asked to hint at my present views. I would say first that the concept of functional autonomy has relevance even at the level of quasiclosed systems. There are now so many indications concerning feedback mechanisms, cortical self-stimulation, self-organizing systems, and the like (Chang, 1950; Hebb, 1949; Olds & Milner, 1954) that I believe we cannot deny the existence of self-sustaining circuit mechanisms which we can lump together under the rubric "perseverative functional autonomy."

But the major significance of the concept lies in a different direction, and presupposes the view that personality is an expanding system seeking progressively new levels of order and transaction. While drive motives remain fairly constant throughout life, existential motives do not. It is the very nature of an open system to achieve progressive levels of order through change in cognitive and motivational structure. Since in this case the causation is systemic we cannot hope to account for functional autonomy in terms of specific reinforcements. This condition I would call "propriate functional autonomy."

Both perseverative and propriate autonomy are, I think, indispensable conceptions. The one applies to the relatively closed part-systems within personality; the other to the continuously evolving structure of the whole.

A last example. It is characteristic of the quasiclosed system outlook that it is heavily nomothetic. It seeks response and homeostatic similarities among all personality systems (or, as in general behavior systems theory, among *all* systems). If, however, we elect the open system view we find ourselves forced in part toward the idiographic outlook. For now the vital question becomes "what makes the system hang together in any one person?" (cf. Taylor, 1958). Let me repeat this question, for it is the one that more than any other has haunted me over the years. *What makes the system cohere in any one person?* That this problem is pivotal, urgent, and relatively neglected, will be recognized by open-system theorists, even while it is downgraded and evaded by those who prefer their systems semi-closed.

Final word

If my discourse has seemed polemical I can only plead that personality theory lives by controversy. In this country we are fortunate that no single party line shackles our speculations. We are free to pursue any and all assumptions concerning the nature of man. The penalty we pay is that for the present we cannot expect personality *theory* to be cumulative—although, fortunately, to some extent personality *research* can be.

Theories, we know, are ideally derived from axioms, and if axioms are lacking, as in our field they are, from assumptions. But our assumptions regarding the nature of man range from the Adlerian to the Zilborgian, from the Lockean to the Leibnitzian, from the Freudian to the Hullian, and from the cybernetic to the existentialist. Some of us model man after the pigeon; others view his potentialities as many splendored. And there is no agreement in sight.

Nils Bohr's principle of complementarity contains a lesson for us. You recall that he showed that if we study the position of a particle we cannot at the same time study its momentum. Applied to our own work the principle tells us that if we focus on reaction we cannot simultaneously study proaction; if we measure one trait we cannot fix our attention on pattern; if we tackle a subsystem we lose the whole; if we pursue the whole we overlook the part-functioning. For the single investigator there seems to be no escape from this limitation. Our only hope is to overcome it by a complementarity of investigators and of theorists.

While I myself am partisan for the open system, I would shut no doors. (Some of my best friends are quasi-closed systematists.) If I argue for the open system I plead more strongly for the open mind. Our condemnation is reserved for that peculiar slavery to fashion which says that conventionality alone makes for scientific respectability. We still have much to learn from our creative fumblings with the open system. Among our students, I trust, there will be many adventurers. Shall we not teach them that in the pastures of science it is not only the sacred cows that can yield good scientific milk?

16 Personality, character, and the self

J. MILTON YINGER

No concept is more important to a behavioral science than that of personality. And none is more difficult to develop in field theoretical terms. Personality can well be thought of as the central concept, the area where all the sciences of man meet; but if this point of view is adopted, personality must be defined in such a way that the several factors studied by the various disciplines are brought to bear upon it.

One can readily find hundreds of definitions of personality, and these vary so widely that classification is difficult. Disregarding most of the variations for the moment, however, we can roughly divide the definitions into those which refer to processes and structures inside the individual and those which refer to behavior. Valuable use can be made of either of these types of definition, provided the limitations imposed by a given concept are accepted. But many theorists have been unwilling to do this.

For example, the point of departure for many psychologists is personality as the internal tendency system: that which "lies *behind* specific acts and *within* the individual" (Allport, 1937, p. 218), "the more or less stable and enduring organization of a person's character, temperament, intellect, and physique" (Eysenck, 1953, p. 2). Yet Allport says in another place (1937, p. 49): "The systems that constitute personality are in every sense *determining tendencies*" (his italics); and the last phrase of the sentence from Eysenck states, ". . . which determines his unique adjustment to his environment." It is exceedingly difficult, after adopting an internal definition, to hold to an abstract conception and to avoid the temptation to think of behavior as being determined by personality. Thus Child (1963, p. 593) states: "For the present discussion, personality will be defined as comprising consistencies of individual differences in behavior which are internally determined. In substance, this agrees with much recent usage, such as that of Allport and Eysenck."

Other students of personality prefer a behavioral definition: "Personality is considered here as a flowing continuum of organism-environment events" (Murphy, 1947, p. 21). It is the totality of behavior during a lifetime (Adler, 1960). ". . . personality is the relatively enduring pattern of recurrent interpersonal situations which characterize a human life" (Sullivan, 1953, pp. 110–111). The problem in this kind of definition is the tendency, on the part of some who use it, to blur the *analytic* distinction between individual and situation, rather than simply to emphasize their empirical interaction. There is an inclination to assume a one-to-one relationship between individual tendency

Excerpted from Chapter 7 of **Toward a Field Theory of Behavior** by J. Milton Yinger (Copyright © 1965 by McGraw-Hill Book Company), with permission of the author and the publisher, McGraw-Hill Book Company.

and social norms, or to infer the structure of the inner tendency system directly from observation of behavior.

Different definitions of personality are possible, but one must accept the implications of his own definition. If one prefers an intraindividual definition, then personality cannot be used as a direct explanation of behavior, but only as one component in behavior determination. If personality is defined as behavior, it must be treated as a field construct, with full awareness of the facilitating and inhibiting influences of the situation, the tendencies of the individual, and the patterned results of their interaction. If both types of definition are used, whichever one is intended should be clear beyond doubt in each context. Only confusion has come both from the tendency to define personality in intraindividual terms while using it to account directly for behavior, and from the opposite tendency to define it as behavior while using it to infer, or to minimize the importance of, inner structure.

No one who has read this far will be surprised to learn that I prefer, for what I believe are sound theoretical reasons, a behavioral definition of personality. Personality is the totality of the behavior of an individual with a given tendency system, interacting with a sequence of situations. This is scarcely more than a restatement of Murphy's definition given above. It suggests the range, the variation in behavior, and the extent of the personality's involvement with the environment, thus calling attention to part of the common-sense meaning of the term. When we say, "That is his personality," our judgment is based on observed behavior in certain settings. If we see the same person in an unaccustomed setting and behaving differently, we are likely to say, "That's a side of his personality I was not familiar with." As personae we do not wear the same masks continuously.

The common-sense meaning, however, has another side which is not covered by a behavioral definition: Individuals have characteristic ways of behaving that appear over some range of situations; there is continuity as well as variation. We have all exclaimed at one time or another, "Now isn't that just like John!" when we have witnessed activity that seems to demonstrate a persistent tendency even in the face of an apparently unsupporting environment. This is the emphasis in such definitions of personality as Hilgard's, which refers to the "total of individual characterstics and ways of behaving which in their organization or patterning describe an individual's unique adjustment to his environment" (1953, p. 407).

Few behavioral scientists deny the importance of the individual tendency system, however they may account for it. If we use the term "personality" for the flow of behavior, therefore, we need another term to designate what Newcomb calls "the individual's organization of predispositions to behavior." For this I shall use the word "character." The character of a person is what he brings into the behavioral situation.

Now these are only words, and we can assign them the meanings we find useful; but they can serve as scientific concepts only if they are used in a way that clarifies our understanding of nature. There is such a strong tendency for personality to take on behavioral connotations that it seems wise to accept this factor in the definition. If we define personality wholly in intraindividual terms, we tend to reify it, to make it more "real" than the group or the setting; we tend to assume or to exaggerate consistency, and to treat personality simply as an independent variable—as the cause of behavior.

We shall not avoid these difficulties, of course, simply by calling "the individual's organization of predispositions to behavior" character instead of personality. But by giving attention to the need for both concepts, we may avoid more successfully the tendency to "smudge over boundaries," to use Sanford's phrase (1963). The need for both an intraindividual term and a behavioral term is what requires emphasis, not the particular choice of words.

The self

Character as I have defined it is a complex system, not a homogeneous unit. Full examination of its significance for the student of human behavior requires a description of its internal structure and of its several functions. I shall do that here only with reference to what is perhaps the central unit of character, the self; but this will permit discussion of many issues related to questions of inner structure and function.

No concept dealt with by the sciences of human behavior touches upon more significant issues, yet entails more ambiguities, than that of the self. It is a concept of interest to many philosophers, theologians, and humanists, as well as to social scientists; yet to others in the same fields it is useless or misleading. Psychologists with strong behavioristic leanings believe the whole concept to be at best an unnecessary construct, and at worst a source of pseudo "explanations" of behavior that are purely tautological. Yet other psychologists regard it as an essential, even

if slippery, concept and focus their attention upon it. Some sociologists believe that study of the self is wholly outside their discipline, while others in the *Mind, Self, and Society* tradition (cf. Strauss, 1956) consider such study to be fundamental. One might hope that the cross-cutting of disciplines with regard to interest in self would lead to helpful confrontation and eventual clarification of concepts; but for the most part the separate groups have moved along in dignified isolation, so far as theory is concerned. Some of the recent research, however, overrides disciplinary boundaries and can help us to explore the value of the self concept for a behavioral science.

For half a century or more, the great weight of experimental psychology supported the view that "self" and "ego" and the many smaller motivational concepts associated with them were of little value. The point was more often made by complete disregard than by direct critical attack. In recent years, however, the theoretical influence of psychoanalysis (both Freudian and other versions), the rise of an "ego psychology," and the increasing interest in using the findings of the science of man for clinical purposes, indicate changes in emphasis.

Although the social scientists involved in this new wave of interest in the person are more aware of the scientific dangers of relying heavily on constructs of inferred properties or processes, they have not avoided all such difficulties. In a development which brings the study of personality close to the humanities, research interest in the self shades off into a partially valuative interest in defining or discovering the "real self," "identity," "self-actualization," the "mature" or "autonomous" person. (One thinks readily of Erich Fromm, Kurt Goldstein, Carl Rogers, Gordon Allport, Erik Erikson, Carl Jung, A. H. Maslow, and Alfred Adler in this connection.) Since I share the values from which this concern springs, I do not mean to suggest that this is an unhappy development. Risks are involved, however, in the failure to define scientific and value questions separately.

Some of the work in personality psychology is so closely tied to the existential search for meaning, to the affirmation of the individual in the face of the presumed depersonalizing forces of industrial society, that barriers are imposed on the ways in which questions can be raised. If questions cannot be asked in such a way that we are alerted to the forces at work, they cannot be answered satisfactorily. Yet the deep lament over the crushing of the individual, from Marx and earlier philosophers to those thinkers particularly sensitive to the tragedies of the twentieth century, can easily lead to assumptions about the individual *versus* society. In a day of totalitarian powers, it is not difficult to accept the belief, variously expressed and interpreted by Thoreau, Nietzsche, Freud, Camus, and many others, that society is the enemy of man.

The affirmation by Cooley, for example, that social life can be the source of freedom and expression sounds almost Pollyannaish. In our time, the liberals and the intellectuals typically fight the structures around them as the "cause" of man's difficulties. One of the ways this tendency expresses itself among many humanists and psychologists is an antisociological bias, for it is sociology's professional task to call attention to and study those structures. (People who study a phenomenon are often blamed for its existence.)

The mixing of evaluation and analysis in some of the writings on the "self" tends to retard both moral and scientific development of the subject. The propensity to set self against social structures sometimes leads to utopian rejection of structure. But the state does not wither away; or traditional structures are broken only to be replaced by peer-group structures scarcely less limiting; or the burden of freedom leads to many efforts to escape it. An adequate formulation of the relationship of the individual to society can scarcely be developed on the basis of an a priori assumption of their essential antipathy. The need, rather, is to ask the prosaic but central scientific question: What are the conditions under which various consequences flow from the range of interactions between self and society?

This brief commentary may have indicated the range of interpretations of the concept of the self. Removing the qualifications that most scholars would use, we can describe three basic approaches in these terms:

1. The concept of a self is unnecessary and harmful to the development of a science of human behavior. It is based on inferences that cannot be measured. It generally becomes tautological, because it is used to explain behavior which has already been employed to ascertain the existence and the presumed qualities of the self. A more parsimonious approach is to measure behavior directly.

2. The concept of the self is essential to a science of man. It corresponds with our intuitive grasp of experience. It explains consistency of behavior more readily than alternative concepts. It gives adequate recognition to the unique qualities in each person and to the basic human capacity for continuous inner

activity through thought. In many situations, self is the independent variable that accounts for the sequence of events.

3. The concept of the self is a valuable link between the individual and the significant others who surround him. It appears, develops, and expresses itself only in social interaction and cannot be defined or understood, therefore, independently of that interaction. Its major components are the various role specifications learned in interaction with the significant others in one's experience.

While these conceptions are, to an important degree, mutually incompatible, elements can be drawn from each to design a fourth construct of self that is harmonious with the field approach of this book [1] and is, in my judgment, theoretically more adequate than most current usages. From the first point of view expressed above, we can draw the emphasis on self as a construct to be used on the basis of its contribution to research. We can also be alerted to the dangers of circular reasoning in the use of such a concept.

A strictly psychological approach, as in the second point of view above, brings recognition of the system properties at the individual level. The paradoxical fact is that a field view, which in one sense obscures boundaries by designing a multilevel system, at the same time demands analytic clarity in the specification of separate systems. The self, as I shall use the term, is an individual fact. It is not, however, the behavior of an individual, or the independent cause of his behavior; it is the name for certain qualities of the individual. This distinction is lost in some psychological work. The significance of those qualities for behavior cannot be measured independ-

[1] [Yinger, 1965.]—Eds.

ently of the total field in which they are located.

A strictly sociological approach, as in the third point of view, emphasizes the social origin of those qualities of the individual called self. The self as agent is primarily a role performer and is deeply affected, therefore, by the structure of relationships into which he is bound. These are essential elements in a field view, although the field researcher would also warn against disregarding that which an individual brings into an interaction. Such disregard may spring from a failure to distinguish between the social origin of self and the social context with which self, once formed (or partially formed, since this is a continuing process), interacts.

It is difficult to write a brief definition of self that carries the full range of meanings implied in this discussion. The definition used by Murphy and Newcomb violates none of the criteria of a field term and is a good starting point: "Self . . . refers to the individual as perceived by that individual in a socially determined frame of reference" (Newcomb, 1950, p. 328). This is expressed somewhat more fully by Deutsch and Solomon (1959). They define self as the symbolic representations one makes of his various biological, psychological, ethical, and social characteristics.

Lindesmith and Strauss emphasize a different point when they designate self "as (1) a set of more or less consistent and stable responses on a conceptual level, which (2) exercise a regulatory function over other responses of the same organization at lower levels" (1956, p. 416). Thus they introduce the idea of structure into self and suggest the processes whereby some order is imposed on the multiplicity of tendencies that might be brought into a given interaction. Many resources valued by the individual—time, energy, money, etc.—are scarce; selections must be made among alternative ways of spending those resources. One aspect of self, then, is the organizing, regulating process of hierarchization of values. The order of preference is continually being redefined as a result of cyclical and other changes in needs and as a result of the opportunities furnished and costs imposed by others.

The strict behaviorist is not happy with such comments. He is likely to say, "Why not merely indicate that when certain measurable conditions prevail, an observable individual behaves in a stated way?" Somewhat uncomfortably—for the danger of reification is great—I would reply that the *construct* of self is a useful shorthand description of consistent orientations toward behavior.

The social behaviorist of the Mead tradition (cf. Strauss, 1956) is likely to say that the inferred consistency of self is based on observations of behavior under conditions where continuity of social positions, with their roles, is also an outstanding fact. Unless the "manager of scarce resources" can be shown to produce consistency over and beyond that which one would expect from position continuity, no self concept is needed. This is a valid criticism, or source of redefinition, of the self idea. I shall comment below on some of the efforts to measure possible gains in prediction that come from positing a self construct as one of a series of interacting variables. It is probably more on intuitive than on experimental grounds, however, that I find the concept of self useful in the study of man, the conscious, remembering, valuing, future-planning creature.

Although terminology is highly incon-sistent in the literature, I shall use the term "ego" to refer to those "managing" processes of self which attempt to shape events toward maximum need satisfaction in a given physical and social "reality." This is, of course, close to Freud (cf. Freud, 1933; Rieff, 1959), although I would emphasize the degree to which the managing processes are affected by the context in which they are expressed. For this reason I would modify somewhat Murphy's definition of ego as a "group of activities concerned with enhancement and defense of self" (1947, p. 984). Ego is a group of inner tendencies the outcome of which depends upon a transaction with the outer world.

Ego thus defined is not synonymous with self. The self includes also the ways in which an individual answers to himself the questions "Who am I?" (self concept) and "What do I want to be?" (self ideal). There are numerous demonstrations that the answers to these questions are social products, closely related to the positions one occupies and the "others" with whom one interacts (cf. Kuhn & McPartland, 1954; Kuhn, 1960; Miller, 1963; Reeder et al., 1960). Nevertheless, as aspects of self, they are individual tendencies, not social facts.

Just as ego, self concept, and self ideal are aspects of self, self is an aspect of character, that total system of tendencies and capabilities of an individual. There is more to character than the reflexive "individual as known to the individual." The self is embedded in a character, and the three processes I have identified with the term "self" are influenced by the system of which they are a part. Tendencies and potentialities of which an individual is completely unaware characterize him no less than the qualities which he can articulate.

On the basis of this discussion, can

self be defined in a way that harmonizes with field theory? Self often has anti-field connotations (e.g., the self, as an independent force, determines behavior). Full "explanation" by reference to individual motives and decisions is a commonplace of everyday speech and thought: "He dropped out of basketball because he was falling behind in his lab work." I.e., an individual, weighing comparative values, independently arrives at a decision which causes behavior. Non-self values and tendencies that influenced the decision—significant others who helped to determine motivation, for example—are absent from this explanation. No harm may come from such common-sense formulations of the kind of statement illustrated here; but the reification of self as an independent cause can be a great barrier to scientific understanding and clinical work. If we continue to be content, for example, with explanations that our enemies do what they do because of what they "are," or "because" of various motives which they express, we shall neither understand them nor be effective in changing our interactions with them.

In short, self concepts and related motivational concepts are incorporated into a field view only with difficulty. Nevertheless they seem to me to be valuable when properly conceived. By "self" I shall mean those processes by which an individual internally answers the questions: "Who am I?" "What do I want to be?" and "How shall I rank my various desires?" Self, so conceived, is an individual construct; it refers to tendencies; it is largely the product of interaction with others and continues to be closely associated with the positions one occupies; and it has structure, including a hierarchy of desires. It is known only in behavior, and therefore can never be perceived "by itself" but must be inferred from patterns of behavior in different contexts. In research it can be treated as both an independent and a dependent variable; a priori assumptions that it is one or the other are unwarranted.

17 Negro American personality: the role and its burdens

THOMAS PETTIGREW

Playing the role of "Negro"

Like all human interactions, discriminatory encounters between whites and Negroes require that both parties "play the game." The white must act out the role of the "superior"; by direct action or subtle cue, he must convey the expectation that he will be treated with deference. For his part, the Negro must, if racist norms are to be obeyed, act out the role of the "inferior"; he must play the social role of "Negro." And if he should refuse to play the game, he would be judged by the white supremacist as "not knowing his place," and harsh sanctions could follow.

The socially-stigmatized role of "Negro" is the critical feature of having dark skin in the United States. "It is part of the price the Negro pays for his position in this society," comments James Baldwin, "that, as Richard Wright points out, he is almost always acting" (1955, p. 68). At the personality level, such enforced role adoption further divides the individual Negro both from other human beings and from himself. Of course, all social roles, necessary as they are, hinder to some extent forthright, uninhibited social interaction. An employer and employee, for example, may never begin to understand each other as complete human beings unless they break through the formality and constraints of their role relationship, unless they "let their hair down." Likewise, whites and Negroes can never communicate as equals unless they break through the role barriers. As long as racial roles are maintained, both parties find it difficult to perceive the humanity behind the façade. Many whites who are by no means racists confuse the role of "Negro" with the people who must play this role. "Negroes are just like that," goes the phrase, "they are born that way." Conversely, many Negroes confuse the role of "white man" with whites. "Whites are just like that, they are born thinking they should be boss."

Intimately associated with this impairment of human relatedness is an impairment of the individual's acceptance and understanding of himself. Both whites and Negroes can confuse their own roles as being an essential part of themselves. Whites can easily flatter themselves into the conviction that they are in fact "superior"; after all, does not the deferential behavior of the role-playing Negro confirm this "superiority"? And Negroes in turn often accept much of the racists' mythology; for does not the imperious behavior of the role-playing white confirm this "inferiority"?

These are not mere speculations of existentialist philosophy. A large body of psychological research convincingly dem-

Abridged from Chapter 1 of **A Profile of the Negro American**, pp. 3–23 (Copyright © 1964, by Litton Educational Publishing, Inc.), with permission of the author and Van Nostrand Reinhold Company.

onstrates the power of role-playing to change deeply-held attitudes, values, and even conceptions of self. Moreover, these remarkable changes have been rendered by temporary role adoptions of an exceedingly trivial nature when compared to the life-long role of "Negro." Imagine, then, the depth of the effects of having to play a role which has such vast personal and social significance that it influences virtually all aspects of daily living. Indeed, the resulting confusion of self-identity and lowering of self-esteem are two of the most serious "marks of oppression" upon Negro American personality.

Self-identity and self-esteem

The quest for self-identity is the search for answers to the all-important questions: Who am I? What am I like as a person? And how do I fit into the world? These are not easy questions for anyone to answer in our complex, swiftly-changing society. Yet they offer even greater difficulties for Negro Americans.

We learn who we are and what we are like largely by carefully observing how other people react to us. But this process is highly structured for the Negro by the role he is expected to play. When he attempts to gain an image of himself on the basis of his typical contacts with white America and the general culture, he often receives a rude jolt. While he is totally American in every conceivable meaning of the term, he finds that most Americans are white and that somehow the mere color of his skin puts him into a unique and socially-defined inferior category. And when the Negro looks around him—except in the spheres of athletics and entertainment—he discovers very few Americans with his skin color who hold important positions in

his society. Save for the mass media expressly tailored for Negro audiences, he sees only white models in advertisements and only whites as heroes of stories (Berelson & Salter, 1946; Logan, 1954; Shuey, et al., 1953; Writer's War Board, 1945). When he does see Negroes in the general mass media, they are likely to be cast in low-status roles and appear as "amusingly ignorant." Little wonder, then, that the question, who am I?, raises special difficulties for him.

Identity problems are unusually acute during certain periods in a person's life. These periods, these identity-crises, often occur in the preschool years, later in adolescence, and again in young adulthood. All three of these periods impose additional stress on Negroes. Negro parents confess to great anxiety and ambivalence over telling their preschool children what it means to be a Negro in American society. Should youngsters be shielded from the truth as long as possible? Or should they be prepared early for blows that are sure to come?

The importance of identity problems for young Negro children has been demonstrated by a series of ingenious investigations. Following the classical work of Kenneth and Mamie Clark (1963, 1947), these researches have utilized a wide assortment of techniques in a variety of segregated Southern and integrated Northern nursery and school settings and have consistently arrived at the same critical conclusions (Goodman, 1952; Landreth & Johnson, 1953; Morland, 1958; Stevenson & Stewart, 1958; Trager & Yarrow, 1952). Racial recognition in both white and Negro children appears by the third year and rapidly sharpens each year thereafter. Of special significance is the tendency found in all of these studies for Negro children to prefer white skin. They are usually slower than white children to make racial distinctions, they frequently prefer white dolls and white friends, and they often identify themselves as white or show a tense reluctance to acknowledge that they are Negro. Moreover, young children of both races soon learn to assign, realistically, poorer houses and less desirable roles to Negro dolls. This early "mark of oppression" is illustrated by the behavior of a small Negro boy who participated in one of these studies conducted in Lynchburg, Virginia. Asked if he were white or colored, he hung his head and hesitated. Then he murmured softly, "I guess I'se kinda colored." (Morland, 1958, p. 137)

Some of this direct manifestation of "self-hate" disappears in later years (Koch, 1946), though similar studies of older Negro children find residual symptoms (Johnson, 1941; Seeman, 1946). One investigation of children aged eight to thirteen years in an interracial summer camp found that Negroes tended at first to be oversensitive to unfavorable behavior of their Negro peers and to avoid choosing other Negroes as friends (Yarrow, 1958). A successful experience in an egalitarian, interracial setting, however, can alleviate these inclinations. In this study, a two-week experience in interracial camping is shown to have significantly modified these expressions of self-hate in the young Negro campers.

In the teens, sex becomes an acute issue. This is a period of great strain for most American adolescents, but for the Negro child in the North who has close friendships with white children, it frequently means a sudden parting of paths. After puberty, the Negro child is no longer invited to his white friends' parties, for at this time the deep racist fears of miscegenation harbored by many white parents enter on the scene. For the majority of Negro youth of this age who have no white friends, the early teens introduce their own version of identity-crisis. From his teachers, his peer group, his contacts with the white world beyond his immediate neighborhood, the Negro teenager encounters new shocks. The full awareness of his social devaluation in the larger society in addition to the sharp strains felt by all teenagers in a complex society can assume the dimensions of a severe emotional stress-situation (Milner, 1953).

If the ambitious Negro has successfully weathered these earlier crises, he must face yet another series of identity-shocks in young adulthood. Employment discrimination may keep him from the job for which he trained, and housing segregation may restrict him from securing the type of housing he wants for his family. Who am I? What am I like as a person? And how do I fit into the world? The old questions from childhood continue to require answers when he is refused a job for which he is qualified and a house for which he has the purchase price.

These identity problems are inextricably linked with problems of self-esteem. For years, Negro Americans have had little else by which to judge themselves than the second-class status assigned them in America. And along with this inferior treatment, their ears have been filled with the din of white racists egotistically insisting that Caucasians are innately superior to Negroes. Consequently, many Negroes, consciously or unconsciously, accept in part these assertions of their inferiority. In addition, they accept the American emphases on "status" and "success." But when they employ these standards for judging their own worth, their lowly positions and their relative lack of success lead to further self-disparagement. Competition with successful whites is especially threatening. Laboratory experimentation demonstrates that even when Negroes receive objective evidence of equal mental ability in an interracial situation they typically feel inadequate and respond compliantly (Katz & Benjamin, 1960).

The sweeping changes of recent years, however, have begun to alter this situation. The old wounds of confused identity and damaged self-esteem have not sufficiently healed, but recent events are potent medicines. Supreme Court decisions, in particular, brought new hope. A 1963 *Newsweek* national poll found that two-thirds of all Negroes credited the Supreme Court for their biggest breakthroughs. "It started the ball rolling," voiced one respondent. And another added, "The Supreme Court gave us heart to fight." (*Newsweek*, 1963, p. 27) Moreover, the Negro's own protests and assertion of civil rights, his increasing educational and economic opportunities, the findings of social science, and the emergence of proud new African nations all have salved the old wounds.

It is difficult for white Americans to grasp the full personal significance of these events for Negro Americans. But imagine how a Negro feels today. All of his life he has been bombarded with white-supremacy ideas and restrictions. Moreover, he has shared much of the naive conception of Africa as the dark continent of wild and naked savages. Now he is greeted with evidence from all sides that the white supremacists are wrong. On television, he sees segregationists desperately defying his national government in their losing battle to maintain Jim Crow, he sees his President conferring with black chiefs of state with full pomp and circumstance, and he sees his nation's representatives wooing the all-important black delegates to the United Nations. He sees all this, and his wounds begin to heal. The special role of "Negro" remains, but is undergoing drastic change.

The hostile environment

Another widespread reaction to racism is a generalized perception of the world as a hostile, threatening place. Horace Cayton considers this a critical feature of the "oppression phobia" experienced by many Negro Americans: an expectancy of violent mistreatment combined with a feeling of utter helplessness (Cayton, 1951). Negroes questioned in *Newsweek's* national poll groped for words to describe this phobia: "the feeling of being choked," said one; "feels like being punished for something you didn't do," said another (*Newsweek*, 1963, p. 18). Such feelings are also experienced by other minority groups. Many Jews, for instance, have reported a preoccupation with anti-Semitism and a vague sense of impending doom, of haunting anxiety, hovering over them (Allport, 1954).

Reality testing is involved here, of course, for the world *is* more often a treacherous, threatening place for Negroes. Consider the social scars of discrimination throughout Negro American history that make this true. Slavery cast the longest shadow. Compared with the institution in Latin America, slavery in the United States had an unusually crushing impact upon Negro personality, because it did not recognize the slave as a human being (Elkins, 1959; Tannenbaum, 1947). Spain and Portugal had centuries of experience with slavery prior to the founding of the New

World, hence Iberian law had evolved a special place for the slave as a human being with definite, if limited, rights. By contrast, England had no previous involvement with the "peculiar institution," and so its law, adopted by the American colonies, treated the slave as mere property—no different legally from a house, a barn, or an animal (Tannenbaum, 1947).

Recently, one historian ventured a parallel between Southern slavery on the large, cotton plantations and the concentration camps of Nazi Germany (Elkins, 1959). Both were closed systems, with little chance of manumission, emphasis on survival, and a single, omnipresent authority. The profound personality change created by Nazi internment, as independently reported by a number of psychologists and psychiatrists who survived, was toward childishness and total acceptance of the SS guards as father-figures—a syndrome strikingly similar to the "Sambo" caricature of the Southern slave. Nineteenth-century racists readily believed that the "Sambo" personality was simply an inborn racial type. Yet no African anthropological data have ever shown any personality type resembling Sambo; and the concentration camps molded the equivalent personality pattern in a wide variety of Caucasian prisoners. Nor was Sambo merely a product of "slavery" in the abstract, for the less devastating Latin American system never developed such a type (Elkins, 1959).

Extending this line of reasoning, psychologists point out that slavery in all its forms sharply lowered the need for achievement in slaves (McClelland, 1961, pp. 376–377). Negroes in bondage, stripped of their African heritage, were placed in a completely dependent role. All of their rewards came, not from individual initiative and enterprise, but from absolute obedience—a situation that severely depresses the need for achievement among all peoples. Most important of all, slavery vitiated family life (Bastide, 1950, pp. 240–247; Frazier, 1957). Since many slaveowners neither fostered Christian marriage among their slave couples nor hesitated to separate them on the auction block, the slave household often developed a fatherless, matrifocal (mother-centered) pattern.

Strong traces of these effects of slavery, augmented by racial discrimination, have persisted since Emancipation because of bitter poverty and the uprooted life of migrants far from home. Poverty is not limited to Negroes, of course, but it takes on a special meaning when due in part to the color of one's skin. Though a substantial number of Negroes have improved their status economically, a much greater percentage of Negroes than whites comprise the nation's most destitute citizens. For these Negroes, poverty means living in the degraded slums of our largest cities in close proximity to the worst centers of the nation's vice and crime. Poverty means less education, less opportunity, and less participation in the general culture. And it means less ability to throw off the effects of past oppression.

Furthermore, Negro Americans are often lonely, recent arrivals to huge metropolitan areas, strangers detached from their home moorings. Between 1950 and 1960, over one-and-a-half million Negroes left the South and came to cities in the North and West; others came to Southern cities from the farms. These migrants are frequently ill prepared for the demands of urban life, with only an inferior Southern rural education and few if any job skills. Consequently, they must fit onto the lowest rungs of the occupational ladder and hope for economic survival in an age when automation is dramatically reducing the number of jobs for unskilled workers. Small wonder such individuals come to view the world as a hostile place.

Family disorganization and personality

Both poverty and migration also act to maintain the old slave pattern of a mother-centered family. Not only does desperate poverty disturb healthy family life through dilapidated housing, crowded living conditions, restricted recreational facilities, and direct contact with the most corrupting elements of urban disorganization, but it makes the ideal American pattern of household economics practically impossible. Employment discrimination has traditionally made it more difficult for the poorly-educated Negro male to secure steady employment than the poorly-educated Negro female. In many areas of the nation, North as well as South, this is still true, with Negro females always able to obtain jobs as domestics if nothing else is available. When the unskilled Negro male does manage to secure a job, he generally assumes an occupation that pays barely enough to support himself— much less a family. Such conditions obviously limit the ability of lower-class Negroes to follow the typical American pattern—that is, a stable unit with the husband providing a steady income for his family.

The Negro wife in this situation can easily become disgusted with her financially-dependent husband, and her rejection of him further alienates the male from family life. Embittered by their experiences with men, many Negro mothers often act to perpetuate the mother-centered pattern by taking a greater interest in their daughters than their sons. For example, more Negro females graduate from college than Negro males, the reverse of the pattern found among white Americans.

Family stability also suffers from the effects of migration, with its tensions over relocation and its release of the migrant from the sanctions of his home community. When all of these factors are considered, the prevalence of divorce, separation, and illegitimacy among poor Negroes should not come as a surprise. For when American society isolates the lower-class Negro from contact with the general norms and prevents him from sharing in the rewards which follow from abiding by these norms, it guarantees the emergence of a ghetto subculture with different standards of conduct, motivation, and family life.

Census data for 1960 illustrate the depth of this family disorganization among Negroes: over a third (34.3 per cent) of all non-white mothers with children under six years of age hold jobs as compared with less than a fifth (19.5 per cent) of white mothers with children under six (U.S. Bureau of the Census, 1962); only three-fourths (74.9 per cent) of all non-white families have both the husband and the wife present in the household as compared with nine-tenths (89.2 per cent) of white families (U.S. Bureau of the Census, 1962); and only two-thirds (66.3 per cent) of non-whites under eighteen years of age live with both of their parents as compared with nine-tenths (90.2 per cent) of such whites (U.S. Bureau of the Census, 1962). These data do not cancel out the effects of social class differences between the two groups; rough comparisons between the lower classes of each race, however, still reveal a greater prevalence of father-absence among Negroes. The scar of slavery upon Negro family life, perpetuated through poverty and migration, is still evident.

Recent psychological research vividly demonstrates the personality effects upon children of having been raised in a disorganized home without a father. One such study reveals that eight-and-nine-year-old children whose fathers are absent seek immediate gratification far more than children whose fathers are present in the home. For example, when offered their choice of receiving a tiny candy bar immediately or a large bar a week later, fatherless children typically take the small bar while other children prefer to wait for the larger bar (Mischel, 1961c). This hunger for immediate gratification among fatherless children seems to have serious implications. Regardless of race, children manifesting this trait also tend to be less accurate in judging time, less "socially responsible," less oriented toward achievement, and more prone toward delinquency (Mischel, 1961a; 1961b). Indeed, two psychologists maintain that the inability to delay gratification is a critical factor in immature, criminal, and neurotic behavior (Mowrer & Ullman, 1945).

The reasons for these characteristics of father-absent children seem clear. Negro girls in such families model themselves after their mothers and prepare to assume male as well as female responsibilities. And various investigations have demonstrated the crucial importance of the father in the socialization of boys (Bandura & Walters, 1959; Mussen & Distler, 1959). Mothers raising their children in homes without fathers are frequently overprotective, sometimes even smothering, in their compensatory attempts to be a combined father and mother. Burton and Whiting persuasively contend that the boys whose fathers are not present have initially identified with their mothers and must later, in America's relatively patrifocal society, develop a conflicting, secondary identification with males (1961). In other words, they must painfully achieve a masculine self-image late in their childhood after having established an original self-image on the basis of the only parental model they have had—their mother.

The "psychologically vulnerable" Negro, crippled by weak ego development from earlier family disorganization, is more likely to fall prey to mental illness, drug addiction, or crime, depending on his particular life history. He has few personality resources to withstand the gale winds of discrimination that strike him full force in adolescence. Thus, segregation has its most fundamental influence on Negro personality in the manner in which it affects Negro family functioning (Jones & Arrington, 1945).

18   The achievement motive

DAVID C. McCLELLAND

Assessing human motives

At least from the time of Plato and the Bhagavad-Gītā, Western philosophers have tended to see reason and desire as two distinctly different elements in the human mind. There would be little point here in giving a history of the various ways in which the "desiring" element has been conceived in the last 2,000 years, but suffice it to say that it always represented a kind of "motivational force" often opposed to but ultimately controllable by reason. At about the dawn of modern scientific psychology, in the middle of the nineteenth century, the relationship between these two psychic elements took on a very specific meaning largely under the influence of Darwin and the wide interest he and others aroused in the theory of evolution. Man was conceived as an animal engaged in a struggle for survival with nature. It was an obvious corollary to assume that because man struggled he had a desire or wish to survive. Biologists and psychologists were quick to point out how such a desire was mechanically controlled by the organism, since unmet physiological needs ordinarily triggered certain danger signals which would irritate or disturb the organism until the needs were satisfied.

The most obvious example is the hunger need. If the organism does not get food, it does not survive; therefore, it is equipped with danger signals (controlled perhaps by contractions of the empty stomach) which would be activated in the absence of food and so cause the organism to be active until it obtains food. The more or less "intelligent" activities of the organism, representing the old reasoning element in man, were conceived as originated and guided by the hunger drive, not in the teleological sense that the organism "knows" it needs food, but purely in the mechanical sense that hunger keeps the organism going until it manages to find some food substance which shuts off the danger signals. The most important theoretical advance made by psychologists who thought of human adaptation in these terms was the conceptual distinction they ultimately made between eating and hunger (the desire to eat). Common-sense psychology might suggest that the more a man eats, the more he wants to eat, in exactly the same sense that the more a man achieves, the more he must *want* to achieve. If, in fact, the two variables are so closely connected that desire to eat can be inferred without error from eating activity, then there is no need for the motive concept at all.

Since science is a parsimonious enterprise using as few concepts as it possibly can to explain what it tries to explain, it can get along without a variable which is always perfectly associated with another. But what behavioral scientists did at this juncture in history was to estab-

Excerpted from Chapter 2 of **The Achieving Society**, pp. 32–62, (Copyright © 1961, by Litton Educational Publishing, Inc.), with permission of the author and Van Nostrand Reinhold Company.

lish an *independent set of operations* for defining the strength of the hunger drive—independent that is, of the activity of eating. They defined the strength of the hunger drive in terms of the number of hours of food deprivation. They assumed that the longer an organism had been without food, the hungrier it would be, and they could then go about determining how different strengths of the hunger drive, as independently measured in this way, would influence various types of behavior, including even eating. They found, not too surprisingly, that when the strength of hunger was measured by hours of deprivation, it did not correlate at all perfectly with the tendency to eat. There were, and are, many disagreements, of course, as to the best method of measuring the hunger drive, but the only point of real significance here is that the way was opened to measure motivation independently of consummatory action. So psychologists have tended by and large to distinguish between motivation and action—between hunger and eating, and between the desire to achieve and actual achievement.

Nevertheless, much remained to be done. There was as yet no interest in the unique effects of particular drives. It is true that American psychologists studied not only the hunger drive, but also the thirst drive, the pain-avoidance drive, and other basic drives. Yet all these were conceived as functionally equivalent forces acting to energize human behavior until the organism managed to remove them by something it did. As might also be expected, there was no particular interest in individual differences in the strength of various motives. In fact the model of the hunger drive suggested that motive potentialities might be pretty much alike in all people and that their actual strength was pri-

marily determined by changes in the external environment (e.g., lack of food). There was not much interest in the possibility that some particular person might have an especially strong hunger drive either because of biological endowment or because of some special learning experiences that had reinforced it. It remained for those more directly interested in human behavior and social motives to fill out the picture somewhat.

Many of them took their cue from Freud. Oddly enough he, too, had been strongly influenced by Darwin. He recognized the importance of survival needs like hunger, but concentrated his attention on the force that perpetuated the species—namely, sexual love. His general "model of motivation" remained not unlike the one adopted by the American psychologists of the functional school. A general motive force—the libido—drives man to invent through reason a variety of techniques or stratagems for diverting or satisfying it. But while the general model stayed the same, he made important empirical contributions that markedly influenced the direction research was to take.

For one thing he destroyed forever (except, perhaps, in the minds of economic theorists) the notion that motives are rational or can be rationally inferred from action. By concentrating his attention on notable irrationalities in behavior—slips of the tongue, forgetting of well-known facts, dreams, accidents, neurotic symptoms—he demonstrated over and over again that motives "are not what they seem." In fact they might be just the opposite. It could no longer be safely assumed that a man walks across the street because he wants to get to the other side. He might, in fact, want just the opposite—to enter a tavern on this side, a desire revealed indirectly by his exaggerated avoidance behavior. Since Freud, psychologists have accepted the fact that a simple act may be variously motivated. In the economic sphere, advertisers have long since taken advantage of Freud's findings in recognizing that a man doesn't buy a car just because he "needs" one in a rational sense, but because the possession of a particular kind of car may satisfy other motives— for power, prestige, or even sexual display. But how is one to know exactly what these other motives are? Here again, Freud provided us with an important clue in the method he himself used for discovering certain motives. He searched in dreams and free associations —in short, in fantasy—for clues to irrational motives. The limitation of his method was that it was always ad hoc. He proceeded, like the doctor he was, to analyze each symptom, for each person, or each dream as it came along, but did not provide scientists with measures of particular motives that would (1) enable different observers to agree what motives were operating with the degree of consensus necessary for science, (2) permit individuals to be compared as to the strength of a given motive, and (3) provide at least crude estimates of group levels or differences in human motives that would be of use to economists and other social theorists in dealing with the behavior of large groups of people.

Measuring the achievement motive

The next step was to develop a method of measuring individual differences in human motivation firmly based on the methodology of experimental psychology and on the psychoanalytic insights of Freud and his followers. How this was accomplished might just as well be illustrated by reviewing briefly the history of the development of a measure of the achievement motive, since we are to study its connection with economic growth throughout the rest of the book. The procedure, which has been described in full elsewhere (McClelland, et al., 1953), may be briefly summarized as follows. First the achievement motive was aroused in a group of subjects to see what its effects on behavior might be. In this way we could avoid the mistake of assuming a priori that the strength of the achievement motive may be inferred simply and directly from some particular type of behavior. For example, actual achievement cannot be considered a safe index of the strength of the need to achieve any more than eating can be considered a safe measure of the strength of the hunger drive. In fact actual achievement is controlled by many more forces than eating—desires for social approval, power, or knowledge—to say nothing of ability factors, so that it is far less a reliable index of the need to achieve than eating is of hunger.

Instead we need some more unique index of the presence of an aroused desire for achievement. Ideally, of course, we might favor something like a "psychic X-ray" that would permit us to observe what was going on in a person's head in the same way that we can observe stomach contractions or nerve discharges in a hungry organism. Lacking such a device, we can use the next best thing— a sample of a person's spontaneous thoughts under minimum external restraints, in short, of his waking fantasies and free associations, as already used by Freud and many others to assess human motives. The question then narrows down quite specifically to: What "unique" effects on fantasy does an aroused state of achievement motivation have? If we can discover any, we can use these effects to infer the strength of "inner concerns" for achievement in subsequent studies.

Deciding how to arouse the achievement motive already involves to a certain extent at least a rough definition of the motive being investigated. It is therefore important to report just how it was done. The subjects initially were all male college students who were given a series of tasks to perform that were introduced in the following way:

The tests which you are taking directly indicate a person's general level of intelligence. These tests have been taken from a group of tests which were used to select people of high administrative capacity for positions in Washington during the past war. Thus, in addition to general intelligence, they bring out an individual's capacity to organize material, his ability to evaluate crucial situations quickly and accurately—in short, these tests demonstrate whether or not a person is suited to be a leader. (McClelland, Atkinson, Clark & Lowell, 1953, p. 105.)

The important point about these instructions is that they stress the fact that the individual is about to be evaluated in terms of standards of excellence—intelligence and leadership capacity—which are ordinarily of considerable importance to men in American culture. It is assumed that such instructions will arouse in most of the people to whom the tests were given a desire to do well, a desire to appear intelligent and demonstrate some leadership capacity. It is, of course, unnecessary to assume that these motives were conscious, or even present, in all of the subjects tested. It is only necessary to assume that consciously or unconsciously a motive to do well was aroused in more of the subjects to whom the instructions were given than in a comparable group of subjects to whom

the tests and instructions were not given. Any differences in the subsequent fantasy behavior of the two groups might then be attributed to the difference in the level of arousal of the achievement motive in the two groups.

After the above tests had been completed, samples of the subjects' fantasies were collected by having them write brief five-minute stories suggested by pictures flashed on a screen for a few seconds. The pictures represented a variety of life situations centering particularly around work, because it was not known in advance exactly what associations would be most likely to be affected by arousing the achievement motive. In non-technical language, the stories represented short samples of the things people are most likely to think about or imagine when they are in a state of heightened motivation having to do with achievement. It may be worth considering for a moment why fantasy as a type of behavior has many advantages over any other type of behavior for sensitively reflecting the effects of motivational arousal. In fantasy anything is at least symbolically possible—a person may rise to great heights, sink to great depths, kill his grandmother, or take off for the South Sea Islands on a pogo stick. Overt action, on the other hand, is much more constrained by limits set by reality or by the person's abilities. Furthermore, fantasy is more easily influenced than other kinds of behavior. Contrast it with problem-solving, for example. One might assume that how hard a person works would directly reflect the strength of his achievement motive. Yet how hard a person works is not easy to influence experimentally. Apparently most people develop a problem-solving "set" which is sufficient to keep them working at a more or less constant rate despite wide variations in feeling, such as those induced by extreme fatigue. In producing work, one motive can substitute for another so that even though the achievement motive may be weak in some people, their output may well be the same as somebody else's because of a stronger desire to please the experimenter.

This points to a third advantage of fantasy over any "overt" behavioral measure—namely, the way in which it gives clues as to *what motive* is aroused. Even if working behavior were more sensitive to experimental influences, one could not determine from the mere fact that a person was working harder what his motive was in working harder. It might be the achievement motive, or it might be the need for social approval, or the desire to get out of a situation as fast as possible and do something else. It is the fantasies of the person, his thoughts and associations, which give us his real "inner concerns" at the time he is working.

The next step was to compare the stories written by subjects whose achievement motives had presumably been aroused with those written by subjects under normal conditions. Certain differences immediately became apparent. The stories written under "aroused" conditions contained more references to "standards of excellence" and to doing well, or wanting to do well, with respect to the standards. A couple of actual stories will illustrate the point best. One of the pictures frequently used shows a boy sitting at a desk with a book open in front of him. Under normal conditions, it evokes a story like this one:

A boy in a classroom who is daydreaming about something. He is recalling a previously experienced incident that struck his mind to be more appealing than being in the classroom. He is thinking about the experience and is now imagining himself in the situation. He hopes to be there. He will probably get called on by the instructor to recite and will be embarrassed.

Nothing in this story deals with achievement or with standards of excellence, but compare it with the following story:

The boy is taking an hour written. He and the others are high-school students. The test is about two-thirds over and he is doing his best to think it through. He was supposed to study for the test and did so. But because it is factual, there were items he saw but did not learn. He knows he has studied the answers he can't remember and is trying to summon up the images and related ideas to remind him of them. He may remember one or two, but he will miss most of the items he can't remember. He will try hard until five minutes is left, then give up, go back over his paper, and be disgusted for reading but not learning the answers.

Obviously, here the boy is concerned about doing his best on the examination ("he is doing his best to think it through" and he is "disgusted for reading but not learning the answers"). Furthermore, there are a number of aspects of an achievement sequence specifically mentioned such as the fact that it is his fault that he is not doing well ("he saw but did not learn") and that he is trying out various ways of solving his problem ("trying to summon up the images and related ideas to remind him of them"). The fact that he is not successful in his achievement efforts is *not* taken to mean that the student who composed this story has a weaker achievement motive than someone who wrote a story in which his problem-solving activities were successful. In fact, the precise advantage of the experimental method adopted is that it makes it unnecessary to make such decisions on "rational" grounds. One might make a case *a priori* for regarding images of success as more likely to be indicative of a strong and successful achievement drive than images of failure. One might also make a good a priori case for the exact opposite conclusion—that people who daydream about success are the very ones whose achievement motive is too weak to engage in actual attempts to do something in real life. To decide such a question on the grounds of what is most reasonable would be to fall into the error that plagued the psychology of economists and philosophers in the 19th century. The experimental approach makes no assumptions as to how the achievement motive is going to affect fantasy in advance: it simply takes whatever differences appear in fact between stories written under "aroused" and normal conditions so long as they make some kind of theoretical sense, and uses them as a means of detecting the presence of the achievement motive.

For example, it was thought in advance that arousal of the achievement motive might affect the outcome of the story, perhaps producing more successful or unsuccessful outcomes as compared with vague or indecisive ones. But in fact there were no differences in the frequency of various types of outcomes of the stories written under "aroused" conditions as compared with those written under normal conditions. So the outcome of the story, or of the achievement sequence in it, cannot be considered a sign of the presence of heightened achievement motivation, no matter how good an a priori case might be made for using it in this way. The point cannot be stressed too much. It was not logic that decided what aspects of fantasy would reflect achievement motivation. It was experimental fact. There is no need to list and define here the several different aspects of fantasy that did

change under the influence of achievement arousal in college students, since they have been fully described elsewhere (McClelland, et al., 1953; Atkinson, 1958). It might be questioned though how general these effects would be. Perhaps an aroused achievement motive would influence the thoughts of Chinese, or Ancient Greeks, or Navaho Indians in quite different ways. Are the results obtained restricted to the male college population on which they were obtained? Ancient Greeks have not, of course, been tested, but Navahos have and their stories change in exactly the same ways under the influence of achievement arousal (McClelland, et al., 1953). So do those written by Brazilian students (Angelini, 1955), or high-school students in our culture from more unselected socioeconomic backgrounds. There may be cultural differences, but the data to date point to major similarities—inducing achievement motivation increases in all types of subjects thoughts of doing well with respect to some standard of good performance, of being blocked in the attempt to achieve, of trying various means of achieving, and of reacting with joy or sadness to the results of one's efforts.

The next step was to obtain a score for an individual by assuming that the more such thoughts he had under normal conditions, the stronger his motive to achieve must be, even in the absence of special instructions and experiences designed to arouse it. What the experiments had demonstrated was what channels peoples' thoughts turned to under achievement pressure. But suppose a person's thoughts run in those same channels without any external pressure. It seems reasonable to infer that he has a strong "inner concern" with achievement. Under normal testing conditions, the pictures used to elicit stories are sufficiently ambiguous to evoke a variety of ideas. If someone, however, in writing his stories consistently uses achievement-related ideas of the same kind as those elicited in everyone under achievement "pressure," then he would appear to be someone with a "bias," a "concern," or a "need" for achievement. So it was decided that a simple count of the number of such achievement-related ideas in stories written under normal testing conditions could be taken to represent the strength of a man's concern with achievement. The count has been called the score for n Achievement (abbreviation for "need for Achievement"), in order to have a technical term which points unmistakably to the fact that the measure was derived in a very particular way, and has an operational meaning quite distinct from estimates one might arrive at by inferring the strength of a person's achievement motive from his actual successful achievements, or from his frequent assertions that he is interested in getting ahead in the world. It remains only to say that the method just described for deriving the n Achievement measure can be applied to measuring n Affiliation, n Power (see Atkinson, 1958), and any other motive that an experimenter can demonstrate influences fantasy in regular and predictable ways.

But of what use are such measures? What good does it do us to know that a person's n Achievement score is high? The answer lies in dozens of research projects which have contrasted the behavior of subjects with high and low n Achievement scores. American males with high n Achievement come more often from the middle class than from the lower or upper class, have better memory for incompleted tasks, are more apt to volunteer as subjects for psychological experiments, are more active in college and community activities, choose experts over friends as working partners, are more resistant to social pressure, cannot give accurate reports of what their "inner concern" with achievement is, etc. (McClelland, et al., 1953; Atkinson, 1958). It is not necessary to review the many such findings in detail here, but it is directly relevant to consider how subjects with high n Achievement actually perform when confronted with a working situation.

Figure 1 presents an early result obtained by Lowell. Obviously the subjects with high n Achievement scores, while they start at about the same level of performance as the subjects with low n Achievements scores, do progressively better as they proceed with the rather complex task of unscrambling words. In common-sense language, they appear to be concerned enough about doing the task well to learn how to do it better as they go along. It might, therefore, be assumed that such subjects—the "highs"—would always do better at any kind of task under any circumstances. Such is not the case. They do not ordinarily do better at routine tasks like canceling the number of "e's" and "o's" in a long string of unrelated letters where no standard of improvement with respect to the performance itself is present. That is, one can really not do such a task "better"—only faster. Furthermore, the "highs" perform better only when performance has achievement significance for them. The point can best be made with the results in Table 1 as adapted from an experiment by French (1955).

In the "relaxed" experimental condition, the subjects with high n Achievement did not do significantly better at a decoding task, presumably because the experimenter removed all achievement

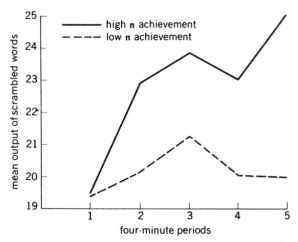

Figure 1. Mean output of scrambled words per four-minute period for subjects with high and low n Achievement scores.

significance from what they were doing with the following instructions: "We are just experimenting today and we appreciate your cooperation very much. We want to find out what kinds of scores people make on these tests." Other research has suggested that appealing for cooperation leads those in the group who have strong n Affiliation to work harder, rather than those with high n Achievement.

In the "task" experimental condition, the subjects were told that the test "measures a critical ability—the ability to deal quickly and accurately with unfamiliar material. It is related to general intelligence, and will be related to your future career. Each man should try to perform as well as possible." Under these instructions, the subjects with high n Achievement as measured some months earlier, performed significantly better than those with low n Achievement. Finally, in the "extrinsic" experimental condition, the subjects were told that "we want to see how fast it is possible to work on a code test . . . with-

out making errors. . . . The five men who make the best scores in five minutes will be allowed to leave right away—as soon as I can check the papers. The others will have more practice periods and more tests." These instructions introduced specific pressure for speed with the extra incentive of time off from work for those who get through as fast as possible. Under these conditions, again the subjects with high n Achievement do not perform better than those with low n Achievement. If anything, the "lows" do a little better on the average, suggesting that the possibility of getting out of the working situation appeals to them the most!

All of these facts together suggest that high n Achievement will lead a person to perform better when achievement in the narrow sense is possible. If the task is just routine, or if finishing it sooner implies cooperating with someone or getting some special reward like time off from work or a money prize (Atkinson & Reitman, 1958), subjects with other motives will perform better. The achieve-

TABLE 1

MEAN PERFORMANCE SCORES AS A FUNCTION OF INITIAL MOTIVATION LEVEL AND
EXPERIMENTAL CONDITIONS (*After French, 1955*)

	EXPERIMENTAL CONDITIONS		
	Relaxed orientation	Task orientation	Extrinsic reward
Initial motivation:			
High n Achievement	17.73	29.80	18.20
Low n Achievement	15.40	16.66	22.47
Correlations with initial motivation	.03	.48*	.02

* A correlation this large could have arisen by chance less than 1 out of 100 times ($p < .01$).

ment motive is apparently not strongly "engaged" under such conditions. Furthermore, we might legitimately expect that people with strong achievement motives would seek out situations in which they could get achievement satisfaction. They ought to be the kind of people who set achievement standards for themselves rather than relying on extrinsic incentives provided by the situation, and they should try harder and more successfully to reach the standards they set for themselves. It does not take a great stretch of imagination to assume further that if a number of people with high n Achievement happened to be present in a given culture at a given time, things would start to hum. They might well start doing things better, as in Fig. 1, or what is even more important, they might start doing them differently by trying to get achievement satisfaction out of what they were doing. What had been done out of a desire to please, to make money, or to get time off from work, might now be converted into an activity in which standards of excellence were defined and pursued in their own right. Viewed in this light it would not be at all surprising to imagine that an increase in n Achievement should promote economic or cultural growth.

19 Some consequences of taking Machiavelli seriously

RICHARD CHRISTIE and FLORENCE GEIS

What are the characteristics of individuals who manipulate others? Reflection led to four hunches which should not be dignified by being termed hypotheses but which seemed consistent with an "ideal type":

1. Manipulators are not basically concerned with morality in the conventional sense.

2. They are basically "cool" in interpersonal relationships. Once one becomes emotionally involved with another person it becomes difficult to treat him as an object to be manipulated.

3. Since those who manipulate are more concerned with means rather than ends, they might be of any ideological persuasion, but are more concerned with conning others than what they are conning them for.

4. Whether or not this behavior might suggest that those who display it should be candidates for a psychiatrist's couch, they do function successfully in the contemporary world. They should not display the type of irrationality commonly or technically viewed as neurotic or psychotic; if anything, they would be over-rational in dealing with others.

Since men have speculated about the characteristics of manipulators or operators from the dawn of recorded history we thought it prudent to examine the writings of power theorists. Many of these theorists gave advice on how to govern a kingdom, but the assumptions underlying the sort of people who would follow their advice seemed more implicit than explicit. The exception appeared to be Machiavelli. It was a revelation to reread *The Prince* and *The Discourses*.

Machiavelli had a convenient habit of giving advice in what was essentially a series of short essays, each oriented around a specific point. This made it fairly easy to convert his precepts into statements that would fit into opinion inventories. For example, "Most men mourn the loss of their patrimony more than the death of their fathers" was edited to read, "Most men forget more easily the death of their father than the loss of their property," on the grounds that it didn't change the basic meaning and the revision would be more meaningful to current populations. In an attempt to get around the problem of response set some statements were reversed, e.g., "Most men are cowards" became "Most men are brave." Some items which seemed congruent with Machiavelli were added, such as, "Barnum was probably right when he said there's a sucker born every minute."

Abridged from Chapter 18 in E. A. Borgatta and W. W. Lambert (Eds.), **Handbook of Personality Theory and Research**, pp. 960–972 (Copyright © by Rand McNally & Company, Chicago), with permission of the authors and the publisher.

The items were typed on cards, and colleagues were asked to respond to them and then asked how they interpreted each item. This procedure had two results. One was that we edited the items for clarity of meaning. The second was that the extent of agreement or disagreement with Machiavelli on the part of the individual respondent had a higher than chance correlation with peer evaluations of "operating" ability.

There are several reasons for spending this amount of time on the development of the concept. With few exceptions the published rationale behind a given paper-and-pencil test is not spelled out. A second reason is that the use of the word "Machiavellianism" to describe the content of the scales has been questioned. Every statement that could be pruned from the translations of Machiavelli's writings that appeared to have a relevance to the way in which one person views another or others, ways of controlling or influencing their behavior, and even more philosophical ways of viewing the history of mankind, were thrown into the hopper. It may be possible to derive in logical fashion a philosophically tighter and more parsimonious set of axioms which condense Machiavelli's writings. Our concern was primarily with ways of identifying those individuals who gravitate to power positions in the contemporary rather than the Renaissance world, so we interpreted Machiavelli's writings in view of thousands upon thousands of responses to questionnaires and interviews.

The next step was empirical. Seventy-one statements were dittoed and given in a Likert format (agree strongly, agree somewhat, no opinion, disagree somewhat, disagree strongly) to three aggregates of undergraduates. They were not selected upon any scientific theory of sampling. They were simply as diverse a group as could be obtained at the time since the early work on this study did not fall within the scope of any foundation program and was done out of curiosity. The items were given to 518 students in sociology courses at the State University of Iowa, 427 in political science at the University of North Carolina, and 251 in psychology at Hofstra College on Long Island.

Part-whole phi coefficients were computed separately on each sample. Surprisingly, 50 of the 71 items discriminated at the .05 level between high and low scorers in all three samples. Elation was somewhat dampened when it was found that statements lifted or modified from those enunciated by Machiavelli hundreds of years ago came through the item analysis more strongly than those we had devised.

A subsequent set of findings was also cause for reflection. The mean reliability on a 20-item scale (Mach IV) on nine samples was .79. Mach IV consisted of the best ten items worded in the Mach direction and the ten best worded in the opposite direction. A similarly long and counterbalanced revision of the F scale (Christie, Havel, & Seidenberg, 1958) had a mean reliability of only .68 on the same nine samples. This is interesting for several reasons. The F scale had gone through a number of revisions, reworking of items, retestings, and various other refinements, and it has proved to be one of the most popularly used and psychologically meaningful scales in recent times. The F scale is based upon a Freudian interpretation of behavior, Mach IV upon an interpretation of Machiavelli. One is tempted to conclude that the dimension in which Machiavelli was interested is more relevant to current undergraduates than that of Freud, or that there is a greater internal consistency in Machiavelli's theorizing than in Freud's.

In the California F scale just mentioned, the "F" stands for potential fascism (Adorno *et al.*, 1950). Because the Mach scale is not ideologically oriented, it was reassuring to find that in various samples there was no significant correlation between F and Mach IV or V. The average correlation was about —.10.

Some psychologists are surprised that there is not a positive correlation between the F and Mach scales. One possible reason is that those who are disenchanted with others should make high scores on both scales. A hunch is that there is a qualitative difference in agreeing with statements representing the two viewpoints. High scorers on both scales should agree with a simple statement, "Most people are no damn good." Underlying the F scale, however, is a moralistic and judging predisposition: "Most people are no damn good *but they should be*"; whereas a high Mach might say, "People are no damn good, why not take advantage of them." Those high in authoritarianism tend to evaluate others in moralistic terms, those high in manipulativeness in opportunistic terms.

The path of research is not always logical. Ideal samples for testing theoretically based hypotheses often do not exist or if they do they may be unavailable. There are, perhaps, some benefits in having to deal with the world as it is. For better or worse, by chance rather than choice, the burgeoning interest in Machiavelli coincided with a study of medical school students. They were given Mach scales in addition to hundreds of other questions which included choice of a medical specialty.

The major intended specialties ranked from highest to lowest, on Mach IV scores, and as follows:
1. Psychiatry
2. Pediatrics
3. Internal Medicine
4. Obstetrics and Gynecology
5. Surgery

Although the difference in Mach scores between specialties was statistically significant, it was not predicted, and essentially it described the orientation of students in three elite medical schools who intended to specialize. (If it is at all relevant, the minority of the samples who wanted to be general practitioners had low scores.) Kurt Back and his associates administered Mach IV to students in eight medical schools carefully selected for their diversity. Again it was found that potential psychiatrists were highest and those opting for surgery and OBGY were lowest (Back, Personal communication, 1959).

This particular finding interested Back and his colleagues enough to follow it up and give Mach IV to faculty members in medical schools as well as practitioners. Psychiatrists, in this case actual rather than potential, scored highest with surgeons and obstetricians being lowest.

Regularities in data, even if unpredicted, deserve attention. One post hoc interpretation is that a relationship appears to exist between the hypothesized number of hours a physician spends with an individual patient and Mach scores. Most patients, for example, are referred to surgeons by other doctors, have a diagnostic hour or two, are worked up in the hospital by a resident, and are under anaesthesia during treatment, while post-operative interchange with the surgeon is often perfunctory. If a non-random sample of mothers is correct, they frequently feel that they are part of an assembly line in obstetricians' offices.

At the other extreme, psychiatrists typically spend at least an hour a week with a patient and this process has been known to endure for years. Pediatricians are also likely to have a continuing relationship with the families that choose them.

Another aspect is the degree of interpersonal manipulation involved. By definition a psychiatrist is attempting to influence the behavior of his patients, i.e., manipulate them. A surgeon is an "operator" in the technical but not the popular sense.

Such speculations led to the hunch that individuals who were involved in formal social roles would tend to become "cooler" and more impersonal in dealing with others than persons whose life was spent in less formalized roles.

Some early findings which supported the hunch that people agreeing with Machiavelli succeeded in the world better than low scorers were by-products of research in which Mach scale items were included in questionnaires. Weinstock found a significant positive correlation between these items and the extent to which Hungarian refugees after the abortive rebellion in 1956 acculturated to American life. In this instance, however, it was difficult to disentangle cause and effect. Did more Machiavelli-like Hungarians find it easier to adapt to the United States, or did successful acculturation raise their scores? A similar problem of interpretation exists with data collected by Milbrath (Personal communication, 1958) on Washington lobbyists. Those lobbyists who served more than one client were, as predicted, higher in agreement with items from Mach IV than those

who had only one client. The most satisfying data were those obtained by Singer (1964) on freshmen at Pennsylvania State University. He correlated Mach V scores with grade point average and statistically controlled for ability, as measured by the admission test battery. A significant positive correlation was found among male undergraduates between Mach V scores at the beginning of college and first-semester grade point average. It should be noted that this relationship held only for males. Despite their aberrance in making comparatively high Mach scores, the coeds displayed the typical feminine pattern. Their Mach V scores did not correlate significantly with other behavioral measures. Singer did find a significant relationship, however, between ratings of physical attractiveness and grade point average, with ability held constant, among the female undergraduates.

Although we had not uncovered any relationship between IQ and Mach scores, the relationship between Mach and interpersonal role orientation intrigued us. An examination of Back's, Silverstein's (Personal Communication, 1959), and some of our own data indicated a significant positive relationship between the judged eliteness of medical schools and Mach scores of students. It is impossible to say whether highly manipulative students choose elite schools or elite schools tend to recruit them. The relationship between eliteness of schools and Mach scores was further investigated among a group of Peace Corps trainees. In this case, an index (known locally as the "fat cat" index) was computed. It was composed of four ratios: student/faculty, number of books in the library/students, annual budget/students, and number of scholarships/students. The average intercorrelation between these measures was roughly +.60 so that we felt justified in combining them.

These trainees came from highly diverse colleges. The things they had in common were a bachelor's degree and the fact that they were going to teach in secondary schools in Nigeria and had been carefully screened. They could in no way be considered representative of the colleges they had attended. Our suspicion is that an Ivy League graduate who volunteers for the Peace Corps is probably lower on Mach than his classmates, whereas a volunteer from a state agricultural college is higher than his peers. Despite this possible built-in bias against the relationship between Mach scores and the fat-catness of the schools they had attended, a significant correlation of +.33 was found.

In candor, a failure to corroborate this finding was found in a different context. Graduating seniors from a private prep school had taken Mach IV. There was no relationship between their scores and Astin's (1962) Affluence ranking of the college at which they were accepted.

In a broader sense, some of the implications of bits and drabs of data collected haphazardly were provocative. The majority of attitude and personality inventories are correlated with measures of intelligence. The Mach scales were not (with the only marginally significant correlation among Tennessee female undergraduates). These results were all based upon captive audiences in such institutional settings as colleges or the Navy where a degree of homogeneity as far as age and institutional selective procedures were operative. What was more puzzling was the finding based upon samples collected for class training purposes: there seemed to be no relationship between years of education and Mach scores.

Other bits of data led to speculations about the social conditions that might foster manipulative orientations. Back's data indicated that physicians on medical school staffs and in practice were less likely to endorse Machiavellian statements than students intending to go into medical specialties. Milbrath's sample of Washington lobbyists scored lower than samples of college students, and a wildly unrepresentive clutch of top-level but over 60-year-old business executives scored lower still.

There appeared to be at least one common denominator differentiating these groups and college students—age. In pondering the fact that older respondents tended to be lower on Mach scales than younger ones of comparable socio-economic status, several notions occurred:

1. Lazarsfeld, Berelson, and Gaudet (1944) have pointed to the fact that there are generational differences in voting. Those who first cast ballots for a presidential candidate in the 20's were more likely to persist in choice of Republican candidates; those first voting in the 30's were more likely to have first voted for and persist in voting for Democratic candidates. More recently, Newcomb (1963) found remarkable attitudinal consistency in a 25-year followup of former students at Bennington College.[1] Although political ideology is involved in both instances, one inference is that values internalized at or about the time of attaining majority persist more frequently than not.

2. The weight of evidence indicates that individuals who spend more of their

[1] This paper appears in Section VI here.—Eds.

time interacting with others in a formal set of roles are more likely to be Machiavellian than those who do not. American society has been characterized by an increasing percentage of the population engaged in precisely these professional and service functions with a concomitant decrease in the proportion of people in farming and on the assembly line. If the postulated relationship is true, it can be hypothesized that a random sample of American adults in 1924 would have been less Machiavellian in orientation than in 1964, because of a less complex web of role sets.

If these two assumptions are made —that the prevalence of manipulative orientations is greater now than was true a generation or more ago, and that people's values tend to stabilize around those they acquire when 20 or so years of age—a prediction can be (and was) made. A representative sample of adults in the United States should be expected to show a negative correlation between age and Mach scores. To be more specific, the greatest change in the societal net of role relationships in the United States probably occurred at the time of the outbreak of World War II. If the preceding assumptions are true, it might be expected that not only is there a negative relationship with age but that the sharpest break should be between contemporary (as of 1963) adults 40 years of age or under who became adults in the early 40's, and those over 40.

These speculations were put to the test. Ten Mach IV items, ten from Mach V, were included in interviews of a representative nation-wide sample of 1482 American adults in 1963, in a study conducted by the National Opinion Research Center. Each respondent was presented a card with the question

printed on it to peruse while the interviewer read the question aloud. The interviewer recorded the response.

The responses to these questions were factor analyzed using a varimax solution. The second factor is more relevant to the generational difference hypothesis. Items from the forced-choice Mach V scale designed to control for social desirability which hung together in this sample (Table I) appear to refer more to what might be termed interpersonal tactics—honesty is *not* the best policy in dealing with others, it *is* wise to flatter more important people, etc. The age categories in this representative nation-wide sample were coded by decades, i.e., 21–30, 31–40, 41–50, 51–60, and 60 and over. Those respondents who attained majority in or after 1941–42 fell in the first two aggregates. A one-way analysis of variance indicates a statistically significant negative relationship between age and scores on this factor. The single most significant difference between age groups is between those 40 or younger early in 1963 and those 41 or older.

Although it is gratifying to find confirmation in survey data of a hunch based upon assumptions that seemed reasonable but not firmly established, it should be reported that some expectations based upon more tenuous and even less firmly established assumptions were not supported. For example, we did not find any significant relation (in the statistical sense) between Mach score and education or socio-economic status, as measured by the Hollingshead SES index. This corroborated results from pilot studies which suggested no such relationship. What was shattering to the investigator's ego was the fact that a discrepancy score computed on the father's reported SES and that of the

TABLE I

MACHIAVELLIAN TACTICS

Loading	Item No.	
.63	28	A. It is best to give others the impression that you can change your mind easily.
		B. It is a good working policy to keep on good terms with everyone.
		ᵃC. Honesty is the best policy in all cases.
.58	30	ᵃA. Barnum was probably right when he said that there's at least one sucker born every minute.
		B. Life is pretty dull unless one deliberately stirs up some excitement.
		C. Most people would be better off if they controlled their emotions.
.53	22	ᵃA. Never tell anyone the real reason you did something unless it is useful to do so.
		B. The well-being of the individual is the goal that should be worked for before anything else.
		C. Once a truly intelligent person makes up his mind about the answer to a problem he rarely continues to think about it.
.48	24	A. The world would be a much better place to live in if people would let the future take care of itself and concern themselves only with enjoying the present.
		ᵃB. It is wise to flatter important people.
		C. Once a decision has been made, it is best to keep changing it as new circumstances arise.
.39	26	ᵃA. All in all, it is better to be humble and honest than to be important and dishonest.
		B. A man who is able and willing to work hard has a good chance of succeeding in whatever he wants to do.
		C. If a thing does not help us in our daily lives, it isn't very important.

ᵃ Indicates items keyed to Machiavelli [Note: Items 28 and 26 above are keyed negatively.—Eds.]

respondent did not indicate that respondents who were upwardly mobile in society were more in agreement with Machiavelli. Even a perverse hunch (that married female respondents whose husbands were higher on the social ladder than the respondent's father would score higher than ladies who did not marry "up") didn't work.

One of the advantages of data such as these is that they jibe with previous findings and hunches based upon them just enough to convince one that something valid is being measured. At the same time, they are not in accord with other, less firmly grounded stereotypes about the prevalance of Machiavellian orientations in American society. It is easy to discount the finding that Machiavellian women (as measured by these scales) do not marry "up." After all, Mach scales do not seem to tap consistently anything meaningful which discriminates individual differences in behavior among women. But other problems are not so easily, or glibly, evaded. Why aren't upwardly-mobile males in this sample higher on the scale than SES-stable or downward-mobiles? Can an honest man get ahead as well in the American social system as a manipulator? Or are agreers with Machiavelli sons of those in the establishment so that they have nowhere to go socioeconomically but to stay the same or go down in SES?

To return for a moment to the problem of why there was not the expected relationship between upward social mobility and Mach scores: it was suggested earlier that the relationship between manipulative orientation and professional preferences depended not so much on education level or the SES of an individual as on the interpersonal role context of such behavior. The occupational classifications used in the survey were designed to describe the social level rather than their role relations vis à vis others. Successful morticians and professors of classics might end up in the same SES category despite a different relationship with dead subjects, just as psychiatrists and surgeons whose patterns of interaction with others might be different.

In the terminology of sociologists, we had measures of statuses rather than of roles or role sets.

This finding prepared us to accept another that we had not anticipated. An analysis of size of place of residence by Mach scores did not yield a consistent relationship. This might seem to run counter to the general hypothesis that the greater the degree of urbanization, the greater the number of role-sets and the greater the Mach scores. Demographic data collected on respondents in the NORC sample were checked against 1960 census data and were found to fit amazingly closely. In 1960, however, the old differentiation between city slicker and the rube did not fit neatly into census data on size of community. Many presumably successful

manipulators did not live in populous metropolitan areas but had moved to less crowded suburbs, and many refugees from the countryside, especially unsuccessful members of minority groups, had moved to urban centers. This reciprocal migration probably diluted rural-urban differences that would have been found a generation or more ago, when city dwelling was associated with interpersonal "sharpness" and rural populations were "hicks" in the time before radio and television became accessible and commonplace among members of all social classes. In short, the blanketing effects of mass communications and the migration of social elites away from residence in census-defined cities and the countermovement of nonelites into core urban areas makes the simple equation of the more urban and complex society with interpersonal manipulation less likely than in times past.

Actually the data described have dealt with only the beginnings of the idea, and a few of many attempts to investigate it. A second major approach has led to a series of laboratory studies. These will be described in a separate report (Christie & Geis, 1970).

Data collected to date indicate the following tentative conclusions:

1. There is a long historical tradition of interest in the individual characteristics of those who manipulate others and in those who permit themselves to be manipulated.

2. Translations of items relating to interpersonal manipulation appear to be relevant enough to differentiate reliably among respondents who are given an opportunity to agree or disagree with them.

3. Endorsement of such items does not appear to be systematically correlated

with known measures of psychopathology, political ideology, or social class.

4. Data to date suggest that the greater the involvement of an individual in a complex of formalized role relationships with others, the greater the endorsement of manipulative tactics.

5. Respondents in agreement with Machiavellian or manipulative state-ments seem to have greater success in meeting the demands of American society—including getting ahead in college.

6. College students who were selected as subjects for laboratory studies succeeded in out-manipulating their partners roughly in proportion to their agreement with Machiavellian precepts.

IV LANGUAGE AND COMMUNICATION

Subhuman species regularly emit and respond to vocal stimuli, often with appropriately differentiated behavior. This "passive" language, as Klineberg once called it (1954), is widely distributed among animals. "Active" language—the use of sounds made by animals themselves as means for controlling others—is, however, sharply limited in distribution and, at best, is only rudimentary even at phylogenetic levels adjacent to man; consequently, the communicative capabilities necessary to support variegated social patterns exist only at the human level (see Smith & Miller, 1966). Furthermore, what Korzybski called the "time-binding" (1941) aspect of communicative modalities, referring to accumulations and transmissions from the past to the present and on to the future, is crucial to the existence of culture, and, so far as we know, is unique to man.

The idea that language is uniquely human is basic to Chomsky's "mentalistic" view of it as outlined in the paper beginning this Section. In it he firmly rejects the notion that human language is continuous with lower forms of communication and offers as a key to comprehension of language and language behavior the concept of "linguistic competence." As Chomsky construes it, linguistic competence signifies distinctive mental or cognitive organizations and operations not simply or directly apparent in behavior, but, nonetheless, underlying and at least partly determining it.

For Chomsky, then, the essence of language is mental, quite as, for him, the essence of human nature is mental (cf. 1966, 1968). He thus explicitly sets himself apart from associationist-behaviorist and "descriptive" linguistic approaches to language study, arguing that both of these, in common with most others as well, have dealt more with manifestations of language than they have with its basic cognitive nature.

Viewpoints such as Chomsky's constitute something of a new wave of thinking about language, but with distinct soundings from a remoter past. If these viewpoints sometimes seem to imply that little real progress has been made in understanding language, many linguistic phenomena nevertheless have been studied to good effect, and social psychological interest in problems of language and communication has a long history (see Osgood and Sebeok, 1954, Ch. 2; Carroll, 1955; Jakobovits & Miron, 1967; Oldfield & Marshall, 1968). Aspects of communicative interaction have been extensively studied, and the selections in Section V directly or indirectly attest to that. Especially in recent years, increasingly frequent investigation can be noted of the modalities by which these interactions progress, notably in language and verbal behavior in general. Both as a vehicle and as a condition for social behavior, therefore, language and communication have been and continue to be major objects for scientific investigation. Osgood and Sebeok make this evident in their descriptive schema reprinted here.

Since communication entails processes of transmitting "coded" messages, its complete understanding requires comprehension of the "nature" of the message. For convenience the problem can be partitioned in two; first, the *content*, or meaning, of the message and its units can be considered and, second, the *structure* of the message, the properties of the "code," can be considered separately. In fact, analyses of behavior in relation to language necessarily assume prior description of language units. Early research in language-behavior relations suffered from the unavoidable primitiveness and naïveté of the means for description and analysis of linguistic codes. Today, however, thanks largely to development of the social science of descriptive or structural linguistics, a well-wrought theory and set of procedures guide direct analyses of language, as Markel shows in his overview in this Section. Furthermore, linguistic theory and methods have served as models for the examination of non-vocal communications systems (see Osgood and Sebeok, 1954, p. 84), and Markel suggests that the framework of descriptive linguistics may prove a productive model for the analysis of other aspects of behavior. Hall (1959) has already demonstrated its potential usefulness for the understanding of non-linguistic cultural patterns. Nevertheless, as Chomsky aptly suggests, the paramount application of descriptive linguistic theory and method is to the *structure* of spoken language.

Another well-known approach to the structural analysis of messages—information theory—is mentioned by Osgood and Sebeok, and a comprehensive, relatively non-technical account may be found in an excellent paper by G. A. Miller (1953). Broader application of the same kinds of ideas can be found in the book by Fitts and Posner (1967). Based in mathematical probability theory and drawn originally from the study of inanimate communication systems, information theory is really a theory of information transmission, providing a useful methodology for examining organizational properties in a communication system. The theory has sometimes been applied as a general model for human behavior, but more frequently it has been used selectively in connection with communication processes. Now generally recognized as inadequate as a general schema for human behavior, and even oversimple as a model for human communication (see Toda, 1956), information theory is nevertheless appropriately applied to partial aspects of those processes.

Neither information theory nor descriptive linguistics has much to say about the *content* of messages. Meaning is handled in descriptive linguistics mainly in the limited sense of the equivalences of linguistic usage, illustrated by Markel's discussion of morphemes. It is obvious, however, that relations between language and behavior are fully comprehensible only with reference to the contents of messages. Standard psychological stipulations hold that behavior is not a function of "stimulus" units *per se*, but of the meanings attached to them. Yet, in spite of wide-ranging scholarly interest, the "meaning of meaning" has only recently begun to emerge from the metaphysical mists that had long enveloped it.

Of the contemporary specialties devoted to the study of meaning, *general semantics* is possibly most widely known. Departing from the somewhat eccentric theory of "sign processes" advanced by Korzybski (1941), S. I. Hayakawa, currently the leading figure in the movement, has concerned himself with broad constructions of meaning (1951). For the most part general semantics has tended to be rather focused in its interests and, following Korzybski's lead, has emphasized imprecisions in sign-significant relations and relativities of meaning associated with communication breakdowns, and even pathological states. However, the selection from Hayakawa's writing reprinted here reflects a broad interest in language and its uses.

In this excerpt from his book *Language in Thought and Action* (1964), Hayakawa is occupied with relations between "words and the world," with uses of language as a means for controlling events and influencing social processes. As he develops his ideas about the "directive uses of language," their wider relevance to social behavior becomes clear. In addition to meaning, as such, his approach pertains to matters such as conformity, leadership, and mass media effects, including attitude change—in fact to a whole gamut of issues and problems discussed at various points in this book under such headings as social influence or social organization.

Hayakawa notes that in order for language to function directively it must be "interesting." It must seize attention. To accomplish this, he suggests, emotional loadings are attached to words and often, for further emphasis, language is supplemented with non-verbal signs such as gestures, rituals, etc. Hayakawa describes the operation of these devices, and their effects and ends, by pointing out that because directive uses of language are in the nature of promissory notes, some care should be taken to insure that the promises are understood and kept. In this sense, his approach to language bears directly on the process of social interaction considered in the next section.

There exist other theories of signs similar in many ways to Hayakawa's and most of them will be found well summarized in Osgood's enormously influential paper, "The nature and measurement of meaning" (1952). Osgood's own theory of meaning begins with a distinction between denotative and connotative meanings. The former meaning is broadly shared within the community and perhaps found in dictionaries, where such exist, while the latter is more individualized and personal, deriving from a person's distinctive pattern of life experience. Osgood goes on to develop a conception of connotative meaning based in Hull-type behaviorist learning theory. Modeled after his more general "mediation hypothesis" (Osgood, 1953), he treats meaning as a perceptual process built up by conditioning and resting in "antedating" fragments of larger instrumental responses, comparable to Hull's fractional antedating goal responses. These implicit fractional response components are presumed to be evoked in the course of behavior and, in turn, produce internal stimuli which serve as representations (signs) of larger behavioral complexes. The meaning of an object or an event, thus, becomes a "perception" *mediated* by internal representational fragments conditioned by previous experiences and aroused by the current situation. Since Osgood places connotative meaning at an "ideational" or cognitive level which is not directly observable, to index it he has developed a scaling technique, involving factor analytic procedures, called the "semantic differential." With this "indirect" device, meaning can be specified quantitatively as a point in a multidimensional "semantic space" (see Osgood *et al.*, 1957).

From his modified associationist perspective, Osgood reasons that in language, representational mediation processes become conditioned to "linguistically coded stimuli" (e.g., the English language system), thereby accomplishing an organization in which either may be produced by the other in processes of "encoding" and "decoding" messages. Essentially arbitrary signs come to be labels for "concept classes" that derive their meanings from mediational processes, including conditions of prior reinforcement.

The psycholinguistic discussion presented here by Brown is directly related to these matters in terms of the acquisition of language and the function of "names." Without necessarily relying on associationist presuppositions, Brown points out that in learning referents (meanings) the words presented by the child's "tutors" will tend to be the most common ones relevant. These words then come to control the child's behavior in reference to the objects and events named.

In effect, what Brown is describing is the relevance, in language learning, of the practices of the "verbal community," the construct so effectively developed by Skinner in the Appendix, reprinted here, to his book *Verbal Behavior* (1957). The question is raised by Brown, for example, whether it is simply arbitrary that one word is more common than another. He makes the point that the name *denotes* behavioral equivalences, but equivalences differentiated from other reference categories. How one is expected to behave toward the reference object is differentiated and signaled by the label. In sum, the kinds of behaviors appropriate to given situations are acquired and a system of signals is also acquired which serve as "cues" for the differential identification of conditions appropriate to particular behavior patterns.

Names, in other words, can be thought of as generics. By denoting equivalences they tend to control behavior with reference to nominally different objects. Moreover, the transmission of names from parent to child amounts also to a process of transmitting cognitive structures and so has great relevance to socialization practices, discussed in Section II. Learning names may be a primary device by which cultural practices are transmitted from individual to individual. The importance to behavior and cognition of the varying "communication channels" in which persons participate, is clearly suggested by these ideas.

Implicit in Brown's offering and in his book, *Words and Things* (1958), is an important departure beyond language as such. He shows in some detail correspondences between linguistic and non-linguistic practices and, by suggesting that names are categories people use in ordering their worlds, feeds directly into what has come to be popularly called the *Whorfian hypothesis* (Whorf, 1956). In its general form this hypothesis asserts that, inasmuch as people behave and think in terms of the classifications they use to lend meaning to features of the world, language may not only be a vehicle by which people interact, it may also be an *active* determiner of what they perceive and think and, therefore, of what they interact about. This hypothesis is founded upon the idea that the *forms* of a linguistic system place finite limits upon a person's array of available concept "categories" and hence upon the kinds of perceptual differentiations and equivalences that he can and will be able to make. For a discussion of perception as a process of coding or categorizing, see Bruner (1957) and also Miller, Galanter, and Pribram (1960).

In "The Verbal Community" Skinner concentrates on the broad conditions regulating verbal behavior and offers a *denotational* definition of meaning as the *conditions* under which a response is characteristically reinforced. He comments that the languages studied by linguists are, therefore, the reinforcing practices of verbal communities. In studying these practices, the linguist (among others) has not broached what Skinner calls *verbal behavior*. For Skinner, the verbal community is a *given*; the question to which he directs his much more general analysis has to do with psychological mechanisms by which individuals behave within this community.

In his book *Verbal Behavior* (1957) Skinner, from an operant conditioning model, directs attention to what happens when a person speaks or responds to speech. Speech is treated as part of the total behavior of the speaker and may be studied as such, as Skinner does, or as an "objective" fact apart from the speaker, as when a linguist studies a recording of speech. In Skinner's usage, verbal behavior is behavior reinforced through the mediation of other persons; it includes speech, but much more. To all intents and purposes, verbal behavior becomes coincident wtih general social behavior and its analysis is, therefore, social psychology. Further, Skinner's assertion that verbal behavior is governed by a verbal environment, makes his concept, the verbal community, a label for society and culture, one aspect of which is language.

Superficially Skinner's treatment of verbal behavior as a "dependent" variable seems to stand in opposition to the Whorfian hypothesis and its active view of linguistic elements. Actually there is no necessary contradiction. Language may be an independent variable defining certain features of the verbal environment (as Whorf suggests), but the verbal behavior of the *individual* is always a function of these antecedent conditions. Whether verbal elements are viewed as independent or as dependent variables depends upon where one looks.

The final paper in this section, by Miller, reiterates and develops the theme introduced at the outset by Chomsky. In doing so it covers a variety of large issues vital to an understanding of language, its functions, and its human context. The chief thrust of Miller's essay is to depict the complexity of language and of meaning at the level of the sensible utterance. What Miller grapples with is the phenomenon of "understanding" and the problems and challenges it offers the student of language. He sketches the meaning of "psycholinguistics" (see also Miller, 1965; Osgood, 1963) and makes plain his exacting view of the psycholinguistic task, giving some illustrations of attempts to get on with its performance.

Miller delves into relations between speakers and listeners and is led to a description of a "generative" theory of speech perception and performance that encompasses both. In this he stresses the importance of expectancies and cognitive processes and builds a case against motor-behavioristic accounts of language (Skinner's being an obvious case-in-point). To Miller, such accounts fail to treat adequately the original combination of linguistic elements, and this "combinatorial productivity" he sees as both fundamental and specific to the human species. Stressing the significance of rules and the ability of persons to follow them, Miller voices serious doubt about prospects for reducing these phenomena to behavioral "principles" derived from studies of infra-humans. In this connection, Chomsky's review (1959) of Skinner's *Verbal Behavior* is worth consulting. Miller goes on to speak of linguistic universals and the evidence they provide for a biological basis of language (see Lenneberg, 1964). The point of Miller's message, like Chomsky's, is clear enough: Language must be studied at the human level and such study must concentrate on the mental as well as the social processes that underlie it. There is, however, the further implication in these viewpoints that in their desire for scientific rectitude social theorists have missed much of what is crucial to language; by their failure to attend to those mental processes, social scientists may have allowed themselves to remain bemused by behavioral by-products.

The next section focuses on detailed aspects of social interaction. Communication is a vital part, perhaps the essence of such interaction, as many of the papers there maintain and as has been mentioned here. The present section, therefore, serves as an essential complement to it by specifying the components, conditions, and complications of communicative modalities. In another sense, the present section is *inseparable* from the next, for linguistic codes are fundamental ingredients in the perceptual processes that direct interaction.

20　Language and the mind

NOAM CHOMSKY

I

I arrived at Harvard as a graduate student shortly after B. F. Skinner had delivered his William James lectures, later to be published in his book, *Verbal Behavior* (1957). Among scholars active in research in philosophy or psychology of language there was little doubt, at that time, that although details were missing, and although matters couldn't really be quite that simple, a behavioristic framework of rather the sort that Skinner had outlined would prove quite adequate to accommodate the full range of language use. There was little reason to question the conviction of Leonard Bloomfield, Bertrand Russell, and positivistically oriented linguists, psychologists, and philosophers in general, that the framework of stimulus-response psychology would soon be extended to the point where it would provide a satisfying explanation for the most mysterious of human abilities.

Critical voices, even those that commanded considerable prestige, were simply unheard. For example, Karl Lashley gave a brilliant critique of the prevailing framework of ideas in 1948, arguing that underlying language use and all organized behavior there must be abstract mechanisms of some sort that are not analyzable in terms of association and that could not have developed by any such simple means. But his arguments and proposals, though sound and perceptive, had absolutely no effect on the development of the field, and went by unnoticed even at his (Harvard) university, then the leading center of psycholinguistic research. It was a decade later that Lashley's words began to be quoted, and his contribution appreciated, and then only after his insights had been independently achieved, in another context.

In the United States at least, there is little trace today of the illusions of the early postwar years. If we consider the current status of structural linguistic methodology, stimulus-response psycholinguistics (whether or not extended to "mediation theory"), or probabilistic or automatatheoretic models for language use, we find that in each case a parallel development has taken place. In each case, a careful analysis has shown that insofar as the system of concepts and principles that was advanced can be made precise, it can be demonstrated to be inadequate in a fundamental way. The kinds of structures that are realizable in terms of these theories are simply not those that must be postulated to underlie the use of language, if empirical conditions of adequacy are to be satisfied. What is more, the character of the failure and inadequacy is such as to give little reason to believe that these approaches are on the right track. That is,

From Noam Chomsky, "Language and the Mind," I & II, in **The Columbia Forum**, 1968, XI, pp. 5–10 & 3, pp. 23–25. This material appears in different form in Noam Chomsky's **Language and Mind**, © 1968 by Harcourt Brace Jovanovich, Inc. Reprinted by permission of the author and Harcourt Brace Jovanovich, Inc.

in each case it has been argued—quite persuasively, in my opinion—that the approach is not only inadequate, but misguided in basic and important ways.

It has, I believe, become quite clear that if we are ever to understand how language is used or acquired, then we must abstract for separate and independent study a cognitive system, a system of knowledge and belief, that is acquired in early childhood and that interacts with many other factors to determine the kinds of behavior that we observe; to introduce a technical term, we must isolate and study the system of *linguistic competence* that underlies behavior, but that is not realized in any direct or simple way in behavior.

This system of linguistic competence is qualitatively different from anything that can be described in terms of the taxonomic methods of structural linguistics, the concepts of reinforcement theory, or the notions developed within the mathematical theory of communication or the theory of simple automata. The theories and models that were developed to describe simple and immediately given phenomena cannot incorporate the real system of linguistic competence. No matter how intricately extended, "extrapolation" from simple descriptions cannot approach the reality of linguistic competence. Mental structures are not simply "more of the same," but they are, so it appears, qualitatively different from the complex networks and structures that can be developed by elaboration of the concepts that seemed so promising to many scientists just a few years ago.

What is involved is not a matter of degree of complexity, but rather of quality of complexity. Correspondingly, there is no reason to expect that the available technology can provide significant insight or understanding or useful achievements; it has noticeably failed to do so, and, in fact, an investment of time, energy, and money in the use of computers for linguistic research, which is quite appreciable by the standards of a small field like linguistics, has failed to provide any significant advance in our understanding of the use or nature of language. The judgments are fairly harsh, but I think that they are quite defensible; they are, furthermore, hardly debated any longer among people active in linguistic or psycholinguistic research.

At the same time there have been significant advances, I believe, in our understanding of the nature of linguistic competence and some of the ways in which it is put to use. But these advances, such as they are, have proceeded from assumptions very different from those that were so enthusiastically put forth in the period I have been discussing. What is more, these advances have not narrowed the gap between what is known and what can be clearly seen to lie beyond the scope of present understanding and technique. Rather each advance has made it clear that these intellectual horizons are far more remote than was heretofore imagined. Finally, it has become fairly clear, so it seems to me, that the assumptions and approaches that appear to be productive today have a distinctly traditional flavor to them; and in general, a much-despised tradition has been largely revitalized in recent years, and its contributions given some serious, and I believe, well-deserved attention. From the recognition of these facts flows the general and quite healthy attitude of skepticism mentioned earlier.

It seems to me quite appropriate, at this moment in the development of linguistics and psychology in general, to turn again to classical questions, and to ask what new insights have been achieved that bear on them, and how the classical issues may provide direction for contemporary research and study.

II

The assumption that human language evolved from simpler systems, akin to those we find among animals, is so familiar as to have an almost reflex quality. It takes a real effort of will to question it, and to ask what evidence there really is to suppose it to be true. The idea that human language is just a more complex variant of systems to be found in other organisms is one of a set of "arguments by extrapolation" that I think can no longer be held by any rational person. It is related to the belief that a language is simply a very complex system of habits or fabric of dispositions to respond, established through conditioning and association.

All normal humans acquire language; whereas the acquisition of even its barest rudiments is quite beyond the capacities of an otherwise intelligent ape—a fact that was emphasized correctly in Cartesian philosophy. It is widely thought that the extensive modern studies of animal communication challenge this classical view. And it is almost universally taken for granted that there exists a problem of explaining the "evolution" of human language from systems of animal communication. However, a careful look at recent study of animal communication provides little support for such beliefs as these. Rather, it seems to me that this study brings out even more clearly the extent to which human language is unique, without significant analogue in the animal world. Two recent discussions are typical in

how much they take for granted and in what they succeed in showing.

In his recently published Arthur Compton lecture, "Clouds and Clocks," Karl Popper tries to show how problems of freedom of will and Cartesian dualism can be solved by analysis of the evolution of human language from more primitive systems. I am not concerned with the philosophical conclusions that he draws from this analysis, but with the analysis itself. Popper's discussion of stages of evolution of language suggests a kind of continuity. But if we look carefully at these stages, we find unbridgeable gaps between them. He established no relation between the "lower stages," in which vocal gestures are used as an expression of, say, emotional states, and "higher stages," in which articulated sound is used as an expression of thought for discussion and critical argument. What links these stages is, in fact, only a metaphorical use of the term "language." There is no more basis for assuming an evolutionary development of higher from lower stages, in this case, than there is for assuming an evolutionary development from breathing to walking. The processes have no significant analogy.

As a second example, consider a recent discussion of this matter by the comparative ethologist Willard Thorpe. He, too, argues that there is an evolutionary development of human language from animal communication, and that all such systems share fundamental properties, which he enumerates as the properties of being "purposive," "syntactic," and "propositional." Human language is "syntactic," in his sense, in that an utterance is a performance with an internal organization, with structure and coherence. It is "propositional" in the sense that it is informative. In this sense, then, both human language and animal communication are purposive, syntactic, and propositional.

All of this is true, but it establishes nothing, since when we move to the level of abstraction at which human language and animal communication fall together, almost all other behavior is included as well. Thus consider walking. Clearly, it is "purposive." Equally obviously, it is "syntactic" in the sense just defined, as in fact, Karl Lashley pointed out a long time ago in his important discussion of serial order in behavior. Furthermore, it is certainly informative; for example, I can signal my interest in reaching a certain goal by the speed or intensity with which I walk.

It is, incidentally, precisely in this manner that the examples of animal communication that Thorpe presents are "propositional." Thus he gives the example of a bird song in which the rate of alternation of high and low pitch signals the intention of the bird to defend its territory—the higher the rate of alternation, the greater the intention to defend territory. The example is interesting, but it seems to me to show very clearly the hopelessness of the attempt to analogize to human language from animal communication. Every animal communication system that is known (if we disregard some science fiction about dolphins) uses one of two basic principles: either it consists of a fixed, finite number of signals, each associated with a specific range of behavior or emotional state (as illustrated in the extensive primate studies that have been carried out by Japanese scientists for the past several years), or it makes use of a fixed, finite number of linguistic dimensions, each of which is associated with a particular nonlinguistic dimension in such a way that selection of a point along the linguistic dimension determines and signals a certain point along the associated nonlinguistic dimension. The latter is the principle realized in the bird-song example of Thorpe's. Rate of alternation of high and low pitch is a "linguistic dimension" correlated with the nonlinguistic dimension of intention to defend a territory. The bird signals its intention to defend a territory by selecting a correlated point along the linguistic dimension of pitch alternation —I use the word "select" loosely, of course.

The linguistic dimension is abstract, but the principle is clear. Where a communication system is of the second type, it has an indefinitely large range of potential signals, as does human language. The mechanism and principle, however, are entirely different from those employed by human language to express indefinitely many new thoughts, intentions, feelings, and so on. It is not correct to speak of a "deficiency" of the animal system, in terms of range of potential signals; rather the opposite, since the animal system admits in principle of continuous variation along the linguistic dimension, whereas human language is discreet. Hence the issue is not one of "more" or "less," but rather of an entirely different principle of organization. When I make some arbitrary statement in a human language, say, that "the rise of supranational corporations poses new dangers for human freedom," I am not selecting a point along some linguistic dimension that signals a corresponding point along an associated nonlinguistic dimension; nor am I selecting a signal from a finite behavioral repertoire, innate or learned.

Furthermore, it is wrong to think of human use of language as characteristically informative, in fact or in intention. Human language can be used to inform or mislead, or for clarifying one's own thoughts or for displaying one's cleverness, or simply for play. If I have no intention of modifying your behavior or thoughts, I am not using language any less than if I say exactly the same things *with* such intention. If we hope to understand human language and the psychological capacities on which it rests, we must first ask what it is, not how or for what purpose it is used.

When we ask what human language is, we find no striking similarity to animal communication systems. There is nothing useful to be said about behavior or thought at the level of abstraction at which animal and human communication fall together. This, I think, is an important point, often overlooked by those who approach human language as a natural, biological phenomenon; in particular, it seems rather pointless, for these reasons, to speculate about the possibility that human language may have evolved from simpler systems— perhaps as absurd as it would be to speculate about the "evolution" of atoms from clouds of elementary particles.

It is interesting to note that one of the earliest motivations in comparative ethology was the hope that through the "investigation of the *a priori*, of the innate working hypotheses present in subhuman organisms," it would be possible to shed light on the *a priori* forms of human thought. This formulation of intent is quoted from an early and little-known paper by Konrad Lorenz entitled "Kant's doctrine of the *a priori* in the light of contemporary biology."

One word of caution is necessary in referring to Lorenz, now that he has been discovered by Robert Ardrey and Joseph Alsop and popularized as a prophet of doom. It seems to me that Lorenz' views on human aggression, which are now being publicized in a not entirely accurate form, are perhaps the least persuasive aspect of his thought, and that they have been extended to near-absurdity by some of his expositors. It is no doubt true that there are innate tendencies in human psychic constitution that lead to aggressiveness under specific social and cultural conditions. But there is little reason to suppose that these tendencies are so dominant as to leave us forever tottering on the brink of a Hobbesian war of all against all—as, incidentally, Lorenz at least is fully aware, if I read him rightly. Skepticism is certainly in order when a doctrine of man's "inherent aggressiveness" comes to the surface in a society that glorifies competitiveness, in a civilization that has been distinguished by the brutality of the attack that it has mounted against less fortunate peoples. I suspect that the enthusiasm for this curious view of man's nature is less attributable to evidence or argument than it is a reflection of the limited extent to which the general cultural level has advanced since the days when Clive and the Portuguese explorers taught the meaning of true savagery to the "inferior races" who stood in their way.

In any event, I would not want what I am saying to be confused with other, entirely different attempts to revive a theory of human instinct. What seems to me important in ethology is its attempt to explore the innate properties that determine how knowledge is acquired and what is the character of this knowledge.

Surely the classical questions of language and mind receive no final solution, or even the hint of a final solution, from the work that is being actively pursued today. Nevertheless, these problems can be formulated in new ways and seen in a new light. For the first time in many years, it seems to me that there is some real opportunity for substantial progress in the study of the contribution of the mind to perception and the innate basis for acquisition of knowledge. Still, in many respects, we have not made the first approach to a real answer to the classical problems. For example, the central problems relating to the creative aspect of language use remain as inaccessible as they have always been in the past. And the study of universal semantics, surely crucial to the full investigation of language structure, has barely advanced since the medieval period. Many other critical areas might be mentioned where progress has been slow or nonexistent. Real progress has been made in the study of the mechanisms of language, the formal principles that make possible the creative aspect of language use and that determine the phonetic form and semantic content of utterances. Our understanding of these mechanisms, though only fragmentary, does seem to me to have real implications for the study of human psychology. By pursuing the kinds of research that now seem feasible and by focusing attention on certain problems that are now accessible to study, we may be able to spell out in some detail the elaborate and abstract computations that determine, in part, the nature of percepts, and the character of the knowledge that we can acquire, the highly specific ways of interpreting phenomena that are, in large measure, beyond our consciousness and control and that may be unique to man.

21 Communication and psycholinguistics

CHARLES E. OSGOOD and THOMAS A. SEBEOK

I Models of the communication process

In the most general sense, we have communication whenever one system, a *source*, influences another system, a *destination*, by manipulation of the alternative signals which can be carried in the *channel* connecting them. The information source is conceived as producing one or more messages which must be transformed by a *transmitter* into signals which the channel can carry; these signals must then be transformed by a *receiver* back into messages which can be accepted at the destination. This minimal system, borrowed from Shannon's discussion (1949) of the theory of information and diagrammed in Figure 1, has been applied, with great generality, to information transmission in electrical, biological, psychological and social systems as well as language communication in the strict sense. In a telephone communication system, for example, the messages produced by a speaker are in the form of variable sound pressures and frequencies which must be transformed into proportional

electrical signals by the transmitter; these signals are carried over wire (channel) to a receiver which transforms them back into the variable sound pressures and frequencies which constitute the message to be utilized by the listener. The activity of the transmitter is usually referred to as *encoding* and that of the receiver as *decoding*. Anything that produces variability at the destination which is unpredictable from variability introduced at the source is called *noise*.

This model of the communication process, developed in connection with engineering problems, was not intended to provide a satisfactory picture of human communication. For one thing, it implies a necessary separation of source and destination, of transmitter and receiver, which is usually true of mechanical communication systems but not of human ones. The individual human functions more or less simultaneously as a source and destination and as a transmitter and receiver of messages— indeed, he is regularly a decoder of the messages he himself encodes through

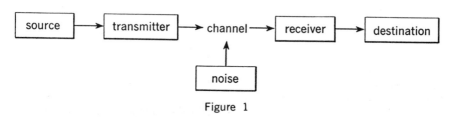

Figure 1

Excerpted from **Psycholinguistics: A Survey of Theory and Research Problems.** Supplement to the **Journal of Abnormal and Social Psychology,** 49, no. 4, Part 2 (Copyright © 1954 by the American Psychological Association), with permission of the authors, the publisher, and the Trustees of Indiana University.

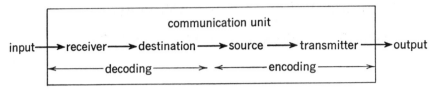

Figure 2

various feedback mechanisms. Each individual in a speech community may be conceived as a more or less self-contained communicating system, encompassing in his nervous apparatus, from receptors to effectors, all of the components shown in Figure 1. If we rearrange the components in Shannon's model in the fashion shown in Figure 2, what might be called a *communication unit* is described, equipped to both receive and send messages. In the process of human decoding, input of some form of physical energy, linguistically or otherwise coded, is first recoded into sensory neural impulses, operated upon by receiving apparatus, and finally "interpreted" at the destination (presumably as some pattern of activity in the higher centers). In the process of human encoding, an "intention" of the source (presumably some pattern of activity in the same centers) is operated upon by transmitting apparatus in the motor areas, is recoded into physical movements, and becomes the output of this unit. Translating into traditional psychological language, *input* becomes equivalent to "stimulus," *receiver* becomes "reception" and "perception," *destination* and *source* become "cognition" (meaning, attitude, and the like), *transmitter* becomes "motor organization and sequencing," and *output* becomes "response."

Another insufficiency of engineering models for human communication purposes is that they are not designed to take into account the *meaning* of signals, e.g., their significance when viewed from the decoding side and their intention when viewed from the encoding side. The research generated by such models has dealt almost exclusively with relations between transmitter and receiver, or with the individual as a single system intervening between input and output signals. This has not been because of lack of awareness of the problem of meaning or its importance, but rather because it is admittedly difficult to be rigorous, objective, and quantitative at this level. Nevertheless, one of the central problems in psycholinguistics is to make as explicit as possible relations between message events and cognitive events, both on decoding and encoding sides of the equation.

Human communication is chiefly a social affair. Any adequate model must therefore include at least two communicating units, a *source unit* (speaker) and a *destination unit* (hearer). Between any two such units, connecting them into a single system, is what we may call the *message*. For purposes of this report, we will define message as that part of the total output (responses) of a source unit which simultaneously may be a part of the total input (stimuli) to a destination unit. When individual A talks to individual B, for example, his postures, gestures, facial expressions and even manipulations with objects (e.g., laying down a playing

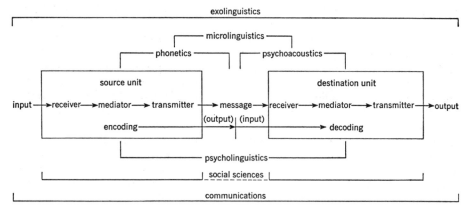

Figure 3

card, pushing a bowl of food within reach) may all be part of the message, as of course are events in the sound wave channel. But other parts of A's total behavior (e.g., breathing, toe-wiggling, thinking) may not affect B at all and other parts of the total stimulation to B (e.g., sensations from B's own posture, cues from the remainder of the environment) do not derive from A's behavior—these events are not part of the message as we use the term. These R-S message events (reactions of one individual that produce stimuli for another) may be either *immediate* or *mediate*—ordinary face-to-face conversation illustrates the former and written communication (along with musical recordings, art objects, and so forth) illustrates the latter.

Figure 3 presents a model of the essential communication act, encoding of a message by a source unit and decoding of that message by a destination unit. Since the distinction between source and destination within the same communicator (as shown in Figure 2) seems relevant only with respect to the direction of information exchange (e.g., whether the communicator is decoding

or encoding), we substitute the single term *mediator* for that system which intervenes between receiving and transmitting operations. The ways in which the various sciences concerned with human communication impinge upon and divide up the total process can be shown in relation to this figure.

II Disciplines concerned with human communication

Microlinguistics (or linguistics proper) deals with the structure of messages, the signals in the channel connecting communicators, as events independent of the characteristics of either speakers or hearers. Once messages have been encoded and are "on the air," so to speak, they can be described as objective, natural science events in their own right. In an even stricter sense, the linguist is concerned with determining the *code* of a given signal system, the sets of distinctions which are significant in differentiating alternative messages. The term *exolinguistics* (sometimes called metalinguistics) has been used rather loosely by linguists to cover all those other aspects of language study which concern relations between the characteristics of messages and the characteristics of individuals who produce and receive them, including both their behavior and culture. Whether or not the grammatical structure of a language influences the thinking of those who speak it is thus an exolinguistic problem. The *social sciences* in general, and psychology, sociology, and anthropology in particular, are concerned with the characteristics of human organisms and societies which influence the selection and interpretation of messages—attitudes, meanings, social roles, values, and so forth. The rather new discipline coming to be known as *psycholinguistics* (paralleling the closely related discipline termed *ethnolinguistics*) is concerned in the broadest sense with relations between messages and the characteristics of human individuals who select and interpret them. In a narrower sense, psycholinguistics studies those processes whereby the intentions of speakers are transformed into signals in the culturally accepted code and whereby these signals are transformed into the interpretations of hearers. In other words,

psycholinguistics deals directly with the processes of encoding and decoding as they relate states of messages to states of communicators. The terminal aspect of human speech encoding, production of speech sounds, is the special province of *phonetics*. Similarly, the initial aspect of human speech decoding, whereby sound pressures and frequencies are transformed into impulses in auditory nerve fibers and relayed to the cortex, is a special field of *psychoacoustics*. Finally, the science of *human communication* would be concerned with relations between sources who select messages and destinations who interpret and are affected by them. In the broadest sense, therefore, human communications as a science includes the other disciplines that have been mentioned; in a narrower sense—and one more in keeping with contemporary activities—students of communications research have usually worked at grosser levels of analysis, concerning themselves with sources such as radio and the newspaper and destinations such as the mass audience, members of another culture, and so on.

22 The basic principles of descriptive linguistic analysis

NORMAN N. MARKEL

Introduction

In the western world the Greek generalizations about language were not improved upon until about 1700. The ancient Greeks took it for granted that the structure of their language embodied universal forms of human thought. They further believed that the origin and true meanings of words could be traced in their shape, and the pursuance of this study they called *etymology*. A Greek etymologist working today on the English language would, for example, note that *goose* is part of *gooseberry*, or that *dog* reversed is *god*, and consider it his proper task to discover the relationship between these words. In their search for universal truths, the Greeks observed their language and discovered its parts of speech and syntactic constructions. But subject and predicate, genders, numbers, cases, persons, tenses and modes were classes defined in terms which were to tell their meaning.

The Romans constructed Latin grammars on the Greek model, and the medieval scholars saw in this classical Latin the logically normal form of human speech, which embodied universally valid canons of logic. An outgrowth of this conception of grammar was that the grammarians, after ascertaining the logical basis of a language, could prescribe how people *ought* to speak. When the students of language came in contact with exotic tongues they proceeded to distort the facts of these languages in order to fit them into the frame of Latin grammar.

It wasn't until the eighteenth century, when Englishmen in India reported on the work of the Hindu grammarians, that a drastic change in European ideas about language occurred. The Brahmin religion held sacred some ancient collections of hymns, and it became the task of a specially trained group of men to insure their correct pronunciation and interpretation. The oldest treatise of this sort that has come down to us is the grammar of Panini. This work records with the greatest detail every inflection, derivation, composition, and syntactic usage of its author's speech. For the first time Europeans saw a complete and accurate description of language based upon observation.

The descriptive linguist is not necessarily a polyglot; indeed, he may not even be fluent in a language which he is analyzing. His primary task is the complete description of each individual language of the world. To accomplish this he has developed a rigorous methodology that enables him to analyze and classify the facts of speech as they are uttered by native speakers.

In recent years there has been an intensification of research in the areas of verbal behavior, verbal learning and psycholinguistics. Workers in the various areas may or may not use a linguistic analysis of speech in their particular research, but they are all coming in contact with linguistic terminology and the results of linguistic analysis. Many participate with linguists in symposia and conferences, and some engage linguists as consultants on their own projects. Furthermore, since the descriptive linguist has developed a methodology for handling what is probably the most complex form of human behavior, the concepts underlying his methodology might prove useful to scientists studying other forms of human behavior. Having these two groups in mind, the social scientists, in general,

tongue, you will demonstrate to yourself a continuum of speech sounds. You will notice that there is continuous movement from the time you start the 'm' until the tip of your tongue reaches the upper teeth. Trying to describe "everything" that happened while you were producing just this one word would take a great deal of time. But, if you will repeat the word slowly you will notice that there are points of maximum closure and maximum openness of the lips and tongue. These crests and troughs are the centers of segments of sounds which have indefinite borders, and it is at these points that we enter the continuum of speech behavior. Schematically:

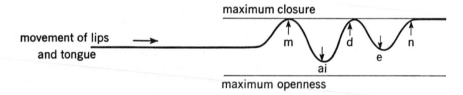

and the students of language, in particular, the following is an attempt to elucidate, in as concise a manner as possible, the basic principles of descriptive linguistic analysis.

Phonology

PHONETICS

In listening to speech one hears a continuous stream of sounds separated into breath groups. Sounds in the stream are not separated from each other in any consistent manner. At this first level of analysis the linguist provides himself with a method of entering this continuum of behavior. If you say the word "maiden" and become very conscious of the movement of your lips and

The arrows point to the centers of the segments.

The next task is to describe the sounds that occur at these centers. All of the sounds are physical events that have three main aspects: (1) *Physiological*, the movements of the organs involved in producing the sound; (2) *Acoustic*, the nature of the sound waves set in motion by the speech apparatus; and (3) *Auditory*, the transformation of the sound wave by the ear and the central nervous system into the perception of speech. Linguists have found the *physiological* aspect the most convenient of the three to describe sounds. The reasons are that the movements and positions of the vocal organs can be directly observed without previous training, that any sound can be unambiguously and simply described in terms of the movements which produce it, and that after some practice it is easy to convert a physiological description of a sound into the sound itself by simply making the movement specified.

The three mechanisms that are primarily involved in producing sounds are used to establish a three dimensional matrix which defines the cardinal value of any sound. These three dimensions are:

1. *The point of articulation.* This is the point of maximum constriction in the mouth or pharynx. For the 'd' in *maiden* it occurs when the apex of the tongue reaches the alveolar ridge.

2. *The degree of air-stream interruption.* If the air-stream is blocked completely during the articulation the sound is a *stop.* If the air-stream is only partially blocked, producing friction, the sound is *fricative.* If the constriction is not narrow enough to produce any degree of friction, and the only function of the mouth and nose is to modify a sound produced by the vocal cords, that sound is called *resonant.*

3. *The vocal cords.* If the vocal cords are active at the time of articulation, the sound is *voiced.* If the cords are not vibrating at the time of articulation, the sound is *voiceless.*

Having decided on a method for segmenting the sound continuum, and providing for the classification of the segments, the linguist now has a frame of reference with which he can describe the vocal products of any speaker. Furthermore, this method for providing *phonetic units* assures him, and any other interested observer, that different

linguists working on the same continuum of speech sounds will arrive at the same conclusions regarding the phonetic units in that continuum.

PHONEMICS

The segmentation of the continuum of speech provides the linguist with his raw data. He next performs a series of operations on these raw data that will reduce their complexity and enable him to describe them parsimoniously. The first level of this analysis, the description of the sound system of a language, is called *phonemics.* The unit of description at this level of analysis is the *phoneme,* which is a class of speech sounds mutually exclusive of any other such class. The member sounds of each phoneme, the *allophones,* share some feature of articulation, or some combination of features, and show characteristic patterns of distribution.

A phonemic analysis can be demonstrated by examining the initial sounds in "keen" and "coat." On close examination the native speaker of English will find that the point of articulation of these sounds is different and distinct. For the 'k' in "keen" the back of the tongue moves forward on the palate. For the 'k' in "coat" the back of the tongue moves up and back to the velum. These two phonetic units are symbolized as [k̟] and [k], respectively. The feature of articulation shared by both these units is the movement of the back of the tongue. The square brackets are always used when referring to phonetic units.

If all occurrences of the 'k' sound in English were examined we would find that [k̟] occurs only before vowels made with the front of the tongue, and [k] occurs only before vowels made with the back of the tongue. These facts demonstrate *complementary distribution* (C.D.); each of the phonetic units occurs in a fixed context in which the other never occurs. On the basis of their phonetic similarity and C.D., [k̥] and [k̟] are analyzed as being members of a class of sounds which are called the phoneme 'k', written /k/. The [k̥] and [k̟] are allophones of /k/. The diagonal lines are used when referring to phonemic units.

There is another pattern of distribution of phonetic units that is created by repeated productions of one unit. If we were to measure everything that could possibly be measured about the [k̟] in repeated occurrences of "keen," we would discover that they are not exactly alike. A plot of the differences of each would result in a normal curve with the unit we call [k̟] as the mean. This type of distribution is called *nondistinctive variation*. The non-distinctive variation of the [k̟] forms a subclass of sounds of the allophone [k̟]. In general, the detection of such non-distinctive variation can only be accomplished by instrumentation or a highly skilled phonetician.

To establish each phoneme of a language as different and distinct from every other phoneme, the principle of *contrast* is invoked. To show contrast, varying phonetic units are substituted at one point in the word while all the other units are held constant. If another word is produced that is distinct and means something else to a native speaker, contrast has been shown and the existence of a distinct phoneme is proven. For example, there is the phoneme /k/ consisting of [k̥]~[k̟]. The ~ means "in complementary distribution with." Similarly, there is a phoneme /g/ consisting of [g̥]~[g̟]. If in the word "till" a [k̟] or a [g̟] is sub-stituted for the 't', or if in the word "tore" a [k̟] or a [g̟] is substituted for the 't', four new words are produced: "kill," "gill," "core" and "gore." To a native speaker of English each of these four words is distinct in the way it sounds and in what it means. This contrast justifies the existence of a /k/ and a /g/ in English.

In the preceding discussion we have been careful to use the qualification "native speaker of English." This was done to emphasize the fact that there is no general /k/ or /g/ for every language. The linguistically unsophisticated native speaker of English is rather hard put to find a difference between the initial sounds of "keen" and "coat," but to a linguistically unsophisticated speaker of Arabic this difference would be immediately apparent. The English speaker has a /k/ with [k̥]~[k̟], but for the Arabic speaker [k̟] is part of a different phoneme, and the /k/ of English and the /k/ of Arabic are not identical.

Prosodic phonemes. The phonetic units of the language that proceed in one dimensional time succession are called *segmental phones*. The analysis of these units yields the *segmental phonemes*. These are what the layman recognizes as the vowels and consonants of the language. But there are also prosodic features of *length, loudness, tone,* and *manner of termination* that occur simultaneously with the segmental phones. The descriptive linguist records the discriminable variations of these prosodic features and subjects them to the same type of analysis as is used for segmental phones. The contrasting classes that result from this analysis are called the *prosodic* or *suprasegmental phonemes* of the language.

If the word "pin" is said a number of times to the speaker of English, each time increasing the amount of time spent on the 'i,' a word is never produced which he will say is different in meaning from any of the other words. As a matter of fact, it is not possible to find any word in English in which, by increasing the length of one of the segmental units, another word can be produced which has a different meaning. Since contrast does not exist, this feature of length is not phonemic in English. This is not true of all languages. In Finnish *peli* means "damper," but increasing the length of the '*l*' produces another utterance meaning "game," and length is phonemic in Finnish.

The loudness of the phonetic unit depends primarily on the force with which air is expelled from the lungs and secondarily on the energy with which the articulation is performed. The degree of loudness is approximately the same for all English monosyllabic utterances said in isolation. This degree of loudness is called "strong" and used as a standard of measurement for other degrees of loudness. If you say *permit*, once stressing the 'e' and once stressing the 'i,' you will produce two words different in sound and meaning, thereby showing that stress is phonemic in English. The degree of loudness on the stressed versions of the 'e' and 'i' is relatively close to that degree of loudness used with monosyllables in isolation. The degree of loudness in the unstressed 'e' and 'i' is much less than that of their stressed versions, or of any monosyllable said in isolation. The degree of loudness on the stressed 'e' and 'i,' and of monosyllables said in isolation, are conditioned variations of the standard "strong loudness," and are allophones of the phoneme *primary stress* (/′/). The weak loudness of the

unstressed 'e' and 'i' are allophones comprising a weak loudness phoneme, /˅/.

The tone of our speech sounds is a function of the tension of the vocal cords and of their consequent rate of vibration. As with loudness, to demonstrate that tone is phonemic in English, multisyllabic words are used, since it is relative tone that is contrasted. The standard is the normal tone of a speaker. This normal tone varies from speaker to speaker and for the same speaker when he is speaking loudly and softly. But every speaker has a recognizable normal tone of voice. Examine, for example, the sentence "he's going home," said as a statement of fact, emphasizing *where* he's going and not the fact that he's going. Using lines to represent tone of voice, the sentence is said like this: he's going home. The line immediately below "he's going" represents the normal tone of voice. The line above the 'h' and part of the 'o' represents a tone of voice about two or three notes above the normal. The line under part of the 'o' and 'me' represents a tone of voice about two or three times below the normal. Humming the words of this sentence will demonstrate this clearly. The examination of many English sentences reveals four levels of tone that are in contrast with each other. These are symbolized as /^{1}/, /^{2}/, /^{3}/, and /^{4}/, and called low, mid, high, and extra-high pitch phonemes.

The phenomena relating to the way in which the sequence of phonetic units of the language are put together are called *junctural phenomena*. The word *nitrate* is an example of a sequence of segmental units with close transition between the members of the sequence. By changing the transition between the *t* and the *r* from close to more distant, another utterance is produced: *night-rate*, which has different sound and meaning. A comparison of such utterances as *I scream* vs. *ice cream, a name* vs. *an aim*, shows that the difference between a close transition and a more open one is phonemic in English. All the allophones of the open transition are classed into the phoneme called "plus juncture," symbolized as /+/.

There is another group of junctural phenomena that occur at places where /+/ would normally occur. These are used by the speaker to signal that he is terminating a sentence, or sequence of sentences. Say the following three sentences in the manner indicated by the conventional punctuation marks:

(1) He's going home.
(2) He's going home?
(3) He's going home for the weekend.

These sentences demonstrate three distinct ways of terminating *home*. In (1) there is a rapid fading away of the voice into silence. In (2) there is a rapid but short rise in pitch, and the voice seems to be sharply cut off. In (3) there is a sustention of pitch and a slight decrease in volume. This contrast shows that there are three terminal juncture phonemes in English: fading, /↘/; rising, /↗/; and sustained, /→/.

Phonemics and orthography. A frequent over-sight on the part of both laymen and scientists studying language behavior, is the fact that the sound system (phonemic structure) of a language is not necessarily isomorphic to the writing system (orthography) of that language. In English there are two major aspects to the discrepancy between sounds and letters of the alphabet. The first is that one sound (phoneme) may be pronounced in response to several different letters or combinations of letters. For example, the phoneme *k* (/k/) is the response to ten different letters or combinations of letters: *car, account, bacchanal, character, back, acquaint, saque, biscuit, kill, liquor.* The second is that one letter of the alphabet may represent several different phonemes. For example, the letter 's' can stand for four different phonemes as in: *see, sugar, has, measure,* which represent the phonemes /s, š, z, ž/, respectively.

A great deficiency in the orthography of English is the almost complete lack of symbols representing the prosodic phonemes. Except for the "marks of punctuation" (, , ., ?), which fairly well indicate the terminal juncture phonemes, there is no systematic method for indicating the stress, pitch, or plus-juncture phonemes.

Morphology

MORPHOPHONEMICS

The phonemic description of a language provides the basis from which the linguist analyzes the various "forms" in which the phonemes occur. The unit of description at this level of analysis is the *morpheme*, which is a class of one or more minimum sequences of phonemes that has a unique function in the *content structure* of the language.

The identification of morphemes proceeds in a manner similar to that used for the identification of phonemes. Words are compared and differences in phonemic form are matched with differences in meaning. Partial similarity both in phonemic form and meaning requires a *morphemic cut* in one or both of the forms compared. This procedure can be demonstrated by examining the words: *boy, boys, boyish; girl, girls, girlish; bear, bears, bearish.* The sequence of phonemes used in *boy, girl,* and *bear,* occur many times in the language. Furthermore, each has a unique meaning attached to it that differs from the other two, or, for that matter, from any other minimum sequence of phonemes in English. The fragments of the words left over from this classification, /-z/, and /-iš/ are also morphemes. They occur many times in the language, and a native speaker will attest to their having unique meaning. We have, then, discovered five morphemes: *boy, girl, bear,* /-z/, and /-iš/.

It is possible for a morpheme to contain within it a sequence of phonemes comprising another morpheme. If removing the contained sequence destroys or drastically alters its unique meaning and leaves a residue *that cannot be accounted for* (i.e., to which no meaning can be attached), then the large sequence retains its status as a morpheme. For example, *boil* contains the phoneme sequence of *boy,* and *bear* contains the phoneme sequence of *air,* but all four are morphemes, because removing *boy* from *boil,* and *air* from *bear* leaves the residue *-l* and *b-,* respectively, to which no meaning can be attached.

If two different minimum sequences of phonemes have the same meaning but can be shown to be in complementary distribution, they are allomorphs of one morpheme.

For example, the /-s/, /-z/, /-iz/ and /-in/, in *hats, boys, glasses,* and *oxen* are allomorphs of one morpheme. Their shared meaning is "plurality." The occurrence of /-s/, /-z/, or /-iz/ depends solely on the phonological characteristics of the *previous phoneme* that has occurred. Their distribution is, therefore, *phonologically conditioned.* The occurrence of /-in/ depends solely on the occurrence of the *previous morpheme* {ox-}, and its distribution is *morphologically conditioned.* Since they all share the same meaning and since they are in C.D., they are allomorphs of one morpheme which is labeled {-Z₁}. Braces are used to indicate morphemes.

Corresponding to the two types of phonemes are segmental and prosodic morphemes. *Segmental morphemes* are sequences of segmental phonemes in close transition. They are either *roots* like *boy, run, to,* or *affixes* like *-s, -ish, -ly, pre-, re-, con-.* The hyphens indicate the manner in which they are affixed. *Prosodic morphemes* are sequences of prosodic phonemes. They are either *superfixes* like { ˊ }, { ˊ ˇ }, and { ˋ + ˊ } respectively; or they are *intonation patterns* like the {231ˎ} that occurs on "He's going home."

Tactics deals with the sequences of morphemes that are used to form the larger significant units of the language, and the classes of morphemes, or sequences of morphemes, that are identical in function. The concept of the *constituent* is important at this stage of analysis. A constituent is any morpheme, or sequence of morphemes, that can be replaced by some other morpheme or sequence of morphemes. For example, the constituents of *boys* are *boy* and *-s; girl* can be substituted for *boy,* and *-ish* can be substituted for *-s.* The constitutents of *the boys are from our school* are 1) *the boys: they* can be substituted; and 2) *are from our school:* the single morpheme *run* can be substituted for this entire sequence. The identification of the constituents of *are from our school* as *are* and *from our school* is facilitated by the fact that a single morpheme, *good,* can be substituted for *from our school.* In this manner the constituents of any sentence can be identified, and the rules for putting them together can be stated.

A *constituent class* is any group of constituents that has an identical function in the content structure of the language. The class is made up of all constituents that can fill the "gap" in an utterance left by the removal of one of its members. For example, in *the —————— saw our school,* all morphemes or sequences of morphemes that can fill the gap are of one class.

It is important in constituent analysis to keep in mind the fact that prosodic morphemes form an essential part of the environment of any constituent, and must be held constant when constituents are substituted at one point in that environment.

Paralanguage

There are identifiable vocal phenomena that accompany the stream of speech, which, because of a limited or unique distribution, cannot be analyzed as being part of the phonemic or morphological structure of language. The systematic observation of these phenomena has led to their classification into two categories: voice qualities and vocalizations.

Voice quality is the category that represents the speaker's control of the overall or background characteristics of the voice. These phenomena would include the speaker's control of articulation, tempo, intensity, quantity, pitch height, and pitch range. When any of these is used in amounts differing from normal, the listener is quite aware that something unusual has occurred. Analysis of the voice qualities has led to the conclusion that they occur in bipolar fashion, differing in a positive or negative way from a mid-point.

Vocalization is the category consisting of sounds which are identifiable segments of the sound continuum, or specifiable modifications of segments. The identifiable segments (e.g., the click in *tsk-tsk*) can be described in terms of the same three dimensions used for describing segmental phones, that is, point of articulation, manner of articulation, and activity in the larynx. These segments are called *vocal segregates,* to emphasize the point that they are segmental sounds, but are not analyzed as being part of the phonemic structure of the language. The specifiable prosodic modifications of segments (either segmental phones or vocal segregates) are intensity, pitch height, and length. These modifications, as a group, are called *vocal qualifiers.*[1]

---

[1] The formulations presented in this paper owe a debt to a number of sources. Among them, the following are certainly prominent: Block & Trager (1942); Bloomfield (1933); Fries (1952); Gleason (1961); McQuown (1954, 1957); Nida (1943); Pike (1943); Pittenger & Smith (1957); Trager (1958); Trager & Smith (1951).

23　The language of social control

S. I. HAYAKAWA

Making things happen

The most interesting and perhaps least understood relationship between words and the world is that between words and future events. When we say, for example, "Come here!" we are not describing the extensional world about us, nor are we merely expressing our feelings; we are trying to *make something happen*. What we call "commands," "pleas," "requests," and "orders" are the simplest ways we have of making things happen by means of words.

There are, however, more roundabout ways. When we say, for example, "Our candidate is a great American," we are of course making an enthusiastic purr about him, but we may also be influencing other people to vote for him. Again, when we say, "Our war against the enemy is God's war. God wills that we must triumph," we are saying something which, though unverifiable, may influence others to help in the prosecution of the war. Or if we merely state as a fact, "Milk contains vitamins," we may be influencing others to buy milk.

Consider, too, such a statement as "I'll meet you tomorrow at two o'clock in front of the Palace Theater." Such a statement about *future* events can only be made, it will be observed, in a system in which symbols are independent of things symbolized. The future, like the recorded past, is a specifically human dimension. To a dog, the expression "hamburger *tomorrow*" is meaningless —he will look at you expectantly, hoping for the extensional meaning of the word "hamburger" to be produced *now*. Squirrels, to be sure, store food for "next winter," but the fact that they store food regardless of whether or not their needs are adequately provided for demonstrates that such behavior (usually called "instinctive") is governed neither by symbols nor by other interpreted stimuli. Human beings are unique in their ability to react meaningfully to such expressions as "next Saturday," "on our next wedding anniversary," "twenty years after date I promise to pay," "some day, perhaps five hundred years from now." That is to say, maps can be made, even though the territories they stand for are not yet actualities. Guiding ourselves by means of such maps of territories-to-be, we can impose a certain predictability upon future events.

With words, therefore, we influence and to an enormous extent *control future events*. It is for this reason that writers write; preachers preach; employers, parents, and teachers scold; propagandists send out news releases; statesmen give addresses. All of them, for various reasons, are trying to influence our conduct—sometimes for our good, sometimes for their own. These attempts to control, direct, or influence the future actions of fellow human beings with words may be termed *directive uses of language*.

Excerpted from Chapter 7 of **Language in Thought and Action**, New Revised Edition (Copyright © 1964 by Harcourt, Brace & World, Inc.), and reprinted with permission of the author and the publisher, and in the British Commonwealth with permission of George Allen & Unwin Ltd.

Now it is obvious that if directive language is going to direct, it cannot be dull or uninteresting. If it is to influence our conduct, it *must* make use of every affective element in language: dramatic variations in tone of voice, rhyme and rhythm, purring and snarling, words with strong affective connotations, endless repetition. If meaningless noises will move the audience, meaningless noises must be made; if facts move them, facts must be given; if noble ideals move them, we must make our proposals appear noble; if they will respond only to fear, we must scare them stiff.

The nature of the affective means used in directive language is limited, of course, by the nature of our aims. If we are trying to direct people to be more kindly toward each other, we obviously do not want to arouse feelings of cruelty or hate. If we are trying to direct people to think and act more intelligently, we obviously should not use subrational appeals. If we are trying to direct people to lead better lives, we use affective appeals that arouse their finest feelings. Included among directive utterances, therefore, are many of the greatest and most treasured works of literature: the Christian and Buddhist scriptures, the writings of Confucius, Milton's *Areopagitica*, and Lincoln's Gettysburg Address.

There are, however, occasions when it is felt that language is not sufficiently affective by itself to produce the results wanted. We supplement directive language, therefore, by *nonverbal affective appeals* of many kinds. We supplement the words "Come here" by gesturing with our hands. Advertisers are not content with saying in words how beautiful their products will make us; they supplement their words by the use of colored inks and by pictures. Newspapers are not content with saying that communism is a menace; they supply political cartoons depicting communists as criminally insane people placing sticks of dynamite under magnificent buildings labeled "American way of life." The affective appeal of sermons and religious exhortations may be supplemented by costumes, incense, processions, choir music, and church bells. A political candidate seeking office reinforces his speech-making with a considerable array of nonverbal affective appeals: brass bands, flags, parades, picnics, barbecues, and free cigars. Often a candidate's smile or, as in the case of President Kennedy, his wife's appearance and charm may be a powerful influence upon the voter.

Now, if we want people to do certain things and if we are indifferent as to *why they do them*, then no affective appeals need be excluded. Some political candidates want us to vote for them regardless of our reasons for doing so. Therefore, if we hate the rich, they will snarl at the rich for us; if we dislike strikers, they will snarl at the strikers; if we like clambakes, they will throw clambakes; if the majority of us like hillbilly music, they may say nothing about the problems of government, but travel among their constituencies with hillbilly bands. Again, many business firms want us to buy their products regardless of our reasons for doing so; therefore, if delusions and fantasies will lead us to buy their products, they will seek to produce delusions and fantasies; if we want to be popular with the other sex, they will promise us popularity; if we like pretty girls in bathing suits, they will associate pretty girls in bathing suits with their products, whether they are selling shaving cream, automobiles, summer resorts, ice-cream cones, house paint, or hardware. Only the law keeps them from presenting pretty girls without bathing suits. The records of the Federal Trade Commission, as well as the advertising pages of many magazines, show that some advertisers will stop at practically nothing.

The promises of directive language

Almost all directive utterances say something about the future. They are "maps," either explicitly or by implication, of *"territories" that are to be.* They direct us to do certain things with the stated or implied promise that if we do these things, certain consequences will follow: "If you adhere to the Bill of Rights, your civil rights too will be protected." "If you vote for me, I will have your taxes reduced." "Live according to these religious principles, and you will have peace in your soul." "Read this magazine, and you will keep up with important current events." "Take Lewis's Licorice Liver Pills and enjoy that glorious feeling that goes with regularity." Needless to say, some of these promises are kept, and some are not. Indeed, we encounter promises daily that are obviously incapable of being kept.

There is no sense in objecting as some people do to advertising and political propaganda—the only kind of directives they worry about—on the ground that they are based on "emotional appeals." Unless directive language has affective power of some kind, it is useless. We do not object to campaigns that tell us, "Give to the Community Chest and enable poor children to enjoy better care," although that is an "emotional appeal." Nor do we resent being reminded of our love of home, friends, and nation when people issue moral or patriotic directives at us. The important question to be asked of any directive utterance is, "Will things happen as promised if I do as I am directed to do? If I accept your philosophy, shall I achieve peace of mind? If I vote for you, will my taxes be reduced? If I use Lifeguard Soap, will my boy friend really come back to me?"

We rightly object to advertisers who make false or misleading claims and to politicians who ignore their promises, although it must be admitted that, in the case of politicians, they are sometimes compelled to make promises that later circumstances prevent them from keeping. Life being as uncertain and as unpredictable as it is, we are constantly trying to find out what is going to happen next, so that we may prepare ourselves. Directive utterances undertake to tell us how we can bring about certain desirable events and how we can avoid undesirable events. If we can rely upon what they tell us about the future, the uncertainties of life are reduced. When, however, directive utterances are of such a character that things do *not* happen as predicted—when, after we have done as we were told, the peace in the soul has not been found, the taxes have not been reduced, the boy friend has not returned, there is disappointment. Such disappointments may be trivial or grave; in any event, they are so common that we do not even bother to complain about some of them. They are, nevertheless, all serious in their implications. *Each of them serves, in greater or lesser degree, to break down that mutual trust that makes cooperation possible and knits people together into a society.*

Every one of us, therefore, who utters directive language, with its concomitant promises, stated or implied, is morally obliged to be as certain as he can, since there is no absolute certainty, that he is arousing no false expectations. Politicians promising the immediate abolition of poverty, national advertisers suggesting that tottering marriages can be restored to bliss by a change in the brand of laundry detergent used in the family, newspapers threatening the collapse of the nation if the party they favor is not elected—all such utterers of nonsense are, for the reasons stated, menaces to the social order. It does not matter much whether such misleading directives are uttered in ignorance and error or with conscious intent to deceive, because the disappointments they cause are all similarly destructive of mutual trust among human beings.

The foundations of society

But propaganda, no matter how persuasive, does not create society. We can, if we wish, ignore its directives. We come now to *directive utterances that we cannot ignore if we wish to remain organized in our social groups.*

What we call society is a vast network of mutual agreements. We agree to refrain from murdering our fellow citizens, and they in turn agree to refrain from murdering us; we agree to drive on the right-hand side of the road, and others agree to do the same; we agree to deliver specified goods, and others agree to pay us for them; we agree to observe the rules of an organization, and the organization agrees to let us enjoy its privileges. This complicated network of agreements, into which almost every detail of our lives is woven and upon which most of our expectations in life are based, consists essentially of *statements about future events which we are supposed, with our own efforts, to bring about.* Without such agreements, there would be no such thing as society. We would all be huddling in miserable and lonely caves, not daring to trust anyone. With such agreements, and a will on the part of the vast majority of people to live by them, behavior begins to fall into relatively predictable patterns; cooperation becomes possible; peace and freedom are established.

Therefore, in order that we shall continue to exist as human beings, we *must* impose patterns of behavior on each other. We must make citizens conform to social and civic customs; we must make husbands dutiful to their wives; we must make soldiers courageous, judges just, priests pious, and teachers solicitous for the welfare of their pupils. In early stages of culture the principal means of imposing patterns of behavior was, of course, physical coercion. But such control can also be exercised, as human beings must have discovered extremely early in history, by *words*—that is, by directive language. Therefore, directives about matters which society as a whole regards as essential to its own safety are made especially powerful, so that no individual in that society will fail to be impressed with a sense of his obligations. To make doubly sure, society further reinforces the directives by the assurance that punishment, possibly including imprisonment and death, may be visited upon those who fail to heed the words.

Directives with collective sanction

These directive utterances with collective sanction, which try to impose patterns of behavior upon the individual in the interests of the whole group, are among the most interesting of linguistic events. Not only are they usually accompanied by ritual; they are usually the central purpose of ritual. There is probably no kind of utterance that we take more seriously, that affects our lives more deeply, that we quarrel about more bitterly. Constitutions of nations and of organizations, legal contracts, and oaths of office are utterances of this kind; in marriage vows, confirmation exercises, induction ceremonies, and initiations, they are the essential constituent. Those terrifying verbal jungles called *laws* are simply such directives, accumulated, codified, and systematized through the centuries. In its laws, society makes its mightiest collective effort to impose predictability upon human behavior.

Directive utterances made under collective sanction may exhibit any or all of the following features:

1. Such language is almost always phrased in *words that have affective connotations*, so that people will be appropriately impressed and awed. Archaic and obsolete vocabulary or stilted phraseology quite unlike the language of everyday life is employed. For example: "Wilt thou, John, take this woman for thy lawful wedded wife?" "This lease, made this tenth day of July, A.D. One Thousand Nine Hundred and Sixty-three, between Samuel Smith, herein after called the Lessor, and Jeremiah Johnson, hereinafter called Lessee, WITNESSETH, that Lessor, in consideration of covenants and agreements hereinafter contained and made on the part of the Lessee, hereby leases to the Lessee for a private dwelling, the premises known and described as follows, to wit . . ."

2. Such directive utterances are often accompanied by *appeals to supernatural powers*, who are called upon to help us carry out the vows, or to punish us if we fail to carry them out. An oath, for example, ends with the words, "So help me God." Prayers, incantations, and invocations accompany the utterance of important vows in practically all cultures, from the most primitive to the most civilized. These further serve, of course, to impress our vows on our minds.

3. The *fear of direct punishment* is also invoked. If God does not punish us for failing to carry out our agreements, it is made clear either by statement or implication that our fellow men will. For example, we all realize that we can be imprisoned for desertion, nonsupport, or bigamy; sued for "breach of contract"; unfrocked" for activities contrary to priestly vows; "cashiered" for "conduct unbecoming an officer"; "impeached" for "betrayal of public trust"; hanged for "treason."

4. The formal and public utterance of the vows may be preceded by *preliminary disciplines* of various kinds: courses of training in the meaning of the vows one is undertaking; fasting and self-mortification, as before entering the priesthood; initiation ceremonies involving physical torture, as before induction into the warrior status among primitive peoples or membership in college fraternities.

5. The utterance of the directive language may be accompanied by other *activities or gestures calculated to impress the occasion on the mind*. For example, everybody in a courtroom stands up when a judge is about to open a court; huge processions and extraordinary costumes accompany coronation ceremonies; academic gowns are worn for commencement exercises; for many weddings, an organist and a soprano are procured and special clothes are worn.

6. The uttering of the vows may be immediately followed by *feasts, dancing, and other joyous manifestations*. Again the purpose seems to be to reinforce still further the effect of the vows. For example, there are wedding parties and receptions, graduation dances, banquets for the induction of officers and, even in the most modest social circles, some form of "celebration" when a member of the family enters into a compact with society. In primitive cultures, initiation ceremonies for chieftains may be followed by feasting and dancing that last for several days or weeks.

7. In cases where the first utterance of the vows is not made a special ceremonial occasion, the effect on the memory is usually achieved by *frequent repetition*. The flag ritual ("I pledge allegiance to the flag of the United States of America . . .") is repeated daily in most schools. Mottoes, which are briefly stated general directives, are repeated frequently; sometimes they are stamped on dishes, sometimes engraved on a warrior's sword, sometimes inscribed in prominent places such as on gates, walls, and doorways, where people can see them and be reminded of their duties.

The common feature of all these activities that accompany directive utterances, as well as of the affective elements in the language of directive utterances, is the deep effect they have on the memory. Every kind of sensory impression from the severe pain of initiation rites to the pleasures of banqueting, music, splendid clothing, and ornamental surroundings may be employed; every emotion from the fear of divine punishment to pride in being made the object of

special public attention may be aroused. This is done in order that the individual who enters into his compact with society —that is, the individual who commits himself to the "map" of the not-yet-existent "territory"—shall never forget to try to bring that "territory" into existence.

For these reasons, such occasions as when a cadet receives his commission, when a Jewish boy has his *bar mitzvah*, when a priest takes his vows, when a policeman receives his badge, when a foreign-born citizen is sworn in as a citizen of the United States, or when a president takes his oath of office—these are events one never forgets. Even if, later on, a person realizes that he has not fulfilled his vows, he cannot shake off the feeling that he should have done so. All of us, of course, use and respond to these ritual directives. The phrases and speeches to which we respond reveal our deepest religious, patriotic, social, professional, and political allegiances more accurately than do the citizenship papers or membership cards that we may carry in our pockets or the badges that we may wear on our coats. A man who has changed his religion after reaching adulthood will, on hearing the ritual he was accustomed to hearing in childhood, often feel an urge to return to his earlier form of worship. In such ways, then, do human beings use words to reach out into the future and control each other's conduct.

It should be remarked that many of our social directives and many of the rituals with which they are accompanied are antiquated and somewhat insulting to adult minds. Rituals that originated in times when people had to be scared into good behavior are unnecessary to people who already have a sense of social responsibility. For example, a five-minute marriage ceremony performed at the city hall for a mature, responsible couple may "take" much better than a full-dress church ceremony performed for an infantile couple. In spite of the fact that the strength of social directives obviously lies in the willingness, the maturity, and the intelligence of the people to whom the directives are addressed, there is still a widespread tendency to rely upon the efficacy of ceremonies as such. This tendency is due, of course, to a lingering belief in word-magic, the notion that, by *saying* things repeatedly or in specified ceremonial ways, we can cast a spell over the future and force events to turn out the way we said they would. ("There'll always be an England!") An interesting manifestation of this superstitious attitude toward words and rituals is to be found among those members of patriotic societies who seem to believe that the way to educate school children in democracy is to stage bigger and better flag-saluting ceremonies and to treble the occasions for singing "God Bless America."

What are "rights"?

What, extensionally, is the meaning of the word "my" in such expressions as "my real estate," "my book," "my automobile"? Certainly the word "my" describes no characteristics of the objects named. A check changes hands and "your" automobile becomes "mine" but no change results in the automobile. What has changed?

The change is, of course, in *our social agreements covering our behavior* toward the automobile. Formerly, when it was "yours," you felt free to use it as you liked, while I did not. Now that it is "mine," I use it freely and you may not.

The meaning of "yours" and "mine" lies not in the external world, but in *how we intend to act*. And when society as a whole recognizes my "right of ownership" (by issuing me, for example, a certificate of title), it agrees to protect me in my intentions to use the automobile and to frustrate, by police action if necessary, the intentions of those who may wish to use it without my permission. Society makes this agreement with me in return for my obeying its laws and paying my share of the expenses of government.

Are not, then, all assertions of ownership and statements about "rights" directives? Cannot, "This is *mine*," be translated, "I am going to use this object; you keep your hands off"? Cannot, "Every child has a *right* to an education," be translated, "*Give* every child an education"? And is not the difference between "moral rights" and "legal rights" the difference between agreements which people believe *ought* to be made, and those which, through collective, legislative sanction, *have been* made?

Directives and disillusionment

A few cautions may be added before we leave the subject of directive language. First, it should be remembered that, since words cannot "say all" about anything, the promises implied in directive language are never more than "outline maps" of "territories-to-be." The future will fill in those outlines, often in unexpected ways. Sometimes the future will bear no relation to our "maps" at all, in spite of all our endeavors to bring about the promised events. We swear always to be good citizens, always to do our duty, and so on, but we never quite succeed in being good citizens *every* day of our lives or in performing *all* our duties. A realization that directives cannot *fully* impose any pattern on the future saves us from having impossible expectations and therefore from suffering needless disappointments.

Secondly, one should distinguish between directive and informative utterances, which often look alike. Such statements as "A boy scout is clean and chivalrous and brave" or "Policemen are defenders of the weak" *set up goals* and do not necessarily describe the present situation. This is extremely important, because all too often people understand such definitions as descriptive and are then shocked and disillusioned when they encounter a boy scout who is not chivalrous or a policeman who is a bully. They decide that they are "through with the boy scouts" or "disgusted with all policemen," which, of course, is nonsense. They have, in effect, inferred an informative statement from what is to be taken only as a very general directive.

A third source of disappointment and disillusionment arising from the improper understanding of directives results from reading into directives promises that they do not make. A common instance is provided by advertisements of the antiseptics and patent medicines which people buy under the impression that the cure or prevention of colds was promised. Because of the ruling of the Federal Trade Commission, the writers of these advertisements carefully avoid saying that their preparations will prevent or cure anything. Instead, they say that they "help reduce the severity of the infection," "help relieve the symptoms of a cold," or "help guard against sniffling and other discomforts." If after reading these advertisements you feel that prevention or cure of colds has been promised, you are exactly the kind of sucker they are looking for. (Of course, if you buy the product knowing clearly what was promised and what was not, that is a different matter.)

Another way of reading into directives things that were not said is by believing promises to be more specific and concrete than they really are. When, for example, a candidate for political office promises to "help the farmer," and you vote for him, and then you discover that he helps the *cotton* farmer without helping the *potato* farmer (and you grow potatoes)—you cannot exactly accuse him of having broken his promise. Or, if another candidate promises to "protect union labor," and you vote for him, and he helps to pass legislation that infuriates the officials of your union (he calls it "legislation to protect union members from their own racketeering leadership")—again you cannot exactly accuse him of having broken his promise since his action may well have been sincerely in accord with his notion of "helping union labor." The ambiguities of campaign oratory are notorious.

Politicians are often accused of breaking their promises. No doubt many of them do. But it must be remarked that they often do not promise as much as their constituents think they do. The platforms of the major parties are almost always at high levels of abstraction ("they mean all things to all men," as the cynical say), but they are often understood by voters to be more specific and concrete (i.e., at lower levels of abstraction) than they are. If one is "disillusioned" by acts of a politician, sometimes the politician is to blame, but sometimes the voter is to blame for having had the illusion to start with—or, as we shall say, for having *confused different levels of abstraction*.

24   How shall a thing be called?

ROGER BROWN

The most deliberate part of first-language teaching is the business of telling a child what each thing is called. We ordinarily speak of *the* name of a thing as if there were just one, but in fact, of course, every referent has many names. The dime in my pocket is not only a *dime*. It is also *money, a metal object, a thing,* and, moving to subordinates, it is a *1952 dime,* in fact a *particular 1952 dime* with a unique pattern of scratches, discolorations, and smooth places. When such an object is named for a very young child how is it called? It may be named *money* or *dime* but probably not *metal object, thing, 1952 dime,* or *particular 1952 dime.* The dog out on the lawn is not only a *dog* but is also a *boxer,* a *quadruped,* an *animate being;* it is the *landlord's dog,* named *Prince.* How will it be identified for a child? Sometimes it will be called a *dog,* sometimes *Prince,* less often a *boxer,* and almost never a *quadruped,* or *animate being.* Listening to many adults name things for many children, I find that their choices are quite uniform and that I can anticipate them from my own inclinations. How are these choices determined and what are their consequences for the cognitive development of the child?

Adults have notions about the kind of language appropriate for use with children. Especially strong and universal is the belief that children have trouble pronouncing long names and so should always be given the shortest possible names. A word is preferable to a phrase and, among words, a monosyllable is better than a polysyllable. This predicts the preference for *dog* and *Prince* over *boxer, quadruped,* and *animate being.* It predicts the choice of *dime* over *metal object* and *particular 1952 dime.*

Zipf (1935) has shown that the length of a word (in phonemes or syllables) is inversely related to its frequency in the printed language. Consequently the shorter names for any thing will usually also be the most frequently used names for that thing, and so it would seem that the choice of a name is usually predictable from either frequency or brevity. The monosyllables *dog* and *Prince* have much higher frequencies according to the Thorndike-Lorge list (1944) than do the polysyllables *boxer, quadruped,* and *animate being.*

It sometimes happens, however, that the frequency-brevity principle makes the wrong prediction. The thing called a *pineapple* is also *fruit. Fruit* is the shorter and more frequent term, but adults will name the thing *pineapple.* Similarly they will say *apple, banana, orange,* and even *pomegranate;* all of them longer and less frequent words than the perfectly appropriate *fruit.* Brevity seems not to be the powerful determinant we had imagined. The frequency principle can survive this kind

Slightly abridged from the **Psychological Review, 65,** 14–22 (Copyright © 1958 by the American Psychological Association), with permission of the author and the publisher.

of example, but only if it is separated from counts like the Thorndike-Lorge of over-all frequency in the printed language. On the whole the word *fruit* appears more often than the word *pineapple* (and also is shorter), but we may confidently assume that, when pineapples are being named, the word *pineapple* is more frequent than the word *fruit*. This, of course, is a kind of frequency more directly relevant to our problem. Word counts of general usage are only very roughly applicable to the prediction of what will be said when something is named. What we need is referent-name counts. We don't have them, of course, but if we had them it is easy to see that they would improve our predictions. Bananas are called *banana*, apples *apple*, and oranges *orange* more often than any of them is called *fruit*. The broad frequency-brevity principle predicts that *money* and *dime* will be preferred to *metal object*, 1952 *dime*, and *particular* 1952 *dime*, but it does not predict the neglect of the common monosyllable *thing*. For this purpose we must again appeal to imagined referent-name counts, according to which dimes would surely be called *dime* or *money* more often than *thing*.

While the conscious preference for a short name can be overcome by frequency, the preference nevertheless affects the naming act. I have heard parents designate the appropriate objects *pineapple, television, vinegar,* and *policeman*; all these to children who cannot reproduce polysyllabic words. Presumably they use these names because that is what the referents are usually called, but the adult's sense of the absurdity of giving such words to a child is often evident. He may smile as he says it or remark, "That's too hard for you to say, isn't it?"

Some things are named in the same way by all adults for all children. This is true of the apple and the orange. Other things have several common names, each of them used by a specifiable group of adults to specifiable children. The same dog is *dog* to most of the world and *Prince* in his own home and perhaps on his own block. The same man is a *man* to most children, *policeman* to some at some times, *Mr. Jones* to the neighborhood kids, and *papa* to his own. Referent-name counts from people in general will not predict these several usages. A still more particular name count must be imagined. The name given a thing by an adult for a child is determined by the frequency with which various names have been applied to such things in the experience of the particular adult. General referent-name counts taken from many people will predict much that the individual does, but, for a close prediction, counts specific to the individual would be needed.

The frequencies to which we are now appealing have not, of course, been recorded. We are explaining imagined preferences in names by imagined frequencies of names. It is conceivable, certainly, that some of these specific word counts might be made and a future naming performance independently predicted from a past frequency. Probably, however, such frequencies will never be known, and if we choose to explain particular naming performances by past frequencies we shall usually have to infer the frequency from the performance.

Beyond the frequency principle

A frequency explanation is not very satisfying even when the appeal is to known frequencies. The question will come to mind: "Why is one name more common than another?" Why is a dog called *dog* more often than *quadruped* and, by some people, called *Prince* more often than *dog*? Perhaps it just happened that way, like driving on the right side of the road in America and on the left in England. The convention is preserved but has no justification outside itself. As things have worked out, coins are usually named by species as *dime, nickel,* or *penny* while the people we know have individual names like *John, Mary,* and *Jim.* Could it just as easily be the other way around? Might we equally well give coins proper names and introduce people as types?

The referent for the word *dime* is a large class of coins. The name is equally appropriate to all members of this class. To name a coin *dime* is to establish its equivalence, for naming purposes, with all other coins of the same denomination. This equivalence for naming purposes corresponds to a more general equivalence for all purposes of economic exchange. In the grocery one dime is as good as another but quite different from any nickel or penny. For a child the name given an object anticipates the equivalences and differences that will need to be observed in most of his dealings with such an object. To make proper denotative use of the word *dime* he must be able to distinguish members of the referent category from everything else. When he learns that, he has solved more than a language problem. He has an essential bit of equipment for doing business. The most common names for coins could not move from the species level to the level of proper names without great alteration in our nonlinguistic culture. We should all be numismatists preparing our children to recognize a particular priceless 1910 dime.

Many things are reliably given the same name by the whole community. The spoon is seldom called anything but *spoon,* although it is also a piece of *silverware,* an *artifact,* and a *particular ill-washed restaurant spoon.* The community-wide preference for the word *spoon* corresponds to the community-wide practice of treating spoons as equivalent but different from knives and forks. There are no proper names for individual spoons because their individuality seldom signifies. It is the same way with pineapples, dimes, doors, and taxicabs. The most common name for each of these categorizes them as they need to be categorized for the community's nonlinguistic purposes. The most common name is at the level of usual utility.

People and pets have individual names as well as several kinds of generic name. The individual name is routinely coined by those who are disposed to treat the referent as unique, and is available afterwards to any others who will see the uniqueness. A man at home has his own name to go with the peculiar privileges and responsibilities binding him to wife and child. But the same man who is a one-of-a-kind *papa* to his own children is simply a *man* to children at large. He is, like the other members of this large category, someone with no time to play and little tolerance for noise. In some circumstances, this same man will be given the name of his occupation. He is a *policeman* equivalent to other policemen but different from *bus drivers* and *Good Humor men.* A policeman is someone to "behave in front of" and to go to when lost. To the kids in the neighborhood the man is *Mr. Jones,* unique in his way—a crank, bad tempered, likely to shout at you if you play out in front of his house. It is the same way with dogs as with people. He may be a unique *Prince* to his owners, who feed and house him, but he is just a *dog* to the rest of the world. A homeless dog reverts to namelessness, since there is none to single him out from his species. Dimes and nickels have much the same significance for an entire society, and their usual names are fixed at this level of significance. People and pets function uniquely for some and in various generic ways for others. They have a corresponding variety of designations, but each name is at the utility level for the group that uses it. Our naming practices for coins and people correspond to our nonlinguistic practices, and it is difficult to imagine changing the one without changing the other.

The names provided by parents for children anticipate the functional structure of the child's world. This is not, of course, something parents are aware of doing. When we name a thing there does not seem to be any process of choice. Each thing has its name, just one, and that is what we give to a child. The one name is, of course, simply the usual name for us. Naming each thing in accordance with local frequencies, parents unwittingly transmit their own cognitive structures. It is a world in which *Prince* is unique among dogs and *papa* among men, *spoons* are all alike but different from *forks*. It may be a world of *bugs* (to be stepped on), of *flowers* (not to be picked), and *birds* (not to be stoned). It may be a world in which *Niggers*, like *spoons* are all of a kind. A division of caste creates a vast categorical equivalence and a correspondingly generic name. *Mr. Jones* and *Mr. Smith* do not come out of racial

anonymity until their uniqueness is appreciated.

Adults do not invariably provide a child with the name that is at the level of usual utility in the adult world. An effort is sometimes made to imagine the utilities of a child's life. Some parents will, at first, call every sort of coin *money*. This does not prepare a child to buy and sell, but then he may be too young for that. All coins are equivalent for the very young child in that they are objects not to be put into the mouth and not to be dropped down the register, and *money* anticipates that equivalence. A more differentiated terminology can wait upon the age of storegoing. Sometimes an adult is aware of a child's need for a distinction that is not coded in the English lexicon. A new chair comes into the house and is not going to be equivalent to the shabby chairs already there. A child is permitted to sit on the old chairs but will not be permitted on the new one. A distinctive name is created from the combinational resources of the language. *The new chair* or *the good chair* is not to be assimilated to *chairs* in general.

Eventually, of course, children learn many more names for each thing than the one that is most frequent and useful. Sometimes a name is supplied in order to bring forward an immediately important property of the referent. A child who starts bouncing the coffee pot needs to be told that it is *glass*. Sometimes a name is supplied to satisfy the child's curiosity as to the place of a referent in a hierarchy of categories. Chairs are *furniture* and so are tables; carrots are a *vegetable* but apples are not. Probably, however, both children and adults make some distinction among these various names. *The* name of a thing, the one that tells what it "really" is, is the name that constitutes the referent as it needs to be constituted for most purposes. The other names represent possible recategorizations useful for one or another purpose. We are even likely to feel that these recategorizations are acts of imagination, whereas the major categorization is a kind of passive recognition of the true character of the referent.

The child's concrete vocabulary

It is a commonplace saying that the mind of a child is relatively "concrete" and the mind of an adult "abstract." The words "concrete" and "abstract" are sometimes used in the sense of subordinate and superordinate. In this sense a relatively concrete mind would operate with subordinate categories and an abstract mind with superordinate categories. It is recorded in many studies of vocabulary acquisition (e.g., International Kindergarten Unit, 1928; Smith, 1926) that children ordinarily use the words *milk* and *water* before the word *liquid*; the words *apple* and *orange* before *fruit*; *table* and *chair* before *furniture*; *mamma* and *daddy* before *parent* or *person*; etc. Very high-level superordinate terms like *article, action, quality,* and *relation*, though they are common in adult speech (Thorndike-Lorge, 1944), are very seldom heard from preschool children (International Kindergarten Unit, 1928). Presumably this kind of vocabulary comparison is one of the sources of the notion that the child's mind is more concrete than the mind of the adult. However, the vocabulary of a child is not a very direct index of his cognitive preferences. The child's vocabulary is more immediately determined by the naming practices of adults.

The occasion for a name is ordinarily some particular thing. In the naming it is categorized. The preference among possible names seems to go to the one that is most commonly applied to the referent in question. That name will ordinarily categorize the referent so as to observe the equivalences and differences that figure in its usual utilization. There are not many purposes for which all liquids are equivalent or all fruits, furniture, or parents; and so the names of these categories are less commonly used for denotation than are the names of categories subordinate to them. It is true that words like *article, action, quality* and *relation* are rather common in adult written English, but we can be sure that these frequencies in running discourse are not equaled in naming situations. Whatever the purposes for which all articles are equivalent, or all actions or qualities, they are not among the pressing needs of children.

It is not invariably true that vocabulary builds from concrete to abstract. *Fish* is likely to be learned before *perch* and *bass; house* before *bungalow* and *mansion; car* before *Chevrolet* and *Plymouth* (Smith, 1926). The more concrete vocabulary waits for the child to reach an age where his purposes differentiate kinds of fish and makes of cars. There is much elaborately concrete vocabulary that is not introduced until one takes courses in biology, chemistry, and botany. No one has ever proved that vocabulary builds from the concrete to the abstract more often than it builds from the abstract to the concrete. The best generalization seems to be that each thing is first given its most common name. This name seems to categorize on the level of usual utility. That level sometimes falls on the most concrete categories in a hierarchy (proper names for significant people), and vocabulary then builds toward the more abstract categories (names for ethnic groups, personality types, social classes). Utility sometimes centers on a relatively abstract level of categorization (fish) and vocabulary then builds in both directions (perch and vertebrate). Probably utility never centers on the most abstract levels (thing, substance, etc.), and so probably there is no hierarchy within which vocabulary builds in an exclusively concrete direction.

In the literature describing first-language acquisition (McCarthy, 1946) there is much to indicate that children easily form large abstract categories. There are, to begin with, the numerous cases in which the child overgeneralizes the use of a conventional word. The word *dog* may, at first, be applied to every kind of four-legged animal. It sometimes happens that every man who comes into the house is called *daddy*. When children invent their own words, these often have an enormous semantic range. Wilhelm Stern's (1920) son Günther used *psee* for leaves, trees, and flowers. He used *bebau* for all animals. Lombroso (Werner, 1948) tells of a child who used *qua qua* for both duck and water and *afta* for drinking glass, the contents of a glass, and a pane of glass. Reports of this kind do not suggest that children are deficient in abstracting ability. It even looks as if they may favor large categories.

There are two extreme opinions about the direction of cognitive development. There are those who suppose that we begin by discriminating to the limits of our sensory acuity, seizing each thing in its uniqueness, noting every hair and flea of the particular dog. Cognitive development involves neglect of detail, abstracting from particulars so as to group similars into categories. By this

view abstraction is a mature rather than a primitive process. The contrary opinion is that the primitive stage in cognition is one of a comparative lack of differentiation. Probably certain distinctions are inescapable; the difference between a loud noise and near silence, between a bright contour and a dark ground, etc. These inevitable discriminations divide the perceived world into a small number of very large (abstract) categories. Cognitive development is increasing differentiation. The more distinctions we make, the more categories we have and the smaller (more concrete) these are. I think the latter view is favored in psychology today. While there is good empirical and theoretical support (Gibson, *et al.*, 1955; Lashley, *et al.*, 1946; Lewin, 1935) for the view that development is differentiation, there is embarrassment for it in the fact that much vocabulary growth is from the concrete to the abstract. This embarrassment can be eliminated.

Suppose a very young child applies the word *dog* to every four-legged creature he sees. He may have abstracted a limited set of attributes and created a large category, but his abstraction will not show up in his vocabulary. Parents will not provide him with a conventional name for his category, e.g., *quadruped*, but instead will require him to narrow his use of *dog* to its proper range. Suppose a child calls all elderly ladies *aunt*. He will not be told that the usual name for his category is *elderly ladies* but, instead, will be taught to cut back *aunt* to accord with standard usage. In short, the sequence in which words are acquired is set by adults rather than children, and may ultimately be determined by the utility of the various categorizations. This will sometimes result in a movement of vocabulary toward higher abstraction and sometimes a movement toward greater concreteness. The cognitive development of the child may nevertheless always take the direction of increasing differentiation or concreteness.

The child who spontaneously hits on the category four-legged animals will be required to give it up in favor of dogs, cats, horses, cows, and the like. When the names of numerous subordinates have been mastered, he may be given the name *quadruped* for the superordinate. This abstraction is not the same as its primitive forerunner. The schoolboy who learns the word *quadruped* has abstracted from differentiated and named subordinates. The child he was abstracted through a failure to differentiate. Abstraction after differentiation may be the mature process, and abstraction from a failure to differentiate the primitive. Needless to say, the abstractions occurring on the two levels need not be coincident, as they are in our quadruped example.

25   The verbal community

B. F. SKINNER

The "languages" studied by the linguist are the reinforcing practices of verbal communities. When we say that *also* means *in addition* or *besides* "in English," we are not referring to the verbal behavior of any one speaker of English or the average performance of many speakers, but to the conditions under which a response is characteristically reinforced by a verbal community. (The lexical definition simply mentions other responses reinforced under the same circumstances; it does not describe the circumstances.) In studying the practices of the community rather than the behavior of the speaker, the linguist has not been concerned with verbal behavior in the present sense.

A functional analysis of the verbal community is not part of this book, but a few standard problems call for comment. One of them is the old question of the origin of language. Early man was probably not very different from his modern descendants with respect to behavioral processes. If brought into a current verbal community, he would probably develop elaborate verbal behavior. What was lacking was not any special capacity for speech but certain environmental circumstances. The origin of language is the origin of such circumstances. How could a verbal environment have arisen out of nonverbal sources? Other classical problems have their parallels. How is a verbal community perpetuated, and why and how does it change? How do new forms of response and new controlling relations evolve, so that a language becomes more complex, more sensitive, more embracing, and more effective?

How the first verbal environment arose will probably always remain a matter for speculation. Theoretically it should be possible to rear a group of human infants in social isolation to discover whether verbal behavior would develop, and if so what it would be like, but there are obvious ethical problems. An experiment appears to have been tried by Frederick the Great in which children were reared in isolation with the object of discovering whether they would naturally speak Hebrew. The experiment failed when all the subjects died. Occasionally, through accidental circumstances, two or more children have grown up in partial isolation from established verbal communities and have developed fairly extensive idiosyncratic verbal systems, but the isolation has never been complete enough to prove that a verbal environment will arise spontaneously in the absence of prior verbal behavior.

Animal cries

A superficial resemblance between verbal behavior and the instinctive signal systems of animals (many of them vocal) has been the source of much confusion. The imitative vocal behavior of parrots, cat-birds, and so on, which duplicates the *forms* of human speech, has added to the confusion. It is true that vocal and other responses of animals constitute "systems of communication." The lost lamb bleats and in so doing "tells its mother where it is." The grazing animal "cries out in alarm" and "warns the rest of the flock of approaching danger." Mating calls bring male and female together. The mother drives predators away from her young with growls or cries of anger. Animal gestures have their place in this system of communication and have recently received special attention from the ethologists (Tinbergen, 1951). The language of bees has been analyzed by Von Frisch (1950).

Such responses appear to be elicited (or "released") by characteristic situations as part of the behavioral equipment of a given species. To say that they are instinctive is merely to say that each form of behavior is observed in most members of a given species, when there has been no opportunity for individual learning. In such cases we must fall back on an evolutionary explanation. Like other activities of the organism, such as digestion, respiration, or reproduction, some behavior with respect to the environment is acquired through natural selection because of its consequences in preserving the species.

There is a parallel between natural selection and operant conditioning. The selection of an instinctive response by its effect in promoting the survival of a species resembles, except for enormous differences in time scales, the selection of a response through reinforcement. The similarity is seen in the apparent purposiveness of both forms. Innate and acquired responses both appear to be emitted "in order to achieve effects"— in order to promote the welfare of the species or the individual. (In both cases it can be shown, of course, that only *prior* instances of such consequences are needed to explain the behavior.) When the instinctive response gains its advantage by affecting the behavior of another organism (when, for example, it is a cry), the parallel with verbal behavior is marked. The mother bird cries out in alarm "in order to" warn her young of approaching danger, as the human mother calls to her child in the street in order to save him from an approaching car. The young bird reacts to its mother's cry "in order to" escape danger, as the child responds to his mother's warning to avoid being hurt. But the interlocking systems in the two cases must be explained in quite different ways. The mother bird cries out not "in order to warn her young" but because the young of earlier members of the species who have cried out have survived to perpetuate the behavior. The young bird does not run for cover upon hearing the cry "in order to escape danger" but because earlier birds who have run under these circumstances have lived to bear their own young, possibly showing the same behavior. The behaviors of the human mother and child, on the other hand, are acquired during their life-times. De Laguna (1927) has ingeniously traced parallels between the two systems, identifying the circumstances under which a cry (or other vocal or nonvocal response) may be classed as a command, a proclamation, a declaration, and so on. As in the present analysis, the distinctions depend upon the situations of "speaker" and "listener" and upon the consequences for both. But the analogy remains an analogy.

It is unlikely, moreover, that verbal behavior in the present sense arose from instinctive cries. Well-defined emotional and other innate responses comprise reflex systems which are difficult, if not impossible, to modify by operant reinforcement. Vocal behavior

below the human level is especially refractory. Although it is easy to condition a cat to assume various postures, move its limbs, and manipulate features of the environment through operant reinforcement, it appears to be impossible to get it to miaow or to purr exclusively through the same process. Apparent exceptions prove upon examination to be samples of a different process. The cat at the door, miaowing "to be let out," may actually be miaowing because it is *not* being let out. The miaow is an emotional response in a frustrating situation. It occurs at approximately the same time and with the same frequency as such an operant as scratching the door, but the two forms of behavior are under different forms of environmental control. Such refractory material does not seem propitious as a precursor of verbal behavior in the present sense. Whether innate *nonverbal* responses can be conditioned in the operant pattern is difficult to say, because the same musculature can be brought under operant control. The experimenter may succeed merely in producing an operant which imitates the innate response. (Since innate responses are commonly associated with emotional situations, the parallel with verbal behavior has been most compelling in explaining emotional "expression." Indeed, the doctrine of expression is sometimes reserved for verbal or nonverbal behavior under the control of emotional variables. Expressive theories of the origin of language build on this pattern.)

This is not to say that lower organisms are incapable of verbal behavior in the present sense. With sufficient exposure to relevant variables vocal verbal behavior could conceivably be set up. But the verbal behavior acquired by the individual under the reinforcing practices of a verbal community does not appear to be a modification of vocalizations acquired by the species because of specific consequences having survival value. The relatively undifferentiated babbling of the human infant from which vocal verbal behavior develops is undoubtedly an evolutionary product, but it is not the sort of behavior which is evoked (or "released") in specific forms on specific occasions. The same may be said of nonverbal behavior. In general, operant behavior emerges from undifferentiated, previously unorganized, and undirected movements.

We can account for the origin of a verbal response in the form of a mand [1] if any behavior associated with a state of deprivation is an important stimulus for a "listener" who is disposed to reinforce the "speaker" with respect to that state of deprivation. Consider, for example, a nursing mother and her baby. It is possible that there is an innate response of the human female to innate cries of the hungry human infant, similar to the systems of communication in other species, but we do not need to assume that this is the case. If a hungry infant behaves in some distinctive fashion—let us say, by crying or squirming in response to painful stimulation of the stomach—and if a mother is inclined to nurse her child, perhaps to escape from the aversive stimulation of a full breast, then the baby's cry (correlated, as it is, with a tendency to suck) will

eventually control the mother's behavior of putting the baby to her breast. Once the mother has acquired this discrimination, her behavior of nursing her baby is contingent upon the baby's cry, and this may be reinforcing. Where the baby first cried as a reflex response to painful stimulation, it may now cry as an operant. It is probably not the reflex response which is reinforced but behavior resembling it. The form of the response is free to undergo a change provided the mother maintains the reinforcement. Eventually the response may not closely resemble the reflex pattern.

Such a response is reinforced with food, and its strength is a function of deprivation. The controlling relation which survives is characteristic of a full-fledged mand. Since we assumed a predisposition on the part of the mother to reinforce, it is the species of mand called a request. But eventually the mother may no longer be predisposed to reinforce with food, and the baby must compensate by creating an aversive condition from which the mother can escape only by supplying appropriate reinforcement. The baby's cry becomes "annoying," and the mother reinforces because the baby then stops crying. The response is no longer a request but a command.

A nonverbal environment may produce another kind of mand concerned with the "attention of the listener." Let us say that A is pouring drinks for a group, but has overlooked B. Any conspicuous movement by B, particularly if this produces a noise, will get the attention of A who may then reinforce B with a drink. Once this has happened, the behavior becomes verbal, similar to explicit mands of the form *Look here!* Verbal communities commonly rein-

[1] "A 'mand,' then, may be defined as a verbal operant in which the response is reinforced by a characteristic consequence and is therefore under the functional control of relevant conditions of deprivation or aversive stimulation. Adjectival and verbal uses of the term are self-explanatory. In particular, and in contrast with other types of verbal operants to be discussed later, the response has no specified relation to a prior stimulus" (Skinner, 1957).—Eds.

force mands which cannot have departed very far from the original nonverbal forms. Knocking at the door of a house is a conventional verbal response, which is easily traced to nonverbal origins, for it must have been originally close to the behavior of a dog scratching at the door "to be let in." It acquires a special style (the number, speed, and intensity of the knocks approach a standard) under appropriate reinforcement by the verbal environment. Rapping on an empty glass or table at a restaurant is comparable, as is the vocal *Har-rumph!*

Any behavior which has an effect upon another person as a mechanical object (pulling, pushing, striking, blocking, and so on) may acquire a behavioral effect if incipient stages of the behavior serve as stimuli. The contingent reinforcement is usually avoidance of, or escape from, the later stages of the behavior. For example, A stops the approach of B by holding out his arm and placing the palm of his hand against B's chest. At this stage the behavior of A would be roughly the same if B were an inanimate object (if B were swinging toward A, for example, at the end of a long rope). But if being stopped by A is aversive to B, or if A stops B only when likely to treat B aversively, B eventually responds to A's outstretched arm to avoid actual contact. When this change has occurred in B, A's response is reinforced not by its mechanical effect on B but by B's behavior. It becomes a "gesture" and is classified as verbal. Every listener and speaker need not pass through similar changes, for the gesture is eventually set up by the community. The traffic policeman's gestured "stop" is as culturally determined as a red light or the vocal response *Stop!*

Such gestures may gain current strength from similar nonverbal contingencies. The "speaker" may be readier to respond in a given way and achieve a more consistent effect upon the listener because of related mechanical effects. Even the railroad semaphore in its "stop" position probably borrows strength from the resemblance to an actual barring of the way. Familiar gestures having roughly the same effects as *Go away!*, *Come here!* (gestured with either the whole arm or the index finger), *Pass by!*, *Sit down!* (as to an audience), and *Stand up!* are subject to similar interpretations. These are all mands which specify behavior resembling the mechanical effect of the nonverbal responses from which they are derived. (Putting a finger on one's *own* lips shows something like the metaphorical extension of putting a finger on the lips of someone else. The latter may occur if the parties are close together.)

If, for purely physical reasons, A cups his hand behind his ear in order to hear B more clearly this becomes for B a stimulus in the presence of which louder behavior (vocal or nonvocal) is differentially reinforced. If B increases the intensity *because A cups his hand*, cupping the hand becomes a "gesture" and may be classed as verbal.

If B can avoid punishment at the hands of A by engaging in a particular form of activity, A may shape B's behavior by delivering or withholding aversive stimulation. For example, if A drives B away from a supply of food by beating him, A's raised fist eventually causes B to withdraw in order to *avoid* blows rather than to wait to *escape* from them. When this has happened, A may *gesture* rather than strike. If A sometimes allows B to eat, B eventually responds to A's fist as a stimulus upon which punishment for approach is contingent. A may eventually use a raised fist for finer shaping of behavior. For example, B may be kept active if A responds as soon as B stops. The contingencies are the same as in keeping a horse moving by *cracking* a whip. In addition to starting and stopping, B's behavior may also be *guided* in direction or intensity level.

If B is predisposed to reinforce A, A may shape B's behavior with any reaction indicating its reinforcing effect upon him. For example, conspicuous ingestive behavior on the part of A may reinforce B for cooking or serving a special kind of food. A's behavior in licking his chops may become a gesture equivalent to *Give me some more of that* as his vocal *m-m* may become the equivalent of the *Yum-yum* shaped by a particular verbal community. The unconditioned behavior of an audience which has been reinforced by an entertainer reinforces the entertainer in turn. Part of the reinforcing effect is the contrast between the intense quiet of the enthralled audience and the noisy release as the entertainer stops. If the audience can induce the entertainer to continue by heightening this contrast, the noise may become a gesture. Clapping, stamping, whistling, and other forms of applause are verbal responses equivalent to *Again!*, *Encore!*, or *Bis!* Eventually such a response may be used to shape up the behavior of a speaker —as in parliamentary debate.

Most of the mands we can account for without assuming a prior verbal environment are gestures. Paget (1930) has tried to derive vocal parallels by pointing to the fact that movements of the tongue are likely to accompany movements of the hand. A child, engrossed in some manual skill, may be observed to chew his tongue or move it about his lips. Paget has suggested that movements of the tongue accompanying manual gestures could modify breathing sounds or primitive vocalizations to supply vocal responses. But even such a process makes little progress in accounting for the diversity of vocal responses which specify kinds of reinforcement.

In explaining verbal behavior in the form of the tact,[2] we must look for different sources of nonverbal materials for the behavior of the "speaker" must be related to *stimulating circumstances* rather than to aversive stimulation or deprivation.

The behavior of a hunting dog may be said to "signal" the presence of game to the human hunter, as the barking of a watch dog "signals" the approach of an intruder. In so far as these are relatively invariable and unconditioned, the hunter and the householder respond to them as to any stimulus associated with a given event—say, the noise produced by the game or the intruder. It is only when the dog is trained as a "speaker" that new phenomena arise. As soon as the hunting dog is *reinforced* for pointing, or the watch dog for barking, the topography of the behavior may come to depend upon the contingencies of reinforcement rather than upon unconditioned reflex systems. In these examples the behavior is never greatly changed, but in others the form is eventually determined by

[2] "A tact may be defined as a verbal operant in which a response of given form is evoked (or at least strengthened) by a particular object or event or property of an object or event. We account for the strength by showing that in the presence of the object or event a response of that form is characteristically reinforced in a given verbal community" (Skinner, 1957).—Eds.

the community—that is, it becomes conventional. It has often been pointed out that the frequency of initial *m's* in words for *mother* may have some relation to the frequency of that sound as an unconditioned response in situations in which mothers frequently figure, where the rest of each word is presumably shaped by the particular community. The shortage of unconditioned vocal responses appropriate to specific situations is an obvious limitation in explaining an extensive repertoire in this way.

Another common explanation appeals to onomatopoeia. The old "bow-wow" theory of the origin of language emphasized formal similarities between stimulus and response which survive in onomatopoetic or "model-building" repertoires. We can "warn someone of the approach of a dog" by imitating its bark, as the tourist draws a picture of the article he wants to buy but cannot name, or as the Indian guide announces good fishing by moving his hand sinuously. The vocal, pictorial, or gestured response is effective because it is physically similar to "the situation described." But the "use of such signs" by either "speaker" or "listener" is not thereby accounted for. If we assume, however, that certain listeners-to-be run away when they hear a dog bark and that this is reinforcing to certain speakers-to-be, we have only to wait—a few thousand years if necessary—for someone to emit a vocal response similar enough to the bark of a dog to be reinforced by its effect on a listener. The result is at best an impure tact, scarcely to be distinguished from a mand. All onomatopoetic responses suffer from the fact that their distinguishing formal properties affect the listener in a way which is closely tied to a particular situation.

But listeners may react to dogs in many ways and for many reasons, and some sort of generalized reinforcement could conceivably follow.

The origins of most forms of response will probably always remain obscure, but if we can explain the beginnings of even the most rudimentary verbal environment, the well-established processes of linguistic change will explain the multiplication of verbal forms and the creation of new controlling relationships. Fortunately changes in reinforcing contingencies can be traced historically and observed in current communities. On the side of form of response, we do not need to suppose that changes follow any particular pattern (such as that of Grimm's Law); indeed, to explain the creation of large numbers of forms, the more accidental changes there are the better. On the side of "meaning" modern historical linguistics has identified many sources of variation. Some are concerned with accidents or faults in transmission. Others arise from the structure of the verbal community. New controlling relations arise when a literal response is taken metaphorically or when a metaphorical response through subsequent restricted reinforcement becomes abstract. As an example of the latter process, if we assume that the standard response *orange* has been brought under the stimulus control of oranges, then we can imagine a first occasion upon which some other object of the same color evokes the response. If it is effective upon the listener, as it may be without special conditioning, it may be reinforced with respect to color alone. If this is sufficiently useful to the community, the relatively abstract color-term *orange* emerges.

More subtle abstractions seem to

emerge in the same way. The *fall* of a coin or die leads at last to the concept of *chance* when the defining properties are free of instances in which something falls. The method of John Horne Tooke is relevant here. A *Sequel to the Diversions of Purley* by John Barcley (London, 1826) examines the origins of terms concerning spirit and mind in an early anticipation of twentieth-century behaviorism, tracing them back etymologically to more robust concepts in human behavior.

It has often been. pointed out, particularly in explaining the origin of myths, that this process works in reverse—that a metaphorical response may be taken literally. The metaphorical report that a man became *beastly* when drunk gives rise to the stoty of a man transformed into an animal upon drinking a magic potion. In the elaboration of such stories, new variables gain control of old responses.

The study of the verbal behavior of speaker and listener, as well as of the practices of the verbal environment which generates such behavior,˙ may not contribute directly to historical or descriptive linguistics, but it is enough for our present purposes to be able to say that a verbal environment could have arisen from nonverbal sources and, in its transmission from generation to generation, would have been subject to influences which might account for the multiplication of forms and controlling relations and the increasing effectiveness of verbal behavior as a whole.

26   The psycholinguists: on the new scientists of language

GEORGE A. MILLER

Psychologists have long recognised that human minds feed on linguistic symbols. Linguists have always admitted that some kind of psycho-social motor must move the machinery of grammar and lexicon. Sooner or later they were certain to examine their intersection self-consciously. Perhaps it was also inevitable that the result would be called "psycholinguistics."

In fact, although the enterprise itself has slowly been gathering strength at least since the invention of the telephone, the name, in its unhyphenated form, is only about ten years old. Few seem pleased with the term, but the field has grown so rapidly and stirred so much interest in recent years that some way of referring to it is urgently needed. *Psycholinguistics* is as descriptive a term as any, and shorter than most.

Among psychologists it was principally the behaviourists who wished to take a closer look at language. Behaviourists generally try to replace anything subjective by its most tangible, physical manifestation, so they have had a long tradition of confusing thought with speech—or with "verbal behaviour," as many prefer to call it. Among linguists it was principally those with an anthropological sideline who were most willing to collaborate, perhaps because as anthropologists they were sensitive to all those social and psychological processes that support our linguistic practices. By working together they managed to call attention to an important field of scientific research and to integrate it, or at least to acquaint its various parts with one another, under this new rubric.[1]

The integration of psycholinguistic studies has occurred so recently that there is still some confusion concerning its scope and purpose; efforts to clarify it necessarily have something of the character of personal opinion.[2] In my own version, the central task of this new science is to describe the psychological processes that go on when people use sentences. The real crux of the psycholinguistic problem does not appear until one tries to deal with sentences, for only then does the importance of productivity become completely obvious. It is true that productivity can also appear with individual words, but there it is not overwhelming. With sentences, productivity is literally unlimited.

Before considering this somewhat technical problem, however, it might be

[1] A representative sample of research papers in this field can be found in **Psycholinguistics, a Book of Readings,** edited by S. Saporta (1962). R. Brown provides a readable survey from a psychologist's point of view in **Words and Things** (1957).

[2] My own opinions have been strongly influenced by Noam Chomsky. A rather technical exposition of this work can be found in Chapters 11–13 of the second volume of the **Handbook of Mathematical Psychology,** edited by R. D. Luce, R. R. Bush, and E. Galanter (1963), from which many of the ideas discussed here have been drawn.

Abridged from **Encounter,** 1964, 23, No. 1, 29–37, with permission of the author and the publisher.

well to illustrate the variety of processes that psycholinguists hope to explain. This can best be done if we ask what a listener can do about a spoken utterance, and consider his alternatives in order from the superficial to the inscrutable.

The simplest thing one can do in the presence of a spoken utterance is to listen. Even if the language is incomprehensible, one can still *hear* an utterance as an auditory stimulus and respond to it in terms of some discriminative set: how loud, how fast, how long, from which direction, etc.

Given that an utterance is heard, the next level involves *matching* it as a phonemic pattern in terms of phonological skills acquired as a user of the language. The ability to match an input can be tested in psychological experiments by asking listeners to echo what they hear; a wide variety of experimental situations —experiments on the perception of speech and on the rote memorisation of verbal materials—can be summarised as tests of a person's ability to repeat the speech he hears under various conditions of audibility or delay.

If a listener can hear and match an utterance, the next question to ask is whether he will *accept* it as a sentence in terms of his knowledge of grammar. At this level we encounter processes difficult to study experimentally, and one is forced to rely most heavily on linguistic analyses of the structure of sentences. Some experiments are possible, however, for we can measure how much a listener's ability to accept the utterance as a sentence facilitates his ability to hear and match it; grammatical sentences are much easier to hear, utter or remember than are ungrammatical strings of words, and even nonsense (*pirot, karol, elat,* etc.) is easier to deal with if it looks grammatical (*pirots kar-*

olise elatically, etc.) (Epstein, 1961). Needless to say, the grammatical knowledge we wish to study does not concern those explicit rules drilled into us by teachers of traditional grammar, but rather the implicit generative knowledge that we all must acquire in order to use a language appropriately.

Beyond grammatical acceptance comes semantic interpretation: we can ask how listeners *interpret* an utterance as meaningful in terms of their semantic system. Interpretation is not merely a matter of assigning meanings to individual words; we must also consider how these component meanings combine in grammatical sentences. Compare the sentences: *Healthy young babies sleep soundly* and *Colourless green ideas sleep furiously.* Although they are syntactically similar, the second is far harder to perceive and remember correctly—because it cannot be interpreted by the usual semantic rules for combining the senses of adjacent English words (Miller & Isard, 1963; see also Katz & Fodor, 1963). The interpretation of each word is affected by the company it keeps; a central problem is to systematise the interactions of words and phrases with their linguistic contexts. The lexicographer makes his major contribution at this point, but psychological studies of our ability to paraphrase an utterance also have their place.

At the next level it seems essential to make some distinction between interpreting an utterance and understanding it, for understanding frequently goes well beyond the linguistic context provided by the utterance itself. A husband greeted at the door by "'I bought some electric light bulbs to-day" must do more than interpret its literal reference; he must understand that he should go to the kitchen and replace that burned-out lamp. Such contextual information lies well outside any grammar or lexicon. The listener can *understand* the function of an utterance in terms of contextual knowledge of the most diverse sort.

Finally, at a level now almost invisible through the clouds, a listener may *believe* that an utterance is valid in terms of its relevance to his own conduct. The child who says "I saw five lions in the garden" may be heard, matched, accepted, interpreted, and understood, but in few parts of the world will he be believed.

The boundaries between successive levels are not sharp and distinct. One shades off gradually into the next. Still the hierarchy is real enough and important to keep in mind. Simpler types of psycholinguistic processes can be studied rather intensively; already we know much about hearing and matching. Accepting and interpreting are just now coming into scientific focus. Understanding is still over the horizon, and pragmatic questions involving belief systems are presently so vague as to be hardly worth asking. But the whole range of processes must be included in any adequate definition of psycholinguistics.

I phrased the description of these various psycholinguistic processes in terms of a listener; the question inevitably arises as to whether a different hierarchy is required to describe the speaker. One problem a psycholinguist faces is to decide whether speaking and listening are two separate abilities, coordinate but distinct, or whether they are merely different manifestations of a single linguistic faculty.

The mouth and ear are different organs; at the simplest levels we must distinguish hearing and matching from vocalising and speaking. At more complex levels it is less easy to decide whether the two abilities are distinct. At some point they must converge, if only to explain why it is so difficult to speak and listen simultaneously. The question is where.

It is easy to demonstrate how important to a speaker is the sound of his own voice. If his speech is delayed a fifth of a second, amplified, and fed back into his own ears, the voice-ear asynchrony can be devastating to the motor skills of articulate speech. It is more difficult, however, to demonstrate that the same linguistic competence required for speaking is also involved in processing the speech of others.

Recently Morris Halle and Kenneth Stevens (1962) of the Massachusetts Institute of Technology revived a suggestion made by Wilhelm von Humboldt over a century ago. Suppose we accept the notion that a listener recognises what he hears by comparing it with some internal representation. To the extent that a match can be obtained, the input is accepted and interpreted. One trouble with this hypothesis, however, is that a listener must be ready to recognise any one of an enormous number of different sentences. It is inconceivable that a separate internal representation for each of them could be stored in his memory in advance. Halle and Stevens suggest that these internal representations must be generated as they are needed by following the same generative rules that are normally used in producing speech. In this way the rules of the language are incorporated into the theory only once, in a generative form; they need not be learned once by the ear and again by the tongue. This is a theory of a language-user, not of a speaker or a listener alone.

The listener begins with a guess about the input. On that basis he generates an internal matching signal. The first attempt will probably be in error; if so, the mismatch is reported and used as a basis for a next guess, which should be closer. This cycle repeats (unconsciously, almost certainly) until a satisfactory (not necessarily a correct) match is obtained, at which point the next segment of speech is scanned and matched, etc. The output is not a transformed version of the input; it is the programme that was followed to generate the matching representation.

The perceptual categories available to such a system are defined by the generative rules at its disposal. It is also reasonably obvious that its efficiency is critically dependent on the quality of the initial guess. If this guess is close, an iterative process can converge rapidly; if not, the listener will be unable to keep pace with the rapid flow of conversational speech.

A listener's first guess probably derives in part from syntactic markers in the form of intonation, inflection, suffixes, etc., and in part from his general knowledge of the semantic and situational context. Syntactic cues indicate how the input is to be grouped and which words function together; semantic and contextual contributions are more difficult to characterise, but must somehow enable him to limit the range of possible words that he can expect to hear.

How he is able to do this is an utter mystery, but the fact that he can do it is easily demonstrated.

The English psychologist David Bruce (1956) recorded a set of ordinary sentences and played them in the presence of noise so intense that the voice was just audible, but not intelligible. He told his listeners that these were sentences on some general topic—sports, say—and asked them to repeat what they heard. He then told them they would hear more sentences on a different topic, which they were also to repeat. This was done several times. Each time the listeners repeated sentences appropriate to the topic announced in advance. When at the end of the experiment Bruce told them they had heard the same recording every time—all he had changed was the topic they were given—most listeners were unable to believe it.

With an advance hypothesis about what the message will be we can tune our perceptual system to favour certain interpretations and reject others. This fact is no proof of a generative process in speech perception, but it does emphasise the important role of context. For most theories of speech perception the facilitation provided by context is merely a fortunate though rather complicated fact. For a generative theory it is essential.

Note that generative theories do not assume that a listener must be able to articulate the sounds he recognises, but merely that he be able to generate some internal representation to match the input. In this respect a generative theory differs from a motor theory (such as that of Sir Richard Paget) which assumes that we can identify only those utterances we are capable of producing ourselves. There is some rather compelling evidence against a motor theory. The American psychologist Eric Lenneberg (1962) has described the case of an eight-year-old boy with congenital anarthria; despite his complete inability to speak, the boy acquired an excellent ability to understand language. Moreover, it is a common observation that utterances can be understood by young children before they are able to produce them. A motor theory of speech-perception draws too close a parallel between our two capacities as users of language. Even so, the two are more closely integrated than most people realise.

I have already offered the opinion that productivity sets the central problem for the psycholinguist and have even referred to it indirectly by arguing that we can produce too many different sentences to store them all in memory. The issue can be postponed no longer.

To make the problem plain, consider an example on the level of individual words. For several days I carried in my pocket a small white card on which was typed UNDERSTANDER. On suitable occasions I would hand it to someone. "How do you pronounce this?" I asked.

He pronounced it.

"Is it an English word?"

He hesitated. "I haven't seen it used very much. I'm not sure."

"Do you know what it means?"

"I suppose it means 'one who understands.'"

I thanked him and changed the subject.

Of course, understander *is* an English word, but to find it you must look in a large dictionary where you will probably read that it is "now rare." Rare enough, I think, for none of my respondents to have seen it before. Nevertheless, they all answered in the same way. Nobody seemed surprised. Nobody wondered how he could understand and pronounce a word without knowing whether it was a word. Everybody put the main stress on the third syllable and constructed a meaning from the verb "to understand" and the agentive suffix "er." Familiar morphological rules of English were applied as a matter of course, even though the combination was completely novel.

Probably no one but a psycholinguist captured by the ingenuous behaviouristic theory that words are vocal responses conditioned to occur in the presence of appropriate stimuli would find anything exceptional in this. Since none of my friends had seen the word before, and so could not have been "conditioned" to give the responses they did, how would this theory account for their "verbal behaviour"? Advocates of a conditioning theory of meaning—and there are several distinguished scientists among them—would probably explain linguistic productivity in terms of "conditioned generalisations." [3] They could argue that my respondents had been conditioned to the word understand and to the suffix—*er*; responses to their union could conceivably be counted as instances of stimulus generalisation. In this way, novel responses could occur without special training.

Although a surprising amount of psychological ingenuity has been invested in this kind of argument, it is difficult to estimate its value. No one has carried the theory through for all the related combinations that must be explained simultaneously. One can speculate, however, that there would have to be many different kinds of generalisation, each with a carefully defined range of applicability. For example, it would be necessary to explain why "'understander" is acceptable, whereas "erunderstand" is not. Worked out in detail, such a theory would become a sort of Pavlovian paraphrase of a linguistic description. Of course, if one believes there is some essential difference between behaviour governed by conditioned habits and

[3] A dog conditioned to salivate at the sound of a tone will also salivate, though less copiously, at the sound of similar tones, the magnitude declining as the new tones become less similar to the original. This phenomenon is called "stimulus generalisation."

behaviour governed by rules, the paraphrase could never be more than a vast intellectual pun.

Original combinations of elements are the life blood of language. It is our ability to produce and comprehend such novelties that makes language so ubiquitously useful. As psychologists have become more seriously interested in the cognitive processes that language entails, they have been forced to recognise that the fundamental puzzle is not our ability to associate vocal noises with perceptual objects, but rather our combinatorial productivity—our ability to understand an unlimited diversity of utterances never heard before and to produce an equal variety of utterances similarly intelligible to other members of our speech community. Faced with this problem, concepts borrowed from conditioning theory seem not so much invalid as totally inadequate.

Some idea of the relative magnitudes of what we might call the productive as opposed to the reproductive components of any psycholinguistic theory is provided by statistical studies of language. A few numbers can reinforce the point. If you interrupt a speaker at some randomly chosen instant, there will be, on the average, about ten words that form grammatical and meaningful continuations. Often only one word is admissible and sometimes there are thousands, but on the average it works out to about ten. (If you think this estimate too low, I will not object; larger estimates strengthen the argument.) A simple English sentence can easily run to a length of twenty words, so elementary arithmetic tells us that there must be at least 10^{20} such sentences that a person who knows English must know how to deal with. Compare this productive potential with the 10^4 or 10^5 individual words we know—the reproductive component of our theory—and the discrepancy is dramatically illustrated. Putting it differently, it would take 100,000,-000,000 centuries (one thousand times the estimated age of the earth) to utter all the admissible twenty-word sentences of English. Thus, the probability that you might have heard any particular twenty-word sentence before is negligible. Unless it is a cliché, every sentence must come to you as a novel combination of morphemes. Yet you can interpret it at once if you know the English language.

With these facts in mind it is impossible to argue that we learn to understand sentences from teachers who have pronounced each one and explained what it meant. What we have learned are not particular strings of words, but *rules* for generating admissible strings of words.

Consider what it means to follow a rule; this consideration shifts the discussion of psycholinguistics into very difficult territory. The nature of rules has been a central concern of modern philosophy and perhaps no analysis has been more influential than Ludwig Wittgenstein's. Wittgenstein remarked that the most characteristic thing we can say about "rule-governed behaviour" is that the person who knows the rules knows whether he is proceeding correctly or incorrectly. Although he may not be able to formulate the rules explicitly, he knows what it is to make a mistake. If this remark is accepted, we must ask ourselves whether an animal that has been conditioned is privy to any such knowledge about the correctness of what he is doing. Perhaps such a degree of insight could be achieved by the great apes, but surely not by all the various species that can acquire conditioned reflexes. On this basis alone it would seem necessary to preserve a distinction between conditioning and learning rules.

As psychologists have learned to appreciate the complexities of language, the prospect of reducing it to the laws of behaviour so carefully studied in lower animals has grown increasingly remote. We have been forced more and more into a position that non-psychologists probably take for granted, namely, that language is rule-governed behaviour characterised by enormous flexibility and freedom of choice.

The first thing we notice when we survey the languages of the world is how few we can understand and how diverse they all seem. Not until one looks for some time does an even more significant observation emerge concerning the pervasive similarities in the midst of all this diversity.

Every human group that anthropologists have studied has spoken a language. The language always has a lexicon and a grammar. The lexicon is not a haphazard collection of vocalisations, but is highly organised; it always has pronouns, means for dealing with time, space, and number, words to represent true and false, the basic concepts necessary for propositional logic. The grammar has distinguishable levels of structure, some phonological, some syntactic. The phonology always contains both vowels and consonants, and the phonemes can always be described in terms of distinctive features drawn from a limited set of possibilities. The syntax always specifies rules for grouping elements sequentially into phrases and sentences, rules governing normal intonation, rules for transforming some types of sentences into other types.

The nature and importance of these common properties, called "linguistic universals," are only beginning to emerge as our knowledge of the world's languages grows more systematic (Greenberg, 1963). These universals appear even in languages that developed with a minimum of interaction. One is forced to assume, therefore, either that (*a*) no other kind of linguistic practices are conceivable, or that (*b*) something in the biological makeup of human beings favours languages having these similarities. Only a moment's reflection is needed to reject (*a*). When one considers the variety of artificial languages developed in mathematics, in the communication sciences, in the use of computers, in symbolic logic, and elsewhere, it soon becomes apparent that the universal features of natural languages are not the only ones possible. Natural languages are, in fact, rather special and often seem unnecessarily complicated.

A popular belief regards human language as a more or less free creation of the human intellect, as if its elements were chosen arbitrarily and could be combined into meaningful utterances by any rules that strike our collective fancy. The assumption is implicit, for example, in Wittgenstein's well-known conception of "the language game." This metaphor, which casts valuable light on many aspects of language, can, if followed blindly, lead one to think that all linguistic rules are just as arbitrary as, say, the rules of chess or football. As Lenneberg (1960) has pointed out, however, it makes a great deal of sense to inquire into the biological basis for language, but very little to ask about the biological foundations of card games.

Man is the only animal to have a combinatorially productive language. In the jargon of biology, language is "a species-specific form of behaviour." Other animals have signalling systems of various kinds and for various purposes— but only man has evolved this particular and highly improbable form of communication. Those who think of language as a free and spontaneous intellectual invention are also likely to believe that any animal with a brain sufficiently large to support a high level of intelligence can acquire a language. This assumption is demonstrably false. The human brain is not just an ape brain enlarged; its extra size is less important than its different structure. Moreover, Lenneberg (1962) has pointed out that nanocephalic dwarfs, with brains half the normal size but grown on the human blueprint, can use language reasonably well, and even mongoloids, not intelligent enough to perform the simplest functions for themselves, can acquire the rudiments. Talking and understanding language do not depend on being intelligent or having a large brain. They depend on "being human."

Serious attempts have been made to teach animals to speak. If words were conditioned responses, animals as intelligent as chimpanzees or porpoises should be able to learn them. These attempts have uniformly failed in the past and, if the argument here is correct, they will always fail in the future—for just the same reason that attempts to teach fish to walk or dogs to fly would fail. Such efforts misconstrue the basis for our linguistic competence: they fly in the face of biological facts.

Human language must be such that a child can acquire it. He acquires it, moreover, from parents who have no idea how to explain it to him. No careful schedule of rewards for correct or punishments for incorrect utterances is necessary. It is sufficient that the child be allowed to grow up naturally in an environment where language is used.

The child's achievement seems all the more remarkable when we recall the speed with which he accomplishes it and the limitations of his intelligence in other respects. It is difficult to avoid an impression that infants are little machines specially designed by nature to perform this particular learning task.

I believe this analogy with machines is worth pursuing. If we could imagine what a language-learning automaton would have to do, it would dramatise—and perhaps even clarify—what a child can do. The linguist and logician Noam Chomsky (1962) has argued that the description of such an automaton would comprise our hypothesis about the child's innate ability to learn languages or (to borrow a term from Ferdinand de Saussure) his innate *faculté de langage*.

Consider what information a language-learning automaton would be given to work with. Inputs to the machine would include a finite set of sentences, a finite set of non-sentences accompanied by some signal that they were incorrect, some way to indicate that one item is a repetition or elaboration or transformation of another, and some access to a universe of perceptual objects and events associated with the sentences. Inside the machine there would be a computer so programmed as to extract from these inputs the nature of the language, i.e., the particular syntactic rules by which sentences are generated, and the rules that associate with each syntactic structure a particular phonetic representation and semantic interpretation. The important question, of course, is what programme of instructions would have to be given to the computer.

We could instruct the computer to discover any imaginable set of rules that might, in some formal sense of the term, constitute a grammar. This approach—the natural one if we believe that human languages can be infinitely diverse and various—is doomed from the start. The computer would have to evaluate an infinitude of possible grammars; with only a finite corpus of evidence it would be impossible, even if sufficient time were available for computation, to arrive at any unique solution.

A language-learning automaton could not possibly discover a suitable grammar unless some strong *a priori* assumptions were built into it from the start. These assumptions would limit the alternatives that the automaton considered —limit them presumably to the range defined by linguistic universals. The automaton would test various grammars of the appropriate form to see if they would generate all of the sentences and none of the non-sentences. Certain aspects would be tested before others; those found acceptable would be preserved for further evaluation. If we wished the automaton to replicate a child's performance, the order in which these aspects would be evaluated could only be decided after careful analysis of the successive stages of language acquisition in human children.

The actual construction of such an automaton is, of course, far beyond our reach at the present time. That is not the point. The lesson to learn from such speculations is that the whole project would be impossible unless the automaton—and so, presumably, a child—knew in advance to look for particular kinds of regularities and correspondences, to discover rules of a rather special kind uniquely characteristic of human language in general.

The features that human infants are prepared to notice sharply limit the structure of any human language. Even if one imagines creating by decree a Newspeak in which this generalisation were false, within one generation it would have become true again.

Psycholinguistics does not deal with social practices determined arbitrarily either by caprice or intelligent design, but with practices that grow organically out of the biological nature of man and the linguistic capacities of human infants. To that extent, at least, it is possible to define an area of empirical fact well within the reach of our scientific methods.

Another line of scientific investigation is opened up by the observation that we do not always follow our own rules. If this were not so, of course, we would not speak of rules, but of the laws of language. The fact that we make mistakes, and that we can know we made mistakes, is central to the psycholinguistic problem. Before we can see the empirical issue this entails, however, we should first draw a crucial distinction between theories of language and theories of the users of language.

There is nothing in the linguistic description of a language to indicate what mistakes will occur. Mistakes result from the psychological limitations of people who use the language, not from the language itself. It would be meaningless to state rules for making mistakes.

A formal characterisation of a natural language in terms of a set of elements and rules for combining those elements must inevitably generate an infinitude of possible sentences that will never occur in actual use. Most of these sentences are too complicated for us. There is nothing mysterious about this. It is very similar to the situation in arithmetic where a student may understand perfectly the rules for multiplication, yet find that some multiplication problems are too difficult for him to do "in his head," i.e., without extending his memory capacity by the use of pencil and paper.

There is no longest grammatical sentence. There is no limit to the number of different grammatical sentences. Moreover, since the number of elements and rules is finite, there must be some rules and elements that can recur any number of times in a grammatical sentence. Chomsky has even managed to pinpoint a kind of recursive operation in language that, in principle, lies beyond the power of any finite device to perform indefinitely often. Compare these sentences:

(R) *Remarkable is the rapidity of the motion of the wing of the hummingbird.*
(L) *The hummingbird's wing's motion's rapidity is remarkable.*
(E) *The rapidity that the motion that the wing that the hummingbird has has has is remarkable.*

When you parse these sentences you find that the phrase structure of (R) dangles off to the right; each prepositional phrase hangs to the noun in the prepositional phrase preceding it. In (R), therefore, we see a type of recurring construction that has been called right-branching. Sentence (L), on the other hand, is left-branching; each possessive modifies the possessive immediately following. Finally, (E) is an onion; it grows by embedding sentences within sentences. Inside "The rapidity is remarkable" we first insert "the motion is rapid" by a syntactic transformation that permits us to construct relative clauses, and so we obtain "The rapidity that the motion has is remarkable." Then we repeat the transformation, this time inserting "the wing has motion" to obtain

"The rapidity that the motion that the wing has has is remarkable." Repeating the transformation once more gives (E).

It is intuitively obvious that, of these three types of recursive operations, self-embedding (E) is psychologically the most difficult. Although they seem grammatical by any reasonable standard of grammar, such sentences never occur in ordinary usage because they exceed our cognitive capacities. Chomsky's achievement was to prove rigorously that any language that does *not* restrict this kind of recursive embedding contains sentences that cannot be spoken or understood by devices, human or mechanical, with finite memories. Any device that uses these rules must remember each left portion until it can be related to its corresponding right portion; if the memory of the user is limited, but the number of admissible left portions is not, it is inevitable that some admissible sentences will exceed the capacity of the user to process them correctly (Chomsky, 1957).

It is necessary, therefore, to distinguish between a description of the language in terms of the rules that a person *knows* and uses and a description of that person's *performance* as a user of the rules. The distinction is sometimes criticised as "psycholatry" by strict adherents of behaviourism; "knowing" is considered too mentalistic and subjective, therefore unscientific. The objection cannot be taken seriously. Our conception of the rules that a language-user knows is indeed a hypothetical construct, not something observed directly in his behaviour. But if such hypotheses were to be forbidden, science in general would become an empty pursuit.

Given a reasonable hypothesis about the rules that a language-user knows, the exploration of his limitations in following those rules is proper work for an experimental psychologist. "Psychology should assist us," a great linguist once said, "in understanding what is going on in the mind of speakers, and more particularly how they are led to deviate from previously existing rules in consequence of conflicting tendencies." Otto Jespersen (1924, p. 344) made this request of psychology in 1924; now at last the work is beginning.

One example. Stephen Isard and I asked Harvard undergraduates to memorise several sentences that differed in degree of self-embedding. For instance, the twenty-two words in the right-branching sentence, "We cheered the football squad that played the team that brought the mascot that chased the girls that were in the park," can be re-arranged to give one, two, three, or four self-embeddings; with four it becomes, "The girls (that the mascot (that the team (that the football squad (that we cheered) played) brought) chased) were in the park." One self-embedding caused no difficulty; it was almost as easy to memorise as the sentence with none. Three or four embeddings were most difficult. When the sentence had two self-embeddings—"The team (that the football squad (that we cheered) played) brought the mascot that chased the girls that were in the park"—some subjects found it as easy to memorise as sentences with zero or one embedding, others found it as difficult as sentences with three or four. That is to say, everybody can manage one embedding, some people can manage two, but everybody has trouble with three or more.

Records of eye movements while people are reading such sentences show that the trouble begins with the long string of verbs, "cheered played brought," at which point all grasp of the sentence structure crumbles and they are left with a random list of verbs. This is just what would be expected from a computer executing a programme that did not make provision for a sub-routine to refer to itself, i.e., that was not recursive. If our ability to handle this type of self-embedded recursion is really as limited as the experiment indicates, it places a strong limitation on the kinds of theories we can propose to explain our human capacities for processing information.

V   SOCIAL INTERACTION AND ROLE

Social interaction describes a nucleus around which most other matters encompassed by this book orbit. Psychological, sociological, and anthropological manifestations all coalesce about it producing its particular colorations. For most social psychologists, phenomena of social interchange are central points of reference in their scientific enterprise. Comprehension of the nature of social interaction is therefore a basic challenge for social psychology (cf. Lindzey & Aronson, 1968, vol. 4).

Among the most important tasks in understanding the character of social interaction is to observe and record the specific actions which go to make up the flow of interaction. This has been the major focus of Bales's influential work on "interaction process analysis." In his paper beginning this section, he considers this method both as a procedure for recording interaction and also as a basis for assessing the characteristic participation which individuals display differentially in groups. After treating the nature and development of his procedure, he illuminates basic dimensions along which interaction can vary, and discusses their functional implications for group behavior.

A fuller statement of Bales's most recent views will be found in his new book *Personality and Interpersonal Behavior* (1970). The thrust of that work grows out of his three-dimensional spatial metaphor of upward-downward, positive-negative, and forward-backward. These correspond to the three major variables of power, affection, and contribution to group tasks, by which he says people usually evaluate others. In his paper here, he considers the relationship of those variables to the twelve categories

245

of interaction, thereby making a tie between the individual's characteristic modes of interaction and the way he is perceived by others. The implications of this work for understanding personality in interaction terms are apparent (see Section III).

It is generally agreed that interactions are a function both of factors external and internal to the person, though the immediate interests of a particular social analyst may understate the one or the other. But, as the papers in this section make plain, no simple categorical separation between the two can be maintained consistently. In this connection one may also recall Yinger's observations in Section III. External and internal conditions sound a continual counterpoint to one another, with harmony the rule rather than the exception.

This fact is clearly revealed in Vinacke's pointed review of recent "game" approaches to the analysis of social interaction, a portion of which is reprinted here. In it Vinacke presents pertinent material showing the interactional interplay of task, situational, and personality variables in game behavior. In line with Bales, he indicates that the behavior of participants in social relations depends heavily on their perceptions of one another, so that it is rarely susceptible to simple "rational" interpretation. Vinacke concludes by stressing the need for theory—like Lewinian field theory—capable of dealing realistically with transactions among situational and personal variables.

When looking at phenomena of interaction, psychological theorists have long tended to accord a pre-eminent explanatory position to processes of perception. How a person behaves in the course of interaction is widely held to be a consequence of constructions or perceptions of the situation, including other persons. It is virtually axiomatic that a person behaves according to what the situation "means" to him, or in W. I. Thomas's felicitous phrase, his "definition of the situation" (cf. Volkart, 1951). Perception, in turn, depends upon the characteristics of the person himself and upon the information communicated to him, intentionally and unintentionally, in the situation. As Tagiuri has noted (1960, p. 569), a person's impressions of a situation including another person are a result of three major elements: the situation, the other person, and the perceiver. All of these are considered in the selections that follow, as they are also in Tagiuri's later writing on the subject (1969).

There are, of course, conditions of a less "perceptual" nature, in the sense of being less personalized, that can and do mold interaction. They reside in the fabric of the social system, its modal patterns of conduct, and in the general "life situation." Until recently, such factors have perhaps received somewhat less attention from social psychologists than have the kinds of perceptual conditions already mentioned, but psychological interest has been growing with reference to a complex of elements signaled by the terms social and behavioral ecology. These interests are exemplified in the discussion by Sommer in this section.

Following the lead of such investigators as Barker (see Section I) and the anthropologist Hall, Sommer demonstrates in a variety of settings how the distribution of actors in space relates to patterns of social interchange (Jackson's paper in Section II is a further illustration). He shows both how the ecology of groups follows from the motives, purposes, and interests of their members and how the processes and outcomes of interaction vary with group structure. Other social psychologists besides those mentioned have in the past contributed observations on the significance to group interaction of spatial-structural phenomena. There is, for example, Newcomb's (1956) work on propinquity as an important starting mechanism for social attraction, and also the well-known studies on the effects of varying communication networks (see, e.g., Leavitt, 1964, Ch. 15). But it has only been lately that systematic study of behavioral ecology has begun to attract wider attention. As Sommer makes clear, it not only serves as a basis for understanding the character of interactions, but also as a fundamental point of reference for purposive environmental engineering designed to facilitate or inhibit selected interaction patterns in the interest of serving designated social objectives.

Another class of structural influences basic to social relations are the long familiar coordinate concepts of *position* (or sometimes status) and *role*—concepts that R. G. Hunt considers at some length in this section. In Hunt's account, positions may be roughly described as aggregations of functions standardized within a social system and "cued" by some set of conventionalized symbols. Roles are the behavioral expectancies usually associated with given positions and evoked by the appropriate symbols. Most analyses of roles, including Hunt's, emphasize the frequent complementary quality of positional differentiation in society and the resulting interlocking features of roles and their enactments. Consequently roles contribute not only to the integration of individual behavior, they are fundamental to general social organization (see Miller, 1963).

The significance of position-role concepts was well described by Rommetveit (1954) when he characterized role as a theoretical point of intersection between psychology and sociology. To paraphrase Rommetveit, role is the largest possible research unit within psychology and the smallest possible within sociology (1954, p. 31). Therefore, despite its "theoretical inelegance" and "lack of conceptual consistency" detected by Deutsch and Krauss (1965), it is easy to understand why role remains a primary reference point in analyses of social processes.

A more comprehensive and detailed review of role concepts may be found in Bredemeier and Stephenson's useful book (1962), in Sarbin and Allen's chapter (1968), and in Biddle and Thomas's reader (1966), but Hunt's discussion here is representative and captures the richness and complexity of the idea. Along with his differentiated definitions of position and role and his classification of varieties of role conflict, Hunt takes note of the relevance of role to questions of personal identity or self which we discussed in Section III. As Goffman has p'.t it, roles come with ready-made identities (1961). But it must be kept in mind that individuals play many roles and so, in a sense, have many identities; but, since they are never wholly included in any one role, aspects of other roles they play can be expected to influence how each separate role is performed. Moreover, so intimately does the social structure and the person mesh in interaction that the aggregation of all the roles a person plays and the synthesis of all the identities he holds will also somehow shape every role performance he executes.

Contributions to the development of self and personality, in terms of the parts one plays in society, were recognized by William James (1892) in his distinction between the self, as known ("Me") and the self as knower ("I"), and by the sociologist C. H. Cooley (1902) in his notion of the "looking glass self." Both James and Cooley realized that one's conception of self derived, partly at least, from the ways others responded to him and that this in turn related to social expectancies or roles. But it remained for George Herbert Mead (1934) with his emphases upon language, communication, and "symbol" and, more recently, Merton

(1957) and Goffman (1959, 1961) to articulate systematically the vital relation of role to personality. It is in this context that Hunt's paper should be seen. What then becomes clear is that major portions of interpersonal relations are regulated by "institutionalized" patterns of relation and the situational definitions they imply. Several of the other papers in the pages that follow, notably those by Gouldner and Goffman, also deal with this aspect of interactional influence.

Integrating the classes of interaction determinants mentioned in the preceding passages, social scientists have often spoken of different *levels* at which the same process may be analyzed; here, Goffman speaks of three—personality, interactions, and society—and suggests coordinations among them. Most popular, however, has been a distinction between *formal* and *informal* levels of analysis, though other terms with comparable meanings may be used (see, for an alternative formulation, Blau's discussion of "macro-structures" and "micro-structures," 1964). Formal analysis points most directly to an account of social behavior in terms of general patterns and widespread norms within a social system, with "society" and/or "culture" as the points of reference for analysis. Role theory, as one example, is often employed formalistically.

An analysis of social processes at an informal level lays stress upon aspects of the immediate interactional setting and participants, including their individual attributes, as determinants of events. Most phenomenological-perceptual-cognitive approaches to interaction concentrate upon analyses at informal levels.

These levels are not rigidly separable, they "interpenetrate" one another extensively, to borrow Parsons's (1959) term. As levels, they represent different selections of variables for study, variables having perhaps differing degrees of generality. Actual social behavior is a complex, multi-determined happening any instances of which involves processes that may be conceptualized at both levels. Psychological analyses correctly convey a preference for specifications at a more informal level, invoking processes operative "in" the individual, though not necessarily uniquely to a given person. Nonetheless it is convenient and highly useful to consider variables at another level.

Whenever well-structured role systems are operative in a situation, social behavior will tend to "run-off" in terms of their prescriptions.

Under such conditions the personal attributes of the parties to the relation and their mutual appreciations of those attributes are of little moment. Steiner (1955), for one, has shown that there are times when detailed and accurate perception of the other is not only unnecessary, but actually disruptive of ordered interaction.

At any rate, when role relations are well defined, interaction can be formalistically conceptualized, as the so-called "symbolic interactionists" do (see Rose, 1962; Strauss, 1964), as an interplay of positions and roles. Persons are only incidentally relevant as the "players of roles." But, when role systems are not clearly defined, informal influences will be stronger and the importance of perceptual accuracy increases proportionately. In a total interaction "episode" certain segments are likely to vary with respect to the weighting of formal-informal determinants. Which class or level is then more important depends upon the particular interaction segment looked at.

That particular interpersonal relations are subject to influences "outside" the unique individualities of the actors is plain, and Gouldner's contribution here takes this matter a step further, proposing a norm of reciprocity as a cultural universal working to both stabilize and initiate relations in a social system. The norm of reciprocity is presumed to be of such generality that it will constitute a broad formal influence governing social systems even in the relative absence of clearly defined status-role stipulations.

Gouldner, in developing his thesis, systematically distinguishes between reciprocity and complementarity from a viewpoint of functional theory and a conception of interaction as exchange. He details the implications of these constructs for power relations, conditions of unequal exchange, and for role systems as well. As he does so, he notes that the norm of reciprocity, as a modal cultural fact, becomes personally internalized as a moral sanction entailing sentiments of obligation and debt and otherwise functioning as a useful check upon "egoism." Gouldner also makes a point of the relative indeterminacy of the norm as a stabilizer, something March (1954) has also emphasized.

It is noteworthy that, while postulated as a cultural universal, Gouldner comments that the norm is not "unconditional." Psychologically, the internalization of reciprocity *sentiments* may vary across groups, such as social classes, and between individuals, and thereby lend markedly distinctive appearances to the interactions of given individuals. A generalized cultural norm of reciprocity may operate as an important source of dispositions relevant to interaction, but it is the individual representation of this norm that is directly relevant to immediate interaction. Nonetheless, Gouldner sees interpersonal interaction as highly relative to circumstances characterizing the larger social world.

Thus, human interaction is subject to a number of broadly constraining social elements residing apart from the immediate relationship. However, the argument can be sustained that the actual implementation of interaction is directly dependent upon processes taking place within and between the actors. It may well be that not every interaction requires personalized perceptions of others as persons, but some minimal perceptual reference is required. Even if the particular behaviors that occur are strictly role-linked, it is still necessary for the interacting parties to "perceive" the positional cues signaling their performance. This is something Banton (1965), for one, has discussed at length with reference to "terms of address" and other signaling devices; what is more, a de-emphasis upon perceptual *accuracy* does not contradict the axiom that *persons* behave chiefly in response to the *perceived* attributes of others and of the situations in which they are encountered.

Indeed, the dependence of behavior upon perception is widely asserted as is the idea that perception is "our own creation" (cf. Cantril, 1957). By classifying events and persons, people create "reality worlds" which then control their percepts and, subsequently, their performance. Once things are classified (as Goffman notes here) the situation becomes stabilized and behavior proceeds according to the significance (meanings) of the classes used. Thus reality, what people perceive to be true, depends upon the classification schemas they bring with them to situations. What one perceives, therefore, is very much related to prior dispositions or sets —a consideration as germane to the perception of persons as to things.

Phenomenally, then, things are literally what they seem. A question remains, though, concerning the "causation" of experience, and especially as this applies to impressions of others. The burden of Heider's distinguished book *The Psychology of Interpersonal Relations* (1958) is to provide just such a causal analysis. The flavor of Heider's endeavor, along with his basic Gestalt-derived perspective and a number of key concepts, is well represented in the selection from that volume reprinted here. In it he features the dynamic interplay of processes in perception and focuses upon "coordination between stimulus conditions outside the person and his experience or phenomenal representation of them." He finds it analytically useful to break the total perceptual process into "stages" or cumulative sequences, as follows: distal stimulus–mediation–proximal stimulus–constructive processes of perception or, if one prefers, cognition.

Heider also treats the import of constancy phenomena, with "meaning" occupying a central position integrating perception and controlling behavior. The discernment of dispositional characteristics (sentiments, motives, etc.) of others serve as major factors structuring a person's perception and his interpersonal relations. Perception of the attributes of others controls the way a person behaves toward them and what he expects from them, and, for Heider, the specific behavior patterns by which these percepts are "cued" is psychologically of minor importance.

Thus Heider construes social perception in a "non-behavioristic" manner as a process between the center of one person and the center of another, all the while allowing due latitude to the contextual effects of the "stimulus field." Interpersonal relations are framed by mutual perceptions of the psychological attributes of others and interaction proceeds from these perceptual premises.

This continued interplay of perceptions and the interactional accommodations to them, especially as relations extend through time, is much in evidence in Goffman's provocative book *The Presentation of Self in Everyday Life* (1959), excerpts from which provide the next to last selection in this section. He begins with the premise that what is perceived is important, then goes on to a penetrating focus upon the person as an agent purposefully influencing what is perceived. The "presentations" that persons make, whether deliberately or not, says Goffman, work to define and control the situation, thus contributing to orderly social processes; expectancies people develop vis-à-vis one another are determined by the mutual "impressions" they receive, and Goffman delineates ways in which information is presented, their varying effects upon behavior, and the motivations for their management.

He distinguishes between two kinds of sign-activity in which persons may engage, but concentrates mainly on those less "deliberate" varieties that tend to be "symptomatic" of what a person is like. His engaging book shows the utility of viewing from a theatrical perspective general interpersonal performances and the settings in which they take place. Interpersonal interactions are regulated and molded by mutual "stagings" and "readings" by the parties. These are influenced by numerous factors, as we have seen, but the course of their transactions depends upon the "script" upon which they collaborate.

Examination of interpersonal sentiments, perceptions of the other, interpersonal attraction, and interaction processes have become a prominent thread in social psychological research. A representation of this focus can be found in the anthology edited by Tagiuri and Petrullo (1958) and in the extensive work of Newcomb, the fullest statement of which is to be found in his book *The Acquaintance Process* (1961), which builds on earlier publications of 1950, 1953, 1956, and 1959. In his paper in Section VI of this volume, for instance, Newcomb comments on the importance to interpersonal attraction of attitudinal similarity, arguing that it is principally perceptions of similarity that are decisive in the process and not actual similarity. Since interaction will vary with attraction it is evident that interaction depends heavily upon interpersonal perceptions. However, the intertwining of attraction and interaction has often been noted. Both Newcomb and Homans, for instance, have pointed out that interaction enhances similarity, so that interaction and attraction are likely to be progressive phenomena, perceptually mediated.

Like Newcomb in Section VI, Blau (1964) develops the argument that attraction leads to interaction by a process (not necessarily rational) of selecting among available alternatives on the basis of expected reward. Together with Gouldner in this section—and Homans and Thibaut and Kelley in Section VI—Newcomb and Blau both look upon social interaction as a form of exchange. They are thus in the tradition of those concerned with transactional processes of social attraction which sustain ongoing social relations.

27　Interaction process analysis

ROBERT FREED BALES

Interaction process analysis is an observational method for the study of the social and emotional behavior of individuals in small groups—their approach to problem solving, their roles and status structure, and changes in these over time. The method is sometimes treated as a type of content analysis, because, like content analysis, it is employed to estimate the relative strength of various underlying determinants of overt behavior. It is distinguished from content analysis, however, in that the observer abstracts from the content, in the ordinary sense of "what is talked about," and focuses attention instead upon the form of the behavior and the changing patterns of action and reaction among individuals by which the content is communicated.

The term "interaction process analysis" was introduced into the literature as the title of a book by Bales (1950). It was presented as a generic designation for a number of similar methods. Some of these methods were then being used in experimental studies of groups, particularly studies by researchers in group dynamics; others were being used in studies of counseling and therapy, particularly research in nondirective therapy, and in studies of classroom groups. Earlier methods for the study of child play and for the study of discussion groups had appeared as much as twenty and thirty years previously. Theoretically, therefore, there is justification for using "interaction process analysis" as a generic term, but in practice it has been closely associated with the particular method and set of categories advanced by the present author.

The method to be described here was the first to be self-consciously developed as a general-purpose descriptive and diagnostic procedure designed to produce theoretically relevant measures for all sorts of small groups, thus encouraging the development of empirical norms. The method has been used by a number of different investigators, and norms as well as a number of useful empirical generalizations have resulted. In a survey of the usage of the method, Bales and Hare (1965) describe the setting, type of group, and other details, and report the total summary profile for each of 21 different studies. The revised set of categories resulting from these studies is shown in Figure 1 (Bales, 1970, p. 92).

Procedure

The observer studies the list of categories and definitions until he is thoroughly familiar with them, not only singly, but as an ordered scheme. Prior to the interaction he assigns and memorizes an identification number for each of the participants. In observing he keeps his eyes on the group as much as

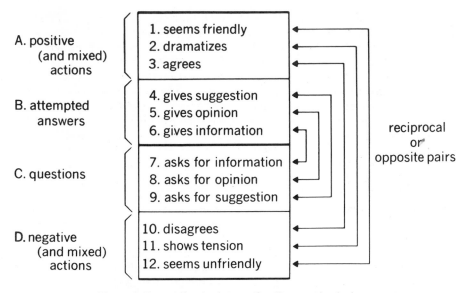

Figure 1. Categories for Interaction Process Analysis.

possible. He divides the ongoing behavior, nonverbal as well as verbal, into separate acts, each of which is recorded by entering the identification number of the person speaking, followed by the identification number of the person spoken to, under the category which best describes the act. The criterion as to how much behavior constitutes an act is pragmatic—enough to allow the observer to make a classification. A single act is essentially equivalent to a single simple sentence. Tone of voice, facial expression, bodily movement, and cues of all kinds, nonverbal as well as verbal, are used in making the classification and in determining to whom the act is directed. The group as a whole is recognized as a recipient of communication, as well as specific other individuals. But the group as a whole is not recognized as an actor. Acts performed in unison (notably laughing) are recorded by a single score but later credited back to individual actors. The observer scores continuously, usually at a rate of ten to twenty scores per minute. Comparable methods differ from each other not only as to the list of categories but also on all these points of procedure. The issues have been discussed in several standard works on methods (see Jahoda, Deutsch, & Cook, 1951; Festinger & Katz, 1953; Lindzey, 1954).

Interaction process analysis is designed for on-the-spot concurrent recording of the behavior, but it may be applied to a sound recording or a written transcript of interaction. The method was developed and is most easily applied with the aid of a laboratory observation room, connected to the group meeting room by one-way mirrors, with sound monitoring, tape recording, and a paper-moving device called an interaction recorder to enable the observer to keep scores in time sequence. None of these aids is strictly necessary, however. Hare

(1957) has applied the method to observation of the leadership behavior of boys on a playground; he used nothing more elaborate than a pencil and a pad of scoring forms. For a field study Strodtbeck (1951) used a pickup truck with a portable sound recorder. Husband-and-wife couples sat in the front seat and talked. The sound recordings were translated, where necessary, by local assistants, Strodtbeck added notations of sighs, laughs, and the like, and the interaction scoring was done by a third person from the written transcript. In an experimental study of jury deliberations Strodtbeck and Mann (1956) noted a few words of content as well as who-to-whom and nonverbal signs at the time of interaction, and the scoring was done later from these notes plus the sound recording. Some researchers may prefer a two-step method like this for the sake of higher reliability or to ease the training problem, but many successful studies have been made using on-the-spot scoring. Learning the method may require one or two months. Through training, correlation between two observers of rates in a given category over a series of sessions may be as high as .90 for some pairs of observers on the categories of higher frequency, but the same observers may find it difficult to obtain correlations higher than .60 for the categories of lower frequency.

Frame of reference

In order to present the correlates of measures to be obtained from interaction process analysis it is helpful to make reference to a three-dimensional "property space" (for which see Barton 1955) that has turned up repeatedly in factor analyses of interpersonal behavior, perceptions, and ratings persons make of each other in small groups. The space was first recognized as rather general by Carter (1954) and Couch (1960), who factor-analyzed data of their own and reviewed a series of other factor analytic studies. The work of Borgatta, Cottrell, and Meyer (1956) and Borgatta (1960) has been particularly notable in carrying on this inquiry. Hare (1962) has presented a review of the relevant studies, to which should be added the work of Leary (1957), who constructed an interpersonal diagnostic system around two of the dimensions. It has not yet been shown that the different property or factor spaces cited are all indicators of the same fundamental evaluative tendencies of persons as they view other persons and actions, but the assumption is plausible. A factor analysis by Couch (1960), which employed an exceptionally large number of measures from a study conducted with the present author, turned up as the three most important factors the same three found most important in previous studies. Couch's factor loadings form the factual basis for the description and interpretation employed here. The types of variables included overt social interaction (the present categories), personality tests, interpersonal perceptions and ratings, value statements, and observer's ratings.

DIMENSIONS OF SOCIAL EVALUATION
Let us suppose that there are at least three fundamental *dimensions of social evaluation* involved as one person views another in a group setting. The first is concerned with the degree of power, dominance, ascendance, or individual prominence of the person as perceived by the evaluator. In ordinary language this dimension is often referred to as if it were vertical in physical space: a

person is said to move "upward" in the group as his power, dominance, or prominence increases and "downward" as his power decreases.

The second dimension is concerned with the pleasant or unpleasant quality of feeling aroused by the person. If the feeling aroused in the evaluator is pleasant, one of acceptance and liking, the evaluation may be called "positive." If it is unpleasant, one of rejection and disliking, it may be called "negative." For purposes of visualization one may think of this dimension as horizontal, with positive to the right-hand side and negative to the left-hand side.

The third dimension is concerned with the value of the other person in the performance of group tasks and the achievement of group goals—that is, those tasks and goals given by acceptance of whatever authority the group recognizes. A spatial metaphor is often used to refer to this dimension: the direction toward achievement of group goals is said to be "forward"; the direction away from achievement is said to be "backward." The person who moves forward may be said to conform to the values given by acceptance of the authority that is effective within the group, while the person who moves backward may be said to deviate.

The spatial metaphors should not be taken too seriously—they are suggested here as an aid to visualization and memory. It may be, of course, that the spatial metaphors continue to be used because they provide an effective, though primitive, way of remembering a complicated set of relationships. It is not easy to find a better model for a three-dimensional set of relationships than the physical space that surrounds us. If the reader wishes to think in terms of the theory, he is urged to adopt the

physical space model. He may then think of the directions in relation to his head as the center of the space.

According to this theory, then, persons judge or evaluate each other according to their significance in relation to power, affection, and contribution to group tasks. The dimensions of social evaluation must be understood broadly as correlated clusters of more concrete attitudes of persons toward others, not as single well-defined attitudes. But so far as they can be thought of as variables, the factor studies suggest that we ought to think of the dimensions as unrelated to each other—as uncorrelated ("orthogonal" in the language of factor analysis). If the variables were actually uncorrelated, individuals would be found about equally distributed in all positions described by all combinations of the directions. Thus, the factor analytic findings imply that the possession of a position of power by a person in a small group should not lead us to expect that the possessor will be either positively or negatively evaluated (liked or disliked), or that he will be either conforming or deviant with regard to the task-oriented common values of the group. We should not expect that the task-oriented conformist is necessarily well liked, nor that the socially–emotionally oriented deviant is necessarily disliked. Knowing the person's position on any one dimension we should not expect to be able to predict his position on either of the other two dimensions.

The conception of three independent dimensions or scales along which any person or any act within the group may be given a position by the social evaluation of group members is, if truly sound and typical, a useful basis for classifying not only positions within the group but also directions of motivational movement, types of values, types of acts, types of roles—in fact anything which may be considered an object of social-psychological evaluation. Properly understood, such a dimensional space is an appropriate starting point for a classification of the functional problems of small groups (the a priori base from which the interaction categories of the present system were originally derived). The classes of functional problems as originally presented (Bales, 1950) were four in number: adaptive, integrative, instrumental, and expressive. Unfortunately, their relations to each other were not very clear. The empirical results of factor analysis now suggest that the adaptive direction may be identified as the downward direction of yielding power or submitting. Its opposite is upward or dominating. The integrative direction may be identified as the positive direction. Its opposite is disintegrative or negative. Finally, the instrumental and expressive directions turn out to be the two opposite directions of the *same* dimension, here called forward and backward.

Thus, to move upward rather than downward in the social evaluation of another person or the group means to acquire the connotation in the minds of others of overcoming by possession of power rather than of *adapting* because of lack of power. To move positively rather than negatively means to acquire the connotation of promoting feelings of social acceptance and *integration* rather than feelings of antagonism and rejection. To move forward rather than backward means to acquire the connotation of contributing *instrumentally* to the achievement of group goals rather than of encouraging deviance by the *expression* of fantasies, tensions, or feelings in such a way as to hamper achievement.

STATUS AND LEADERSHIP

Is "higher social status" the primitive meaning of "upward"? Probably what most sociologists mean by "higher status" is not simply "upward" but a combination of "upward," "positive," and "forward," in the present dimensional system. High status of an individual in the small group, as in the large, is probably best thought of as an additive combination of high evaluation on several components, not necessarily correlated with each other. In the present case, the components are uncorrelated with each other over a population of many individuals in many groups. Leadership, like high status, is a complex direction. Apparently what most group members mean when they rate a member high on leadership is that he combines the components of "upward," "positive," and "forward" movement. The traits which make for each of the components are uncorrelated over a population of many individuals in many groups. Hence, "great men" who combine them are rare. They must be simultaneously high on "activity," "likeability," and "taskability," to use the language of an earlier formulation (Bales, 1958).

The interaction profile

An interaction profile is an array of the rates of activity in each category. The profile of acts initiated by an individual is obtained by calculating the percentage of his total acts falling in each of the categories. The profile of acts received by an individual may be obtained as well as the profile of acts initiated. Individuals may be compared to each other or to general norms and scores can be translated into judgments of the individual as high, medium, or low on each category. These judgments in turn can be used as diagnostic indicators for placement of the individual on the three dimensions described above. Table 1 shows the placements most consistent with empirical evidence so far. Norms and detailed interpretations of individual placements are given in Bales (1970).

The interaction matrix

An interaction matrix is a tabulation of the number of acts addressed by each individual in a group to each other individual, and to the group as a whole, with appropriate subtotals and totals. The symbol ΣI is used to indicate the subtotal of acts addressed to specific individuals by a given actor. The symbol ΣO is used to indicate the subtotal of acts he addresses to the group as a whole rather than to specific individuals. The symbol ΣR is used to indicate the subtotal of acts he receives from all others. Finally, the term "total participation" is used to designate the sum of these three subtotals—that is, the total number of acts initiated plus the total number of acts received by that individual.

In most groups the amount initiated by a given actor to a specific other

TABLE 1

KEY FOR INTERPRETATION OF HIGH AND LOW RATES ON THE INTERACTION PROFILE[a]

	INTERACTION INITIATED		INTERACTION RECEIVED	
Interaction category	Directional components[b] indicated if the rate of initiating is:		Directional components[b] indicated if the rate of receiving is:	
1. Seems friendly	Low = N	High = P	Low = N	High = P
2. Dramatizes	Low = DF	High = UB	Low = NF	High = PB
3. Agrees	Low = NB	High = PF	Low = B	High = F
4. Gives suggestion	Low = DB	High = UF	Low = DN	High = UP
5. Gives opinion	Low = B	High = F	Low = NB	High = PF
6. Gives information	Low = U	High = D	Low = N	High = P
7. Asks for information	Low = DN	High = UP	Low = UF	High = DB
8. Asks for opinion	Low = N	High = P	Low = UP	High = DN
9. Asks for suggestion	Low = UB	High = DF	Low = B	High = F
10. Disagrees	Low = P	High = N	Low = DPB	High = UNF
11. Shows tension	Low = UF	High = DB	Low = DPF	High = UNB
12. Seems unfriendly	Low = P	High = N	Low = DPB	High = UNF

[a] High and low rates of interaction in all categories of interaction initiated and received by an individual may be combined to predict the attitudes other members may have toward that individual, that is, where they place him in the three-dimensional evaluative space. The combination is performed by addition of the directional components.

[b] A directional component is an indicator of a direction of movement in the three-dimensional evaluative space. The dimensions and directions are:

Dimension I	Dimension II	Dimension III
U = Upward	P = Positive	F = Forward
D = Downward	N = Negative	B = Backward

No movement in any direction is indicated by 0. Directional components are considered to be algebraically additive as they are in three-dimensional physical space. U and D are of opposite sign and cancel each other. The same is true of P and N, and again of F and B. Thus, U + U = 2U, but U + D = 0, and similarly for the other dimensions. The prediction of actual movement is obtained by summing all components to a single resultant direction. A resultant direction may name one, two, or three components, such as: U, UP, UPF. Thus U + P + F = UPF. A number of personality and role traits related to each resultant direction are known.

person tends to be of the same order of magnitude as the amount the other addresses to the actor. But more exactly, it is generally true that the lower of the two participators addresses a little more to the higher participator than the higher participator addresses to him. It is generally true that persons in uncontested higher power positions address a relatively large part of their total participation to the group as a whole (ΣO) rather than to specific individuals. For the highest participator in many groups the amount they address to the group as a whole (ΣO) exceeds the sum they address to all individuals specifically (ΣI). For the lowest participators, on the contrary, the amount they address to the group as a whole tends to fall short of the amount they address to specific individuals. When, for a given individual, the amount he addresses to the group as a whole exceeds the amount he addresses to specific individuals, it may be inferred that he is at least trying to move "upward." Conversely, when the amount he addresses to specific individuals exceeds the amount he addresses to the group as a whole, it may be inferred that he is tending to move "downward."

An act addressed to the group as a whole may be taken as a bid for power; an act received in return which does not require an answer or an argument may be taken as an agreement or vote of confidence. The actual power position of a given person in the group may be roughly estimated, then, by counting the number of other persons who will regularly respond to his bids for power with agreement, thus leaving him free to continue further bids for power by speaking to the group as a whole, instead of arguing with each of them specifically. The person who is successful in this way will build up a high total participation. For most individuals there is no better indicator of relative power or position in the upward–downward evaluation of the group than his total participation compared to that of others.

Phase movements

Under certain conditions of organization, and when there is a clear-cut but complex task of group decision to be arrived at within a given session, groups tend to move through an orbit of directional movement over the course of the session (Bales & Strodtbeck, 1951). They may start with preliminary pleasantries that average toward the positive side. As they begin with the task proper they move downward with high rates of giving information, then forward and upward as rates of information fall and rates of giving opinion and suggestion rise. The movement tends toward the negative side as giving opinion rises accompanied by disagreement. (Actually, rates of agreement as well as disagreement tend to rise, but on the average the negative movement is at first stronger.) Some groups, especially those which begin with low status consensus, may hang in this phase indefinitely. Others, particularly if their status problems are not severe, pass through the crisis as the group begins a period of joking and laughing. As the laughter grows and spreads, the movement swings backward, positive and downward, completing the orbit at about the same place as the starting position, on the positive side.

Somewhat similar cycles can be described for longer time spans for groups (Heinicke & Bales, 1953). It seems probable that a similar orbital model could be useful for examining successful as compared to unsuccessful episodes in child socialization, as well as other social processes which have a basic phasic character. This remains to be seen. It also seems likely that the conceptualization of evaluative space as a theory will have many applications in which actual observation of interaction may play only a minor part. It should be noted that estimates of position in the space may be made from many bases other than interaction.

28 Variables in experimental games: toward a field theory

W. EDGAR VINACKE

In recent years, the literature on experimental games expanded at an enormous rate. Most experiments concentrated on the dyad; a smaller number dealt with the triad, and still fewer looked at tetrads or larger groups. The systematic character of this research was more apparent in the painstaking manipulation of specific variables within particular game-situations than in sampling different kinds of games or in seeking to relate one type of variable to another.

Game-situations

A game may be defined as a contest conducted under specified rules, in which the outcome is not known in advance, but depends upon the actions of the participants. This definition is rather broad. However, there appears to be an advantage in adopting an inclusive definition because, ultimately, gaming must be brought within the general context of social interaction. To do so, we must seek for relationships of experimental game-situations to group discussion and problem solving, interpersonal influence and decision making, etc. Definite rules, sequences of acts, contingencies of one player on another, and the striving for definite outcomes (or payoffs), the allocation of which depends on what players do, are features particularly characteristic of games. They should not, however, obscure the fact that the fundamental issues still concern social interaction processes.

General evaluation

The present survey [1] indicates that numerous variables influence behavior in experimental games. It would be difficult

[1] The extensive coverage of literature has been omitted here, for the sake of an emphasis on Professor Vinacke's major concepts and conclusions.—Eds.

Excerpted from the **Psychological Bulletin**, 71, 293–318 (Copyright © 1969 by the American Psychological Association), with permission of the author and the publisher.

at this juncture to decide whether task, situational, or personality variables are most influential. In fact, all three are clearly important, and, therefore, theory must take this fact into account.

Consider that if we wished to influence choices in matrix games, we could use variables in any of the three categories. With respect to *task variables*, payoffs could be altered (if the range is sufficiently wide), with consequent effects on the frequency of defections and joint outcomes; or the payoff functions could be cast in a form which influences the subjects' perceptions of their advantages and disadvantages; or, finally, the length of run could be varied, thus affecting the overall level of cooperation. With respect to *situational variables*, choices could be influenced by controlling the opponent's strategy, although it appears that a sharp change in this respect is more crucial than a consistent pattern of play; choices could be strongly affected by varying the instructions, thus determining the subjects' understanding of the goal of the game; communication between players could be permitted, thus affecting not only how players perceive the general aim of the game, but also how they interpret their opponents' choices in immediate events or sequences of events; the characteristics of the opponent could be manipulated, thus also leading to special ways of viewing the situation in relation to one's own aims; and, finally, the reward could be varied, with effects as yet not wholly clear—but, at least, under high reward the subject seems to orient himself more directly to the actual consequences of his choices, possibly pays more attention to risks, self-interest, and final total outcome. With respect to *personality variables*, important differences are found between the two sexes, between age groups, and between cultures, all suggesting the general effects of perceptual, attitudinal, and motivational influences; similar implications stem from differences in family background; it is evident that attitudes relevant to the game and its goals markedly influence play, especially attitudes and values that might be labeled "exploitative-accommodative"; motives also help to determine game-behavior.

From this mass of research, many interesting problems emerge. Some of them are suggested here.

1. *The game-situation.* It is quite evident that investigators have been content with a very narrow range of games, with emphasis placed disproportionately on the Prisoner's Dilemma. It would be very desirable, at the very least, to include in experiments two or more different matrix games, rather than limiting play to only one. Such variations are especially necessary if a better understanding of personality variables is to be achieved. Throughout the present paper there recurs the significance of players' perception of the game and their interpretation of the goal. It is certainly reasonable to suppose that antecedent intrinsic properties of the subjects (together with relevant arousal conditions) partly determine the perceptions and actions of players.

Even more interesting is the question of differences between kinds of games. Preoccupation with simple matrix games may have blinded investigators to the patent fact that such games have definite characteristics which may override general behavioral processes. That is, we need to know whether findings generalize to other kinds of situations. In the triad experiments, the present investigator has tried to use a variety of games, and, in general, the exploitative-accommodative dimension appears to cut across them. However, it is obvious that the particular effects may differ in different games. Since there are interesting 2 × 2 games, in addition to Prisoner's Dilemma and Chicken, there clearly is much to be done even within the narrow scope of the matrix situation. There is no reason to suppose that "internationalists," say, differ from "isolationists" in the same fashion in different games. Indeed, Marwell and Schmitt (1968) pointed out that so-called "trivial games" [2] may be especially suitable for revealing motives and altruism (or other attitudes).

2. *Constraints of the situation.* It is clear that when the game presents very limited and formal conditions, individual differences among the subjects have little scope to manifest themselves. Geis, for example, discovered in triad experiments that Machiavellianism is related to performance under free and ambiguous conditions, but not under ambiguous conditions. It is likely that the sex differences found in triad experiments depend, in large degree, on the great freedom allowed the subjects to negotiate and to reach decisions. The highly constrained matrix game is unusually convenient for the experimenter, but it is also important to provide freer scope for subjects to behave in accordance with their perceptions, expectations, and wishes.

3. *Demand characteristics.* Preceding remarks have made it amply clear that explicit attention should be paid to the special cues of the game. Many investigators seek to reduce such effects by

carefully avoiding reference to "competition," "game," etc., in their instructions. It is difficult to say, at this point, whether this device actually eliminates the implied cues. The foregoing discussion of sex differences in the Prisoner's Dilemma illustrated the possibility that the perceptions and aims of players should be considered more explictly, even when these factors are not directly manipulated.

4. *Social interaction.* So far, investigators have gone to considerable pains to rule out actual interaction between players, although the communication variable previously discussed is certainly a step in this direction. Except for dealing with a few basic problems, there is little virtue in the artificial technique in which a stooge, experimenter, or computer takes the part of one player. By this procedure, one only eliminates what is perhaps the most important feature of the game. The simulation technique, in fact, interposes an additional obstacle between findings and extension to new areas—especially, of course, natural settings. Games are social interaction situations, and negotiation is a crucial feature. Matrix games may not be as suitable as other kinds of games for the study of negotiation (but note Beck, 1968), and, therefore, the dominant interest in them results in the postponement of information about the effects of negotiation. In any case, much more attention should be paid to games in which social interaction is permitted to occur—under such conditions, personality variables very probably will emerge more sharply.

5. *Relevance of variables.* As research with motivational variables develops, various traditions tend to become established. Thus, in the realm of social motives, which appear to be more signif-

[2] An example is a matrix in which only one player can gain at the expense of the other, as in this situation: 10,1   2,2
                      1,1   2,2

icant in game situations than do bio-genic motives, we seldom hear of any-thing but achievement and affiliation. And yet game-situations may call just as much on other motives. In addition to nurturance and power, one can mention deference, abasement, exhibition, auton-omy, recognition—to say nothing of a peculiarly disregarded motive: *play*. Why do people play games (aside from the experimenter's request)? And what rewards do they obtain from them? Cer-tainly much remains to be done to explore the personality variables most relevant to games.

Much the same point might be ad-vanced with respect to the notion that experimental games may contribute to our knowledge of international relations. There is much activity in pursuing pos-sible parallels between experimental games and problems of international conflict. In fact, these situations repre-sent one of the few meaningful avenues to an empirical treatment of problems of conflict. However, it is naive to sup-pose that international relations are really being studied in the laboratory, no matter how imaginatively various aspects of the game are labeled. It becomes important, therefore, to exam-ine closely the relevance of one to the other, and to seek for the variables which presumably are involved in both situa-tions. In this quest, attitudinal variables, such as altruism, self-interest, exploita-tiveness, etc., may be important, but we must be cautious in assuming that these labels apply similarly (if at all) to both laboratory and international conflict.

6. *Interaction.* Perhaps an obvious im-plication of this review is that even a simple game situation is influenced by multiple variables, which have inter-active effects on performance (Vinacke, 1962). It would be nice if we could follow the practice of patiently testing out one variable at a time in the classic experimental fashion. It, however, has become obvious in research on person-ality variables that we must examine interaction effects. It seems typical, in game experiments, as in other kinds, that, when two or more variables are manipulated, significant interactions are found. Thus, there appears a complex area in which systematic research must be conducted.

7. *Group size.* Finally, one of the most striking features of game experi-ments is the paucity of research with more than two players. The dyad is grossly inadequate as a model, for several reasons.

In the first place, there is a discon-tinuity between dyads and larger groups, as pointed out by Simmel (1965). A subdivision of a dyad results in an elimination of the group, whereas sub-division of any larger group does not. Thus, coalitions become a major prob-lem of investigation. To this extent, generalization about behavior from dyads is impossible without, at least, conduct-ing adequate comparisons with larger groups. Although there have been a number of studies of group size in the area of group discussion and group prob-lem solving, this topic is almost un-touched with respect to experimental games. Presently experiments are being developed with three-person matrix games, as a step in this direction. Be-yond the triad, Willis (1962) and Shears (1967) dealt with tetrads, with important implications for coalition-formation. For example, they found that alliances typically involve the *strongest* member, in contrast to his comparative disadvantage in the triad. These issues are beyond the scope of this paper, and this illustration merely serves to point out the fruitfulness of examining variations in size.

In the second place, personality variables probably may operate in a less constrained fashion in groups larger than the dyad. There may be, of course, some upper limit, but certainly phenomena attributable to personality may appear more clearly in triads, tetrads, or pentads than in dyads.

Finally, social interaction itself becomes potentially a more significant factor as groups increase in size. Probably, group properties of various kinds —role differentiation, leadership structure, cohesiveness, status, pressures to conform—exert influences not readily seen in the dyad (if they operate at all). One example comes from the ingenious experiment by Jacobs and Campbell (1961), in which a group norm was transmitted from one generation of laboratory subjects to another. Such a tradition surely is more significant for the behavior of a triad than for a dyad, in which possible influence of only one person is involved. Another example comes from an experiment (Vinacke, 1968) in which groups of three through nine played the same politics game.

Certain aspects of behavior show a systematic change with increasing size— particularly the tendency for male groups to become more exploitative. Some evidence proves that even-numbered groups (at least those of four and six persons) differ from other sizes (Bales & Borgatta, 1965).

In sum, there is a great need to break free from the dyad and to investigate larger groups.

Theory

A discussion of some of the theoretical implications of game research is in order.

FORMAL OR RATIONAL THEORIES

The theory of games has provided an important impetus to research with experimental games. This theory rests on two major assumptions: (a) a person will obtain and process all available information in a situation; and (b) response is strictly determined by this information. To these points could be added a utility principle: The person acts to maximize gain and minimize

TABLE 1

COALITIONS PREDICTED BY THE THEORY OF PERCEPTION OF STRENGTH
AND BY THE THEORY OF STRICTLY RATIONAL ANALYSIS

Power pattern	Players and weights	Coalitions based on perception of strength[a]	Coalitions based on rational analysis[b]
All-Equal	A = 1, B = 1, C = 1	Any	Any
All-Powerful	A = 3, B = 1, C = 1	None or few	None
All-Different	A = 4, B = 3, C = 2	BC[c]	Any

[a] Caplow (1956).
[b] Theory of games.
[c] This coalition typically occurs.

loss. Choices in a game are, from this standpoint, a function of the task and situational variables described above, especially the former. This approach sees behavior as wholly rational in a formal sense—that is, where facts and their interpretation are independent of the person,[3] and can be fully described without reference to the actor. Extending these principles a little, allowance for considerable variation in strategy is possible. For example, choices other than the optimal ones are aspects of performance intended to promote, in the long run, the best interests of the player in achieving the rational solution.

The influence of this type of theory has made it extremely difficult for many theorists to accept the fact that cooperation in the Prisoner's Dilemma game is typically not greater than it is. Lieberman (1962), among others, noted that the assumptions of game theory are not borne out in research. In one of his experiments, players apparently varied their strategies simply to alleviate boredom or to make the game more interesting (Lieberman, 1960). The foregoing survey of research also demonstrates how frequently experimental results fail to agree with a strictly rational viewpoint. In general, cooperation is less than 50%, under standard conditions, and may fall as low as 10%. Under appropriate conditions, it may rise to a very high level. Even if we discard conditions which may be regarded as facilitating the discovery of the rational outcome, there remain factors that cannot be explained solely on the basis of the assumptions stated above.

Our triad experiments also reveal that actual behavior often fails to agree

[3] Failure to act in accordance with information thus defined is treated as failure, error, irrational, etc.

with a strictly rational view. Table 1 summarizes predictions based on derivations from game theory and from Caplow's (1956) theory of power differences, together with coalitions typically found. Obviously, players act more on the basis of their *perceptions* of the power relations than on a rational analysis of their significance. Beyond that, females represent a number of puzzling kinds of behavior which reveal the importance of special attitudes. Whereas males appear typically to treat the game as a competition in which individual gain is salient, associated with a desire to win at whatever cost, females appear to treat the game as a social interaction situation in which equitable outcomes are sought. Especially striking evidence of this orientation is provided by a significant tendency by female triads to establish triple alliances (hardly predictable from any "rational" theory) and to make altruistic offers. Offers of this latter kind are those in which one member proposes that two other members form a coalition to *their* advantage —a phenomenon that practically never occurs in male triads. It is a mistake to say that females are not competitive or that they do not enjoy winning. Rather, it is a matter of how problems are perceived and solved. It is better to say that males tend to be exploitative and females tend to be accommodative.

Gamson (1961) suggested an alternative interpretation to account for the occurrence of alliances between weak players. He called it the "cheapest winning" alliance, and it represented essentially another rational or formal interpretation, as shown in Table 2. In this case, the players are assumed to act in accordance with their analysis of relative gains in each possible coalition. Weaker players can ostensibly gain more in alli-

TABLE 2
COALITIONS AS PREDICTED BY GAMSON'S THEORY OF CHEAPEST
WINNING COALITION

Power pattern	Players and weights	Comparative advantages of coalitions, if based on proportional gain	Gain to B	Gain to C
All-Different	$A = 4, B = 3, C = 2$	AB (43) = 57% + 43%	43%	—
		AC (42) = 67% + 33%	—	33%
		BC (32) = 60% + 40%	60%	40%
		Net for BC	17%	7%

ance with each other than either can gain in alliance with the strong player. Unfortunately, this theory cannot be tested in triads, because the outcomes generally agree with those based on the perception-of-strength theory. A proper test requires that the cheapest winning coalition be different from the weak winning coalition, a condition that needs more than three players. Table 3 sets forth this condition for tetrads and pentads. Note that the cheapest winning coalition involves the stronger player in a two-person alliance, but the weak winning coalition is a three-person alliance. Both Willis (1962) and Shears (1967) carried out experiments with tetrads. They determined that the two-person strong alliance very often occurs, but the weak three-person alliance also occurs frequently. Here, of course, we must consider that a coalition among three members is more difficult to reach than a two-person coalition, since the former usually requires more negotiation and demands greater trust, points which indicate the necessity for additional types of experimental manipulation. In any case, obviously, the Gamson version of a strictly rational theory is not sufficient.

In general, then, the implication of rational theories that every sensible person ought to act in a formally predicted fashion, given certain stated conditions, is unjustified. Apparently, game theory *could* incorporate situational and personality variables as components, but to do so might violate the basic assump-

TABLE 3
PREDICTIONS IN TETRADS AND PENTADS FOR
GAMSON CHEAPEST WINNING COALITION
AND COALITION BASED ON PERCEPTION
OF STRENGTH

Size	Players and weights	Cheapest winning coalition	Perception of strength (weakest coalition)
Tetrad	$A = 4$ $B = 3$ $C = 2$ $D = 1$	AB (43) AC (42)	BCD (321)
Pentad	$A = 5$ $B = 4$ $C = 3$ $D = 2$ $E = 1$	AB (54) AC (53)	BCDE (4321)

Note.—The All-Different power pattern is shown. This pattern does not fully distinguish the position of Player B, who stands to gain more from coalition with A than from the weakest coalition. However, it does yield a distinction between the smaller strong coalition and the larger weak coalition. In the Tetrad, C would receive the same gain in either coalition.

tions or render the analysis overly complex. Indeed, some game theorists seem convinced that differences between subjects are accidental or trivial and, therefore, should be dismissed or ignored. This attitude would make sense only if such differences could be accounted for by task and well-defined situational variables. The evidence runs counter to this possibility, except when bothersome personality variables are ruled out by task constraints or by various control procedures.

PERSONALITY VARIABLES

As an alternative, a theory could be developed based on the motives, attitudes, and perceived goals of the persons who play the game. Such a theory would be based on assumptions that intrinsic properties of the person determine the perception of goals, the interpretation of task and situational conditions, and that motivational states determine the responses that will be made. A need factor could be added, to the effect that people act to satisfy their motives. In this case, task and situational variables could be treated as incidental conditions. If there were no differences among subjects, they would be explained on the grounds that inappropriate tasks have been chosen or that the subjects have not been sufficiently aroused, and so on. We could then search for new tasks and new conditions to differentiate persons, which could lead to an infinite regression. Instead, we could search for general attitudes and motives especially relevant to the game-situation.

Studies previously cited attest to the role played by personality variables. An instance comes from the present experimenter's studies with triads, in which the occurrence of sex differences led to the formulation of contrasting exploitative and accommodative attitudes. Some male groups act much like females, and some female groups resemble male groups. This consideration led to the development of a simple questionnaire, a Test of Strategy, intended to measure these attitudes in both sexes. Samples of the two sexes score significantly differently on this test. In a recent experiment, Vinacke et al. (1968) preselected triads on the basis of this test. They composed for each sex sets of three triads, one with all members high in accommodativeness, one with all three high in exploitativeness, and one with all three intermediate in these tendencies. These triads of triads engaged in three games, both under intragroup and intergroup conditions of negotiation. All three games displayed differences between highly accommodative and highly exploitative groups in the expected direction.

It, therefore, would be quite possible to adduce as strong evidence in favor of a personality theory as in favor of a strictly rational theory. But however clearly personality variables enter into games, it is easy to establish conditions in which significant differences between groups do not appear. One reason lies in the possible selection of a variable which is not relevant to the situation; another reason lies in the possibility that the experimental conditions fail to activate sufficiently an attitude or motive. The major reason, no doubt, lies in the fact that task and situational variables are also important, and may either attenuate or override personality variables. Thus, a theoretical approach based primarily on personality variables is no more satisfactory than one based on task and situational variables.

FIELD THEORY

People are neither wholly rational in the game-theoretical sense, nor wholly guided by antecedent intrinsic characteristics. Rather, behavior is a function of those forces—whatever they may be in their relative intensity—that operate at the time response occurs. Something like Lewinian field theory holds the best promise for interpreting experimental games. We need to look comprehensively at the interaction between person and environment, identifying variables from both directions and seeking to determine how they are related in producing behavior. It is grossly artificial to believe that subjects can be treated as if they were all alike. It is equally artificial to eliminate variations in the situations where behavior takes place. Thus, emphasis needs to be placed on the interpretation of interactions between the forces that can meaningfully be measured in both person and situation.

29   Spatial factors in face-to-face interaction

ROBERT SOMMER

Small group ecology

As early as 1931, the sociologist Bogardus had stated, "It is only as social and physical facts can be reduced to, or correlated with, spatial facts that they can be measured at all" (Bogardus, 1931). However, the systematic study of spatial factors in face-to-face groups did not begin until 1950 with the study by Steinzor. As a leader of discussion groups, Steinzor had noticed one man change his seat in order to sit directly opposite another man with whom he had previously had a verbal altercation. Steinzor then went back through the past interaction records to see if group members were more likely to interact with people whom they could see. He found that when one person in the group finished speaking, it was the man opposite rather than someone alongside who was the next to speak (Steinzor, 1950). Hearn found that the type of leadership within a group interacted with spatial effects to influence participation. With minimal leadership, people directed more comments to those sitting opposite (the Steinzor effect), but when a strong leader was present, people directed more com-

Excerpted from Chapter 5 of **Personal Space: The Behavioral Basis of Design** (© 1969 by Prentice-Hall, Inc., Englewood Cliffs, N.J.), and reprinted with permission of the author and publisher.

ments to adjacent seats (Hearn, 1957). This illustrates the role played by eye contact in face-to-face groups. Based on studies of dominance (see Sommer, 1969, Ch. 2), we can hypothesize that with a strong leader close by, the individual restricts his gaze to adjacent seats, but when leadership is weak or absent, he can look anywhere and the stimulus value of people opposite becomes heightened.

Textbooks of group dynamics and ap-

plied psychology frequently allude to the idea that certain arangements of people are more suited to certain activities than others. We decided to investigate this problem, not from the standpoint of specific practical tasks such as might occur in a work situation, but from that of certain attitudes (cooperation, competition, or separate action) and observe how people arranged themselves.

a. *Rectangular tables.* Each student

PERCENTAGE OF Ss CHOOSING THIS ARRANGEMENT

Seating arrangement	Condition 1 (conversing)	Condition 2 (cooperating)	Condition 3 (co-acting)	Condition 4 (competing)
	42	19	3	7
	46	25	32	41
	1	5	43	20
	0	0	3	5
	11	51	7	8
	0	0	13	18
TOTAL	100	100	100	99

Figure 1. Seating preferences at rectangular tables.

was asked to indicate his own seating and that of a friend on diagrams showing a rectangular table (1–2–1–2). Students overwhelmingly chose a corner-to-corner or face-to-face arrangement for casual conversation (see Fig. 1). The explanation emphasized both physical proximity and visual contact in these arrangements. The students selected a side-by-side arrangement for cooperative activity and explained that it was easier to share things this way. Competing pairs generally chose face-to-face seating, although some used a distant seating pattern. Those who chose the face-to-face arrangement maintained that this stimulated competition. Various distant or catty-corner arrangements were selected by students who worked separately at the same table (co-acting pairs). The students cited the minimal eye contact in a catty-corner

arrangement—e.g.: "It allows staring into space and not into my neighbor's face."

b. *Round tables.* A similar questionnaire was used with another group, except that a diagram showed a round table surrounded by six chairs. Most pairs who wanted to converse or work together used adjacent chairs. Again the reasons emphasized psychological closeness: "I want to chat with my friend, not the whole cafeteria, so I sit next to her," and "more intimate, there are no physical barriers between us." The competing pairs chose to sit directly across from one another to keep from seeing each other's work, and to stimulate competition by being able to see how the other was doing. The students working separately left empty chairs between one another.

c. *Psychological intimacy.* A question

PERCENTAGE OF Ss CHOOSING THIS ARRANGEMENT

Seating arrangement	Condition 1 (conversing)	Condition 2 (cooperating)	Condition 3 (co-acting)	Condition 4 (competing)
	63	83	13	12
	17	7	36	25
	20	10	51	63
TOTAL	100	100	100	100

Figure 2. Seating preferences at round tables.

of some relevance in seating behavior is the psychological closeness of different arrangements. We asked groups of approximately 100 college students each in the United States, England, Holland, Sweden, and Pakistan to rate a series of 37 arrangements of pairs seated at square, round, and rectangular tables along a scale from "very intimate and psychologically close," to "very distant and psychologically remote." The rank order of closeness was identical in all five countries. Side-by-side seating was always the most intimate, followed by corner seating, face-to-face seating, and various distant or catty-corner arrangements.

d. *Distance and intimacy.* Russo (1967) asked students to rate diagrams of seating arrangements at a rectangular table (2–1–2–1). She found that increased distance produced ratings of less acquaintance, less friendliness, and lower talkativeness, except where increased eye contact counteracted the effects of increased distance. Even though the physical distance was greater between two people at the head and foot of the table, there was more psychological closeness between them than between people in a diagonal arrangement. The cultural influence of the head position was evident on the equality dimension. When one person was at the head of the table, the pair was considered less equal than if both members were at the ends of the table or both were at the sides.

e. *Children's seating arrangements.* An attempt was made to verify experimentally some of the questionnaire results from Studies A and B. We wanted to test children in cooperative competitive, and co-acting activities to determine how they would arrange themselves. Cooperating pairs sat side by side, competing pairs used a corner arrange-

ment, and children working on separate tasks used a catty-corner arrangement. Very few children sat directly opposite one another, a widely used arrangement in studies of adults, second only in popularity to corner seating. It is likely that a 30-inch distance across the table was a much longer psychological distance on the children's scale than it would be for adults. As in previous studies, girls made more use than boys of side-by-side seating (Norum, *et al.*, 1967). Elkin also found that sitting across was uncommon among young children but increased in frequency with age, while sitting side by side decreased with age (Elkin, 1964).

f. *Adult pairs.* Since the previous study used children with a specific task, an additional study using adults with a different task seemed warranted. Each subject was told nothing about the task he was to perform, but only that his partner (or opponent) had already arrived and was waiting in the experimental room. The room contained a large rectangular table (4–1–4–1), and the decoy always occupied the same chair—one from the end along the side of the table. The perceived relationship of cooperation or competition had a significant effect on seating. In the cooperative condition, 13 people sat on the same side of the table as the decoy and 11 sat opposite. In the competitive condition, only four sat on the same side as the decoy, and 19 sat opposite. There was a trend, not statistically reliable, for females to make greater use of side-by-side seating.

g. *Approval seating motives.* Rosenfeld (1965) asked students to enter a room (in which a decoy was already seated) and to behave in such a way as to show the seated person that "you want to become friendly with her."

Other subjects were told to imagine that the decoy was a girl they did not like and "you want to let her know that you don't want to become friendly with her." In both cases the subject was instructed not to come right out and tell the other person how he felt, but to communicate his feelings in other ways. The average distance the subject remained from the decoy in the approval-seeking condition was 57 inches, compared to an average of 94 inches in the avoidance condition.

h. *Discussion topic*. Michael McNeill attempted to test the effects of discussion topics on seating arrangements at a rectangular table (1–3–1–3). Forty pairs of college girls were given topics that ranged from those very personal (Sex as Communication) to those that were relatively impersonal. The results showed that the topic made almost no difference in seating. Twenty pairs sat corner to corner, 12 sat opposite, and eight sat side by side [1] and this was composed of a perfect 5–3–2 for each of the four discussion topics. It seems apparent that it is the nature of the relationship between the individuals rather than the topic itself that characterizes a discussion as personal or impersonal. Two lovers discussing the weather can have an intimate conversation, but a zoology professor discussing sex in a lecture hall containing 300 students would be having an impersonal session regardless of the topic.

i. *Personal space on long benches.* Brian Talcott studied seating patterns at three 12-foot long benches at a Berkeley bus stop. Each bench could conceivably accommodate six people (allowing two feet per person), but it was typical to find two people, one at each

[1] This ratio is similar to that found in our cafeteria studies (cf. Sommer, 1959).

end, "filling" the bench to the extent that other people would stand around or sit on a nearby stone wall rather than occupy a center position. Mr. Talcott concluded that these long bus benches were inefficient and alternatives such as smaller sizes, or the introduction of armrests as barriers should be tested. As in the library, the first occupant of the bench gravitated to an end position, and the second occupant went to the opposite end. It is noteworthy that the sex of the person seated at the other end of the bench was irrelevant to the second occupant. A male was just as likely to sit down at one end of the bench with a female at the other end as when a male was at the other end. The lack of any sexual segregation indicates that the incumbent was able to remain a nonperson. Although this can be considered a desirable feature from the standpoint of maintaining privacy, the efficiency of 12-foot benches that accommodate a maximum of two people can be questioned.

j. *The limits of comfortable conversation.* This study was based on the previous observation that people conversing prefer to sit across from one another, although at some slight angle, rather than side by side. However, it is obvious that this must be qualified by the size of the gap between the people. If two men are given the choice of conversing across from one another at a distance of 30 feet or sitting side by side on a sofa, they will select the sofa. This means that people will sit across from one another until the distance between them exceeds the limit for comfortable conversation. By noting the point at which people begin to sit side by side, we can learn the limits of comfortable conversation under the particular conditions used. Two sofas in an attractively furnished lounge were placed at prearranged distances from one another before each session. Pairs of subjects were asked to enter the lounge and discuss various impersonal topics. When the couches were placed one to three feet apart, people sat opposite one another. This does not mean they sat directly opposite one another since one person may have sat on the left side of one couch whereas the other sat on the right side of the other couch. However, the people did sit on different couches. From three-and-one-half feet and beyond, people sat side by side. It can be noted that, with couches like these, people's heads are usually one foot behind the front of the couch. Using the architect's concept of nose-to-nose distance, our subjects began to sit side by side when they were five-and-one-half feet apart. Under the particular conditions we used—two people who knew each other slightly discussing an impersonal topic in a large lounge—this can be considered the upper limit for comfortable conversation. In many private homes, however, conversational distance is much longer. One difference is the room scale is smaller in private homes, and there is some evidence that as room size becomes larger, people sit closer together. The same occurs when noise level and distraction increase.

k. *Conversational distance side by side and across.* The couches used in Study J permitted distance across to be varied systematically. It seemed desirable to conduct a further investigation in which four chairs were substituted for the two couches, which meant that the side-by-side distance could be varied, too. If people are given a choice between sitting five feet apart and across from one another or five feet apart but alongside one another, how will they sit? The results support the idea that people who want to converse will sit across from one another rather than side by side. However, the preference for sitting opposite is true only when the distance across is equal to or less than the side-by-side distance. When the distance across was greater than the distance side by side, most pairs sat side by side.

l. *Conversational and co-acting groups.* On one college campus, we found a cafeteria that served a number of different functions. During meal hours it was a crowded eating place, but between meals it was a half-empty lounge and study place for assorted students and employees. This made it possible to study spatial arrangements in the same setting by people who were eating, conversing, or studying. The observations took place over a one-year period during nonmeal hours, and a distinction was made between people who were interacting (conversing or studying together) and those who were co-acting (occupying the same table but studying or drinking coffee separately). At the small square tables, interacting pairs showed a definite preference for corner seating, whereas co-acting pairs sat opposite one another. At the rectangular tables interacting pairs preferred corner seating and, to a lesser extent, opposite seating. However, more than two-thirds of the co-acting pairs chose distant arrangements that separated the two people spatially and visually.

Discussion and implications

We have seen that the spacing of individuals in small groups is not random but follows from the personality and cultural backgrounds of the individuals involved, what they are doing, and the nature of the physical setting. Stated more simply, we can say that spatial arrangements in small groups are functions of personality, task, and environment. Anthropologist Edward Hall has described how people from different countries interpret the language of space. What Americans experience as crowded, Latin Americans may perceive as spacious. A Latin American official who gave Hall a tour of a factory remarked, upon opening the door of an 18 × 20 foot office that contained seventeen clerks at individual desks, "See, we have nice spacious offices. Lots of space for everyone." Furniture in the American's home is placed around the edges, but the Japanese family gather in the middle of the room. An American in the Middle East or Latin America is likely to feel crowded and hemmed in—people come too close, lay their hands on him, and crowd against his body. He doesn't feel this in England or Scandinavia where it is the American who perceives the local residents as cold and aloof (Hall, 1966). Small group ecology is particularly suited to cross-cultural studies since spatial arrangement can be easily and reliably recorded using inexpensive photographs as well as diagrams and moving pictures, and such recordings do not depend on the use of language or extensive familiarity with the culture. Questionnaires using diagrams and drawings with minimum reliance on language are also practicable. Whether there are general principles of spacing that apply in most cultures is an interesting question. Humans everywhere have a similar arrangement of sense organs, although they may use them differently. Since our eyes are at the front of our heads, since we have simple rather than compound eyes, and since we locate things spatially by sound as well as sight, certain consistencies in spatial arrange-

ments could arise regardless of culture. On the other hand, Westerners are communicating to an increasing extent by telephone, letter, and teletype, which frees interaction from spatial constraints.[2]

Personality differences as distinct from cultural factors have been the subject of less investigation. Several studies have shown that introverts remain further away from other people than do extroverts, which is another way of saying that spatial distance as well as social distance are aspects of what we call introversion (see Williams, 1963; Leipold, 1963). Fear of rebuke tends to increase individual distance but approval seeking reduces it. A shared fear such as that produced by a ghost story reduces social distance (Feshbach & Feshbach, 1963), and it seems probable that internal threat—some danger originating within the group itself—would increase the average spatial distance between individuals. The most extreme form of withdrawal from other people is manifested by schizophrenic individuals who are fearful of being hurt in social intercourse. Our studies have shown that they not only remain too far from others but on occasions come too close (Sommer, 1959). This was particularly evident in decoy studies in which male and

[2] Most of these studies have been concerned with the arrangement of people vis-à-vis one another rather than with respect to barriers, borders, and boundaries. There is a line of research typified by the work of de Jonge that has focused on the way people arrange themselves in parks, recreational areas, and buildings. He has found a preference for areas that are marked, bounded, and make possible visual contact with surrounding areas. Other studies by de Jonge (see 1967–68) in Dutch railway stations, cafeterias, and reading rooms show clearly that people gravitate to wall locations that have privacy and the opportunity for visual contact with the outside in preference to exposed tables in central areas.

female schizophrenics sat immediately alongside a male decoy whom they knew slightly or not at all, which happened rarely if ever among the normal group. This behavior on the part of the schizophrenic violates the personal space of others who become offended by his excessive closeness. One can speculate on whether this relates to the schizophrenic's lack of a stable self-image and clear self-boundaries. A person unsure of who he is may not be clear as to where he ends and the next person begins.

Kleck and his associates have undertaken an interesting series of studies on the effect of stigma upon interaction distance. College students were asked to go into a room and converse with another person who was sometimes described as an epileptic. They sat further from the other person when he was described as an epileptic than when he was not. The experiment was repeated with the other person described either as "warm and friendly" or "cold and unfriendly." It was found that people sat further away from the "unfriendly" person than from the "friendly" person (see Kleck, 1970). A further study was done to learn how far people would remain from an amputee. In this case a young man in a specially adapted wheel chair simulated the amputee. College students were asked to enter the room and teach either the amputee or a normal person to fold paper figures. The students sat further from the amputee than from a supposedly normal individual (Kleck et al., 1969). These studies were supported by grants from an association to aid crippled children, which was interested in exploring the isolation experienced by stigmatized individuals. The fact that a person in a wheel chair is kept at a greater distance would be likely to have some effect upon his motivation, attitudes, and feelings of belonging with normal individuals.

There is a definite need for studies of the ecology of natural work groups, not only as a complement for laboratory studies, but from the standpoint of determining how task affects physical arrangements. Whyte studied the ecology of 12 Chicago restaurants where friction between the dining room and the kitchen employees was commonplace. He attributed some conflict to the role reversal that occurred when female waitresses handed orders to male cooks who were more highly paid and skilled than the waitresses. Whyte found the difficulty could be resolved by eliminating direct face-to-face contact between waitresses and cooks (Whyte, 1956). Some restaurants reduce the friction by having the waitresses place the customers' orders on slips that are attached on a clipboard to the window between kitchen and dining room. The men pick off the order slips, fill them, and put the plates in the compartment where the waitresses pick them up, thus eliminating all face-to-face contacts. In the code of the American West, a face-to-face encounter constituted a challenge that could not be ignored. The prudent man stepped aside when the top guns walked down the street. Dwight Eisenhower describes this code in a speech delivered in November 1953:

I was raised in a little town . . . called Abilene, Kansas. We had as our Marshal a man called Wild Bill Hickok. Now that town had a code, and I was raised as a boy to prize that code. It was: Meet anyone face-to-face with whom you disagree. You could not sneak up on him from behind, or do any damage to him, without suffering the penalty of an enraged citizenry. If you met him face-to-face and took the same risks as he did, you could get away with almost anything, as long as the bullet was in front (see Aurthur, 1966).

The studies described here tell us many things about the way that people in face-to-face groups, predominately Americans, use space. It will only be a matter of time before comparable studies of other cultures begin to appear in the literature. Certainly the work of Hall (1959, 1966) and Birdwhistell (1952) augurs well in this regard. However, it is important to ask how these findings can be applied in practice—how they can be marketed to do some good and increase the sum total of human happiness. If one finds that French Canadian students are able to tolerate closer presence than can their English Canadian counterparts, does this mean that a Quebec architect can (a) use a smaller room for the same number of students, (b) double the number of students in ordinary size classrooms, or (c) attempt to change the students' spatial preferences by increasing the distances between chairs? The answers must be given in terms of goals, objectives, and values rather than technical specifications. The architect can develop the present trends even further—take advantage of the closeness of French-Canadian students and use smaller classrooms —or make the classroom more sociofugal in order to keep the students away from one another—or he can disregard this finding completely. What he *should* do is a question of value that involves something which he creates himself or accepts from others; it does not flow out of the problem itself. It is possible to treat symmetry and harmony as absolute values and arrange the classrooms in terms of a spatial esthetic under the assumption that schoolchildren are exceedingly plastic and should be molded

in line with universal and logical spatial principles. I prefer to begin with the idea that man himself and what he wants to do (his value system) represents the yardstick by which design solutions must be measured.

This still leaves open the question of how studies of *what is* can help in deciding *what should be*. These two conditions are not necessarily independent; what presently exists tends to become sacred (i.e., valuable in its own right). A designer is rarely criticized for doing what has been done in the past; he may not get much praise for it either, but there will be few cries of indignation or outrage. There are reasons—historical, cultural, economic, and functional —why things developed as they did. The schoolhouse is not simply the result of accident and inadequate theorizing; it arose in response to a certain type of teaching (sit and learn) in a certain type of society. Studying the nature of nature has always been an important part of any scientific field although one finds it occasionally labeled as a preliminary or "pre-experimental" activity.

Observational data can also be used in teaching people who must work in various settings. An English-Canadian teacher may feel uncomfortable at the close proximity of her French-Canadian pupils and her French-Canadian colleagues. Not being aware that this is part of their culture, she may feel personally affronted and assaulted—on the edge of panic. The Jewish child from New York's lower East Side where close contact is the rule is likely to feel that people in the Midwest are cold and distant. Apart from the idea of designing schools for Puerto Rican or Jewish children that take into account the way these children use time and space— and I want to emphasize that I am not sure how this can be done—there seems the more practical possibility of using knowledge of the ethnic group to prepare teachers from other backgrounds who will work with the children. One teaches *what is* to people who must deal with the present situation rather than, in the case of building a school for X group of children, equating what is with what should be.

From a practical standpoint, knowledge of how groups arrange themselves can assist in fostering or discouraging relationships. A library that is intended to be sociofugal space, where interaction is discouraged, requires knowledge of how to arrange people to minimize unwanted contact. One possibility is to use the rank order of preferred arrangements by interacting groups as arrangements to be avoided in sociofugal space. On this basis, corner seating would be less satisfactory than opposite or distant seating in the sociofugal setting. An Emily Post or Amy Vanderbilt may know these principles intuitively, and diplomatic protocol may codify them, but there is need to make them explicit and subject them to empirical test. To an increasing extent we find ourselves being arranged by impersonal environments in lecture halls, airports, waiting rooms, and lobbies. Many aspects of the proximate environment have been placed for ease of maintenance and efficient cleaning with little cognizance given to their social functions. These principles will be of most help in institutional settings where the occupants have little control over their surroundings. The study of small group ecology is important, not only from the standpoint of developing an adequate theory of human society that takes into account the context of social relationships, but also from the practical standpoint of designing and maintaining functional spaces where human relationships can develop.

30 Role and role conflict

RAYMOND G. HUNT

Conceptual framework

Any social system, and especially a formal organization, may be viewed structurally as an at least partially interlocking complex of *positions*. These positions represent the functional divisions of labor deemed useful to achievement of the system's goals and are populated by a collection of particular individuals each of whom occupies at least one but commonly more than one of them (cf. Gross, *et al.*, 1958, and in connection with much of what follows).

Organizationally the positional structure of social systems follows a general "principle" of complementarity. Positions tend to be grouped as dyadic units around a set of complementary rights and duties—complementary in that the "rights" of a given or *focal-position* are the "duties" of some other or *counter-position* and the "rights" of the latter are the "duties" of the former. Thus the focal-position "child" may be analyzed in relation to complementary counter-positions "mother" and/or "father." Each position in a system, therefore, is differentiated with reference to one or more other positions in relation to which it stands in complementary contrast.

This complementary contrast is, of course, a function basically of the complex patterns of behavior organized around these positions and embodying the relevant mutual expectations (the rights and duties) *vis à vis* one another

held by occupants of positions. It is possible, therefore, to regard social process as an interaction of positions patterned in terms of these complementary expectations which are themselves called *roles*.

It will be seen that a role represents the content of a position or the behavioral implications of positional occupancy and that, for a given social system, the shape of social interaction will depend heavily upon the position-role differentiations and definitions current within it. Moreover, because roles entail expectations for attributes (i.e., personal characteristics) as well as for behavior, they also contribute to definitions of personal identity (self) and thereby further influence interaction indirectly (see Goffman, 1959, 1961).

It is important to remember that a role can be comprehensively described only with reference to other roles associated with positions complementary to that occupied by the "role player." In most instances a given focal-position or role (e.g., teacher) will stand in organizational relation to more than a single counter-position (e.g., pupil, colleague, principal, etc.). The totality of counter-positions that can be set in meaningful complementary contrast with a given focal-position is therefore said to describe that focal-position's *role-set* (cf. Kahn, *et al.*, 1964). Thus, the role-set

Abridged from Chapter 4 of H. J. Hartley & G. E. Holloway (Eds.), **Focus on Change and the School Administrator**, Buffalo, N.Y.: State University of New York, School of Education, 1965, pp. 37–46, with permission of the publisher.

of a "teacher" includes, among others, the counter-positions "pupil," "colleague," "principal," etc. Taking these counter-positions one at a time, the particular array of expectations associated with the relationship between a given focal-position (teacher) and a single counter-position (principal) is termed a *role-sector* (cf. Gross, *et al.*, 1958). The idea of the role-sector makes plain the fact that roles vary somewhat depending upon the particular counter-position comprising the other half of the dyad at a given time. In other words, the "teacher" role is different in relation to "principal" from what it is in relation to "pupil."

We might observe that some theorists (e.g., Sarbin, 1954) regard positions as the units of *society* (structure) and roles as the units of *culture* (content or function). It is also useful to point out that the term position is here used as some earlier theorists (Linton, 1945) used the term *status*.[1] We shall see later, however, that it is useful to reserve the term *status* for another purpose and so avoid much confusion.

The differentiation of roles

We may assume that through the complex processes of socialization individuals develop modes for representing the panoply of positional differentiations and role patternings defining the social system in which they operate. Some of these representations they will acquire as a result of direct experience and others will develop as a consequence of indirect influences. At all events these representations will be *individualized* matters and

[1] The term "office" has also been used to signify the same structural notion, but with some differences in connotation (see Gerth & Mills, 1946).

so will entail some variation between persons even within the same social system. Therefore, our conceptualization of roles must be sufficiently discriminated to accommodate the fact and ramifications of variation.

Hence it is helpful to consider the following role varieties:

1. *Role prescriptions:* These may be thought of as the "cultural requirements" within a social system. A description of a role prescription is an *abstraction* drawn from aggregating the behaviors of a number of occupants of comparable positions. Thus it represents some sort of behavioral central tendency among the several positional occupants distributed through space and time. Consequently, a role prescription, once stated, is extremely unlikely to be exemplified by any specific single individual. This is why, of course, the anthropologist commonly employs a number of informants before constructing a "model" of a society's role patterns.

2. *Role stereotypes:* While we can take role prescriptions to be abstractly defined cultural givens, we must recognize that individuals encounter concrete representations of them in a manifold of ways and contexts. These we can call variant manifestations. From these, we postulate, the individual synthesizes personalized representations of the cultural requirements which may exhibit considerable variation as between persons. These personal role constructions we call *role stereotypes*. It is important to bear in mind that the word stereotypes here implies no judgment of the adequacy of the construction. A given person's stereotype *may* be highly idiosyncratic or it may be largely shared. The point is that it is necessarily stereotypic psychologically for there is no determinate evidential base for its evalu-

ation. It is a cognitive or mediational process built up from a "sample" from the universe of possible exposures.

3. *Role expectations:* We have already observed that any construction of a role includes specifications concerning the behavior both of the person himself and also of the behavior of the occupants of positions complementary to his own. It is common practice to refer to that aspect of a total role construction that refers to the behavior of another as a "role expectation." While we have talked of this matter in terms of complementarities of positions it would be perfectly legitimate to use the term "role expectation" to refer to any anticipation of particular behavior patterns contingent upon another's occupancy of any given position regardless of any relationship to one's own.

Persons holding expectations concerning the role performances of others commonly strive to communicate their expectations to the focal-person in hopes of influencing the latter to conform to them. Each of the counter-persons communicating such expectations can be thought of as a *role-sender* and his communicated expectations can be called a *sent-role* (cf. Kahn, *et al.*, 1964). A focal-person's perceptions of the totality of sent-roles respecting his position will weigh heavily in shaping his role stereotype—indeed, if we define any source of information (including mass media, films, etc.) concerning a role as a role-sender, then we could define role stereotypes as synthesized perceptions of sent-roles.

With these statements in mind, it can be seen that any social system constitutes a more or less complex mutual influence network. Organizationally, the system is describable and definable in terms of the temporally-relative functional relations or influence patterns among the positions into which the system has been structurally differentiated.

4. *Role enactments:* The constructs we have stated thus far have been cognitive or mediational in form.[2] We may posit that they will operate among the determinants of the actual behavior manifested by a given positional occupant. However, as these cognitive aspects of roles are abstract and/or stereotypic they function as schemas or behavior models and not as exclusive causal agents. In short, the actual role *behavior* exhibited by a person will be associated with a variety of antecedent conditions and variables among which the cognitive components of roles will be only one (though highly important ones). Thus we shall refer to a person's actual role behavior as a "role enactment." Now from what we have already said it is plain that role enactments can vary between individuals occupying similar positions either as a result of variations in their cognitive role constructions, or because of variations in the "stimulus" field in which they behave, or, of course, both. Furthermore, the role enactments of a single person can vary through time as a function of the same factors.

5. *Counter-role expectations:* While this label is unfortunately cumbersome, it refers to another highly important aspect of role phenomena that requires mention; from his perceptions of sent-roles, and also from more subtle sources (see Goffman, 1959), each person not only develops constructions pertaining to his own behavior and expectations of others' behavior, he likewise forms con-

---

[2] We have not and will not consider how roles are sent, but obviously they must be sent behaviorally. However, the role **expectation** communicated in the sent-role is itself cognitive.

structions of what others expect of him. Indeed, in practice these several conceptualizations mutually reinforce and modify one another and some theorists have even held that the latter one is a prime determiner of the former two (Mead, 1934). In any event, a person's conceptualization of others' expectations will be an important influence upon his behavior.

Salience and definiteness of role constructions

The *salience* of a role refers to its prominence and/or importance in a person's life situation. By implication, the more salient a role the greater will be a person's "investment" in it and its components, the more will he tend to organize his "view of things" around it, the more will he strive to augment its clarity, the more will he tend to resist change in it once cognitively organized, and, hence, the more will it tend to dominate his behavior. For present purposes we can view salience as a dimension of role that refers to the quantitative emotional involvement in it of the person. Anticipating subsequent discussion a bit, conflict among elements of salient roles will be more intense than any involving less salient roles.

Definiteness of a role refers to the clarity and/or articulation of elements in a differentiated role construction. The clearer and more articulated a role construction the more significant will it be as a behavior determinant. And the more a definite construction is articulated with other role constructions the more flexible will be the person's behavior. Finally, the more indefinite and inarticulate a role construction the greater will be the possibility for conflict

involving it and the greater will be the person's anxiety in performing it.

Many factors influence the definiteness of a role construction, but we have need to mention only two: positional awareness and experience. Obviously the most basic requirement for a definite role construction is awareness of the positional differentiation defining the distal social system in which the person functions. As a corollary we may observe that it is also necessary that the person allocate position occupants with some precision. It should be clear that awareness of the positional structure of a system is, by itself, insufficient to effective social behavior without accompanying awareness of the distribution of particular others among these positions. Hence, without adequate and comprehensive positional awareness, a person's social behavior is likely to be less than apt— even inept.

The second factor of interest to us as a contributor to role definition is experience. It is highly credible that, in general, the more "practice" a person has in role playing the clearer and more differentiated will these roles become. Furthermore, their reciprocal features are likely to be sharpened with the result that greater consensus among role constructions is likely to be achieved. No less important is a growth in "sophistication" entailing a relaxation in the rigidity of role construction and enactment. This proceeds from greater awareness of and sensitivity to the variations in role construction and enactment common in the community and the functional interrelationships between these variations and other system components. Sophistication also implies a continued awareness of the fundamental invariance of the role as a positional attribute with observed variations being represented as variant forms of the same role structure.

Role conflict

In any complex social system involving a large number of interrelated positional differentiations and with individuals simultaneously occupying a variety of positions, some related and some not, there is obviously wide latitude for confusion and conflict. This will be especially true in any setting where normative guides are uncertain or inconsistent —a condition akin to what Durkheim and Merton have called *anomie*.

Actually there are a variety of conditions that can produce role conflict. None of these will be discussed in exhaustive detail, but we shall inventory certain prominent circumstances. Before doing so, however, we must be clear about the usage of the term "conflict" in this discussion. We shall use the term to denote one or both of two conditions, the second of which is not typical of psychological discussions of conflict.

In the first, and usual, sense conflict refers to a condition where an individual *experiences* the simultaneous arousal of two or more incompatible behavioral tendencies. In this case the person is likely to be "aware" of the conflict, though not necessarily able to resolve it or even to identify clearly its sources. In the second, atypical, sense "conflict" may refer to a situation in which the objective social *requirements* would be such as to demand simultaneous, incompatible responses from the person. In this case, the person himself might not be aware of the "conflict" owing to an inadequate definition of the situation or because of indefinite, inarticulate position-role differentiation. Thus the term

conflict is used here to denote any condition wherein the person functions in a field the requirements of which are in conflict whether he perceives it so or not. The reason for this broad usage rather than the more usual "intrapersonal" formulation is that the focus of our interest in dealing with role concepts is *interpersonal* and conflict may exist if not, strictly speaking, within either of the participants, then *in the relationship* where the resulting "tension" may be expected to have behavioral consequences of great disruptive potential because its sources are unrecognized and therefore difficult to cope with adaptively.

With this preface we can turn to a survey of some prominent circumstances productive of conflict.

1. The most obvious of these is represented by a situation in which the person perceives himself to, or does in fact, occupy two or more positions, both of which are relevant to the situation and the role constructions of which are incompatible. An illustration of this variety of role conflict can be seen in the well-worn Hollywood plot theme in which a dedicated policeman is called upon to arrest his miscreant brother.

2. A second condition is one wherein an individual's role expectations are incompatible. In this case the conflict involves the projected performances of the occupants of counter-positions. Exemplification frequently can be found in the demands of parents that their adolescent offspring behave at once independently and subordinately.

3. A third condition is one wherein an individual's role stereotype is incom-

patible with his construction of the other's role expectations. This form of role conflict, involving perceptions of sent-roles, is authentically interpersonal whether the person's constructions are accurate or not for it refers explicitly to the matter of one's behavior in relation to others. In some ways this species of conflict is similar to the first type and, indeed, either or both kinds could be aroused by the same circumstances. What differentiates them is that in the first type the person perceives himself as occupying *multiple* and conflicting positions whereas in this third form he perceives himself as occupying a *single* position the counter-role expectations of which are inconsistent with his role stereotype. For instance, the policeman in our first example might regard the conflict as entirely one of his "duty" and his brother's expectations that he will subordinate duty to familial sentiment.

4. Another condition would be represented by a circumstance wherein an individual's role expectations are incompatible with the role enactments of the other or vice versa. This form of conflict hardly needs further elaboration; it simply refers to those frequent circumstances when another person's behavior is not what we think it should be.

5. A final circumstance, not typically included in these discussions, is one wherein some constraining element of a role is behaviorally inconsistent with some other non-role-related feature of the stimulus field. For example, a conscientious teacher concerned over his economic circumstances might be cast into conflict by perceiving his role-linked "professionalism" to be inconsistent with

a seeming necessity to strike and picket as a means to produce change in an unsympathetic school board. This condition does not represent a role conflict *per se* perhaps, but one entailing conflict among behavior determinants. It is of great import, however, because of its relevance to problems of status to which we shall come presently.

Although we shall not discuss the matter, it is to be expected that different kinds of conflict will entail different implications for social process and it should be evident now that the varieties of role conflict and of role-linked conflict are many. What is important to keep in mind is that role-conflict can arise from actual requirements of the behavioral field whether veridically perceived or not, or from perceptual error, or from failure to achieve an adequately definite and articulated construction of position-role.

Status

Status in this discussion is not synonymous with position but is conceived as an attribute of positions. Without laboring the point, status can be thought of as referring to the "rank order" of a position within a system of positions. These rankings are a result of a number of factors a consideration of which would take us too far afield. Suffice it to say that any position may rank high or low relative to others and that this status connotes variations in the power and/or prestige-respect accruing to a position.

Now, there are a few complicating matters. In the first place, since status accrues to a position, any occupant of the position acquires or is *ascribed* that status. However, even within a given position, an individual's *achieved* status may vary upward or downward from this base, depending upon features of his performance in the position. To be brief, a person's role enactments serve to "validate" his status and so may modify it. Consequently, ineptness in role enactment will lead to a loss in status.

The second complicating factor is perhaps of even greater significance: There is a frequent tendency to think of status as a sort of unitary monolith. However, while it is true that we can grossly characterize a *person* as having a certain status, strictly speaking status is associated with positions, not persons. Since each person will occupy multiple positions, each of which accords him a status, we can with justice think of persons as being characterized by *statuses*. And Homans (1961), for one, has reasoned, there is an interpersonal tendency to maintain congruence among these statuses and any interaction involving incongruencies among statuses

will be strained and conflictful, independently of any *specifics* of role behavior.

Conclusion

From the preceding remarks it can be seen that a large part of the variance in interpersonal relations and organizational functioning can be understood in terms of interactions among persons as occupants of positions and players of roles. In fact, many phenomena appearing in such relations and regularly ordered to personality traits and peculiarities of the individual parties involved are probably more properly viewed in terms of aspects and relations of positions and roles and their correlative status. In other words, it must of needs be recognized that large parts of individual social behavior are formally determined and have little to do with the specific intrapsychic aspects of the behaver.

31   The norm of reciprocity: a preliminary statement

ALVIN W. GOULDNER

The aims of this paper are: (1) to indicate the manner in which the concept of reciprocity is tacitly involved in but formally neglected by modern functional theory; (2) to clarify the concept and display some of its diverse intellectual contents, thus facilitating its theoretical employment and research utility; and (3) to suggest concretely ways in which the clarified concept provides new leverage for analysis of the central problems of sociological theory, namely, accounting for stability and instability in social systems.

Reciprocity and functional theory

My concern with reciprocity developed initially from a critical reexamination of current functional theory, especially the work of Robert Merton and Talcott Parsons. The fullest ramifications of what follows can best be seen in this theoretical context. Merton's familiar paradigm of functionalism stresses that analysis must begin with the identification of some problematic pattern of human behavior, some institution, role, or shared pattern of belief. Merton stipulates clearly the basic functionalist assumption, the way in which the problematic pattern is to be understood: he holds that the "central orientation of functionalism" is "expressed in the practice of interpreting data by establishing their consequences for larger structures in which they are implicated" (1957).

The functionalist's emphasis upon studying the *existent* consequences, the on-going functions or dysfunctions, of a social pattern may be better appreciated if it is remembered that this concern developed in a polemic against the earlier anthropological notion of a "survival." The survival, of course, was regarded as a custom held to be unexplainable in terms of its existent consequences or utility and which, therefore, had to be understood with reference to its consequences for social arrangements no longer present.

Functionalism, to repeat, explains the persistence of social patterns in terms of their ongoing consequences for existent social systems. If social survivals, which by definition have no such consequences, are conceded to exist or to be possible, then it would seem that functionalism is by its own admission incapable of explaining them. To suggest that survivals do not help us to understand other patterns of social behavior is beside the mark. The decisive issue is whether existent versions of functional theory can explain social survivals, not whether specific social survivals can explain other social patterns.

It would seem that functionalists have but one of two choices: either they must dogmatically deny the existence or possibility of functionless patterns (survivals), and assert that all social behavior is explainable parsimoniously on the basis of the same fundamental

Excerpted from the American Sociological Review, 1960, 25, 161–79, with permission of the author and the American Sociological Association.

functionalist assumption, that is, in terms of its consequences for surrounding social structures; or, more reasonably, they must concede that some social patterns are or may be survivals, admitting that existent functional theory fails to account for such instances. In the latter case, functionalists must develop further their basic assumptions on the generalized level required. I believe that one of the strategic ways in which such basic assumptions can be developed is by recognizing the manner in which the concept of *reciprocity* is tacitly involved in them, and by explicating the concept's implications for functional theory.

The tacit implication of the concept of reciprocity in functional theory can be illustrated in Merton's analysis of the latent functions of the political machine in the United States. Merton inquires how political machines continue to operate, despite the fact that they frequently run counter to both the mores and the law. The *general* form of his explanation is to identify the consequences of the machine for surrounding structures and to demonstrate that the machine performs "positive functions which are at the same time not adequately fulfilled by other existing patterns and structures" (1957, p. 73). It seems evident, however, that simply to establish its consequences for other social structures provides no answer to the question of the persistence of the political machine (cf. Gouldner, 1959b). The explanation miscarries because no explicit analysis is made of the feedback through which the social structures or groups, whose needs are satisfied by the political machine, in turn "reciprocate" and repay the machine for the services received from it. In this case, the patterns of reciprocity, implied in the notion of the "corruption" of the machine, are well known and fully documented.

To state the issue generally: the demonstration that A is functional for B can help to account for A's persistence only if the functional theorist tacitly assumes some principle of reciprocity. It is in this sense that some concept of reciprocity apparently has been smuggled into the basic but unstated postulates of functional analysis. The demonstration that A is functional for B helps to account for A's own persistence and stability only on two related assumptions: (1) that B *reciprocates* A's services, and (2) that B's service to A is *contingent* upon A's performance of positive functions for B. The second assumption, indeed, is one implication of the definition of reciprocity as a transaction. Unless B's services to A are contingent upon the services provided by A, it is pointless to examine the latter if one wishes to account for the persistence of A.

It may be assumed, as a first approximation, that a social unit or group is more likely to contribute to another which provides it with benefits than to one which does not; nonetheless, there are certain general conditions under which one pattern may provide benefits for the other despite a *lack* of reciprocity. An important case of this situation is where power arrangements constrain the continuance of services. If B is considerably more powerful than A, B may force A to benefit it with little or no reciprocity. This social arrangement, to be sure, is less stable than one in which B's reciprocity *motivates* A to continue performing services for B, but it is hardly for this reason sociologically unimportant.

The problem can also be approached

in terms of the functional autonomy (see Gouldner, 1959b) of two units relative to each other. For example, B may have many alternative sources for supplying the services that it normally receives from A. A, however, may be dependent upon B's services and have no, or comparatively few, alternatives. Consequently, the continued provision of benefits by one pattern, A, for another, B, depends not only upon (1) the benefits which A in turn receives from B, but also on (2) the power which B possesses relative to A, and (3) the alternative sources of services accessible to each, beyond those provided by the other. In short, an explanation of the stability of a pattern, or of the relationship between A and B, requires investigation of mutually contingent benefits rendered and of the manner in which this mutual contingency is sustained. The latter, in turn, requires utilization of two different theoretical traditions and general orientations, one stressing the significance of power differences and the other emphasizing the degree of mutual dependence of the patterns or parties involved.

Functional theory, then, requires some assumption concerning reciprocity. It must, however, avoid the "Pollyanna Fallacy" which optimistically assumes that structures securing "satisfactions" from others will invariably be "grateful" and will always reciprocate. Therefore it cannot be merely hypostatized that reciprocity will operate in every case; its occurrence must, instead, be documented empirically. Although reciprocal relations stabilize patterns, it need not follow that a lack of reciprocity is socially impossible or invariably disruptive of the patterns involved. Relations with little or no reciprocity may, for example, occur when power disparities

allow one party to coerce the other. There may also be special mechanisms which compensate for or control the tensions which arise in the event of a breakdown in reciprocity. Among such compensatory mechanisms there may be culturally shared prescriptions of one-sided or unconditional generosity, such as the Christian notion of "turning the other cheek" or "walking the second mile," the feudal notion of "noblesse oblige," or the Roman notion of "clemency." There may also be cultural prohibitions banning the examination of certain interchanges from the standpoint of their concrete reciprocity, as expressed by the cliché, "It's not the gift but the sentiment that counts." The major point here is that if empirical analysis fails to detect the existence of functional reciprocity, or finds that it has been disrupted, it becomes necessary to search out and analyze the compensatory arrangements that may provide means of controlling the resultant tensions, thereby enabling the problematic pattern to remain stable.

The "exploitation" problem

It was not only the functionalist polemic against the concept of survivals that obscured the significance and inhibited the study of unequal exchanges. A similar result is also produced by the suspicion with which many modern sociologists understandably regard the concept of "exploitation." This concept of course is central to the traditional socialist critique of modern capitalism. In the now nearly-forgotten language of political economy, "exploitation" refers to a relationship in which unearned income results from certain kinds of unequal exchange.

The continued use of the concept of

exploitation in sociological analyses of sexual relations stems largely from the brilliant work of Willard Waller on the dynamics of courtship. Waller's ambivalent comments about the concept suggest why it has fallen into sociological disrepute. "The word exploitation is by no means a desirable one," explains Waller, "but we have not been able to find another which will do as well. The dictionary definition of exploitation as an 'unfair or unjust utilization of another' contains a value judgment, and this value judgment is really a part of the ordinary sociological meaning of the term" (1951, p. 163). In short, the concept of exploitation may have become disreputable because its value implications conflict with modern sociology's effort to place itself on a value-free basis, as well as because it is a concept commonly and correctly associated with the critique of modern society emphasized by the political left. But the concept *need* not be used in such an ideological manner; it can be employed simply to refer to certain transactions involving an exchange of things of unequal value. It is important to guarantee that the ordinary value implications of a term do not intrude upon its scientific use. It is also important, however, to prevent our distaste for the ideological implications of exploitation from inducing a compulsive and equally ideological neglect of its cognitive substance.

The unsavory implications of the concept of exploitation have *not* excluded it from studies of sexual relations, although almost all other specializations in sociology eschew it. Why this is so remains a tempting problem for the sociology of knowledge, but cannot be explored here. In the present context, the important implications are the following: If the possible sexual exploitation of daughters by fathers gives rise, as Davis (1949) suggests, to mechanisms that serve to prevent this, then it would seem that *other* types of exploitation may also be controlled by *other* kinds of mechanisms. These may be no less important and universal than the incest taboo. If the exploitation of women by men (or men by women) is worthy of sociological attention, then also worth studying is the exploitation of students by teachers, of workers by management or union leaders, of patients by doctors, and so on. If the notion of exploitation, in a value-free sense, is useful for the analysis of sexual relations then it can be of similar aid in analyzing many other kinds of social relations.

Doubtless "exploitation" is by now so heavily charged with misleading ideological resonance that the term itself can scarcely be salvaged for purely scientific purposes and will, quite properly, be resisted by most American sociologists. This is unimportant. Perhaps a less emotionally freighted—if infelicitous—term such as "reciprocity imbalance" will suffice to direct attention once again to the crucial question of unequal exchanges.

Complementarity and reciprocity

The question of the meaning of the concept of reciprocity should be re-examined. Consideration of some of the ways in which the reciprocity problem is treated by Parsons helps to distinguish reciprocity from other cognate concepts. "It is inherent in the nature of social interaction," writes Parsons, "that the gratification of ego's need-dispositions is contingent on alter's reaction and vice versa" (1951, p. 21). Presumably, therefore, if the gratification of either party's needs is not contingent upon the other's reactions, the stability of their relation is undermined. This, in turn, implies that if a social system is to be stable there must always be some "mutuality of gratification" (Parsons & Shils, 1951, p. 107). Social system stability, then, presumably depends in part on the mutually contingent exchange of gratifications, that is, on reciprocity as exchange.

This, however, remains an insight the implications of which are never systematically explored. For example, the implications of differences in the *degree* of mutuality or in the symmetry of reciprocity are neglected. Again, while the concept of "exploitation" assumes *central* importance in Parsons' commentary on the patient-doctor relation, it is never precisely defined, examined, and located in his *general* theory.

One reason for Parson's neglect of reciprocity is that he, like some other sociologists, does not distinguish it from the concept of complementarity. Parsons uses the two concepts as if they are synonymous and, for the most part, centers his analysis on complementarity to the systematic neglect of reciprocity rigorously construed. The term complementarity, however, is itself an ambiguous one and is not, in all of its meanings, synonymous with reciprocity. Complementarity has at least four distinct meanings:

Complementarity$_1$ may mean that a right (x) of Ego against Alter implies a duty (−x) of Alter to Ego. Given the often vague use of the term "right," it is quite possible that this proposition, in one aspect, is only an expansion of some definition of the concept "right." To that degree, of course, this is simply an analytic proposition. The interesting

sociological questions, however, arise only when issues of empirical substance rather than logical implication are raised. For example, where a group shares a belief that some status occupant has a certain right, say the right of a wife to receive support from her husband, does the group in fact also share a belief that the husband has an obligation to support the wife? Furthermore, even though rights may logically or empirically imply duties, it need not follow that the reverse is true. In other words, it does not follow that rights and duties are always transitive. This can be seen in a second meaning of complementarity.

Complementarity$_2$ may mean that what is a duty (−x) of Alter to Ego implies a right (x) of Ego against Alter. On the *empirical* level, while this is often true, of course, it is also sometimes false. For example, what may be regarded as a duty of charity or forebearance, say a duty to "turn the other cheek," need not be *socially* defined as the *right* of the recipient. While a man may be regarded as having an unconditional obligation to tell the truth to everyone, even to a confirmed liar, people in his group might not claim that the liar has a *right* to have the truth told him.

The other two meanings of complementarity differ substantially. Complementarity$_3$ may mean that a right (x) of Alter against Ego implies a duty (−y) of Alter to Ego. Similarly, complementarity$_4$ may mean that a duty (−x) of Ego to Alter implies a right (y) of Ego against Alter.

In these four implications of complementarity—sometimes called reciprocal rights and obligations—there are two distinctive types of cases. Properly speaking, *complementarity* refers only to the first two meanings sketched above, where what is a right of Ego implies an obligation of Alter, or where a duty of Alter to Ego implies a right of Ego against Alter. Only the other two meanings, however, involve true instances of *reciprocity*, for only in these does what one party receives from the other require some return, so that giving and receiving are mutually contingent.

In short, complementarity connotes that one's rights are another's obligations, and *vice versa*. Reciprocity, however, connotes that *each* party has rights *and* duties. This is more than an analytic distinction: it is an *empirical* generalization concerning role systems the importance of which as a datum is so elemental that it is commonly neglected and rarely made problematic. The English philosopher MacBeath suggests that this empirical generalization may be accounted for by the principle of reciprocity (1952). This would seem possible in several senses, one of which is that, were there only rights on the one side and duties on the other, there need be no exchange whatsoever. Stated differently, it would seem that there can be stable patterns of reciprocity *qua* exchange only insofar as *each* party has both rights and duties. In effect, then, reciprocity has its significance for *role systems* in that it tends to structure *each* role so as to include both rights and duties. It is now clear, at any rate, that reciprocity is by no means identical with complementarity and that the two are confused only at theoretical peril.

The norm of reciprocity

Contrary to some cultural relativists, it can be hypothesized that a norm of reciprocity is universal. As Westermarck stated, "To requite a benefit, or to be grateful to him who bestows it, is probably everywhere, at least under certain circumstances, regarded as a duty" (1908, vol. 2, p. 154). A norm of reciprocity is, I suspect, no less universal and important an element of culture than the incest taboo, although, similarly, its concrete formulations may vary with time and place.

Specifically, I suggest that a norm of reciprocity, in its universal form, makes two interrelated, minimal demands: (1) people should help those who have helped them, and (2) people should not injure those who have helped them. Generically, the norm of reciprocity may be conceived of as a dimension to be found in all value systems and, in particular, as one among a *number* of "Principal Components" universally present in moral codes. (The task of the sociologist, in this regard, parallels that of the physicist who seeks to identify the basic particles of matter, the conditions under which they vary, and their relations to one another.)

To suggest that a norm of reciprocity is universal is not, of course, to assert that it is unconditional. Unconditionality would, indeed, be at variance with the basic character of the reciprocity norm which imposes obligations only contingently, that is, in response to the benefits conferred by others. Moreover, such obligations of repayment are contingent upon the imputed *value* of the benefit received. The value of the benefit and hence the debt is in proportion to and varies with—among other things—the intensity of the recipient's need at the time the benefit was bestowed ("a friend in need . . ."), the resources of the donor ("he gave although he could ill afford it"), the motives imputed to the donor ("without thought of gain"), and the nature of the constraints which are perceived to exist or to be absent ("he gave of his own free will . . ."). Thus the obligations imposed by the norm of reciprocity may vary with the *status* of the participants within a society.

Similarly, this norm functions differently in some degree in different *cultures*. In the Philippines, for example, the *compadre* system cuts across and pervades the political, economic, and other institutional spheres. *Compadres* are bound by a norm of reciprocity. If one man pays his *compadre's* doctor's bill in time of need, for example, the latter may be obligated to help the former's son to get a government job. Here the tendency to govern all relations by the norm of reciprocity, thereby undermining bureaucratic impersonality, is relatively legitimate, hence overt and powerful. In the United States, however, such tendencies are weaker, in part because friendship relations are less institutionalized. Nonetheless, even in bureaucracies in this country such tendencies are endemic, albeit less legitimate and overt. Except in friendship, kinship, and neighborly relations, a norm of reciprocity is not imposed on Americans by the "dominant cultural profile," although it is commonly found in the latent or "substitute" culture structure in all institutional sectors, even the most rationalized, in the United States.

In otherwise contrasting discussions of the norm of reciprocity one emphasis is notable. Some scholars, especially Homans (1958), Thurwald (1932), Simmel (1950), and Malinowski (1932), assert or imply that the reciprocity norm stipulates that the amount of the return to be made is "roughly equivalent" to what had been received. The problem

of equivalence is a difficult but important one. Whether in fact there is a reciprocity norm specifically requiring that returns for benefits received be *equivalent* is an empirical question. So, too, is the problem of whether such a norm is part of or distinct from a more general norm which simply requires that one return some (unspecified) benefits to benefactors. Logically prior to such empirical problems, however, is the question of what the meaning of equivalence would be in the former norm of equivalent reciprocity.

Equivalence may have at least two forms, the sociological and psychodynamic significance of which are apt to be quite distinct. In the first case, heteromorphic reciprocity, equivalence may mean that the things exchanged may be concretely different but should be equal in *value*, as defined by the actors in the situation. In the second case, homeomorphic reciprocity, equivalence may mean that exchanges should be concretely alike, or identical in form, either with respect to the things exchanged or to the circumstances under which they are exchanged. In the former, equivalence calls for "tit for tat"; in the latter, equivalence calls for "tat for tat." Historically, the most important expression of homeomorphic reciprocity is found in the *negative* norms of reciprocity, that is, in sentiments of retaliation where the emphasis is placed not on the return of benefits but on the return of injuries, and is best exemplified by the *lex talionis*.

Finally, it should be stressed that equivalence in the above cases refers to a definition of the exchangeables made by actors in the situation. This differs of course, from holding that the things exchanged by people, in the long run, will be *objectively* equal in value, as measured by economists or other social scientists. Here, again, the adequacy of these conceptual distinctions will be determined ultimately by empirical test.

Reciprocity and social systems

As mentioned above, sociologists have sometimes confused the notion of complementarity with that of reciprocity and have recently tended to focus on the former. Presumably, the reason for this is because of the importance of complementarity in maintaining the stability of social systems. Clearly, if what one party deems his right is accepted by the other as his obligation, their relation will be more stable than if the latter fails to so define it. But if the group stabilizing consequences of complementarity are the basis of its theoretical significance, then the same consideration underwrites with equal potency the significance of reciprocity. For reciprocity has no less a role in maintaining the stability of social systems.

Note that there are at least two ways, not merely one, in which complementarity as such can break down. In the one case, Alter can refuse to acknowledge Ego's rights as his own duties. In the other case, however, Ego may not regard as rights that which Alter acknowledges as duties. The former is commonly viewed as the empirically more frequent and as the theoretically more significant case. That this often seems to be taken as a matter of course suggests the presence of certain tacit assumptions about basic human dispositions. It seems to assume, as Aristotle put it, that people are more ready to receive than to give benefits. In short, it premises a common tendency toward what used to be called "egoism," a salient (but not exclusive) concern with the satisfaction of one's own needs.

This or some cognate assumption appears to be eminently reasonable and empirically justified. There can be no adequate systematic sociological theory which boggles at the issue; indeed, it is one of the many virtues of Parsons' work that it confronts the egoism problem. His solution seems to be sidetracked, however, because his overwhelming focus on the problem of complementarity leads to the neglect of reciprocity. If assumptions about egoistic dispositions are valid, however, a complementarity of rights and obligations should be exposed to a persistent strain, in which each party is somewhat more actively concerned to defend or extend his own rights than those of others. There is nothing in complementarity as such which would seem able to control egoism.

One way out may be obtained by premising that socialization internalizes complementary rights and obligations in persons, before they fully assume responsible participation in a social system. Even if socialization were to work perfectly and so internalize such rights and obligations, there still remains the question as to what mechanism can sustain and reinforce these during full participation in the social system. The concept of complementarity takes mutually compatible expectations as given; it does not and cannot explain how they are maintained once established. For this we need to turn to the reciprocities processes because these, unlike pure complementarity, actually mobilize egoistic motivations and channel them into the maintenance of the social system. Benthamite utilitarianism has long understood that egoism can motivate one party to satisfy the expectations of the other, since by doing so he induces the latter to reciprocate and to satisfy his own. As Max Gluckman might put it with his penchant for Hegelian paradox, there is an altruism in egoism, made possible through reciprocity.

A full analysis of the ways in which the whole reciprocities complex is involved in the maintenance of social systems would require consideration of the linkages between each of its various elements, and their relation to other general properties of social systems. There is no space for such consideration here. Instead, I examine only one part of the complex, namely, the generalized *norm* of reciprocity, and suggest some of the ways in which it contributes to social system stability.

If, following Parsons, we suppose that social systems are stable to the extent that Ego and Alter conform with one another's expectations, we are confronted with the problem of why men *reciprocate* gratifications. Parsons holds that once a stable relation of mutual gratification has been established the system is self-perpetuating; presumably, no special mechanisms are necessary to maintain it. Insofar as this is not simply postulated in analogy with the principle of inertia in physics, apparently reciprocity is accounted for by Parsons, and also by Homans, as a result of the development of a beneficent cycle of mutual reinforcement. That is, Ego's conformity with Alter's expectations reinforces Alter's conformity with Ego's expectations, and so on.

This explanation of reciprocity *qua* transaction is particularly strange in Parsons' case since he often stresses, but here neglects, the significance of shared values as a source of stability in social systems. So far as the question here is

not simply the general one of why men conform with the expectations of others but, rather, the more specific problem of why they *reciprocate* benefits, part of the answer would seem to be that they have commonly internalized some general *moral norm*. In short, the suggestion is that the motivation for reciprocity stems not only from the sheer gratification which Alter receives from Ego but also from Alter's internalization of a specific norm of reciprocity which morally obliges him to give benefits to those from whom he has received them. In this respect, the *norm* of reciprocity is a concrete and special mechanism involved in the maintenance of any stable social system.

Why should such a norm be necessary? Why is it that expedient considerations do not suffice to mobilize motivations to comply with other's expectations, thereby inducing them to provide reciprocal compliances? One major line of analysis here would certainly indicate the disruptive potentialities of power differences. Given significant power differences, egoistic motivations may seek to get benefits without returning them. The situation is then ripe for the breakdown of reciprocity and for the development of system-disrupting exploitation. The norm of reciprocity, however, engenders motives for returning benefits even when power differences might invite exploitation. The norm thus safeguards powerful people against the temptations of their own status; it motivates and regulates reciprocity as an exchange pattern, serving to inhibit the emergence of exploitative relations which would undermine the social system and the very power arrangements which had made exploitation possible (see Gouldner, 1959a).

As we have seen, Parsons stresses that

the stability of social systems largely derives from the *conformity* of role partners to each other's expectations, particularly when they do their duty to one another. This formulation induces a focus on conformity and deviance, and the degrees and types of each. Presumably, the more that people pay their social debts the more stable the social system. But much more than conformity and deviance are involved here.

Insofar as men live under such a rule of reciprocity, when one party benefits another, an obligation is generated. The recipient is now *indebted* to the donor, and he remains so until he repays. Once interaction is seen as taking place over time, we may note that the norm of reciprocity so structures social relations that, between the time of Ego's provision of a gratification and the time of Alter's repayment, falls the shadow of indebtedness. An adequate analysis of the dynamics of social interaction is thus required to go beyond the question of deviance from or conformity with the parties' obligations to one another. A second basic dimension needs to be examined systematically, namely, the time period when there is an obligation still to be performed, when commitments which have been made are yet to be fulfilled.

These outstanding obligations, no less than those already given compliance, contribute substantially to the stability of social systems. It is obviously inexpedient for creditors to break off relationships with those who have outstanding obligations to them. It may also be inexpedient for *debtors* to do so because their creditors may not again allow them to run up a bill of social indebtedness. In addition, it is *morally* improper, under the norm of reciprocity, to break off relations or to launch hostilities against those to whom you are still indebted.

If this conclusion is correct, then we should not only look for mechanisms which constrain or motivate men to do their duty and to pay off their debts. We should also expect to find mechanisms which induce people to *remain* socially indebted to each other and which *inhibit* their complete repayment. This suggests another function performed by the requirement of only *rough* equivalence of repayment that may be involved in one of the norms of reciprocity. For it induces a certain amount of ambiguity as to whether indebtedness has been repaid and, over time, generates uncertainty about who is in whose debt. This all hinges, however, on a shared conception of the moral propriety of repayment, engendered by the norm of reciprocity.

Still another way in which the general norm of reciprocity is implicated in the maintenance of social system stability is related to an important attribute of the norm, namely, its comparative indeterminancy. Unlike specific status duties and like other general norms, this norm does not require highly specific and uniform performances from people whose behavior it regulates. For example, unlike the status duties of American wives, it does not call upon them to cook and to take care of the children. Instead, the concrete demands it makes change substantially from situation to situation and vary with the benefits which one party receives from another.

This indeterminancy enables the norm of reciprocity to perform some of its most important system-stabilizing functions. Being indeterminate, the norm can be applied to countless *ad hoc* transactions, thus providing a flexible moral sanction for transactions which might not otherwise be regulated by specific status obligations. The norm, in this respect, is a kind of plastic filler, capable of being poured into the shifting crevices of social structures, and serving as a kind of all-purpose moral cement.

Not only does the norm of reciprocity play a stabilizing role in human relations in the *absence* of a well developed system of specific status duties, but it contributes to social stability even when these are *present* and well established. Status duties shape behavior because the status occupant believes them binding in their own right; they possess a kind of *prima facie* legitimacy for properly socialized group members. The general norm of reciprocity, however, is a second-order defense of stability; it provides a further source of motivation and an additional moral sanction for conforming with specific status obligations. For example, the employer may pay his workers not merely because he has contracted to do so; he may also feel that the workman has earned his wages. The housewife may take pains with her husband's meals not merely because cooking may be incumbent on her as a wife; she may also have a particularly considerate husband. In each case, the specific status duties are complied with not only because they are inherent in the status and are believed to be right in themselves, but also because each is further defined as a *"repayment."* In sum, the norm of reciprocity requires that if others have been fulfilling their status duties to you, you in turn have an additional or second-order obligation (repayment) to fulfill your status duties to them. In this manner, the sentiment of gratitude joins forces with the sentiment of recti-

tude and adds a safety-margin in the motivation to conformity.

Starting mechanisms

Two distinct points have been made about the social functions of the norm of reciprocity. One is that this norm serves a group *stabilizing* function and thus is quite familiar in functional theory. The second point, however, is the view that the norm is not only in some sense a defense or stabilizing mechanism but is also what may be called a "starting mechanism." That is, it helps to initiate social interaction and is functional in the early phases of certain groups before they have developed a differentiated and customary set of status duties.

In speaking of the norm of reciprocity as a "starting mechanism," indeed in conceiving of starting mechanisms, we find ourselves outside the usual perspective of functional theory. Functional theory commonly focuses on already-established, on-going systems, and on the mechanisms by means of which an established social system is enabled to maintain itself. Although functional theory is concerned with the problems of how individual actors are prepared by socialization to play a role in social systems, its general theoretical models rarely, if ever, include systematic treatment of the beginnings of a social system as such and, consequently, do not formally raise the question of the nature of the mechanisms needed to start such a system.

Every social system of course has a history, which means that it has had its beginnings even if these are shrouded in antiquity. Granted that the question of origins can readily bog down in a metaphysical morass, the fact is that many concrete social systems do have determinate beginnings. Marriages are not made in heaven, and whether they end in divorce or continue in bliss, they have some identifiable origins. Similarly, corporations, political parties, and all manner of groups have their beginnings. (Recent studies of friendship and other interpersonal relations in housing projects have begun to explore this problem.)

People are continually brought together in new juxtapositions and combinations, bringing with them the possibilities of new social systems. How are these possibilities realized? Is such realization entirely a random matter? These are the kinds of questions that were familiar to the earlier students of "collective behavior," who, in focusing on crowds, riots, and rumors, were often primarily concerned with investigating the development of groups in *statu nascendi*. Although this perspective may at first seem somewhat alien to the functionalist, once it is put to him, he may suspect that certain kinds of mechanisms, conducive to the crystallization of social systems out of ephemeral contacts, will in some measure be institutionalized or otherwise patterned in any society. At this point he would be considering "starting mechanisms." In this way, I suggest, the norm of reciprocity provides one among many starting mechanisms.

From the standpoint of a purely economic or utilitarian model (cf. Schelling, 1956), there are certain difficulties in accounting for the manner in which social interaction begins. Let us suppose two people or groups, Ego and Alter, each possesses valuables sought by the other. Suppose further that each feels that the only motive the other has to conduct an exchange is the anticipated gratification it will bring. Each may then feel that it would be advantageous to lay hold of the other's valuables without relinquishing his own. Furthermore, suppose that each party suspects the other of precisely such an intention, perhaps because of the operation of projective or empathic mechanisms. At least since Hobbes, it has been recognized that under such circumstances, each is likely to regard the impending exchange as dangerous and to view the other with some suspicion (cf. Deutsch, 1955). Each may then hesitate to part with his valuables before the other has first turned his over. Like participants in a disarmament conference, each may say to other, "You first!" Thus the exchange may be delayed or altogether flounder and the relationship may be prevented from developing.

The norm of reciprocity may serve as a starting mechanism in such circumstances by preventing or enabling the parties to break out of this impasse. When internalized in both parties, the norm *obliges* the one who has first received a benefit to repay it at some time; it thus provides some realistic grounds for confidence, in the one who first parts with his valuables, that he will be repaid. Consequently, there may be less hesitancy in being the first and a greater facility with which the exchange and the social relation can get underway.[1]

[1] Certain elaborations, illustrations (e.g., a discussion of Malinowski), and historical references in Prof. Gouldner's original article are omitted.—Eds.

32   Perceiving the other person

FRITZ HEIDER

Through perception we come to cognize the world around us, a world made up of things and people and events. Obviously, the existence of the other person, o, as an object with not only physical and spatial particulars, but also with complex psychological properties, must be mediated in some way to the subject, that is perceived by p, if o is to feature in p's thinking, feelings, and actions. Likewise, if p is to influence o, he must create changes that in some way can be perceived by o, barring, of course, internal reactions such as those instigated by drugs that affect o. The nature of this perception, in particular the principles that underlie the coordination between the stimulus conditions outside the person and his experience or phenomenal representation of them, is the topic to which we shall address ourselves here.

Our orientation is directed toward explicating some of the naïve, implicit principles that underlie perception, principles that connect the stimulus configurations presented to the person with his apprehension of them. During the course of this explication, we shall leave the realm of naïve psychology and make use of knowledge gained from the scientific causal analysis of the perceptual process. Moreover, because many of the principles underlying social perception have parallels in the field of nonsocial or thing perception, and because in many instances their significance has first been recognized in this field, we shall frequently have recourse to knowledge about the perception of things. We shall speak of "thing perception" or "nonsocial perception" when we mean the perception of inanimate objects, and of "person perception" or "social perception" when we mean the perception of another person. The term "object perception" which has been traditionally used in discussions of the perception of things is avoided in this chapter, since the word "object" is also used in its more general sense—"the object of perception" or "the distal object"—which includes persons as well as things. Brunswik's (1934) conclusion, that the objects of social and nonsocial perception are similar in regard to their formal characteristics as well as in regard to the processes by which they are perceived, is in general a valid framework for discussion (p. 211).

This is not to say, of course, that there are no differences between the perception of things and people. It is a commonplace that inanimate objects differ from persons in important ways. In discussing thing perception, we assume that there are real, solid objects with properties of shape and color, things placed in particular positions in real space, having functional properties making them fit or interfere with our purposes, and in general defining their place in the space of means-end relations. There is a chair on which one

Excerpted from Chapter 2 of **The Psychology of Interpersonal Relations**, New York: Wiley, 1958, with permission of the author and the publisher.

can sit; there is an object with which one can cut paper, tie a package, or write a note.

In discussing person perception, we also assume that these "objects" have color and occupy certain positions in the environment. They are, however, rarely mere manipulanda; rather they are usually perceived as action centers and as such can do something to us. They can benefit or harm us intentionally, and we can benefit or harm them. Persons have abilities, wishes and sentiments; they can act purposefully, and can perceive or watch us. They are systems having an awareness of their surroundings and their conduct refers to this environment, an environment that sometimes includes ourselves. And yet, just as the contents of the non-social environment are interrelated by certain lawful connections, causal or otherwise, which define what can or will happen, we assume that there are connections of a similar character between the contents of the social environment.

Phenomenal and causal description in perception

By phenomenal description is meant the nature of the contact between the person and his environment as directly experienced by the person. By causal description is meant the analysis of the underlying conditions that give rise to perceptual experience. There is no a priori reason why the causal description should be the same as the phenomenal description, though, of course, the former should adequately account for the latter. We shall see, however, that though there are differences between the two, the parallels are marked.

It has often been stressed, especially by phenomenologists, that the person

feels that he is in direct contact with things and persons in his environment. He sees objects directly, just by focusing his eyes upon them. He acts on objects directly by touching them and lifting them. The same is true of person perception. He not only perceives people as having certain spatial and physical properties, but also can grasp even such intangibles as their wishes, needs, and emotions by some form of immediate apprehension.

In contrast to phenomenal description is the causal analysis which, instead of revealing the person as being in direct contact with the objects of perception, distinguishes a number of steps. A somewhat technical vocabulary has been built up to describe these steps. According to causal analysis, the perceptual process may be conceived of as a perceptual arc (Brunswik, 1952) encompassing two end points—the object, i.e., the part of the environment toward which perception is directed; and the percept, i.e., the way the object appears to us. The former has been referred to by Brunswik (1952) as the *initial focus* inasmuch as it is the starting point of the perceptual arc. It has also been referred to as the *distal stimulus* since it pertains to something "outside the person's skin," at a distance from the person. It is the chair "out there" that is seen or the melody coming from the violin that is heard. Whatever its designation, it refers to the environmental reality, an objective stimulus defined by properties perceivable by everyone.

The distal stimulus, however, does not directly affect the person. Rather it is mediated, for example, by light or sound-wave patterns that excite his sensory organs. This stimulus pattern, impinging as it does directly upon the sense organs, has been designated the *proximal stimulus;* it is the stimulus that is physically in direct proximity to the person. With touch or taste the object must come in direct contact with the sensory receptors, and the starting point of the perceptual process is the proximal rather than the distal stimulus; nonetheless the distinction between the two is still meaningful inasmuch as the sensory quality is attributed to the distal object—the object as separate from the person.

The perceptual process thus far involves distal stimuli, and mediation ending in the proximal stimuli. Within the organism there is, then, the constructive process of perception which leads to some event corresponding to the awareness of the object, the reality as perceived. The terms, *representation* or *image* of the object have been used to describe this awareness. It has also been referred to as the percept, the phenomena, and the terminal focus, the latter pointing to the fact that it is the end point of the perceptual arc, completing its function of providing an awareness of the "environmental reality." The constructive part of the perceptual process within the person is sometimes spoken of as involving central or higher phenomena, processes, or layers, whereas the proximal stimuli entering the organism, the so-called raw material, involve more peripheral or lower layers. The proximal stimuli, being unorganized and uninterpreted are also described as being more superficial.

With person perception, causal analysis also divides the phenomenally given immediate presence of the other person into steps. The other person, with his psychological processes such as needs and intentions, functions as the distal stimulus. He is the "object" toward which p's perception is directed. The mediation consists of the manifestations of the personality of the other, as they determine the proximal stimulus pattern. Often the manifestations of o's inner psychological processes are behavioral though they may be data gained from other sources, such as verbal communication from a third person. Finally, there is the perceptual construction within the person that leads from this raw material to the awareness of the other.

However, the process does not proceed in a one-way fashion from peripheral to central excitation. There is an interaction between the central processes in the brain and the more peripheral data, the "raw material" from the outside, so that the former determine, in some cases more, in some cases less, how the raw material is organized. What is of primary importance is that the central processes provide the "terms" in which the lower layers are interpreted, making it possible, for instance, for a movement to be perceived as a personal action. Often only the contents of the higher levels are directly present, and the lower levels —the raw material of peripheral data —are either not given at all, or are already in terms of the higher levels.

Summarizing, we can say that in many cases of both thing and person perception the raw material remains phenomenally unidentifiable, the only fact that appears ready-made in our life space being the percept, the end product of the organizing process. In other cases the raw material is phenomenally given, or at least can become so as we concentrate on the "visual field" instead of the "visual world," to use Gibson's (1950) expression. It is then that the whole process of perception seems more visible, more spread out for our inspection. It is probably fair to say that the less one depends on direct visual properties such as size and shape, and the more on events or behavior, the more the mediation becomes accessible to awareness.

Coordination between distal object and percept

CONSTANCY PHENOMENA

In perception, the percepts (or impressions or representations) of the environment largely furnish an adequate picture of the surroundings. That is to say, there is a high degree of coordination between the percept and the distal object. According to a phenomenal description of naïve psychology this is to be expected, for if the person is in direct contact with his environment, a true correspondence is naturally expected.

But the causal analyst quickly realizes that the object as perceived is not equal to the stimuli that are actually in direct contact with the person, namely the proximal stimuli mediated, for example, by light waves. Thus, even though the light waves from the surface of a table form varying patterns on my retina depending on my position with respect to the table—sometimes a trapezoid, sometimes a parallelogram, sometimes a large retinal image, sometimes a tiny one—I still perceive the table as rectangular and do quite well at approximating its size. Or, even though the stimuli on the retina are affected by illumination, the color of an object appears surprisingly little influenced. In other words, perception of the object remains fairly constant in spite of the enormous variation in the proximal

stimuli which mediate it through the excitation of sensory organs. This phenomenon is referred to as the problem of perceptual constancy. It should be noted, however, that constancy does not hold completely.

The term constancy phenomenon is usually applied to the perception of color, brightness, size, and shape, but it is also applicable in the social perception of such crucial distal stimuli as wishes, needs, beliefs, abilities, affects, and personality traits. If we assert that a "wish constancy" is possible just as there is a size, shape, or color constancy, that means we recognize a wish as being the same in spite of its being mediated by different cues. The same wish may be conveyed, for example, by an innumerable variety of word combinations, ranging from "I want that" to the lengthy and complicated reflections transmitted to the therapist in a psychonalytic session. Or, the same wish may be conveyed by a colorful array of actions, as when a child, wanting a red wagon above all else, goes up and takes it, pushes a competing child from it, and even angrily kicks it in a fit of frustration.

Thus, again we see that the interaction between the person and his environment, in this case between a person and someone he is observing, can best be described as going on between two foci separated by the mediation which can, to some extent, be neglected in the description. Later we shall examine the conditions that impede veridical perception, but in a first approach we will assume that the significant features of the other person (distal objects) are more or less invariantly connected with the perception of them, while neither object nor phenomenon show invariant relations to the mediation.

COORDINATION WITH DISPOSITIONAL PROPERTIES

A further point, closely related to the constancy phenomenon, also concerns the comparison between the way we experience the environment and the way a causal analysis presents it: The parts or characteristics of the environment that are directly given phenomenally and towards which perception (or action) is directed, are those parts that either themselves show an invariance (i.e., do not change very much in their properties), or which, when they change, change mostly in ways that follow macroscopically visible laws. Such properties have been referred to as *dispositional properties*. Here we should like to emphasize that the object as we perceive it is not coupled with just any arbitrarily selected part of the environment; rather it is coupled with such properties as shape, color, and size, properties that are relatively invariant features of the object and show consistent relations with other events. The shape of a solid object, for instance, is relatively enduring. It is something one can rely upon finding again. It is connected with important and lasting possibilities of the object. It allows us to predict to a certain degree how the object will behave when we handle it; for instance, if I see an object is spherical, I predict it can be rolled. This prediction is possible because shape is connected in an invariant way with a possible event, namely all spherical solid objects can be rolled. It is because these intrinsically invariant properties belong so often to distant objects, that is, objects separated in space from the person, that distal perception plays such an important role in interaction with the environment.

It is interesting that in social perception, also, the direct impressions we form of another person, even if they are not correct, refer to dispositional characteristics. At least, relative to the events that mediate these impressions, the characteristics show a high degree of intrinsic invariance. For instance, the impression that a person is friendly, which may be conveyed in any number of ways, points to a relatively enduring characteristic of the person. In fact, any personality trait refers to something that characterizes the person, that is, holds over time in spite of irregularities of circumstance and behavior. As a dispositional property, a personality characteristic enables one to grasp an unlimited variety of behavioral manifestations by a single concept, e.g., friendliness. A description of a manifold of interpersonal relations becomes far more systematically simple by reference to such enduring characteristics. Furthermore, insofar as personal dispositions are connected in lawful ways with other features, predictions about behavior of the other person become possible. Just as one can predict the rolling behavior of the ball because its spherical shape is a persisting property, so one can predict (albeit with less confidence) that *o* will help *p* because of his friendly nature, an enduring personality trait.

PSYCHOLOGICAL DISPOSITIONAL PROPERTIES IN SOCIAL PERCEPTION

The dispositional properties that are the important distal stimuli in social perception frequently refer to psychological or mental entities, to concepts that are not defined in a physical sense. The preceding example of friendliness is a case in point. Without the aid of such psychological, dispositional prop-

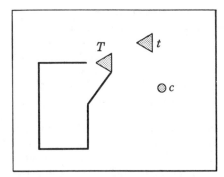

Figure 1. Geometrical figures in apparent behavior (Heider and Simmel, 1944, p. 244).

erties, the behavior of persons mediated by the proximal stimuli would remain largely unintelligible.

Experimentally, this has been demonstrated by the use of a film in which, physically speaking, only an enclosure with a movable part in the upper right-hand corner plus the movements of three geometrical figures are seen (Heider and Simmel, 1944). A still of this film is presented in Fig. 1. As long as the pattern of events shown in the film is perceived in terms of movements as such, it presents a chaos of juxtaposed items. When, however, the geometrical figures assume personal characteristics so that their movements are perceived in terms of motives and sentiments, a unified structure appears.

For social perception on the human level, the uses of "mental" dispositional concepts in the understanding and even description of interactions between persons are legion. Let us suppose that person A likes person B and that he wants to do him a favor. He takes into account B's wishes, and also what B can do: perhaps there is something B desires very much but cannot get by himself. A also has to consider the possibility that the benefit might embarrass B, or that B might feel that it implies a lack of respect. Finally, A, deciding on a particular action, goes through with it. B is overjoyed. He concludes that A, about whose attitudes he had been in doubt, really likes him; he appreciates especially the tactful way in which A handled the matter.

Descriptions of this kind seem to capture the essential features of an interpersonal event. One might go even further and try to discover the reasons why A likes B, or why B was questioning A's sentiments; or one might try to assess the personality characteristics that played a role in this event. Though the description as it stands does not go far back into the history of the relation between A and B, nor into deep psychological motivations, within its limits it is a meaningful episode.

If we examine the concepts that are used in making this episode intelligible, we find sentiments, wishes, abilities, and emotions. The particular behavioral data on which the judgments or perceptions of the other person's wishes, abilities, or traits are based are not mentioned. One may even feel that the description of the essential interpersonal process would not gain very much in exactitude if they were specified. Neither would a more detailed report of A's particular actions change very much our understanding of the main features of the event. The particular action by which A benefited B is of importance only insofar as it is judged by B and is related by him to his self-evaluation. To be sure, we might describe the event by concentrating on the surface, on the overt behavior, on what can be seen from the outside. But even then the reader would certainly translate the overt syndromes into concepts very much like the ones used in the description given above. These concepts provide the nodal points in terms of which the event can be described most economically, which allow for extrapolation to other possible events and which allow for prediction.

Social perception in general can best be described as a process between the center of one person and the center of another person, from life space to life space. When A observes B's behavior, he "reads" it in terms of psychological entities (and his reactions, being guided by his own sentiments, expectations, and wishes, can again be understood only in terms of psychological concepts). A, through psychological processes in himself, perceives psychological processes in B.

One might say psychological processes such as motives, intentions, sentiments, etc., are the core processes which manifest themselves in overt behavior and expression in many variable ways. The manifestations are then directly grasped by p, the observer, in terms of these psychological core processes; they would otherwise remain undecipherable. By looking through the mediation, p perceives the distal object, the psychological entities that bring consistency and meaning to the behavior; p's reaction is then to this meaning, not to the overt behavior directly, and this reaction is then carried back by the mediation to o, etc.

However, though the main process of social perception goes on between person and person spanning the mediation, and though often a first over-all description can catch the essentials without considering the mediation, we also want to know how the mediation carries the process. After all, the perceiving person gets information about the environment only through the proximal stimuli. This,

then, poses the important problem of relating the proximal stimuli to two end points (the foci of the perceptual arc), namely the contents of the environment on the one hand and the phenomena, the way these contents appear to us, on the other. Only then will we also be able to explain cases in which one person misunderstands another, or in which an action (a primary medium for the transmission of psychological characteristics) does not correspond to the intention of the agent.

The mediation

ITS GRAMMATICAL STRUCTURE
The simplest model for the coordination of mediation to distal stimuli would be one in which a specific offshoot is coordinated to each content or property. The organism would then only have to learn the specific connections between offshoots and contents. He would, so to speak, have to memorize a vocabulary of mediation consisting only of nouns. If the organism perceived one of the offshoots, he would react to it as if he were perceiving the content, the offshoot being an unambiguous sign of the content. This would be the case, if, for example, a raised eyebrow were the necessary and sufficient indication that o was dubious.

However, the language of nature is more complicated. It offers its contents to us not merely through patterns comparable to univocal nouns but also through patterns that are in some way analogous to ambiguous words and synonyms, or to adjectives and verbs, and which even contain something of a grammatical structure. A parallel to ambiguous messages is seen when an offshoot is coordinated to two or more different contents. Then, of course, the manifestation taken by itself can be a sign of any one of these contents.

EMBEDDEDNESS

Carrying the analogy of grammatical structure further, we can say that, just as ambiguous words become more specifically defined when they are placed in sentences that give them a contextual setting the ambiguity of mediation events is reduced when the stimuli or manifestations referring to the distal stimulus are *embedded* in the total situation. In discussions of embeddedness, the term "local stimulus" is sometimes used to refer to a part of the stimulus pattern as distinct from the total stimulus which includes the surroundings as well.

Very often in social perception, what a person says and does provides important cues for such distal properties as motivations, intentions, abilities, etc. But this raw material is also not univocally coordinated to these important properties of the person. Corresponding to the surrounding in thing perception is the situation in social perception, with the consequence that the ambiguity of behavior as a local stimulus is reduced when it is seen in a situational context.

It is probably fair to say that the stimulus fields basic for person perception are usually *more extended in time* than those relevant to thing perception. Let us assume that we enter an unfamiliar room for the first time, and that in it we find a few people we have never met before. A glance around the room will suffice to get an approximately correct idea of the shape of the room and of the objects in it. We shall be much more insecure in our judgments of the people. We may get a global first impression of them but we do not perceive the relevant properties of the social situation as quickly. We do not know whether A likes or dislikes B, whether C intends to thwart D, and so on. Many more data, a much wider manifold of stimuli, are needed to give us this information. We have to get acquainted with these people. We have to interact with them and observe how they interact with each other. We might say that person perception will be like reduction screen vision (familiar in experiments on color constancy) if we exclude the perception of events and actions. Although we believe that we get to know something about a person from the shape of his face, or even the color of his hair, these physiognomic properties are far outweighed by his actions as cues to his personality. In most cases we cognize a person's traits, and especially his wishes, sentiments, or intentions from what he does and says, and we know considerably less when we are limited to what we can see of him as a static object.

STIMULUS CONFIGURATIONS

At first glance it seems difficult to arrive at scientific generalizations concerning the stimulus field mediating perception, for if we have to consider the total field in order to achieve good coordination between distal stimulus and percept, the task seems complex indeed.

But in social perception, the influence of additional data that resist geometrical definition is often essential, and it seems that the most fruitful way to treat the process of perception is to assume stages that intervene between the proximal stimulus and the percept. This would lead to the notion of a hierarchical process, in which the proximal stimulus gives rise to more peripheral meanings, which in turn play the role of data for the higher levels of construction.

Constructive processes within the observer

MEANINGS AS DATA

The proposition that meanings as "intervening variables" are necessary in order that stimulus patterns may be co-ordinated with phenomena is significant enough to warrant further explications. Let us suppose that o is perceived as being "courageous." This impression can be produced by many different concrete stimulus configurations. We can conceive of all these stimulus configurations as making up a manifold which is defined by the fact that each member of it produces the impression "o acts courageously." Then each configuration has the position of a synonym. Yet it is impossible to find a geometrical pattern, an ordinal stimulus definable by a figural feature, which would distinguish the members of this manifold from, let us say, stimulus patterns producing the impression "o acts in a cowardly way." It is even unlikely that one can point to a limited number of figurally identifiable subgroups of this manifold, as is possible to a certain extent, with the ordinal stimuli producing the impression "this surface is slanting." This, of course, does not preclude the possibility of finding a figural parameter coordinated to the impression "courageous" in a particular situation. Thus, if one presents different motion picture scenes in which an obviously dangerous animal is shown with different persons, the impression that person A is more cou rageous than B might be produced by simple motions of approach or

withdrawal. But one cannot say that motions of approachment or withdrawal defined in a temporal and spatial way, are *generally* coordinated with these impressions. Only when the level of meaning is included can a feature common to all the cases producing the impression "courageous" be found. The meaning might be something like: going ahead or not withdrawing in spite of danger ahead. Bear also in mind that in this case "going ahead" does not have to be defined spatially in the physical sense; it can be defined "hodologically," as doing something that is a condition for coming into contact. The actions can be in social space. Also "danger" cannot be defined figurally.

Perception through speech provides another area where the crucial data are meanings, and not simply stimulus patterns reduced to spatial coordinates. This is even clear in cases in which a person reports his thoughts and feelings literally, as when he says, "I am angry" or "I think thus and so." But it is even more sharply brought out when we infer his thoughts and feelings indirectly from what he says and how he says it. In either case we immediately are in the realm of meaning, but in the latter the direct or concrete meaning of the sentence is only one factor in understanding. Many other factors are taken into account, such as knowledge about the person uttering the sentence, to whom it is said, the relation between speaker and the one spoken to, the situation that provoked to utterance, etc. Again there is no simple coordination between a particular utterance and the impression produced by it: a particular utterance can have many different meanings in different situations and one and the same impression can be produced by many different utterances. Nevertheless, the hearer has the feeling of being directly in the presence of anger or other feelings of o, and it would be hard to find a difference between this feeling of presence and the feeling of being in the presence of directly, visually seen objects. There certainly does not have to intervene a "judgment" or an "inference" just because meanings are essential data in the perceptual process.

MEANINGS AS INTEGRATING FACTORS

The role of meanings in perception becomes even more central because the consistent representation of the world towards which perception tends depends upon meanings (or beliefs or interpretations or evaluations, to indicate a wider scope of connotations) as organizing factors. The integrative phenomenon may be expressed in general as follows: Let us assume that a certain stimulus, x, is ambiguous. It can be seen as a or b. Whether a or b is seen depends upon the *meaning* to which any additional stimuli give rise and how these meanings fit with a or b. We can even assume that the additional stimulus, y, is also ambiguous, that is, it can be seen as c or d. If meaning b fits with meaning c, while neither fits with a or d, nor d with a or b, then the first stimulus will be seen as b, the second as c. The world we perceive has to be consistent, and the equivocal stimuli, even ordinal stimuli, will give rise to percepts that fit together and produce an integrated picture.

That the valuations of different parts of the stimulus manifold are put together in such a way as to form an integrated impression leads to the assumption of a hierarchy of structures interposed between the stimulus manifold and the resulting impressions, of stages of intervening variables that help

us to analyze in a fruitful manner the correlations between the total stimulus field and the total phenomenal field. The parts of the stimulus manifold are evaluated, and these evaluations combine to produce still more encompassing evaluations, and so on—though in considering this process we must never forget that its direction is not all one way, from stimuli to impressions, but that the evaluations or meanings of the higher levels in turn influence the meanings of the low er levels. We are aware of the fact that this description is still very inexact; however one can trust that it can be made more objective. A promising beginning in this direction has been made by Hayek (1952) with his ideas about a hierarchy of evaluations.

Within the hierarchy of required relations, conflicts arise when relations that hold between parts of the visual world are incompatible with relations required by other parts or by the total visual field. Such conflict is in evidence, for example, when I can see through an object which casts a shadow, or when Object A seems nearer than B, and B nearer than C, but also C nearer than A.

ECONOMY OF INTERPRETATION—
REDUNDANCY

We have seen that a stimulus which is ambiguous as long as it is given singly, may become unequivocal with the addition of further data. It is important to stress that this specificity is established through the meaningfulness of the integrated perceptual field. But of two equally meaningful integrations, the one that is less complex, the one that requires fewer assumptions, fewer data in general, seems in general to be preferred. This is sometimes referred to as the principle of parsimony, a principle well known in the philosophy of science, and which may have its analogue in perception.

Social perception also has systems of implied facts, with the possibility that certain data may be superfluous for providing additional information. If, for example, one already knows that A is superior in power to B, then the fact that A is chasing B does not add much information about the power relation between A and B. Such behavior is "just what one expected." The motion of A moving behind B [as, for example, when T moves behind t in the Heider-Simmel film illustrated in Figure 1.—Eds.] will be seen as "chasing" and not "following" just because of the principle of economy of interpretation. If, however, the observer was told that A, though superior in power, is in fact following B (or that B is leading A) then additional information is presented, information that is not at all redundant and therefore sheds a new light on the relation between A and B. The integrative process then presses for a sensible explanation, one that brings order into the array of facts. One might conclude, for instance, that though A is more powerful than B, he is trying to teach B to assume qualities of leadership, or that he is engaged in a friendly game with B. But if the only fact at hand is the power superiority of A, such explanations are clearly more expensive than perceiving the notion of A and B as chasing. In these examples, the integration of only two data is required. The expense difference between the simplest and the most complicated hypothesis mounts very rapidly when examples with a greater manifold of data are considered.

In the first part of this chapter, it was pointed out that in person perception, the manifold of incoming messages (the proximal stimuli of perception) is encoded in terms of the motives, sentiments, beliefs, and personality traits of other persons. There we mentioned that these are dispositional properties, the relatively stable distal features that are relevant to us. We now should like to add that it is through the process of construction within the central layers of the observer that these dispositional features serve to integrate a bewildering mass of data in the most economical terms.

Misperception

The coordination between the percept and the distal stimulus in spite of ambiguities of the local proximal stimulus is, of course, of vital importance for an efficient interaction on the part of the person with his environment. To say that it would be confusing if the shape of objects were transformed with every positional shift, or if persons were perceived as changing character with every action, or if what I perceive as o's desires might just as easily be his antipathies, is but a great understatement of how much more disturbing the world would be. We need to perceive things and people with their invariant properties more or less as they are, even though these properties are mediated to us in a complicated way and not simply by the local proximal stimulus.

As has already been stressed, the principle of embeddedness refers to a process essential to this coordination, namely the integration between the local stimulus and its surroundings. Moreover, the meaning of the local stimulus is often, if not always, a function of the integration of the perceptual field. As examples of this kind of constructive embeddedness, we have noted the perceptual constancies in which the surrounding helps determine the properties of the object by eliminating the ambiguity of the local stimulus. For social perception, it is the surrounding situation that makes it possible to determine the motivations and intentions that lie behind a specific overt behavior.

Unfortunately (or fortunately if distortion and pretense aid and abet one's intentions), though the surrounding influences the appearance of a subpart of the perceptual field, it does not always improve cognition. It may be so misleading as to interfere with the coordination between the distal object and the perception of it.

Many examples of the inadequate apprehension of the significant conditions surrounding behavior appear in Ichheiser's essay "Misunderstandings in human relations." He points out that a mother and teacher may have very different pictures of the personality of a child because they do not take into account the fact that the home situation is different from the school situation. Moreover, they tend to overestimate the unity of the child's personality because of a tendency to think that the child will behave in the same way in all situations.

Thus, the father always sees his son in the role of son, the employer sees the employee only as an employee behaving in front of the employer, etc. Varying somewhat an analogy of Ichheiser, we might say it is as if we always carried a flashlight with a filter of red color when examining an empty room; we would then ascribe the color to the room. We are reminded of discussions regarding the influence of the method of observation on what is observed in science.

Another case of misjudging the factor of situation occurs when the situation is perceived egocentrically, that is, if the situation of the other person is silently presupposed to be the same as the situation of the observer. Ichheiser (1949) quotes the example of Marie Antoinette who, upon being told that the people were hungry because they had no bread, asked why they did not eat cake instead.

Sometimes the raw materials of social perception are the things that belong to a person. We form an idea of a person when we see his room, his books, his pictures, etc. (Ichheiser, 1949, p. 5). If we are sure that the person himself selected the things because he likes them, then this idea may be more or less adequate. But again, in many cases other factors besides personal preference determined the ownership of the things, and we are misled by this raw material.

Misperceptions also occur when the properties of a person are mediated to us through what other people say or write about him, through gossip, newspapers, etc. Consequently, the interpretation of new behavioral data may also be in error because of its integration with false beliefs.

In all of the cases discussed, the reason for the misperceptions or differences in interpretations concerning another person lies in the lack of correlation between the raw material and the intended object of perception. We take the raw material too literally without taking into account additional factors that influence it.

Perceptual styles

The fact that there is a lack of correspondence between the raw material of perception and the intended object of perception allows idiosyncratic approaches to the world on the part of the observer a much freer reign in the organization and interpretation of incoming proximal stimuli. The issue here does not concern errors of perception as much as it does perceptual styles—what the person extracts from his world because of his manner of perceiving.

A striking case is the calculating prodigy who was so prone to perceive the world in terms of numerical combinations that, after seeing a play, he was entirely unaffected by the scene but instead "informed his hosts of the exact number of words uttered by the various actors, and of the number of steps taken by others in their dances" (Ball, 1956, p. 469).

Physiognomic perception, the mode of perception in which things appear animate, shows interesting individual differences. From Werner's (1948) writings, the proposition that physiognomic perception "plays a greater role in the primitive world than in our own" (p. 69) has become familiar. Children, for example, show more physiognomic perception than adults. Chronic schizophrenics, in a study by Ihrig (1953) produced fewer animistic responses to the Heider-Simmel film than the control groups. Even with normal adults there seem to be differences in the tendency to interpret stimulus configurations in terms of personal behavior.

Another case in point concerns depth of personal contact with one's environment. We know that the degree of intimacy of contact between two people depends on the situation, how long the persons have known each other, and on individual differences. Some people perceive the more superficial layers of personality in interpersonal relations and act accordingly, whereas the perceptions and actions of others are more concerned with central layers, the deeper and sometimes more covert psychological aspects of the person. Karl Buehler (1929), in his interesting analysis of interactions in a dyad, discusses examples of different degrees of depth of contact. Lewin (1948) has extended individual differences concerning this dimension to differences in national character, notably to differences between the United States and Germany (especially p. 24). Interesting differences in social perception between Russian displaced persons and Americans are described by Hanfmann (1957).

Phenomenologically oriented psychologists in particular have stressed that for one person to be in contact with another and to perceive and react to the other's sentiments and wishes, it is not enough that he is exposed to certain stimulus configurations. A general readiness to perceive psychologically is necessary; this receptivity makes possible the arousal of such percepts as "he is angry," or "he wants to tell me something." As we know, people vary widely in such social-psychological perceptivity.

The inclination of the observer to perceive his world according to individual perceptual styles could also be elaborated by reference to such concepts as "levelers" versus "sharpeners" (Klein, 1951), "authoritarians" versus "nonauthoritarians" (Titus and Hollander, 1957), the optimist who sees a rosy glow to everything versus the pessimist who extracts the negative values. All these are perceptual attitudes, general ways of "being in the world" which lead to the arousal of different percepts in spite of the fact that the stimulus configurations presented are the same.[1]

[1] Many comparative and documenting references in Prof. Heider's original chapter are omitted.—Eds.

33   The presentation of self in everyday life

ERVING GOFFMAN

When an individual enters the presence of others, they commonly seek to acquire information about him or to bring into play information about him already possessed. They will be interested in his general socio-economic status, his conception of self, his attitude toward them, his competence, his trustworthiness, etc. Although some of this information seems to be sought almost as an end in itself, there are usually quite practical reasons for acquiring it. Information about the individual helps to define the situation, enabling others to know in advance what he will expect of them and what they may expect of him. Informed in these ways, the others will know how best to act in order to call forth a desired response from him.

For those present, many sources of information become accessible and many carriers (or "sign-vehicles") become available for conveying this information. If unacquainted with the individual, observers can glean clues from his conduct and appearance which allow them to apply their previous experience with individuals roughly similar to the one before them or, more important, to apply untested stereotypes to him. They can also assume from past experience that only individuals of a particular kind are likely to be found in a given social setting. They can rely on what the individual says about himself or on documentary evidence he provides as to who and what he is. If they know, or know of, the individual by virtue of experience prior to the interaction, they can rely on assumptions as to the persistence and generality of psychological traits as a means of predicting his present and future behavior.

However, during the period in which the individual is in the immediate presence of the others, few events may occur which directly provide the others with the conclusive information they will need if they are to direct wisely their own activity. Many crucial facts lie beyond the time and place of interaction or lie concealed within it. For example, the "true" or "real" attitudes, beliefs, and emotions of the individual can be ascertained only indirectly, through his avowals or through what appears to be involuntary expressive behavior. Similarly, if the individual offers the others a product or service, they will often find that during the interaction there will be no time and place immediately available for eating the pudding that the proof can be found in. They will be forced to accept some events as conventional or natural signs of something not directly available to the senses. In Ichheiser's terms (1949, pp. 6–7), the individual will have to act so that he intentionally or unintentionally *expresses* himself, and the others will in turn have to be *impressed* in some way by him.

The expressiveness of the individual

Excerpted from **The Presentation of Self in Everyday Life**, New York: Doubleday-Anchor, 1959, with permission of the author and copyright owner, Erving Goffman.

(and therefore his capacity to give impressions) appears to involve two radically different kinds of sign activity: the expression that he *gives*, and the expression that he *gives off*. The first involves verbal symbols or their substitutes which he uses admittedly and solely to convey the information that he and the others are known to attach to these symbols. This is communication in the traditional and narrow sense. The second involves a wide range of action that others can treat as symptomatic of the actor, the expectation being that the action was performed for reasons other than the information conveyed in this way. As we shall have to see, this distinction has an only initial validity. The individual does of course intentionally convey misinformation by means of both of these types of communication, the first involving deceit, the second feigning.

Let us now turn from the others to the point of view of the individual who presents himself before them. He may wish them to think highly of him, or to think that he thinks highly of them, or to perceive how in fact he feels toward them, or to obtain no clear-cut impression; he may wish to ensure sufficient harmony so that the interaction can be sustained, or to defraud, get rid of, confuse, mislead, antagonize, or insult them. Regardless of the particular objective which the individual has in mind and of his motive for having this objective, it will be in his interests to control the conduct of the others, especially their responsive treatment of him. This control is achieved largely by influencing the definition of the situation which the others come to formulate, and he can influence this definition by expressing himself in such a way as to give them the kind of impression that will lead them to act voluntarily in accordance with his own plan. Thus, when an individual appears in the presence of others, there will usually be some reason for him to mobilize his activity so that it will convey an impression to others which it is in his interests to convey.

Of the two kinds of communication —expressions given and expressions given off—this report will be primarily concerned with the latter, with the more theatrical and contextual kind, the non-verbal, presumably unintentional kind, whether this communication be purposely engineered or not.

I have said that when an individual appears before others his actions will influence the definition of the situation which they come to have. Sometimes the individual will act in a thoroughly calculating manner, expressing himself in a given way solely in order to give the kind of impression to others that is likely to evoke from them a specific response he is concerned to obtain. Sometimes the individual will be calculating in his activitiy but be relatively unaware that this is the case. Sometimes he will intentionally and consciously express himself in a particular way, but chiefly because the tradition of his group or social status require this kind of expression and not because of any particular response (other than vague acceptance or approval) that is likely to be evoked from those impressed by the expression. Sometimes the traditions of an individual's role will lead him to give a well-designed impression of a particular kind and yet he may be neither consciously nor unconsciously disposed to create such an impression. The others, in their turn, may be suitably impressed by the individual's efforts to convey something, or may misunderstand the situation and come to conclusions that are warranted neither by the individual's intent nor by the facts. In any case, in so far as the others act *as if* the individual had conveyed a particular impression, we may take a functional or pragmatic view and say that the individual has "effectively" projected a given definition of the situation and "effectively" fostered the understanding that a given state of affairs obtains.

There is one aspect of the others' response that bears special comment here. Knowing that the individual is likely to present himself in a light that is favorable to him, the others may divide what they witness into two parts; a part that is relatively easy for the individual to manipulate at will, being chiefly his verbal assertions, and a part in regard to which he seems to have little concern or control, being chiefly derived from the expressions he gives off. The others may then use what are considered to be the ungovernable aspects of his expressive behavior as a check upon the validity of what is conveyed by the governable aspects. In this a fundamental asymmetry is demonstrated in the communication process, the individual presumably being aware of only one stream of his communication, the witnesses of this stream and one other. For example, in Shetland Isle one crofter's wife, in serving native dishes to a visitor from the mainland of Britain, would listen with a polite smile to his polite claims of liking what he was eating; at the same time she would take note of the rapidity with which the visitor lifted his fork or spoon to his mouth, the eagerness with which he passed food into his mouth, and the gusto expressed in chewing the food, using these signs as a check on the stated feelings of the eater.

Now given the fact that others are likely to check up on the more control-lable aspects of behavior by means of the less controllable, one can expect that sometimes the individual will try to exploit this very possibility, guiding the impression he makes through behavior felt to be reliably informing.[1] For example, in gaining admission to a tight social circle, the participant observer may not only wear an accepting look while listening to an informant, but may also be careful to wear the same look when observing the informant talking to others; observers of the observer will then not as easily discover where he actually stands.

This kind of control upon the part of the individual reinstates the symmetry of the communication process, and sets the stage for a kind of information game—a potentially infinite cycle of concealment, discovery, false revelation, and rediscovery. It should be added that since the others are likely to be relatively unsuspicious of the presumably unguided aspect of the individual's conduct, he can gain much by controlling it. The others of course may sense that the individual is manipulating the presumably spontaneous aspects of his behavior, and seek in this very act of manipulation some shading of conduct that the individual has not managed to control. This again provides a check upon the individual's behavior, this time his presumably uncalculated behavior, thus re-establishing the asymmetry of the communication process.

When we allow that the individual projects a definition of the situation when he appears before others, we must also see that the others, however passive their role may seem to be, will them-

[1] The widely read and rather sound writings of Stephen Potter are concerned in part with signs that can be engineered to give a shrewd observer the apparently incidental cues he needs to discover concealed virtues the gamesman does not in fact possess.

selves effectively project a definition of the situation by virtue of their response to the individual and by virtue of any lines of action they initiate to him. Ordinarily the definitions of the situation projected by the several different participants are sufficiently attuned to one another so that open contradiction will not occur. I do not mean that there will be the kind of consensus that arises when each individual present candidly expresses what he really feels and honestly agrees with the expressed feelings of the others present. This kind of harmony is an optimistic ideal and in any case not necessary for the smooth working of society. Rather, each participant is expected to suppress his immediate heartfelt feelings, conveying a view of the situation which he feels the others will be able to find at least temporarily acceptable. The maintenance of this surface of agreement, this veneer of consensus, is facilitated by each participant concealing his own wants behind statements which assert values to which everyone present feels obliged to give lip service. Further, there is usually a kind of division of definitional labor. Each participant is allowed to establish the tentative official ruling regarding matters which are vital to him but not immediately important to others, e.g., the rationalizations and justifications by which he accounts for his past activity. In exchange for this courtesy he remains silent or non-committal on matters important to others but not immediately important to him. We have then a kind of interactional *modus vivendi*. Together the participants contribute to a single over-all definition of the situation which involves not so much a real agreement as to what exists but rather a real agreement as to whose claims concerning what

issues will be temporarily honored. Real agreement will also exist concerning the desirability of avoiding an open conflict of definitions of the situation. I will refer to this level of agreement as a "working consensus." It is to be understood that the working consensus established in one interaction setting will be quite different in content from the working consensus established in a different type of setting. Thus, between two friends at lunch, a reciprocal show of affection, respect, and concern for the other is maintained. In service occupations, on the other hand, the specialist often maintains an image of disinterested involvement in the problem of the client, while the client responds with a show of respect for the competence and integrity of the specialist. Regardless of such differences in content, however, the general form of these working arrangements is the same.

In noting the tendency for a participant to accept the definitional claims made by the others present, we can appreciate the crucial importance of the information that the individual *initially* possesses or acquires concerning his fellow participants, for it is on the basis of this initial information that the individual starts to define the situation and starts to build up lines of responsive action. The individual's initial projection commits him to what he is proposing to be and requires him to drop all pretenses of being other things. As the interaction among the participants progresses, additions and modifications in this initial informational state will of course occur, but it is essential that these later developments be related without contradiction to, and even built up from, the initial positions taken by the several participants. It would seem that an individual can more easily make a choice as to what line of treatment to demand from and extend to the others present at the beginning of an encounter than he can alter the line of treatment that is being pursued once the interaction is underway.

When the interaction that is initiated by "first impressions" (Whyte, 1946, pp. 132–3) is itself merely the initial interaction in an extended series of interactions involving the same participants, we speak of "getting off on the right foot" and feel that it is crucial that we do so.

Given the fact that the individual effectively projects a definition of the situation when he enters the presence of others, we can assume that events may occur within the interaction which contradict, discredit, or otherwise throw doubt upon this projection. When these disruptive events occur, the interaction itself may come to a confused and embarrassed halt. Some of the assumptions upon which the responses of the participants had been predicated become untenable, and the participants find themselves lodged in an interaction for which the situation has been wrongly defined and is now no longer defined. At such moments the individual whose presentation has been discredited may feel ashamed while the others present may feel hostile, and all the participants may come to feel ill at ease, nonplussed, out of countenance, embarrassed, experiencing the kind of anomy that is generated when the minute social system of face-to-face interaction breaks down.

In stressing the fact that the initial definition of the situation projected by an individual tends to provide a plan for the co-operative activity that follows —in stressing this action point of view

—we must not overlook the crucial fact that any projected definition of the situation also has a distinctive moral character. It is this moral character of projections that will chiefly concern us in this report. Society is organized on the principle that any individual who possesses certain social characteristics has a moral right to expect that others will value and treat him in a correspondingly appropriate way. Connected with this principle is a second, namely that an individual who implicitly or explicitly signifies that he has certain social characteristics ought to have this claim honored by others and ought in fact to be what he claims he is. In consequence, when an individual projects a definition of the situation and thereby makes an implicit or explicit claim to be a person of a particular kind, he automatically exerts a moral demand upon the others, obliging them to value and treat him in the manner that persons of his kind have a right to expect. He also implicitly forgoes all claims to be things he does not appear to be and hence forgoes the treatment that would be appropriate for such individuals. The others find, then, that the individual has informed them as to what is and as to what they *ought* to see as the "is."

One cannot judge the importance of definitional disruptions by the frequency with which they occur, for apparently they would occur more frequently were not constant precautions taken. We find that preventive practices are constantly employed to avoid these embarrassments and that corrective practices are constantly employed to compensate for discrediting occurrences that have not been successfully avoided. When the individual employs these strategies and tactics to protect his own projections, we may refer to them as "defensive practices"; when a participant employs them to save the definition of the situation projected by another, we speak of "protective practices" or "tact." Together, defensive and protective practices comprise the techniques employed to safeguard the impression fostered by an individual during his presence before others. It should be added that while we may be ready to see that no fostered impression would survive if defensive practices were not employed, we are less ready perhaps to see that few impressions could survive if those who received the impression did not exert tact in their reception of it.

In addition to the fact that precautions are taken to prevent disruption of projected definitions, we may also note that an intense interest in these disruptions comes to play a significant role in the social life of the group. Practical jokes and social games are played in which embarrassments which are to be taken unseriously are purposely engineered. Fantasies are created in which devastating exposures occur. Anecdotes from the past—real, embroidered, or fictitious—are told and retold, detailing disruptions which occurred, almost occurred, or occurred and were admirably resolved. There seems to be no grouping which does not have a ready supply of these games, reveries, and cautionary tales, to be used as a source of humor, a catharsis for anxieties, and a sanction for inducing individuals to be modest in their claims and reasonable in their projected expectations.

To summarize, then, I assume that when an individual appears before others he will have many motives for trying to control the impression they receive of the situation. This report is concerned with some of the common techniques that persons employ to sustain such impressions and with some of the common contingencies associated with the employment of these techniques. The specific content of any activity presented by the individual participant, or the role it plays in the interdependent activities of an on-going social system, will not be at issue; I shall be concerned only with the participant's dramaturgical problems of presenting the activity before others.

For the purpose of this report, interaction (that is, face-to-face interaction) may be roughly defined as the reciprocal influence of individuals upon one another's actions when in one another's immediate physical presence. An interaction may be defined as all the interaction which occurs throughout any one occasion when a given set of individuals are in one another's continuous presence; the term "an encounter" would do as well. A "performance" may be defined as all the activity of a given participant on a given occasion which serves to influence in any way any of the other participants. Taking a particular participant and his performance as a basic point of reference, we may refer to those who contribute the other performances as the audience, observers, or co-participants. The pre-established pattern of action which is unfolded during a performance and which may be presented or played through on other occasions may be called a "part" or "routine." [2] These situational terms can easily be related to conventional structural ones. When an individual or performer plays the same part to the

[2] For comments on the importance of distinguishing between a routine of interaction and any particular instance when this routine is played through, see John von Neumann and Oskar Morgenstern, **The Theory of Games and Economic Behavior** (1947).

audience on different occasions, a social relationship is likely to arise. Defining social role as the enactment of rights and duties attached to a given status, we can say that a social role will involve one or more parts and that each of these different parts may be presented by the performer on a series of occasions to the same kinds of audience or to an audience of the same persons.

The framework

A social establishment is any place surrounded by fixed barriers to perception in which a particular kind of activity regularly takes place. I have suggested that any social establishment may be studied profitably from the point of view of impression management. Within the walls of a social establishment we find a team of performers who co-operate to present to an audience a given definition of the situation. This will include the conception of own team and of audience and assumptions concerning the ethos that is to be maintained by rules of politeness and decorum. We often find a division into back region, where the performance of a routine is prepared, and front region, where the performance is presented. Access to these regions is controlled in order to prevent the audience from seeing backstage and to prevent outsiders from coming into a performance that is not addressed to them. Among members of the team we find that familiarity prevails, solidarity is likely to develop, and that secrets that could give the show away are shared and kept. A tacit agreement is maintained between performers and audience to act as if a given degree of opposition and of accord existed between them. Typically, but not always, agreement is stressed and

opposition is underplayed. The resulting work consensus tends to be contradicted by the attitude toward the audience which the performers express in the absence of the audience and by carefully controlled communication out of character conveyed by the performers while the audience is present. We find that discrepant roles develop: some of the individuals who are apparently teammates, or audience, or outsiders acquire information about the performance and relations to the team which are not apparent and which complicate the problem of putting on a show. Sometimes disruptions occur through unmeant gestures, *faux pas*, and scenes, thus discrediting or contradicting the definition of the situation that is being maintained. The mythology of the team will dwell upon these disruptive events. We find that performers, audience, and outsiders all utilize techniques for saving the show, whether by avoiding likely disruptions or by correcting for unavoided ones, or by making it possible for others to do so. To ensure that these techniques will be employed, the team will tend to select members who are loyal, disciplined, and circumspect, and to select an audience that is tactful.

These features and elements, then, comprise the framework I claim to be characteristic of much social interaction as it occurs in natural settings in our Anglo-American society. This framework is formal and abstract in the sense that it can be applied to any social establishment; it is not, however, merely a static classification. The framework bears upon dynamic issues created by the motivation to sustain a definition of the situation that has been projected before others.

An establishment may be viewed

"technically," in terms of its efficiency and inefficiency as an intentionally organized system of activity for the achievement of predefined objectives. An establishment may be viewed "politically," in terms of the actions which each participant (or class of participants) can demand of other participants, the kinds of deprivations and indulgences which can be meted out in order to enforce these demands, and the kinds of social controls which guide this exercise of command and use of sanctions. An establishment may be viewed "structurally," in terms of the horizontal and vertical status divisions and the kinds of social relations which relate these several groupings to one another. Finally, an establishment may be viewed "culturally," in terms of the moral values which influence activity in the establishment—values pertaining to fashions, customs, and matters of taste, to politeness and decorum, to ultimate ends and normative restrictions on means, etc. It is to be noted that all the facts that can be discovered about an establishment are relevant to each of the four perspectives but that each perspective gives its own priority and order to these facts.

It seems to me that the dramaturgical approach may constitute a fifth perspective, to be added to the technical, political, structural, and cultural perspectives. The dramaturgical perspective, like each of the other four, can be employed as the end-point of analysis, as a final way of ordering facts. This would lead us to describe the techniques of impression management employed in a given establishment, the principal problems of impression management in the establishment, and the identity and interrelationships of the several performance teams which operate in the establishment. But, as with the facts utilized in each of the other perspectives, the facts specifically pertaining to impression management also play a part in the matters that are a concern in all the other perspectives.

Personality-interaction-society

In recent years there have been elaborate attempts to bring into one framework the concepts and findings derived from three different areas of inquiry: the individual personality, social interaction, and society. I would like to suggest here a simple addition to these inter-disciplinary attempts.

When an individual appears before others, he knowingly and unwittingly projects a definition of the situation, of which a conception of himself is an important part. When an event occurs which is expressively incompatible with this fostered impression, significant consequences are simultaneously felt in three levels of social reality, each of which involves a different point of reference and a different order of fact.

First, the social interaction, treated here as a dialogue between two teams, may come to an embarrassed and confused halt; the situation may cease to be defined, previous positions may become no longer tenable, and participants may find themselves without a charted course of action. The participants typically sense a false note in the situation and come to feel awkward, flustered, and, literally, out of countenance. In other words, the minute social system created and sustained by orderly social interaction becomes disorganized. These are the consequences that the disruptions have from the point of view of social interaction.

Secondly, in addition to these disorganizing consequences for action at the moment, performance disruptions may have consequences of a more far-reaching kind. Audiences tend to accept the individual's particular performance as evidence of his capacity to perform the routine and even as evidence of his capacity to perform any routine. In a sense these larger social units— teams, establishments, etc.—become committed every time the individual performs his routine; with each performance the legitimacy of these units will tend to be tested anew and their permanent reputation put at stake. This kind of commitment is especially strong during some performances. Thus, when a surgeon and his nurse both turn from the operating table and the anesthetized patient accidentally rolls off the table to his death, not only is the operation disrupted in an embarrassing way, but the reputation of the doctor, as a doctor and as a man, and also the reputation of the hospital may be weakened. These are the consequences that disruptions may have from the point of view of social structure.

Finally, we often find that the individual may deeply involve his ego in his identification with a particular part, establishment, and group, and in his self-conception as someone who does not disrupt social interaction or let down the social units which depend upon that interaction. When a disruption occurs, then, we may find that the self-conceptions around which his personality has been built may become discredited. These are consequences that disruptions may have from the point of view of individual personality.

Performance disruptions, then, have consequences at three levels of abstraction: personality, interaction, and social structure. While the likelihood of disruption will vary widely from interaction to interaction, and while the social importance of likely disruptions will vary from interaction to interaction, still it seems that there is no interaction in which the participants do not take an appreciable chance of being slightly embarrassed or a slight chance of being deeply humiliated. Life may not be much of a gamble, but interaction *is*. Further, in so far as individuals make efforts to avoid disruptions or to correct for ones not avoided, these efforts, too, will have simultaneous consequences at the three levels. Here, then, we have one simple way of articulating three levels of abstraction and three perspectives from which social life has been studied.

Underlying all social interaction there seems to be a fundamental dialectic. When one individual enters the presence of others, he will want to discover the facts of the situation. Were he to possess this information, he could know, and make allowances for, what will come to happen and he could give the others present as much of their due as is consistent with his enlightened self-interest. To uncover fully the factual nature of the situation, it would be necessary for the individual to know all the relevant social data about the others. It would also be necessary for the individual to know the actual outcome or end product of the activity of the others during the interaction, as well as their innermost feelings concerning him. Full information of this order is rarely available; in its absence, the individual tends to employ substitutes—cues, tests, hints, expressive gestures, status symbols, etc.—as predictive devices. In short, since the reality that the individual is concerned with is unperceivable at the moment, appearances must be relied upon in its stead. And, paradoxically, the more the individual is concerned with the reality that is not available to perception, the more must he concentrate his attention on appearances.

We come now to the basic dialectic. In their capacity as performers, individuals will be concerned with maintaining the impression that they are living up to the many standards by which they and their products are judged. Because these standards are so numerous and so pervasive, the individuals who are performers dwell more than we might think in a moral world. But, *qua* performers, individuals are concerned not with the moral issue of realizing these standards, but with the amoral issue of engineering a convincing impression that these standards are being realized. Our activity, then, is largely concerned with moral matters, but as performers we do not have a moral concern with them. As performers we are merchants of morality. Our day is given over to intimate contact with the goods we display and our minds are filled with intimate understandings of them; but it may well be that the more attention we give to these goods, then the more distant we feel from them and from those who are believing enough to buy them. To use a different imagery, the very obligation and profitability of appearing always in a steady moral light, of being a socialized character, forces one to be the sort of person who is practiced in the ways of the stage.

Staging and the self

The general notion that we make a presentation of ourselves to others is hardly novel; what ought to be stressed in conclusion is that the very structure of the self can be seen in terms of how we arrange for such performances in our Anglo-American society.

In this report, the individual was divided by implication into two basic parts: he was viewed as a *performer*, a harried fabricator of impressions involved in the all-too-human task of staging a performance; he was viewed as a *character*, a figure, typically a fine one, whose spirit, strength, and other sterling qualities the performance was designed to evoke. The attributes of a performer and the attributes of a character are of a different order, quite basically so, yet both sets have their meaning in terms of the show that must go on.

In analyzing the self then we are drawn from its possessor, from the person who will profit or lose most by it, for he and his body merely provide the peg on which something of collaborative manufacture will be hung for a time. And the means for producing and maintaining selves do not reside inside the peg; in fact these means are often bolted down in social establishments. There will be a back region with its tools for shaping the body, and a front region with its fixed props. There will be a team of persons whose activity on stage in conjunction with available props will constitute the scene from which the performed character's self will emerge, and another team, the audience, whose interpretive activity will be necessary for this emergence. The self is a product of all of these arrangements, and in all of its parts bears the marks of this genesis.

Scaffolds are to build other things with, and should be erected with an eye to taking them down. This report is not concerned with aspects of theater that creep into everyday life. It is concerned with the structure of social encounters; the structure of those entities in social life that come into being whenever persons enter one another's immediate physical presence. The key factor in this structure is the mainte- nance of a single definition of the situation, this definition having to be expressed, and this expression sustained in the face of a multitude of potential disruptions.

VI ATTITUDES AND COGNITION

Although Gordon Allport called the concept of attitude ". . . the most distinctive and indispensable concept in contemporary American social psychology" (1935, p. 798), it has had an elusive history. Reflecting this are the controversies surrounding the nature and specificity of attitudes, their bearing on behavior, and their relationship to other constructs, such as beliefs, values, motives, norms, and roles. In the current scene, with many of the older issues reformulated, or waning in importance, the nature of attitudes is generally agreed to lie in the direction of learned sets or dispositions to respond, often *evaluatively* (see Campbell, 1963; Scott, 1968). As Katz notes here, attitudes include affective (like-dislike) as well as cognitive (belief-disbelief) components. From this point of departure, there is a fair convergence of attention on three interrelated aspects of attitudes: source, in the sense of development; function, related to the way in which attitudes are integrated in personality; and change, having to do most expressly with the way in which new experience becomes incorporated into an already existing belief system.

While the interest in studying attitudes gave way in the 1940's and 1950's to an upsurge in small groups' research, attitude change in particular has now regained a prominent place in the field. Dissonance, congruity, consistency, and balance, are the bywords reflecting the new age given special impetus by Leon Festinger with his influential work, A *Theory of Cognitive Dissonance* (1957), and by Osgood and Tannenbaum (1955) with their congruity theory. The tradition represented by the Yale attitude change studies, under the inspiration of the late Carl Hovland, also contributed importantly to the hearty interest in these phenomena (see, e.g., Hovland *et al.*, 1949, 1953, 1957; Hovland and Janis, 1959).

The wealth of material becoming available now on attitudes, and attitude change especially, is exemplified by many noteworthy books and other publications. The most ambitious of these is the recent collection of papers entitled *Theories of Cognitive Consistency: A Sourcebook* (1968), edited by Abelson, Aronson, McGuire, Newcomb, Rosenberg, and Tannenbaum. Another notable collection, with an orientation different from consistency theories *per se*, is the book *Psychological Foundations of Attitudes* (1968), edited by Greenwald, Brock, and Ostrom. For a comprehensive treatment of the area, Insko's *Theories of Attitude Change* (1967) and the book by Kiesler, Collins, and Miller on *Attitude Change* (1969) are worthwhile sources.

What gives the attitude concept its appeal is easy to understand. It serves, in the first place, as a simple, manageable representation of something quite complex: a brief summary of what has gone before in the individual's experience that may affect his present behavior. But, secondly, attitude is essentially a neutral concept which permits virtually any and all content to be contained within it; moreover, historically, it provided a way of retaining some content of "mind," despite the climate of behaviorism prevailing over many years (see McClelland, 1955).

Several other points of reference are useful in treating attitudes. They are both elements of perception ("cognitive structures" is a way of characterizing them in the aggregate), and they are elements of motivational force, insofar as they direct behavior. Put simply, they represent our outlooks and our inclinations toward action. However, not all attitudes are equally potent across time or situations, and indeed may be in conflict, as is considered at greater length in the papers in this section by Osgood and Rokeach. This leads to the conclusion that while people "hold" attitudes, they may be variously cued to "manifest" them, depending upon the social context and their relationship to it (see, e.g., Hyman & Singer, Section II).

Three lines in particular appear to be sources of attitudes; these are, direct experience with the object, explicit and implicit learning from others, and personality development. The latter source involves the effect of recurring interaction with others in establishing certain general "sets" to respond. Largely based in a psychoanalytic model, this position asserts than an individual, as a function of early experience, develops characteristic reactions as enduring orientations (see Fromm, 1941, 1947). The most notable research on this is to be found in *The Authoritarian Personality* (Adorno *et al.*, 1950) and some associated endeavors, e.g., Rokeach (1960, 1968), and the work on Machiavellianism (see Christie and Geis, Section III, and 1970). The work on "authoritarianism," especially, presents the relationship between such predisposing personality factors and manifest attitudes of prejudice (see Allport, Section X).

The two other categories of source are more obvious. One considers attitudes toward some "thing" in the outside world to be a function of *contact* with that thing. A dramatic experience, for example, might instigate an individual's attitudes and response patterns toward a category of similar things over a long time span. Secondly, people may learn attitudes quite apart from literal contact with the object of the attitude, by having contact with those holding the attitude. A substantial body of research supports the contention that children, without actually having experienced elements of the environment, take on prevailing attitudes toward them. Statements uttered by parents, encountered from the mass media, or conveyed in endless other ways, often serve to yield implicit learning of this sort. Subsequently, appropriate attitudes are bolstered by the person's attachment to groups. But beneath this feature, an attitude must be understood to provide some psychological utility for the individual.

In his paper in this section, Katz speaks to this question, i.e., the function which attitudes fulfill for the individual. This so-called functional approach refers to the role of attitudes in personality, although the term "function" is sometimes used concerning the construct's service in social psychological thought. The reasons for holding or for changing attitudes, Katz suggests, are found in the part attitudes play in personality for such functions as adjustment, ego defense, value expression, and knowledge. By making these distinctions, broader implications for the mechanics of attitude change come into focus (cf. Katz and Stotland, 1959). It will be seen that Katz considers the learned nature of attitudes and the necessity in attitude change for relearning under appropriate motivational conditions.

Osgood presents an overview here of several models of cognitive consistency, by way of considering the broad area of attitude change. He is known for his own "mediation theory" (Osgood, 1952) in which he accommodates cognitive processes in behavior; thus, the meaning of an object or event becomes a perception which is mediated by internal representations, conditioned by previous experiences, and aroused by the current situation. It is within this framework that he developed the measurement technique known as the "semantic differential" (Osgood *et al.*, 1957). In his paper here, he includes a comparison of several theories of cognitive consistency, among them Festinger's dissonance theory, Heider's balance theory, and the Osgood and Tannenbaum (1955) congruity theory. Pointing out the similarities between these, insofar as they deal with direction or sign, he proceeds to a searching consideration of what it means to speak of congruity between elements which are "signed" or labeled positively or negatively and by magnitude. A particularly useful feature of the Osgood discussion is the application he draws from these processes to the world of everyday events. His formulation with Tannenbaum (1955) of "congruity" affords predictions about the degree of change which will occur as a function of exposure to incongruous elements. The significant feature of this formulation is the lawful fashion in which the dynamics of interaction among cognitive elements are predicted, as a contribution to the understanding of attitude change phenomena.

In his widely known cognitive dissonance approach, Festinger also is concerned with cognitive elements that have a "non-fitting" relationship with one another. In effect, he postulates a motive for consonance, that is, the avoidance of dissonance, and then considers the ways by which people seek to reduce dissonance. His theory has encouraged a good deal of experimentation, based upon predictions which frequently are not of an obvious variety. Aronson's paper here provides an overview and evaluation of much of the research sparked by the theory and, from the vantage point of a former co-worker of Festinger's, considers some of the criticism which has been leveled at the dissonance formulation. For example, in his discussion of the "nothing but" critique, he sharpens the distinction between conflict and dissonance, pointing out that while conflict occurs before a decision, dissonance occurs after it. He also provides a provocative discussion of why the dissonance prediction of greater attitude change with smaller rewards is sometimes reversed by a high incentive. He indicates that the main condition which is optimal for the dissonance effect is high commitment, especially in a face-to-face situation. Moreover, he also makes the point that dissonance is more likely to operate when a firm expectancy is involved as one of the cognitions in question.

Another approach to the organization of attitudes, or "beliefs" as he prefers to conceive them, is represented in Rokeach's paper here. His contribution is vitally based in the concept of a cognitive organization which synthesizes the affective and belief components (see Rokeach, 1968). Beliefs are *not* retained, says Rokeach, ". . . in an unorganized, chaotic state within our minds." Rather, they cohere in cognitive structures. Moreover, in Rokeach's view, beliefs vary in their importance to the individual along a dimension of centrality-peripherality. From this and several related concepts, he delineates implications for attitude change. His depiction of "primitive beliefs" as central to cognitive structures is especially important in terms of resistance to change. Thus, it may be relatively easy to alter a peripheral belief without affecting the broader structure in which it is imbedded. But changing—or even challenging—a primitive belief regarding, for instance, a person's identity, encounters considerable resistance coupled with negative feeling. This is in harmony with Katz's position regarding the functions in personality that central attitudes hold.

Because many studies of attitude change have dealt with essentially trivial and peripheral beliefs, Rokeach's work raises some question about their generalizability to more central beliefs. It is also noteworthy that Rokeach's view suggests by implication that cognitive dissonance would be differentially produced depending upon the degree of centrality of the dissonant beliefs which were paired, thus sustaining a contention made by Aronson here, concerning the importance of a firm expectancy in producing dissonance effects.

As we have already noted, an individual's attitudes are generally reinforced through some group to which he belongs, or to which he refers himself (see Sections I, II, and VII). To the extent that he is motivated to retain this affiliation, those attitudes are unlikely to change, whatever their initial source. Attitudes, then, are quite distinctively social psychological variables by virtue of their genesis in and linkage to social processes and groups.

This social linkage in the persistence of attitudes is nicely conveyed by

Newcomb's report here. In it he presents the results of his follow-up study, after more than twenty years, of the women who were subjects in his now classic research in the 1930's at Bennington College. In that Bennington study he found that shifts toward the prevailing campus climate of liberal political attitudes, among these girls from mainly conservative homes, occurred from the freshman to senior years. Furthermore, these shifts were associated with social acceptance in terms of popularity and leadership. His follow-up study now supports the broader conclusion that such attitudes persist by the selection of a sustaining social environment. In particular, he finds that these women married men whose attitudes were more liberal than the conservative norm of the socio-economic stratum from which they came.

As Newcomb points out, his findings mesh well with the ideas of "balance" in Heider's work, discussed here by Osgood. Newcomb has dealt with this himself in terms of his "A-B-X Model" (1953). The essential point of this model is that a state of balance exists when persons A and B are mutually attracted to one another and share the same attitude toward object X. Imbalance can develop in various ways, including mutual liking with an opposite attitude toward the same object, or mutual disliking with the same attitude toward the object. Evidently, Newcomb's subjects achieved balance by findings spouses with attitudes similar to their own on political and social issues.

Carl Hovland was another major initiator of research on factors influencing attitude change who, together with his coworkers, contributed a rich array of concepts and experimental studies (e.g., Hovland *et al.*, 1949, 1953, 1957). As a way of characterizing personality factors associated with attitude change, he had a particular interest in the variable of persuasibility (see especially Hovland & Janis, 1959). He saw this as a persisting individual disposition related psychodynamically to central attitudes regarding one's self, such as self-esteem. In Section VII, a one-time coworker of Hovland's, Herbert Kelman, offers a conceptual scheme concerning social influence which is partly derivative of the persuasibility construct and also bears upon Katz's functional viewpoint discussed above.

In Hovland's work with Muzafer Sherif, *Social Judgment* (Sherif & Hovland, 1961), they advanced their view that an attitude should be considered a range or latitude of acceptable positions, not as a single point on a continuum. As indicated in the selection from the first chapter of that book here, the "social judgment-involvement approach" considers that a person's own stand on an issue serves as an anchor point which influences the person's evaluation of alternative positions. The Sherif-Hovland view is associated with classical psychophysics and more recently with the work of Helson (1948) on "adaptation level." The essential feature of this newer approach to attitudes is its emphasis on the person's *own position* as a determinant of his latitudes of acceptance, rejection, and noncommitment on an issue. In this view, attitudes are cognitive structures, related to self perceptions and reference group affiliations of the individual, which determine his response to communications. This point is pursued further in the more recent work by Sherif, Sherif, and Nebergall entitled *Attitude and Attitude Change: The Social Judgment-Involvement Approach* (1965).

For the most part, laboratory experimentation on attitude change has shown greater effects than have survey studies. In discussing this disparity, Hovland (1959) considered such factors as the selection of subjects and the focused intensity of the experimental situation to be potent determiners of this enhanced effect, as against the more diffuse context of the survey. He pointed to the major independent variables which yield communication effects, among them, the communicator, the nature and sequence of communication, and the position of the recipient of the communication. The paper here by Bauer is a departure from this traditional scheme.

Bauer's emphasis is upon social communication as a two-way influence process. He reviews the typical approach to communication, in terms of propaganda and attitude change through advertising, and concludes that it is inadequate to an understanding of what actually transpires. In referring to Hovland's (1959) comparison of laboratory and survey findings on attitude change, he says that it is quite clear that people receiving communications in their natural habitat are much less likely to attend to them and be influenced by them than they would be as subjects in a laboratory experiment. From a range of research findings, Bauer proceeds to bolster the view that individuals are selective in what they attend to and seek a fair exchange when accepting influence assertions from a communicator. This approach is very much in keeping with the idea of social exchange considered in the work of Homans and of Thibaut and Kelley in Section VII. Bauer also raises questions regarding the appropriateness of seeing persuasibility as a function of low self-esteem, since the importance of the issue for the person must also be taken into account. He thus implicitly deals with the centrality-peripherality dimension considered by Rokeach, and underscores its importance in understanding an individual's receptivity to attitude change.

Though attitudes have implications on various levels of analysis, they continue to be important to social psychology in terms of manifest behaviors, such as voting. A fair amount of interdisciplinary study, involving political scientists with social psychologists, has been conducted on the bases for voting phenomena (see, e.g., A. Campbell *et al.*, 1960; Sears, 1968). While easily confused with it, the nature of this research is not the same as public opinion polling directed at *predicting* the outcome of an election; it may, however, hold implications for understanding shifts in political attitudes which have a bearing subsequently on election results. Furthermore, the data obtained from public opinion polling during a political campaign can be studied in retrospect to check on the adequacy of the conceptual model dealing with factors affecting the vote.

Abelson's paper here treats the basis for failures in public opinion polling, notably in primary elections and local referenda. He dismisses the belief that errors are explicable by a "secret vote," and contends that campaigns of this kind are exceptional cases with distinctive elements. In primaries, disinterest creates difficulty for the candidate in making a clear impression until the very end of the campaign. In referenda, there is a particular vulnerability, he says, to having some abstract principle pitted against a very concrete fear or desire which overwhelms it as the campaign nears its conclusion. Because of their volatility, these campaigns are more hazardous to predict than are national campaigns where accuracy is far greater.

Abelson then describes the procedures by which computers, with data from just a few districts, can make almost miraculously instantaneous predictions about an election outcome over a large area. He concludes that the effectiveness of these rather simple projection models indicates the generality of major forces working on the electorate and how little most people concern themselves with the consistency of the political ideas they hold. In an echo of Katz's functional view, as well as Rokeach's belief system, Abelson postulates the existence of "opinion molecules," which bestow conversational and cognitive security on individuals, and which are closed and relatively impervious to other arguments.

Unless an individual is educated and concerned with the necessity for being prepared for counterarguments, he goes along, as Abelson puts it, with just "a fact and a feeling." On the other hand, knowing the refutation for counterarguments to one's position solidifies resistance to influence, according to the work of McGuire (1964, 1968) with his "inoculation model." Thus, he finds that hearing only one's own position expressed reduces the capacity to deal with counterarguments. The implication of McGuire's work is that the thoroughly committed "true believer," in Hoffer's (1951) phrase, is more vulnerable to a shift in attitude than the person who assesses the alternative arguments and is inoculated against them.

In the aggregate, the study of attitudes, and cognitive processes more generally, has aided the understanding of a broad range of topics in social psychology. Among these are intra-group and inter-group phenomena, considered in the sections which follow. The persisting interest in the attitude concept is also evident in the amount of attention devoted to attitude measurement. The recent book by Shaw & Wright (1967) provides a compendium of attitude scales. Other approaches to the assessment of attitudes include surveys, interviews and questionnaires, projective techniques, content analyses, semantic differential ratings, and even unobtrusive measures. Some useful treatments of these methodological approaches will be found in Edwards (1957), Holsti (1969), Hyman (1955), Osgood *et al.* (1957), Richardson *et al.* (1965), Scott (1968), and Webb *et al.* (1966), which the reader would do well to consult as primary sources.

34 The functional approach to the study of attitudes

DANIEL KATZ

Early approaches to the study of attitude and opinion

There have been two main streams of thinking with respect to the determination of man's attitudes. The one tradition assumes an irrational model of man: specifically it holds that men have very limited powers of reason and reflection, weak capacity to discriminate, only the most primitive self-insight, and very short memories. Whatever mental capacities people do possess are easily overwhelmed by emotional forces and appeals to self-interest and vanity. The early books on the psychology of advertising, with their emphasis on the doctrine of suggestion, exemplify this approach. One expression of this philosophy is in the propagandist's concern with tricks and traps to manipulate the public. A modern form of it appears in *The Hidden Persuaders,* or the use of subliminal and marginal suggestion, or the devices supposedly employed by "the Madison Avenue boys." Experiments to support this line of thinking started with laboratory demonstrations of the power of hypnotic suggestion and were soon extended to show that people would change their attitudes in an uncritical manner under the influence of the prestige of authority and numbers. For example, individuals would accept or reject the same idea depending upon whether it came from a positive or negative prestige source (Sherif, 1936).

The second approach is that of the ideologist who invokes a rational model of man. It assumes that the human being has a cerebral cortex, that he seeks understanding, that he consistently attempts to make sense of the world about him, that he possesses discriminating and reasoning powers which will assert themselves over time, and that he is capable of self-criticism and self-insight. It relies heavily upon getting adequate information to people. Our educational system is based upon this rational model. The present emphasis upon the improvement of communication, upon developing more adequate channels of two-way communication, of conferences and institutes, upon bringing people together to interchange ideas, are all indications of the belief in the importance of intelligence and comprehension in the formation and change of men's opinions.

Now either school of thought can point to evidence which supports its assumptions, and can make fairly damaging criticisms of its opponent. Solomon Asch (1952) and his colleagues, in attacking the irrational model, have called attention to the biased character of the old experiments on prestige suggestion which gave the subject little opportunity to demonstrate critical

Excerpted from the **Public Opinion Quarterly,** 1960, 24, 163–77, with permission of the author and publisher.

thinking. And further exploration of subjects in these stupid situations does indicate that they try to make sense of a nonsensical matter as far as possible. Though the same statement is presented by the experimenter to two groups, the first time as coming from a positive source and the second time as coming from a negative source, it is given a different meaning dependent upon the context in which it appears. Thus the experimental subject does his best to give some rational meaning to the problem. On the other hand, a large body of experimental work indicates that there are many limitations in the rational approach in that people see their world in terms of their own needs, remember what they want to remember, and interpret information on the basis of wishful thinking. H. H. Hyman and and P. Sheatsley (1947) have demonstrated that these experimental results have direct relevance to information campaigns directed at influencing public opinion. These authors assembled facts about such campaigns and showed conclusively that increasing the flow of information to people does not necessarily increase the knowledge absorbed or produce the attitude changes desired.

The major difficulty with these conflicting approaches is their lack of specification of the conditions under which men do act as the theory would predict. For the facts are that people do act at times as if they had been decorticated and at times with intelligence and comprehension. And people themselves do recognize that on occasion they have behaved blindly, impulsively, and thoughtlessly. A second major difficulty is that the rationality-irrationality dimension is not clearly defined. At the extremes it is easy to point to examples, as in the case of the acceptance of stupid suggestions under emotional stress on the one hand, or brilliant problem solving on the other; but this does not provide adequate guidance for the many cases in the middle of the scale where one attempts to discriminate between rationalization and reason.

Reconciliation of the conflict in a functional approach

The conflict between the rationality and irrationality models was saved from becoming a worthless debate because of the experimentation and research suggested by these models. The findings of this research pointed toward the elements of truth in each approach and gave some indication of the conditions under which each model could make fairly accurate predictions. In general the irrational approach was at its best where the situation imposed heavy restrictions upon search behavior and response alternatives. Where individuals must give quick responses without adequate opportunities to explore the nature of the problem, where there are very few response alternatives available to them, where their own deep emotional needs are aroused, they will in general react much as does the unthinking subject under hypnosis. On the other hand, where the individual can have more adequate commerce with the relevant environmental setting, where he has time to obtain more feedback from his reality testing, and where he has a number of realistic choices, his behavior will reflect the use of his rational faculties (cf. Scott, 1958). The child will often respond to the directive of the parent not by implicit obedience but by testing out whether or not the parent really meant what he said.

The theory of psychological consonance, or cognitive balance, assumes that man attempts to reduce discrepancies in his beliefs, attitudes, and behavior by appropriate changes in these processes. While the emphasis here is upon consistency or logicality, the theory deals with all dissonances, no matter how produced. Thus they could result from irrational factors of distorted perception and wishful thinking as well as from rational factors of realistic appraisal of a problem and an accurate estimate of its consequences. Moreover, the theory would predict only that the individual will move to reduce dissonance, whether such movement is a good adjustment to the world or leads to the delusional systems of the paranoiac. In a sense, then, this theory would avoid the conflict between the old approaches of the rational and the irrational man by not dealing with the specific antecedent causes of behavior or with the particular ways in which the individual solves his problems.

In addition to the present preoccupation with the development of formal models concerned with cognitive balance and consonance, there is a growing interest in a more comprehensive framework for dealing with the complex variables and for bringing order within the field. The thoughtful system of Ulf Himmelstrand [presented in his 1960 paper], is one such attempt. Another point of departure is represented by two groups of workers who have organized their theories around the functions which attitudes perform for the personality. Sarnoff, Katz, and McClintock, in taking this functional approach, have given primary attention to the motivational bases of attitudes and the processes of attitude change (Sarnoff & Katz, 1954). The basic assumption of this group is that both attitude forma-

tion and attitude change must be understood in terms of the needs they serve and that, as these motivational processes differ, so too will the conditions and techniques for attitude change. Smith, Bruner, and White (1956) have also analyzed the different functions which attitudes perform for the personality. Both groups present essentially the same functions, but Smith, Bruner, and White give more attention to perceptual and cognitive processes and Sarnoff, Katz, and McClintock to the specific conditions of attitude change.

The importance of the functional approach is threefold. (1) Many previous studies of attitude change have dealt with factors which are not genuine psychological variables, for example, the effect on group prejudice of contact between two groups, or the exposure of a group of subjects to a communication in the mass media. Now contact serves different psychological functions for the individual and merely knowing that people have seen a movie or watched a television program tells us nothing about the personal values engaged or not engaged by such a presentation. If, however, we can gear our research to the functions attitudes perform, we can develop some generalizations about human behavior. Dealing with nonfunctional variables makes such generalization difficult, if not impossible.

(2) By concerning ourselves with the different functions attitudes can perform we can avoid the great error of oversimplification—the error of attributing a single cause to given types of attitude. It was once popular to ascribe radicalism in economic and political matters to the psychopathology of the insecure and to attribute conservatism to the rigidity of the mentally

aged. At the present time it is common practice to see in attitudes of group prejudice the repressed hostilities stemming from childhood frustrations, though Hyman and Sheatsley (1954) have pointed out that prejudiced attitudes can serve a normative function of gaining acceptance in one's own group as readily as releasing unconscious hatred. In short, not only are there a number of motivational forces to take into account in considering attitudes and behavior, but the same attitude can have a different motivational basis in different people.

(3) Finally, recognition of the complex motivational sources of behavior can help to remedy the neglect in general theories which lack specification of conditions under which given types of attitude will change. Gestalt theory tells us, for example, that attitudes will change to give better cognitive organization to the psychological field. This theoretical generalization is suggestive, but to carry out significant research we need some middle-level concepts to bridge the gap between a high level of abstraction and particularistic or phenotypical events. We need concepts that will point toward the types of motive and methods of motive satisfaction which are operative in bringing about cognitive reorganization.

Before we attempt a detailed analysis of the four major functions which attitudes can serve, it is appropriate to consider the nature of attitudes, their dimensions, and their relations to other psychological structures and processes.

Nature of attitudes: their dimensions

Attitude is the predisposition of the individual to evaluate some symbol or object or aspect of his world in a favorable or unfavorable manner. Opinion is the verbal expression of an attitude, but attitudes can also be expressed in nonverbal behavior. Attitudes include both the affective, or feeling core of liking or disliking, and the cognitive, or belief, elements which describe the object of the attitude, its characteristics, and its relations to other objects. All attitudes thus include beliefs, but not all beliefs are attitudes. When specific attitudes are organized into a hierarchical structure, they comprise *value systems*. Thus a person may not only hold specific attitudes against deficit spending and unbalanced budgets but may also have a systematic organization of such beliefs and attitudes in the form of a value system of economic conservatism.

The dimensions of attitudes can be stated more precisely if the above distinctions between beliefs and feelings and attitudes and value systems are kept in mind. The *intensity* of an attitude refers to the strength of the *affective* component. In fact, rating scales and even Thurstone scales deal primarily with the intensity of feeling of the individual for or against some social object. The cognitive, or belief, component suggests two additional dimensions, the *specificity* or *generality* of the attitude and the *degree of differentiation* of the beliefs. Differentiation refers to the number of beliefs or cognitive items contained in the attitude, and the general assumption is that the simpler the attitude in cognitive structure the easier it is to change (cf. Krech & Crutchfield, 1948, pp. 160–63). For simple structures there is no defense in depth, and once a single item of belief has been changed the attitude will change. A rather different dimension of attitude is the *number and strength of its linkages to a related value system.* If an attitude favoring budget balancing by the Federal government is tied in strongly with a value system of economic conservatism, it will be more difficult to change than if it were a fairly isolated attitude of the person. Finally, the relation of the value system to the personality is a consideration of first importance. If an attitude is tied to a value system which is closely related to, or which consists of, the individual's conception of himself, then the appropriate change procedures becomes more complex. The *centrality* of an attitude refers to its role as part of a value system which is closely related to the individual's self-concept.

An additional aspect of attitudes is not clearly described in most theories, namely, their relation to action or overt behavior. Though behavior related to the attitude has other determinants than the attitude itself, it is also true that some attitudes in themselves have more of what Cartwright (1949) calls an action structure than do others. Brewster Smith (1947) refers to this dimension as policy orientation and Katz and Stotland (1959) speak of it as the action component. For example, while many people have attitudes of approval toward one or the other of the two political parties, these attitudes will differ in their structure with respect to relevant action. One man may be prepared to vote on election day and will know where and when he should vote and will go to the polls no matter what the weather or how great the inconvenience. Another man will only vote if a party worker calls for him in a car. Himmelstrand's work is concerned with all aspects of the relationship between attitude and behavior, but

he deals with the action structure of the attitude itself by distinguishing between attitudes where the affect is tied to verbal expression and attitudes where the affect is tied to behavior concerned with more objective referents of the attitude (cf. 1960). In the first case an individual derives satisfaction from talking about a problem; in the second case he derives satisfaction from taking some form of concrete action.

Attempts to change attitudes can be directed primarily at the belief component or at the feeling, or affective, component. Rosenberg theorizes that an effective change in one component will result in changes in the other component and presents experimental evidence to confirm this hypothesis (cf. 1960). For example, a political candidate will often attempt to win people by making them like him and dislike his opponent, and thus communicate affect rather than ideas. If he is successful, people will not only like him but entertain favorable beliefs about him. Another candidate may deal primarily with ideas and hope that, if he can change people's beliefs about an issue, their feelings will also change.

Four functions which attitudes perform for the individual

The major functions which attitudes perform for the personality can be grouped according to their motivational basis as follows:

1. *The instrumental, adjustive, or utilitarian function* upon which Jeremy Bentham and the utilitarians constructed their model of man. A modern expression of this approach can be found in behavioristic learning theory.

2. *The ego-defensive function* in which the person protects himself from acknowledging the basic truths about himself or the harsh realities in his external world. Freudian psychology and neo-Freudian thinking have been preoccupied with this type of motivation and its outcomes.

3. *The value-expressive function* in which the individual derives satisfactions from expressing attitudes appropriate to his personal values and to his concept of himself. This function is central to doctrines of ego psychology which stress the importance of self-expression, self-development, and self-realization.

4. *The knowledge function* based upon the individual's need to give adequate structure to his universe. The search for meaning, the need to understand, the trend toward better organization of perceptions and beliefs to provide clarity and consistency for the individual, are other descriptions of this function. The development of principles about perceptual and cognitive structure have been the contribution of Gestalt psychology.

Stated simply, the functional approach is the attempt to understand the reasons people hold the attitudes they do. The reasons, however, are at the level of psychological motivations and not of the accidents of external events and circumstances. Unless we know the psychological need which is met by the holding of an attitude we are in a poor position to predict when and how it will change. Moreover, the same attitude expressed toward a political candidate may not perform the same function for all the people who express it. And while many attitudes are predominantly in the service of a single type of motivational process, as described above, other attitudes may serve more than one purpose for the individual. A fuller discussion of how attitudes serve the above four functions is in order.

1. THE ADJUSTMENT FUNCTION

Essentially this function is a recognition of the fact that people strive to maximize the rewards in their external environment and to minimize the penalties. The child develops favorable attitudes toward the objects in his world which are associated with the satisfactions of his needs and unfavorable attitudes toward objects which thwart him or punish him. Attitudes acquired in the service of the adjustment function are either the means for reaching the desired goal or avoiding the undesirable one, or are affective associations based upon experiences in attaining motive satisfactions (Katz & Stotland, 1959). The attitudes of the worker favoring a political party which will advance his economic lot are an example of the first type of utilitarian attitude. The pleasant image one has of one's favorite food is an example of the second type of utilitarian attitude.

In general, then, the dynamics of attitude formation with respect to the adjustment function are dependent upon present or past perceptions of the utility of the attitudinal object for the individual. The clarity, consistency, and nearness of rewards and punishments, as they relate to the individual's activities and goals, are important factors in the acquisition of such attitudes. Both attitudes and habits are formed toward specific objects, people, and symbols as they satisfy specific needs. The closer these objects are to actual need satisfaction and the more they are clearly perceived as relevant to need satisfaction, the greater are the probabilities of positive attitude formation. These principles of attitude formation are often observed in the breach rather than the compliance. In industry, management frequently expects to create favorable attitudes toward job performance through programs for making the company more attractive to the worker, such as providing recreational facilities and fringe benefits. Such programs, however, are much more likely to produce favorable attitudes toward the company as a desirable place to work than toward performance on the job. The company benefits and advantages are applied across the board to all employees and are not specifically relevant to increased effort in task performance by the individual worker.

Consistency of reward and punishment also contributes to the clarity of the instrumental object for goal attainment. If a political party bestows recognition and favors on party workers in an unpredictable and inconsistent fashion, it will destroy the favorable evaluation of the importance of working hard for the party among those whose motivation is of the utilitarian sort. But, curiously, while consistency of reward needs to be observed, 100 per cent consistency is not as effective as a pattern which is usually consistent but in which there are some lapses. When animal or human subjects are invariably rewarded for a correct performance, they do not retain their learned responses as well as when the reward is sometimes skipped (Jenkins & Stanley, 1950).

2. THE EGO-DEFENSIVE FUNCTION

People not only seek to make the most of their external world and what it offers, but they also expend a great deal of their energy on living with themselves. The mechanisms by which the individual protects his ego from his own unacceptable impulses and from the knowledge of threatening forces from without, and the methods by which he reduces his anxieties created by such problems, are known as mechanisms of ego defense. A more complete account of their origin and nature will be found in Sarnoff (1960). They include the devices by which the individual avoids facing either the inner reality of the kind of person he is, or the outer reality of the dangers the world holds for him. They stem basically from internal conflict with its resulting insecurities. In one sense the mechanisms of defense are adaptive in temporarily removing the sharp edges of conflict and in saving the individual from complete disaster. In another sense they are not adaptive in that they handicap the individual in his social adjustments and in obtaining the maximum satisfactions available to him from the world in which he lives. The worker who persistently quarrels with his boss and with his fellow workers, because he is acting out some of his own internal conflicts, may in this manner relieve himself of some of the emotional tensions which beset him. He is not, however, solving his problem of adjusting to his work situation and thus may deprive himself of advancement or even of steady employment.

Defense mechanisms, Miller and Swanson (1960) point out, may be classified into two families on the basis of the more or less primitive nature of the devices employed. The first family, more primitive in nature, are more socially handicapping and consist of denial and complete avoidance. The individual in such cases obliterates through withdrawal and denial the realities which confront him. The exaggerated case of such primitive mechanisms is the fantasy world of the paranoiac. The second type of defense is less handicapping and makes for distortion rather than denial. It includes rationalization, projection, and displacement.

Many of our attitudes have the function of defending our self-image. When we cannot admit to ourselves that we have deep feelings of inferiority we may project those feelings onto some convenient minority group and bolster our egos by attitudes of superiority toward this underprivileged group. The formation of such defensive attitudes differs in essential ways from the formation of attitudes which serve the adjustment function. They proceed from within the person, and the objects and situation to which they are attached are merely convenient outlets for their expression. Not all targets are equally satisfactory for a given defense mechanism, but the point is that the attitude is not created by the target but by the individual's emotional conflicts. And when no convenient target exists the individual will create one. Utilitarian attitudes, on the other hand, are formed with specific reference to the nature of the attitudinal object. They are thus appropriate to the nature of the social world to which they are geared. The high school student who values high grades because he wants to be admitted to a good college has a utilitarian attitude appropriate to the situation to which it is related.

All people employ defense mechanisms, but they differ with respect to the extent that they use them and some of their attitudes may be more defensive in function than others. It follows that the techniques and conditions for attitude change will not be the same for ego-defensive as for utilitarian attitudes.

Moreover, though people are ordinarily unaware of their defense mechanisms, especially at the time of employing them, they differ with respect to the amount of insight they may show at some later time about their use of defenses. In some cases they recognize that they have been protecting their egos without knowing the reason why. In other cases they may not even be aware of the devices they have been using to delude themselves.

3. THE VALUE-EXPRESSIVE FUNCTION

While many attitudes have the function of preventing the individual from revealing to himself and others his true nature, other attitudes have the function of giving positive expression to his central values and to the type of person he conceives himself to be. A man may consider himself to be an enlightened conservative or an internationalist or a liberal, and will hold attitudes which are the appropriate indication of his central values. Thus we need to take account of the fact that not all behavior has the negative function of reducing the tensions of biological drives or of internal conflicts. Satisfactions also accrue to the person from the expression of attitudes which reflect his cherished beliefs and his self-image. The reward to the person in these instances is not so much a matter of gaining social recognition or monetary rewards as of establishing his self-identity and confirming his notion of the sort of person he sees himself to be. The gratifications obtained from value expression may go beyond the confirmation of self-identity. Just as we find satisfaction in the exercise of our talents and abilities, so we find reward in the expression of any attributes associated with our egos.

Value-expressive attitudes not only give clarity to the self-image but also mold that self-image closer to the heart's desire. The teenager who by dress and speech establishes his identity as similar to his own peer group may appear to the outsider a weakling and a craven conformer. To himself he is asserting his independence of the adult world to which he has rendered childlike subservience and conformity all his life. Very early in the development of the personality the need for clarity of self-image is important—the need to know "who I am." Later it may be even more important to know that in some measure I am the type of person I want to be. Even as adults, however, the clarity and stability of the self-image is of primary significance. Just as the kind, considerate person will cover over his acts of selfishness, so too will the ruthless individualist become confused and embarrassed by his acts of sympathetic compassion. One reason it is difficult to change the character of the adult is that he is not comfortable with the new "me." Group support for such personality change is almost a necessity, as in Alcoholics Anonymous, so that the individual is aware of approval of his new self by people who are like him.

The socialization process during the formative years sets the basic outlines for the individual's self-concept. Parents constantly hold up before the child the model of the good character they want him to be. A good boy eats his spinach, does not hit girls, etc. The candy and the stick are less in evidence in training the child than the constant appeal to his notion of his own character. It is small wonder, then, that children reflect the acceptance of this model by inquiring about the characters of the actors in every drama, whether it be a television play, a political contest, or a war, wanting to know who are the "good guys" and who are the "bad guys." Even as adults we persist in labeling others in the terms of such character images. Joe McCarthy and his cause collapsed in fantastic fashion when the telecast of the Army hearings showed him in the role of the villain attacking the gentle, good man represented by Joseph Welch.

A related but somewhat different process from childhood socialization takes place when individuals enter a new group or organization. The individual will often take over and internalize the values of the group. What accounts, however, for the fact that sometimes this occurs and sometimes it does not? Four factors are probably operative, and some combination of them may be necessary for internalization. (1) The values of the new group may be highly consistent with existing values central to the personality. The girl who enters the nursing profession finds it congenial to consider herself a good nurse because of previous values of the importance of contributing to the welfare of others. (2) The new group may in its ideology have a clear model of what the good group member should be like and may persistently indoctrinate group members in these terms. One of the reasons for the code of conduct for members of the armed forces, devised after the revelations about the conduct of American prisoners in the Korean War, was to attempt to establish a model for what a good soldier does and does not do. (3) The activities of the group in moving toward its goal permit the individual genuine opportunity for participation. To become ego-involved so that he can internalize group values, the new member must find one of two conditions. The group activity open to him must tap his talents and abilities so that his chance to show what he is worth can be tied into the group effort. Or else the activities of the group must give him an active voice in group decisions. His particular talents and abilities may not be tapped but he does have the opportunity to enter into group decisions, and thus his need for self-determination is satisfied. He then identifies with the group in which such opportunities for ego-involvement are available. It is not necessary that opportunities for self-expression and self-determination be of great magnitude in an objective sense, so long as they are important for the psychological economy of the individuals themselves. (4) Finally, the individual may come to see himself as a group member if he can share in the rewards of group activity which includes his own efforts. The worker may not play much of a part in building a ship or make any decisions in the process of building it. Nevertheless, if he and his fellow workers are given a share in every boat they build and a return on the proceeds from the earnings of the ship, they may soon come to identify with the ship-building company and see themselves as builders of ships.

4. THE KNOWLEDGE FUNCTION

Individuals not only acquire beliefs in the interest of satisfying various specific needs, they also seek knowledge to give meaning to what would otherwise be an unorganized chaotic universe. People need standards or frames of reference for understanding their world, and attitudes help to supply such standards. The problem of understanding, as John Dewey (1910) made clear years ago, is one "of introducing (1) *definiteness* and *distinction* and (2) *consistency* and *stability* of meaning into what is otherwise vague and wavering." The definiteness and stability are provided in good measure by the norms of our culture, which give the otherwise perplexed individual ready-made attitudes for comprehending his universe. Walter Lippmann's classical contribution to the study of opinions and attitudes was his description of stereotypes and the way they provided order and clarity for a bewildering set of complexities (1922). The most interesting finding in Herzog's familiar study of the gratifications obtained by housewives in listening to daytime serials was the unsuspected role of information and advice (1944). The stories were liked "because they explained things to the inarticulate listener."

The need to know does not of course imply that people are driven by a thirst for universal knowledge. The American public's appalling lack of political information has been documented many times. In 1956, for example, only 13 per cent of the people in Detroit could correctly name the two United States Senators from the state of Michigan and only 18 per cent knew the name of their own Congressman (Katz & Eldersveld, 1961). People are not avid seekers after knowledge as judged by what the educator or social reformer would desire. But they do want to understand the events which impinge directly on their own life. Moreover, many of the attitudes they have already acquired give them sufficient basis for interpreting much of what they perceive to be important for them. Our already existing stereotypes, in Lippmann's language, "are an ordered, more or less consistent picture of the world, to which our habits, our tastes, our capacities, our comforts and our hopes have adjusted themselves. They may not be a complete picture of the world, but they are a picture of a possible world to which we are adapted" (1922). It follows that new information will not modify old attitudes unless there is some inadequacy or incompleteness or inconsistency in the existing attitudinal structure as it relates to the perceptions of new situations.

Determinants of attitude arousal and attitude change

The problems of attitude arousal and of attitude change are separate problems. The first has to do with the fact that the individual has many predispositions to act and many influences playing upon him. Hence we need a more precise description of the appropriate conditions which will evoke a given attitude. The second problem is that of specifying the factors which will help to predict the modification of different types of attitude.

The most general statement that can be made concerning attitude arousal is that it is dependent upon the excitation of some need in the individual, or some relevant cue in the environment. When a man grows hungry, he talks of food. Even when not hungry he may express favorable attitudes toward a preferred food if an external stimulus cues him. The ego-defensive person who hates foreigners will express such attitudes under conditions of increased anxiety or threat or when a foreigner is perceived to be getting out of place.

The most general statement that can be made about the conditions conducive to attitude change is that the expression of the old attitude or its anticipated expression no longer gives satisfaction to its related need state. In other words, it no longer serves its function and the individual feels blocked or frustrated. Modifying an old attitude or replacing it with a new one is a process of learning, and learning always starts with a problem, or being thwarted in coping with a situation. Being blocked is a necessary, but not a sufficient, condition for attitude change. Other factors must be operative and will vary in effectiveness depending upon the function involved.[1]

[1] **Prof. Katz's further elaboration of these latter points will be found in the original paper. —Eds.**

35 Cognitive dynamics in the conduct of human affairs

CHARLES E. OSGOOD

Over the past two decades a great deal of social-psychological research has been converging on a conclusion about human thinking that common sense had already isolated as the consistency which is the "hobgoblin of little minds." It appears, however, that "consistency" can plague big minds as well as little, in high places as well as low. Indeed, the difficulties we face today on both national and international levels can be traced, in part at least, to these dynamics of human thinking. Research that is relevant to our problem cuts a wide swathe through the social sciences—attitude formation and change; the effects of context upon the interpretation of both perceptual and linguistic signs; interpersonal perception and group dynamics; the interactions among beliefs, decisions, and social behavior; and even public affairs. The researchers have come from a diversity of theoretical molds. Accordingly, the purposes of this paper are to provide a brief purview of this research on cognitive dynamics, to indicate the essential similarities in the theoretical notions that have been proposed, and to point up the significance of such cognitive dynamics for contemporary human affairs. But first we need a few specimens of the phenomena we wish to study.

Specimen 1: International affairs. Before the delegates to the United Nations Khrushchev makes sweeping proposals for world disarmament. A large segment of the American press editorializes about the deceptive nature of these proposals, that, rather than sincere overtures toward peaceful solutions of problems, his proposals are carefully planned moves in the Cold War. It is cognitively inconsistent for us to think of people we dislike and distrust making honest, conciliatory moves, behaving as human beings ought to behave, and assuming noble postures.

Specimen 2: Internal affairs. A noted counterspy is invited to speak in the high school auditorium of a university town. In the course of his talk, he emphasizes the fact that the university hasn't invited any *anti*-Communists (including himself) to make public appearances in its halls. Although no allegations are directly made, many people in his audience are led to conclude (a) that the university has invited *pro*-Communists (which it hasn't), or at least (b) that the university must include some powerful Communist supporters.

Specimen 3: Individual behavior and belief. Some time after stories in the mass media about the relation between smoking and lung cancer had saturated the public, a survey in Minneapolis inquired about both the smoking habits of respondents and whether they thought the relationship between smoking and lung cancer had been proven or not proven. The results showed that 29 per

Reprinted with slight abridgment from the **Public Opinion Quarterly**, 1960, 24, 341–65, with permission of the author and publisher.

cent of nonsmokers, 20 per cent of light smokers, but only 7 per cent of heavy smokers believed it had been proven. It is cognitively inconsistent to believe one way and behave another; people who smoke heavily find it easier to *disbelieve* information that it is damaging to their health (Festinger, 1957).

Specimen 4: Interpersonal affairs. Fraternity men were asked to (a) name the men in their group they liked best and liked least, (b) rate themselves on a series of traits, and (c) rate the other men on the same series of traits. The results showed that these men *assumed* greater similarity in personality traits between people they liked and themselves than actually existed (Fiedler, Warrington, & Blaisdell, 1952). It has also been shown that husbands and wives attribute more similarity between them than actually exists, and this is more true for happily married than for unhappily married couples (Preston, *et al.*, 1952). It is "natural" to assume that people we like must think and feel as we do—at least, to the extent that we like ourselves.

Specimen 5: Making inferences about people. If we observe, or are told, that so-and-so is *intelligent* and *considerate*, and this is all the information we have, we are nevertheless able to generate many inferences about him—he is also likely to be *sensitive, socially adept, alert*, and so forth, we assume. The traits we infer are not haphazard: they are generated from the region of intersection of the meanings of the traits we know about, according to laws of cognitive interaction (Bruner & Tagiuri, 1954). Many of the predictions we make about people and the expectations we have of them are based on inferences of this type.

Specimen 6: Perceptual affairs. In his *Film Technique and Film Acting* Pudovkin (1954) describes a little experiment in film editing. A simple, passive close-up of the well-known Russian actor, Mosjukhin, was joined to three different strips of film. In one this close-up was followed by a shot of a bowl of soup on the table; in another it was followed by shots showing a dead woman in a coffin; in the third it was followed by shots of a little girl playing with a funny toy bear. The effects on an unsuspecting audience were terrific, according to Pudovkin. "The public raved about the acting of the artist. They pointed out the heavy pensiveness of his mood over the forgotten soup, were touched and moved by the deep sorrow with which he looked at the dead woman, and admired the light, happy smile with which he surveyed the girl at play. But we knew that in all three cases the face was exactly the same."

Specimen 7: A matter of naming. "A rose by any name would smell as sweet," we have been told—but would it? I do not know of any experiments on the influence of labels upon perception of odors, but this should be easily demonstrated, smells being the elusive, subjective business they are. But from the myth of suburbia we can gather many examples of the same sort—the cramped, standardized, insignificant little house with its postage-stamp yard in "Briarwood Valley," in "Larchmont Hills," or in "Sunnyvale Downs" somehow assumes a splendor and grace it could never have in "Southside Brighton Avenue, subdivision No. 7." The cheap panel-and-paste bedroom set, produced by the hundreds of thousands but garnished with the name "Beverley Charm by Rudet," acquires a distinction far beyond its cost and worth.

Specimen 8: Attitudinal affairs. Suppose that we are favorably disposed toward Eisenhower, both as a person and as the President of our country. In Uruguay, let us say, he is greeted with flowers and smiles, but in Paraguay an unruly mob of students boos him and has to be dispersed with tear gas. Having little information, and generally neutral attitudes, toward both Uruguay and Paraguay, we find ourselves considerably more favorable toward the former than toward the latter. Subsequent news that Uruguay lives under a harsh dictatorship will be discounted—it must really be "benevolent"—and the fact that Paraguay has a democratic form of government, much like our own, is somehow difficult to assimilate. As this hypothetical example shows, we strive to maintain internal consistency among our attitudes and beliefs, often at the price of doctoring reality.

So much for specimens of cognitive interaction in human affairs. Such examples could be elaborated *ad infinitum.* The important thing is that they are all cut from the same cloth; they are all instances of a basic dynamism according to which human judgment, belief, perception, and thought are transformed in midflight, so to speak.

Some theory of cognitive interaction

Insight into the dynamics of human thinking has been available in the writings of brilliant men of all periods. Certainly Aristotle was aware of these dynamics when he dealt with the principles of rhetoric; Shakespeare imposes the rules of psycho-logic (Abelson & Rosenberg, 1958) on the thought and behavior of his characters; and Machiavelli could not have had the understanding he did of politics without an intuitive grasp of the same rules. But intuitive grasp and common sense—essential though they may be to discovery in science—are not the same thing as explicit and testable principles of human behavior.

Among psychologists who have dealt with cognitive interaction in recent times, Fritz Heider undoubtedly has given the earliest and richest analysis, in his two papers in the middle forties (1944, 1946) and particularly as elaborated in his new book, *The Psychology of Interpersonal Relations* (1958), which is a much broader study of human perception and thinking than the title implies. Working in the area of human communication, particularly in small groups, Theodore Newcomb (1953) has utilized very similar theoretical notions to Heider's. In his *A Theory of Cognitive Dissonance*, Leon Festinger (1957) has probably given the clearest statement of this type of theory and, through his own ingenious experiments, has extended it into the whole area of relations between cognitions and overt behavior. Osgood and Tannenbaum (1955), working in the area of attitude change, have presented what they call "the congruity hypothesis"—which again has similar features to the Heider-Newcomb-Festinger approaches. The most explicit statement of this hypothesis appears in *The Measurement of Meaning* in the context of Osgood's mediation theory of meaning and the measurement procedures of the semantic differential (Osgood, Suci, & Tannenbaum, 1957). Rather than try to describe each of these theories in isolation, it will be more useful to describe them comparatively in terms of certain common and differential features.

1. *Cognitive modification results from*

the psychological stress produced by cognitive inconsistencies. We have here a kind of motivation, analogous to other drive states like hunger, sex, and anxiety, but purely cognitive in origin. It is necessary, of course, to define the states of cognitive "consistency" and "inconsistency" and in terms as close as possible to observables. Heider himself speaks in terms of *balance and imbalance* (from within a gestalt framework), but he does not provide us with a very clear statement, beyond the fact that "a balanced state is . . . a situation in which the relations among the entities fit together harmoniously; there is no stress toward change." In order to give meaning and order to the flux of distal stimuli (things, persons, events), the individual strives to maintain balance among the proximal signs (cognitions) of these external affairs.

Newcomb sees human communication as a means of achieving or maintaining *symmetry* in the orientations of individuals with respect to objects or events. Festinger's theory is expressed in terms of *consonance and dissonance.* These terms refer to the relations which may exist between pairs of cognitive elements (bits of knowledge about the world, other people, the self, one's own behavior).

Where Heider has not attempted a formal definition of balance in his system, Cartwright and Harary (1956) have done so in terms of the mathematical theory of linear graphs. To handle Heider's types of situation in graph theory requires, according to these authors, *signed, directed graphs of type* 2. We start with the cognitive elements (people, objects, etc.) defined as points. If these elements are involved in interactions (and they need not be, cf. section 2 below), then we connect them

with a line; the line must be *directed* by means of an arrow in order to take into account Heider's distinction between agent and recipient. Since Heider talks about both sentiments (liking vs. disliking) and cognitive units (belonging vs. not belonging) as being two-valued, we also require a *signed* line— which Cartwright and Harary accomplish by means of solid vs. dashed lines. Finally, since Heider distinguishes the two types of relations, "liking" vs. "belonging," it is suggested that a type 2 graph, using two colors, for example, should be employed. However, Cartwright and Harary make little use of this last distinction and, in fact, criticize the ambiguity in Heider's "cognitive unit" conception (see section 2 below). In a more recent paper Harary (1959) has further elaborated this type of analysis, with special reference to the measurement of structural balance in small groups.

This brings up a source of confusion in this field that has hardly been recognized, as far as I am aware, but must be cleared up before we proceed. Cognitive interactions, obviously, transpire within the nervous systems of single individuals. The "maps" we draw to represent such interactions necessarily reflect person-person and person-object relations *as some individual perceives them.* Festinger is clearly aware of this; Heider also seems to be working on this basis—to the extent that his book might better have been titled "The Psychology of Interpersonal *Perceptions.*" But both Newcomb and Cartwright and Harary seem to shift too easily from the subjective (cognitive interactions in individuals) to the objective (group structure and dynamics) frame of reference. Now it may be that the laws which apply to the interactions, stresses, and resolutions among the cognitive processes of individuals can be directly transferred to interactions within groups of people—where persons are the elements rather than cognitions—but this remains to be proven. The bridge between the two levels presumably lies in the fact that the structuring of a group depends upon the cognitive "maps" individual members have of it.

Osgood *et al.* (1957) equate "cognitive elements" with the *meanings* of signs, and these are indexed in terms of *n* bipolar dimensions or factors. However, since interactions are assumed to occur on each dimension independently of the others, we may restrict our attention to the dominant evaluative factor of the meaning space—which is the one which has interested all other investigators. In the measurement system provided by the semantic differential, the evaluative factor runs from +3 (extremely good) through o (neutral) to −3 (extremely bad). The *evaluative meaning* of a concept (cognitive element) is its location along such a scale; the *polarization* of a concept is its distance from o, regardless of sign. Now, it is assumed that evaluative meanings are mediated by a representational reaction system (perhaps here the autonomic nervous system and its connections with the central nervous system) which can only do one thing, assume one "posture," at one time. It must follow, therefore, that if two (or more) signs associated with different evaluative meanings occur near-simultaneously, only one cognitive reaction can occur in the system, and this must be a compromise. According to Osgood *et al.*, *congruity* exists when the evaluative meanings of interacting signs are equally polarized or intense—either in the same or opposite evaluative directions (see section 2 on types of *assertions*). To the extent that there are differences in polarization, some degree of *incongruity* must exist to be resolved in the process of cognizing these signs.

Although this theory will be shown to lead to similar conclusions about human thinking, it developed from a very different conceptual background than the others we have been considering, and certain critical differences should be noted at this point. First, *it attributes degrees of incongruity to single pairs of elements* rather than the all-or-nothing relations found in Heider and Festinger. Coupled with a measuring device like the semantic differential, this can lead to more refined predictions. Second, *it assigns affective or attitudinal values to the cognitive elements themselves*, and not to their relations, whereas Heider, at least, assigns both affective and connecting properties to the relations between cognitive elements. This double function of the relational variable is, to my mind, the major weakness in Heider's theory.

2. *If cognitive elements are to interact, they must be brought into some relation with one another.* Contiguity is a necessary, but not a sufficient, condition for interaction among cognitive elements. In "Tom is a thief; Paul will catch him," "Paul" is spatially and temporally closer to "thief" than is "Tom," but the *structure* of the sentence brings "Tom" and "thief" into interaction. We have varying attitudes toward myriad people, things, and events, many of them *potentially* incongruent, imbalanced, or dissonant as one's theory would have it, but these cognitions are not continuously interacting—only when they are brought together in some way.

Festinger's theory fails to give explicit

recognition to this variable. Implicit recognition of the need for linkage in some unit appears in the design of his experiments, however—dissonance only occurs when a person has been forced to make a choice between two gifts, when he has been exposed to information consistent or inconsistent with his beliefs, and so on. Analysis into "relevant" and "irrelevant" pairs of cognitive elements is not sufficient; cognitions of the attractiveness of an electric toaster and an electric clock are always potentially relevant, but only become effectively relevant when, by forced choice, the implied negative assertion that one is better than the other is made.

Heider, on the other hand, does give explicit recognition to this variable (1958, pp. 176ff) treating it in terms of gestalt perceptual factors. "Separate entities comprise a unit when they are perceived as belonging together. For example, members of a family are seen as a unit; a person and his deed belong together." Such factors as similarity, proximity, common fate, good continuation, set and past experience are cited as contributing to the formation of cognitive units, but it is evident in his examples that much more than perceptual organization in the traditional sense is involved. The difficulty with Heider's analysis, as Cartwright and Harary have implied, is that belonging in a unit (U or not U) is given the same status as liking (L vs. DL), both as relations between cognitive elements. Thus the triad, P *worships* O (P L O), O *told a lie* (O U X), and P *disapproves of lying* (P DL X), is said to be unbalanced because it has only one negative relation. One could also say that since O is + in evaluation and X is − in evaluation for P, the single assertion that O *told a lie*

(i.e., +O + −X) is itself cognitively unbalanced or dissonant for P.

Osgood *et al.* (1957) make an absolute distinction between structure and content in the representation and analysis of cognitive interactions. In order for two cognitive elements to interact, they must be related in some kind of *assertion*. Assertions may be linguistic ("Eisenhower *favors* Big Business," as read in an editorial) or behavioral (a picture of Eleanor Roosevelt *patting the head of* a little colored boy), and they may be either associative (X *favors, likes, owns, is a member of*, etc., Y) or dissociative (X *attacks, dislikes, throws away, is excluded from*, etc., Y). But whether a particular cognitive pattern is congruent or not depends on both the structure *and* the content. Thus, in contradistinction to Heider, the assertion P *likes* O merely indicates an associative or positive structure; if both P and O have the same sign evaluatively, the assertion is congruent (e.g., "God is on our side" and "The Devil aids the enemy" are both congruent assertions), but if P is + and O −, or vice versa, then P *likes* O becomes incongruent (e.g., "God is with the enemy").

Although it is significant that Heider came to his theory via a very penetrating study of the ordinary *language* of human relations—which he calls a "naïve psychology"—it does not seem to me that he has fully explored the possibilities in rigorous linguistic (structural) analysis. Osgood, Saporta, and Nunnally (1956) have developed a technique for abstracting the affective content of messages, called *evaluative assertion analysis*: (1) Objects of attitude are isolated from common-meaning terms and then masked by substituting nonsense letter pairs like AZ, BY, and CW for them.

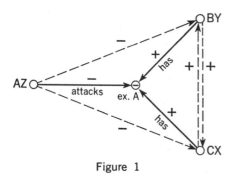

Figure 1

(2) Complex utterances in the masked message are broken down into component assertions of the actor-action-complement form. (3) Evaluative weights are given to the symbols for attitude objects in terms of their structural relations to evaluative common-meaning terms and other attitude objects. (4) The attitudinal consistency of the original utterances is checked by applying the congruity test (an even number of negative signs in each assertion).

Take, for example, the masked sentence, "AZ attacks *the expansionist ambitions* of both BY and CX." This breaks into three component assertions: /AZ/attacks/*expansionist ambitions*/, /BY/has/*expansionist ambitions*/, and /CX/has/*expansionist ambitions*/. The circles and solid lines in Figure 1 provide a signed di-graph of the structural relations actually given. However, if one is also given the valence of the common-meaning cognitive element, "expansionist ambitions," he can fill in by the rules of inference of psycho-logic what the valences of all of the attitude-object circles must be: AZ must be +, BY must be −, and CX must be −, otherwise we would have an assertion line with an odd number of negatives. But note that we still cannot decide whether

or not this is a congruent or incongruent pattern until we know that, in fact and for some particular language user, AZ *is* + in evaluation, BY is −, and so forth. If AZ (e.g. Franco Spain) is in fact somewhat negative for a person, then it is incongruous psycho-logically for it to be "attacking" something (e.g. the "expansionist ambitions") belonging to two bad things (e.g. Russia and the Arab League), and he is under some pressure to modify his cognitive map.

The process of inference through psycho-logic—hence the possibility of predicting the effects of implicit assertions in linguistic and behavioral situations—is also illustrated in Figure 1 by the dashed lines. Given that AZ is +, BY is −, and CX is − (i.e. a balanced situation), even though nothing is *said* about other relations, we can predict (1) that AZ should be against BY and vice versa, (2) that AZ should be against CX and vice versa, and (3) that BY should be in favor of CX and vice versa. Much of what is communicated attitudinally by messages and by behavior is based on such inferences; this is, of course, the chief tool of the propagandist, the technique of "innuendo." The syntax of language and of behavior provides a structural framework within which meaningful contents are put; the structure indicates what is related to what, and how, but only when the meaningful values are added does the combination of structure and content determine psycho-logical congruence or incongruence.

It was Abelson and Rosenberg (1958) who introduced the term "psycho-logic" and contrasted it with "logic." They give a number of the rules of psycho-logic: rule 1—A *likes* B and B *likes* C implies that A likes C also; rule 2—A *likes* B and B *dislikes* C implies that

A dislikes C; rule 3—A *dislikes* B and B *dislikes* C implies that A likes C, and so forth. It is important to point out that the inferences from psycho-logic are not necessarily invalid; they are simply illogical. For example, if Krushchev were to indicate that he favors a particular American presidential hopeful —the so-called "kiss of death"—many people would, psycho-logically, become suspicious of this candidate. Now, Khrushchev's support might be valid grounds for suspicion, but the inference is not logically necessary.

Abelson and Rosenberg also make an assertional analysis of linguistic statements, very much as Osgood, Saporta, and Nunnally have done, and they extend this type of analysis to interlocking sets of statements on the same topic. If the connectives (positive, p, and negative, n) in the following assertions— "I'm for having *coeds* at Yale," "I want *good grades*," and "Having *coeds* would undoubtedly interfere with getting *good grades*"—are arranged in a matrix in this fashion,

	Ego	Coeds	Good Grades
Ego	p	p	p
Coeds	p	p	n
Good Grades	p	n	p

the degree and locus of incongruity can be clearly indicated. Since we cannot change the signs of any corresponding row and column in the matrix (always leaving the diagonal entries signed p) and thereby reduce the number of n's in one half of the matrix, the minimum complexity or imbalance is 1. If the first statement were changed to "I am against having coeds at Yale," similar analysis shows that all entries could be changed to the same sign, and hence the matrix of state-

ments would then be congruent. This approach is similar to that of Cartwright and Harary, but is based on matrix algebra rather than the mathematical theory of graphs.

3. *Magnitude of stress toward modification increases with the degree of cognitive inconsistency.* Most of the theories we have been considering express this relation, but it only becomes useful when a theory permits quantification. Heider's own statements remain essentially qualitative. Newcomb, on the other hand, states his principles in quantitative form, e.g., "the stronger the forces toward A's co-orientation in respect to B and X, . . . the greater A's strain toward symmetry with B in respect to X . . . ," (1953) but the units in which "forces toward co-orientation" and "strain toward symmetry" are to be measured remain obscure. Festinger specifies that the magnitude of dissonance increases (1) with the importance of the dissonant elements and (2) with the weighted proportion of all elements in a cognitive cluster that are dissonant. But again it is not clear how "importance" or "weighted proportion of elements that are dissonant" are to be quantified.

Association of the Osgood and Tannenbaum congruity hypothesis with the semantic differential provides quantification of cognitive inconsistency, but it also limits the types of situation that can be studied. Total *pressure toward congruity*, P, is stated to be equal to the difference between the initial scale position of a cognitive element (prior to interaction) and its location of perfect congruence (under the conditions of interaction). Perfect congruence between two elements was defined earlier as equal polarization (intensity), either in the same evaluative direction (for associative assertions) or in opposite evaluative directions (for dissociative assertions). Thus, for a hypothetical individual for whom Eisenhower is $+3$ and Uruguay is $+1$, the assertion "Eisenhower was greeted with flowers in Uruguay" *would* be congruent *if* Eisenhower were only $+1$ or Uruguay were $+3$. We therefore have 2 units of pressure toward congruity, P, in this situation—and it may be noted in passing that the *P's* associated with the various interacting elements are always equal according to this hypothesis.

Cartwright and Harary arrive at the *degree of balance* of an S-digraph by taking the ratio of the number of positive semicycles to the total number of semicycles (cf., above). They state that such an index makes it possible to deal with cognitive inconsistencies in probabilistic and statistical fashions; they do *not* state any relation between degree of balance and the total stress toward consistency, however. Abelson and Rosenberg define the *complexity of imbalance* as the minimum number of changes of relations necessary to achieve balance. In the example given earlier about having coeds at Yale, the sign of one of the three assertions would have to be changed to achieve psycho-logical consistency. Again, however, there is no statement to the effect that amount of stress toward consistency varies with the "complexity of imbalance." It is possible, of course, that total pressure toward cognitive modification does *not* vary in any simple way with degree of inconsistency. This may be the case particularly when only the structural relations and not the affective values of the contents are considered. Both Festinger and Osgood, who express the magnitude principle explicitly, deal with the properties of the cognitive elements themselves, not just their structural relation to each other.

4. *The dynamics of cognitive interaction are such that modifications under stress always reduce total cognitive inconsistency.* We have here a kind of "mental homeostasis" (Stagner, 1951) —cognitive inconsistencies set up pressures toward their own elimination. But we must say at the outset that modifications do not necessarily occur at all. People simply may not think about the matter or, as Festinger has shown, they may avoid exposing themselves to dissonance-arousing information. Furthermore, as Heider points out, some people seem to be able to "live with it" or even actively seek cognitively disturbing situations; they are more "tolerant of ambiguity," to borrow an older phrase. Such tolerance probably increases with intelligence and education, and it certainly decreases under states of heightened emotion. But even here there may be a larger consistency operating: it may be intrinsically disturbing for some people to follow the simple-minded dictates of psycho-logic, at least to the extent they are aware of them.

But let us assume that our subjects are exposed to inconsistency, that they are thinking about it, and that they are susceptible to psycho-logic—what are the alternative resolutions available and how can we decide which will occur? We will find that theories in this field have been better at stating alternatives than at deciding among them.

a. *The sign, or even existence, of a relationship may be changed.* For theories like Heider's that deal only with relations and not with the values of the included elements, this is the only type of resolution. However, since he deals with several types of relations, e.g. *L* vs. *DL* and *U* vs. *notU*, the situation is complicated. In the simplest diadic case, if P L O but also P *notU* O, either P may decide he doesn't like O or he may try to join O in some unit— what happens presumably depends upon the relative strengths of L vs. *notU*.

b. *The sign, or even existence, of a cognitive element may be changed.* Although Festinger does not attribute evaluations per se to cognitive elements, he does deal with changes of these elements in the direction of consonance. By making certain assumptions about the importance of different elements and other factors in particular experimental situations, Festinger is able to select among alternative resolutions.

Osgood and Tannenbaum have formulated a general law governing interactions among cognitive events: *Interacting elements are modified in inverse proportion to their intensity or polarization*, i.e. the congruity formula,

$$mc_1 = \frac{|p_2|}{|p_1| + |p_2|} P$$

$$mc_2 = \frac{|p_1|}{|p_1| + |p_2|} P$$

in which *mc* refers to *meaning change* on some dimension (e.g. attitude), *p* refers to *polarization* (deviation from neutrality regardless of sign), P refers to total *pressure toward congruity* (cf. section 3 above), and the subscripts 1 and 2 refer to the interacting cognitive elements. Given the assertion, "Eisenhower was greeted with flowers in Uruguay," and known values of $+3$ for Eisenhower and $+1$ for Uruguay, we can predict that three-fourths of the attitude change should be exerted on Uruguay and only one-fourth on Eisenhower. Similarly, in Heider's triadic P L O, P L X, O DL X, imbalance situa-

tion, if the attitude toward O were more intensely favorable than that toward X the formula would have to predict that most of the pressure in this dissociative assertion would be on making X much less favorable. The Eisenhower/Uruguay example illustrates another characteristic of the congruity hypothesis— it predicts changes on a quantitative basis even where relations are qualitatively balanced (here a + associated with a +).

However, some insufficiencies of the congruity hypothesis of Osgood and Tannenbaum appear when it is applied experimentally. First, although the associative or dissociative nature of assertions (relations) determines the direction of congruence (and hence the sign of P) in this model, the formula deals entirely with the changes in the meanings of the cognitive elements. Yet change in sign or even denial of the assertion itself is obviously one type of resolution. The assertion that Eisenhower is a card-carrying Communist produces incredulity and is denied. In order to generate accurate predictions in his attitude-change experiment, Tannenbaum had to apply a "correction for incredulity" that increased with the magnitude of P between values of 3 and 6, i.e. highly incongruous assertions. Second, the formula gives no weight to the direction of an assertion (cf. Heider's distinction between agent and recipient)—P *praises* O has the same effects upon the elements as O *praises* P, as far as the formula is concerned. Yet Tannenbaum's evidence, where Sources come out for or against Concepts, suggests that a greater share of the impact is exerted upon the recipient than the agent. The inverse proportionality formula underlying the congruity hypothesis may be valid in the "other things equal" sense, but there are certainly other factors to be considered.

In a recent paper titled "Modes of Resolution of Belief Dilemmas," Abelson (1958) presents a considerable variety of resolution types. He limits his consideration to the simplest diadic situations, in which A is either associated with or dissociated from B by assertions, but follows Osgood *et al.* (1957) in attributing positive or negative values to the cognitive elements A and B, themselves. His first type—which he unfortunately calls *denial*—includes both the major forms of resolution discussed above, (1) where the sign of the relation is changed and (2) where the sign of one or both of the cognitive elements is changed. The term "denial" implies an all-or-nothing quality and a consciousness of decision which certainly do not apply to many of the interactions we would like to handle, e.g. in perceptual modification or in semantic adjustments to word mixtures. But let us now look at some of these other resolution types.

c. *Other cognitive elements that are in balanced relation with one or the other of the dissonant elements may be adduced (bolstering).* As Abelson points out, this does not eliminate the imbalance but tends to "drown it out." This is a type of resolution stressed by Festinger, e.g. the heavy smoker who says that one is more likely to die in an automobile accident, that he has a large chest expansion, that he wouldn't be among the unlucky 15 per cent anyway, and so forth. Abelson also points out that it is usually the more strongly entrenched (attitudinally polarized?) element that receives bolstering: if one is a devout Catholic, yet intellectually agrees with the use of contraceptives, he is likely to react to the Church's condemnation of this practice by thinking of the Church's long history of being right, of God relying on him to exercise will power, and so on.

d. *Other cognitive elements that are in a relation of imbalance with one or the other of the dissonant elements may be adduced (undermining).* Abelson does not distinguish this type of resolution from "bolstering," perhaps because it is the converse. Here new cognitive elements that have a dissociative (imbalance) relation to the less firmly entrenched element are adduced—the familiar process of rationalization.

In most real-life situations we are dealing with complex clusters of cognitive elements, each with its valence and each connected with others by an interlocking set of assertions, explicit or implicit. Patterns of bolstering and undermining relations already exist, without need for adducing them. We may, following Abelson's analysis, suggest a general rule for resolution in complex cases: *those cognitive modifications* (changes in assertions or in element valences) *will occur which require the minimum restructuring of the entire cognitive map.*

e. *One or the other of the dissonant cognitive elements may be split into two parts, these parts being of opposed valence and dissociatively related (differentiation).* It may be interesting to note that what is involved in differentiation is a denotative reclassification of cognitive units forced by a connotative (affective) stress. Behaving the same way, having the same attitude, toward all members of a class (racial group, religious group, teachers, students, fried foods, sport-car owners, cats, etc.) often runs us into cognitive conflicts of an affective, psycho-logical sort, and intellectual redifferentiation provides one way out.

f. *Dissonant cognitive elements may be combined into a larger unit which, as a whole, is in balance with other cognitive elements (transcendence).* Abelson gives as an example of this the typical resolution of the dissonance between "rational man" (A) and "spiritual man" (B): joined together in a larger unit, "the whole man," they become congruent with positive concepts (C) like "the full life," "a balanced education," and so forth. Or another example: Cain and Abel are always squabbling with each other; their father manages to avoid choosing between them by saying, "You are both my sons, and I love my sons." In itself, transcendence does not resolve incongruities —it merely hides them. However, as Heider has pointed out, simply being included within a common unit implies a consonant relation among the dissonant elements, and this must weaken the total dissonance—the father is impelled toward believing that Cain and Abel really love one another, and our educator is impelled toward believing that religion can be rationalized.

Some evidence on cognitive interaction

Here some indication will be given of the diversity of phenomena which appear to follow the rules of cognitive interaction. These rules may be summarized as follows: When, in the course of human thinking, inconsistent cognitive elements are forced together by linguistic or behavioral assertions, stress is produced in proportion to the magnitude of the inconsistency, this stress producing cognitive modifications which —by changing the nature of the assertion, changing the connotative meanings of the elements, differentiating or integrating the denotations of the elements—serve to re-establish cognitive consistency. No attempt will be made to cover the experimental literature exhaustively; it has become quite extensive.

1. ATTITUDE CHANGE

Whenever a person reads a book or newspaper, listens to the belief statements of others, or even ruminates within his own storehouse of concepts, he is exposing himself to assertions which are likely to be incongruent to some degree with his existing frame of reference. In experiments we try to measure some part of his existing attitude structure, produce messages which are congruent or incongruent to some definable degree, predict what the effects on him should be, and then measure his attitude structure again to determine the correctness of these predictions (see Tannenbaum, 1953; Kerrick, 1959b).

2. COGNITION AND BEHAVIOR

Pressures toward consistency in what one believes and how one behaves have been studied most intensively by Festinger and his associates in a variety of ingeniously contrived, realistic experiments (1957). Two examples will have to suffice.

a. *Consequences of decisions.* The need for making a decision implies that there are dissonant elements in either course; therefore, to a degree dependent on the importance of the decision, the relative attractiveness of the unchosen course, and the degree of overlap of elements in the two courses, decisions will leave some dissonance to be reduced.

b. *Exposure to information.* Dissonance theory also leads to the prediction that people will avoid exposure to dissonance-increasing information and seek exposure to dissonance-decreasing information; if exposure to dissonant information is forced, they will defend against fully cognizing it.

3. INTERPERSONAL PERCEPTION

Although Heider himself has not contributed heavily on the experimental side, many other people have done research either inspired by or at least relevant to his theoretical notions. Jordan (1953) directly tested Heider's prediction that people prefer balanced to imbalanced situations. Sixty-four hypothetical (and, unfortunately, very abstract) triadic situations were given to subjects to rate for degree of pleasantness, half of them being cognitively balanced and half unbalanced. An example would be: "I dislike O; I have a sort of bond or relationship with X; O likes X." The ratings for balanced triads were significantly more "pleasant" than ratings for unbalanced triads, and Cartwright and Harary have shown that if the ambiguous *notU* situations are eliminated, the difference becomes even greater.

4. COMMUNICATION AND GROUP COHESIVENESS

Newcomb cites experiments by Festinger and Thibaut (1951), by Schachter (1951), and by Back (1951), which demonstrate (a) that attempts to influence others increase with the attractiveness of the others to Ego, (b) that communications in cohesive groups tend to be directed toward those perceived as most deviant (up to the point where the sign of the relation shifts and a deviate is ejected from the group), and (c) that communications within groups typically result in both increased uniformity (co-orientations toward relevant X's) and increased cohesiveness (co-attractions among members). There are many other experiments in which the role of interpersonal communication can legitimately be inferred even though it was not directly observed, e.g. in a study by Festinger, Schachter, and Back (1950) where a correlation of +.72 was found between a measure of interpersonal attractiveness and a measure of attitudinal conformity among people in a housing project.

5. SEMANTIC INTERACTIONS

Finally, we will look briefly at a series of experiments which—precisely because of their remoteness from familiar everyday matters like attitudes, beliefs, and interpersonal relations—may serve to indicate the generality of our principles. All these studies are alike in that *meaning* as measured with a form of semantic differential is the dependent variable. They are also alike in general design: subjects first judge the meanings of a set of component stimuli and then judge the meanings of various combinations of these stimuli; predicted meanings of the combinations, derived from applying the congruity formula to the component meanings, are checked against the actual meanings of the combinations derived from subject ratings.

a. *Word mixture.* All subjects first rated the meanings of eight adjectives ("sincere," "breezy," "listless," etc.) and eight nouns ("nurse," "husband," "prostitute," etc.). Then they rated eight of the sixty-four possible combinations ("sincere husband," "breezy prostitute," "listless nurse," etc.), eight groups being required to complete the design (Osgood, Suci, & Tannenbaum, 1957, pp. 275–84). Problem: Can the meanings of the combinations be predicted from the measured meanings of the components? Correlations between predicted and obtained meanings were high, .86, .86, and .90 for the evaluative, potency, and activity factors respectively. A constant error appeared for the evaluative factor, however—obtained evaluations of the mixtures were consistently less favorable than predicted evaluations. No obvious explanation for this error is at hand.

b. *Fusion of facial expressions.* The affective meanings of five facial expressions posed by the same person (intended to convey glee, rage, optimistic determination, complacency, and passive adoration) were obtained from thirty subjects in terms of two dominant factors, *pleasantness* and *activation* (Hastorf & Osgood, unpublished). Then the same subjects viewed all possible combinations of these expressions when fused in a steroscope under conditions designed to minimize eye dominance. The apparent meanings of these fused expressions proved to be predictable via the congruity formula to a high degree. The median intrasubject correlation (across the ten combinations) between predicted and obtained scores was .84 for pleasantness and .82 for activation. Furthermore, as must be predicted from the congruity hypothesis, the semantic profiles for combinations regularly correlated more highly with the more polarized component; that is, the more intensely meaningful expression dominated in the process of interaction.

c. *News photos and captions.* Kerrick (1959a) devised two unrelated captions ("A Quiet Minute Alone" and "Exiled Communist") to go with each of five pictures (e.g. a full profile shot of a well-dressed man on a park bench). Subjects judged the captions and pictures alone and then in combination (the design was such that subjects judging one set of captions alone would get the other set linked with the pictures). The results were strikingly different from those of (a) and (b) above: if picture and caption in isolation had opposed meaning, the meaning of their combination was predictable via congruity; but if picture and caption in isolation had similar meanings, their effects *summated* in combination, contrary to the congruity principle. In other words, combining a slightly "happy" picture with a slightly "happy" caption produced a very "happy" whole.

d. *Sound movies.* A similar summation effect was found by Gregory in an unpublished study on the combinations of words with sight in sound movies. Five short "takes" of an actor saying five phonetically similar things with different meanings, with appropriate facial expressions and gestures, were recorded on sound film (e.g., "I can't get over the death of my wife," or, "This is the happiest day of my life"). Subjects judged the heard words alone, the viewed movies alone, the original combinations, and crossed combinations produced by splicing the words of one "take" with the sight of another. The results of the crossed combinations were generally predictable from the components via congruity, but the meanings of the "natural" combinations were more polarized than either component alone. We can only guess at why meaningful summation occurs in experiments (c) and (d) but not in experiments (a) and (b); both situations (c) and (d) involve interactions *across modalities*, and it may be that in such situations something other than simple congruity is operating.

Cognitive dynamics in public affairs
In the absence of a science of public affairs, national and international, we can at least hypothesize that laws governing the thinking and behaving of individuals also govern the "thinking" and "behaving" of groups. The leap from individual cognitive maps to the structuring of relations within small groups has already been made—in some cases apparently without any self-consciousness of the shift in reference. However, application of the laws of cognitive dynamics to public affairs can be justified on several grounds: first, with nothing but communication to bind us together, it is clear that "decisions" and "behaviors" of nations must come down to myriad decisions in individual nervous systems and myriad behaviors of individual human organisms. Second, to the extent that government is popular, we can work on the basis of averaging over individuals, and to the extent that government is not, we are back to individuals anyhow. Finally, evidence abounds that we do "personalize" groups and issues—not so much by an error of oversimplification as by an intuitive grasp of the underlying laws.

The analogue of a cognitive element for an individual is what we may call a *cultural meaning* (stereotype, public image, etc.) for a group. Although individuals within groups may be expected to vary in their private meanings, it is characteristic of cohesive groups, as Newcomb has shown, for interpersonal communication to produce increased uniformity of opinion and attitude. Mass communications have this function for the larger groupings of individuals in modern society, such as nations. Many of the applications of the semantic differential—in the study of

information about mental health and illness, of images of political personalities and issues, of commercial institutions and products, and so forth—have dealt with cultural meanings based on reasonably representative groups of people. The degree of conformity on issues is often striking, 90 to 100 per cent of subjects frequently choosing the same side, if not the same intensity. This happens both for common meanings (tornadoes are *active*) and for attitude objects (the Bible is *good*).

Now, to the extent that the cultural meanings of two socially significant referents have different evaluative locations, increasing proportions of individuals will necessarily experience pressures toward congruity when these items are forced into interaction by assertions in the mass media. If, under accusation by his rival or perhaps a mantle of honesty, a candidate for public office admits that he, John Jones, *does not believe in* God, we have for large numbers of people a somewhat unfamiliar and neutral source making a negative assertion about a deeply entrenched and favorably polarized concept. The result is inevitable—all the pressure toward consistency is on John Jones to move in a negative direction. Whenever political candidates, particularly unfamiliar ones, run into conflict with the mores—become associated with bad things, like gambling, call girls, and divorce, or become dissociated from good things, like Mother, God, and Country—they lose out. Conversely, political candidates themselves try to establish associative assertions with good things and dissociative assertions with bad, by their statements and by their behavior. Even if the private attitudes and beliefs of the elites in popular governments may be at variance with such a simple-minded organization of the universe, they rarely run counter to the tide. These are all very familiar facts about public affairs, but I think they illustrate the underlying laws.

Among our store of cultural meanings are a large number of "personalized" national stereotypes. Whether it is valid or not, populations in various countries do react to nations *as if* they were a collection of people, having certain "personality" traits and being organized into unstable group structures. The findings of Buchanan and Cantril (1953) in their book, *How Nations See Each Other*, are quite consistent with this idea. Following Heider, if P *likes* O (e.g. O *is an ally* of P) and P *dislikes* X (e.g. X *is an enemy* of P), then P should attribute favorable characteristics to O and unfavorable ones to X. We find that Americans most often attribute to the British the traits of being *intelligent, hard-working, brave,* and *peace-loving,* whereas they most often attribute to the Russians the traits of being *cruel, backward, hard-working,* and *domineering* (being "hard-working" is obviously independent of general evaluation). We would also expect people to view their own countrymen favorably, in the interest of cognitive balance; the four most frequent self-attributions (across the eight countries sampled) were *peace-loving, brave, intelligent,* and *hard-working.* Although Buchanan and Cantril did not get into this matter, Heider's notions of cognitive balance would lead us to expect that if P *likes* O and P *likes* Q, but P *dislikes* X, then P would infer that O *likes* Q and that O and Q *dislike* X, and vice versa. Americans expect the British to favor the French, and vice versa, but they expect both to be as antagonistic to the Russians as we are. If P *likes* O, he also must infer that O *likes* P reciprocally; but as studies like *The Ugly American* (Lederer & Burdick, 1958) show only too clearly, this doesn't necessarily follow.

The operation of psycho-logic in national and international affairs shows up quite generally once you start to look for it. All nations in time of conflict, for example, create "bogey men" on this basis. If we are *good, kind,* and *fair* and they are our enemy, then psycho-logic dictates that they must be *bad, cruel,* and *unfair.* However, when we are exposed to live Russians, as tourists in their country or as hosts to them in our homes and farms, and we find them in many ways *just like us,* cognitive disturbance is produced; it may be eliminated by the technique of differentiation—it is the Russian *leaders* who are bad, not the Russian *people.* And we confidently wait for the good Russian *people* to overthrow the bad Russian *leaders*—just as the Russians, no doubt, confidently wait for the good American *workers* to begin the revolution against their bad *capitalist leaders.* Abelson illustrates how differentiation works with a different example, the conflict over hydrogen bomb testing (+) being associated with poisonous fallout (−): if one can accept a distinction between using "clean bombs" and "dirty bombs," then a cognitively consistent resolution is achieved (Abelson, 1958).

Such examples could be adduced *ad infinitum,* but they would not further prove the thesis. The essential argument of this paper has been as follows: (1) there has been a considerable *confluence* (if not unanimity) *in theories* of cognitive interaction, sufficient at least to make it possible here to formulate several general principles; (2) there is a great deal of evidence for the operation of such principles *in the thinking and behaving of human individuals,* in areas as diverse as interpersonal relations and the semantics of word combination; and (3) we can at least hypothesize the operation of the same laws *at the level of groups, national and international,* and find illustrations which seem to support the hypothesis. How useful such a model would be for predicting in the area of public affairs remains to be seen.

36 Dissonance theory: progress and problems

ELLIOT ARONSON

As a formal statement, Festinger's theory of cognitive dissonance (1957) is quite primitive; it lacks the elegance and precision commonly associated with scientific theorizing. Yet its impact has been great. As McGuire has observed in his recent survey in the *Annual Review of Psychology* (1966a, p. 492), "Over the past three years, dissonance theory continued to generate more research and more hostility than any other one approach." I will allude to the "hostility" part of this statement from time to time throughout this chapter; but first let us discuss the research.

The research has been as diverse as it has been plentiful; its range extends from maze running in rats (Lawrence & Festinger, 1962), to the development of values in children (Aronson & Carl-smith, 1963); from the hunger of college sophomores (Brehm, Back & Bogdonoff, 1964), to the proselytizing behavior of religious zealots (Festinger, Riecken, & Schachter, 1956). For descriptive summaries of dissonance experiments, the reader is referred to Festinger, 1957; Festinger and Aronson, 1960; Brehm and Cohen, 1962; Festinger and Bramel, 1962; Festinger and Freedman, 1964.

The proliferation of research testing and extending dissonance theory is due for the most part to the generality and simplicity of the theory. Although it has been applied primarily in social psychological settings, it is not limited to social psychological phenomena such as interpersonal relations or feelings toward a communicator and his com-

Abridged from Chapter 1 in R. P. Abelson et al. (Eds.), Theories of Cognitive Consistency: A Sourcebook. Chicago: Rand McNally & Co., 1968, 5-27, with permission of the author and the publisher.

munication. Rather, its domain is in the widest of places: the skull of an individual organism.[1]

The core notion of the theory is extremely simple: Dissonance is a negative drive state which occurs whenever an individual simultaneously holds two cognitions (ideas, beliefs, opinions) which are psychologically inconsistent. Stated differently, two cognitions are dissonant if, considering these two cognitions alone, the opposite of one follows from the other. Since the occurrence of dissonance is presumed to be unpleasant, individuals strive to reduce it by adding 'consonant' cognitions or by changing one or both cognitions to make them 'fit together' better—i.e., so that they become more consonant with each other.[2] To use Festinger's time-worn (but still cogent) example, if a person believes that cigarette smoking causes cancer and simultaneously knows that he himself smokes cigarettes, he experiences dissonance. Assuming that the person would rather not have cancer, his cognition "I smoke cigarettes" is psychologically inconsistent with his cognition "cigarette smoking produces cancer." Perhaps the most efficient way to reduce dissonance in such a situation is to stop smoking. But, as many of us have discovered, this is by no means easy. Thus, a person will usually work

on the other cognition. There are several ways in which a person can make cigarette smoking seem less absurd. He might belittle the evidence linking cigarette smoking to cancer ("Most of the data are clinical rather than experimental"); or he might associate with other cigarette smokers ("If Sam, Jack, and Harry smoke, then it can't be very dangerous"); or he might smoke filter-tipped cigarettes and delude himself that the filter traps the cancer-producing materials; or he might convince himself that smoking is an important and highly pleasurable activity ("I'd rather have a shorter but more enjoyable life than a longer, unenjoyable one"); or he might actually make a virtue out of smoking by developing a romantic, devil-may-care image of himself, flaunting danger by smoking. All of these behaviors reduce dissonance, in effect, by reducing the absurdity involved in going out of one's way to contract cancer. Thus, dissonance theory does not rest upon the assumption that man is a *rational* animal; rather, it suggests that man is a rational-*izing* animal—that he attempts to appear rational, both to others and to himself. To clarify the theoretical statement and to illustrate the kind of research generated by the theory, I will briefly describe a few experiments.

DISSONANCE FOLLOWING A DECISION

One of the earliest experiments testing derivations from dissonance theory was performed by Brehm (1956). Brehm gave individuals their choice between two appliances which they had previously evaluated. He found that following the decision, when the subjects reevaluated the alternatives, they enhanced their liking for the chosen appliance and downgraded their evaluation of the unchosen one. The derivation is

---

[1] An additional reason for the great number of experiments on dissonance theory is completely ad **hominem:** Leon Festinger has an unmatched genius for translating interesting hypotheses into workable experimental operations and for inspiring others to do so. He has produced a great deal of research irrespective of any particular theoretical approach.

[2] Although dissonance theory is an incredibly simple statement, it is not quite as simple as a reading of this chapter will indicate. Many aspects of the theory (for example, the propositions relevant to the magnitude of dissonance) will not be discussed here because they are peripheral to the major focus of this chapter.

clear. After making a difficult choice, people experience dissonance; cognitions about any negative attributes of the preferred object are dissonant with having chosen it; cognitions about positive attributes of the unchosen object are dissonant with *not* having chosen it. To reduce dissonance, people emphasize the positive aspects and deemphasize the negative aspects of the chosen objects while emphasizing the negative and deemphasizing the positive aspects of the unchosen object (see also Festinger, 1964).

DISSONANCE RESULTING FROM EFFORT

Aronson and Mills (1959) reasoned that, if people undergo a great deal of trouble in order to gain admission to a group which turns out to be dull and uninteresting, they will experience dissonance. The cognition that they worked hard in order to become members of the group is dissonant with cognitions concerning the negative aspects of the group. One does not work hard for nothing. To reduce dissonance, they will distort their perception of the group in a positive direction. In the Aronson-Mills experiment, college women underwent an initiation in order to become a member of a group discussion on the psychology of sex. For some of the girls the initiation was very embarrassing—it consisted of reciting a list of obscene words in the presence of the male experimenter. For others the initiation was a mild one. For still others there was no initiation at all. All of the subjects then listened to the same tape-recording of a discussion being held by the group they had just joined. As predicted, the girls in the Severe Initiation condition rated the discussion much more favorably than did those in the other two conditions (see also Aronson, 1961;

Zimbardo, 1965; Lewis, 1964; Gerard & Mathewson, 1966).

INSUFFICIENT JUSTIFICATION

Aronson and Carlsmith (1963) predicted that if threats are used to prevent people from performing a desired activity, the *smaller* the threat, the greater will be the tendency for people to derogate the activity. If an individual refrains from performing a desired activity, he experiences dissonance: The cognition that he likes the activity is dissonant with the cognition that he is not performing it. One way to reduce dissonance is by derogating the activity—in that way he can justify the fact that he is not performing it. However, any threat provides cognitions that are consonant with not performing the activity; and the more severe the threat, the greater the consonance. In short, a severe threat provides ample justification for not performing the activity; a mild threat provides less justification, leading the individual to add justifications of his own in the form of convincing himself that he *doesn't like* to perform the activity. In their experiment, Aronson and Carlsmith found that children who were threatened with *mild* punishment for playing with a desired toy *decreased* their liking for the toy to a greater extent than did children who were severely threatened (see also Turner & Wright, 1965; Freedman, 1965).

What is psychological inconsistency?

The very simplicity of the core of the theory is at once its greatest strength and its most serious weakness. We have already discussed the heuristic value of its simplicity. It should be emphasized that many of the hypotheses which are obvious derivations from the theory are *unique* to that theory—i.e., they could not be derived from any other theory. This increases our confidence in dissonance theory as an explanation of an important aspect of human behavior. The weakness occurs primarily in the difficulty involved with defining the limits of the theoretical statement. While at the 'center' of the theory it is relatively easy to generate hypotheses that are clear and direct, at its 'fringes' it is not always clear whether or not a prediction can be made from the theory and, if so, exactly what that prediction will be.[3] Although investigators who have had experience working with the theory seem to have little difficulty intuiting its boundary conditions, they have had considerable difficulty communicating this to other people; indeed, a situation has evolved which can best be described by the statement: "If you want to be sure, ask Leon." This has proved to be both a source of embarrassment for the proponents of the theory as well as a source of annoyance and exasperation to its critics.

Why is it so difficult to make a more precise theoretical statement? Perhaps the most basic reason has to do with the nature of the inconsistency involved in the core definition of dissonance theory. It would be easy to specify dissonant situations if the theory were limited to *logical* inconsistencies. There exist relatively unequivocal rules of logic which can be applied without ambiguity or fear of contradiction. But recall that the inconsistency that produces dissonance, although it can be logical inconsistency, is not necessarily logical. Rather, it is *psychological* inconsistency. While this aspect of the theory increases

<hr>

[3] Further along in this chapter some attempt will be made to specify exactly what we mean by 'center' and 'fringes.'

its power, range, and degree of interest, at the same time it also causes some serious problems. Thus, returning to our friend the cigarette smoker, the cognition regarding smoking cigarettes is not logically inconsistent with the cognition linking cigarette smoking to cancer; i.e., strictly speaking, having information that cigarette smoking causes cancer does not make it illogical to smoke cigarettes. But these cognitions do produce dissonance because, taken together, they do not make sense psychologically. Assuming that the smoker does not want cancer, the knowledge that cigarettes cause cancer should lead to *not* smoking cigarettes. Similarly, none of the research examples mentioned above deals with logical inconsistency; e.g., it is not illogical to go through hell and high water to gain admission to a dull discussion group; it is not illogical to choose to own an appliance that one considers slightly more attractive than the unchosen alternative; it is not illogical to refrain from playing with a toy at the request of an adult.

Festinger (1957) lists four kinds of situations in which dissonance can arise: (1) logical inconsistency, (2) inconsistency with cultural mores, (3) inconsistency between one cognition and a more general, more encompassing cognition, (4) past experience.

1. Logical inconsistency: Suppose a person believed that all men are mortal but also held the belief that he, as a man, would live forever. These two cognitions are dissonant because they are logically inconsistent. The contrary of one follows from the other on strict logical grounds.

2. Cultural mores: If a college professor loses his patience with one of his students and shouts at him angrily, his knowledge of what he is doing is dis-

sonant with his idea about what is the proper, acceptable behavior of a professor toward his students—in our culture. In some other cultures this might be appropriate behavior and, therefore, would not arouse dissonance.

3. Inconsistency between one cognition and a more encompassing cognition: In a given election, if a person who has always considered himself to be a Democrat votes for the Republican candidate, he should experience dissonance. The concept "I am a Democrat" encompasses the concept "I vote for Democratic candidates."

4. Past experience: If a person stepped on a tack while barefoot and felt no pain, he would experience dissonance because he knows from experience that pain follows from stepping on tacks. If he had never had experience with tacks or other sharp objects, he would *not* experience dissonance.

The illustrations presented above are clear examples of dissonance. Similarly, the situations investigated in the experiments I have described above are clearly dissonant. But there *are* situations where for all practical purposes it is not perfectly clear whether two cognitions are dissonant or merely irrelevant. Because dissonance is *not* limited to logical inconsistencies, it is occasionally difficult to specify a priori whether or not a cultural more is being violated, whether or not an event is markedly different from past experience, or whether or not it is different from a more general cognition. Recall the basic theoretical statement: Two cognitions are dissonant if, considering these two cognitions alone, the opposite of one follows from the other. The major source of conceptual ambiguity rests upon the fact that Festinger has not clarified the meaning of the words "follows from."

For example, if I learn that my favorite novelist beats his wife, does this arouse dissonance? It is difficult to be certain. Strictly speaking, being a wife-beater is not incompatible with being a great novelist. However, there may be a sense in which the term "great novelist" implies that such a person is wise, sensitive, empathic, and compassionate —and wise, sensitive, empathic, and compassionate people do not go around beating their wives. This is not a logical inconsistency; nor is it a clear violation of a cultural more; moreover, it may have nothing to do with past experience—and it is not *necessarily* imbedded in a more general cognition. Thus, a knowledge of the kinds of situations in which dissonance *can* occur is not always useful in determining whether dissonance *does* occur.

A rule of thumb which I have found useful is to state the situation in terms of the violation of an expectancy. For example, one might issue the following instructions: "Consider Thurgood Marshall. I'm going to tell you something about his beliefs about the native I.Q. of Negroes relative to that of Caucasians. What do you expect these beliefs to be?" I imagine that most people would have a firm expectancy that Justice Marshall would have said that there are no innate differences. Consequently, one could then conclude that if individuals were exposed to a statement by Justice Marshall to the effect that Negroes were innately stupider than Caucasians, most would experience dissonance. Let us try our difficult example: Suppose we confronted a large number of people with the following proposition: "Consider the great novelist X. I am about to tell you something about whether or not he beats his wife. What do you expect me to say?" My guess is that most people would shrug; i.e., they would not have a strong expectancy (but, again, this is an empirical question; I am not certain that it would come out this way). If this occurred, one could conclude that X's wife-beating behavior is irrelevant to his status as a novelist. An empirical rule of thumb may be of practical utility but is, of course, no substitute for a clearer, less ambiguous, more precise theoretical statement. Near the end of this chapter we will elaborate upon this rule of thumb and indicate how it might be used conceptually.

The "nothing but" critique

Scientists tend to be conservative, parsimonious creatures. This is generally a healthy attitude which most frequently manifests itself in a reluctance to accept a new theory or a novel explanation for a phenomenon if the phenomenon can be squeezed (even with great difficulty) into an existing approach. In this regard, dissonance theory has been referred to as nothing but a new name for an old phenomenon. This has been most persistently stated in regard to that aspect of the theory related to decision making. In this context dissonance theory has been referred to as nothing but another name for conflict theory.

In fact, there are several differences. Conflict occurs before a decision is made, dissonance occurs after the decision. During conflict it is assumed that an individual will devote his energies to a careful, dispassionate, and sensible evaluation and judgment of the alternatives. He will gather all of the information, pro and con, about all of the alternatives in order to make a reasonable decision. Following the decision, a person is in a state of dissonance—all

negative aspects of X are dissonant with having chosen X; all positive aspects of Y are dissonant with *not* having chosen Y. Far from evaluating the alternatives impartially (as in conflict), the individual experiencing dissonance will seek biased information and evaluations designed to make his decision appear more reasonable. As in Brehm's (1956) experiment, he will seek to spread the alternatives apart. The more difficulty a person had making a decision, the greater the tendency toward this kind of behavior as a means of justifying his decision.

But how can we be certain that the spreading apart of the alternatives in Brehm's experiment occurred after the decision? Could it not have occurred during the conflict stage? That is, it is conceivable that, in order to make their decision easier, subjects in Brehm's experiment began to reevaluate the appliances in a biased manner *before* the decision. If this were the case, then there is no essential difference between predecisional and postdecisional processes; if so, this behavior can be considered part of conflict—and there is, indeed, no need to complicate matters by bringing in additional terminology.

Brehm's experiment does not allow us to determine whether the evaluation of chosen and unchosen alternatives was spread apart before or after the decision. Recent experiments by Davidson and Kiesler (1964) and by Jecker (1964) serve to clarify this issue (see Jecker, 1968). In Jecker's experiment, subjects were offered their choice between two phonograph records. In three conditions there was *low conflict*; i.e., subjects were told that there was a very good chance that they would receive *both* records no matter which they chose. In three other conditions, *high conflict* was produced by telling them that the probability was high that they would be given only the record that they chose. All of the subjects rated the records before the instructions; in each of the conflict conditions subjects rerated the records either (a) after they discovered that they received both records, (b) after they discovered that they received only the one record they chose, or (c) before they were certain whether they would get one or both. The results are quite clear: No spreading apart occurred when there was no dissonance; i.e., when the subject actually received both records or when he was not certain whether he would receive one or both he did *not* reevaluate the alternatives systematically. Where dissonance did occur there was a systematic reevaluation; i.e., subjects spread their evaluation of the alternatives when they received only one record—this occurred independently of the degree of conflict. This experiment provides clear evidence that conflict and dissonance are different processes; whatever else dissonance theory might be, it is *not* "nothing but conflict theory."

Dissonance theory and reward-incentive theory

One of the intriguing aspects of dissonance theory is that it frequently leads to predictions which stand in apparent contradiction to those made by other theoretical approaches—most notably, to a general reward-incentive theory. The words "stand in apparent contradiction" were carefully chosen, for as we shall see, these theories are not mutually exclusive on a conceptual level. No advocate of dissonance theory would take issue with the fact that people frequently perform actions in order to obtain rewards or that activities associated with rewards tend to be repeated. What they would suggest is that under certain carefully prescribed conditions, cognitive events are set in motion which result in behaviors quite different from what one would except from reward-incentive theories. Moreover, they might also suggest that such situations are not rare and, therefore, such behaviors are not flukey. Rather, they are quite common; one reason that they seem strange or 'uncommonsensical' to us is that total reliance on other theoretical approaches (explicitly or implicitly) has blinded us to alternative possibilities or has made us disinclined to look beyond the obvious events generated by reward-reinforcement theories. The much discussed 'nonobvious' predictions generated by dissonance theory are only nonobvious in an apparent sense; they become obvious and make sense—once we gain an understanding of the dissonance-reducing process.

When discussing alternative ways of reducing dissonance, I have tried to make the point that it is not very fruitful to ask what the mode of dissonance reduction is; rather, it is far more meaningful and instructive to isolate the various modes of reducing dissonance and to ask what the optimum conditions are for each. Similarly, rather than ask whether dissonance theory or reward-incentive theory is the more valid, one should attempt to determine the optimal conditions for the occurrence of processes and behaviors predicted by each theory.

In Gerard and Mathewson's (1966) conceptual replication of the Aronson-Mills (1959) experiment, they found that when dissonance was eliminated from the experimental situation (in the No Initiation condition), subjects tended to rate the group discussion as being less attractive if it followed severe electric shock. This is opposite to the "feelings of accomplishment" interpretation proposed by Chapanis and Chapanis (1964); rather, it can be considered as consistent with a general reward theory—i.e., stimuli contiguous with severe shock are considered to be unattractive. Similar findings relevant to reward theory are reported by Aronson (1961).

Another example of this approach can be found in an experiment by Freedman (1963), who had subjects perform a dull task after first informing them that either (a) the data would definitely be of no value to the experimenter—since his experiment was already complete, or (b) the data would be of *great* value to the experimenter. According to dissonance theory, performing a dull task is dissonant with the fact that it is not very valuable; in order to reduce dissonance, subjects should attempt to convince themselves that they actually enjoyed performing the task for its own sake. However, if the data are valuable, there is little dissonance, hence little need to convince oneself that the task was enjoyable. Freedman's results confirmed his prediction: Subjects in the "No-Value" condition enjoyed the task to a greater extent than did subjects in the "High-Value" condition. In addition, he ran a parallel set of conditions except that he withheld information about how valuable the task performance was for the experimenter until *after* the subjects had completed the task. With this modification he found the opposite effect: Those who were told the task was valuable enjoyed it more than those who were told it was useless. A moment's reflection should indicate that there is little or no dissonance in the above situation (see Carlsmith & Freedman, 1968). No subject can have

any reason to suspect that an experimenter is running him for no reason at all. If the subject performed the task in good faith, he had no way of knowing his data would not be used by the experimenter. That is, experimenters do not generally collect data that they have no intention of using. Accordingly, the subject does not need to seek justification for performing the task—the fact that his performance turned out to be futile was nothing that he could have possibly foreseen. On the other hand, if, in advance, he had some reason for believing that his efforts might be futile (as in the previous condition), he *does* need additional justification—he must convince himself that he chose to do it for its own sake. The point I want to stress here is that where little or no dissonance exists, an incentive effect emerges: The more valuable the task, the 'better' it is; the 'better' it is, the more subjects enjoyed doing it. This experiment clearly demonstrates that dissonance effects and incentive effects can exist side by side. Moreover, it helps define some of the limiting conditions of each.

In a similar vein, a recent experiment by Carlsmith, Collins, and Helmreich (1966) has taken us a long way toward an understanding of the conditions optimal for the emergence of incentive and dissonance phenomena following counterattitudinal advocacy.

According to dissonance theory, if a person says something he feels is untrue, he experiences dissonance: The cognition "I said X" is dissonant with the cognition "I believe *not*-X." In order to reduce dissonance, he might attempt to convince himself that what he said was not so very untrue. Thus, dissonance theory suggests that advocating an opposite position increases one's tendency to believe in that position. However, if one is provided with a great deal of justification for advocating an opposite position (for example, if one is paid a great deal of money for telling a lie), one experiences less dissonance. That is, if I told a small lie for $53,000, I would have ample justification for having lied: The cognition that I received $53,000 is consonant with having lied. Consequently, I would have less need to justify my action by convincing myself that I really believed what I said than if I had been paid a mere 53 cents for lying. This type of prediction has been confirmed by several experiments (e.g., Festinger & Carlsmith, 1959; Cohen, 1962; Nuttin, 1964; Lependorf, 1964). These experiments have shown greater attitude change for less reward across a wide range of topics; moreover, it has been confirmed across a wide range of rewards, from $20.00 (high) and $1.00 (low) in the Festinger-Carlsmith experiment, to 50 cents (relatively high) and 5 cents (relatively low) in the Lependorf experiment. Thus, it would appear that this is a sturdy finding. On the other hand, there is some evidence that, under certain conditions, the opposite effect might emerge (Janis & Gilmore, 1965; Elms & Janis, 1965; Rosenberg, 1965d).[4] Briefly, under certain conditions, offering a high incentive for advocating a given position may lead to a better performance—i.e., thinking up more and better arguments. This could lead to greater attitude change; i.e., a person changes his attitude *because* he has exposed himself to more arguments *because* he has looked harder *because* he was paid more money.

But what are these conditions? Or, better still, what conditions are optimal

[4] For a more detailed critical analysis of all of these experiments, see Aronson, 1966.

for the dissonance effect and what conditions are optimal for the incentive effect? The experiment by Carlsmith, Collins, and Helmreich (1966) provides us with a solid clue. In their experiment subjects were put through a dull task and were then asked to describe the task as interesting. The dependent variable was the extent to which the subjects convinced themselves that the task really was interesting. The results showed a dissonance effect (the smaller the reward, the greater the opinion change) only under conditions where subjects lied to another person in a highly committing face-to-face situation. In other conditions, subjects wrote an essay, were assured complete anonymity, and were told that only bits and pieces of their argument would be used. Here an incentive effect emerged: The greater the reward, the greater the opinion change. In the early experiments (e.g., Festinger & Carlsmith, 1959) the importance of the face-to-face situation was not fully appreciated by the investigators because this variable was not systematically manipulated. In a recent analysis of this area (Aronson, 1966) I suggested that the important distinction between the above conditions is "degree of commitment." That is, in the face-to-face situation, the subject was saying things to a person which he himself believed were untrue. As I see it, this situation involves much more commitment and, hence, arouses much more dissonance than the writing of an anonymous essay which the subject had been told would not be used in its original form.

At the same time, it should be noted that the complexity of the experimental operations employed by Carlsmith, Collins, and Helmreich (1966) allows for alternative explanations. One of the most serious of these alternative explanations is in terms of the complexity of the counterattitudinal task involved. Rosenberg (1966) has argued that dissonance theory may be limited to situations where not much cognitive elaboration is required; he contends that where the task is more complex, incentive effects might occur. In analyzing the Carlsmith, Collins, and Helmreich study, Rosenberg makes the reasonable point that writing an essay and telling a lie not only differ in degree of commitment, but also may differ in the degree of cognitive complexity required. Consequently, this experiment cannot be taken as offering unambiguous support for my suggestion that degree of commitment is the decisive factor.

Two very recent experiments shed some additional light on this problem. In one, Linder, Cooper, and Jones (1967) were careful to hold the complexity of the task constant. The task was a complex one in all conditions—college students were asked to write an essay favoring more stringent paternalistic supervision of students by the college administration. The experimenters varied (a) the degree of commitment (in terms of whether or not the subjects were allowed to feel that they had a clear choice as to whether or not to write the essay) and (b) the magnitude of monetary incentive for writing the essay. The results are quite clear: When commitment was high there was a dissonance effect; i.e., the smaller the incentive, the greater the opinion change. When commitment was relatively low there was an incentive effect. A different experiment (Helmreich & Collins, 1968, in press) produced similar clear results. Here the task was also held constant, but instead of being complex (as in the Linder, Cooper, & Jones study), it was a simple one. Subjects were asked to re-

cord a statement which would be played to a large classroom of other students. In two relatively high-commitment conditions the subject's simple statement was put on *video* tape along with his name, class, major, and hometown. In a low-commitment condition the subjects made statements anonymously on *audio* tape. The results paralleled those obtained by Linder, Cooper, and Jones. In the high-commitment conditions the smaller the incentive, the greater the opinion change (dissonance effect); in the low-commitment condition the greater the incentive, the greater the opinion change (incentive effect).

The "underlying cognition" problem

The importance of commitment emerges most clearly when we scrutinize the phenomenon of the white lie more thoroughly. Clearly, every time we say something that we do not believe, we do *not* experience dissonance. Under certain conditions there are some underlying cognitions which serve to prevent the occurrence of dissonance. For example, if we stated a counterattitudinal position in the context of a formal debate, we would not experience dissonance (see Scott, 1957, 1959; Aronson, 1966). It is clearly understood both by the speaker and the audience that a debator's own personal views have nothing to do with the opinions he expresses. The rules of the game of debating provide an underlying cognition which prevents the occurrence of dissonance. Similarly, as teachers we frequently are exposed to a great many stupid ideas from our students. I think that unless we know the student well—know that he is capable of better ideas and know that he is capable of 'taking it'—most teachers refrain from tearing the idea to pieces. Instead, we tend to give the student our attention, nod and smile, and suggest that it is not such a bad idea. We do this because we have a general underlying cognition that we should not discourage students early in their careers and that it is wrong to be unkind to people who are relatively powerless to fight back. It would be ludicrous to suggest that teachers begin to believe that a student's poor idea is really a pretty good one simply because the teacher had said "pretty good idea" to the student. The underlying cognition prevents the occurrence of dissonance. But observe how commitment can make it a dissonant situation: If, on the basis of the teacher's statement, the student had decided to read his paper at the state psychological convention, the teacher might begin to convince himself that it was not such a bad idea—because the teacher has now been committed—he has misled the student into taking some action. This increases the teacher's commitment to the situation and is probably more powerful than the underlying consonant cognition "this is how we treat students." The teacher now seeks additional justification for having misled the student, perhaps by convincing himself that it was not such a bad idea after all.

The general point to be made here is an important one. Inconsistency is said to arise between two cognitive elements if, "considering these two alone, the [opposite] of one element follows from the other" (Festinger, 1957, pp. 260–261). But we know that in most situations two cognitions are almost never taken by themselves. Occasionally, two cognitions which in the abstract would appear to be dissonant fail to arouse dissonance because of the existence of a neutralizing underlying cognition. For example, suppose I know a brilliant fellow who is married to an incredibly stupid woman. These cognitions are inconsistent but I would contend that they do not necessarily produce dissonance. I can tolerate this inconsistency—it does not cause me pain, it does not necessarily lead me to change my opinion about the brilliant fellow or his wife, I do not conclude that he is dumber than I thought or that she is smarter. Why? Because I have a general, underlying, pervasive cognition that there are a multitude of factors which determine mate selection—similarities of intelligence being only one of them. Moreover, I know that it is extremely rare for all of these to be matched in a marital relationship. Therefore, although taken by themselves the above two cognitions are incompatible, I simply do not ever take them by themselves.

Festinger suggests that one way to reduce dissonance is to martial consonant cognitions—thus, he might say that the above reasoning is one way of reducing dissonance. But it is a moot and important point whether I martialed the above cognitions as a result of the inconsistency, or whether I walked around with these cognitions about mate selection before the fact. If the latter is the case, then it can hardly be said that I dredged up this overriding cognition as a means of reducing dissonance. For example, let us look at the finding (Aronson & Carlsmith, 1963; Turner & Wright, 1965; Freedman, 1965) that children threatened with mild punishment for playing with a toy tend to derogate that toy after refraining from playing with it. Suppose that many children entered the situation with the strong feeling that adults must be obeyed always, even when commands are arbitrary and threats are nonexistent ("My mother, right or wrong!"). Put another way (which will become important in a moment), suppose that part of the self concept of these children was "obedience to adult authority." If this were the case there would have been no dissonance—even though, *taken by itself*, the cognition "I like that toy" is dissonant with the cognition "I'm not playing with it." If this were *not* already a part of the person's self concept, it might have become one as a function of the experiment—i.e., developing a belief in the importance of obedience is one way of reducing dissonance in the above situation. But if it were already there—there would have been no dissonance to begin with.

This added complexity should not lead us to throw our hands up in despair. Rather, it should lead us to a more careful analysis of the situations we are dealing with and perhaps even to a greater concern with individual differences.

The importance of the self concept and other expectancies

In discussing the difficulties in making precise predictions from dissonance theory in some situations, we have purposely tiptoed around the problem of individual differences. The fact that all people are not the same presents intriguing problems for dissonance theory as it does for all general motivational theories. Of course, one man's 'problem' is another man's primary datum; i.e., psychologists who are interested in personality regard individual differences as being of great interest. For those who are primarily interested in establishing nomothetic laws, individual differences usually constitute nothing more than an annoying source of error variance. Never-

theless, whether or not we are interested in individual differences *per se*, an understanding of the way people differ in dissonant situations can be an important means to clarify and strengthen the theory. Basically, there are three ways that individuals differ which should be of concern to people investigating dissonance theory:

1. People differ in their ability to tolerate dissonance. It seems reasonable to assume that some people are simply better than others at shrugging off dissonance; i.e., it may take a greater *amount* of dissonance to bring about dissonance-reducing behavior in some people than in others.

2. People probably differ in their preferred mode of dissonance reduction. E.g., some people may find it easier to derogate the source of a communication than to change their own opinion. Others may find the reverse resolution easier.

3. What is dissonant for one person may be consonant for someone else; i.e., people may be so different that certain events are regarded as dissonant for some but not for others.

Dissonant or consonant with what? Recall the earlier discussion wherein I described a rule of thumb based upon an expectancy (e.g., the Thurgood Marshall and wife-beating novelist illustrations). In my judgment, dissonance theory makes a clear prediction when a firm expectancy is involved as one of the cognitions in question. Thus, our cognition about Thurgood Marshall's *behavior* can be dissonant with our expectancy about how Justice Marshall *will* behave. Dissonance theory is clearer still when that firm expectancy involves the individual's self concept, for—almost by definition—our expectancies about our own behavior are firmer than our expectancies about the behavior of another person. Thus, at the very heart of dissonance theory, where it makes its clearest and neatest prediction, we are not dealing with just any two cognitions; rather, we are usually dealing with the self concept and cognitions about some behavior. If dissonance exists it is because the individual's behavior is inconsistent with his self concept.

As an empirical refinement this self concept notion is probably trivial. The experimenters who made the tacit assumption that people have high self concepts achieved positive results—which indicates that this assumption is valid for most people in these situations. But it may constitute a valuable and interesting *theoretical* refinement. A theory becomes infinitely more meaningful when its domain is clearly demarcated; i.e., when it states clearly where it does not apply. If it is the case that dissonance theory makes unequivocal predictions only when the self concept or another strong expectancy is involved, then an important set of boundary conditions has been drawn. What I described earlier as a rule of thumb may actually be a conceptual clarification.

I stated early in this chapter that "at the 'center' of the theory" predictions are unequivocal, but at the 'fringes' they are somewhat fuzzy. At this point, we can say that 'at the center' means situations in which the self concept or other firm expectancies are involved —and in which most people share the same self concepts or other firm expectancies. Thus, most people have self concepts about being truthful and honest so that we can make clear predictions intuitively, as in the Carlsmith, Collins, and Helmreich (1966) experiment. Most people have self concepts involving making reasonable and wise decisions so that we can intuit clear predictions, as in the Brehm (1956) or Jecker (1964) experiments. Also, most people have firm expectancies about what Thurgood Marshall would say about Negro intelligence, so that a dissonance theory prediction makes sense and can be made clearly, even though a self concept is not involved. The prediction about the great novelist who beats his wife gives the theory trouble precisely because people differ tremendously with regard to whether or not they expect a particular novelist to be a gentle and considerate man. In a specific instance, the knowledge of whether or not individual X has this expectancy would increase the accuracy of the prediction. I do not regard this of great importance. What I do regard as important is merely the recognition of the fact that dissonance theory may be best suited for making general predictions in situations where expectancies are firm and nearly universal.

37 The organization and modification of beliefs

MILTON ROKEACH

Most everyone would agree that the total number of beliefs which a grown person possesses is probably very large. By the time we have grown into adulthood we have formed tens, and possibly hundreds, of thousands of beliefs concerning what is, and what is not, true and beautiful and good about the physical and social world in which we live.

It is inconceivable that all these countless beliefs which we each possess would be retained in an unorganized, chaotic state within our minds. Rather, it must be assumed that man's beliefs—like the physicist's electrons and protons, like the astronomer's moons and planets and suns, like the geneticist's chromosomes and genes—become somehow organized into architectural systems having describable and measurable structural properties which, in turn, have observable behavioral consequences.

When I use the term belief I am not necessarily referring to a believer's verbal reports taken at face value; beliefs are inferences made by an observer about underlying states of expectancy. When a person says: "This I believe . . . ," he may or may not represent accurately to us what he truly believes because there are often compelling personal and social reasons, conscious and unconscious, why he will not or cannot tell us. For these reasons, beliefs—like motives, genes, and neutrons—cannot be directly observed but must be inferred as best one can, with whatever psychological devices available, from all the things the believer says or does.

A belief system may be defined as having represented within it, in some organized psychological—but not necessarily logical—form, each and every one of a person's countless beliefs about physical and social reality. By definition, we do not allow beliefs to exist outside the belief system for the same reason that the astronomer does not allow stars to remain outside the universe.

There are at least seven major kinds of interrelated questions which it is possible to ask about the nature of man's systems of belief. First, what are the structural properties which all belief systems have in common, regardless of content? Second, in what structural ways do belief systems differ from one another? Third, how are they developed and learned? Fourth, what motivational functions do belief systems serve? Fifth, what is the relation between belief and emotion or, in other terms, between cognition and affection? Sixth, how do belief systems guide perceiving, thinking, remembering, learning, and action? And, finally, what conditions facilitate and hinder the modification of belief systems?

It is not my intent to discuss all these questions here; they are mentioned only to point to the broader theoretical framework for the present concern, which is to focus particular attention on theory, method, and findings relevant to

Abridged from the **Centennial Review**, 1963, 7, No. 4, 375–95, with permission of the author and the publisher. An elaborated version of this paper appears as Chapter I in Professor Rokeach's book **Beliefs, Attitudes, and Values**, 1968.

the first and last of the seven questions mentioned, namely, those mainly concerned with the organization and modification of systems of belief. In doing so, it is my hope that the discussion will serve to increase an understanding of a variety of situations in real life in which man's belief systems would seem to undergo change. For example, changes in systems of beliefs are often said to occur as a result of successful therapy, or as a result of political or religious conversion, or conversely, as a result of undergoing processes of ideological disillusionment and defection. Mention might be made also of various coercive attempts to alter belief systems, such as the "thought reform" procedures employed in Communist China and the so-called "brainwashing" techniques employed in North Korean prisoner-of-war camps and, somewhat earlier, by Khrushchev's own admission, in the great Soviet purge trials of the mid-thirties.

I

I will begin the analysis with three simple assumptions: first, not all beliefs are equally important to the individual; beliefs vary along a central-peripheral dimension; second, the more central— or, in our terminology, the more primitive—a belief, the more it will resist change; third, the more central the belief change, the more widespread the repercussions in the rest of the belief system. These assumptions are not unlike the assumptions made by the atomic physicist who conceives of a central nucleus within the atom wherein the particles within the nucleus are held together in a stable structure, and contain vast amounts of potential energy. Under some circumstances, for example, through processes of fission or fusion, the potential energy contained within

the nucleus will be released, thus changing the structure of the nucleus and, thereby, the structure of the whole atom. Is it possible, in a roughly analogous fashion, to conceive also of belief systems as having "nuclear" beliefs which, if we only understand their nature and how to alter that nature, might lead us to better understand why it is that belief systems are typically in a relatively stable state highly resistant to change, and under what conditions they will change?

By what logical criteria can one decide which ones of a person's countless beliefs are central or primitive and which ones are not? To deal with this question, we have assumed that every one of a person's beliefs, whether conscious or unconscious, is at least in one sense a social belief. For every belief a person forms, he also forms some notion about how many others in a position to know believe it too. We define primitive beliefs as taken-for-granted, uncontroversial beliefs supported by a unanimous social consensus among those in a position to know. It is as if the believer says to himself: "I believe, and everyone else who could know believes it too."

Primitive beliefs can be thought of as being represented within the innermost core of the belief system. Such beliefs are called primitive because they are meant to be roughly analogous to the primitive terms of an axiomatic system in mathematics or science. A person's primitive beliefs represent his "basic truths" about physical reality, social reality, and the nature of the self; they represent a subsystem within the total system in which the person has the heaviest of commitments. In the ordinary course of life's events, they are so much taken for granted that they do not even come up as a subject for discussion or controversy. *I believe this is a table, I believe this is my mother, I believe my name is so-and-so* are examples, respectively, of primitive beliefs about the physical world, the social world, and the self supported by a unanimous consensus among those in a position to know.

Another way of describing primitive beliefs about physical reality, the social world, and the self is to talk about *object constancy, person constancy*, and *self-constancy*. Even though I see this rectangular table from many angles, I continue to believe (primitively) that it remains a table and that it remains rectangular. What many perception psychologists have overlooked thus far is that object constancy is also a social phenomenon, built up in childhood side-by-side with person constancy, both object and person constancy being necessary prerequisites for developing a sense of self-constancy. Not only does a child learn that objects maintain their constancy, but also that other people constantly experience physical objects as he does. Thus, two sets of primitive beliefs are built up together, one about the constancy of physical objects and the other about the constancy of people with respect to physical objects.

Object constancy and person constancy seem to serve an important function for the growing child. They build up within him a basic minimum of *trust* that the physical world will stay put and also that the world of people can at the very least be depended on to react constantly to physical objects as he does. It is as if nature and society had conspired to provide the child with a minimum guarantee of stability on the basis of which to build his own sense of self-constancy.

Actually, the child seems to need and to strive for far more person constancy than that provided by the physical contexts within which he learns object constancy. A child depends on his mother to remain his mother (with all that is meant by mother), and his family and social groups to remain his family and social groups, no less than on a table to remain a table.

It may be supposed that any inexplicable disruption of these taken-for-granted constancies, physical or social or self, would lead one to question the validity of one's own senses, one's competence as a person who can cope with reality, or even one's sanity. Put another way, violation of any primitive beliefs supported by unanimous consensus may lead to serious disruptions of beliefs about self-constancy or self-identity and from this other disturbances should follow.

In the beginning all beliefs are probably primitive ones, the young child not yet being capable of understanding that some beliefs are not shared by everybody. The young child's mental capacities and his experience are as yet too circumscribed for him to grasp the fact that he lives in a world in which there is controversy, or even armed conflict, over which authorities are positive and which negative, and which beliefs and ideologies associated with authority are the most valid. In the very beginning there is only one authority the infant looks to for information and nurturance —the mother; somewhat later, the father. These parental referents are the only referents which exist for the young child, and there does not yet exist for him either the conception that there are other positive referents, or that there exist negative referents.

As the infant develops toward maturity, one of three things can happen to his primitive beliefs:

1. Many of his primitive beliefs will continue to remain primitive throughout life, if they do not arise as subjects of controversy. As the child grows and broadens the range of his interactions with others outside the family, his authority base becomes gradually extended to include virtually everyone in a position to know. Thus, should any doubt arise about the validity of such a primitive belief—for example, is today Wednesday or Thursday?—he can check it by asking virtually any stranger who happens along.

2. But not all primitive beliefs owe their primitiveness to the universalization of social support. Through adverse experience, some primitive beliefs (about the self and about others) may become transformed into a second kind of primitive belief, in which support from external authority is abandoned altogether. A primitive belief originally supported by 100 per cent consensus may become transformed through adverse or traumatic learning experiences into a primitive belief supported by zero consensus. For example, a child may come to believe through intense experience or through an accretion of less intense experiences that he lives in a totally hostile world, or that he is unlovable or, phobically, that certain heretofore benign objects or places are now dangerous. In this second kind of primitive belief, it is as if the believer says: "I believe, but nobody else could know. It, therefore, does not matter what others believe." Or, to quote from a more popular refrain: "Nobody knows the troubles I've seen."

3. Finally, as the child interacts with others, his expanding repertoire of primitive beliefs is continually brought into play and he thus stands to discover at any moment that a particular belief he had heretofore believed everyone else believed, such as the belief in God or Country or Santa Claus, is not shared by everyone. At this point the child is forced to work through a more selective conception of positive and negative authority, and this point marks the beginning of the development of the non-primitive parts of the child's ever-expanding belief system.

Non-primitive beliefs are conceived to develop out of the primitive beliefs and to be in a functional relationship with them. They seem to serve the purpose of helping the person to round out his picture of the world, realistically and rationally to the extent possible, defensively and irrationally to the extent necessary. In using the concept of non-primitive beliefs, I am trying to point to a class of beliefs which do not seem to have the same taken-for-granted character as primitive beliefs. We learn to expect differences of opinion and controversy concerning them, however much we might cherish them. Such beliefs, while important and generally resistant to change, are nevertheless conjectured to be less important and easier to change than those I have called primitive beliefs.

Most important of these non-primitive beliefs would seem to be those concerning positive and negative authority—what the sociologists call reference persons or reference groups. Such beliefs concern not only which authorities are those who *could* know but also which authorities *would* know. Which authorities, positive and negative, are we to trust and distrust, to look to and not look to, as we go about our daily lives seeking information about the world? The particular authorities relied on for information, in order to have a basis for action, differ from one person to the next and would depend upon learning experiences within the context of the person's social structure—family, class, peer group, ethnic group, religious and political group, country, et cetera.

If we know about a person only that he believes in a particular authority, we should be able to deduce a great number of his other beliefs, those which emanate or derive from the authorities he happens to identify with. Because they are derived from other beliefs, I have called them peripheral beliefs. They are less important, dynamically, than beliefs about authority, and therefore a change of belief with respect to authority, or a direct communication from one's authority, should lead to many other changes in beliefs deriving from authority. It is these peripheral beliefs which form what is ordinarily referred to as an ideology and, along with the identifications with reference persons and groups on which such ideologies are based, provide one with a sense of group identity.

In summary, a person's total belief system includes peripheral beliefs, pre-ideological beliefs about specific authority, and pre-ideological primitive beliefs about the nature of the physical world, society, and the self. All such beliefs are assumed to be formed and to develop very early in the life of a child. They are undoubtedly first learned in the context of interactions with parents. As the child grows older, he somehow learns that there are certain beliefs which virtually all others believe, other beliefs which are true for him even though no one else were to believe them, and still other beliefs about which men differ.

Taken together, the total belief system may be seen as an organization of beliefs varying in depth, formed as a result of living in nature and in society, designed to help a person maintain, insofar as possible, a sense of ego and group identity, stable and continuous over time, an identity which experiences itself to be a part of, and simultaneously apart from, a stable physical and social environment.

II

To be discussed next is a series of investigations designed to test various hypotheses stemming from our theoretical formulations. The full details of these investigations are too complex to present here; they will be reported in separate publications. Instead, I will have to content myself here with a relatively brief discussion of the different types of phenomena studied, the methods employed, as well as some of the major findings and their implications for everyday life.

In one study, done in collaboration with Albert Zavala, we tried to ascertain whether primitive beliefs, as defined, are indeed more resistant to change than other beliefs, as would be expected by our theory. Table 1 shows nine statements which were presented to about 70 subjects representing the three kinds of beliefs designated as primitive, authority, and peripheral beliefs. They were asked to rank these nine statements in terms of which one they would be most reluctant to relinquish under any circumstance, which one they would be next most reluctant to relinquish, and so on. The subjects were also asked to indicate how strongly they agreed with each of the nine beliefs and to estimate how many others believed as they did with respect to each of the nine beliefs.

The first column of Table 1 shows the rank order of resistance to change of the nine beliefs, as judged by our subjects. It is seen that the three primitive ones are ranked highest in resistance to change. These are followed by the three authority beliefs and, finally, by the three peripheral beliefs. The rankings of all nine beliefs conform to theoretical expectations without exception. Moreover, as shown in the second column of Table 1, the vast majority of our subjects adhere to primitive beliefs with absolute intensity while considerably fewer subjects do so with respect to authority and peripheral beliefs. Finally, as shown in the last column of Table 1, about three-fourths of our subjects report that all others unanimously believe as they do with respect to primitive beliefs while only a scattered few claim unanimous social consensus for authority and peripheral beliefs. Thus, the theoretical distinctions drawn among central, authority, and peripheral beliefs are opera-

tionally demonstrated. Naive subjects who know nothing of our theory seem to behave as if they, too, can tell the difference among the three kinds of beliefs.

These results suggest that beliefs about such things as the Bible, the fallibility or infallibility of the Pope, or the United States Constitution are not among the most deeply held of man's beliefs. More deeply held and possibly more resistant to change are those beliefs which all men would share with one another, which rarely come up for discussion or controversy, namely, primitive beliefs. These results would further suggest that in the event there is a conflict between two beliefs varying in centrality, that the more central belief would win out. Such a conflict is neatly exemplified in a slogan we are all familiar with, a political slogan first made famous by Bertrand Russell: *Better red than dead*

TABLE 1

DEGREE OF RESISTANCE TO CHANGE, INTENSITY OF AGREEMENT, AND PERCEIVED
CONSENSUS OF PRIMITIVE, AUTHORITY, AND PERIPHERAL BELIEFS

	Mean rank	% who absolutely accept or reject belief	% reporting unanimous social consensus
Primitive beliefs			
1. Death is inevitable	2.47	92	72
2. We cannot live unless we have oxygen	2.67	91	74
3. My name is _____	2.86	98	83
		93.7	76.3
Authority beliefs			
4. There is only one true Bible	4.17	50	4
5. The U. S. Constitution is the best constitution ever framed	5.30	21	7
6. The Pope is infallible in matters of faith and morals	5.97	55	2
		42.0	4.3
Peripheral beliefs			
7. I favor birth control	6.37	48	2
8. Adam had a navel	7.22	28	9
9. It is wrong to smoke	7.89	34	0
		36.7	3.7

and the counter-slogan *Better dead than red*. These slogans become theoretically interesting precisely because they seem to pit two beliefs against each other, one a primitive belief which is shared by everybody, *It is better to be alive than dead*, and the other an ideological belief, in our terms, a peripheral belief, *It is better to be anti-Communist than Communist*. In line with our theory, we would have to predict, contrary to what many Americans would undoubtedly predict, that most people, even anti-Communist Americans, would prefer the state of redness to the state of deadness, simply because of the greater potency of primitive beliefs over peripheral beliefs.

To find out if this is indeed so, a study was recently conducted at Michigan State University in collaboration with Irwin Horowitz in which subjects were simply asked to agree or disagree with the statement: "Death is preferable to living under a Communist regime." Only 40% reported that they would rather be dead than red, while 60% reported they would rather be red than dead. But even the finding of 40% who prefer being dead seems questionable in the light of some additional data which were available for the subjects.

We found further that a majority of the better-dead-than-red group believes that no one would be mad enough to start a nuclear holocaust and a majority of them does not believe that war is probable in the next decade. The subjects are college students, as I have already indicated, and it may be assumed that a decade represents for such subjects a very long time. In other words, the subjects who say they prefer death to life under Communism do not seem to conceive of their own death as a realistic or immediate possibility: they would rather be dead than red, but no one would be mad enough to start a nuclear war; and, besides, it won't come within the next decade. In contrast, a sizable majority of the better-red-than-dead group admits to the fear that a madman can start an atomic war at any moment. On the basis of these additional data, it may be doubted that even 40% of our sample really prefer death to life under Communism.

Following a similar line of reasoning, it may be suggested that whenever people have been given a choice between such alternatives as death and life under Fascism, between death and religious conversion, as was the case during the Spanish Inquisition, their belief systems and psyches have been so constituted that, by and large, they have preferred life to death. Thus on psychological grounds, I would not be inclined to accept seriously an invitation to die for this or that cause because it is doubtful that those who advocate dying for causes would, when the chips are down, themselves die for that cause. The deliberate choice of death over life under an alien ideology is probably an extremely rare event in human history, and martyrdom is probably better understood as a state conferred *a posteriori* rather than freely chosen *a priori*.

All the preceding is not to deny, of course, that most of us possess primitive beliefs regarding conditions under which we would prefer death to life, which would serve as genuine guides to action. For example, most mothers primitively believe that they would prefer to sacrifice their own lives to save the life of a loved child. Most of us primitively believe that we would prefer to die rather than betray a comrade to death at the hands of an enemy. But such instances are altogether different from those previously discussed. What seems to be involved in the examples just cited is not a primitive belief pitted against a peripheral belief but primitive beliefs supported by unanimous social consensus, or one altogether independent of social consensus, about the value of the life of one's own child as compared with one's own, or about the utter worthlessness of one's own life when bought at the expense of a comrade's.

In addition to the three kinds of beliefs already discussed—primitive beliefs, authority beliefs, and peripheral beliefs —we have recently found it necessary to posit a fourth kind of belief not previously discussed, called inconsequential beliefs. The latter refers to beliefs involving matters of taste which, if changed, are not expected to lead to any important consequences in the rest of the belief system.

Some examples of peripheral beliefs, that is, ideological beliefs derivable from authority, are: "The Russians were justified in putting down the Hungarian revolt in 1956." "The Gettysburg Address does not really say anything important," and "I think this country would have been better off if the South had won the Civil War."

Finally, let me give some examples of inconsequential beliefs, beliefs which if changed, are not expected to produce any significant changes in other beliefs: "There is no doubt in my mind that Elizabeth Taylor is more beautiful than Dinah Shore," and "I think summertime is a much more enjoyable time of the year than winter."

Consider next several instances in which there is a violation of primitive beliefs about physical reality. The television program *Candid Camera* often achieves its "entertaining" effects precisely because the audience is observing the reactions of persons whose primitive beliefs are being violated. Another ex-

ample comes from the well-known Asch experiments, in which a subject overhears five other subjects in a group experiment report that two lines are of equal length when in fact they are clearly of unequal length. The subject does not know that these other five subjects are really confederates of the experimenter, instructed in advance to give the same wrong answer when comparing lines of varying length. This experiment is typically emotionally upsetting to the subject because all the other subjects are clearly in a position to know, yet they all disagree with him. There has been a violation of primitive belief which is relieved only when, at the end, the subject is let in on the nature of the experiment.

Ethical considerations clearly forbid social scientists from conducting "thought control" experiments or tampering with a normal child's or adult's primitive beliefs for prolonged periods. It was because of such considerations that it was necessary to turn away from further investigations with normal persons to focus instead on psychotic persons holding delusional belief systems. It is the object of psychotherapy and social policy to alter the psychotic's delusional beliefs and to readjust him to reality insofar as possible. Thus, experimental attempts over prolonged periods to change beliefs become ethically more justifiable when they serve therapeutic rather than destructive or "thought control" or "brainwashing" ends.

Such considerations culminated in our bringing together for study over a two-year period three chronic paranoid schizophrenic patients, each believing he was the re-incarnation of Jesus Christ. Leon, in his mid-thirties, had been hospitalized five years before. Joseph was in his late fifties and Clyde was about seventy years of age. Both had been institutionalized almost two decades before. The three delusional Christs were assigned to adjacent beds in one ward, ate at one table in the dining room, worked together on the same job, and met daily for group discussions. Each one was thus confronted with two others laying claim to the same identity within a controlled environment for a prolonged period. In addition, other experimental procedures were employed with Leon and Joseph. They received written suggestions to change their beliefs and behavior from authority figures they looked up to, figures who existed only in their imagination. Actually these communications were written and sent by me. All such procedures were designed to test the following hypotheses: first, having to live with others claiming the same identity over a prolonged period is as dissonance-producing a situation as is humanly conceivable and, consequently, changes in delusional beliefs and in behavior designed to reduce this dissonance should result; second, a persuasive communication emanating with one's positive authority figure can only be responded to in one of two ways: either the suggestion to change is accepted from the positive authority or, if it is unacceptable, the attitude toward the positive authority figure will undergo change. In either event, changes in delusions should result.

The full story of what happened as a result of these experimental procedures is reported in *The Three Christs of Ypsilanti* (Rokeach, 1964). At the risk of over-simplification let me here try to summarize briefly the main findings. First, the effect of confrontations over identity produced changes in the identity and in the delusional beliefs of the youngest of the three delusional Christs, the changes involving the destruction of existing delusions and the formation of new delusions concerning identity, bolstered by additional delusions emerging for the first time. Second, the effect of the persuasive communications from delusional authority figures was that it produced many changes in the delusions and in the behavior of Leon and Joseph, including eventually the destruction of both Leon's and Joseph's delusional authority figures. In general, it may be said that Leon, the youngest of the three, changed most as a result of our experimental procedures and Clyde, the oldest, changed the least.

It should perhaps be most emphasized in closing, that although each of our investigations has served to increase our understanding of the internal architecture of belief systems and of the conditions for their modification, we have not yet learned how to control experimentally induced modifications in belief systems in order to achieve socially desirable, therapeutic effects. In the last experiment referred to, we were indeed able to produce changes but we were not able to control the direction the changes took. It would thus seem that the nuclear physicists are way ahead of us in this respect; they have not only learned how to produce a schizophrenic shattering of the atom which destroys everything in its path but also how to slow down and control its nuclear reaction in order to achieve socially desirable ends. The task for psychology is a roughly similar one: to learn enough about the structure of belief systems in order to know how to form them in the first place and how to modify them in the second place so that they will best serve to increase the happiness and freedom of the individual and his society.

38　Persistence and regression of changed attitudes: long-range studies

THEODORE M. NEWCOMB

I

One's attitude toward something is not only a resultant of one's previous traffic with one's environment but also a determinant of selective response to present and future environments. Viewed in the latter way, existing attitudes may determine one's selection among alternative environmental settings, and these in turn may serve to preserve or undermine the very attitudes that had been initially responsible for one's selection among the alternatives. Insofar as attitudes are self-preserving, such tendencies to select a supportive environment would, if empirically supported, provide an important explanation of their persistence. In its most general form, the hypothesis would run somewhat as follows: Existing attitudes are most likely to persist, other things equal, when one's environment provides most rewards for their behavioral expression. But this platitudinous proposition ("things persist when conditions are favorable to their persistence") is not very interesting, and is probably not even testable. A more interesting and more testable form of the proposition would take account of both change and persistence, both of attitudes and of environmental supportiveness. In particular, it would say something about a changed selection of environments fol-

lowing attitude change, about the ways in which the recently formed attitude is or is not reinforced by the new environment, and about the persistence of the attitude in both supportive and hostile environments. Such a proposition, in its simplest form, would run somewhat as follows: A recently changed attitude is likely to persist insofar as it leads to the selection of subsequent environments that provide reinforcements for the behavioral expression of the changed attitude.

Among the many possible forms of environmental reinforcements of behavioral expressions of attitudes, I shall consider a single class: behavior on the part of other people that one perceives as supportive of one's own attitudes. With few exceptions, such support comes from persons or groups toward whom one is positively attracted, according to the principles of what is perhaps most frequently known as balance theory (cf. Heider, 1958; Brown, 1962; Newcomb, 1963). I am, in short, about to defend the limited proposition that a recently changed attitude is most likely to persist if one of its behavioral expressions is the selection of a social environment which one finds supportive of the changed attitude. This proposition differs from the one about autistic hostility primarily in that persistence of

Reprinted with slight abridgment from the **Journal of Social Issues**, 1963, 19, 3–14, with permission of the author and the Society for the Psychological Study of Social Issues.

a recently acquired attitude depends upon continuing rather than cutting off sources of information about the attitude-object.

II

There are various ways in which such a proposition might be tested in the laboratory. But insofar as one is interested, as I have been, in long-range effects, one will make use of "natural" settings. I shall therefore cite a few findings from two of my own studies, mentioning only briefly the less immediately relevant one (1961), which involved the daily observation of two populations of 17 male students, all initial strangers to one another, who lived intimately together for four-month periods. The only attitudes of these subjects that showed much change, from first to last, were their attractions toward each other —attitudes which had not even existed, of course, before their initial encounters in this research setting. Expressions of interpersonal attraction during the first week or two were highly unstable, but after about the fifth week they showed only slow and slight changes (cf. Newcomb, 1963).

Under the conditions of this research, imposed environments (in the form of arbitrarily assigned rooms, roommates, and floors) had no consistent effects beyond the first week or two in interpersonal preferences. That is, one could predict little or nothing about interpersonal attraction from the fact of being roommates or floormates. Self-selected interpersonal environment, however, was closely associated with interpersonal attraction. At all times later than the first week or two, pairs of subjects who were reported by others to belong to the same voluntary subgroups were almost invariably pairs whose members chose each other at very high levels of attraction. If this seems to be a commonplace observation (as indeed it is), let me remind you of my reason for reporting it; interpersonal environments are not only consequences of existing attraction but also sources of future attraction. It is an everyday phenomenon that, having developed differential attitudes toward one's several acquaintances, one manipulates one's interpersonal environment, insofar as one can, to correspond with one's interpersonal preferences. And insofar as one is successful, chances are that the preferences will be further reinforced. My data, showing stability both of preferences and of voluntarily associating subgroups following the first month or so, indicate that exactly this was occurring. The fact that it is an everyday occurrence enhances rather than negates the importance of the principle involved, namely, that a recently acquired attitude will persist insofar as it results in the selection of an environment that is supportive of that attitude.

III

I now turn to a totally different set of data, or rather to two sets of data from the same subjects, obtained over an interval of more than 20 years. The earlier responses were obtained between 1935 and 1939 at Bennington College (Newcomb, 1943); the later ones, obtained in 1960 and 1961, were from almost all of the subjects who had been studied for three or more consecutive years during the 1930's. To be specific, out of 141 former students in this category who in 1960 were alive, resident in continental United States, and not hopelessly invalided, 130 (scattered in 28 states) were interviewed, and 9 of the remaining 11 completed more or less parallel questionnaires. The interview dealt primarily with their present attitudes toward a wide range of public-affairs issues, with attitudes of their husbands and other contemporary associates, and with their histories and careers since leaving the College.

Before telling you some of the follow-up findings, I ought to report a few of the original ones. During each of four consecutive years (1935–36 through 1938–39), juniors and seniors were on the average markedly less conservative than freshmen in attitude toward many public issues of the day. Studies of the same individuals over three- and four-year intervals showed the same trend, which was not attributable to selective withdrawal from the College. Comparisons with other colleges showed almost no intercollege differences in freshmen attitudes, but much less conservatism at Bennington than at the other institutions on the part of seniors. Individual studies showed that at Bennington nonconservatism was rather closely associated with being respected by other students, with participation in college activities, and with personal involvement in the College as an institution. The relatively few malcontents were, with surprisingly few exceptions, those who held conservative attitudes toward public issues.

Given these initial findings, one of my concerns in planning the follow-up study was the following: Under what conditions would individuals who had become less conservative during their college years remain relatively nonconservative 20-odd years later, and under what conditions would they "regress" to relatively conservative positions? (As to the problem of comparing attitudes toward one set of issues in the 1930's with those toward quite different issues

in the 1960's, I shall for present purposes note only that at both times we used indices of relative, not absolute standing: each subject is compared with the same set of peers.)

By way of noting the general pattern of persistence vs. regression on the part of the total population, I shall first compare one early with one later datum. In the 1940 presidential election, 51% of our interview sample who reported a preference for either major candidate chose the Democrat, F. D. Roosevelt, and 49% the Republican, W. Willkie. Twenty years later, the comparable figures were 60% for J. F. Kennedy and 40% for R. M. Nixon. No single election, of course, provides a very good test of what might be termed "general conservatism concerning public affairs," but at any rate this particular comparison does not suggest any conspicuous regression toward freshman conservatism. This conclusion is also supported by the following finding: In six consecutive presidential elections (1940 through 1960), an outright majority of our interviewees (51%) reported that they had preferred the Republican candidate either once or never, whereas only 27% of them had preferred that candidate as many as five times out of the six times.

The problem of regressive effects can also be approached by comparing relative conservatism on the part of the same individuals over the interval of 20-odd years. In terms of party or candidate preference in 1960, the degree of individual stability is startling. As shown in Table 1, individuals who were in the least conservative quartile of the total population, on graduating, preferred Kennedy by frequencies of 30 to 3, and those in the next quartile by 25 to 8; 83% of this half of the population preferred Kennedy 20 years

TABLE 1

PRESIDENTIAL PREFERENCES IN 1960, ACCORDING TO QUARTILES OF PEP * SCORES
ON LEAVING COLLEGE IN THE LATE 1930'S

PEP quartile	Nixon preferred	Kennedy preferred	Total
1 (least conservative)	3	30	33
2	8	25	33
3	18	13	31
4 (most conservative)	22	11	33
TOTAL	51	79	130

* Political and Economic Progressivism—Eds.

later, while 37% of the initially more conservative half preferred Kennedy after 20 years. Political party preferences, and also an index of general political conservatism, showed about the same relationship to political conservatism more than two decades earlier. These data provide no support for a prediction of general regression— either toward previous conservatism or in the statistical sense of regression toward the mean.

Other evidence concerning the general nonconservatism in this population in the early 1960's includes the following:

77% of them considered themselves "liberal" or "somewhat liberal," as compared with 17% who were "conservative" or "somewhat conservative";

76% "approved" or "strongly approved" of "Medicare" for the aged under Social Security;

61% "approved" or "strongly approved" of admitting Red China into the United Nations.

These and other data suggest that the population as a whole is now far less conservative than is to be expected in view of its demographic characteristics. Its socio-economic level may be judged from these facts: (1) 77% of the 117 respondents who were or had been married were judged by the interviewer to be at least "fairly well-to-do," with annual incomes of not less than $20,000; and (2) of 113 mothers in the population, 65% had sent at least one of their children to a private school. In religious background, about three-quarters of them were Protestants (more than half of whom were Episcopalian), and less than 10% were either Catholic or Jewish. According to information assembled for me by the Survey Research Center of the University of Michigan,* the proportion of Protestant women college graduates at the income level of this population who in 1960 expressed a preference for Kennedy over Nixon was less than 25—as compared with 60% of this alumnae population.

I shall now revert to my earlier theme: If this population is now less conservative than one might expect, to what extent is this explainable in terms of its members' selection of post-college environments that were supportive of nonconservative attitudes? It proves to be very difficult to categorize total environments from this point of view, and so for the present I shall limit myself to a single aspect of post-college environments: husbands. I am making no assumptions here except that (1)

* By my colleague Philip Converse, to whom I am most grateful.

husbands were indeed a part of their wives' environments; (2) wives had had something to do with selecting this part of their environments; and (3) husbands, as environmental objects, were capable of being either supportive or nonsupportive of their wives' attitudes.

Nearly 80% of our respondents both had a husband and were able to report on his attitudes toward most of the issues with which we were concerned, during all or most of the past 20 years; one reason for placing a good deal of confidence in their reports is that they seem highly discriminating, as indicated by such responses as these: "I don't think I know how he'd feel on that particular issue," or "Now on *that* one he doesn't agree with me at all." Here are some summaries concerning all husbands whose wives were willing to attribute attitudes toward them (nearly all wives on most issues):

54% of the husbands in 1960 favored Kennedy over Nixon;

64% of them either "approved" or "strongly approved" of "Medicare" for the aged under Social Security;

57% of them either "approved" or "strongly approved" of admitting Red China into the United Nations.

And so it is almost as true of husbands as of wives that they are less conservative than is to be expected in view of their demographic characteristics: husbands' and wives' demographic characteristics are taken to be identical except for a very few couples differing in religious background, and their present attitudes are highly similar (90% of 1960 presidential preferences by pairs of spouses, for example, being reported as the same in 1960). It would hardly seem to be a matter of sheer chance that a set of men who are less conservative than is to be expected are married

to a set of women of whom just the same thing is true. It seems necessary, therefore, to assume that attitudes toward public affairs had something to do with husbands' and wives' reciprocal selection of one another, or with postmarital influence upon one another, or with both. Here is one statistical support for this assumption: the correlation between wives' scores on an instrument labeled Political and Economic Progressivism, as of their graduating from college in the late 1930's, with the number of Republican candidates that their subsequent husbands voted for between 1940 and 1960 was .32; this does not account for much of the variance, but its p value is $< .0005$.

Another interesting finding has to do with the number of women in our interview sample whose husbands had attended Ivy League colleges; one would expect this proportion to be high, since so many of the women's fathers and brothers had attended these colleges. The actual frequency turned out to be just 50%. These Ivy League husbands' voting preferences in 1960, however, turned out to be much more like their wives' preferences than like their classmates' preferences: 52% of husbands whose wives were able to state a preference were for Kennedy—which is to say that they did not differ at all in voting preferences from all non-Ivy League husbands. This total set of facts can best be interpreted as follows: Our Bennington graduates of the late 1930's found their husbands in the kinds of places where their families expected them to be found, but they selected somewhat atypical members of these "proper" populations of eligibles; they tended not to have conservative attitudes that were then typical of these populations.

One evidence of this atypical selection is to be seen in the occupational distribution of these women's husbands. Only 38% of all husbands are classifiable as "in management or business," the remaining 62% representing for the most part a wide range of professions (especially college teaching, entertainment, and the arts) and public employment (especially in government). Husbands in these two general categories (management and business vs. all others) differed sharply in their voting preferences in 1960; of the 113 husbands whose wives attributed preferences to them, 26% of those in management and business preferred Kennedy, and 68% of all other husbands preferred Kennedy. In sum, these women's husbands had typically come from "the right" places but a majority of them did not have "the right" attitudes or occupational interests.

If, therefore, I were to select a single factor that contributed most to these women's maintenance of nonconservative attitudes between the late 1930's and early 1960's, I think it would be the fact of selecting husbands of generally nonconservative stripe who helped to maintain for them an environment that was supportive of their existing attributes.

IV

Now I shall turn from the total population of interviewees to some comparisons of subpopulations. The most crucial of these, from the point of view of my proposition about supportive environments, are to be found within the population of nonconservatives on leaving college in the late 1930's: What seems to be the differences between those who do and those who do not remain nonconservative in the early 1960's? Such comparisons will have to be impressionistic, since numbers of cases are small.

Among 22 individuals previously labeled as clearly nonconservative in their third or fourth year of attendance at the College, just half belong in the same category now. Only three of them are clearly conservative today, the remaining eight being classified as intermediate. Here are these wives' descriptions of their husbands' political positions over the years:

3 presently conservative wives: 3 Republican husbands (100%)
7 presently intermediate wives: 3 Republican husbands (42%)
8 presently nonconservative wives: 2 Republican husbands (25%)

Of the three presently conservative women, none mentions having engaged in activities related to political or other public issues; of the eight who are intermediate, six mention some activity of this kind, but they identify their activity only in such general terms as "liberal" or "Democratic Party"; of the 11 still nonconservative women, eight mention such activities, more than half of them specifying such "causes" or organizations as labor unions, civil liberties, the ADA, or the NAACP.

Each interviewee was also asked about the general orientation of "most of your friends" toward political and other public affairs. More than half (12) of the 22 women originally labeled as clearly nonconservative described their environment of friends as "liberal," in spite of the fact that most of them lived in suburbs or other geographical areas not generally renowned for liberalism. Interestingly enough, those who are now relatively conservative answered this question in just about the same way as did those who are still relatively nonconservative. The 16 women originally labeled as clearly conservative, on leaving college, answered this question somewhat differently; more than half of them (9) described their environment of friends as predominantly "conservative," but answers differed with the present attitudes of the respondents. That is, those who are now, in fact, relatively conservative with near-unanimity describe their friends as conservative, whereas those who are now relatively nonconservative consider a substantial proportion or even most of their friends to be "liberal." Thus only those who were quite conservative in the late 1930's and who still remain so see themselves surrounded by friends who are primarily conservative.

In sum, nearly all of the still nonconservative women mention either husbands or public activities (most commonly both) that have served to support and maintain previously nonconservative attitudes, while none of the three formerly nonconservative but presently conservative women mentions either husband or public activities which have served to maintain earlier attitudes.

What about attitude persistence on the part of those who, after three or four years in college, were still relatively conservative? Sixteen of those who were then labeled conservative were interviewed in the early 1960's, ten of them being categorized as still conservative and three as now nonconservative. Only one of the nonchangers reported having a husband who was a Democrat, and in this lone case he turned out to have voted for Nixon in 1960. Two of the three changers, on the other hand, report husbands who were Democrats and Kennedy voters in 1960. Only two of the persistent conservatives mentioned public activities presumably sup-

portive of their attitudes (in behalf of the Republican Party, in both cases); eight of the ten described most of their friends either as conservative or as Republicans. The conditions that favor the persistence of conservatism over the 20-odd years are thus about the same as those that favor the persistence of nonconservatism: supportive environments in the form of husbands, local friends, and (for the nonconservatives but not the conservatives) in the form of associates in activities related to public issues.

There is a special subpopulation of students who, as of graduating in the late 1930's, were candidates for regression; that is, they became much less conservative during their college years. Of these, about one-third (9 of 28) were among the most conservative half of the same population in the early 1960's, and may be regarded as regressors, in some degree at least. Eight of these potential regressors were, for various reasons, unable to report on husbands' preferences. Among the remaining 19 respondents, five were actual regressors, four of whom reported their husbands to be Republicans or "conservative Republicans." Among 14 actual non-regressors reporting, ten described their husbands as Democrats or "liberal Democrats," two referred to them as "Republicans who have been voting Democratic," and only two call their husbands Republicans. These are highly significant differences: the actual regressors can pretty well be differentiated from the nonregressors merely by knowing their husbands' present attitudes. By this procedure only 3 of 19, or 16% of all predictions would not have been correct.

This total set of data suggests that either regression and persistence of attitudes as of leaving college are, over the years, influenced by husbands' attitudes, or early post-college attitudes had something to do with the selection of husbands, or both. In either case, both regression and persistence are facilitated by the supportiveness of husbands.

v

If there is any very general principle that helps to account for this whole range of phenomena (both my 1946 and my 1963 versions), I believe that it is to be found in an extended version of "balance theory," as originally outlined by Heider (1946, 1958). Heider's formulations are formulated in individual and phenomenological terms; a balanced state is a strictly intrapersonal, psychological state. But it is also possible to conceptualize an objective, multi-person state of balance, referring to the actual relationships among different persons' attitudes, regardless of the person's awareness of each other. Such a concept is psychologically useful not only because it describes an actual, existing situation—an environment of which each person is himself a part, as suggested by Asch (1952)—but also because it describes a relationship which, given reasonably full and accurate communication, comes to be accurately perceived. My own recent work on the acquaintance process has been interesting to me primarily because it inquires into the processes by which and the conditions under which *intra*personal states of balance come to correspond with *inter*personal ones. As outlined by Heider, and subsequently by many others (cf. Brown, *et al.*, 1962), the processes by which imbalanced states serve as goals toward

the attainment of balanced ones include both internal, psychological changes and external modifications of the environment. Thus, one may achieve a balanced state with the important figures in one's social environment—whether by selecting those figures, by modifying one's own attitudes, or by influencing others' attitudes—and at the same time continue to perceive that environment accurately.

According to such an extended, *inter*personal concept of balance, an imbalanced state under conditions of continued interaction is likely to be an unstable one, simply because when it is discovered it arouses *intra*personal imbalance on the part of one or more of the interactors, and this state arouses forces toward change. Given marked attitude change on the part of one but not the other member of a dyad actually in balance with respect to that attitude, imbalance results. This was what typically happened to students at Bennington College vis-à-vis their parents, in the 1930's. A common way in which they attempted to reduce imbalance was by avoidance—not necessarily of parents but of the divisive issues as related to parents. As Heider might say, unit formation between issue and parents was broken up, and psychological imbalance thus reduced. Such a "solution" resembles autistic hostility in that it involves a marked restriction of communication.

But this solution, as many of my subjects testified, was not a particularly comfortable one. Hence, it would hardly be surprising if many of them, during early post-college years, were in search of environments that would provide less uncomfortable solutions—or, better yet, more positively rewarding ones. An ideal one, of course, would be a husband who was rewarding as a supporter of one's own attitudes as well as in other ways.

And so, vis-à-vis parents and fellow-students at first, and later vis-à-vis husbands (or perhaps working associates), forces toward balance were at work. Specifically, support from important people concerning important issues came to be the rule, and its absence the exception. Support sometimes came about by changing one's own attitudes toward those of needed supporters, or, more commonly, by selecting supporters for existing attitudes. The latter stratagem represented not merely an automatic tendency for attitudes to perpetuate themselves. More significantly, I believe, it represents an adaptation to a world that includes *both* persons and issues. Such a dual adaptation can be made, of course, by sacrificing one's stand on the issues (regression). But if the dual adaptation is to be made without this sacrifice, then an interpersonal world must be selected (or created) that is supportive—in which case we can say that the attitude has been expressed by finding a supportive environment.

An existing attitude may be maintained by creating environments in which *either* new information can be avoided *or* in which other persons support one's own information. In either case, the fate of an attitude is mediated by the social environment in which the individual attempts to maintain or to restore balance regarding that same attitude. Insofar as that environment excludes disturbing information or provides reinforcing information, the attitude persists. And insofar as the selection or the acceptance of that environment is a consequence of holding the attitude, we have a steady-state, self-maintaining system.

39 Judgmental processes and problems of attitude

MUZAFER SHERIF and CARL I. HOVLAND

Traditional approaches to attitude and attitude change

Studies of attitude conducted during the twenties and thirties were mainly of the "survey" type in which individuals were asked to check prepared categories on an issue. The primary concern was with the extent to which different groups held particular attitudes, for example the difference between attitudes toward war of student and nonstudent populations. Relatively little concern was manifested in regard to the psychological processes underlying the individual's expression of his attitudes or to the pattern of stimulus conditions under which the responses were obtained. Thurstone (1929) and his associates made a major contribution in providing more systematic means for scaling attitudinal responses. But their underlying assumption, that the intervals between various positions on an attitude scale are independent of the position of the individual who is making the judgments, has been called into question by the research of the writers (Hovland & Sherif, 1952; Sherif & Hovland, 1953). It now appears that distances between different points on an attitude scale derived by the method of equal appearing intervals are affected by the position of the individual making the evaluation.

During the same span of years interest in the effect of communications on attitudes was largely in showing that changes in questionnaire or "attitude scale" checkings occur as a consequence of exposure to communication. There was much less concern with the psychological processes underlying the changes. Considerable divergence in results was obtained, some showing change in the direction of the communication and others showing shifts in the opposite direction. Thus while a number of studies showed that lecturers, pamphlets, and motion pictures could produce changes in attitude, few studies were made until the forties to show how specific content transmitted by specific communicators affects particular audiences (cf. e.g., Hovland, Lumsdaine, & Sheffield, 1949).

The change which has taken place in the analysis of attitudes is well illustrated by the studies presented in the recent special issue of the *Public Opinion Quarterly* (Katz, ed., 1960). It will be seen that in the fifties there has been an increased concern with fundamental factors underlying attitudes and their modification. Illustrative of recent approaches to these problems are the studies of Heider (1958) and Festinger (1957). It is the writers' belief, however, that attitude research should be more solidly based on previous work in basic psychological processes, particu-

Abridged from Chapter 1 of Social Judgment, New Haven, Conn.: Yale University Press, 1961, pp. 2–14, with permission of the first author and the publisher.

larly of judgment. What appears to be seriously needed is more extensive exploration of the underlying principles governing attitudinal evaluations by the individual and the factors by which such evaluations are modified. It is to this type of analysis that the present volume is addressed.

Relevance of judgment processes to attitude problems

Our underlying assumption is that the processes of judgment are critical for understanding research findings in the area of attitude and attitude change. A few illustrations may serve to give substance to our assumption.

During the baseball season, one may observe judgments from thousands of spectators relative to the decisions of the umpire. When he declares the verdict "You're out" against their favored team, the boos from the partisans are resounding expressions of their own judgment of the event. Of course, the fans are capable of making objectively correct judgments if they have the opportunity to examine all the details of the episode through slow-motion pictures. However, in complex stimulus situations such as that in a crowded stadium, "committed" individuals with a strong attitude on an issue do not wait: they readily *pass judgments* and *act* in terms of them.

As the above example implies, a person's attitude on an issue may well influence the way he appraises relevant behavior and events. Thus individuals who straddle the fence in public life are frequently judged differently by people holding one extreme position than by people taking an extreme stand on the opposite side. For example, the vacillating labor lead, Samuel Gompers,

was judged as rather radical by the conservatives of his day, but he was dubbed a conservative by left-wingers in the labor movement. Supreme Court justices Charles Evans Hughes and (probably to a lesser extent) Owen J. Roberts balanced between the "conservatives" and "liberals" of the "Roosevelt court" in the thirties. Evaluations rendered by various authors of these two justices are strongly colored by the attitudes of the writer passing judgment. Liberal writers tend to place these justices on the conservative side, but this is not the judgment of writers who are not liberals.

As discussed in earlier volumes of this series, an attitude toward an object, person, group, or social issue is not directly observable but is inferred from a persistent and *characteristic* mode of reaction to that stimulus or stimulus class. This characteristic mode of reaction signifies differential treatment of the object of attitude. It is inferred that the object of attitude is placed in a category or class favorable or unfavorable in some degree, high or low in some degree, acceptable or unacceptable in some degree in the individual's scheme of things. In short, one essential aspect of the attitudinal reaction is a categorization process, whether or not the individual is aware that he is passing a judgment.

Categorization as an essential aspect of attitudinal response

When one solicits an expression of an individual's attitude toward some social issue, person, or group, one typically finds that the process involves placement of the issue in a framework and assignment to a category. Thus if a person (who is a practicing member of one of the religious groups that use some kind of baptism as part of the initiation of new members) is asked to express his attitude toward baptism, he is likely to place baptismal ceremonies into differentiated rankings, the preferred practice of his own group probably being at the top and serving as the standard. Likewise, if one asks an individual for his opinion as to acceptability of various groups, he is likely to place them in a certain number of categories ranging from encouragement of close personal association, through the category of tolerating residence in his own neighborhood, all the way to the category of desiring their exclusion from the country. We typically find that the individual has internalized categories designating relative positions or "social distance" for placement of the individual in a group, and that each category is endowed with certain qualities. A person's attitude is revealed in his favorable or derogatory reactions regulated by the category in question and by the attributes attached to that category. If the X group is "endowed" by the Y group with qualities a, b, and c (favorable or unfavorable) the representative members of the Y group will tend to see these qualities in the collective or individual behavior of the X group and react accordingly in a characteristic way.

Differentiation of judgment processes: discrimination, placement, and acceptance-rejection

From the point of view of conceptual analysis and experimental specification, it is feasible to differentiate the judgment process in various ways. A conceptual differentiation can be made in terms of item discrimination, placement

of items, and acceptance-rejection of items. A great deal of experimental work has accumulated along each of these three lines.

Discrimination refers to the task of identifying a stimulus item (a weight, a tone, a statement) as different from another item. The tremendous amount of work dealing with just noticeable differences (j.n.d.s) between two stimuli differing along the same dimension is representative.

It is convenient to refer to that kind of discrimination which locates a given stimulus relative to more than two other discriminable items as *placement* or *categorization* of the item. Studies dealing with scaling of neutral items, like weights or tones, are representative of this approach. Our concern in this [account] is primarily with reactions to motivationally relevant items, as exemplified by statements evaluating a social issue or a group of people. However, even in placement of motivationally neutral items, variations occur as a function of the stimulus arrangements and procedures of the experimental conditions. Therefore, if the effects of attitudes upon placement of items are to be assessed adequately, it is necessary first to consider judgmental variations attributable to such stimulus arrangements and procedures. In particular, such consideration will yield methodological guides for evaluating the conditions in which attitudinal factors are maximally or minimally effective in producing judgmental variations, such as displacements, over- and under-estimations. The general problem was illustrated earlier with reference to judgments concerning an umpire's verdict at the baseball stadium or on the basis of slow-motion pictures after the game.

The judgment task carried out under *acceptance-rejection* instructions also requires placement or categorization of items (statements, objects, human groups) in terms of the preferences of the individuals. Scales of judgment instructing the subjects to place the most acceptable items at one end, the most objectionable ones at the other extreme, and other items in appropriate places between the extremes, are representative of this line of analysis. Placement of groups along a social-distance scale and rank-order scales based on preference (such as ranking of composers or painters) are representative of placement in terms of affectively charged attitudes.

Motivational and learning factors relevant to placement of items

A judgment always involves a comparison between two or more stimuli. For purposes of conceptual analysis, psychologists devise laboratory experiments in which judgment consists of the comparison of only two objects or items. One of the objects is just noticeably heavier, brighter, louder, or longer than the comparison object. Or one stimulus item is noticeably more pleasant or more favorable than another item. The items may be compared simultaneously or successively with a very short interval between presentations. In such experiments, the task is discrimination and the main psychological problem is the keenness of discrimination. When keenness of discrimination (keenness of tactual, visual, auditory, or kinesthetic sense, or keenness in discriminating the dictionary meaning of words) is the principal problem, experimental procedures requiring the subject to make this kind of comparison are suitable.

However, if the primary problem of research concerns the judgmental activity ordinarily involved when a person judges stimuli related to an attitude, the above procedures and analysis may not be appropriate. Procedures suitable for the study of simple discrimination circumscribe the stimulus pattern drastically and thereby constrict the operation of attitudinal factors in the judgment process.

Learning factors. Judgment of a stimulus item relevant to an individual's attitude is necessarily related to other similar items to which the individual has been exposed. The individual forms an attitude as a consequence of repeated encounters with objects, persons, or communications. Comparison of an item related to an attitude is made against a whole background of similar objects which constitutes the range of such objects perceived and categorized on the basis of the individual's prior encounters with them. Therefore, the process of comparison in judgment of a relevant stimulus is not represented by having the individual compare two objects presented simultaneously or in close succession.

We shall refer to the background for a particular comparison as the *reference scale* of the individual in that respect. Placement of stimulus items is made relative to a reference scale formed by the individual. The formation of reference scales by the individual whether in relation to objects, human groups, or social norms is clearly a problem of *learning.*

Motivational factors. As stated above, the judgment of an item relevant to an attitude involves comparison with an appropriate reference scale, rather than a simple comparison between two items as in a typical laboratory experiment on discrimination. It follows that attitudinal judgments are typically of the *placement* type, and this has definite implications for fruitful research practice in this area.

In the study of judgment processes underlying attitudinal reactions, the identification of judgment categories in an individual's reference scale and placement of items within it are crucial problems. For example, in a study of attitudes toward the segregation-desegregation issue, it is necessary to learn what kind and how many categories individuals actually use in judging behavior or verbal statements ranging from the most extreme segregationist position to the most extreme desegregationist position. In assessing an individual's attitude on this issue, it is necessary to know that a person with a desegregationist stand on the issue places statements advocating segregation on the bus or on the train in the unfavorable category. From the outset, research in this area involves the problem of *placement*.

Research on the problem of scaling items relevant to social attitudes has frequently been facilitated by circumscribing the stimuli to be compared in the manner of discrimination experiments. As useful as this procedure may be for test construction, it cannot be regarded as appropriate for studying judgment of items related to attitudes as this activity typically occurs in actual life. The inadequacy of such procedures can be illustrated. Faced with the task of discrimination between the relative favorableness of segregation applied on the train and on the bus, a desegregationist can render a judgment. The fact remains that both examples are in an objectionable category for him. In the discrimination task which requires the individual with a strong attitude on an issue to choose one of two objectionable statements as more favorable than the other, the subject's reactions to such a task and toward the experimenter subjecting him to it may be more significant psychologically than the choice itself.

When the problems of research pertain to the judgmental process underlying specific attitudinal reactions, it is appropriate to use procedures which allow motivational factors to be manifested. If keenness of discrimination is the primary research problem, it is possible, as we have seen, to minimize the effect of attitude or past experience (learning) by circumscribing the judgment situation to the comparison of two clearly defined items and requiring a choice. However, the latter procedure does not represent typical conditions in which the individual judges an attitude-related item. A stimulus related to an attitude is necessarily judged against the reference scale which the individual has formed relative to the particular class of stimulus items in question.

On a scale of positions on a social issue ranging from one extreme to the opposite extreme, for example, one of the positions is appropriated to represent the individual's own stand or commitment. This stand on the issue is a major factor in regulating his relationships with other individuals involving that issue. His acceptances and rejections in that regard are regulated accordingly. As experiments show, placement of items related to the issue is significantly affected by their relative proximity or distance from the individual's own stand. In short, the judgment of items related to an attitude involves placement in terms of the individual's reference scale, but it becomes placement in which the degree of acceptance or rejection is significant.

Psychological reference scales and the stimulus conditions during their formation

Laboratory findings on judgment have shown that placement of a particular stimulus in a series is not made solely in terms of the discrete physical properties of that stimulus. A judgment is rendered in terms of the psychological reference scale which the individual has formed on the basis of his previous encounters with similar stimuli.

In other words, judgment of a particular stimulus in a series involves placement in categories, and it is influenced by the whole background of similar stimuli which constitutes the basis for an appropriate reference scale. Analysis of the stimulus conditions on the basis of which the individual forms a psychological reference scale has far-reaching implications for the study of judgment of social issues and communication concerning them.

In laboratory studies of judgment, psychological scales are usually formed during repeated presentations of a well-graded series of stimuli (weights, tones, statements). The reference scale consists of categories whose labels are ordinarily provided through instructions. In the traditional experiments, each stimulus to be judged is presented with a *standard* stimulus, which serves as a salient reference point or anchorage in the formation of a psychological scale. However, it was found that the use of a formal standard is not necessary for the formation of a reference scale. If each stimulus is presented singly throughout several presentations of a definite series of stimuli, the individual still forms a scale of judgment consisting of a number of categories. In the latter case, the stimuli at the ends of the particular series are utilized by the individual as anchorages in the formation of a psychological scale.

Once a psychological scale is formed, subsequent judgment of a similar stimulus is greatly affected by the position of that stimulus relative to the prevailing reference scale. When stimuli are presented with values greater than or less than any in the series which was the basis of the reference scale, the categories of the scale are subject to alterations. These phenomena constitute the area of research investigating reciprocal relationships between psychological scales and anchorages.

When psychological scales are based on encounters with a well-graded stimulus series such as a definite range of discriminable physical stimuli, there is a close relationship between the stimulus series and the psychological scale. The psychological scale is readily susceptible to adjustments with the addition of new stimuli to the series or with shifts of the total range of the objective stimulus series. This may be one reason why psychological scales related to technological developments in various societies change somewhat more readily than scales related to socio-political and religious values.

Let us go a step further. It is not necessary to have a definitely graded series of stimuli for the formation of psychological scales. Even when the stimulus series is not well-graded, individuals still form psychological scales. In these instances, the range of the scale and the number of categories within it are significantly influenced by the judgments of other people. As a result, the stimulus conditions affecting the formation of a reference scale have to include the social setting: established norms, the properties of the interaction among the individuals involved, the general setting of their interaction, the prevailing pattern of relationships among them, and so on.

Once established, psychological scales initially based on *psycho-social actualities* serve a function similar to those based on series of physical gradations. Namely, they serve as a basis for comparison and appraisal of relevant stimulus items on subsequent encounters. Social reference scales that individuals in human groups use in judging political, religious, ethical, and aesthetic matters cannot be gauged against an objectively graded stimulus series. They are psycho-social in origin and can be gauged against social realities. They define and regulate one's relationship to other individuals, groups, social objects, and institutions. A certain category in such a reference scale becomes the individual's preferred category. This position within the scale represents his own stand on the issue and serves as a major anchor in judgment. If the issue is a significant one to him, he is willing to tolerate only slight deviation from this category and finds further deviation obnoxious.

On a social reference scale, we may refer to the range of positions that includes an individual's stand and other positions that he will tolerate as his *latitude of acceptance*. Beyond this, other positions on the issue are rejected, and that range of positions is his *latitude of rejection*.

The individual's reactions to a communication and the effect of that communication on his attitude can be studied relative to his established categorizations of the issue, that is, his reference scale for judgment of the issue. Investigation of these problems must determine the location of his latitudes of acceptance and rejection relative to the stand advocated in communication. The resulting information about the individual's placement of the communication and his evaluation of it may clarify problems of attitude change.

40   The obstinate audience: the influence process
from the point of view of social communication

RAYMOND A. BAUER

The model held by the general public, and by social scientists when they talk about advertising, and somebody else's propaganda, is one of the exploitation of man by man. It is a model of one-way influence: The communicator *does* something to the audience, while to the communicator is generally attributed considerable latitude and power to do what he pleases to the audience. This model is reflected—at its worst—in such popular phrases as "brainwashing," "hidden persuasion," and "subliminal advertising."

The second model—which *ought* to be inferred from the data of research—is of communication as a transactional process in which two parties each expect to give and take from the deal approximately equitable values. This, although it *ought* to be the scientific model, is far from generally accepted as such, a state of affairs on which W. Philips Davison (1959) makes the comment:

the communicator's audience is not a passive recipient—it cannot be regarded as a lump of clay to be molded by the master propagandist. Rather, the audience is made up of individuals who demand something from the communications to which they are exposed, and who select those that are likely to be useful to them. In other words, they must get something from the manipulator if he is to get something from them. A bargain is involved. Sometimes, it is true, the manipulator is able to lead his audience into a bad bargain by emphasizing one need at the expense of another or by representing a change in the significant environment as greater than it actually has been. But audiences, too, can drive a hard bargain. Many communicators who have been widely disregarded or misunderstood know that to their cost (p. 360).

Davison does not contend that all the exchanges are equitable, but that the inequities may be on either side. He only implies that neither the audience nor the communicator would enter into this exchange unless each party expected to "get his money's worth," at least most of the time. After all, Davison is not speaking as a social philosopher nor as an apologist for the industry, but as an experienced researcher trying to make sense out of the accumulated evidence.

Whether fortunately or unfortunately, social criticism has long been associated with the study of communication. The latter was largely stimulated by the succession of exposés of propaganda following World War I, particularly of the munitions-makers' lobby and of the extensive propaganda of the public utilities. There was also social concern over the new media, the movies and radio, and the increasingly monopolistic control of newspapers. Propaganda analysis, which is what research communication was called in those days, was occupied with three inquiries: the structure of the media (who owns and controls them, and what affects what

Abridged from the **American Psychologist**, 19, 319–28 (Copyright © 1964 by the American Psychological Association), with permission of the author and the publisher.

gets into them); content analysis (what was said and printed); and propaganda techniques (which are the devil's devices to influence people). In this period, *effects* for the most part were not studied: They were taken for granted. Out of this tradition evolved Laswell's (Smith, Laswell, & Casey, 1946) formulation of the process of communication that is the most familiar one to this day: "Who says what, through what channels [media] of communication, to whom [with] what . . . results [p. 121]." This apparently self-evident formulation has one monumental built-in assumption: that the initiative is exclusively with the communicator, the effects being exclusively on the audience.

While the stimulus and the model of research on communication were developing out of the analysis of propaganda, survey research, relatively independently, was evolving its technology in the commercial world of market research and audience and leadership measurement. As is well known, Crossley, Gallup, and Roper each tried their hands at predicting the 1936 presidential election and whipped the defending champion, the *Literary Digest*. By 1940, Lazarsfeld was ready to try out the new technology on the old model with a full-scale panel study of the effects of the mass media on voting in a national election, having tested his strategy in the New Jersey gubernatorial race in 1938.

The results of this study, again, are well known. Virtually nobody in the panel changed his intention, and most of the few who did so attributed it to personal influence (Lazarsfeld, Berelson, & Gaudet, 1948). The mass media had had their big chance—and struck out. Negative results had been reached

before but none which had been demonstrated by such solid research. A number of equally dramatic failures to detect effects of campaigns carried on in the mass media followed, and by the end of the decade Hyman and Sheatsley (1947) were attempting to explain why. No one could take the effects of communication for granted.

As a matter of fact a considerable number of the sociologists studying communication grew discouraged with inquiring into the immediate effects of the mass media, and went looking for "opinion leaders," "influentials," the "web of influence," and so on. At the same time, a few here and there began doing something we now call "functional studies." They were curious to know how the audience was behaving.

In the meantime, at just about the time that the students of the effect of communication in a natural setting were beginning to wonder if communication ever had effects, experimental studies were burgeoning under essentially laboratory conditions. Experiments had been conducted before, but the tradition of experimenting on the effects of communication was vastly enhanced by the War Department's Information and Education Division, and after the war by Hovland and his associates at Yale (Hovland, Lumsdaine, & Sheffield, 1949). The Yale group's output, and that of colleagues and students of Kurt Lewin, account for a very high proportion of the experimental work on the subject in the past two decades.

The experimenters generally had no trouble conveying information or changing attitudes. Of course nobody stopped to record very explicitly the main finding of all the experiments: that communication, given a reasonably large audience, varies in its impact. It affects some one way, some in the opposite way, and some not at all. But nevertheless the experimenters got results.

By the end of the fifties it was quite clear that the two streams of investigation needed reconciling, and Carl Hovland (1959) did so. More recently, pursuing the same theme, I stated Hovland's major point as being that the audience exercises much more initiative outside the laboratory than it does in the experimental situation (Bauer, 1962). The audience selects what it will attend to. Since people generally listen to and read things they are interested in, these usually are topics on which they have a good deal of information and fixed opinions. Hence the very people most likely to attend to a message are those most difficult to change; those who can be converted do not look or listen. A variety of studies attribute to this circumstance alone the fact that actual campaigns have often produced no measurable results, while quite marked effects could be produced in a laboratory.

Two favorite problems of the laboratory experimenters take on quite a different aspect when considered in a natural setting. One is the question of the order of presentation of arguments. Is it an advantage to have your argument stated first (the so-called law of primacy) or stated last (the so-called law of recency)? In a laboratory the answer is complex but it may be quite simple in a natural situation: He who presents his argument first may convert the audience and they in turn may exercise their oft-exercised prerogative of not listening to the opposing case. Hence to have the first word rather than the last could be decisive in the real world, but for a reason which may seem irrelevant to the relative merits of primacy versus recency.

Of course, another important variable is the credibility of the source. By creating an impression of the credibility of the stooge or experimenter in the laboratory, it is often possible to convert a person to a position far removed from his original one. But in real life, the audience usually does its own evaluation of sources, and at a certain point sometimes arrives at a result quite the opposite of that reached experimentally. If the audience is confronted with a communicator trying to convert it to a position opposed to its own it is likely to see him as "biased," and the like, and come away further strengthened in its own convictions.

It was quite clear from Hovland's piece, and should have been even earlier, that the characteristic behavior of the audience in its natural habitat is such as to bring about crucial modifications of the results seen in the laboratory. In general, these modifications are strongly in the direction of suppressing effect.

In a sense, Joseph Klapper's 1960 book, *The Effects of Mass Communication*, marks the end of an era. Twenty years earlier, a social scientist would have taken effects for granted and specified the devices the propagandist employed to achieve them. But Klapper (1960) makes statements like these: "[my position] is in essence a shift *away* from the tendency to regard mass communication as a necessary and sufficient cause of audience effects, toward a view of the media as influences, working amid other influences, in a total situation [p. 5]." He sees communications as operating through mediating factors—group membership, selective exposure, defense mechanisms—"such that they typically render mass communication a contributory agent, but not the sole cause in a process of reinforcing the existing conditions. (Regardless of the condition in question . . . the media are more likely to reinforce [it] than to change) [p. 8]." Change takes place, according to Klapper, in those rare circumstances when mediating forces are inoperative, when they are occasionally mobilized to facilitate change, or in certain residual situations. He reviews the literature on the effect of variation in content, mode of presentation, media, and so on, but rather than taking effects for granted, he searches for the exceptional case in which the mass media change rather than fortify and entrench.

Klapper recommends what he calls the "phenomenalistic" and others have called the functional approach. The study of communication has traditionally (although not exclusively) been conducted from the point of view of the *effects intended by the communicator*. From this perspective, the disparity between actual and intended results has often been puzzling. The answer has come increasingly to be seen in entering the phenomenal world of the audience and studying the functions which communication serves. The failure in research to this point has been that the audience has not been given full status in the exchange: The intentions of its members have not been given the same attention as those of the communicator.

Some will argue that these generalizations do not hold true of advertising. They do. But until now no one has undertaken to match the effects of communication in various areas according to comparable criteria and against realistic expectation.

Actually much more is expected of the campaigns with which academic psychologists are associated than is expected of commercial promotion. For example, a paper on governmental informational campaigns concluded with these words (Seidenfeld, 1961): "while people are willing to walk into a drugstore and buy low calorie preparations and contraceptives, they are not very anxious to take shots for protection against polio or attend a clinic dealing with sexual hygiene." By the author's own figures, 60% of the public had had one or more polio shots and 25% had had the full course of four. According to his expectations, and probably ours, these were hardly satisfactory accomplishments.

Yet, what about the highly advertised product, low in calories, with which he was comparing polio inoculations? Presumably he had heard that it was a smashing commercial success, or had seen some dollar volume figure on gross sales. Actually, it was being bought by 4% of the market—and 60% and even 25% are larger figures than 4%. Our unacknowledged expectations must be reckoned with.

These differences in expectation and criteria produce much confusion, usually on the side of convincing people that commercial campaigns are more successful than others. Yet, consistently successful commercial promotions convert only a very small percentage of people to action. No one cigarette now commands more than 14% of the cigarette market, but an increase of 1% is worth $60,000,000 in sales. This means influencing possibly .5% of all adults, and 1% of cigarette smokers. This also means that a successful commercial campaign can alienate many more than it wins, and still be highly profitable.

Equally misleading is the frequent reference to percentage increase on some small base. This device has been a particular favorite of both the promoters and the critics of motivation research: One party does it to sell its services, the other purportedly to warn the public; both exaggerate the effect. Thus, for example, the boast, "a 300% increase in market share," means that the product increased; but it may easily be from 1% of the market to 3%. Or we may have a 500% gain in preference for "the new package" over the old one. That there is that much consensus in the esthetic judgment of the American public is a matter of interest, but it tells nothing about the magnitude of consequences on any criterion in which we are interested. I have made some computations on the famous Kate Smith war-bond marathon, which elicited $39 million in pledges. Kate Smith moved apparently a maximum of 4% of her audience to pledge to buy bonds; the more realistic figure may be 2%! In the commercial world this is a rather small effect as judged by some expectations, but yet an effect which often adds up to millions of dollars.

But commercial promotions often do not pay their way. The word is currently being circulated that a mammoth corporation and a mammoth advertising agency have completed a well-designed experiment that proves the corporation has apparently wasted millions of dollars on promoting its corporate image. Some studies have shown that an increase in expenditures for advertising has, under controlled experimental conditions, produced a decrease in sales.

The truth is now out: that our social model of the process of communication is morally asymmetrical; it is concerned almost exclusively with inequities to the advantage of the initiators, the manipulators. From the social point of view this may be all to the good. The answer to the question whether our social and scientific models should be identical is that there is no reason why we should be equally concerned with inequities in either direction; most of us consider it more important to protect the weak from the powerful, than vice versa. However, no matter how firmly committed to a morally asymmetrical social model, investigators should note that inequities fall in either direction and in unknown proportions.

The combination of this asymmetry and the varying expectations and criteria mentioned earlier fortifies the model of a one-way exploitative process of communication. And it is probably further reinforced by the experimental design in which the subject is seen as *reacting* to conditions established by the experimenter.

Traditionally, the name "functional studies" has been applied to any work concerned with a range of consequences wider than or different from those intended by the communicator. Two early classics, both done in the forties, are studies of listening to daytime radio serials: one by Herta Herzog (1944), and the other by Warner and Henry (1948). They established that women used the radio serials as models for their behavior in real life. In the late forties, Berelson (1949) studied how people reacted to not having newspapers during a strike, work which Kimball (1959) replicated in the newspaper strike of 1948. The variety of functions the newspapers proved to serve is amazing, including the furnishing of raw material for conversation. "The radio is no substitute for the newspaper. I like to make intelligent conversation [Kimball, 1959, p. 395]." There was also research on the adult following of comics (Bogart, 1955), children's use of TV (Maccoby, 1954), and the reading of *Mad* magazine (Winick, 1962).

Meanwhile, new trends have been developing in psychological research on communication. Until about a decade ago, the failure of experimental subjects to change their opinions was regarded as a residual phenomenon. Little systematic or sympathetic attention was paid to the persistence of opinion. The considerable volume of recent research using what the Maccobys (Maccoby & Maccoby, 1961) call a homeostatic model is dominated by theories based on the psychology of cognition, Heider's balance theory, Festinger's dissonance theory, Osgood and Tannenbaum's congruity theory, and Newcomb's strain for symmetry. While the proponents of each theory insist on adequate grounds on their distinctiveness, all agree that man acts so as to restore equilibrium in his system of belief. In any event, homeostatic studies do finally accord some initiative to the audience. Specifically, they reveal individuals as deliberately seeking out information on persons either to reinforce shaken convictions or consolidate those recently acquired. Festinger, for example, is interested in the reduction of dissonance following upon decisions—which means he views people as reacting to their own actions as well as to the actions of others. This influx of new ideas and new research is a valuable and welcome addition to both the theory and practice of social communication.

Restoring cognitive equilibrium is, however, only one of the tasks for which man seeks and uses information. Furthermore, the homeostatic theories, while according initiative to the audience, make it peculiarly defensive. They do little to counteract the notion of a one-way flow of influence—although it must be conceded that a scientific model is under no moral obligation to correct the defects, if any, of the social model.

Much is gained by looking upon the behavior of the audience as full-blown problem solving. Such a viewpoint requires the assumption that people have more problems to solve than simply relating to other people and reducing their psychic tension, among them being the allocation and conservation of resources.

The necessity for taking explicit cognizance of the audience's intention was forced on us when we were studying Soviet refugees. We knew that virtually every Soviet citizen was regularly exposed to meetings at which were conveyed a certain amount of news, the party line on various issues, and general political agitation and indoctrination. In free discussion our respondents complained endlessly of the meetings so we knew they were there. But when we asked them, "From what sources did you draw most of your information about what was happening?" only 19% specified them, in contrast to 87% citing newspapers, 50% citing radio, and another 50% word of mouth (Inkeles & Bauer, 1959, p. 163). Gradually the obvious dawned on us; our respondents were telling us where they learned what *they* wanted to know, not where they learned what the regime wanted them to know.

A similar perplexity arose with respect to the use of word-of-mouth sources of information. It was the least anti-Soviet of our respondents who claimed to make most use of this unofficial fountain of information. Rereading the interviews, and further analysis, unraveled the puzzle. It was the people most involved in the regime, at least in the upper social groups, who were using word-of-mouth sources the better to understand the official media, and the better to do their jobs (Inkeles & Bauer, 1959, p. 161)! As a result we had to conduct analysis on two levels, one where we took into account the intentions of the regime, the other, the intentions of the citizen. Thus, viewed from the vantage point of the regime's intention, the widespread dependence upon word of mouth was a failure in communication. From the point of view of the citizen and what he wanted, his own behavior made eminent sense.

At the next stage, we benefited from the looseness of our methods, the importance of the people we were studying, and from highly imaginative colleagues from other disciplines. We were studying the processes of decision, communication, and the like, in the business and political community. As we studied "influence" by wandering around and getting acquainted with the parties of both camps, and kept track of what was going on, the notion of a one-way flow became preposterous. It became clear that men in influential positions did a great deal to determine what sort of communication was directed toward them (Bauer, Pool, & Dexter, 1963). At this juncture, Ithiel de Sola Pool crystallized the proposition that the audience in effect influences the communicator by the role it forces on him. This idea became the organizing hypothesis behind the Zimmerman and Bauer demonstration (1956) that individuals process new information as a function of their perceived relationship to future audiences. Specifically, they are less likely to remember information that would conflict with the audience's views than they are to remember information to which the audience would be hospitable.

The final crystallization of my present views began several years ago when a decision theorist and I together reviewed the studies by motivation researchers of the marketing of ethical drugs to doctors. Surprisingly, I found the level of motivation discussed in these reports quite trivial, but the reports provided perceptive cognitive maps of the physician's world and the way he went about handling risk. The now well-known studies of the adoption of drugs by Coleman, Menzel, and Katz (1959) contributed data consistent with the following point: Physicians become increasingly selective in their choice of information as risk increases either because of the newness of the drug or difficulty in assessing its effects. Thereupon, a group of Harvard Business School students (in an unpublished manuscript) established by a questionnaire survey that as the seriousness of the disease increased, physicians were increasingly likely to prefer professional to commercial sources of information.

Why doesn't the physician always prefer professional to commercial sources of information? The physician is a busy man whose scarcest resources are time and energy, two things which commercial sources of information, on the whole, seem to help him conserve. Even so, he is selective. Let us assume two components in the choice of source of information: social compliance and the reduction of risk. Consider, then, that the doctor may be influenced by his liking either for the drug company's salesman who visits his office, or for the company itself. We may assume that, of these two components of influence, social compliance will be more associated with his sentiments toward the salesman and risk reduction with the company's reputation.

In a study conducted with the Schering Corporation (Bauer, 1961), I found that in the case of relatively riskless drugs, the correlation of preference for drugs with preference for salesman and for company was about equal. However, with more hazardous drugs—and with large numbers of subjects—preference for the company carried twice the weight of preference for the salesmen: The physicians selected the source closest associated with reduction of risk.

In the latest and fullest development of this point of view, Cox (1962) asked approximately 300 middle-class housewives to evaluate the relative merits of "two brands" of nylon stockings (Brand N & Brand R) as to over-all merits and as to each of 18 attributes. After each rating the subject was asked to indicate how confident she was in making it. The subjects then listened to a tape-recorded interview with a supposed salesgirl who stated that Brand R was better as to six attributes, whereupon they were asked to judge the stockings again and to evaluate the salesgirl and their confidence in rating her. Finally, they completed a questionnaire which included three batteries of questions on personality, one of which was a measure of self-confidence.

The findings of interest here bear upon personality and persuasibility. Male subjects low in generalized self-confidence are generally the more persuasible. Females are more persuasible in general but on the whole this is not correlated with self-confidence or self-esteem.

The reigning hypotheses on the relationship of self-confidence to persuasibility have been based either on the concept of ego defense (Cohen, 1959) or social approval (Janis, 1954), and Cox chose to add *perceived self-confidence in accomplishing a task*. He was dealing, then, with two measures of

self-confidence: generalized self-confidence, presumably an attribute of "personality"; and specific self-confidence, that is, perceived confidence in judging stockings.

It has been suggested that the reason that in women personality has not been found correlated with persuasibility is that the issues used in experiments have not been important to them. And importance may account for the strong relationship Cox found when he gave them the task of rating stockings.

The virtue of Cox's data is that they enable us to relate the problem-solving dimensions of behavior to social relationships and ego defensive. It is interesting that—in this study—the more "psychological" processes come into play only at the point at which felt self-confidence in accomplishing the task falls below a critical point. Thus, tendency to accept the suggestions of the alleged salesgirl in Cox's experiment must be seen as a function of both ability to deal with the task and personality.

The difficulty of the task may either fortify or suppress the more "social-psychological" processes, depending on the specific circumstances. Thus, study of drug preference shows that as the task gets easier, the individual can indulge in the luxury of concurring with someone whom he likes, whereas when risk is great he has to concentrate on the risk-reducing potentialities of the source of information.

Thus the full-blown, problem-solving interpretation of the behavior of an audience in no sense rules out the problems with which students of communication have recently concerned themselves: ego defense and social adjustment. As a matter of fact, such problems seem explorable in a more profitable fashion if, simultaneously, attention is paid to the more overt tasks for which people use information. Yet, while there has been a consistent drift toward granting the audience more initiative, it cannot be said that the general literature on communication yet accords it a full range of intentions.

Of course, the audience is not wholly a free agent: It must select from what is offered. But even here, the audience has influence, since it is generally offered an array of communications to which it is believed it will be receptive. The process of social communication and of the flow of influence in general must be regarded as a transaction. "Transactionism," which has had a variety of meanings in psychology, is used here in the sense of an exchange of values between two or more parties; each gives in order to get.

The argument for using the transactional model for *scientific* purposes is that it opens the door more fully to exploring the intention and behavior of members of the audience and encourages inquiry into the influence of the audience on the communicator by specifically treating the process as a two-way passage. In addition to the influence of the audience on the communicator, there seems little doubt that influence also operates in the "reverse" direction. But the persistence of the one-way model of influence discourages the investigation of both directions of relationship. With amusing adroitness some writers have assimilated the original experiment of Zimmerman and Bauer (1956) to establish concepts such as reference groups, thereby ignoring what we thought was the clear implication of a two-way flow of influence.

At our present state of knowledge there is much to be said for the transactional model's pragmatic effect on research, but at the same time it is the most plausible description of the process of communication as we know it. Yet there seems to be a tendency to assume that words such as "transaction," "reciprocity," and the like imply exact equality in each exchange, measured out precisely according to the value system and judgment of the observer. This is nonsense. Obviously there are inequities, and they will persist, whether we use our own value systems as observers or if we have perfect knowledge of the people we observe.

The rough balance of exchange is sufficiently equitable in the long run to keep *most* individuals in our society engaged in the transactional relations of communication and influence. But some "alienated" people absent themselves from the network of communication as do, also, many businessmen who have doubts about the money they spend on advertising. The alienation is by no means peculiar to one end of the chain of communication or influence.

This point of view may be taken as a defense of certain social institutions such as advertising and the mass media. There is a limited range of charges against which *impotence* may indeed be considered a defense. Once more, ironically, both the communicator and the critic have a vested interest in the exploitative model. From the point of view of the communicator, it is reassuring that he will receive *at least* a fair return for his efforts; to the critic, the exploitative model gratifies the sense of moral indignation.

41   When the polls go wrong and why

ROBERT P. ABELSON

The man who doesn't feel he has a real justification for holding a socially undesirable attitude is in much the same psychological position in the voting booth as he is in the interview situation, albeit one is by appearances more private than the other. In both cases, he must either allow himself to be trapped into making the socially desirable response, or else suffer the social discomfort associated with making an undesirable response.

I do not mean to assert that there are no differences at all between interview and voting-booth situations. There might be a number of people who would vote differently from the way they would poll, but not necessarily all would vote in favor of the less socially desirable response. Some individuals might even use the privacy of the voting booth to guiltily register a conforming response (for example, a pro-minority group vote) that they would be too embarrassed to support in public. This orientation might especially apply to moderate Negro candidates such as Massachusetts Senator Edward Brooke and Cleveland Mayor Carl Stokes. The matter deserves further analysis and study, but there is no evidence for massive "secret votes" in recent Presidential campaigns. I would further assert that in general the validity of surveys is quite high, although there is a certain kind of exception to which I refer below.

Primary elections

Many of the most spectacular apparent failures of polls have been in primaries. "Pollsters Fooled Again," declared the *New York Times* on page 1 of its News of the Week section the Sunday after Eugene McCarthy's stunning showing in the New Hampshire primary, which began the incredible 1968 political season. The idea that pollsters have been tricked by a shrewd electorate makes appealing journalism, but it can tend to perpetuate a serious misrepresentation, as I shall try to show.

In 1964, there were three key Republican primaries, and the polls were wrong in all three cases. In New Hampshire, Rockefeller was supposed to be slightly ahead, but Lodge won easily. In Oregon, Lodge was supposed to be ahead, but Rockefeller won easily. And in crucial California, the final poll had Rockefeller the winner but, of course, Goldwater won.

In 1968, only one primary winner was miscalled by the polls (Robert Kennedy's loss to McCarthy in the close Oregon race), but the percentage predictions were occasionally way off, as in New Hampshire.

The percentage errors in two of the three 1964 cases were much too large to be accounted for by sampling variation, but the clue to what might have gone wrong was that the eventual

Excerpted from "Computers, polls, and public opinion—some puzzles and paradoxes" (Copyright © 1968 by **Trans-action Magazine**, New Brunswick, N.J.), Vol. 5, 9, 20–27.

winner gained five percentage points between the next-to-last poll and the last poll. A late trend was also evident in McCarthy's New Hampshire showing in 1968. This is the basis for what I like to call the First Law of Poll-Watching: *If in a dull primary you see a trend in the polls a week before the election, extrapolate to the result by tripling this trend in the final week.*

The psychological basis for this carefree, slightly tongue-in-cheek rule of thumb is that unless the issues are sharply drawn early, the attributes of the candidates do not usually make a clear impression until the last two weeks before the election. As the day of decision nears, however, any compelling, pithy argument may create a wave of social endorsement for the lucky candidate in whose behalf the argument can be made. With Lodge in the 1964 New Hampshire primary, the pithy argument was that Lodge, unlike the other candidates, was after all a New Englander. With Rockefeller in Oregon, it was that Rockefeller was at least campaigning while Lodge wasn't even clearly interested. In California, the situation was rather more complicated. The campaign commanded sharper interests and loyalties, and no sweeping overall trend was discernible just before the last poll, so the First Law did not apply.

In 1968 in New Hampshire, the simple idea of registering a protest against President Johnson gained rapid currency (though less than half of the voters knew that McCarthy was a "dove"). And in Oregon and elsewhere Robert Kennedy apparently suffered near voting time from the charge that he was ruthless.

Local referendum campaigns

With local referendum campaigns, sim-ilarly, there is every indication that a strong last-minute amplification of simple, possibly trivial, arguments occurs, carrying the day for one side or the other. Here, too, there are some notable examples of polls seeming to be incorrect. National samples typically show sentiment in favor of water fluoridation at around 60 percent. Yet three out of four local fluoridation referenda lose. The explanation seems to be that before the referendum campaign starts, more positive than negative arguments are known, but during the last two weeks the negative arguments gain wider currency, and a sufficient number of people change from weak pro to weak anti opinions to ensure defeat. I have some very detailed data from a study I did of the water-fluoridation referendum in Berkeley in 1964, which clearly showed this effect.

Two other cases, both notorious, in which polls were accurate in predicting the referendum outcome but were seriously incorrect in calling the percentage margin of victory, were the Proposition 14 vote against fair housing in California in 1964, and the repeal in New York of a civilian police review board in 1966. And lest anyone think from these examples that the illiberal side always wins referenda when the chips are down, I hasten to mention a contrary instance: In California in 1966, a very strict provision (called CLEAN) against obscene literature was leading slightly in the polls yet lost on election day, even while Reagan was romping away with the governorship.

These examples suggest a Second Law of Poll-Watching: *If in a referendum an abstract principle is pitted against a very concrete fear or desire, the concrete side will gain heavily as the campaign nears its conclusion.*

Ordinarily, polls are not taken frequently enough in referendum campaigns to allow extrapolation of last-minute trends. If they were, the experienced poll-watcher could add to this Second Law the triple-trend principle of the First Law—that is, take the percentage gain of the concrete side of the issue in the next-to-last week of the campaign and triple it to predict the final outcome. The reason I suspect that this would work is that the psychological processes involved in last-minute trends are probably similar in referenda and primaries: Just when public attention finally begins to focus lazily on the imminence of voting on a complex matter, a compelling little summarization of what it's all about makes the social rounds.

The feelings involved may range widely in intensity, and the arguments may vary in content from one issue to the next, without disturbing the generalization that in a public confrontation the concrete side of an issue gains voters from the abstract side. The principle of preventive dental hygiene is rather abstract, whereas the various alarms that can be conjured up about fluoride poisoning and impure water are immediate and concrete. In parallel fashion, it is all well and good to declare in principle against pornography, but if it means that someone is going to censor what you read, or worse, take away your copy of *Playboy*, well, then one must stand and be counted.

Now, the discrepancies between abstract and concrete can, to the outside observer, look like sheer hypocrisy, and, on racial issues, conniving bigotry as well. Yet the voter himself may be blissfully unaware of a discrepancy as he switches from his bland early endorsement of a general principle in an interview to his later concerned support of an application of its contrary, under the stimulus of a pointed campaign exposing him largely to the latter side. Even if he is aware of the discrepancy, it may not disturb him. As political scientist Robert Dahl puts it, "[It is] a common tendency of . . . mankind . . . to qualify universals in application while leaving them intact in rhetoric."

As my preceding remarks have indicated, local campaigns possess a volatility not characteristic of national campaigns. Computerizing local public opinion is therefore more hazardous than computerizing national public opinion. Furthermore, it is an expensive proposition because data-bank information cannot be transferred from one locale to another. Extensive background on the local issues and voters in Berkeley doesn't help you much in predicting the outcome of an election in Indianapolis.

There are quite a number of very interesting psychological questions to be investigated in local referenda or mass public controversies, however, and the construction of computer models whose predictions can be checked against responses from local survey panels is at least one useful way to proceed with such an investigation. To check the predictions of one computer model devised a few years ago by Alex Bernstein and me, I have assembled intensive data from three cities on fluoridation and school-segregation controversies. In this endeavor, we have encountered one peculiar problem that deserves mention, though I will not explore it in detail here. In a local computer model, it is necessary to predict *individual* rather than group opinion changes because there are not enough respondents to construct a large bank of voter types; but when we examine some of these individual changes, however, we find strong evidence of unreliable pseudo-change. Many respondents hop wildly back and forth on the attitude scales from one time to the next, while reporting no exposure to any conversations or persuasive appeals on the issue. It is as if their interview responses are given randomly. This is the phenomenon that sociologists Paul Lazarsfeld and James Coleman refer to as "turnover," and political social psychologists Philip Converse and Milton Rosenberg call "non-attitudes." It is especially prevalent on topics that for uninformed voters are essentially "nonsense issues," such as water fluoridation, but it occurs to some extent on all issues. And computer simulation models, obviously, will have difficulty in tracing something that isn't there.

Most of what I have said thus far paints a picture of public opinion as disorganized and wishy-washy. But in fact I believe that there are definite simple patterns at work. The forces acting upon public opinion may be viewed as gravitational masses pulling upon a shallow body of water. If more than one force is applied, then the resultant response is often a simple sum of the various appropriate responses. Thus, although the published account of our 1960 and 1964 computer analyses invoke so-called cross-pressure theory, the theory that opposing decisional elements impinging on the voter interact to produce strong motivational effects, I am much more inclined in retrospect to take the view that different issues superpose upon one another *without* mutual interference. Characterizing this view are four simple assumptions:

1. Most issues have so little effect that for practical purposes one may ignore them;

2. One or two issues may have the same effect across all voter types;

3. One or two issues may have different effects across major voter types, effects proportional to measurable susceptibilities to the issue among the various types; and

4. These effects combine additively to determine the final outcome.

What convinces me most strongly of the accuracy of this simple "gravitational" model is the great success of another kind of computer analysis—the election-night computer projections by the television networks of final vote outcomes (see Skedgell, 1966). In the early projection attempts, a number of pratfalls occurred, but in 1964 and again in 1966 the speed and accuracy of projection were awesome. In the 229 races called in those two election years, each of the two major networks made but two errors. The successful pattern is by now familiar: The bemused announcer, without the slightest understanding of how it's done, and not knowing whether he should believe it himself, reports, "With the polls closed only 20 minutes, and 0 percent of the vote tabulated, the computer already predicts that incumbent Governor Sam Smurch of Idaho will lose to his opponent, Runaway Roberts." And sure enough, when the tabulation is finally in four hours later, Sam Smurch loses.

Observation in a few key districts

On the basis of my experience at NBC in 1964, I can suggest how these minor miracles can be performed. One basic and extremely simple supposition is that a trend observed in a few districts generalizes to a large portion of states or even to the whole state. Since the early observation of trends is clearly important to early projection, key districts can be chosen from among those known to have early returns available. But another crucial property of key districts is whether their shifts in voting from election to election have corresponded to the state's shifts over corresponding elections—that is, whether these districts are "swingometric." Suppose that in a state that voted 47 percent Democratic in a previous comparable election, a swingometric precinct that last time went 30 percent Democratic now goes 38 percent Democratic, and one that went 50 percent Democratic now goes 58 percent Democratic. On the basis of only these two pieces of early information, the best guess about the outcome would be a statewide 8 percent swing toward the Democratic side from the previous state results; thus, if in the previous election the Democrats had captured 47 percent of the statewide vote, they would now be predicted to capture 55 percent. Of course, the accuracy depends upon whether these key precincts are in some sense representative of the state, unless *all* precincts have swung the same 8 percent, in which case it doesn't matter which ones you choose for early projection.

If one party's campaign exerts equal attraction on all voter types, it will produce roughly the same amount of swing in all precincts. The projection procedure will then be very "robust," that is, insensitive to the choice of key early precincts. But consider the slightly more subtle situation where the campaign exerts different effects across the state's major population types, say urban versus rural. In that case, the key precincts must be carefully selected to give a balanced picture of swings in both groups.

Ideally the selection of key precincts should be deliberately balanced on the basis of the population characteristics known or thought to be important in a swing. Thus, if the state is divided 50-50 between urban and rural population, and key precincts show a 4 percent swing to the Democrats in urban areas and a 6 percent swing to the Republicans in rural areas, then the projected swing in the state as a whole would be 2 percent in favor of the Republicans.

There are many variations on this basic scheme. Instead of previous voting records, polls throughout the state and in the key precincts can provide the baseline for calculating a probable swing. This polling approach is especially useful in party primaries lacking a historical precedent. The networks have managed to project primary as well as final election results, although in 1964 and again in 1968 CBS almost goofed in mercurial California with overly quick declarations based too heavily on Southern California key precincts.

That rather simple election-night projection models can work so well is testimony to the simplicity of the major forces operating on the electorate. If a unique constellation of many different forces combined to produce the vote outcome in each separate district, then geographical variation of outcomes would be so high and so apparently unsystematic that any prediction would be hazardous.

Is the view of public opinion I am espousing, with its emphasis on bland simplicity, an unusual view? No, indeed. Professional politicians, and lay and academic analysts of the public mind, have long sounded closely related themes. Herbert McClosky, following an analysis that revealed weak and self-contradictory clusters of public beliefs about

Democratic norms and practices, put the matter quite sharply. He said, "As intellectuals and students of politics we are disposed both by training and sensibility to take political ideas seriously. . . . We are therefore prone to forget that most people take them less seriously than we do, that they pay little attention to issues, rarely worry about the consistency of their opinions, and spend little or no time thinking about the values, presuppositions and implications which distinguish one political orientation from another."

It seems to me that we can understand and perhaps even sympathize with the general public's failure to organize the political world very well if we realize that there are limits on the typical man's intellectual reach—that his organizing capacities and efforts are usually applied only over a small content area.

Opinion molecules

To see this pattern, let us postulate the existence of self-contained cognitive units called opinion *molecules*. Each molecule functions for the person holding it by serving most of the purposes an opinion serves. Much has been written about the expressive purposes of opinions and about the psychodynamic functions of more general attitude orientations, but there is a more homey and widespread function that opinions satisfy. Opinions bestow conversational and cognitive security—they give you something to say and think when the topic comes up. To serve this function, as well as some of the deeper psychological functions, the usual minimum-sized, stable opinion molecule seems to require a *fact*, a *feeling*, and a *following* —that is, some item of "information"

(which may or may not be objectively correct); some emotional orientation; and some sense that there are others who hold the same opinion.

It is easy to give examples of such molecules: "It's a fact that when my Uncle Charlie had back trouble, he was cured by a chiropractor. You know, I feel that chiropractors have been sneered at too much, and I'm not ashamed to say so, because I know a lot of people who feel the same way." Or again, "Nobody on this block wants to sell to Negroes, and neither do I. The property values would decline." These sorts of opinions are often quite impervious to other levels of argumentation because of their complete, closed, molecular character. It is as if the opinion-holder were saying, "What else could there possibly be to add?"

Certainly the opinion molecule's size will vary, from individual to individual, depending upon habit, education, intelligence, personality, and social context. Sometimes a molecule will have only two components, say just a fact and feeling with no following, as in private little delusions, or a feeling and a following with no essential dependence on variations in fact, as in "Burn, baby, burn." On the other hand, it is quite possible to have larger molecules that include arguments to counter the opposition, qualifications of the opinion, and an organized account of the facts, feelings, and following on the other side.

How elaborate the structure housing an opinion will be depends upon how elaborate the individual requires it to be to serve his purposes. For example, if no counter-arguments are expected, then there is no need to prepare for them. But this is also a matter of cognitive style, varying according to a self-imposed question, "How much do I have to know to be entitled to an opinion?" Presumably, highly educated individuals feel some embarrassment when and if their opinions are revealed as superficial, and therefore are at pains to try to construct them well. But most of the general public feels no such pressure, and there is no realistic reason why they should. Without question, this is a source of great frustration to all those who in some way work to try to increase the public's level of sophistication.

VII   NORMATIVE BEHAVIOR, CONFORMITY, AND INTRA-GROUP PROCESSES

Social psychology has had a long-standing concern with conformity and influence processes in groups. Indeed, because these processes constitute one of the main traditional interests in the field, a considerable amount of experimentation has devolved about the mechanisms which produce adherence to group norms. The breadth of this research is represented in such significant works as *Group Dynamics: Research and Theory* (Cartwright & Zander, 1968), *The Handbook of Small Group Research* (Hare, 1962), *Small Groups* (Hare, Borgatta, & Bales, 1965), and *Small Group Research* (McGrath & Altman, 1966).

A major locus for studying group processes is the small group, in which, by definition, members share a common function, or task, and have an associated "structure" for achieving it. Structure includes some division of labor and status differentiation, a pattern of communication, a sense of identity, and expectations for conformity to normative demands. Though our interest in this section is directed especially toward intra-group processes related to conformity, the leadership of the group serves a significant influence function which is considered in the next section. Furthermore, the results which flow from research on conformity in small groups may hold various implications for the wider society.

Social interaction within any social framework implies demands for regularized behaviors, in the form of patterned actions or attitudinal expressions, as has been pointed out in previous sections. Gouldner in his paper in Section V, illustrates one such persisting demand, "the norm of reciprocity," but apart from that kind of broad societal expectation, norms frequently originate and reside in the functional group. The question of why individuals conform to the expectations of these groups is at the heart of social psychological concern, and a range of emphases, some at times more dominant than others, has been suggested by way of answer. One thing is, however, certain: groups could not effectively achieve their goals without conforming behavior, nor could societies be sustained. A word is in order then on the motivational basis for conformity and some misconceptions that prevail about it, before we examine some of these emphases.

Affiliation with functional groups is frequently based upon a voluntary desire by the individual to take part in the group's activity; it is also true though, that the individual thereby gains a number of social rewards which sustain his participation, i.e., recognition, a shared pride in achievement, and a sense of belonging and approval. In addition, groups may provide individuals with a frame of reference for perceiving their world which they might lack alone, what Festinger (1950) dubbed "social reality," and what Cantril here, in Section I, speaks of as the "reality world." Many viewpoints in social psychology proceed from the idea of a group's common perspective on the world (see Newcomb, 1950). One function of a reference group, for example, is to provide a standard of judgment (see Hyman and Singer, Section II). Furthermore, individuals tend to find relationships more rewarding with another person when important attitudes are shared by the other (see Newcomb, Section VI). Conformity thus affords various inducements to the individual as a consequence of his continued acceptance as a member in good standing. If membership in a group is not forced, then a person who loses interest, or changes his outlook, or becomes attracted to other sources of reward, or finds the membership composition of the group no longer to his taste, may move away from it and not be concerned, other things being equal, about the rejection he may engender.

Individuals therefore gain quite directly from conforming, despite the view that they give up some precious individuality in the process, and the related commonplace that conformity is inimical to individuality. A way of clarifying this point is to think of true individuality not as slavish nonconformity (or *anti*conformity), but rather as involving a range of choices *not* relying at either extreme upon a norm as the determinant of conduct, whether *pro* or *anti*. Therefore, as Willis (1963, 1965) has pointed out, what is called nonconformity is comprised of two quite distinct patterns: *anticonformity*, which is fixed to a norm as much as is overconformity, and *independence*, which is a freer expression of individual choice, whether or not it coincides with the norm. Gardner, in Section II, also speaks to this more productive conception of individuality.

Essentially, there are four elements associated with conformity. They may be summarized as: (1) the individual, with his own characteristics, exemplified by personality; (2) the qualities of the group and its setting; (3) the nature of the norm itself; and (4) the past and present interchange between the individual and the others within the situation.

A great deal of attention has been directed to issues raised by the initial two emphases, the person and the situation. In the first place, there is a contention that individuals bring to numerous situations a differential inclination to conform and that, at the extreme, some people are "conformists" and others "nonconformists," in the sense of an attribute of personality. This line of emphasis is represented by Crutchfield's (1955) study of the individual differences in conforming behavior produced by "group pressure" induced in a manner adapted from the original studies of Sherif (1935) and Asch (1952). Another line of work on personality dispositions toward conformity is seen in the studies of "persuasibility" reported by Hovland and Janis (1959). One problem with such results is that the "groups" studied in these various experiments are low on functionality, and normative expectations often are set by the experimenter. Furthermore, little or no interaction occurs between subjects.

In the second view, conformity is treated more as an outgrowth of a group process. It is recognized that persons may react differently to different situations, as a function of how they perceive them. The differing properties of situations, filtered through the perception of individuals, have some effect even if persons bring different dispositions with them to many social settings. And this suggests a range within which people are variously sensitized to the demands for conformity across situations. A formulation of the pressures toward "uniformity" in groups is represented in Festinger's well-known theory of informal social communication (1950). In his position, he accounts for processes which may alter the consensus,

415

in contrast to the "personality disposition" approach which conceives conformity as dependent upon a relatively fixed standard to which compliance is demanded, without reference to change. Viewing norms as fixed standards obscures what is probably more true of group norms, i.e., that they stand as "normative perceptions" of what is expected and that they are neither fixed nor general, as Hollander and Willis note in their paper in this section.

In a related way, Kelman treats the relationship between manifest and underlying aspects of conformity in his paper here. He distinguishes influence processes leading to compliance, identification, and internalization. An individual may not be motivated to conform but be unable to do as he wishes. Accordingly, he may behave in one way but actually have different underlying tendencies. Kelman draws distinctions between these three processes of influence with specific regard to the psychodynamics of their motivational underpinnings. His conception is related to Katz's functional approach to attitudes (see Section VI), with its motivational emphasis.

Though social psychology studies conforming behavior without invoking judgments about the nature of the norm as such, society at large is concerned with deviance as a source of threat to the social order. Becker's paper, drawn from the first chapter of his insightful work *Outsiders* (1963), deals with nonconformity in the tradition of the sociological interest in deviance, defined as the breaking of an agreed-upon rule. As Becker notes, however, this traditional definition can be misleading because a person may break the rules of one group by the very act of abiding by the rules of another. This point corresponds to the idea put forth by Blau (1964, p. 26) that an equilibrium in one set of interpersonal associations is often achieved at the cost of a disequilibrium in other relationships.

Becker contends that the concept of deviance is created by groups in that they make the rules whose infraction constitutes deviance. Moreover, once people have been labeled as "deviants," says Becker, they share something in common—not in the sense of being alike so much as being seen as "outsiders" and being treated as such. This illustrates again the common fact of social life that people and objects are responded to mainly in terms of the social categories to which they are allocated. In this regard Pettigrew's analysis in Section II of the Negro role is especially pertinent as are Brown's paper in Section IV and the general discussion of roles in

Section V. One of the consequences of this process is the alienation from the rules that relatively powerless elements of society come to feel, which Becker views as a wellspring of conflict in society.

In the paper which follows, Hollander and Willis point to the widespread emphasis in social psychology on the study of conforming behavior at the expense of nonconformity. In their review and critique of the current work on these phenomena, they consider the importance of distinguishing between description and explanation as levels of analysis, and between movement conformity, in the classic sense of "convergence" to a common norm, and congruence conformity which relies essentially on past habituation to a social convention.

In treating the differential responses associated with conformity and nonconformity, the Willis distinction between anticonformity and independence provides a better indication of the various options available to the individual in a given influence situation. Let us be clear, however, that this is not a typology of people, in the sense of personality dispositions, so much as it is an indication of possible modes of response by an individual. On the descriptive level, at least, there is a similarity between the Becker view and that represented by the Willis model.

After a review of salient points in the history of research on movement conformity, or "convergence," Hollander and Willis consider various issues raised by a concern with situational versus personality determinants of conformity. They reject this either-or proposition, favoring instead the interactionist position of J. McV. Hunt, in Section III (see also Yinger there). The last major part of their paper moves to a consideration of the effects of conformity, with some particular attention to social exchange. Associated with this perspective is the "idiosyncrasy credit" model (Hollander, 1958, 1964), which emphasizes the interpersonal perceptions which individuals hold of each other that give them latitude, in terms of credit, to take actions eventually which might otherwise be seen as deviant. Thus, conforming or nonconforming produces effects, in the sense of rewards or costs to others, which alter the pattern of subsequent interaction. The three papers which follow in this section are illustrative of this transactional feature of social exchange.

For some years, George Homans has devoted attention to conformity processes, and his book *Social Behavior: Its Elementary Forms* (1961) extends his ideas on social exchange even more broadly. In his recent paper republished here, he lays out the essential features of his rewards-costs conception based upon reinforcement theory, placing special weight on the implicit exchange of a reciprocated response. After presenting his five propositions, he proceeds to the consideration of the applicability of these to social interaction and to processes generating status. Among the more important outgrowths of his position is the concept of "distributive justice" which has ramifications to a number of areas of contemporary concern surrounding equity and the perception of inequity (see, e.g., Adams, 1965). This concept has a certain resonance with the ideas of Heider on "balance" and Festinger on "dissonance," emphasizing as they do a degree of symmetry or aptness between actions and counteractions, as well as actions and perceptions.

Thibaut and Kelley are represented in his section by a discussion from their provocative book *The Social Psychology of Groups* (1959), which serves in particular to underscore the utility of norms for the maintenance of influence independent of the repetitive exercise of personal power. While they use the two-person relationship as a referent, a range of implications is provided in their book for intra-group processes. An important psychological construct which they employ is "comparison level for alternatives," which has to do with other available rewards and is suggestive of adaptation level phenomena (see Helson, 1948). Though the Thibaut and Kelley matrix of rewards and costs resembles Homans's matrix, it is arrived at with somewhat different emphases. The study of interactions by persons involved in various "payoff" matrices has been followed extensively in experimental games (see Vinacke, Section V). Another source for this work is Rapoport's *Two-Person Game Theory* (1966).

There are other similarities in the key concepts of Homans and of Thibaut and Kelley, and some elements of distinction. Both views imply an interchange in the responses of individuals one to another in a diadic relationship, but with implications to larger groups. While the concept of an exchange is implied as well in Hollander's theory of "idiosyncrasy credit," the emphasis there is more upon the interpersonal perceptions which individuals hold of *each other* and the latitude that this comes to provide as one gains "credit" in the eyes of others through positive impressions. An important distinction here is the fact that normative demands become associated with individuals as a feature of ongoing interaction. Acceptable behavior from one person within a stable group context, would therefore not necessarily be acceptable behavior for another.

In his paper here, Jones is also concerned with manifest conformity as it affects others' perceptions. In his book *Ingratiation* (1964) he sees manifest conformity as one tactic of "ingratiation," especially where a person of lower relative status seeks to gain more favorable outcomes from a person of higher status. This viewpoint meshes well with the "idiosyncrasy credit" concept in that they both stress the gains the individual may achieve through observable conformity in social interaction. Given a basis for knowing what is expected, Jones considers such conformity to be motivated especially by a practical desire to secure benefits from another person in a more powerful position. Thus, multiple motivations may be at work in determining the basis for conformity; these are crucially dependent upon the way in which the individual perceives others within his situation, and various rewards must be entertained as possible sources of action whatever conception of conformity is employed.

In the final paper in this section, Latané and Darley consider some of the expectancies and rewards affecting behavior in emergency situations. Because there are evidently few positive rewards for successful action in an emergency, they contend that an implicit norm has grown up toward inaction; they then consider the conditions under which individuals are more likely to violate that norm by acting in a nonconforming fashion. They conclude that a series of decisions is involved. Rather than requiring a single course of action, the individual is faced with a complex matrix of choice alternatives. This is further complicated by the fact that most emergencies begin as ambiguous events, and that there are few firm guidelines to be followed in such situations. Furthermore, the presence of other people may act as a deterrent to the individual's action insofar as he takes a public risk of disfavor, and, in light of the rewards and costs involved, may accordingly conclude that action is unjustified.

The heart of the Latané and Darley paper consists of their report of a series of highly innovative experiments on bystander intervention. These experiments range from a circumstance involving an apparent fire, on through a possible injury, to someone who seems to have fallen in the next room, to the action of customers in a store who observe a case of beer being stolen, and then to an emergency which involves an apparent victim of an epileptic attack. In assessing this rich array of findings, these researchers conclude that social influence and diffusion of responsibility explanations seem valid in accounting for inaction on the part of individuals. Thus, individuals may be influenced by the interpretations that they read into the inaction of others, thereby creating a state of pluralistic ignorance. Furthermore, under the diffusion-of-responsibility view, the costs associated with nonintervention are reduced because of others' inaction, and no one person feels at fault. One key finding from the work of Latané and Darley, bearing on these interpretations, is that knowing another person even casually in advance increases the willingness to help that person in injurious circumstances. These results also fit within the framework of the impersonal, noninvolved character of large city life treated by Milgram in Section X.

The study of conformity and influence processes comes down ultimately to the issue of the social fabric which holds people together in society. Though it proceeds from an immediate concern with group processes, this work has broader ramifications for the nature of social conduct, social responsibility, and commitment to others.

42   Three processes of social influence

HERBERT C. KELMAN

The study of social influence

Social influence has been a central area of concern for experimental social psychology almost since its beginnings. Three general research traditions in this area can be distinguished: (1) the study of social influences on judgments, stemming from the earlier work on prestige suggestion (e.g. see Asch, 1952); (2) the study of social influences arising from small-group interaction (e.g. see Cartwright & Zander, 1953); and (3) the study of social influences arising from persuasive communications (e.g. see Hovland, *et al.*, 1953). In recent years, there has been a considerable convergence between these three traditions, going hand in hand with an increased interest in developing general principles of social influence and socially induced behavior change.

One result of these developments has been that many investigators found it necessary to make qualitative distinctions between different types of influence. In some cases, these distinctions arose primarily out of the observation that social influence may have qualitatively different effects, that it may produce different kinds of change. For example, under some conditions it may result in mere public conformity—in superficial changes on a verbal or overt level without accompanying changes in belief; in other situations it may result in private acceptance—in a change that is more general, more durable, more integrated with the person's own values (Festinger, 1953; Kelman, 1953; French & Raven, 1959; Jahoda, 1959). Other investigators found it necessary to make distinctions because they observed that influence may occur for different reasons, that it may arise out of different motivations and orientations. For example, under some conditions influence may be primarily informational— the subject may conform to the influencing person or group because he views him as a source of valid information; in other situations influence may be primarily normative—the subject may conform in order to meet the positive expectations of the influencing person or group (Deutsch & Gerard, 1955; Thibaut & Strickland, 1956; Jackson & Saltzstein, 1958).

My own work can be viewed in the general context that I have outlined here. I started out with the distinction between public conformity and private acceptance, and tried to establish some of the distinct determinants of each. I became dissatisfied with this dichotomy as I began to look at important examples of social influence that could not be encompassed by it. I was especially impressed with the accounts of ideological conversion of the "true believer" variety, and with the recent accounts of "brainwashing," particularly the Chinese Communist methods of "thought reform" (Lifton, 1956). It is apparent that these experiences do not

Excerpted from "Processes of Opinion Change," **Public Opinion Quarterly**, 1961, 25, 57–78, with permission of the author and publisher.

simply involve public conformity, but that indeed they produce a change in underlying beliefs. But it is equally apparent that they do not produce what we would usually consider private acceptance—changes that are in some sense integrated with the person's own value system and that have become independent of the external source. Rather, they seem to produce new beliefs that are isolated from the rest of the person's values and that are highly dependent on external support.

These considerations eventually led me to distinguish three processes of social influence, each characterized by a distinct set of antecedent and a distinct set of consequent conditions. I have called these processes *compliance, identification,* and *internalization.*

Three processes of social influence

Compliance can be said to occur when an individual accepts influence from another person or from a group because he hopes to achieve a favorable reaction from the other. He may be interested in attaining certain specific rewards or in avoiding certain specific punishments that the influencing agent controls. For example, an individual may make a special effort to express only "correct" opinions in order to gain admission into a particular group or social set, or in order to avoid being fired from his government job. Or, the individual may be concerned with gaining approval or avoiding disapproval from the influencing agent in a more general way. For example, some individuals may compulsively try to say the expected thing in all situations and please everyone with whom they come in contact, out of a disproportionate need for favorable responses from others of a

direct and immediate kind. In any event, when the individual complies, he does what the agent wants him to do—or what he thinks the agent wants him to do—because he sees this as a way of achieving a desired response from him. He does not adopt the the induced behavior—for example, a particular opinion response—because he believes in its content, but because it is instrumental in the production of a satisfying social effect. What the individual learns, essentially, is to say or do the expected thing in special situations, regardless of what his private beliefs may be. Opinions adopted through compliance should be expressed only when the person's behavior is observable by the influencing agent.

Identification can be said to occur when an individual adopts behavior derived from another person or a group because this behavior is associated with a satisfying self-defining relationship to this person or group. By a self-defining relationship I mean a role relationship that forms a part of the person's self-image. Accepting influence through identification, then, is a way of establishing or maintaining the desired relationship to the other, and the self-definition that is anchored in this relationship.

The relationship that an individual tries to establish or maintain through identification may take different forms. It may take the form of classical identification, that is, of a relationship in which the individual takes over all or part of the role of the influencing agent. To the extent to which such a relationship exists, the individual defines his own role in terms of the role of the other. He attempts to be like or actually to *be* the other person. By saying what the other says, doing what he does, believing what he believes, the individual maintains this relationship and the satisfying self-definition that it provides him. An influencing agent who is likely to be an attractive object for such a relationship is one who occupies a role desired by the individual—who possesses those characteristics that the individual himself lacks—such as control in a situation in which the individual is helpless, direction in a situation in which he is disoriented, or belongingness in a situation in which he is isolated.

The behavior of the brainwashed prisoner in Communist China provides one example of this type of identification. By adopting the attitudes and beliefs of the prison authorities—including *their* evaluation of *him*—he attempts to regain his identity, which has been subjected to severe threats. But this kind of identification does not occur only in such severe crisis situations. It can also be observed, for example, in the context of socialization of children, where the taking over of parental attitudes and actions is a normal, and probably essential, part of personality development. The more or less conscious efforts involved when an individual learns to play a desired occupational role and imitates an appropriate role model would also exemplify this process. Here, of course, the individual is much more selective in the attitudes and actions he takes over from the other person. What is at stake is not his basic sense of identity or the stability of his self-concept, but rather his more limited "professional identity."

The self-defining relationship that an individual tries to establish or maintain through identification may also take the form of a reciprocal role relationship—that is, of a relationship in which the roles of the two parties are defined with reference to one another. An individual may be involved in a reciprocal relationship with another specific individual, as in a friendship relationship between two people. Or he may enact a social role which is defined with reference to another (reciprocal) role, as in the relationship between patient and doctor. A reciprocal-role relationship can be maintained only if the participants have mutually shared expectations of one another's behavior. Thus, if an individual finds a particular relationship satisfying, he will tend to behave in such a way as to meet the expectations of the other. In other words, he will tend to behave in line with the requirements of this particular relationship. This should be true regardless of whether the other is watching or not: quite apart from the reactions of the other, it is important to the individual's own self-concept to meet the expectations of his friendship role, for example, or those of his occupational role.

Thus, the acceptance of influence through identification should take place when the person sees the induced behavior as relevant to and required by a reciprocal-role relationship in which he is a participant. Acceptance of influence based on a reciprocal-role relationship is similar to that involved in classical identification in that it is a way of establishing or maintaining a satisfying self-defining relationship to another. The nature of the relationship differs, of course. In one case it is a relationship of identity; in the other, one of reciprocity. In the case of reciprocal-role relationships, the individual is not identifying with the other in the sense of taking over *his* identity, but in the sense of empathically reacting in terms of the other person's expectations, feelings, or needs.

Identification may also serve to maintain an individual's relationship to a group in which his self-definition is anchored. Such a relationship may have elements of classical identification as well as of reciprocal roles: to maintain his self-definition as a group member an individual, typically, has to model his behavior along particular lines and has to meet the expectations of his fellow members. An example of identification with a group would be the member of the Communist Party who derives strength and a sense of identity from his self-definition as part of the vanguard of the proletarian revolution and as an agent of historical destiny. A similar process, but at a low degree of intensity, is probably involved in many of the conventions that people acquire as part of their socialization into a particular group.

Identification is similar to compliance in that the individual does not adopt the induced behavior because its content per se is intrinsically satisfying. Identification differs from compliance, however, in that the individual actually believes in the opinions and actions that he adopts. The behavior is accepted both publicly and privately, and its manifestation does not depend on observability by the influencing agent. It does depend, however, on the role that an individual takes at any given moment in time. Only when the appropriate role is activated—only when the individual is acting within the relationship upon which the identification is based—will the induced opinions be expressed. The individual is not primarily concerned with pleasing the other, with giving him what he wants (as in compliance), but he is concerned

with meeting the other's expectations for his own role performance. Thus, opinions adopted through identification do remain tied to the external source and dependent on social support. They are not integrated with the individual's value system, but rather tend to be isolated from the rest of his values—to remain encapsulated.

Finally, *internalization* can be said to occur when an individual accepts influence because the induced behavior is congruent with his value system. It is the content of the induced behavior that is intrinsically rewarding here. The individual adopts it because he finds it useful for the solution of a problem, or because it is congenial to his own orientation, or because it is demanded by his own values—in short, because he perceives it as inherently conducive to the maximization of his values. The characteristics of the influencing agent do play an important role in internalization, but the crucial dimension here—as we shall see below—is the agent's credibility, that is, his relation to the content.

The most obvious examples of internalization are those that involve the evaluation and acceptance of induced behavior on rational grounds. A person may adopt the recommendations of an expert, for example, because he finds them relevant to his own problems and congruent with his own values. Typically, when internalization is involved, he will not accept these recommendations *in toto* but modify them to some degree so that they will fit his own unique situation. Or a visitor to a foreign country may be challenged by the different patterns of behavior to which he is exposed, and he may decide to adopt them (again, selectively and in modified form) because he finds them more in keeping with his own values than the patterns in his home country. I am not implying, of course, that internalization is always involved in the situations mentioned. One would speak of internalization only if acceptance of influence took the particular form that I described.

Internalization, however, does not necessarily involve the adoption of induced behavior on rational grounds. I would not want to equate internalization with rationality, even though the description of the process has decidedly rationalist overtones. For example, I would characterize as internalization the adoption of beliefs because of their congruence with a value system that is basically *irrational*. Thus, an authoritarian individual may adopt certain racist attitudes because they fit into his paranoid, irrational view of the world. Presumably, what is involved here is internalization, since it is the content of the induced behavior and its relation to the person's value system that is satisfying. Similarly, it should be noted that congruence with a person's value system does not necessarily imply logical consistency. Behavior would be congruent if, in some way or other, it fit into the person's value system, if it seemed to belong there and be demanded by it.

It follows from this conception that behavior adopted through internalization is in some way—rational or otherwise—integrated with the individual's existing values. It becomes part of a personal system, as distinguished from a system of social-role expectations. Such behavior gradually becomes independent of the external source. Its manifestation depends neither on observability by the influencing agent nor on the activation of the relevant role, but on the extent to which the underlying values have been made relevant by the issues under consideration. This does not mean that the individual will invariably express internalized opinions, regardless of the social situation. In any specific situation, he has to choose among competing values in the face of a variety of situational requirements. It does mean, however, that these opinions will at least enter into competition with other alternatives whenever they are relevant in content.

It should be stressed that the three processes are not mutually exclusive. While they have been defined in terms of pure cases, they do not generally occur in pure form in real-life situations. The examples that have been given are, at best, situations in which a particular process predominates and determines the central features of the interaction.

Antecedents and consequents of the three processes

For each of the three processes, a distinct set of antecedents and a distinct set of consequents have been proposed. These are summarized in the table below. First, with respect to the antecedents of the three processes, it should be noted that no systematic quantitative differences between them are hypothesized. The probability of each process is presented as a function of the same three determinants: the importance of the induction for the individual's goal achievement, the power of the influencing agent, and the prepotency of the induced response. For each process, the magnitude of these determinants may vary over the entire range: each may be based on an induction with varying degrees of importance, on an influencing agent with varying degrees of power, and so on. The processes differ only in terms of the *qualitative* form that these determinants take. They differ, as can be seen in the table, in terms of the *basis* for the importance of the induction, the *source* of the influencing agent's power, and the *manner* of achieving prepotency of the induced response.

1. The processes can be distinguished in terms of the basis for the importance of the induction, that is, in terms of the nature of the motivational system that is activated in the influence situation. What is it about the influence situation that makes it important, that makes it relevant to the individual's goals? What are the primary concerns that the individual brings to the situation or that are aroused by it? The

differences between the three processes in this respect are implicit in the descriptions of the processes given above: (a) To the extent that the individual is concerned—for whatever reason—with the *social effect* of his behavior, influence will tend to take the form of compliance. (b) To the extent that he is concerned with the *social anchorage* of his behavior, influence will tend to take the form of identification. (c) To the extent that he is concerned with the *value congruence* of his behavior (rational or otherwise), influence will tend to take the form of internalization.

2. A difference between the three processes in terms of the source of the influencing agent's power is hypothesized. (a) To the extent that the agent's power is based on his *means control*,

SUMMARY OF THE DISTINCTIONS BETWEEN THE THREE PROCESSES

	COMPLIANCE	IDENTIFICATION	INTERNALIZATION
ANTECEDENTS:			
1. Basis for the *importance of the induction*	Concern with social effect of behavior	Concern with social anchorage of behavior	Concern with value congruence of behavior
2. Source of *power of the influencing agent*	Means control	Attractiveness	Credibility
3. Manner of achieving *prepotency of the induced response*	Limitation of choice behavior	Delineation of role requirements	Reorganization of means-ends framework
CONSEQUENTS:			
1. Conditions of performance of induced response	Surveillance by influencing agent	Salience of relationship to agent	Relevance of values to issue
2. Conditions of change and extinction of induced response	Changed perception of conditions for social rewards	Changed perception of conditions for satisfying self-defining relationships	Changed perception of conditions for value maximization
3. Type of behavior system in which induced response is embedded	External demands of a specific setting	Expectations defining a specific role	Person's value system

influence will tend to take the form of compliance. An agent possesses means control if he is in a position to supply or withhold means needed by the individual for the achievement of his goals. The perception of means control may depend on the agent's *actual* control over specific rewards and punishments, or on his *potential* control, which would be related to his position in the social structure (his status, authority, or general prestige). (b) To the extent that the agent's power is based on his *attractiveness*, influence will tend to take the form of identification. An agent is attractive if he occupies a role which the individual himself desires (see Whiting, 1959) or if he occupies a role reciprocal to one the individual wants to establish or maintain. The term "attractiveness," as used here, does not refer to the possession of qualities that make a person likable, but rather to the possession of qualities on the part of the agent that make a continued relationship to him particularly desirable. In other words, an agent is attractive when the individual is able to derive satisfaction from a self-definition with reference to him. (c) To the extent that the agent's power is based on his *credibility*, influence will tend to take the form of internalization. An agent possesses credibility if his statements are considered truthful and valid, and hence worthy of serious consideration. Hovland, Janis, and Kelley (1953, p. 21) distinguish two bases for credibility: expertness and trustworthiness. In other words, an agent may be perceived as possessing credibility because he is likely to *know* the truth, or because he is likely to *tell* the truth. Trustworthiness, in turn, may be related to over-all respect, likemindedness, and lack of vested interest.

3. It is proposed that the three processes differ in terms of the way in which prepotency is achieved. (a) To the extent that the induced response becomes prepotent—that is, becomes a "distinguished path" relative to alternative response possibilities—because the individual's choice behavior is limited, influence will tend to take the form of compliance. This may happen if the individual is pressured into the induced response, or if alternative responses are blocked. The induced response thus becomes prepotent because it is, essentially, the only response permitted: the individual sees himself as having no choice and as being restricted to this particular alternative. (b) To the extent that the induced response becomes prepotent because the requirements of a particular role are delineated, influence will tend to take the form of identification. This may happen if the situation is defined in terms of a particular role relationship and the demands of that role are more or less clearly specified; for instance, if this role is made especially salient and the expectations deriving from it dominate the field. Or it may happen if alternative roles are made ineffective because the situation is ambiguous and consensual validation is lacking. The induced response thus becomes prepotent because it is one of the few alternatives available to the individual: his choice behavior may be unrestricted, but his opportunity for selecting alternative responses is limited by the fact that he is operating exclusively from the point of view of a particular role system. (c) Finally, to the extent that the induced response becomes prepotent because there has been a reorganization in the individual's conception of means-ends relationships, influence will tend to take the form of

internalization. This may happen if the implications of the induced response for certain important values—implications of which the individual had been unaware heretofore—are brought out, or if the advantages of the induced response as a path to the individual's goals, compared to the various alternatives that are available, are made apparent. The induced response thus becomes prepotent because it has taken on a new meaning: as the relationships between various means and ends become restructured, it emerges as the preferred course of action in terms of the person's own values.

Depending, then, on the nature of these three antecedents, the influence process will take the form of compliance, identification, or internalization. Each of these corresponds to a characteristic pattern of internal responses—thoughts and feelings—in which the individual engages as he accepts influence. The resulting changes will, in turn, be different for the three processes, as indicated in the second half of the table. Here, again, it is assumed that there are no systematic quantitative differences between the processes, but rather qualitative variations in the subsequent histories of behavior adopted through each process.

1. It is proposed that the processes differ in terms of the subsequent conditions under which the induced response will be performed or expressed. (a) When an individual adopts an induced response through compliance, he tends to perform it only under conditions of *surveillance* by the influencing agent. These conditions are met if the agent is physically present, or if he is likely to find out about the individual's actions. (b) When an individual adopts an induced response through identification,

he tends to perform it only under conditions of *salience* of his relationship to the agent. That is, the occurrence of the behavior will depend on the extent to which the person's relationship to the agent has been engaged in the situation. Somehow this relationship has to be brought into focus and the individual has to be acting within the particular role that is involved in the identification. This does not necessarily mean, however, that he is consciously aware of the relationship; the role can be activated without such awareness. (c) When an individual adopts an induced response through internalization, he tends to perform it under conditions of *relevance of the values* that were initially involved in the influence situation. The behavior will tend to occur whenever these values are activated by the issues under consideration in a given situation, quite regardless of surveillance or salience of the influencing agent. This does not mean, of course, that the behavior will occur every time it becomes relevant. It may be out-competed by other responses in certain situations. The probability of occurrence with a given degree of issue relevance will depend on the strength of the internalized behavior.

2. It is hypothesized that responses adoped through the three processes will differ in terms of the conditions under which they will subsequently be abandoned or changed. (a) A response adopted through compliance will be abandoned if it is no longer perceived as the best path toward the attainment of social rewards. (b) A response adopted through identification will be abandoned if it is no longer perceived as the best path toward the maintenance or establishment of satisfying self-defining relationships. (c) A response

adopted through internalization will be abandoned if it is no longer perceived as the best path toward the maximization of the individual's values.

3. Finally, it is hypothesized that responses adopted through the three processes will differ from each other along certain qualitative dimensions. These can best be summarized, perhaps, by referring to the type of behavior system in which the induced response is embedded. (a) Behavior adopted through compliance is part of a system of external demands that characterize a specific setting. In other words, it is part of the rules of conduct that an individual learns in order to get along in a particular situation or series of situations. The behavior tends to be related to the person's values only in an instrumental rather than an intrinsic way. As long as opinions, for example, remain at that level, the individual will tend to regard them as not really representative of his true beliefs. (b) Behavior adopted through identification is part of a system of expectations defining a particular role—whether this is the role of the other which he is taking over, or a role reciprocal to the other's. This behavior will be regarded by the person as representing himself, and may in fact form an important aspect of himself. It will tend to be isolated, however, from the rest of the person's values—to have little interplay with them. In extreme cases, the system in which the induced response is embedded may be encapsulated and function almost like a foreign body within the person. The induced responses here will be relatively inflexible and stereotyped. (c) Behavior adopted through internalization is part of an internal system. It is fitted into the person's basic framework of values and is congruent with it. This does not imply complete consistency: the degree of consistency can vary for different individuals and different areas of behavior. It does mean, however, that there is some interplay between the new beliefs and the rest of the person's values. The new behavior can serve to modify existing beliefs and can in turn be modified by them. As a result of this interaction, behavior adopted through internalization will tend to be relatively idiosyncratic, flexible, complex, and differentiated.

43 Outsiders

HOWARD S. BECKER

All social groups make rules and attempt, at some times and under some circumstances, to enforce them. Social rules define situations and the kinds of behavior appropriate to them, specifying some actions as "right" and forbidding others as "wrong." When a rule is enforced, the person who is supposed to have broken it may be seen as a special kind of person, one who cannot be trusted to live by the rules agreed on by the group. He is regarded as an *outsider*.

The outsider—the deviant from group rules—has been the subject of much speculation, theorizing, and scientific study. What laymen want to know about deviants is: why do they do it? How can we account for their rule-breaking? What is there about them that leads them to do forbidden things? Scientific research has tried to find answers to these questions. In doing so it has accepted the common-sense premise that there is something inherently deviant (qualitatively distinct) about acts that break (or seem to break) social rules. It has also accepted the common-sense assumption that the deviant act occurs because some characteristic of the person who commits it makes it necessary or inevitable that he should. Scientists do not ordinarily question the label "deviant" when it is applied to particular acts or people but rather take it as given. In so doing, they accept the values of the group making the judgment.

It is easily observable that different groups judge different things to be deviant. This should alert us to the possibility that the person making the judgment of deviance, the process by which that judgment is arrived at, and the situation in which it is made may all be intimately involved in the phenomenon of deviance. To the degree that the common-sense view of deviance and the scientific theories that begin with its premises assume that acts that break rules are inherently deviant and thus take for granted the situations and processes of judgment, they may leave out an important variable.

Another, sociological view is more relativistic. It identifies deviance as the failure to obey group rules. Once we have described the rules a group enforces on its members, we can say with some precision whether or not a person has violated them and is thus, on this view, deviant.

This view is closest to my own, but it fails to give sufficient weight to the ambiguities that arise in deciding which rules are to be taken as the yardstick against which behavior is measured and judged deviant. A society has many groups, each with its own set of rules, and people belong to many groups simultaneously. A person may break the rules of one group by the very act of abiding by the rules of another group. Is he, then, deviant? Proponents of this definition may object that while ambiguity may arise with respect to the rules peculiar to one or another group in society, there are some rules that are very generally agreed to by everyone, in which case the difficulty does not arise. This, of course, is a question of fact, to be settled by empirical research. I doubt there are many such areas of consensus and think it wiser to use a definition that allows us to deal with both ambiguous and unambiguous situations.

Deviance and the responses of others

The sociological view I have just discussed defines deviance as the infraction of some agreed-upon rule. It then goes on to ask who breaks rules, and to search for the factors in their personalities and life situations that might account for the infractions. This assumes that those who have broken a rule constitute a homogeneous category, because they have committed the same deviant act.

Such an assumption seems to me to ignore the central fact about deviance: it is created by society. I do not mean this in the way it is ordinarily understood, in which the causes of deviance are located in the social situation of the deviant or in "social factors" which prompt his action. I mean, rather, that *social groups create deviance by making the rules whose infraction constitutes deviance*, and by applying those rules to particular people and labeling them as outsiders. From this point of view, deviance is *not* a quality of the act the person commits, but rather a consequence of the application by others of rules and sanctions to an "offender."

The deviant is one to whom that label has successfully been applied; deviant behavior is behavior that people so label.[1]

Since deviance is, among other things, a consequence of the responses of others to a person's act, students of deviance cannot assume that they are dealing with a homogeneous category when they study people who have been labeled deviant. That is, they cannot assume that these people have actually committed a deviant act or broken some rule, because the process of labeling may not be infallible; some people may be labeled deviant who in fact have not broken a rule. Furthermore, they cannot assume that the category of those labeled deviant will contain all those who actually have broken a rule, for many offenders may escape apprehension and thus fail to be included in the population of "deviants" they study. Insofar as the category lacks homogeneity and fails to include all the cases that belong in it, one cannot reasonably expect to find common factors of personality or life situation that will account for the supposed deviance.

What, then, do people who have been labeled deviant have in common? At the least, they share the label and the experience of being labeled as outsiders. I will begin my analysis with this basic similarity and view deviance as the product of a transaction that takes place between some social group and one who is viewed by that group as a rule-breaker. I will be less concerned with the personal and social characteristics of deviants than with the process by which they come to

---

[1] The most important earlier statements of this view can be found in Tannenbaum (1951), and Lemert (1951). An article stating a position very similar to mine is Kitsuse (1962).

be thought of as outsiders and their reactions to that judgment.

The degree to which other people will respond to a given act as deviant varies greatly. Several kinds of variation seem worth noting. First of all, there is variation over time. A person believed to have committed a given "deviant" act may at one time be responded to much more leniently than he would be at some other time. The occurrence of "drives" against various kinds of deviance illustrates this clearly. At various times, enforcement officials may decide to make an all-out attack on some particular kind of deviance, such as gambling, drug addiction, or homosexuality. It is obviously much more dangerous to engage in one of these activities when a drive is on than at any other time. (In a very interesting study of crime news in Colorado newspapers, Davis (1952) found that the amount of crime reported in Colorado newspapers showed very little association with actual changes in the amount of crime taking place in Colorado. And, further, that peoples' estimate of how much increase there had been in crime in Colorado was associated with the increase in the amount of crime news but not with any increase in the amount of crime.)

The degree to which an act will be treated as deviant depends also on who commits the act and who feels he has been harmed by it. Rules tend to be applied more to some persons than others. Studies of juvenile delinquency make the point clearly. Boys from middle-class areas do not get as far in the legal process when they are apprehended as do boys from slum areas. The middle-class boy is less likely, when picked up by the police, to be taken to the station; less likely when taken to the station to be booked; and it is extremely unlikely that

he will be convicted and sentenced (see Cohen & Short, 1961). This variation occurs even though the original infraction of the rule is the same in the two cases. Similarly, the law is differentially applied to Negroes and whites. It is well known that a Negro believed to have attacked a white woman is much more likely to be punished than a white man who commits the same offense; it is only slightly less well known that a Negro who murders another Negro is much less likely to be punished than a white man who commits murder (see Garfinkel, 1949). This, of course, is one of the main points of Sutherland's analysis of white-collar crime: crimes committed by corporations are almost always prosecuted as civil cases, but the same crime committed by an individual is ordinarily treated as a criminal offense (Sutherland, 1940).

Some rules are enforced only when they result in certain consequences. The unmarried mother furnishes a clear example. Vincent (1961) points out that illicit sexual relations seldom result in severe punishment or social censure for the offenders. If, however, a girl becomes pregnant as a result of such activities the reaction of others is likely to be severe. (The illicit pregnancy is also an interesting example of the differential enforcement of rules on different categories of people. Vincent notes that unmarried fathers escape the severe censure visited on the mother.)

Why repeat these commonplace observations? Because, taken together, they support the proposition that deviance is not a simple quality, present in some kinds of behavior and absent in others. Rather, it is the product of a process which involves responses of other people to the behavior. The same behavior may be an infraction of the rules at one time and not at another; may be an infraction when committed by one person, but not when committed by another; some rules are broken with impunity, others are not. In short, whether a given act is deviant or not depends in part on the nature of the act (that is, whether or not it violates some rule) and in part on what other people do about it.

Some people may object that this is merely a terminological quibble, that one can, after all, define terms any way he wants to and that if some people want to speak of rule-breaking behavior as deviant without reference to the reactions of others they are free to do so. This, of course, is true. Yet it might be worthwhile to refer to such behavior as *rule-breaking behavior* and reserve the term *deviant* for those labeled as deviant by some segment of society. I do not insist that this usage be followed. But it should be clear that insofar as a scientist uses "deviant" to refer to any rule-breaking behavior and takes as his subject of study only those who have been *labeled* deviant, he will be hampered by the disparities between the two categories.

If we take as the object of our attention behavior which comes to be labeled as deviant, we must recognize that we cannot know whether a given act will be categorized as deviant until the response of others has occurred. Deviance is not a quality that lies in behavior itself, but in the interaction between the person who commits an act and those who respond to it.

Whose rules?

I have been using the term "outsiders" to refer to those people who are judged by others to be deviant and thus to stand outside the circle of "normal" members of the group. But the term contains a second meaning, whose analysis leads to another important set of sociological problems: "outsiders," from the point of view of the person who is labeled deviant, may be the people who make the rules he had been found guilty of breaking.

Social rules are the creation of specific social groups. Modern societies are not simple organizations in which everyone agrees on what the rules are and how they are to be applied in specific situations. They are, instead, highly differentiated along social class lines, ethnic lines, occupational lines, and cultural lines. These groups need not and, in fact, often do not share the same rules. The problems they face in dealing with their environment, the history and traditions they carry with them, all lead to the evolution of different sets of rules. Insofar as the rules of various groups conflict and contradict one another, there will be disagreement about the kind of behavior that is proper in any given situation.

Italian immigrants who went on making wine for themselves and their friends during Prohibition were acting properly by Italian immigrant standards, but were breaking the law of their new country (as, of course, were many of their Old American neighbors). Medical patients who shop around for a doctor may, from the perspective of their own group, be doing what is necessary to protect their health by making sure they get what seems to them the best possible doctor; but, from the perspective of the physician, what they do is wrong because it breaks down the trust the patient ought to put in his physician. The lower-class delinquent who fights for his "turf" is only doing what he considers necessary and right, but teachers, social workers, and police see it differently.

While it may be argued that many or most rules are generally agreed to by all members of a society, empirical research on a given rule generally reveals variation in people's attitudes. Formal rules, enforced by some specially constituted group, may differ from those actually thought appropriate by most people (Rose & Prell, 1955). Factions in a group may disagree on what I have called actual operating rules. Most important for the study of behavior ordinarily labeled deviant, the perspectives of the people who engage in the behavior are likely to be quite different from those of the people who condemn it. In this latter situation, a person may feel that he is being judged according to rules he has had no hand in making and does not accept, rules forced on him by outsiders.

To what extent and under what circumstances do people attempt to force their rules on others who do not subscribe to them? Let us distinguish two cases. In the first, only those who are actually members of the group have any interest in making and enforcing certain rules. If an orthodox Jew disobeys the laws of kashruth only other orthodox Jews will regard this as a transgression; Christians or nonorthodox Jews will not consider this deviance and would have no interest in interfering. In the second case, members of a group consider it important to their welfare that members of certain other groups obey certain rules. Thus, people consider it extremely important that those who practice the healing arts abide by certain rules; this is the reason the state licenses physicians, nurses, and others, and forbids anyone who is not licensed to engage in healing activities.

To the extent that a group tries to impose its rules on other groups in the society, we are presented with a second question: Who can, in fact, force others to accept their rules and what are the causes of their success? This is, of course, a question of political and economic power. Later we consider the political and economic process through which rules are created and enforced. Here it is enough to note that people are in fact always *forcing* their rules on others, applying them more or less against the will and without the consent of those others. By and large, for example, rules are made for young people by their elders. Though the youth of this country exert a powerful influence culturally—the mass media of communication are tailored to their interests, for instance—many important kinds of rules are made for our youth by adults. Rules regarding school attendance and sex behavior are not drawn up with regard to the problems of adolescence. Rather, adolescents find themselves surrounded by rules about these matters which have been made by older and more settled people. It is considered legitimate to do this, for youngsters are considered neither wise enough nor responsible enough to make proper rules for themselves.

In the same way, it is true in many respects that men make the rules for women in our society (though in America this is changing rapidly). Negroes find themselves subject to rules made for them by whites. The foreign-born and those otherwise ethnically peculiar often have their rules made for them by the Protestant Anglo-Saxon minority. The middle class makes rules the lower class must obey—in the schools, the courts, and elsewhere.

Differences in the ability to make rules and apply them to other people are essentially power differentials (either legal or extralegal). Those groups whose social position gives them weapons and power are best able to enforce their rules. Distinctions of age, sex, ethnicity, and class are all related to differences in power, which accounts for differences in the degree to which groups so distinguished can make rules for others.

In addition to recognizing that deviance is created by the responses of people to particular kinds of behavior, by the labeling of that behavior as deviant, we must also keep in mind that the rules created and maintained by such labeling are not universally agreed to. Instead, they are the object of conflict and disagreement, part of the political process of society.

44   Some current issues in the psychology of conformity and nonconformity

EDWIN P. HOLLANDER and RICHARD H. WILLIS

When Thoreau voiced the suspicion that the apparent nonconformer was merely marching to a more distant drummer, he provided an insight which has been rather surprisingly disregarded in much of the contemporary research on conformity. Cooley (1922), pursuing the same point, asserted that there is no definite line between conformity and nonconformity, and that both should be considered together as normal and complementary phases of human activity.

Despite these long-standing and astute observations, the dominant focus of most current research on social influence has been to ascertain what can be systematically shown to occasion conforming behavior. Nonconformity is typically ignored or at least not considered conscientiously. What makes this a curious emphasis is that conformity is usually the modal response. Hence, this work tells us less than it might about individual differences in reactions to social pressures. Introducing conditions favoring the possibility of nonconformity, by contrast, can reveal a good deal more about the idiosyncratic patterning of responses that we are accustomed to terming "personality," for quite often there are several ways in which one can not conform but only one way of conforming.

Slightly abridged from the **Psychological Bulletin**, 68, 62–76 (Copyright © 1967 by the American Psychological Association), with permission of the authors and the publisher.

An overview

The essential task of this paper is to redress this present imbalance in research on conformity and nonconformity, and to explicate several concepts and distinctions which clarify certain basic features of such research. In documenting the importance of these concepts and distinctions here, we cite a rather large number of studies. However, these citations are illustrative, rather than exhaustive, of what is a considerable literature.

In this connection, it should be noted that although the literature on conformity and closely related topics has reached Brobdingnagian proportions (cf., e.g., Allen, 1965; Berg & Bass, 1961; Graham, 1962; Willis, 1961), it remains disparate in many of its implications. Mann (1959), for example, reported a marked degree of inconsistency concerning the relationship between stable attributes of personality and conformity in the 27 studies he surveyed. Conformity was found to be a positive function of certain personality variables in some of these studies and uncorrelated or a negative function of these same variables in other studies. This strongly suggests the desirability of reexamining most carefully the differential meaning of "conformity" and "noncomformity" as they are currently conceptualized, and as they have been operationalized in psychological research.

Throughout most of this paper we are concerned with conformity-nonconformity as social *response*—that is, we focus on the actor. Toward the latter part of the paper, in the discussion of the assumption of norm homogeneity, we move to a concern with conformity-nonconformity as social *stimulus*. That is, we consider how the actor is perceived by others.

Levels of analysis

Part of the difficulty associated with the study of social influence resides in a confusion of levels of analysis and in definitions. Just as with other categories of response, conformity and nonconformity can be approached on either of two levels—the *descriptive*, and the *inferential* or explanatory. The first deals with manifest behavior, and research at this level studies overt conformity in terms of antecedent situational conditions and personality characteristics. The second deals with the underlying psychological states and processes affecting such overt responses differentially. The descriptive level is exemplified, within conformity research, by Floyd Allport (1934) when he formulated his J curve hypothesis (but not when he accounted for it in psychological terms), or by Solomon Asch (1951, 1956) when he investigated the conformity of a minority of one as a function of various situational parameters (but not when he classified his subjects according to predominant motives, feelings, and cognitions). Examples of recent inferential analysis of social influence processes are Katz, Sarnoff, and McClintock (1956), Kelman (1958, 1961), French and Raven (1959), and Raven (1965). The inferences drawn by these writers relate primarily to the motivational bases of social influence and power.

Operational definitions are employed at the descriptive level, while conceptual definitions are required at the level of explanation. Description is logically prior to explanation in that an adequate scheme for observing and categorizing is usually necessary before a range of phenomena becomes well understood. At the same time, conceptual definitions are logically prior to operational ones in that the latter are customarily suggested by the former. There exists, therefore, a mutual interdependence between the two levels of analysis, and refinements at either level can be expected to facilitate progress at the other. In the remainder of this paper, we consider, first, the analysis of conformity and its alternatives at the descriptive level, turning subsequently to more inferential or psychological aspects of the topic.

Operational definitions of conformity have often been based on observations of a single instance of behavior under such situational variations as ambiguity or nonambiguity of stimuli, or the presence or absence of status differentials between an influence source and recipient. It has also been measured by personality inventories and attitude scales. For the most part, however, conformity is operationally defined in experimental work as essentially a *change* in behavior in the direction of greater agreement with the evident behavior of the other group members. This is conformity in the sense of manifest convergence.

The problem, of course, is that this manifestation of change is not in itself indicative of specifiable underlying changes, for example, in terms of motivation. Indeed, there is need to scrutinize the widespread assumption that conformity in the descriptive sense reflects a motivational intent. Such an assumption appears unwarranted on several grounds. First, an individual may choose to do as others do without being dependent upon their standard in any persisting sense. Second, motivation to conform may be consequent upon a desire to participate in a group activity, not upon seeking approval from others. Third, in the absence of accurate perception of social demands a person could behave in line with a social standard without being motivated to do so. And fourth, apparent conformity may be due to similarity of non-social circumstances, as when one puts on a coat when going out, not because others do so, but because it is cold. If, in this last case, the similar responses have been independently learned, then the phenomenon can be referred to as *coenotropic* behavior (Young, 1956, p. 49).

Without undue formality, we therefore favor for its clarity a conceptual or psychological definition of conformity as behavior *intended* to fulfill normative group expectancies as presently *perceived* by the individual (cf. Hollander, 1959; Willis, 1965a). Thus, we would exclude incidental fulfillment of norms which, descriptively, quality as conformity. In the next section, we consider two descriptive criteria of conformity-nonconformity, congruence and movement, from which a variety of operational definitions can be derived; but for a psychological view of conformity, it is necessary to formulate a definition in terms of motivation and perception-cognition, as the one just given.

Descriptive criteria

Contemporary treatments of conformity usually fail to take account of the kind of distinction illustrated in Halla Beloff's (1958) contrasting of *conventionality* and *acquiescence* as modes of social response. The former is operationally defined as high *agreement* between an individual's response and the mean or modal response of his group or class, while the latter is operationally defined as the amount of *shift* from private to public opinion. Beloff comes as close as anyone known to us to making an explicit distinction between the two basic descriptive criteria of conformity-non-

conformity that have been formally analyzed by Willis (1964) and labeled
congruence and movement. At the
purely descriptive level, the congruence
criterion requires that conformity (or
nonconformity) be measured in terms
of the extent of agreement between a
given response and the normative ideal.
The movement criterion dictates the
measurement of conformity (positive or
negative) in terms of a change in response resulting in a greater or lesser
degree of congruence.

When these two aspects of social response are not conscienciously differentiated, paradoxes can result. This may be
readily shown in the recent work of
Walker and Heyns (1962) in which
conformity was quite explicitly defined
in terms of, and only in terms of, movement: "Let us define conformity as
movement toward some norm or standard and nonconformity as movement
away from such a norm or standard
[p. 5]."

The implication of this definition,
standing alone as it does, is clearly that
an individual complying fully with the
norm or standard from the beginning
cannot be considered to reveal conformity. Walker and Heyns evidently con-
templated this dilemma, since later on
the same page they stated, "To describe
a person or a group as conformist on the
basis of a single observation implies an
earlier state in which the degree of
agreement with the norm was not so
great." This would mean that an individual who had moved only slightly from
a position of extreme nonconformity
would be considered more conforming
than one who had from the outset
matched the norm.

It becomes apparent, then, that congruence conformity and the potential
for movement conformity are actually
perfectly and inversely related! The mixing of these two aspects of conformity,
or the failure to recognize one or the
other, doubtless explains much of the
confusion encountered in attempts to
understand the workings of "conformity" at the global level. For purposes of
understanding, it is accordingly essential
to maintain a strict distinction between
these inversely related aspects of conformity.

At a somewhat more psychological
level, a roughly analogous distinction
can be made between habituation to
past social demands which have some
continuity in the present, as exemplified
by musical preferences and aversions
(Beloff's "conventionality," the congruence criterion), or a reaction to an
immediate influence, as exemplified by
compliance with a request to leave the
room (Beloff's "acquiescence," the movement criterion).

Unidimensional approaches

Another inadequacy in the customary
view of response to social influence is
the tendency to cast it into a single dimension of response, with perfect conformity at one end and perfect something else, usually nonconformity or
independence, at the other. Instructive
in this connection is an observation
made by DeSoto (1961) in reporting on
his work on the predilection for single
orderings: "In the theorizings of social
scientists about society and culture [this
predilection] shows up as a stubborn
urge somehow to reduce discrepant
orderings of people, or classes, or cultures, to single orderings [p. 22]."

These unidimensional approaches
give rise to the classical bipolar conception of conformity-nonconformity, such
as the J curve formulation of Floyd All-

port (1934); or to the conformity-independence variant, seen in the work of Asch (1951, 1956), Marie Jahoda (1959), and many others. Throughout the literature on social influence, one sees a view of perfect conformity as an exact matching of one and only one group-approved position along the response continuum, which stands in contrast to an opposite response location, viewed either as nonconformity or independence. Although Walker and Heyns (1962) constitute an exception, there appears to be some tendency for those adopting the nonconformity contrast to think of conformity as *being* like others, while those employing the independence contrast typically view conformity as *becoming* more like others. Clearly, the first formulation is appropriately addressed to the congruence criterion, whereas the second applies to movement.

In what follows, we are concerned primarily with the movement criterion, the one customarily employed in experimental social psychology, particularly in studies of convergence. Nonetheless, we wish to stress our belief that, ultimately, both criteria must be rigorously analyzed, thoroughly investigated empirically, and fully interrelated with one another.

Bearing in mind specifically the movement criterion, consider the hypothetical case of an individual who consistently responds negatively to any and all social pressures. Where can he be located along the conformity-independence dimension? Obviously he is not a conformist, but, equally apparent, he cannot be considered independent. Nor can he be placed at any intermediate position. Actually, he is maximally dependent, since his behavior is highly predictable from a knowledge of the social pressures to which he is exposed, but

at the same time he is minimally conforming. There is no place for this "anticonformist" and yet a place must be provided—not because such perfect anticonformists are known to exist, but because there is no logical reason that one could not exist, and also because such negativistic behavior tendencies have often been observed in more attenuated form. It can be shown that a two-dimensional model of social response is capable of resolving this dilemma.

A two-dimensional approach

A two-dimensional model of social response, applying to the movement criterion and to binary judgments, has recently been suggested by Willis (1963) and adapted in research by Willis and Hollander (1964a) and Hollander and Willis (1964). This model stipulates two dimensions of response, the first of which is dependence-independence, or merely *independence*. The second is conformity-anticonformity, or *net conformity*. These are orthogonal of one another, not in the sense of being uncorrelated (the extent of the correlation being an empirical matter and varying from situation to situation), but rather in the same sense that one plots two such obviously correlated variables as height and weight against orthogonal coordinates. In the initial conception of the model, the response space, which defines the limits of possible patterns of responding over trials, is an isosceles triangle with vertices labeled Conformity and Anticonformity along the net conformity dimension, and Independence, at the vertex formed by the conjunction of the two equal sides. These vertices represent three basic modes of responding to social pressure, defined descriptively (operationally) as follows:

Pure conformity. Viewed relative to the movement criterion, this consists of maximal and completely consistent movement in the direction of greater congruence. This descriptive definition stands in contrast to the conceptual definition of conformity given earlier.

Pure independence. This behavior is describable within the triangular model as a total lack of movement from pre-exposure to postexposure responses. In psychological terms, such behavior would occur when (but not only when) the individual perceives relevant normative expectancies, but does not rely upon them as guides to his behavior.

Pure anticonformity. This corresponds to movement that is maximal and completely consistent (like pure conformity), but in the direction of *lesser* congruence. Also like conformity, anticonformity implies dependence upon the normative expectancies, but of a negative kind.

Crutchfield has conceived of conformity and its alternatives in similar terms. Although he usually speaks of counterformity rather than anticonformity, essentially the same three modes of responding are considered to be interrelated as the vertices of a triangle (Krech, Crutchfield, & Ballachey, 1962, pp. 506–507). Crutchfield and his associates have not embarked upon experimentation on counterformity behavior, but he has discussed some of the personality characteristics of "the counterforming personality" (Crutchfield, 1962, 1963).

Our own experimentation deriving from the Willis triangular model has revealed significant differences both in the factors producing the various modes of response and in the reactions each has elicited from observers. As a demonstration of the variables producing conformity and nonconformity of both the independence and anticonforming varieties, Willis and Hollander (1964a) induced large and highly significant differences in patterns of responding among three experimental conditions in line with the three modes of this triangular model. The significance of this experiment resides in the fact that it indicates the possibility of evoking in considerable strength *all three* modes of reactions specified by this triangular model, thus supporting the two-dimensional view as more adequate than the usual unidimensional one. In this connection, it should be noted that (*a*) the conformity-independence model is a *special case* of the two-dimensional formulation, and (*b*) it is perfectly satisfactory so long as negativistic tendencies are absent, that is, so long as all movement is in the direction of greater congruence.

Another kind of support comes from an experiment by Hollander and Willis (1964) in which it was found that subjects reacted differently to independence and anticonformity on the part of partners. It follows that these two kinds of nonconformity must be distinguished, not only as modes of social *response*, but also in their differential social *stimulus* values.

A refinement of the triangular model, the diamond model, was subsequently developed. It takes account of a fourth mode of response, Variability or "Self-anticonformity" (Willis, 1965a; Willis & Hollander, 1964b). Pure variability behavior would be exhibited by a subject who *always* changes his mind from initial to subsequent judgments on each trial. It can be considered as a kind of "inverted" independence, insofar as invariable change precludes taking into account normative expectancies. That is, if a subject always changes his response in a two-choice situation, his postexposure responses are predictable from his pre-exposure responses but not from the source of social pressure defining on each trial one of the two responses as correct. Such variability behavior, except in diluted form, is probably rare. Still, a rather dramatic instance of this general kind of behavior has been reported by Aronson and Carlsmith (1962). In their experiment, and one would expect in general, variability or self-anticonformity was associated with negative, or at least very low, self-esteem.

Several experiments have now been conducted within the framework of the diamond model (Willis, 1965b, 1965c, 1966), with results demonstrating its research utility. The most detailed explication of the underlying logic, including the rationale for replacing the triangular response space with the diamond, is to be found in Willis (1965a).

This concludes our descriptive analysis of conformity and nonconformity. In the following sections we turn to a consideration of both earlier and recent conformity research in light of the foregoing but at a more psychological (i.e., inferential or explanatory) level.

Studies of movement conformity

The classic study of Muzafer Sherif (1935) provided a model for much subsequent work on group conformity. Earlier, Arthur Jenness (1932a, 1932b) had conducted experiments in which subjects judged the number of beans in a bottle, then discussed this judgment with others to arrive at a single judgment, after which each made a second set of individual judgments. Results consistently indicated convergence (i.e.,

movement) towards a group standard. Sherif employed a comparable research paradigm but used the autokinetic phenomenon as the basis for his stimulus. In the absence of physical cues to distance and with the requirement for absolute judgments, he found a marked tendency for the perceptual judgments of subjects to converge in this highly ambiguous situation.

A number of studies followed which varied the Sherif procedure, employing a variety of stimuli and tasks, all within the framework of conformity in terms of perceptual convergence (e.g., Asch, 1951, 1956; Crutchfield, 1955; Schonbar, 1945). In a related vein, the studies of Mausner (1953, 1954a), Kelman (1950), and Luchins and Luchins (1961) manipulated the reinforcement of accuracy and the alleged characteristics of a partner in order to determine their effects on the degree of movement. In general, reinforcing the subject for accuracy of his own responses leads to a decrease in conformity as measured by the convergence procedure, and the net effect, therefore, seems to be to increase independence from the partner or group. Conversely, perceptions of the other(s) as more competent or of higher status than the subject usually result in greater conformity.

Such studies highlight the importance of the immediately preceding information supporting one's own accuracy in determining nonconformity. However, the source of this supporting information appears to be critical. Hollander, Julian, and Haaland (1965) have recently demonstrated that prior agreement from *other subjects*, rather than from the experimenter, leads to higher subsequent movement conformity. Furthermore, as predicted, the pattern of conformity varied over time.

Thus, the condition with complete prior support produced more initial conformity than either of two conditions of less prior support, but the decrement in conformity over trials was also most marked for this condition.

Other studies have manipulated the credibility, prestige, or competence of the source of judgments and have found that subjects are affected by sources having these attributes more than by those who do not possess them (e.g., Croner & Willis, 1961; Gerard, 1954; Kidd & Campbell, 1955; Mausner, 1954b; Wolf, 1959). The results consistently indicate predictable situational sources of conformity and nonconformity in terms of the perception of the influence source—whether a co-worker, a group, or an experimenter.

By and large, even with its productive features, this line of investigation (i.e., the Sherif construction of conformity as perceptual convergence, and related approaches) has tended to further a view which is still in popular currency, namely, that there exists a general norm *equally applicable* to all group members. The limitations of this assumption of norm homogeneity, as we can term it, are considered in some detail in a later section. Briefly, it involves the conception of a standard of conduct as a place on a continuum where some consensus rests, and is associated historically with Floyd Allport's J curve description of conforming behavior on a collective level as an accumulation of approved responses at one end of the response continuum (Allport, 1934). A more adequate view allows the definition of conformity to vary as a function of the status of the actor (Hollander, 1958, 1959, 1960, 1961).

A second criticism that can be leveled against the traditional work on perceptual convergence is that it is heavily biased against the elicitation of nonconformity. It shares with almost all psychological experimentation the feature of very high experimenter status as measured relative to the subject. Typically, experimenters create influence assertions directed at producing movement conformity by the constructions of the situations they pose to subjects, especially through instructional sets and task materials. The demand characteristics (Orne, 1962) implicit in this subject-experimenter relationship tend to force one kind of modal response.

Milgram (1965) has recently reported an experiment closer to the substance of a real-life problem and involving a test of experimenter influence. It is illuminating in several ways. As the experimenter, he instructed subjects to administer what was falsely thought to be a painful shock to another (mock) subject. In one set of experimental conditions, two other mock subjects either agreed to administer the shock or refused to do so. He found significantly more subjects refusing to administer shock if the other "subjects" would not than he did when they were instructed to do so with no others present. What is particularly striking is that he found no significant differences in willingness to give shock between subjects run with two other compliant subjects and those run alone. The very presence of the experimenter so biased the situation in favor of compliance that results from the confederates-complying and the confederates-refusing conditions are not directly comparable.

Greater use of experimental procedures in which the experimenter is perceived by the subject as incompetent, obnoxious, vulgar, or *needlessly* cruel (a rationale was provided in the Milgram study) might reveal varieties of behavior that have been to date rarely observed in the psychological laboratory. The question of the ethics of deception, which has deservedly received much attention recently (e.g., Kelman, 1966), is bypassed here because of space limitations. We emphasize, rather, that customary experimental techniques conspire with well-channeled habits of unidimensional thinking to foster a pervasive fixation on the conformity end of the spectrum and a particular neglect of negativistic reactions.

On the more encouraging side, there appears to be increasing attention devoted to the study of *resistance* to influence, which is to say, the independence mode. In addition to the work of Asch and the Milgram experiment just noted, this tack is represented by Vaughan and Mangan (1963), Kiesler and Kiesler (1964), McGuire (1964), and McGuire and Millman (1965).

The situation and conformity

Among the situational variables that have been identified as affecting movement conformity are the ambiguity or difficulty of the stimuli; the greater status, power, or competence of the influence source; the observable unanimity of attractive others; and the general appropriateness of the act of conformity to achieving a desired goal (Asch, 1951, 1956; Blake, Helson, & Mouton, 1956; Goldberg, 1954; Jackson & Saltzstein, 1958; Mausner & Block, 1957; Thibaut & Strickland, 1956; Walker & Heyns, 1962). Further, the effects of these variables have usually been found to be enhanced by the requirement of a public response (e.g., Argyle, 1957; Gorden, 1952; Mouton, Blake, & Olmstead, 1956), although the

seemingly simple distinction between public compliance and private acceptance is in fact a complex one (Asch, 1959; Jahoda, 1959; Kiesler, 1969).

The essential thrust of this work is towards the understanding of conditions in the situation which do lead to predictably greater conformity in the sense of convergence towards a group judgment. Psychologically, all of these effects appear to be explainable in terms of a heightened willingness to accept influence as a feature of dependence (cf. Berkowitz, 1957). In this regard, Blake and Mouton (1961) have said:

conformity behavior increases when it is necessary for an individual to rely more heavily on the responses of others in making his own adjustment. Attitudes are more easily shifted than are reactions to factual or logical items, probably because attitudes are more social in character. Increasing the difficulty of items, reducing external cues which provide objective information, and increasing the strength of command in the direction of the compliant behavior all serve to increase the effectiveness of conformity pressures in shifting a person's response [p. 11].

While all of this may be demonstrably so, a question which requires additional study concerns the situational bases for *nonconformity*. Most theoretical treatments are very lopsided in this respect. French's (1956) otherwise instructive formal model of social power, for example, focuses almost exclusively on pressures towards increased consensus, with only the most oblique concern for factors affecting diversity. Zetterberg's (1957) axiomatic treatment of compliant actions also provides little consideration of motivational or situational factors which would prevent a state of perfect agreement in the long run.

There is another reason for this habitual neglect of nonconformity, over and above the constraints of the traditional experimental paradigm. It is the widespread and highly questionable assumption that the situational and motivational bases of nonconformity are identical to those of conformity, but working in reverse. Taken literally, this assumption leads to the notion that knowledge about conformity means knowledge about nonconformity. This assumption of symmetry, as it might be called, fails to take into account that there are usually multiple ways of not conforming opposed to any particular manner of conforming. Another source of asymmetry arises from the fact that in groups larger than two, perfect consensus (congruence conformity) is always possible in principle, but perfect dissensus is not.

Another entirely different kind of asymmetry that enters into social influence, and which has been very little investigated as yet, concerns the relationship between power *over* another and power to *resist* that other (Cartwright, 1959). It was found by Croner and Willis (1961) that perceptions of differential competence on a prior task within dyads resulted in significant differences in influence transmitted in each direction during a subsequent task, as would be expected, but it was also observed that task similarity was a critical factor. French (1963) has advanced the interesting idea that power to influence and power to resist will be positively correlated in the case of persuasive power but negatively correlated in the case of coercive power.

Personality and conformity

Despite some voices raised to the contrary (e.g., Crutchfield, 1955; Hovland & Janis, 1959; Tuddenham, 1959), it is increasingly clear that the search for sovereign attributes of a conforming personality have not been especially fruitful. True, for any particular situation individual differences are invariably observed, and these are often substantial, but it is also true that conformity in one situation is not generally a very reliable predictor of conformity in other situations. Although Vaughan (1964), for example, found some consistency in conformity or nonconformity for 20% of the subjects he studied across four situations, the remainder were quite clearly affected differentially by the situations in terms of the amount of conformity manifested.

Additional examples are not lacking. Weiner and McGinnies (1961) conducted a study of the relative levels of conformity by authoritarians and nonauthoritarians, finding no confirmation for their hypothesis that authoritarians conform more. Smith (1961) found no relationship between conformity and Barron's Ego-Strength Scale (Barron, 1953). Using several measures growing out of the work of Schroder and Hunt, an investigation by Wilson (1960) supported his predictions regarding personality determinants of conformity for some attitudinal stimuli, but not for a series of perceptual stimuli. These and similar studies often fall back on the necessity to look further at the characteristics of the situation, and how it is defined by the subjects, to account in principle for the apparent inconsistencies in the observed patterns of behavior. One can conform or not conform in the service of such a wide variety of personal needs and perceived instrumentalities as to permit only a very limited validity to the construct of the conforming personality.

The issue is reminiscent of the earlier

one about leadership attributes. It will be recalled that a prolonged search for the general traits of leaders was sufficiently discouraging as to produce a thoroughgoing reorientation of thought on the topic, with the situational determinants of leadership receiving almost exclusive consideration for a time (see, e.g., Gouldner, 1950). Eventually the pendulum swung back to a more moderate position, and today the importance of the situation continues to be stressed while the role of personal attributes (temperamental, intellective, and physical) as group resources is also generally recognized (cf. Hollander & Julian, 1968).

Whether the issue is leadership or conformity, the recent penetrating treatment by Hunt (1965)[1] is especially noteworthy, pointing out as it did that personality factors are more likely to be most important in their *interactions* with situational factors rather than in any sense of total primacy over them. For his data, which serve only an illustrative function, differences among situations accounted for somewhat more variance than differences among persons. More to the present point, however, is the fact that the interactions were more important than either, accounting for 4 to 11 times the variance due to persons! In Hunt's own words, "Thus, it is neither the individual differences among subjects, *per se*, nor the variations among situations, *per se*, that produce the variations in behavior. It is, rather, the interactions among these which are important [p. 83]."

Related to the idea of the conforming personality is that of the "conforming society." At least one experimental study (Milgram, 1961) has demonstrated con-

sistent differences in amount of movement conformity between samples from two countries. Norwegian university students were observed to be more conforming than French university students across all of five situations related to the Crutchfield procedure. Concerning these results, Milgram (1961) said, "No matter how the data are examined they point to greater independence among the French than among the Norwegians [p. 50]." He went on to relate this difference in "independence" to differences in the two national cultures.

Although it *may* be true that the French are the more independent, Milgram's data do not actually allow this conclusion. There exists another equally tenable interpretation. If it is recalled that anticonformity, like conformity, is a variety of *dependence* (cf. the triangular or diamond model of social response), it becomes apparent that one very real possibility is that the French group was exhibiting substantially stronger anticonformity tendencies than the Norwegian group. If so, it could well be that the French subjects were at the same time *less conforming but more dependent*. While the Norwegians felt less free to not conform, the French may have felt less free to conform. Or, if one may put it this way, the French may have been in some degree conforming to a norm of anticonformity.

It should be borne in mind that this interpretation of the Milgram experiment remains speculative, because his data do not allow a direct test of it; and his data do not allow a test because they derive from experimentation based upon the conformity-independence paradigm. However, the main point is that conformity and dependence are not logically equivalent, and the distinction needs to be maintained both in the

[1] This paper appears in Section III here.—Eds.

design of research and in conceptual analyses.

Whether or not Norway does in fact constitute a conforming society, a whole school of social criticism has developed around the theme that American culture can be so described (e.g., Riesman et al., 1950; Whyte, 1956). The most characteristic tack in such critiques is to describe conventional behavior in modern American society, label it conformity, invoke the "self-evident" premise that conformity is oppositional to individuality or independence, and therefore conclude that modern society and its component institutions hamper constructive initiative and are accordingly bad.

Apart from the value-laden feature of this literature, it neglects and indeed often hides the particular psychological utility of conformity behavior. Under many circumstances an objective analysis of possible courses of action leads to the conclusion that conformity will most effectively serve the individual's goals, whether these are social (e.g., need for approval) or nonsocial (e.g., need for food). From the assumption that all that qualifies as conformity, descriptively, is fully explainable in strictly social terms, an unfortunate confounding of description and explanation results which obscures the necessary and distinct place of each.

Although it is true that conformity and individuality are in opposition insofar as the perfect conformist cannot display individuality, they are in *very imperfect* opposition by virtue of the fact that even the most individualistic person often conforms. The hypothetical perfect individualist would not waste his energy and his status by not conforming in trivial ways—such as wearing red silk suits instead of gray flannel. Rather, he would feel free to not conform whenever something of importance to him was at stake, just as he would *feel free to conform* whenever this had instrumental value.

The distinction, already considered, between conventionality and acquiescence (or, more generally, between congruence and movement), is useful for liberating conventional behavior from the blanket stigma of acquiescent conformity. Thus, the convention of wearing clothes in public cannot be treated as slavish conformity in the same sense as accommodating to any and all fads, indiscriminately. The former represents a long-term habituation to a pattern which has obvious advantages as a necessary condition for normal social interaction of almost all kinds; the latter represents a series of short-term yieldings which, taken in the aggregate, do not have any general instrumentality. A mathematician is not considered lacking in initiative just because he adopts the conventional notation of mathematics, for this is obviously a necessary precondition for the demonstration of whatever professional skills he may have.

Clearly, then, much of the social criticism regarding conformity is misplaced in that what an individual's culture teaches him may severely limit alternatives that are socially and psychologically economical. His habits become conventionalized along the lines occasioned by cultural requirements that usually encourage the self-sufficiency of a particular mode of behaving. As Asch (1959) has put it:

Each social order confronts its members with a selected portion of physical and social data. The most decisive feature of this selectivity is that it presents conditions lacking in perceptible alternatives. There is no alternative to the language of one's group, to the kinship relations it practices, to the diet that nourishes it, to the art it supports. The field of the individual is, especially in a relatively closed society, in large measure circumscribed by what is included in the given cultural setting [p. 380].

Like the idea of a conforming personality, the conforming society concept appears to be of limited utility. A realistic assessment of the precise limits of the utility of these concepts will become possible only after the correction of such ambiguities and confusions as have been discussed here lead to a less superficial level of analysis.

Conformity-nonconformity and social exchange

Another, very promising avenue to understanding conformity and nonconformity is to be found in recent conceptions of reciprocity and social exchange (Adams, 1965; Blau, 1964; Gouldner, 1960; Homans, 1958, 1961; Jones, 1964; Thibaut & Kelley, 1959), which has ties both to reinforcement theory and to game theory. The approach is applicable to a study of social behavior either as response or as stimulus, although in this section only the latter is considered.

The social-exchange view construes conformity as a social process in which positive effects are occasioned in interactions with others by manifestations of expected behavior. Seen in this light, conformity becomes either a *deserved reward to others* which smooths the path of interaction and provides for further prospects for rewarding exchange, or as a *payment in advance* for anticipated rewards. In this latter regard, Jones (1965) has called attention again to the various ways in which conformity may be used as a technique of ingratiation. The ingratiation concept indicates one

instrumental basis for displaying conformity in interaction which forms a counterpart to the more basic "deserved reward" conception. Moreover, it emphasizes the potential *alteration* of expectancies which is an essential feature of social interaction in the full sense of the term.

Related to these schemes is the "idiosyncrasy credit" model (Hollander, 1958, 1964), which looks upon conformity as one input to the accumulation of status in the form of positive impressions or "credit" awarded by others. This credit then permits greater latitude for nonconformity under certain conditions. A basic feature of the idiosyncrasy credit model is the view that conformity and nonconformity are *not* invariably defined relative to a fixed norm to which everyone in the group is expected to comply equally, as in the Sherif paradigm. Rather, nonconforming behavior is seen to be variously defined by the group for any given actor depending upon how that actor is perceived. Conformity is thus considered to be to some degree person-specific and functionally related to status. That individuals of higher status or greater esteem have wider latitude for deviation has been widely observed and variously demonstrated in recent experiments by Berkowitz and Macaulay (1961), Hollander (1960, 1961), Julian and Steiner (1961), Sabath (1964), and Wiggins, Dill, and Schwartz (1965).

The consideration that when a person is perceived to have higher status his behavior is evaluated differently provides a useful bridge for understanding the relationship between conformity and the later potential for the kinds of deviancy associated with leadership. Thus, the apparent paradox that leaders are said to be greater conformers to group norms

(Homans, 1950; Merei, 1949), while also being initiators of change reflected in seemingly nonconforming behavior, is handled within the idiosyncrasy credit model as a matter of sequence. Early conformity, in combination with such attributes as perceived competence, enhances acceptance of later nonconformity.

Nonconformity can also be viewed with regard to the distinction between common expectancies of a group regarding its members and those special expectancies associated with high status. While there is more tolerance of nonconformity for the high-status person in some directions, there are greater restrictions in others. These obligations are the particular role obligations associated with his position in the group. There are at least two reasons why the role obligations of high-status persons are more severely delimited (Hollander, 1964, p. 227). First, because high status is perceived to hold greater self-determination, those in high-status positions are assumed to be more responsible for their actions. Second, and no less critical, high status carries with it role demands which are more likely to affect important outcomes for the members of the group.

The visibility associated with higher status also means that the outcome of any given act of nonconformity will be judged not only in terms of intentions but also in terms of the rewards it produces for the group. Other things equal, the high-status group member's behavior is more likely to be perceived as providing good outcomes to the group, rather than bad. Norm violations are more often seen as instances of "productive nonconformity" in the terminology of Pauline Pepinsky (1961). Uppermost here, however, is the consideration that acts of an evidently nonconforming variety will be variously interpreted as a function of others' *perceptions of the actor* based on their past experience with him, and in particular their *imputation of motives* to him (cf. Heider, 1958). Thus it has been found that the high-status person who conforms is seen to do so for internally determined causes while the low-status person is seen to conform for externally determined causes (Thibaut & Riecken, 1955). Accordingly, the motives seen to underlie the action will vary as a function of the actor's perceived status and the related assumption that the high-status person is more in command of initiatives to do as he wishes.

It should follow, too, that when his actions are seen to hurt the group, the high-status person will be held more responsible than would a low-status member. This would hold in particular when some basic role requirement, specific to the position of the individual, is not met. It is true that the acts of the high-status person are less likely to be perceived negatively than those of a low-status person, but *given* that the evaluation of acts is equally unfavorable, the high-status person will pay the higher social price.

In sum, conformity and nonconformity are observed and evaluated as features of interaction which may influence the subsequent action of others toward the actor.

Conclusions and implications

Let us now consider some salient conclusions.

1. *Current research on social influence is preoccupied with conformity to an extent sufficient to produce a relative neglect of nonconformity.* It should be

evident from the numerous studies cited that conceptual and experimental work on nonconformity phenomena has received only a fraction of the attention devoted to the conformity side of the picture. The obvious implication is that a shift of emphasis is much needed.

2. *Current research is characterized by a failure to distinguish consistently between descriptive (phenotypic) and explanatory (genotypic) levels of analysis.* A mutual interdependence exists between the two levels of analysis, and refinements at either level can be expected to facilitate progress at the other. In the area of social influence, however, the distinction has not been maintained as conscientiously as it might. An unfortunate result is that it becomes very easy to overlook the fact that the same overt act, or the same kind of overt act, observed on different occasions, can correspond to a variety of underlying psychological states and processes. A second effect has been the almost total neglect of careful descriptive analysis; this in turn has led to the necessity of making the next point.

3. *Current research is characterized by a nearly universal failure to distinguish between two basically different descriptive criteria of conformity-nonconformity, here termed congruence and movement.* Of writers known to us, only Halla Beloff (1958) has approached an explicit distinction of this kind. Her *conventionality* corresponds to congruence, while her *acquiescence* corresponds to movement—at least so it would seem from the kinds of measures she employed. She, like most others, considered only the conformity side of social influence.

From a strictly descriptive or operational point of view, congruence refers to the proximity between the position of the response along the response continuum and the point defining the normative ideal. Movement refers to changes in level of congruence from one occasion to another. The customary failure to distinguish between the two is roughly analogous to a failure to distinguish between hot and cold, since there is a perfect inverse relationship between the level of congruence and the potential for movement conformity.

4. *Current research is characterized by a persisting tendency to conceptualize conformity and its alternative(s) in an overly restrictive unidimensional manner.* Here two versions of a two-dimensional approach to movement conformity were described. The first, a triangular model, is similar to a less fully articulated conceptualization by Crutchfield and his associates. Conformity, independence, and anticonformity (or counterformity) are considered to be interrelated as the vertices of a triangle. A refinement of the triangular model, the diamond model, introduces a fourth mode of response, variability or self-anticonformity.

The unidimensionality of previous and current research was documented in a selective survey of the literature on movement conformity as a function of situational factors.

5. *Current thinking on conformity and nonconformity often indulges in unwarranted value judgments.* Here the reference was to the related "conforming personality" and "conforming society" points of view. The former fails to recognize that interactions between personality and situational factors are more important than personality variables per se. Both also fail to take into account the fact that nonconformity, as well as conformity, can represent dependency. One must consider both the individual's

freedom to not conform *and his freedom to conform*. At the societal level, a higher level of conformity does not necessarily imply a lower level of psychological freedom or individuality.

6. *Current thinking by social psychologists is frequently characterized by the simplistic and unwarranted assumption that conformity to the general group norms is defined alike for all members of the group*. This assumption of norm homogeneity fails to incorporate the effects of those group processes that produce variations in normative expectations as a function of the status of the actor. These processes were discussed in terms of the idiosyncrasy credit formulation, and related to the social-exchange view of interaction. From extensions of this kind, a more adequate understanding of the mechanisms producing such group phenomena as leadership, innovation, and deviance becomes possible.

45 Fundamental processes of social exchange

GEORGE C. HOMANS

Human institutions and human societies often appear so well established and so powerful that they dominate individual men and escape human control altogether. Yet these leviathans are the products of something that we think of as being weaker than water—individual human choices. Every last one of them consists of human actions, including those uniquely human ones: the things men say. It is not true that these monsters consist of the actions of men and something more. They *are* the actions of men: they can be analyzed into individual actions with nothing left over. And if they consist of individual actions, they must be finally explained by the principles of individual behavior. Here, our purpose is to show how the weak creates the strong, and how human choice creates social institutions.

The basic propositions

Consider a person performing what we call an activity; that is, some intelligible unit of voluntary behavior—voluntary in the sense that it is not a mere reflex action like the familiar knee jerk. Suppose the activity is baiting a hook on a fishing line and casting it into a pool. The first question we ask about such an activity is whether it is successful. Is the cast rewarded by a bite or at least a rise?

Abridged from "Fundamental Social Processes," Chapter 1 in Neil Smelser (Ed.), **Sociology**, New York: Wiley, 1967, pp. 27–78, with permission of the author and the publisher.

If the fisherman does get a bite, he is likely to repeat the activity. We sum up what happens in this and other examples of rewarded activity by stating our first proposition which, like all explanatory propositions, presents a relationship between at least two variables.[1] In this case, the variables are the frequency with which the activity is rewarded and the probability that a person will perform it.

Proposition I   The more often a person's activity is rewarded, the more likely he is to perform the activity.

We call this the *success* proposition. Like our other propositions, it is only approximately true. It implies that if an activity, once rewarded, is never rewarded thereafter, the probability that a person will perform it will, sooner or later, decrease to zero; that is, the person will cease to perform it at all. In the language of psychologists, the activity will become *extinguished*. But the proposition does not specify just how long "sooner or later" will be. Much depends on the pattern in which the reward comes. For a given number of rewards within a given period of time, the evidence is that a person will perform an activity less often if the rewards come at regular ratios—in our case, for example, a bite at every third cast—than if they come at irregular and random ratios. Furthermore, an activity once rewarded at regular ratios will, when the reward ceases, become extinguished sooner than one rewarded at irregular ratios. One of the reasons why people work so hard at fishing and keep on fishing even when

they have little success is that this activity is almost always rewarded at irregular ratios. Yet Proposition I, although only approximately true, is true enough for our purposes.

Proposition II   If in the past the occurrence of a particular stimulus, or set of stimuli, has been the occasion in which a person's activity has been rewarded, then the more similar the present stimuli are to the past ones, the more likely the person is to perform the activity, or some similar activity, now.

We call this the *stimulus* proposition. Like the success proposition, the stimulus proposition is only approximately true. The crucial variable is the similarity of stimuli, but similarity may have many more than one dimension—things may be similar in different ways—and the subtleties of the psychology of perception are beyond the scope of this chapter. Moreover, the proposition as stated here says nothing about the relationship in time between the stimulus and the activity. If the original stimulus coincided with the rewarded activity in time, it is apt to be more effective in eliciting future activity than if it had occurred much earlier or later. If we use ordinary language, we say that the person would be more likely to perceive the connection.

The first two propositions imply an important tendency toward *generalization* in a person's behavior. Both the stimulus and the activity may be generalized. The fisherman, if he has been successful in fishing in a shady pool, will fish in other shady pools or even in pools that are quite dark. If he has been successful at one kind of fishing, he will be more eager to try other kinds, and even sports that are similar to fishing, such as hunting. In time, of course, the tendency toward generalization may run into difficulty. The fisherman may find that he does well in shady pools but poorly in pools that are positively dark, and thus he may, in time, come to discriminate between the stimuli of shadiness and darkness. The process of *discrimination* accompanies the process of generalization.

Propositions I and II imply that a person's behavior is learned, and that his past experience—both his past history of success in his activities and the past circumstances attending them—has an enormous effect on his present behavior. Men, of course, have been aware of this fact for a long time, but modern psychology has reemphasized its importance. We now know that a person's past experiences (such as those of his early childhood) and his unconscious experiences (unconscious in the sense that he cannot talk about them) may influence the likelihood that he will perform certain activities and respond to certain stimuli today. Also his experience may be vicarious rather than immediate. At the outset the fisherman may fish in shady pools because someone has advised him to do this, or because he has read about fishing in a book. Nevertheless, immediate experience must enter the picture at some point. The angler is unlikely to take advice about fishing without question unless he has had an earlier experience in which he took advice and actually found it rewarding.

In stating Propositions I and II we assumed that a person's activity was rewarded, but we did not comment upon the degree of the reward. The fact is, of course, that the degree of a reward is a variable, which we call its *value*, and we must state a proposition describing the effect of this variable on other behavioral variables. If fish is the only food a hungry person can get, fish becomes very valuable to him, and he is likely to work harder at fishing than if he had just eaten his fill. Accordingly, we state the next proposition.

Proposition III   The more valuable the reward of an activity is to a person, the more likely he is to perform the activity.

We call this the *value* proposition. We must recognize that the value in question is the value per unit of the reward, no matter how that unit is defined, since (as we shall see) the values of successive units may change.

The success proposition and the value proposition must be considered together. Some social scientists talk as if the only thing that determines whether a man performs an activity is his motivation: his need for the reward, his drive to get the reward—what we call its *value*. But a man may need a certain reward very much and still take no action to get it if, in his past experience, he never has been successful in getting it. Only if success presents no problem does value alone determine the probability of a man's performing an activity.

The value proposition, simple as it looks, runs into many difficulties. Although it is hard to think of performing an activity at a negative frequency, it is easy to think of rewards of negative values, which we call punishments. Our hypothetical fisherman is punished if he has to struggle through brambles to get to his pool, if he gets his line tangled in a tree, or if he slips off a rock and falls headlong in the water. The value proposition has this implication: the more punishing is the result of an activity (that is, the more negative its value), the more likely a man is *not* to perform it.

What is much more important: any activity that permits a person to escape or avoid the punishment becomes, by that fact, a rewarded activity—and the more painful is the punishment avoided, the more valuable is the reward. Note that I have said *any* activity. This has crucial implications for the use of punishment in controlling behavior. The effect of a positive reward usually is to render the performance of a specific activity more likely, but punishment has the effect of rendering more likely the performance of any activity, and there may be a wide variety of such activities, that allows a person to avoid the punishment. If we propose to get a man to perform a specific action by punishing him if he does *not* do it, we must take care that he cannot perform any other action that might avoid the punishment. Closing the other avenues of escape may be very costly.

Values are always relative. We cannot speak of the degree of reward that a man gets from an activity except in relation to some alternative reward to be obtained from some alternative activity. That is, a man compares activities and their rewards and chooses between them, whether consciously or unconsciously. Our fisherman may either go fishing or stay in camp and play bridge; he may fish in one pool rather than in another. What we mean by an alternative reward is something that he must give up, or forego, if he chooses to do something else. Man's greatest tragedy is that he really cannot do two things at once. In terms of relative values, the value proposition implies that the probability of a man's performing an activity depends on the relation between the reward of the activity that he performs and the

reward to be obtained from some alternative activity, relinquished by the fact that he performs the first one. We call the foregone reward the *cost* of the activity, and the probability that a man will perform the activity depends on its net value, or reward less cost. But we must be careful in interpreting this statement. It does not imply, in the least, that as the reward less the cost of an activity approaches zero, the probability that a man will perform the activity also approaches zero. It implies only that the probability that the man will perform the activity tends to become equal to the probability that he will perform the alternative activity.

There are many activities from which a man cannot reap a reward without, at the same time, incurring some punishment. The fisherman may be unable to fish a certain pool without first scrambling through a bramble patch. Our statement about relative values still applies to such activities. Since any activity that permits a man to avoid punishment is, by that fact, rewarded, the cost of fishing the pool is the foregone value of avoiding the brambles. And the greater the cost (in this case, perhaps, the greater the extent of the brambles), the less likely it is that the man will fish the pool.

The doctrine that all values are relative may seem to imply that a man, when he acts, compares the rewards of all of the activities that he conceivably might perform. In explaining human behavior we can, in practice, forget about this possibility. In practice a man compares only the alternatives open to him at any given time. But what does "open to him" mean? It means, naturally, that once an activity or course of activities has been chosen and started, the act of choosing and starting the activity changes the net rewards of future activities, making the costs of some of them prohibitive. Once our fisherman has committed himself to fishing and has gone upstream, he has, for the moment, greatly increased the cost of his alternative activity—playing bridge—since he must now get back to camp before he can play. The fact that present choices affect future rewards and costs is another inescapable tragedy of the human condition. Think of something more important than fishing, such as commitment to a career. No one should sell his freedom of choice except for a high price.

Proposition IV   The more often in the recent past a person has received a particular reward, the less valuable any further unit of that reward becomes to him.

But suppose that we are not assessing the value to a man of a single type of reward on two separate occasions but the relative value that he sets on two different rewards on the same occasion. Suppose also there is no obvious difference between the rewards in the degree to which the man has been deprived of them or satiated with them. Clearly, the problem is very common. For instance, suppose that the fisherman prefers catching salmon to catching trout. Is it really true that we have no measure of the relative value to him of the two fish other than the fact that he will do more to catch one than the other so that, in this case, the value proposition becomes tautological? It might be true if the fisherman were a member of a native tribe that we had just begun to study, and all we knew about him was his actual fishing habits. But if we knew that he was an Eastern sports fisherman,

and that Eastern sports fishermen assigned a higher prestige to salmon than to trout, then we should have in these facts a measure of the relative value to him of the two fish—at least in the sense of his ranking them in order of value— and the measure would be independent of the fact that he did more to catch one than the other. Someone might argue that we had only driven the problem of tautology back one step. For how can we measure the value that our man sets on prestige? Is not, perhaps, what he is really deprived of prestige and not fish? But one step back is far enough to get the problem out of the way, at least for an approximate treatment like this one.

We have thus far treated man as if he never displayed what we usually call emotional behavior. Actually he is one of the most emotional of animals. Think of the parts played in a man's life, even his social life, by love and hatred, joy and sorrow, hope and fear, euphoria and melancholy, and even ease and constraint. Take, for example, the anxiety that arises when a highly valued result is uncertain and long deferred. Under these conditions almost any activity that is, in fact, followed by the desired result is, by the success proposition, likely to be repeated, no matter how fortuitous the origin of the action and no matter how little it really has to do with producing the result. An old-time seaman longed for a wind to fill his sails; he happened to whistle, and the wind came. It always does come sooner or later. Also whistling as a stimulus is similar to the sound of the wind. Thus whistling became reinforced as an activity that brings wind to seamen. It became established as wind-magic. Think of the part played in society by magic and superstitious behavior in general. It flourishes even today in an age of science, although it is not always recognized as being what it is.

Even though we recognize the enormous range and weight of emotional behavior, we shall introduce here only a single proposition about emotionality. Our justification is a desire not to complicate unnecessarily an introductory treatment. The proposition that follows is particularly important for explaining social processes.

Proposition V   When a person's activity does not receive the reward he expected, or receives punishment he did not expect, he will be angry, and in anger, the results of aggressive behavior are rewarding.

We call this the *frustration-aggression* proposition. Perhaps we should add that when the person *does* get what he expected, he still will have an emotional reaction, which we might call satisfaction. But satisfaction is seldom as spectacular as anger.

The terms in Proposition V need further definition. What a man expects is defined by Proposition II: when a set of stimuli are present, similar to that in which a man's activity was rewarded in the past, he expects that the activity will be rewarded again now, and to the extent that it is not, he will be frustrated and angry. He is apt to be more angry the more often he was successful in these circumstances in the past (Proposition I) and the more valuable the reward is to him (Proposition III). But note that his failure to get the reward now will change his expectations for the future, so that the next time he fails in these circumstances he may well get less angry. Finally, aggressive behavior is behavior that apparently hurts some-

thing or somebody, especially the something or somebody that looks like the source or reason for the frustration, but in a pinch almost anything will do. The proposition says that in anger the results of aggressive behavior become relatively more valuable than they were before.

These five propositions certainly do not exhaust the findings of behavioral psychology. Instead, they represent the very minimum needed in explaining the simpler features of social behavior. Of equal importance with the propositions themselves is the fact that they hold true simultaneously, each limiting, modifying, or masking in particular circumstances the features of behavior that the others would lead us to expect. We have given some examples of this, but let us consider one more. According to Proposition I, the more often a man's activity is rewarded, the more often he performs it. But, by Proposition IV, the more often an activity is rewarded, the less valuable any further unit of the reward becomes and, by Proposition III, the less valuable the reward, the less often a man performs the activity. In effect, the propositions combined imply (which, of course, we know) that if a man's activity is successful often enough, this fact will create the conditions that lead to his ceasing to perform it. The propositions also imply that if a man is to keep on working hardest to get a particular reward, he must be successful just often enough to satiate partly, but not wholly, his need for the reward. If he is working to appease his hunger, he should be just successful enough to keep him a little hungry all the time. No success would lead, by Proposition I, to apathy; too much success would lead, by Proposition IV, to satiation. Since all of the propositions are simultaneously true, we should, in principle, either use them all in explaining any particular feature of behavior or show why, under the circumstances, one or more of them do not apply. In practice we do not make this effort when the reasons for the omissions are obvious.

Social interaction

Although our subject is social behavior (that is, when a man's activity is rewarded or punished directly or indirectly by one or more other men), we have stated our propositions about a man's behavior under the influence of reward as if it made no difference where the reward came from: our fisherman was not rewarded by other men but by fish. And, in one sense, it does indeed make no difference, since no new propositions are needed to explain social behavior. But it does make a difference to the complexity of the explanation. When a man's activity is rewarded by the nonhuman environment, he acts in accordance with the laws of human psychology, but the environment does not. When a man's activity is rewarded by the activity of another man, both are acting in accordance with these laws. The activity of each is influencing the activity of the other, and in human ways. The two are *interacting*, and it is this reciprocal influence that causes complexity.

To replace fishing, let us find a typical example of social interaction. Suppose that at least two men, whom we shall call Person and Other, are working in the same office.[2] Person, who is inexperienced in the job, needs some advice about how to do his paper work. He goes to Other, who is an old hand at the game, and asks for help. Other gives the advice, and Person thanks him. Per-

[2] This example is taken from Blau (1955).

son's activity has been rewarded by advice, and Other's activity by thanks. Or, stated another way, they have exchange advice for thanks.

How do we explain why the interaction—the exchange—takes place? The answers are obvious, but unless we make them explicit we shall never be able to explain the more complicated cases of social interaction. Let us first go back to our propositions, and reexamine the stimulus proposition (II). In social behavior the most important stimuli are those presented by persons. Assume that Person considers Other as being the kind of experienced man who could give him good advice, and that Person has had previous success in getting help of some kind from those more knowledgeable than he is himself. Most of us have had some such experience from childhood onward. Therefore, there is some likelihood that Person will ask Other for help. Assume also that, as far as Other is concerned, there is nothing about Person to suggest that he will be ungrateful.

Now let us turn to the value proposition (III). Since values are relative to alternatives, we must look at the alternative rewards open to each man. Person can either ask for advice or keep on doing his own work. Since he is inexperienced in the ways of the office, we assume that getting advice is more valuable to him than doing his own work —indeed, it will ultimately help him do his own work better—and that, for the time being, he is not satiated with advice (Proposition IV). But we must also consider the costs of getting advice, costs that he would avoid incurring if he simply did his own work. One of the costs is low. Person's friend, Other, is near at hand, so that Person does not have to spend much time finding him.

Physical proximity is one of the chief factors reducing the costs, and thus increasing the probability of human interaction.[3] Another kind of cost may be heavier. If Person asks Other for advice he, by so doing, admits to Other (and, indeed, to any spectator) that, in at least this respect, he is inferior to Other and, for some men, this is a heavy cost indeed. We shall consider this kind of cost in more detail later but, for the moment, assume that it is not too great to prevent Person from asking for advice.

In the same way, Other may either give advice or keep on doing his own work. If he gives advice, he expects to be rewarded by thanks, or, to speak more generally, with social approval. All of the evidence suggests that for many men social approval is a valuable reward, and that it is difficult to satiate them with it. Other's cost in giving advice is, of course, the time he takes off from doing his own work, but this cost may not be great, since he is an experienced man and therefore can do his own work quickly.

Once it has taken place, the exchange —the interaction—has consequences for the future. By Propositions I and II (the success and the stimulus propositions), the probability increases that each party will, in the future, exchange the same rewards with the same other person, so long as the attendant circumstances remain favorable. In the short run, they may not remain favorable. The more advice Other gives Person in the course of a day's work at the office, the less time he has left for doing his own work; the cost of giving advice becomes prohibitive, and he will break off the exchange. In the same way, Person may have gotten all the advice he needs for

[3] For a good example, see Festinger, Schachter, and Back (1950), pp. 33–59.

the time being (Proposition IV). But by the next morning these drawbacks may have disappeared. That is, in the long run the probability that the exchanges will continue has increased. Note that many of the most persistent features of social life consist of repeated interactions between individuals in families, in other small groups, and in large organizations. A repeated exchange of the same kinds of reward between two persons may be called a *relationship* between them.

A repeated interaction also makes a difference to future behavior because it changes expectations. Suppose that Other has been giving Person advice whenever he has asked for it, and then suddenly refuses. Person has come to expect the advice and is angry when he fails to get it. Generally speaking, if Person has performed an activity that has been repeatedly rewarded by Other in the past, and finds on a new and similar occasion that the reward is not forthcoming, he is, by the frustration-aggression proposition (V), apt to be angry; and, in anger, hostile activities become rewarding to him, especially activities that punish Other. Since the withholding of an expected reward is a punishment, these activities may include Person's refusal to enter into future exchanges with Other, even if he still needs advice. He is cutting off his nose to spite his face but, in anger, it is worth it if he can get back at Other. Insofar as Other values his future exchanges with Person, he may learn to avoid the punishment by living up to Person's expectations. He is the more likely to do so, the more the punishment would hurt him, which may mean that there is no alternative way by which he could get the kind of reward (social approval) that Person would deny him. To sum up:

expectations may arouse aggressive reactions if they are not met, and thus bring in a new reward—precisely the reward of avoiding the aggression—that may help maintain the relationship.

Note that we have just introduced a new meaning of *alternative*. Besides alternative rewards, there are alternative ways of getting the same kind of reward. These ways may be activities directed at alternative persons. If there is some third man who can provide Other with the approval that Person denies him, Other will have less to fear from Person's anger.

The elaboration of interaction

Thus far, from our discussion, it would seem as if the two persons in interaction each rewarded the other with only one kind of activity and as if the activities were essentially dissimilar: Other gives advice; Person gives approval. But persons who interact repeatedly are apt to enter into more than one kind of exchange, and some of the activities exchanged may not be entirely dissimilar. In the course of giving and getting advice, Other and Person may begin talking about matters of common interest outside the office, exchanging opinions about the affairs of the day. Sociologists would say that their relationship has become *elaborated*. The reasons for the elaboration should be obvious. A man who rewards another in one way is, by the stimulus proposition, perceived as the kind of man who may be more generally rewarding. And the very fact that the two have already been brought together by one kind of exchange may make it less costly for them to enter into a new kind of exchange with one another than with third parties. Elabora-

tion is a common feature of social relationships.

The new exchanges may affect the original one, and vice versa. Let us examine the exchange of opinions. It may be cynical but it is often true that what rewards a man's expression of opinion is another's agreement with it, and the second party's agreement is more apt to be forthcoming if the first party's opinion is, in fact, similar to that of the second party. Now suppose that in the course of their conversation, Person expresses disagreement with Other's opinion. To some degree he has frustrated Other, deprived him of an expected reward. As usual, in anger, any activity that hurts the offender becomes, by that fact, rewarded. And one way in which Other can now hurt Person is by withdrawing from the original exchange: he may cease to give Person advice. If a man values his own opinions strongly enough, he may break off all previous relations with a person who disagrees with them.

But Person may readily learn to forestall this result. The higher the value he sets on getting advice from Other, the more likely he is to change his expressed opinion in order to make it more like Other's, and he may even, eventually, believe sincerely what he says. The total result of the many situations of this kind is a certain strain toward consistency in human relations: either two persons reward one another in more than one way, like each other on more than one count, and increase their interaction, or they will hurt one another in more than one way, dislike one another, and decrease interaction. It appears to be rather difficult, although not impossible, to keep on interacting with a person who rewards in one way and punishes in another. This strain toward consistency has been widely discussed by psychologists under the heading of *balance theory* (see especially Heider, 1958; Festinger, 1957). It should also be clear why persons who interact frequently with one another are apt to become similar in some respect: to express similar opinions, to share common interests, and even to dress alike. To summarize: the elaboration of a relationship tends either to strengthen it or to weaken it, but not to leave it unchanged.

Status

Among the things that men rank are the things people do and what they get for what they do—their outward and visible signs, if not their inward and spiritual values. They certainly rank the outward and visible signs of differences in power. And from ranking these things, it is but a step to ranking the man himself. Other gives more advice than Person or the Third Man; he gets more approval; he provides them with knowledge they cannot provide for themselves. Therefore, he himself is a "better" or "bigger" or "higher" man than they are. And since both Person and the Third Man need advice and both give approval for it in return, the two men may be called equals. From ranking persons it is another short step to ranking classes of persons. With respect to skill, at least, skilled persons are "better" than unskilled persons, and unskilled persons are "equal" to one another. After actual differences in power, the verbal ranking of persons is the crucial feature of differences in status.

The next question is why, in any group, status differences should form a system. When we talk of a system, we refer to some kind of consistency; in the case of status, two kinds are at stake.

First, why should not a person rank high on one dimension of status but not another, so that it would be difficult to rank him as a whole, so to speak, as higher or lower than other persons? Many cases like this, of course, occur, cases of what sociologists call *status incongruence*; for instance, a person who is wealthy, because he has inherited money, but who appears to have almost no intelligence to go with it. But at least in small groups some tendency toward consistency is built into the underlying power relationships. A powerful person like Other gives more advice and gets more approval than either Person or the Third Man: on the two dimensions, or two counts, if you like—what he gives and what he gets—he is better than they are. There are other forces making for status congruence, including the tendency for persons who command one source of power to acquire additional sources, but we must postpone these other forces until we get further in our argument.

The second problem of consistency is this: Why should all the members of a group rank others in the same way? Why should not one man rank Other high and another man rank him low? Again, perfect consistency of this sort is never attained, but there is a tendency toward it. The origin of differences in status is differences in power, and men are powerful when many want what they, the few, are able to supply or many fear what they, the few, are able to withhold. Consequently, if there are any differences in power in the group, there will be a relatively large number of persons, at least an important nucleus, who will be in no position to deny that the few are of higher rank than they. Generally, the more similar the members of the group are in their values, the more likely they are to be similar in their rankings of others.

But how about other persons, members of the group, perhaps in the sense of being present in the same room, who do not happen to want what the few are able to supply, and who therefore are not in the least in the power of the few? Why should they also accord high status to the few? Status is a matter of the use of language, and one of the forces making for consistency in status is a force that helps bring about consistency in the use of language generally. The uttering of a form of words is an activity like any other, and it is unlikely to be repeated indefinitely if it is not rewarded by assent or at least understanding. If the persons who would not otherwise accord high status to the few, when talking to the persons who do accord it, refer to the few in words implying that they are just ordinary members of the group, they may not command the assent or even the understanding of their listeners, who may not, as we say, know what they are talking about. Accordingly the dissenters have some tendency to shift to a form of words that does communicate. More generally, a status system need not command the emotional assent of every member of a group. All that is needed for a status system is that members talk as if it were generally recognized that people like Other were "big men."

Distributive justice

In connection with status we must now return to Proposition V, which bears repeating. *When a person's activity does not receive the reward he expected, or receives punishment he did not expect, he will be angry, and in anger, the results of aggressive behavior are reward-ing.* In discussing pair relations without differences in power, we observed that the failure of one party to an exchange to provide as much reward as the other expected would tend to complicate the relationship by adding new values: on the one part, the rewards of aggressive behavior, and on the other, the rewards of avoiding the aggression. And it is not just a matter of reward: a cost greater than expected may have the same effect as a reward less than expected. The same certainly holds true of pair relations between persons of unequal power. If Other suddenly implies by his behavior that he wants even more approval as the price of his help, Person may say: "That guy won't help me unless I crawl. I've got too much self-respect to do that any more. It isn't worth it."

The development of status complicates what a man expects in the way of reward. It increases the importance of the outward and visible signs of what men give and get: Other is now established as "better" than Person and the Third Man, both in what he gives (advice) and in what he gets (approval). And it makes the rewards and costs of third parties relevant to the original pair exchange: the fact that the Third Man, as well as Person, now wants what Other alone is ready to supply is the basis for Other's superior status. Whether Person gets angry with the terms of his exchange now depends on the answers to two questions, two comparisons: Am I getting what I expect to get, what I ought to get, in relation to someone who is "better" than I (Other)? And am I getting what I expect to get, what I ought to get, in relation to someone who is similar to me (the Third Man)? The comparison always brings in costs as well as rewards: Am I getting as much from the other as I ought to get, in view of his costs? Naturally the comparison is not made in terms of "subjective values" but in terms of the outward stimuli that behavior presents. This is the problem of distributive justice (justice in the distribution of rewards among members of a group) and of its reverse, *distributive injustice* or, as sociologists call it, *relative deprivation*. Justice is what men expect, and injustice, above all other things in social behavior, is what leads to anger.

What a man expects is determined, above all, by what has actually happened to him: by his own experience and by the experience of others, transmitted to him in words. The more common and general the experience has been, the more firm is the expectation. Now many men have had actual experience, and often many experiences, with differences in power, and they know what the general rule is. It is that a man like Other who gives relatively much of what few are able to supply, like advice, gets relatively much of what many are able to supply, like approval, and that a man who gives relatively little gets relatively little. Of course, not all men have had this experience; some have been rewarded so much at random that they hardly have any expectations at all: life to them is a matter of chance, of getting the breaks. But many men have had it— and what *is* determines what always *ought* to be. It is this actual, common experience that provides the basis for the general rule of justice: If a man is better than I in what he gives, which always entails costs, he ought to be better than I in what he gets, his rewards. But the rule works both ways, and if he is better than I in what he gets, he also ought to be better in what he gives. More generally, if he is better on one count, he

ought to be better on both: his rankings on the two counts should be in line with one another. By the same token, if a man is equal to me in what he gives, he ought to be equal to me in what he gets. Aristotle's is the first general writing on distributive justice to come down to us: these two rules—two aspects of a single rule—appear in his *Nichomachean Ethics*.

When two persons are interacting in isolation, there may be a problem of justice, but often each person can do something to produce what he conceives to be just conditions, because each is dependent on the other. The problem of achieving justice becomes more difficult when three persons are interacting. There are at least two cases. Suppose Other provides advice to both Person and the Third Man, but only the latter gives him approval. Then Person is being unjust to Other: Other is better than Person in the advice he gives, but Person does not recognize his superiority in return. In this case, however, Other is in the position of superior power, and may easily restore just conditions by denying Person advice until he gives approval. If one has power, he need not worry much about getting justice for himself.

Much more common is the case in which the person to whom injustice has been done is in the weaker power position. Suppose both Person and the Third Man are ready and willing to give Other approval, but Other gives advice only to the Third Man. Then injustice has been done to Person: he is similar to the Third Man in what he can give, but inferior to him in what he gets. And, in this case, he is less powerful than Other, so that he is less able to force him to be just. A great deal of experience shows that problems of injustice are especially apt to arise over distributions of rewards made by superiors to inferiors. The superior may not, of course, be an individual but an organized unit like "the company," as when the company is unfair to individuals and groups, as they see it, in the relative wages it pays them.

Again, the rule of justice, as we have stated it, implies a series of rank order correlations, a series of ordinal differences rather than cardinal ones. A man who is better than another man in what he gives should be better than the other in what he gets. But *how much* better in either respect? Here, there is no general rule, but considerable evidence that, in justice, an inch is almost as good as an ell. In one department of a business firm the members of one job group said that they ought to get "just a few dollars" more pay than another group "just to show that our job is more important." Symbolically, it was the ordinal difference that counted (Homans, 1962, pp. 61–74).

Justice is a matter of human expectations; when the expectations are unrealized, men are apt to feel angry and, in anger, the results of aggressive behavior become rewarding—a fact that adds new values and new possibilities of behavior to the original ones. A man who feels he has been unjustly treated may be angry not only at the powerful man who caused the injustice but also at his own equal, who is the beneficiary of injustice by getting more reward than he does himself. A powerful man is better able to maintain injustice than most men, but even he may have good practical reasons for wanting to avoid it insofar as he can. A man to whom the powerful man has done wrong is a fellow who may want to get back at him, and what better way is there than *not* doing what the powerful man says, just because he says it? Insofar as the powerful man wants his inferiors to work well together, he will want to avoid creating jealousies between them. Finally, doing justice is the prerogative of high status, so that a man who is unfair to his inferiors may, to a degree, render his status less legitimate. He is in special danger when he has been unjust to many people in the same way, for then they may not only want to get back at him but combine together to do so. There are many good reasons for doing justice, but when there are good reasons for doing something, there are usually also good reasons for not doing it; and justice is often both difficult to do and costly. How is the best net advantage achieved? Injustice in its multifarious forms has always been the great social problem.

Remember: in the end, and always, the sense of injustice is invariably grounded on a defeat of expectations, and expectations in the long run are always grounded on what actually happens. Reexamining one of our examples: if, over a period of time, older persons do not generally get better jobs than younger ones, then an older man's sense of injustice, when he does not get a good job, will eventually disappear. Whatever is, is right—if only what is will stay put long enough, which it usually does not. It is change that makes the trouble. Thus a person or group that has, for any reason, come to expect a steady increase in rewards will, when the increase is checked or reversed, feel angry, even if they are better off absolutely than they were in the beginning. In psychologists' language, their *level of aspiration* has risen. This is a fertile source of revolt and one very hard to cope with, for how can anyone go on increasing rewards indefinitely?

46 On norms

JOHN W. THIBAUT and HAROLD H. KELLEY

Conceptualization of norms

Consider two people in a dyadic relationship and assume that the pattern of their outcomes is such that they cannot achieve their best outcomes at the same time. For example, this might be a husband and wife whose problem is that the wife likes to go dancing in the evening and the husband prefers that they go to the movies. The outcomes are illustrated in Figure 1. It is apparent that trading is necessary if both are to obtain good outcomes even occasionally.

Trading can be established through exercise of the power that each possesses, if this power is adequate. For example, the husband can use his control over the wife's outcomes by promising to go dancing if she will go with him to the movies. Or he can threaten to go to the movies anyway if she fails to cooperate, in which case she will have poor outcomes. Similar influence opportunities exist for the wife.

The moment-to-moment use of personal power can be obviated if the two can agree upon some rule for trading. For example, they might agree that they will alternate between dancing and attending the movies, making the shift upon some mutually acceptable signal; for example, a word from the momentarily favored person to the effect that he or she is satiated with the present activity. Once agreement is reached on a rule of this sort, shifts are likely to proceed smoothly and predictably and,

in view of the limitations inherent to the relationship (noncorrespondence of high outcomes), each person is likely to feel that his own outcomes are satisfactory.

Agreements of this sort may be matters of mere convenience, repeated for their immediate value in reducing the costs involved in face-to-face influence and in smoothing out the course of the interaction. However, as Waller and Hill (1951) so aptly put it, "The *usual* quickly becomes the *right* . . ." (p. 49). The rule is likely to take on the characteristics of a moral obligation (or even to have them from the start). This means, in brief, that conformity to agreements becomes rewarding in and of itself.

Just how this transformation occurs is a complex matter. It probably has some basis in the fact that conformity to rules and agreements has proven rewarding in past relationships in which some external agent has delivered extrinsic rewards for conformity. For example, two brothers disagree about

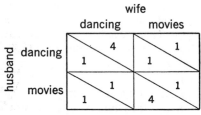

Figure 1. Illustration of relationship requiring trading.

Excerpted from Chapter 8 of **The Social Psychology of Groups**, New York: John Wiley and Sons, Inc., 1959, pp. 127–35, with permission of the authors and the publisher.

what to play because they prefer different games. Their mother steps in and says, "Play what Jimmy wants for awhile, and, after you've done that, give Johnny a chance," and rewards them if they follow her rule. Agreement to rules is also reinforced by the value they have for the relationship in cutting costs and enhancing rewards. We shall elaborate this shortly.

These reinforcing conditions make it likely that the two boys will learn to value "fair play." They will *accept* the rule in the sense that their equitable turn-taking behavior will no longer occur simply as a result of their compliance to external sanctions but also because they have *internalized* the rule [see Kelman, 1961].

Thus a predisposition to value and abide by a trading rule may exist at the outset of the husband and wife relationship. Norms need not be invented anew for each relationship but may often be transferred from other ones. These learning conditions also make it likely that a general value for agreements and rules of this sort will be acquired.

When an agreement about a matter such as trading exists between the members of a dyad and when it is accepted to some degree by both, we would say that a norm exists. This would manifest itself to an outside observer in several ways:

(1) There would be regularity in behavior (in our example, a routinized sequence of shifts in activities of the pair).

(2) In the event of disruption of this regularity, the "injured" person would attempt to restore it by appealing, at least initially, to the rule and he would exercise his personal power as an enforcer of the rule.

(3) The person disrupting the regularity would be likely to feel some obligation to adhere to the agreement and might even exhibit some conflict or guilt about deviating from it, as if he were punishing himself for his nonconformity.

Once a norm exists, it appears to the pair almost as if a third agent had entered the relationship, a feeling which undoubtedly is reinforced by the fact that in earlier relationships the enforcers of rules often actually were third persons (e.g., the mother in the case of the two brothers). The third agent exercises power over each member in the usual sense of making it desirable for him to act in certain ways at certain times and does so in an impartial way without regard to the special interests of either one. This normative power, when the rule has been accepted or internalized, seems to be exclusively behavior control, except in the case we discuss later in which the person is unable to make the necessary discriminations or perform the specified behavior. In one sense this power accrues to the norm because the two persons give up some of their individual power to it. This is evidenced by their exercising personal power in the name of the norm rather than to advance their personal interests. In another sense, the norm may have power over them independently of their enforcement of it: to the degree that the norm is accepted by individuals to whom it applies, conformity is more rewarding, other things being equal, than nonconformity.

From the preceding discussion the reader can deduce our definition of norm. A norm is a behavioral rule that is accepted, at least to some degree, by both members of the dyad. (A rule which one person advances and tries to enforce but which the other person does not accept cannot be called a norm, at least in a dyad. In large groups, on the other hand, acceptance by all members is not an essential part of the concept, although acceptance by a sizable number is.) Thus both members feel some obligation to adhere to it. Nonadherence is met with the use of power to attempt to produce conformity, but the influence appeal is to a supra-individual value ("Do it for the group" or "Do it because it's good") rather than to personal interests ("Do it for me" or "Do it and I'll do something for you").

The reader may wish to compare the present treatment of norm with similar conceptualizations advanced by other social scientists. Most similar is Homans' (1950) definition:

A norm, then, is an idea in the minds of the members of a group, an idea that can be put in the form of a statement specifying what the members or other men should do, ought to do, are expected to do, under given circumstances. . . . A statement of the kind described is a norm only if any departure of real behavior from the norm is followed by some punishment (p. 123).

In the Lewinian tradition, Festinger, Schachter and Back (1950) give a definition in terms of forces: ". . . a uniform set of directions which the group induces on the forces which act on the members of the group" (p. 166). Rommetveit (1954) distinguishes carefully between the individual acting as enforcer of a norm, on the one hand, and the individual subject to it, on the other: "A social norm is a pressure existing between a norm-sender and a norm-receiver's behaviour in a category of recurrent situations" (p. 45). The last phrase excludes accidental and temporary interpersonal pressures. Pressure is said to be manifested in the norm sender's expectations that the norm receiver will behave in a specific way, or in his wish for this behavior, and in overt sanctions applied by the norm sender in response to the norm receiver's actions (pp. 45 ff.).

Norms as substitutes for informal influence

The foregoing discussion illustrates the characteristics of normative processes and also implies what we take to be the major broad functional value of norms —that they serve as substitutes for the exercise of personal influence and produce more economically and efficiently certain consequences otherwise dependent upon personal influence processes. Let us now consider this point in detail by examining the various problems created by the use of informal, interpersonal power and the ways in which norms may avoid or solve them.

In the first place norms may function to prevent or delay the development of any of the dependencies on which interpersonal power is based. Particularly in the very early stages of the relationship, when it is not yet clear whether the relationship will be formed, norms may assist in preventing premature commitments. As Hiller (1947) says ". . . norms supply a means for evading an implication of affectional relations. This is accomplished by treating with strict politeness or rigid etiquette a person who wishes to occupy a position which is too intimate. . . . Formality indicates a categorical rather than a unique personal footing; and unwanted approaches are .repelled by confronting the other with decorous conduct. . . ." (pp. 105–106).

Let us go on though to consider a relationship that has formed. Assume first that A has greater power than B, at least within some limited segment of the matrix. From B's point of view a number of problems exist. If A has behavior control [1] over him, the unbridled use of this power tends to reduce the quality of B's outcomes. If A has fate control [2] and converts it in order to control B's behavior, the unstandardized use of this converted control places B in an uncomfortable situation. A's conversion of his fate control is more or less arbitrary; that is to say, he has several alternative ways in which he can use it. If he shifts among these in an unpredictable way, B may on any given occasion act upon the wrong assumption about what A intends and thereby suffer reduced payoffs. Even without actually making incorrect behavioral choices, B may worry about the possibility of doing so, and this tends to raise his costs for all the activities involved. The uncertainty is most extreme, of course, when A uses his fate control willy-nilly. If A converts and uses his control in one standardized manner, B's situation becomes that of having control over his *own* outcomes.

From the point of view of A, the more powerful individual, there are also problems, but of a different sort. If he is not careful in the use of whatever behavior control he may have, it will be reduced or even lost entirely. Because of the effects of interruptions in reducing B's outcomes, A must use his behavior control sparingly if he is to conserve it. If, on the other hand, A uses converted fate power to induce B to respond differentially, A must often monitor B's action, and such monitoring or surveillance is usually costly.

Given the above problems, both the weaker and the more powerful members of a dyad are likely to be somewhat dissatisfied with the informal exercise of personal power. However, many occasions arise in the course of their interaction in which some sort of control over behavior is necessary. Behavioral norms provide a means of meeting this dilemma: they control behavior but do not entail the difficulties created by the unrestrained use of interpersonal power. For example, they may include a definite and unchanging statement that behavior x is expected from person B, the weaker of the two. Knowing this, B need not worry about a change in the rules; he can always be confident about what to do in order to attain good outcomes or avoid poor ones. Furthermore, if he accepts the norm, B will perform the required behavior even in the absence of surveillance, thus relieving A of the necessity of monitoring him. (In larger groups wide acceptance of a norm has the further consequence that there can be sharing of the task of maintaining whatever surveillance is necessary, thereby reducing the cost to each individual.) The general point is that both weaker and stronger persons stand to gain from the introduction of mutually acceptable rules which introduce regularity and control into the relationship without recourse to the direct interpersonal application of power.

Consistent with this view is evidence obtained by Wispe and Lloyd (1955)

[1] "If, by varying his behavior, A can make it desirable for B to vary his behavior too, then A has behavior control over B" (Thibaut & Kelley, 1957, p. 103).—Eds.
[2] "If, by varying his behavior, A can affect B's outcomes, regardless of what B does, A has fate control over B" (Thibaut & Kelley, 1957, p. 102).—Eds.

that structured normative procedures are preferred to more informal and spontaneous ones by low-power members. Forty-three life insurance agents were interviewed about their preferences for various types of interactions between agents and managers. The main result of the study was that, as compared with highly productive agents, the less productive ones preferred their interaction with managers to be structured and normative rather than informal and spontaneous. Since the productivity of the agents fluctuated over time rather erratically, nearly all of the agents performed poorly from time to time. The authors interpret their findings to mean that those who are currently producing poorly, hence are very vulnerable, experience less anxiety about their vulnerability if there are structured procedures to protect them from managerial power.

The general contention advanced above can be argued from a slightly different point of view. Consider a dyad in which one member, A, performs a certain special behavior that is highly rewarding to B. As long as A continues to perform this sequence, there will be no problem; B will come to *expect* it in the sense of predicting that A is likely to repeat it in the future. However, if A is somewhat undependable or even merely exhibits covert tendencies not to perform his special function, B's dependency upon him is dramatized and becomes somewhat difficult to tolerate. This might be explained by assuming the existence of a need for autonomy (Murray, 1938) that motivates people to avoid interpersonal situations in which they are dependent upon others. Perhaps it is simpler merely to suggest that dependency upon an unreliable person is cost increasing. In interaction

with such a person one often begins behavioral sequences without being able to consummate them, and one frequently does things for him without getting anything in return. On the other hand, dependency is no problem with a perfectly reliable deliverer of rewards, for example, a bountiful environment or the corner grocer with his stable prices.

So B's problem is to strengthen A's tendency to perform the desired sequence without making too apparent his dependency upon A, that is, without suffering power loss. This is done by an appeal to a supra-individual value connected with the welfare of some third agent, set of persons, or organization rather than with B's own welfare. Such appeals as "Do it because it's good," "People expect it of you," or "Do it for the group" are essentially power-maintenance strategies. They play down the value of the behavior to the person making the appeal or request but at the same time insure that the performance will continue. Allport (1954) summarizes an extremely cynical version of this point, advanced by Le Dantec. Moral standards such as those expressed in the Ten Commandments are described as being promulgated merely for the convenience of those who have some interest to protect, as, for example, property owners—"Thou shalt not steal"— and persons who have sexual partners— "Thou shalt not commit adultery." Thus B attempts to change the basis for A's performing the behavior from that of doing B a personal favor to that of satisfying social or moral obligations.

This process of transforming the value basis for compliance is probably supported and reinforced by conflict reduction on the part of A, the performer. If he has impulses not to help his partner, he has a recurring conflict between incompatible activities, those rewarding to B versus those which are not. This conflict is costly and can be reduced by mobilizing powerful instigations to only one kind of behavior. These are provided by the moralistic or social value appeals used by B which give A a justification for overvaluing the desirability of the behavior. Thus acceptance of supra-individual, depersonalized values as the basis for behavior has functional value both for the actor and the one dependent upon his actions.

Norms have similar functional values in many dyads in which power is evenly distributed. In highly cohesive groups the great power the two members have over each other not only gives them ability to carry out strong influence measures but also to resist each other's influence. This situation potentially leads to interpersonal conflicts and unresolved "stand-offs" in which neither one is able to get the other to engage in desired acitivities. This type of conflict can be avoided by procedural rules in which power is transferred, so to speak, from personal agents to the norms. Then, when A tries to induce B to do something, B is expected to perceive the locus of causality for the influence attempt not as internal to a whimsical or self-aggrandizing A but as existing in the depersonalized norm on behalf of which A is acting. We might expect that the counterpower (or resistance) that B might mobilize against A's suggestion would not exist for an impersonal set of rules. Alternatively stated, in a highly cohesive dyad B's counterpower derives from his ability to affect A's fate; this source of resistance is eliminated when power is depersonal-

ized by transfer to a set of procedures or rules. (Note the implication that norms will develop more rapidly and more surely in highly cohesive groups, assuming that the majority of the members have about the same degree of dependence on the group, than in less cohesive groups.) Frank (1944) provides evidence that an appeal to an impersonal value encounters less resistance than does the direct exercise of personal power.

Even if equal power does not lead to interpersonal impasses, the interaction process is likely to be characterized by a good deal of argument and informal litigation. Unless argument and uncertainty happen to be rewarding in themselves, they merely represent unnecessary costs. These costs can be substantially reduced by agreements that enable the individuals to run off their most frequent interaction sequences according to automatic routines, without moment-by-moment decision making. Green (1956) comments on this point, "What an utter chaos human life would be— it could not long endure—if every day we had to settle by family debate or authoritarian decision how many meals we would eat *this* day, at what hour of the day or night" (p. 75). In a similar vein, MacIver and Page (1949) write of norms, "Without them the burden of decision would be intolerable and the vagaries of conduct utterly distracting" (p. 207). It may also be noted that for both members of a dyad the necessity of invoking power on the one hand and the necessity of complying with it on the other tend to bring to mind and dramatize the dependence of each upon the other. As we have stated above, the feeling of dependence is probably something most people would rather avoid. To the extent that there is depersonalization of influence, the source of power and control being external to both individuals, the basic fact of their interdependence goes unstated and probably unnoticed.

In short, we may view norms as social inventions that accomplish more effectively what otherwise would require informal social influence. We do not intend to imply that norms are deliberately developed for this purpose. The contention is merely that there exists a basis for unconscious collusion between weaker and stronger persons, between controllers and the controlled, between persons highly dependent upon each other—a collusion that has the effect of bringing regularity and control into the relationship without the informal exercise of personal power.

Some implications

This point of view has several important implications. *First,* if the central assertion is correct, that norms are means of influence and control which minimize the problems created by informal influence, then from a close examination of informal influence and its problems we should be able to infer the general *properties of norms.* This requires little explanation beyond that contained in the preceding pages. Norms are, in the first place, *rules about behavior.* They tell each person what is expected of him in certain situations, and in so doing they indirectly indicate requests that others may not properly make of him. In this way, he is protected from subjugation to another's whimsically exercised power. Norms are also *stable* so that the individual knows not only what is expected of him today but what

will be expected of him tomorrow. Furthermore, norms are based upon *agreement or consensus* which reduces the necessity for thorough surveillance and, in large groups, distributes the responsibility for surveillance rather widely. The enforcement of norms often involves *appeals to impersonal values or suprapersonal agents,* which reduce the extent to which compliance is viewed as a matter of giving in to a more powerful person and thereby reduces resistance. Also these values are often *widely held* among the group members, so that once they have been associated with compliance it becomes directly rewarding and the need for exercise of external control is greatly reduced. Simmel (1902) puts the last point this way:

In the morality of the individual, society creates for itself an organ which is not only more fundamentally operative than law and custom, but which also spares society the different sorts of costs involved in these institutions. Hence the tendency of society to satisfy its demands as cheaply as possible results in appeals to "good conscience," through which the individual pays to himself the wages for his righteousness, which otherwise would probably have to be assured to him in some way through law or custom (p. 19n).

The *second* implication is this: If norms are to control or replace interpersonal influence, then they should have some relevance to the things about which this influence is exercised. What norms are about, that which is commonly called the *content of norms,* should be inferable from a consideration of the things about which group members find it necessary to influence each other.

47   Conformity as a tactic of ingratiation

EDWARD E. JONES

There seems to be much promise in looking at social interaction with an eye to the unfolding of strategies designed to gain or maintain personal power. There is nothing novel in the suggestion that there is a strategic side to social behavior—that people try to calculate ways to make the most of a particular relationship—but the attempt to study such strategies by laboratory experimentation is a recent development (see Jones, 1964).[1]

All interpersonal relationships involve mutual dependence; this is the equivalent of saying that each party to a social interchange has potential influence over certain rewards available to and costs incurred by the other. If the dependences of one on the other are not only mutual but approximately equal, then there is a balance of power in which each can enforce a certain minimal receipt of rewards through his capacity to enact or fail to enact the responses sought by the other. When the power in a two-person relationship is asymmetrical, however, the more dependent person is somewhat at the mercy of the more powerful one. In any event, we can well understand why the more dependent person is concerned about his poor position and, under most circumstances, tries in various ways to improve it.

[1] Ingratiation is "strategic behaviors . . . designed to influence a particular other person concerning the attractiveness of one's personal qualities" (p. 11).—Eds.

When we look at the strategic alternatives available to the more dependent person, it appears that some of these strategies guarantee him at least a certain minimum of rewards but do so at the expense of confirming or strengthening the power asymmetry which defines his dependence. Other strategies, however, may be effective in modifying the asymmetry itself so that the dependent person's power is, in the long run, increased. Compliance is an example of one kind of dependence-confirming tactic. The dependent person may, through overt obedience, avoid punishment and secure the rewards available to him, but such compliance tends to perpetuate the power differential to which it is a response. For example, the more reliable the worker becomes in meeting the supervisor's demands, the more confident the supervisor will be that these demands are reasonable, and that the worker is happy with the "bargain" symbolized by the difference in their power. In contrast to compliance, we may view ingratiation as power-enhancing or dependence-reducing. By making himself attractive to the more powerful person, the more dependent person increases the value of his own sanctioning responses at the same time that he makes it more difficult for the powerful person to apply the full range of sanctions that were initially part of his repertory. In other words, as the dependent person becomes more attrac-

Excerpted from **Science**, 1965, 149, No. 3680. 144–50, with permission of the author and publisher. Copyright © 1965 by the American Association for the Advancement of Science.

tive, the powerful person cannot punish him without greater cost to himself. This, in effect, means that his power has been reduced.

By what specific tactical means may the dependent person increase his attractiveness? Such tactics are undoubtedly as various as social behavior itself —there is an appealing and an unappealing way of doing almost everything. But I have found it particularly useful to consider three main classes of tactics available to the "ingratiator:" compliments, agreement, and presentation of oneself in a favorable light. We may support and flatter others, convince them that we share their views, or present our characteristics in terms that they can appreciate. In this article, I single out agreement, or conformity of opinion, as the dependent variable of particular interest. The experiments reviewed all show how persons modify their publicly expressed opinions as a way of coping with a condition of social dependence.

First, however, it is appropriate to comment on some of the moral issues involved in the behavior we are studying. *Ingratiation*, like its sister term, *flattery*, is at least mildly pejorative in everyday usage. The word has connotations of dissimulation and deceit in social communication. Am I suggesting, then, that most of us are so concerned with the effects of our behavior on others that we deliberately engage in manipulative and deceitful tactics in order to gain their esteem? I do not know how one could ever obtain actuarial figures on this point, but I would argue—without great alarm—that all of us under·appropriate circumstances do shape our social responses to increase our attractiveness to particular people. The scientific student of such response-

shaping is unlikely to make much progress by interviews or naturalistic observation. In this particular area, I have learned through research experience that people are extremely likely to deceive themselves. Not only do they want to avoid publicizing the extent to which their responses to others are conditioned by approval-seeking motives, they work busily to protect themselves from awareness of the link between wanting to be liked and modifying one's behavior to this end. It is my current belief that only by comparing appropriate experimental and control treatments can we begin to explore the conditions favorable to the tactics of ingratiation and thus begin to specify the variables essential to construction of a theory concerning it. Questions of the frequency of occurrence and the extent of such behavior in the natural environment, and questions concerning individual differences, are not considered here.

The ingratiator's dilemma

Much of the fascination in studying ingratiation comes from the fact that the same situational factors that increase one person's desire to be found attractive by another alert the other (the "target" person) to the likelihood of tactical behavior. Thus, the dependent person will be strongly motivated to be ingratiating, but the fact that his dependence stands revealed reduces the likelihood that his overtures will be effective. His dilemma is magnified further by his natural reluctance to see himself as deceitful or manipulative. Thus, the more dependent he is on another, the more he will be forced to justify to himself any actions conceivably designed to curry favor with the other. These two factors—the target person's alertness to overtures from a dependent person and the dependent person's reluctance to see himself as one who uses manipulative social tactics— would seem almost to rule out ingratiating tactics in those very situations where it is important to be liked. Indeed, there is fairly good evidence that such tactics can boomerang; especially when the "actor" is highly dependent on the target person, the latter is apt to be more attracted to him if he shows some restraint in his praise or in the degree of his agreement. The results of three studies (see Jones, 1965) show that, in the ambiguous area of social responses that may or may not make one seem attractive to another person, the role relation between the ingratiator and the target person is a critical factor which affects the latter's judgments of manipulative intentions or ulterior motivation.

To some extent, however, the ingratiator is protected by the vanity of the target person from having such judgments go against him. Each of us likes to believe the best about himself, and many of us must be exposed to the most blatant praise before we begin to suspect that we are the targets of manipulative intentions. Often, no doubt, the ingratiator joins his target in what might be called an autistic conspiracy, since, for understandable psychological reasons, both the ingratiator and the target person are anxious to believe that the latter is better than he is.

I now feel that this autistic conspiracy may be maintained by the most intricate interpersonal tactics—tactics designed to conceal from both the "tactician" and the target person the former's underlying intentions. Since I believe that not many of us deliberately and consciously calculate such tactical maneuvers, I am suggesting that, from well-learned orientations toward those more powerful than ourselves, we develop patterns of social behavior unwittingly designed to attract, while avoiding the extremes of sycophancy. Such extremes would reveal to both parties the true nature of the autistic conspiracy.

Issue relevance and agreement

My central thesis thus far has been that dependence increases the motivation to make oneself seem attractive, but public knowledge of this dependence makes it more difficult to gain esteem through such simple stratagems as slavish agreement or effusive compliments. In order to be successful, the ingratiator must complicate his tactics and inject some subtlety. One obvious way to increase subtlety is to convey the impression of agreeing in a discerning way. The ingratiator must steer between the Scylla of errant disagreement and the Charybdis of blatant conformity, conveying minor disagreement within the context of a general similarity of position. Beyond this, if we know something about the social context in which opinions are being exchanged, it may be possible to specify the issues on which agreement is most likely and the issues on which moderate disagreement may be expected.

One important aspect of the social context is the relative difference in status between the two persons involved in the interchange. Status differences usually imply asymmetrical power, which is one of the preconditions for ingratiation tactics.[2]

[2] Several research studies (e.g., Jones, Gergen, & Jones, 1963) which are considered at this point in Professor Jones's paper have been omitted in this abridgment.—Eds.

48 Bystander "apathy"

BIBB LATANÉ and JOHN M. DARLEY

On a March night in 1964, Kitty Genovese was set upon by a maniac as she came home from work at 3 A.M. Thirty-eight of her Kew Gardens neighbors came to their windows when she cried out in terror—none came to her assistance. Even though her assailant took over half an hour to murder her, no one even so much as called the police.

This story became the journalistic sensation of the decade. "Apathy," cried the newspapers. "Indifference," said the columnists and commentators. "Moral callousness," "dehumanization," "loss of concern for our fellow man," added preachers, professors, and other sermonizers. Movies, television specials, plays, and books explored this incident and many more like it. Americans became concerned about their lack of concern.

But can these epithets be correct? We think not. Although it is unquestionably true that witnesses in such emergencies have often done nothing to save the victims, "apathy," "indifference," and "unconcern" are not entirely accurate descriptions of their reactions. The 38 witnesses to Kitty Genovese's murder did not merely look at the scene once and then ignore it. Instead they continued to stare out their windows at what was going on. Caught, fascinated, distressed, unwilling to act but unable to turn away, their behavior was neither helpful nor heroic; but it was not indifferent or apathetic either.

Actually, it was like crowd behavior in many other emergency situations; car accidents, drownings, fires, and attempted suicides all attract substantial numbers of people who watch the drama in helpless fascination without getting directly involved in the action. Are these people alienated and indifferent? Are the rest of us? Obviously not. It seems only yesterday we were being called overconforming. But why, then, don't we act?

Even if empathy or sympathy were not strong enough to lead us to help in emergencies, there are a variety of social norms which suggest that each of us has a responsibility to each other, and that help is the proper thing to do. "Do unto others as you would have them do unto you," we hear from our earliest years. Although norms such as these may not have much influence on our behavior in specific situations, they may imbue us with a general predisposition to try to help others.

If people are willing to help in non-emergency situations, they should be even more willing to help in emergencies when the need is so much greater. Or should they? Emergencies differ in many ways from other types of situations in which people need help, and these differences may be important. The very nature of an emergency implies certain psychological consequences.

Abridged from the **American Scientist**, 1969, 57, 244–68, with permission of the authors and the publisher.

Characteristics of emergencies

Perhaps the most distinctive characteristic of an emergency is that it involves threat or harm. Life, well-being, or property is in danger. Even if an emergency is successfully dealt with, nobody is better off afterwards than before. Except in rare circumstances, the best that can be hoped for if an emergency occurs is a return to the status quo. Consequently, there are few positive rewards for successful action in an emergency. At worst, an emergency can claim the lives not only of those people who were initially involved in it, but also of anybody who intervenes in the situation. This fact puts pressures on individuals to ignore a potential emergency, to distort their perceptions of it, or to underestimate their responsibility for coping with it.

The second important feature of an emergency is that it is an unusual and rare event. Fortunately, although he may read about them in newspapers, or watch fictionalized accounts on television, the average person probably will encounter fewer than half a dozen serious emergencies in his lifetime. Unfortunately when he does encounter one, he will have had little direct personal experience in handling such a situation. Unlike the stereotyped patterns of his everyday behavior, an individual facing an emergency is untrained and unrehearsed.

In addition to being rare, emergencies differ widely, one from another. There are few common requirements for action between a drowning, a fire, or an automobile accident. Each emergency presents a different problem, and each requires a different type of action. Consequently, unlike other rare events, our culture provides us with little secondhand wisdom about how to deal with emergencies.

The fourth basic characteristic of emergencies is that they are unforeseen. They "emerge," suddenly and without warning. Being unexpected, emergencies must be handled without the benefit of forethought and planning and an individual does not have the opportunity to think through in advance what course of action he should take when faced with an emergency. He must do his thinking in the immediacy of the situation, and has no opportunity to consult others as to the best course of action or to alert others who are especially equipped to deal with emergencies. The individual confronted with an emergency is thrown on his own resources. We have already seen that he does not have much in the way of practiced responses or cultural stereotypes to fall back upon.

A final characteristic of an emergency is that it requires instant action. It represents a pressing necessity. If the emergency is not dealt with immediately, the situation will deteriorate. The threat will transform itself into damage; the harm will continue or spread. There are urgent pressures to deal with the situation at once. The requirement for immediate action prevents the individual confronted with an emergency from leisurely considering the possible courses of action open to him. It forces him to come to a decision before he has had time to consider his alternatives. It places him in a condition of stress.

The picture we have drawn is a rather grim one. Faced with a situation in which there is no benefit to be gained for himself, unable to rely on past experience, on the experience of others, or on forethought and planning, denied the opportunity to consider carefully his course of action, the bystander to an emergency is in an unenviable position.

It is perhaps surprising that anyone should intervene at all.

A model of the intervention process

If an individual is to intervene in an emergency, he must make, not just one, but a *series* of decisions. Only one particular set of choices will lead him to take action in the situation. Let us now consider the behavioral and cognitive processes that go on in an individual who is in the vicinity of an emergency. What must he do and decide before he actually intervenes? These may have important implications for predicting whether an individual will act.

Let us suppose that an emergency is actually taking place. A middle-aged man, walking down the street, has a heart attack. He stops short, clutches his chest, and staggers to the nearest building wall, where he slowly slumps to the sidewalk in a sitting position. What is the likelihood with which a passerby will come to his assistance? First, the bystander has to *notice* that something is happening. The external event has to break into his thinking and intrude itself on his conscious mind. He must tear himself away from his private thoughts or from the legs of the pretty girl walking down the street ahead of him and pay attention to this unusual event.

Once the person is aware of the event as something to be explained, it is necessary that he *interpret* the event. Specifically, he must decide that there is something wrong, that this ambiguous event is an emergency. It may be that the man slumped on the sidewalk is only a drunk, beyond any assistance that the passerby can give him. If the bystander decided that something is indeed wrong, he must next decide that he has a *re-sponsibility* to act. Perhaps help is on the way or perhaps someone else might be better qualified to help. Even in an emergency, it is not clear that everybody should immediately intrude himself into the situation.

If the person does decide that he should help, he must decide what *form of assistance* he can give. Should he rush in directly and try to help the victim or should he detour by calling a doctor or the police? Finally, of course, he must decide how to *implement* his choice and form of intervention. Where is the nearest telephone? Is there a hospital nearby? At this point, the person may finally begin to act in the situation. The socially responsible act is the end point of a series of decisions that the person makes.

Second, the bystander in an emergency is not a detached and objective observer. His decisions have consequences for himself just as much as for the victim. Unfortunately, however, the rewards and penalties for action and inaction are biased in favor of inaction. All the bystander has to gain from intervention is a feeling of pride and the chance to be a hero. On the other hand, he can be made to appear a fool, sued, or even attacked and wounded. By leaving the situation, he has little to lose but his self-respect. There are strong pressures against deciding that an event is an emergency.

Intervention, then, requires choosing a single course of action through a rather complex matrix of possible actions. The failure to intervene may result from failing to notice an event, failing to realize that the event is an emergency, failing to feel personally responsible for dealing with the emergency, or failing to have sufficient skill to intervene.

Social determinants of bystander intervention, I

Most emergencies are, or at least begin as, ambiguous events. A quarrel in the street may erupt into violence, but it may be simply a family argument. A man staggering about may be suffering a coronary or an onset of diabetes; he may simply be drunk. Smoke pouring from a building may signal a fire; on the other hand, it may be simply steam or airconditioner vapor. Before a bystander is likely to take action in such ambiguous situations, he must first define the event as an emergency and decide that intervention is the proper course of action.

In the course of making these decisions, it is likely that an individual bystander will be considerably influenced by the decisions he perceives other bystanders to be taking. If everyone else in a group of onlookers seems to regard an event as nonserious and the proper course of action as non-intervention, this consensus may strongly affect the perceptions of any single individual and inhibit his potential intervention.

The definitions that other people hold may be discovered by discussing the situation with them, but they may also be inferred from their facial expressions or their behavior. A whistling man with his hands in his pockets obviously does not believe he is in the midst of a crisis. A bystander who does not respond to smoke obviously does not attribute it to fire. An individual seeing the inaction of others, will judge the situation as less serious than he would if alone.

But why should the others be inactive? Unless there were some force inhibiting responses on the part of others, the kind of social influence process described would, by itself, only lead to a convergence of attitudes within a group. If each individual expressed his true feelings, then, even if each member of the group were entirely guided by the reactions of the others, the group should still respond with a likelihood equal to the average of the individuals.

An additional factor is involved, however. Each member of a group may watch the others, but he is also aware that others are watching him. They are an audience to his own reactions. Among American males, it is considered desirable to appear poised and collected in times of stress. Being exposed to the public view may constrain the actions and expressions of emotion of any individual as he tries to avoid possible ridicule and embarrassment. Even though he may be truly concerned and upset about the plight of a victim, until he decides what to do, he may maintain a calm demeanor.

The constraints involved with being in public might in themselves tend to inhibit action by individuals in a group, but in conjunction with the social influence process described above, they may be expected to have even more powerful effects. If each member of a group is, at the same time, trying to appear calm and also looking around at the other members to gauge their reactions, all members may be led (or misled) by each other to define the situation as less critical than they would if alone. Until someone acts, each person sees only other non-responding bystanders, and is likely to be influenced not to act himself. A state of "pluralistic ignorance" may develop.

It has often been recognized (Brown, 1954, 1965) that a crowd can cause contagion of panic, leading each person in the crowd to over-react to an emergency to the detriment of everyone's welfare. What we suggest here is that a crowd can also force inaction on its members. It can suggest, implicitly but strongly, by its passive behavior that an event is not to be reacted to as an emergency, and it can make any individual uncomfortably aware of what a fool he will look for behaving as if it is.

This line of thought suggests that individuals may be less likely to intervene in an emergency if they witness it in the presence of other people than if they see it alone. It suggests that the presence of other people may lead each person to interpret the situation as less serious, and less demanding of action than he would if alone. The presence of other people may alter each bystander's perceptions and interpretations of the situation. We suspect that the presence of other people may also affect each individual's assessment of the rewards and costs involved in taking action, and indeed we will discuss this possibility in some detail later. First, however, let us look at evidence relevant to this initial process.

EXPERIMENT 1. WHERE THERE'S SMOKE, THERE'S (SOMETIMES) FIRE [1]

In this experiment we presented an emergency to individuals either alone, in the presence of two passive others (confederates of the experimenter who were instructed to notice the emergency but remain indifferent to it), or in groups of three. It was our expectation that individuals faced with the passive reactions of the confederates would be influenced by them and thus less likely to take action than single subjects. We also predicted that the constaints on behavior in public combined with social influence processes would lessen the

[1] A more detailed report of this experiment is given in Latané & Darley (1968).

likelihood that members of three-person groups would act to cope with the emergency.

Male Columbia students living in campus residences were invited to an interview to discuss "some of the problems involved in life at an urban university." As they sat in a small room waiting to be called for the interview and filling out a preliminary questionnaire, they faced an ambiguous but potentially dangerous situation as a stream of smoke began to puff into the room through a wall vent. Some subjects filled out the questionnaire and were exposed to this potentially critical situation while alone. Others were part of three-person groups consisting of one subject and two confederates acting the part of naive subjects. The confederates attempted to avoid conversation as much as possible. Once the smoke had been introduced, they stared at it briefly, made no comment, but simply shrugged their shoulders, returned to the questionnaires and continued to fill them out, occasionally waving away the smoke to do so.

As soon as the subjects had completed two pages of their questionnaires, the experimenter began to introduce the smoke through a small vent in the wall. The "smoke" was finely divided titanium dioxide produced in a stoppered bottle and delivered under slight air pressure through the vent. It formed a moderately fine-textured but clearly visible stream of whitish smoke. For the entire experimental period, the smoke continued to jet into the room in irregular puffs. By the end of the experimental period, vision was obscured in the room by the amount of smoke present.

All behavior and conversation was observed and coded from behind a one-way window (largely disguised on the subject's side by a large sign giving preliminary instructions). When and if the subject left the experimental room and reported the smoke, he was told that the situation "would be taken care of." If the subject had not reported the smoke within six minutes of the time he first noticed it, the experiment was terminated.

The typical subject, when tested alone, behaved very reasonably. Usually, shortly after the smoke appeared, he would glance up from his questionnaire, notice the smoke, show a slight but distinct startle reaction, and then undergo a brief period of indecision, and perhaps return briefly to his questionnaire before again staring at the smoke. Soon, most subjects would get up from their chairs, walk over to the vent, and investigate it closely, sniffing the smoke, waving their hands in it, feeling its temperature, etc. The usual Alone subject would hesitate again, but finally walk out of the room, look around outside, and, finding somebody there, calmly report the presence of the smoke. No subject showed any sign of panic; most simply said, "There's something strange going on in there, there seems to be some sort of smoke coming through the wall. . . ." The median subject in the Alone condition had reported the smoke within two minutes of first noticing it. Three-quarters of the 24 people run in this condition reported the smoke before the experimental period was terminated.

The behavior of subjects run with two passive confederates was dramatically different; of ten people run in this condition, only one reported the smoke. The other nine stayed in the waiting room as it filled up with smoke, doggedly working on their questionnaires and waving the fumes away from their faces. They coughed, rubbed their eyes, and

opened the window—but they did not report the smoke. The difference between the response rate of 75% in the Alone condition and 10% in the Two Passive Confederates condition is highly significant ($p < .002$ by Fisher's Exact test, two-tailed).

The results of this study clearly support the predictions. Individuals exposed to a room filling with smoke in the presence of passive others themselves remained passive, and groups of three naive subjects were less likely to report the smoke than solitary bystanders. Our predictions were confirmed—but this does not necessarily mean that our explanation for these results is the correct one. As a matter of fact several alternatives are available. Subjects' behavior might have reflected their fear of fire, with subjects in groups feeling less threatened by the fire than single subjects and thus less concerned to act. It has been demonstrated in studies with humans (Schachter, 1959) and with rats (Latané, 1969; Latané and Glass, 1968) that togetherness reduces fear, even in situations where it does not reduce danger. In addition, subjects may have felt that the presence of others increased their ability to cope with fire. For both these reasons, subjects in groups may have been less afraid of fire and thus less likely to report the smoke than solitary subjects. A similar explanation might emphasize, not fearfulness, but the desire to hide fear.

EXPERIMENT 2. A LADY IN DISTRESS [2]

Although it seems unlikely that the group inhibition of bystander intervention observed in Experiment 1 can be attributed entirely to the fact that smoke represents a danger to the indi-

[2] A more detailed description of this experiment is given in Latané & Rodin (1969).

vidual bystander, it is certainly possible that this is so. Experiment 2 was designed to see whether similar group inhibition effects could be observed in situations where there is no danger to the individual himself for not acting. In addition, a new variable was included: whether the bystanders knew each other.

Male Columbia undergraduates waited either alone, with a friend, or with a stranger to participate in a market research study. As they waited, they heard someone fall and apparently injure herself in the room next door. Whether they tried to help, and how long they took to do so were the main dependent variables of the study. Subjects were telephoned and offered $2 to participate in a survey of game and puzzle preferences conducted at Columbia by the Consumer Testing Bureau (CTB), a market research organization. Each person contacted was asked to find a friend who would also be interested in participating. Only those students who recommended friends, and the friends they suggested, were used as subjects.

In one condition (Alone, $n = 26$) each subject was by himself in the testing room while he filled out the questionnaire and heard the fall. In a second condition (Stooge, $n = 14$), a stranger, actually a confederate of the experimenter, was also present. The confederate had instructions to be as passive as possible and to answer questions put to him by the subjects with a brief gesture or remark. During the emergency, he looked up, shrugged his shoulders, and continued working on his questionnaire. Subjects in the third condition (Strangers, $n = 20$ pairs) were placed in the testing room in pairs. Each subject in the pair was unacquainted with the other before entering the room and they were not introduced. Only

one subject in this condition spontaneously introduced himself to the other. In a final condition (Friends, $n = 20$ pairs), pairs of friends overheard the incident together.

Alone vs. Stooge conditions: Seventy per cent of all subjects who heard the accident while alone in the waiting room offered to help the victim before she left the room. By contrast the presence of a non-responsive bystander markedly inhibited helping. Only 7% of subjects in the Stooge condition intervened. These subjects seemed upset and confused during the emergency and frequently glanced at the passive confederate who continued working on his questionnaire.

Alone vs. Two Strangers: Since 70% of Alone subjects intervened, we should expect that at least one person in 91% of all two-person groups would offer help if members of a pair had no influence upon each other. In fact, members did influence each other. In only 40% of the groups did even one person offer help to the injured woman.

Strangers vs. Stooge: The response rate in the Two Strangers condition appears to be somewhat higher than the 7% rate in the Stooge condition. Making a correction similar to that used for the Alone scores, the expected response rate based on the Stooge condition is 13%.

Alone vs. Two Friends: Pairs of friends often talked about the questionnaire before the accident, and sometimes discussed a course of action after the fall. Even so, in only 70% of the pairs did even one person intervene. While, superficially, this appears as high as the Alone condition, there must again be a correction for the fact that twice as many people are free to act.

Friends vs. Strangers: Although pairs

of friends were inhibited from helping when compared to the Alone condition, they were significantly faster to intervene than were pairs of strangers ($p < .01$).

These first experiments show that in two, widely different types of emergency settings, the presence of other people inhibits intervention. Subjects were less likely to report a possible fire when together than alone, and they were less likely to go to the aid of the victim of an accident when others were present. Is this a general effect? Will it apply to all types of emergency? Are there situations in which the presence of other people might actually facilitate bystander intervention? One possible set of circumstances in which we might expect social facilitation of intervention is when an emergency is caused by a villain. People who fail to intervene in real emergencies sometimes claim they were afraid of the consequences of intervention—afraid of direct attack, afraid of later retribution, afraid of having to go to court. In situations involving a villain, even if one person is afraid to take action, the presence of other people as potential risk-sharing allies might embolden him to intervene. Under these circumstances, there might actually be a group facilitation of intervention. To test this possibility, two Columbia undergraduates, Paul Bonnarigo and Malcolm Ross, turned to a life of crime.

EXPERIMENT 3. THE CASE OF
THE STOLEN BEER

The Nu-Way Beverage Center in Suffern, New York, is a discount beer store. It sells beer and soda by the case, often to New Jerseyans who cross the state line to find both lowered prices and a lowered legal drinking age. During the spring of 1968 it was the scene of a minor crime wave—within one two-week period, it was robbed 96 times. The robbers followed much the same modus operandi on each occasion. Singly or in a pair, they would enter the store and ask the cashier at the checkout counter "What is the most expensive imported beer that you carry?" The cashier, in cahoots with the robbers, would reply "Lowenbrau. I'll go back and check how much we have." Leaving the robbers in the front of the store, the cashier would disappear into the rear to look for the Lowenbrau. After waiting for a minute, the robbers would pick up a case of beer near the front of the store, remark to nobody in particular, "They'll never miss this," walk out of the front door, put the beer in their car, and drive off. On 46 occasions, one robber carried off the theft; on 46 occasions, two robbers were present.

The robberies were always staged when there were either one or two people in the store, and the timing was arranged so that the one or both customers would be at the checkout counter at the time when the robbers entered. On 46 occasions, one customer was at the checkout counter during the theft; on 46 occasions, two customers were present. Although occasionally the two customers had come in together, more usually they were strangers to each other. Sixty-one per cent of the customers were male, 39% female. Since the checkout counter was about 20 feet from the front door, since the theft itself took less than a minute, and since the robbers were both husky young men, nobody tried directly to prevent the theft. There were, however, other courses of intervention available.

When the cashier returned from the rear of the store, he went to the checkout counter and resumed waiting on the customers there. After a minute, if nobody had spontaneously mentioned the theft, he casually inquired, "Hey, what happened to that man (those men) who was (were) in here? Did you see him (them) leave?" At this point the customer could either report the theft, say merely that he had seen the man or men leave, or disclaim any knowledge of the event whatsoever. Overall, 20% of the subjects reported the theft spontaneously, and 51% of the remainder reported it upon prompting. Since the results from each criterion followed an identical pattern, we shall indicate only the total proportion of subjects in each condition who reported the theft, whether spontaneously or not.

Results: Whether there were one or two robbers present made little difference. Customers were somewhat but not significantly more likely to report the theft if there were two robbers (69%) than if there was only one (52%). Sex also made no difference; females were as likely to report as males. The number of customers, on the other hand, made a big difference. Thirty-one of the 48 single customers, or 65%, mentioned the theft. From this, we would expect that 87% of the two-person groups would include at least one reporter. In fact, in only 56% of the two-person groups did even one person report the theft ($p <$ .01). Social inhibition of reporting was so strong that the theft was actually somewhat (though not significantly) less likely to be reported when two people saw it than when only one did.

In three widely differing situations the same effect has been observed. People are less likely to take a socially responsible action if other people are present than if they are alone. This effect has occurred in a situation involving general danger, in a situation

where someone has been the victim of an accident, and in a situation involving one or more villains. The effect holds in real life as well as in the laboratory, and for members of the general population as well as college students. The results of each of these three experiments clearly support the line of theoretical argument advanced earlier. When bystanders to an emergency can see the reactions of other people, and when other people can see their own reactions, each individual may, through a process of social influence, be led to interpret the situation as less serious than he would if he were alone, and consequently be less likely to take action.

Social determinants of bystander intervention, II

So far we have devoted our attention exclusively to one stage of our hypothesized model of the intervention process: noticing the situation and interpreting it. Once an individual has noticed an emergency and interpreted it as being serious, he still has to decide what, if anything, he will do about it. He must decide that he has a responsibility to help, and that there is some form of assistance that he is in a position to give. He is faced with the choice of whether he himself will intervene. His decision will presumably be made in terms of the rewards and costs of the various alternative courses of action open to him.

In addition to affecting the interpretations that he places on a situation, the presence of other people can also alter the rewards and costs facing an individual bystander. Perhaps most importantly, the presence of other people can alter the cost of not acting. If only one bystander is present at an emergency, he carries all of the responsibility for dealing with it; he will feel all of the guilt for not acting; he will bear all of any blame others may level for non-intervention. If others are present, the onus of responsibility is diffused, and the individual may be more likely to resolve his conflict between intervening and not intervening in favor of the latter alternative.

When only one bystander is present at an emergency, if help is to come it must be from him. Although he may choose to ignore them (out of concern for his personal safety, or desire "not to get involved"), any pressures to intervene focus uniquely on him. When there are several observers present, however, the pressures to intervene do not focus on any one of the observers; instead the responsibility for intervention is shared among all the onlookers and is not unique to any one. As a result, each may be less likely to help.

Potential blame may also be diffused. However much we wish to think that an individual's moral behavior is divorced from considerations of personal punishment or reward, there is both theory and evidence to the contrary. It is perfectly reasonable to assume that, under circumstances of group responsibility for a punishable act, the punishment or blame that accrues to any one individual is often slight or nonexistent.

Finally, if others are known to be present, but their behavior cannot be closely observed, any one bystander may assume that one of the other observers is already taking action to end the emergency. If so, his own intervention would only be redundant—perhaps harmfully or confusingly so. Thus, given the presence of other onlookers whose behavior cannot be observed, any given bystander can rationalize his own inaction by con-

vincing himself that "somebody else must be doing something."

These considerations suggest that, even when bystanders to an emergency cannot see or be influenced by each other, the more bystanders who are present, the less likely any one bystander would be to intervene and provide aid. To test this suggestion, it would be necessary to create an emergency situation in which each subject is blocked from communicating with others to prevent his getting information about their behavior during the emergency. Experiment 4 attempted to fulfill this requirement.

EXPERIMENT 4. A FIT TO BE TRIED [3]
Procedure: Thirteen male and 104 female students in introductory psychology courses at New York University were recruited to take part in an unspecified experiment as part of their class requirement. When a subject arrived in the laboratory, he was ushered into an individual room from which a communication system would enable him to talk to the other participants (who were actually figments of the tape recorder). Over the intercom, the subject was told that the experimenter was concerned with the kinds of personal problems faced by normal college students in a high-pressure, urban environment, and that he would be asked to participate in a discussion about these problems. To avoid possible embarrassment about discussing personal problems with strangers, the experimenter said, several precautions would be taken. First, subjects would remain anonymous, which was why they had been placed in individual rooms rather than face-to-face. Second, the experimenter would not listen to the initial discussion him-

[3] Portions of these results have been reported in Darley & Latané (1968).

self, but would only get the subjects' reactions later by questionnaire.

The plan for the discussion was that each person would talk in turn for two minutes, presenting his problems to the group. Next, each person in turn would comment on what others had said, and finally there would be a free discussion. A mechanical switching device regulated the discussion, switching on only one microphone at a time.

The Emergency: The discussion started with the future victim speaking first. He said he found it difficult to get adjusted to New York and to his studies. Very hesitantly and with obvious embarrassment, he mentioned that he was prone to seizures, particularly when studying hard or taking exams. The other people, including the one real subject, took their turns and discussed similar problems (minus the proneness to seizures). The naive subject talked last in the series, after the last prerecorded voice.

When it was again the victim's turn to talk, he made a few relatively calm comments, and then, growing increasingly loud and incoherent, he continued:

I er um I think I I need er if if could er er somebody er er er er er er er give me a little er give me a little help here because er I er I'm er er h-h-having a a a a real problem er right now and I er if somebody could help me out it would it would er er s-s-sure be sure be good . . . because er there er er a cause I er I uh I've got a a one of the er sei-----er er things coming on and and and I could really er use some help so if somebody would er give me a little h-help uh er-er-er-er-er c-could somebody er er help er uh uh uh (choking sounds) . . . I'm gonna die er er I'm . . . gonna die er help er er seizure er (chokes, then quiet).

The major dependent variable of the experiment was the time elapsed from the start of the victim's seizure until the subject left her experimental cubicle. When the subject left her room, she saw the experiment's assistant seated at the end of the hall, and invariably went to the assistant to report the seizure. If six minutes elapsed without the subject's having emerged from her room, the experiment was terminated.

Ninety-five per cent of all the subjects who ever responded did so within the first half of the time available to them. No subject who had not reported within three minutes after the fit ever did so. This suggests that even had the experiment been allowed to run for a considerably longer period of time, few additional subjects would have responded.

Eighty-five per cent of the subjects who thought they alone knew of the victim's plight reported the seizure before the victim was cut off; only 31% of those who thought four other bystanders were present did so. Every one of the subjects in the two-person condition, but only 62% of the subjects in the six-person condition ever reported the emergency.

The effects of prior acquaintance with the victim were also strong. Subjects who had met the victim, even though only for less than a minute, were significantly faster to report his distress than other subjects in the six-person condition. Subjects in this condition later discussed their reactions to the situation. Unlike subjects in any other group, some of those who had accidentally met the victim-to-be later reported that they had actually *pictured* him in the grip of the seizure. Apparently, the ability to *visualize* a specific, concrete, distressed individual increases the likelihood of helping that person.

Subjects who failed to report the emergency showed few signs of the apathy and indifference thought to characterize "unresponsive bystanders."

When the experimenter entered her room to terminate the situation, the subject often asked if the victim were all right. "Is he being taken care of?" "He's all right, isn't he?" Many of these subjects showed physical signs of nervousness; they often had trembling hands and sweating palms. If anything, they seemed more emotionally aroused than did the subjects who reported the emergency.

Why, then, didn't they respond? It is not our impression that they had decided *not* to respond. Rather, they were still in a state of indecision and conflict concerning whether to respond or not. The emotional behavior of these non-responding subjects was a sign of their continuing conflict; a conflict that other subjects resolved by responding.

Social determinants of bystander intervention, III

We have suggested two distinct processes which might lead people to be less likely to intervene in an emergency if there are other people present than if they are alone. On the one hand, we have suggested that the presence of other people may affect the interpretations each bystander puts on an ambiguous emergency situation. If other people are present at an emergency, each bystander will be guided by their apparent reactions in formulating his own impressions. Unfortunately, their apparent reactions may not be a good indication of their true feelings. It is possible for a state of "pluralistic ignorance" to develop, in which each bystander is led by the *apparent* lack of concern of the others to interpret the situation as being less serious than he would if alone. To the extent that he does not feel the situation is an emergency, of course, he will be unlikely to take any helpful action.

Even if an individual does decide that an emergency is actually in process and that something ought to be done, he still is faced with the choice of whether he himself will intervene. Here again, the presence of other people may influence him—by reducing the costs associated with non-intervention. If a number of people witness the same event, the responsibility for action is diffused, and each may feel less necessity to help.

Both the "social influence" and the "diffusion of responsibility" explanations seem valid, and there is no reason why both should not be jointly operative. Neither alone can account for all the data. For example, the diffusion explanation cannot account for the significant difference in response rate between the Strangers and Stooge conditions in Experiment 2. There should be equal diffusion in either case. This difference can more plausibly be attributed to the fact that strangers typically did not show such complete indifference to the accident as did the stooge. The diffusion process also does not seem applicable to the results of Experiment 1. Responsibility for protecting oneself from fire should not diffuse. On the other hand, "social influence" processes cannot account for results in Experiment 4. Subjects in that experiment could not communicate with each other and thus could not be influenced by each other's reactions.

Although both processes probably operate, they may not do so at the same time. To the extent that social influence leads an individual to define the situation as non-serious and not requiring action, his responsibility is eliminated, making diffusion unnecessary. Only if social influence is unavailable or unsuccessful in leading subjects to misinterpret a situation, should diffusion play a role. Indirect evidence supporting this analysis comes from observation of non-intervening subjects in the various emergency settings. In settings involving face-to-face contact, as in Experiments 1 and 2, non-interveners typically redefined the situation and did not see it as a serious emergency. Consequently, they avoided the moral choice of whether or not to take action.

The results of these experiments suggest that social inhibition effects may be rather general over a wide variety of emergency situations. In four different experiments, bystanders have been less likely to intervene if other bystanders are present. The nature of the other bystander seems to be important: a non-reactive confederate provides the most inhibition, a stranger provides a moderate amount, and a friend, the least. Overall, the results are consistent with a multiprocess model of intervention; the effect of other people seems to be mediated both through the interpretations that bystanders place on the situation, and through the decisions they make once they have come up with an interpretation.

Is there safety in numbers? If so, why? Two reasons are often suggested. Individuals are less likely to find themselves in trouble if there are others about, and even if they do find themselves in trouble, others are likely to help them deal with it. While it is certainly true that a victim is unlikely to receive help if nobody knows of his plight, the experiments above cast doubt on the suggestion that he will be more likely to receive help if more people are present. In fact, the opposite seems to be true. A victim may be more likely to get help, or an emergency be reported, the fewer people who are available to take action.

Although the results of these studies may shake our faith in "safety in numbers," they also may help us begin to understand a number of frightening incidents where crowds have listened to, but not answered, a call for help. Newspapers have tagged these incidents with the label "apathy." We have become indifferent, they say, callous to the fate of suffering others. Our society has become "dehumanized" as it has become urbanized. These glib phrases may contain some truth, since startling cases such as the Genovese murder often seem to occur in our large cities, but such terms may also be misleading. Our studies suggest a different conclusion. They suggest that situational factors, specifically factors involving the immediate social environment, may be of greater importance in determining an individual's reaction to an emergency than such vague cultural or personality concepts as "apathy" or "alienation due to urbanization." They suggest that the failure to intervene may be better understood by knowing the relationship among bystanders rather than that between a bystander and the victim.

Our results may explain why the failure to intervene seems to be more characteristic of large cities than rural areas. Bystanders to urban emergencies are more likely to be, or at least to think they are, in the presence of other bystanders than witnesses of non-urban emergencies. Bystanders to urban emergencies are less likely to know each other or to know the victim than are witnesses of non-urban emergencies. When an emergency occurs in a large city, a crowd is likely to gather; the crowd members are likely to be strangers; and it is likely that no one will be acquainted with the victim. These are exactly the conditions that made the helping response least likely in our experiments.

VIII   LEADERSHIP, POWER, AND CHANGE

Leadership is a phenomenon of enduring interest in social psychology. It was initially studied in terms of the leader's attributes, and more recently as an outgrowth of the effects induced by the demands of the situation. While evidences of these "trait" and "situational" viewpoints persist in some approaches to leadership, it is being seen increasingly as a process of interaction involving an influence person and those who are influenced. Furthermore, refined empirical procedures have been applied to its study, and a number of concepts have been stimulated through this effort. One of these distinguishes between the leader who gains his authority by consent of followers, the so-called emergent leader, and the leader whose authority is imposed by an external source, the appointed leader found in most organizations. Bridging these concepts are related questions of concern directed at the maintenance of leader status and the processes defining successful leadership and the exercise of power. There are also implications in current research for understanding innovation and change.

Though a main focus for studying leadership has been in experiments with small groups, increasing attention is being turned to leadership phenomena in ongoing organizational settings. Much of this work is taken up with supervisory and executive effectiveness, in regard to the decision processes and interpersonal relations associated with productivity and morale. Some of these considerations are treated in the next section, on organizational processes.

The paper by Hollander which begins this section is drawn from his book *Leaders, Groups, and Influence* (1964) and serves as an introduction to modern developments. It distinguishes the two classic approaches to leadership and notes the waning of earlier attention to the "mystique" of the leader's personality. Relatedly, Hollander emphasizes the extension of interest into the interactive characteristics of leadership as these bear upon both the emergence of leadership as well as its maintenance. Of particular importance is the present impetus toward a view of leader-follower relations in terms of interpersonal perception. Thus, Hollander sees the leader's influence to be affected by the perceptions followers hold of his actions as well as the motives which underlie them. This process appears to be a relevant feature of leader-follower interaction, whether the leader emerges by group consent or is imposed from above.

In looking at imposed leadership within organizations, there are, however, some distinguishing features that require attention. In his paper here, Bavelas considers a number of these. His analysis updates the "man vs. situation" issue by stressing that the *function* to be fulfilled is an essential element in the organizational situation in which the leader operates. Thus, the leader's individual characteristics must mesh with these functional demands. It is therefore no longer sensible, he says, to ask merely who the leader is but rather to ask how leadership functions are distributed. The book *Organizations* by March and Simon (1958) provides a worthwhile expansion of this issue (see also Nealey & Fiedler, 1968; Katz & Kahn, 1966; March, 1964).

While Bavelas recognizes that differences exist between organizational requirements and, indeed, in their unique "personalities," he feels that the functions of leadership have a core of similarity calling forth characteristics of a distinctive sort. It is the nature of these functions that stamps organizations uniquely. Within the broader demands made by these functions, however, the leader provides for what Bavelas considers "uncertainty reduction." This definition is suggestive of Hemphill's (1958) concept of the leader as one who "initiates structure," discussed in the Hollander paper. Both the Bavelas and Hemphill conceptions lend themselves to a study of the maintenance of leadership in terms of some criteria of individual performance, which is by way of saying that "effective leadership" is assessed both from below and from above within organizational constraints.

Fiedler is concerned with the interaction of leaders and followers as it is affected by several situational variables. The extensive empirical work with which Fiedler has been identified gives a special place to the leader's social perception, in the special sense of a measure of perceptual discrimination (see Fiedler, 1958, 1967). This measure is based on a simple scale indicating the degree to which the rater describes favorably or unfavorably his least preferred coworker, hence the designation LPC. Fiedler's research, over a considerable range of subjects and contexts, indicates ". . . that a person who describes his least preferred coworker in a relatively favorable manner tends to be permissive, human relations oriented, and considerate of the feelings of his men. But a person who describes his least preferred coworker in an unfavorable manner—who has what we have come to call a low LPC rating—tends to be managing, task-controlling, and less concerned with the human relations aspects of the job" (p. 116).

In discussing styles of leadership here, Fiedler finds support for his conception that LPC is a leader characteristic which interacts with various situational factors in determining his effectiveness. The research he reports represents a significant melding of leader attributes and situational circumstances, as represented in the latter instance by quality of leader-member relations, the degree of task structure, and the leader's power. Depending upon the combination of these elements and the leader's permissiveness as measured by the LPC, Fiedler finds striking differences in the leader's ability to achieve productive outcomes. Thus the leader's style is a function of his construction of his relationship with followers (see G. A. Kelly, 1963), and its appropriateness to such situational factors as those Fiedler has studied.

In the paper which follows next, Hollander and Julian provide an analysis and critique of current trends in leadership research. They note the failings and limitations of the trait and situational approaches, and point to several developments which link them, including the work of Fiedler and the growing interest in processes of power. Within a transactional framework, they emphasize the implicit exchange between leaders and followers, whereby the resources provided by the leader are reciprocated in terms of his status and heightened influence. They see the legitimacy of the leader, in terms of how he attains and maintains his position, as a pivotal element in determining the character of leader-follower relations. And they especially urge consideration of the entire interpersonal system implicated in leadership when assessing its effectiveness. Perhaps the most important point of departure for the papers to come is the Hollander and Julian emphasis on how the structure of group or organizational contexts affects perceptions and expectancies about leadership, power, and authority. Though these terms are often used interchangeably, they may usefully be distinguished from one another, as the subsequent papers here reveal.

It is, of course, somewhat artificial to speak of dimensions of leadership as if they were independent—such things as power, innovation potential, or effectiveness traits. These are intermingled and serve only as guidelines for hypothesis testing, just as conceptions of "emergent leaders" and "imposed leaders" represent a form of typology which deals in abstractions that may in the real world have considerably greater congruence. It seems clear that what is found to typify the effective "imposed leader" might parallel qualities found in those who emerge as leaders under prevailing situational conditions. There is, however, a great deal of validity in looking at the differential bases of power.

In their book, *The Social Psychology of Groups* (1959), an excerpt from which is presented in the preceding section, Thibaut and Kelley present a useful conception concerning power by distinguishing between "behavior control" and "fate control." By fate control they mean that "A can affect B's outcomes *regardless of what B does* . . ." while in behavior control, "by varying his behavior, A can make it desirable for B to vary his behavior too . . ." They point out that power of the behavior control variety may be thought of in the sense of a statistical interaction, i.e., B's outcomes are determined not as a function either of A's behavior nor his own, but as a result of the joint effects of these. Note, however, that in the case of fate control, A can provide high rewards to B at low cost to himself, though he need not. The choice is his; but, as Thibaut and Kelley suggest, in most functional groups the fact that the members are to a degree dependent upon one another for satisfactions tends to place limits upon each person's "usable power" even under conditions where fate control prevails. Untrammeled exploitation of less powerful by more powerful group members may occur, though a more likely pattern is the fostering of various kinds of mutually profitable bargaining relations—

especially when these are supported by the kind of reciprocity orientations discussed by Gouldner in Section V.

French and Raven present an analysis here of the differential bases for power. They make a distinction parallel to the one by Thibaut and Kelley just noted, but also extend their concern with reward power and coercive power to a consideration of legitimate power, referent power, and expert power. All of these have characteristics which are distinctive, though they may occur together. In any case, power need not be translated directly into leadership, in the more interactive sense of that term.

Reward power and coercive power are counterparts of one another. The first represents gains, the other potential losses, for compliance and non-compliance, respectively. Referent power is an extension of reward power through a process of identification which does not require continuous surveillance for its effectiveness. The less powerful person incorporates as his own the demands of the more powerful one. Expert power arises from conditions of specialized knowledge that is valued. Legitimate power is based upon the assimilation of norms which require the acceptance of influence by one person from another, as in employer-employee relations viewed broadly.

In connection with the fate control conception, there is the significant central question of the means at the disposal of a person to reject the demand for compliance, which casts the problem of power in terms of the "resisting force" accessible to a person. A clear relationship is evident between this and the considerations of conformity touched on in the previous section and in French and Raven's discussion.

Olsen provides an extension of these conceptions of power into all kinds of organizational settings. In his paper here, drawn from his new book, *The Process of Social Organization* (1968), he sees power as occurring in any organized relationship. His emphasis upon the nature and functioning of power affords several useful distinctions. Thus, he sees both influence and control as embodying power, but varying on a continuum in the degree to which they predetermine outcomes. His conception of "control" follows the essential lines of "fate control" in that it can be exercised regardless of the wishes of the recipient.

In his wide-ranging analysis of the functioning of power, Olsen classifies it along several other dimensions, including: purposeful versus nonpurposeful power; positive versus negative power; internal versus external power; and direct versus indirect power. These cut across a number of other distinctions, including several that implicate dimensions roughly paralleling those of French and Raven. While they are concerned with the sources of power, however, the main thrust of Olsen's presentation is in its exercise. His treatment of legitimacy, for example, is similar to the legitimate power concept of French and Raven. His own fourfold typology of social power attempts to assimilate its functional versus normative aspects with its independent versus organizational aspects.

While Olsen, as well as French and Raven, concern themselves mainly with organizations as a model for the exercise of power, there is also the vast reach of political activity which clearly implicates power and influence. In the selection here by Gamson, taken from his new book, *Power and Discontent* (1968), the focus is aimed directly at the world of political affairs.

Gamson considers the relationship of public authorities to "partisans," that is, those who wish to influence authority in behalf of a particular change in policy. In his terms, "influence" is directed by partisans toward authority, and "social control" is employed by authority ". . . to achieve societal goals most efficiently while at the same time avoiding costly side effects . . ." (Gamson, 1968, p. 11). Though persons in authority may be disposed to employ the means of social control, they need not. It is incorrect, says Gamson, to view their position as either entirely free or entirely constrained. Social control tends to operate through routinized mechanisms, usually conscious in nature, sometimes with explicit decision-making, but social change may proceed without these processes as a result of the inexorability of a set of societal and environmental forces (see Murdock, Section II). An essential problem raised by Gamson's analysis is the capability to maintain a structure for social change. This problem also involves a number of issues relevant to Turner's paper on public protest in Section X.

One consequential function of leadership is to facilitate innovation and change. All societies and the groups within them face the need for some alteration of past practices to meet new demands, and this appears to be an elementary fact of survival. Yet changes are resisted, however beneficial, for a host of reasons including the security of the familiar, particularly the maintenance of congenial social practices. An imbalance, disequilibrium, or "dissonance," is created by a challenge to prevailing structures and belief systems. Weick (1969) has recently observed that perhaps too much is made of change at the expense of recognizing the importance of maintaining the routine or even mundane. He contends that the study of change has often occurred in times of turbulence when resistance is heightened; thus, behind the seductive phrase "people resist change," lie some important unanswered questions.

Planning for change is a field receiving ever-growing attention. As Cartwright (1951) pointed out in his classic formulation, following on Lewin's "group dynamics" conceptions, the group is the basic agent of change: the greater the attractiveness of a group to its members, the more it can exert influence toward change; external "change agents" may facilitate this process, but they must gain the acceptance of the group members; attempts to effect changes which would cause members to be in violation of the group's norms will occasion strong resistance; group members must have a common perception of the need for change; and, plans for change and their consequences must be shared by relevant group members. Uppermost, Cartwright views these preconditions for change as dependent upon a leadership process, whether that process is instigated from within, or by agents brought from outside. Two useful source books in this vein are Lippitt, Watson, & Westley, *The Dynamics of Planned Change* (1958), and Bennis, Benne, & Chin, *The Planning of Change* (1969).

An exemplification of the important role of leadership in change is found in studies of diffusion of information (e.g., Lazarsfeld *et al.*, 1948; Katz and Lazarsfeld, 1955; Menzel and Katz, 1955). The "two-step flow of communication" concept embodied in this work indicates that "opinion leaders" interpret information from outside sources for group members. Rather than being directly affected by communications emanating from the mass media, political speakers, or advertisers, people are affected, in a reference group fashion, by the construction which these opinion leaders place on the information's meaning and implications for action (see Hyman and Singer, Section II). The work on *Personal Influence* (Katz and Lazarsfeld, 1955) indicates that opinion leaders operate as agents of innovation or change in such diverse reaches of society as politics and fashion, and that they are very much like their followers, not definably different kinds of people.

Leadership phenomena, therefore, exist all around us, often in undramatic forms. In practical terms, however, they take on a pervasive and self-conscious quality in formal organizational settings where people are assigned to perform leader roles. What is learned from the study of emergent or informal leaders, including those who help shape the opinions and propensities of others about them, may nonetheless have considerable relevance to the improvement of leadership in organizations. It is appropriate then that in the next section we extend our view of leadership to organizational processes.

49 Leadership, innovation, and influence: an overview

EDWIN P. HOLLANDER

As a current focal point for studying influence effects from social interaction, leadership has ramifications to many other concerns relevant to group process, including conformity, morale, and social change. The study of leadership accordingly contributes to knowledge about the dynamics of influence processes because, in a strict sense, leadership is neither a unique personal attribute, nor is it separable from social influence more generally. Speaking to this point, Thibaut and Kelley have said, "In virtually all cases, leadership seems to be analyzable in terms of other, simpler concepts . . . [every] member of the group can be considered as exhibiting leadership insofar as he exercises power effectively, promotes organization along functional lines, or has symbolic value" (1959, p. 289).

The trait approach to leadership

In the most traditional study of leadership, unique characteristics of "leaders" were sought. The emphasis was placed upon what "made" a leader. But this obscured some important distinctions including the source of authority and the nature of the function to be fulfilled in diverse situations. Leadership had been interwoven for so long with notions of the "man on horseback" and associated images that the more common and pedestrian, work-a-day exercise of leadership was left aside as a process unworthy of attention under the same heading.

Why an emphasis on traits should have prevailed is easy to understand. The literary, prescientific conception of the leader as a special person, a "great man," called attention to inherent qualities that one either possesses or does not, in short, "leadership traits" in the traditional usage. Illustrations of this viewpoint abound, especially in popular literature. Emerson has said, "He is great who is what he is from Nature. . . ." And Thomas Heggen, in introducing the hero of his novel about naval leadership, *Mister Roberts*, says of him: "He was a born leader; there is no other kind."

In psychology, furthermore, the trait approach found a congenial reception because of the psychologist's essential interest in individual characteristics. To measure and assess the personality of "leaders" seemed eminently appropriate to the psychologically-oriented investigator. What was overlooked, however, in the view that leaders are uniquely endowed, was the actual fact of daily life, that is, that persons function as leaders in a particular time and place, and that these are both varying and delimiting conditions; that there are several pathways to leadership, sometimes from higher authority, other times from group consent, and at times from both; and that a good many leadership events transpire routinely between individuals in reciprocal relationships, as illustrated by husband and wife, work partners, and playmates. To speak therefore of "the leader" or of leadership as if those terms conveyed an immutable "state of being" from genetics or social tradition, was to leave out a great deal of real-life social process. Indeed, if any point stands forth in the modern day view of leadership it is that leaders are made by circumstance even though some come to those circumstances better equipped than others. It is this line of development which led ultimately to the so-called "situational approach" to the study of leadership.

The situational approach to leadership

The distinctive asset in the situational view lies in the way it frames leadership events in the life context in which they occur. If a leader—let us take the fictional Mr. Roberts, for example—is effective, this is a relevant datum only insofar as it speaks of his setting, a ship's crew, and its associated conditions, as a time-space-person complex. His responsiveness to those men, in their circumstances, at that time, is what helps us to know and understand his effectiveness; and characteristics which make him effective there in securing a willing, responsive group support might not carry through to other situations with different demands.

It is in the nature of situational requirements that they call forth certain expectations for leadership, and these may be fulfilled by various individuals in the situation. Cartwright and Zander

(1960) have put it this way: ". . . while certain minimal abilities are required of all leaders, these are widely distributed among nonleaders as well. Furthermore, the traits of the leader which are necessary and effective in one group or situation may be quite different from those of another leader in a different setting" (p. 492). Thus, the situational approach conceives of leadership in terms of function performed, rather than in terms of persisting traits of the leader. Closely related to this is the importance attached to the source of authority as a leader, a matter which is often discussed in terms of so-called "emergent" as contrasted with "imposed" leadership.

Emergent and imposed leadership

The distinction made in contemporary social psychology between emergent and imposed leadership has a broad significance for the nature of groups and their internal dynamics. The acceptance of influence, which is conditional upon the consent of followers, produces "emergent" leadership. "Imposed" leadership tends to be determined by superior authority; it is also possible to have an interlocking state of affairs where these reside in the same person, as in many institutions whose imposed leaders have characteristics which would make them acceptable as emergent leaders as well. In addition, much that has been learned about emergent leaders has applicability to the maintenance of status by those who are imposed leaders (see Hollander, 1961a).

"INFORMAL" AND "FORMAL" LEADERSHIP

Another way this emergent-imposed differentiation is made is in terms of "informal" as against "formal" leadership.

The former suggests emergence and the latter imposition; but using them as if they sharply defined different functions is unrealistic in light of what Homans (1961) calls "elementary social behavior," which he considers to have rules of social interaction applicable all the time. However, the terms formal and informal do have utility *not* with reference to definable modes of interaction as much as to the source of the "structure" which determines the pattern of authority of influence persons. These terms represent, in brief, situational forces rather than categories of mutually exclusive behavior.

WHAT FUNCTIONS ARE TO BE FULFILLED?

Clearly much leadership in the world is of an institutional or "imposed" variety such that task requirements are frequently set by an organization and the structure which it establishes. This means that "leaders" may be people who have highly confined, programmed functions, e.g., decision-making, within the determination of organizational constraints and expectations. This carries operational implications quite different from the usual conception of those interpersonal qualities we think of in the leader-follower relation involving freer personal interaction and "social exchange." This kind of imposed leader makes choices within tightly-limited organizational guidelines, entirely apart from being the traditional "supervisor." On this point Alex Bavelas says that the *function* of the organizational leader may be definably different from his personal characteristics (1960). He suggests that in the aggregate such "leaders" are those who perform certain categories of task rather than share characteristic attributes of personality. The question

in organizational leadership, says Bavelas, is not "Who is the leader?" but "What functions are to be fulfilled?" This viewpoint of common functional requirements in institutional situations reveals the expectation of an interchangeability of managerial personnel.

Interactive characteristics of leadership

Granting the demands of the situation, the question nonetheless persists whether there are characteristics of leadership which *do* cut across and pervade many situations in our society. And there appear to be some, although they must be understood in finer detail. Gibb (1954), for example, has said that where situations are limited in certain ways leaders do exhibit various "outstanding qualifications." What these may be, and whether they refer to the task or interpersonal demands, is another matter. In either event, if these existed, that would not in and of itself contradict the potency of situational factors since their content may in fact be determined by those features of the social context which have high priority or thrust. As a case in point, competence in providing for some group function is one kind of requirement for group acceptance; but *what* that competence should be is necessarily linked to the social forces at work in that time and place. Because many groups operate in terms of verbal communication, it is hardly surprising that many studies should point up verbal effectiveness as an attribute of those who are leaders. Consequently, strangers brought together in a common plight may be expected to coalesce about the one among them who speaks out suggesting a course of action; on that same probability basis he also has a high likelihood of becoming influential in the sense of taking on a leadership role (cf. Riecken, 1958).

A further point to consider is that leaders must be aware of the circumstances which prevail in order to affect group activity. Where the leader is out of touch with the group's situation and its inclinations about it, he is ill-equipped to meet the expectations for action. Clearly then leaders must be attuned to what is expected of them, recognizing that they can and do initiate changes, including those in the social expectations themselves. It follows therefore that social perceptiveness is a feature that is demanded of leaders in many circumstances, but this need not be a "trait" since it has been found to be moderated by other elements. The leader's motivation and the nature of the group are among them. Also, where a person is *more* motivated to be aware of the happenings in a social context, he is more likely to perceive what is occurring. This holds true whenever persons have a desire to be accepted in a group, to use it as a model for action, or to identify with it even at a distance, as with some "reference groups." Therefore, if leaders are said to be more socially perceptive, this should be understood to involve not just a capacity for perceptiveness alone but quite likely some impelling motivation as well.

Status emergence and status maintenance

The relationships producing leadership can be further distinguished by studying the interrelated processes of status emergence, concerning factors at work in the *achievement* of influence, and status maintenance, covering those which allow the *retention* of influence. A failure to make this distinction has led to findings which appear contradictory on the face of it. These processes not only differ from one another but they also differ from the informal-formal distinction. Imposing authority and forcing compliance by followers to the formal structure does not eliminate the need for influence to be retained. Even with a mandate from above, as in most organizations, imposed leadership must also rest on the responsiveness of followers, and their willingness to comply. This is a lesson that organizationally imposed leaders learn at times with regret. The retention of leadership necessarily depends somewhat upon others' perceptions of competence and effectiveness.

STRUCTURE AND FUNCTION: PROCESS AND EFFECT

Since the idea of "structure" is central to what has been said and what follows, it is useful here to place it in the broader picture of the dynamics of groups. Toward that end, two pairs of distinctions are required: (1) *structure* and *function*; and (2) *process* and *effect*. While these terms are often used arbitrarily, more usually a group's "structure" refers to its organization including distribution of labor, status differentiation, patterns of communication, and such normative expectations as procedures, roles, and the like. On the other hand, a group's "function" refers to the activities or behaviors carried on mutually for the achievement of some common goal, reflecting the purpose or *raison d'être* of the group. Thus, structure by definition includes influence patterns, which optimally are supposed to be harmonious with the function to be fulfilled and, in turn, the goal to be commonly attained.

In the case of emergent leadership, the structure arises from the group's perception of its function, and if that function should change grossly then the structure must also be altered for the group to act effectively. Effective leadership therefore is a structural feature of the functional or task requirements presented to the group (see Hollander, 1964, Ch. 20). However, structures have a self-sustaining quality which, as will be noted, supports the maintenance of present leadership. This tendency is all the more marked in institutional settings where the structure is imposed from above, and where leadership is anchored in the prevailing structure. But in either case, whether structures are informal or formal, leaders are beneficiaries of the present structure, even though a change in situational conditions may instigate alterations in the structure. The basis for the leader's hold on the structure lies significantly in his role in molding it to his design, or to his exemplification of its associated function by his competence in a focal group task.

In the other distinction noted, group "process" may be thought of as the ongoing nature of intra-group activities, including for example goal-seeking behavior and related patterns of interaction. In an important sense, process encompasses the inter-relationship over time between function and structure. Group "effects" refer to the *products* of process, including member attitudes seen in such things as cohesiveness, or shifts in leadership expectations, or in broad social change.

INITIATING STRUCTURE

Structure is vital in, for example, Hemphill's (1958, 1961) view that leadership involves the "initiation of structure" in the group. He sees leadership not simply as a part of structure, but rather as an instrumental agent determining the shape it should take. In his terms, *attempted* leadership is based on such initiations of new structure; however, the leadership act is incomplete unless that initiation is *accepted*. A completed sequence in Hemphill's phrase is "successful leadership"; and "effective leadership" occurs when a contribution is made to the solution of the group's mutual problem. Hemphill and his co-workers, Pepinsky and Shevitz (1958), have reported at least one study where the degree of initiation of structure by a subject is significantly raised or lowered by the acceptance that person is led to believe he has, through a form of social reinforcement. This serves as a demonstration of the situational constraints or enhancements which shape leadership acts. And most importantly, it speaks to processes which determine an individual's *attempts* at influence assertion.

On the other side of this process there is the broader issue of conditions which determine the *acceptance* of influence. Several kinds of approaches may be fruitful in highlighting one or more variables which have potency in this respect. High in contemporary interest are the interaction characteristics of leader-follower relationships. Here the focus rests upon what conditions permit acceptable assertions of influence. Several clusters of elements are bound up in this interest. One of these is the nature of the group context, suggesting variables in the group's function and structure, its cohesiveness, communication, and the like.

PERCEPTION OF THE LEADER

Also of key importance is the perception "relevant others" hold of the potential leader, the influence-person, in that setting. Considering leadership as an interpersonal encounter necessarily involving person perception, three categories of qualities appear to be in the nature of distinctions made. Though variously labeled, these are: (1) the perceived competence of the individual, broadly conceived in terms of the specific task of the group at the time; (2) the adherence of the individual to agreed upon procedures, that is, what he does to demonstrate his identification with the group; and (3) those of his personal characteristics or attributes perceived as valued for their own sake, though they may contribute less specifically to the function of the group. The first two factors appear to have prime significance in the attainment of a position of influence where emergence is possible. This suggests that the individual must be in a group sufficiently long to develop in others a degree of trust or esteem for him, and for them to note his part in helping to fulfill group goals.

While this process of status attainment goes on, the group's prevailing social forms must be adhered to, unless the potential influence person is extremely competent, or is in the category of an expert, which presents special circumstances. Generally speaking, it is unlikely that just any member of a group could achieve leadership by a suggestion for innovation very early in his exposure to a group. The context is simply not yet favorable. And this is the common observation made in connection with the newcomer to a group: he

is considerably more restricted in behavior than the person who has established himself there over a longer time and has gained "idiosyncrasy credit" by proving himself.

Once attained, the maintenance of leadership requires innovation and change as acceptable, indeed often expected, functions on the part of the leader. Having accorded high acceptance to this individual, the group may receive his suggested innovations more favorably. This is related to a number of formulations, including Homans's (1961) concept of "status congruence," that is, the appropriateness of behaviors and functions in relation to hierarchical status.

Power and influence

A frequently made assumption is that influence necessarily involves the exercise of power. This would suggest that any act of influence would represent power over the person actually influenced; however, in this sense, the terms influence and power are not synonymous. Another questionable assumption is that imposed leadership, with authority vested from above, must operate in terms of the assertion of power.

There are several factors which should be borne in mind to qualify these beliefs. In the first place, power may be both influence potential as well as resistance potential as Cartwright (1959, Ch. 1) has pointed out. Second, the absence of influence acceptance in the face of an assertion of influence does not necessarily mean that the influence agent is powerless but could mean that he does not fully assert the influence potential at his command. This matter of restraint in the use of power available in imposed organizational structures is a necessarily vital condition for smooth relationships. Where the person in authority consistently uses the full power of his position this undercuts his long-term effectiveness because of the resistance built up over time, as well as other disadvantages. Unfettered use of power obviously does occur, but a greater likelihood exists that bargaining relationships of a jointly rewarding nature will develop to offset resistance, as Thibaut and Kelley (1959) have contended in their model of social exchange.

Another consideration then is that power may be employed by degrees. It is not an all-or-nothing matter. Even in the most authoritatively oriented structures, it is not identical to exercising "effective leadership." Indeed, imposed leaders must reckon with the structure of the emergent group which serves as a base of security for the individual and provides power in the form of a mutual resistance potential to the dictatorial use of power. This is by way of saying that power to avoid untrammeled exploitation rests with the work group and that this must be recognized as a counterforce by the supervisor. Even in extreme conditions, where power is founded on physical force which overdetermines the outcome, power is *not* an instrument of successful leadership in its own right.

The key consideration to be emphasized is that the influence assertions of the imposed leader are evaluated by the group in the context of the perceived motivation involved and the consequences for some common good represented in a group goal. It is in this sense that the maintenance of leadership, even by an imposed leader, requires a regard for the working relationships which are affected by assertions of power.

Social change

An expansion of these points leads to the consequential issue of social change. All societies, and the groups comprising them, must continually undergo some change as an elemental fact of nature. There are, however, forces resisting change, whatever the desirability of the new course offered. Very often these arise because of the essential security provided by the familiar. Accordingly, a central question in considering social change is how groups come to recognize that some well-entrenched social form ought to be altered. It is especially useful to employ terms associated with status emergence in pursuing this further.

For social change to be instigated there must be a comparison between things as they are and things as they might be. This suggests a flow of information through some channel of communication, and calls attention to the work on diffusion and innovation by Katz and Lazarsfeld (1955) and Menzel and Katz (1955) in which the leader is found to be a person who provides an interpretation of the world outside the immediate group. It is he who conveys a structure in terms of "social reality," and the acceptance of innovation. Partly because of this, social change no longer can be cast in the tidy terms of the venerable historical controversy of "the man *or* the times." More accurately, in contemporary social psychology, this problem seems a matter of studying the combined impact of the leader and the social context upon the view that followers will hold of their world. This is significant to their associated willingness to undertake change. In short, neither man nor the situation exists independently of the other since, in the *emergence* aspect of leadership, group members operate from the base of a situation and the particular demands it makes for "task requirements."

In a related vein, it is also true that suggestions offered are variously reacted to depending upon the status of the person from whom they come, a point already noted here (see Hollander, 1961b). This offers a tie with balance or congruity theories of attitude change which suggest the cognitive aptness of similarly "signed" terms, i.e., leader positively signed, his recommended course of action positively signed, then "balanced." The work of Osgood and Tannenbaum (1955) and of Heider (1958), among others, is suggestive of this line of analysis. If we take the relatively simple case of the leader as a positively signed term, his neutral idea or negatively signed idea may carry the day: it is cognitively consistent for him to be identified with positive things, and so balancing occurs. Still, equally possible, a negatively signed person, or a neutral person, may gain status by espousing a potent "positive" idea with which he becomes associated and from which he then draws residual benefits.

An expansion of these considerations would lead to a somewhat richer, more nuance-laden conception of social influence involving the leader as the emitter of complex multi-signed stimuli which become relevant to the follower, as recipient, in terms of the motivational and reference group contexts of which he partakes at a given time.

The leader's emergence or waning of status is thus inextricably linked to the prevailing situation, both as group members understand it from the information at hand and as they hold attachments to persons or orientations, present but also past. A change of the influence structure must necessarily overcome the resistance which these factors erect and encourage. It is not so much, then, the "man or the times" as it appears to be the perception of the man and what he represents himself to be and to stand for in the context of the already enveloping situation. Yet, once having achieved status of high influence, what he does may not and indeed need not fit past expectations for, in the maintenance of his position, he is obliged to fulfill new expectations which arise as the situation inevitably is altered.

50   Leadership: man and function

ALEX BAVELAS

There is a useful distinction to be made between the idea of leadership as a personal quality and the idea of leadership as an organizational function. The first refers to a special combination of personal characteristics; the second refers to the distribution throughout an organization of decision-making powers. The first leads us to look at the qualities and abilities of individuals; the second leads us to look at the patterns of power and authority in organizations. Both of these ideas or definitions of leadership are useful, but it is important to know which one is being talked about, and to know under what conditions the two must be considered together in order to understand a specific organizational situation.

Early notions about leadership dealt with it almost entirely in terms of personal abilities. Leadership was explicitly associated with special powers. An outstanding leader was credited not only with extensions of the normal abilities possessed by most men but with extraordinary powers such as the ability to read men's minds, to tell the future, to compel obedience hypnotically. These powers were often thought of as gifts from a god, as conditional loans from a devil, or as the result of some accidental supernatural circumstance attending conception, birth, or early childhood. Today, claims of supernatural powers are made more rarely, but they are not entirely unknown. Of course, milder claims—tirelessness, infallibility

of intuition, lightning-quick powers of decision—are made in one form or another by many outstandingly successful men. And when they do not make them for themselves, such claims are made for them by others who, for their own reasons, prefer such explanations of success to other more homely ones.

Outright supernatural explanations of leadership have, in recent times, given way to more rational explanations. Leadership is still generally thought of in terms of personal abilities, but now the assumption is made that the abilities in question are the same as those possessed by all normal persons: individuals who become leaders are merely presumed to have them to a greater degree.

For many years, attempts to define these abilities and to measure them failed. This was not only because the early techniques of measurement were primitive and unreliable but for a more important reason. The traits that were defined as important for leadership were often nothing more than purely verbal expressions of what the researcher felt leaders *ought* to be like. Few of the many lists of traits that were developed had very much in common. Typical of the items that frequently appeared on such lists were piety, honesty, courage, perseverance, intelligence, reliability, imagination, industriousness. This way of thinking about leadership is still very common. It persists, not because it is helpful in analyzing and understanding the phenomenon of leadership, but be-

Reprinted from the **Administrative Science Quarterly,** 1960, 4, 491-98, with permission of the author and publisher.

cause it expresses a deep and popular wish about what leaders *should* be like.

Modern trait research proceeds in a very different way. Leadership traits are no longer selected arbitrarily. They are, instead, largely derived from the results of tests that are carefully designed, administered, and interpreted. And the techniques of measurement and analysis which are applied to the data that are gathered have been extensively developed and refined. Numerous trait studies have been made of the physical, intellectual, and social characteristics of leaders. On various tests, persons who are leaders tend to be brighter, tend to be better adjusted psychologically, and tend to display better judgment. Studies that have concentrated on the social behavior of leaders show that they "interact" more than nonleaders. They tend to give more information, ask for more information, and to take the lead in summing up or interpreting a situation.

Despite these accomplishments, the trait approach has in recent years been subjected to increasing criticism. A common objection is that the results are obtained by a method that requires an initial separation of people into "leaders" and "nonleaders" or "good leaders" and "not-so-good leaders." The validity of the distinguishing traits that come out of such work, the argument goes, can only be as good as the validity of the preliminary grouping of the persons being studied. All of this leads to the question, "On what basis is the initial separation of subjects made, and how is it justified?"

At first glance, this may appear a trivial and carping question. In fact, however, it is one of the most serious obstacles in the way of all leadership research. It is obviously impossible to define "good leaders" without reference to a system of values. To say that a man is a "good leader" means that his behavior and its consequences are held to be of greater worth than other behaviors and results.

What system of values shall the researcher adopt that is both scientifically acceptable and socially useful in distinguishing good or successful leaders from others? Many attempts have been made to find a suitable criterion, but the results have been generally unsatisfactory —not that it is difficult to find standards which are desirable and inspiring, but that such standards tend to be based, just as the early lists of traits were, on qualities that are difficult or impossible to measure. And often they just do not seem to "work." For example, there have been attempts to distinguish leaders from nonleaders in terms that rest essentially on moral and ethical consideration;. It may be a significant commentary on our society that there appears to be no particular correlation between a man's ethics and morals and his power to attract followers.

It has been suggested that many of the philosophical difficulties that attend the definition of "good leader" can be avoided if one accepts the more limited task of defining "good executive." In business and industry, one would like to think, there should be practical, quantitative ways of making the distinction. Many attempts have been made in this direction. Reputation, financial success, hierarchical position, influence, and many other criteria have been tried without much satisfaction. The inadequacies of such standards are obvious to any experienced executive.

There is a second and more interesting objection that has been made to the trait approach. It is based not on the question of the accuracy or the validity of the assumptions that are made but upon the nature of the "traits" themselves. Traits are, after all, statements about personal characteristics. The objection to this is that the degree to which an individual exhibits leadership depends not only on *his characteristics*, but, also, on the *characteristics of the situation* in which he finds himself. For example, a man who shows all the signs of leadership when he acts as the officer of a well-structured authoritarian organization may give no indication of leadership ability in a less-structured, democratic situation. A man may become influential in a situation requiring deliberation and planning but show little evidence of leadership if the situation demands immediate action with no opportunity for weighing alternatives or thinking things out. Or, to take still another instance, a man may function effectively and comfortably in a group whose climate is friendly and co-operative but retreat and become ineffective if he perceives the atmosphere as hostile.

The case for the situational approach to leadership derives its strength from this fact: while organizations in general may exhibit broad similarities of structure and function, they also, in particular, show strong elements of uniqueness.

It is a matter of common observation that within any normal industrial organization, providing there has been a sufficient past, there will be found patterns of relationships and interaction that are highly predictable and highly repetitive. Some of these reoccurring situations will be unique to that organization. It is this uniqueness that is referred to when one speaks of the "personality" of a company. This is what a management has in mind when

it selects a new member with an eye to how he will "fit in." The argument of the researcher who stresses the situational aspects of leadership is that these unique characteristics of an organization are often crucial in determining which of two equally competent and gifted men will become a "leader," and further that in the very same organization these unique patterns may change significantly at different levels of the hierarchy. The very same "leadership abilities" that helped a man rise to the top may, once he is there, prove a positive detriment.

The status of trait and situational leadership research can be summed up in this way: (1) the broad similarities which hold for a great number of organizations make it possible to say useful things about the kind of person who is likely to become a leader in any of those organizations, and (2) the unique characteristics of a particular organization make it necessary to analyze the situational factors that determine who is likely to become a leader *in one particular organization*. To put it another way, when specific situational patterns are different from organization to organization, one cannot say what personal traits will lead to acknowledged leadership. Instead, one must try to define the leadership functions that must be performed in those situations and regard as leadership those acts which perform them. This point of view suggests that almost any member of a group may become its leader under circumstances that enable him to perform the required functions of leadership and that different persons may contribute in different ways to the leadership of the group.

In these terms we come close to the notion of leadership, not as a personal quality, but as an *organizational func-*

tion. Under this concept it is not sensible to ask of an organization "who is the leader?" Rather we ask "how are the leadership functions distributed in this organization?" The distribution may be wide or narrow. It may be so narrow—so many of the leadership functions may be vested in a single person—that he is the leader in the popular sense. But in modern organizations this is becoming more and more rare.

What are these "leadership functions?" Many have been proposed: planning, giving information, evaluating, arbitrating, controlling, rewarding, punishing, and the like. All of these stem from the underlying idea that leadership acts are those which help the group achieve its objectives, or, as it is also put, to satisfy its "needs." In most face-to-face groups, the emergence of a leader can well be accounted for on this basis. That person who can assist or facilitate the group most in reaching a satisfactory state is most likely to be regarded as the leader. If one looks closely at what constitutes assistance or facilitation in this sense, it turns out to be the making of choices or the helping of the group to make choices—"better" choices, of course.

But can the function of leadership be reduced simply to decision making or the facilitation of decision making? The objection can be raised that such a definition is much too wide to be useful. Every action, even every physical movement one makes, is after all "chosen" out of a number of possible alternatives. If when I am at my workbench I pick up a screwdriver in preference to a hammer, I am clearly making a choice; am I, by virtue of that choice, displaying leadership? Something is obviously wrong with a definition of leadership which imputes it to any act that can be shown to have involved a choice. Common sense would argue that customary, habitual, and "unconscious" actions, although they may logically contain elements of choice, should be separated from actions that are subjectively viewed by the person taking them as requiring a decision. Common sense would also argue that questions of choice that can be settled on the basis of complete information should be considered differently from questions of choice in which decisions must be taken in the face of uncertainty. And common sense would argue that some distinction should be made between decisions that, although made on equally uncertain grounds, involve very different orders of risk.

This is, of course, the implicit view of the practicing manager, and although it may contain very knotty problems of logic it is the view that will be taken here. Stated in general terms, the position that will be taken is that organizational leadership consists of *uncertainty reduction.* The actual behavior through which this reduction is accomplished is the making of choices.

We saw above that not all choices are equally difficult or equally important. Some choices are considered unimportant or irrelevant and are ignored, and of course whole areas may be seen as so peripheral to the interests of the organization that they are not perceived as areas of choice at all. Other choices that *must* be made are so well understood that they become habitual and automatic. Some of these are grouped into more or less coherent bundles and given a job name. The employee learns to make them correctly as he becomes skilled in the job. In most job evaluation plans, additional credit is given if the job requires judgment. This is a way of saying that there are choices remaining in the job that cannot be completely taken care of by instructions but must be made by the employee as they come along.

There are other choices which, although they are equally clear and habitual, are of a more general nature and do not apply just to a specific job but apply to all. These are customarily embodied in rules and procedures. Rules and procedures are, in this sense, decisions made in advance of the events to which they are to be applied. Obviously, this is possible and practical only to the extent that the events to which the rules and procedures apply can be foreseen, and the practical limit of their completeness and specificity depends on how these future events can be predicted.

Following this line of analysis, it is theoretically possible to arrange all the logically inherent choices that must be made in operating an industrial organization along scales of increasing uncertainty and importance. At some level in this hierarchy of choices, it is customary for management to draw a line, reserving for itself from that point on the duty and the privilege of making the required decisions.

Precisely where a management draws this line defines its scope. The way in which a management distributes the responsibility for making the set of choices it has thus claimed to itself defines its structure. What organizational leadership *is* and what kinds of acts constitute it are questions that can be answered only within this framework of scope and structure. In these terms leadership consists of the continuous choice-making process that permits the organization as a whole to proceed toward its objectives despite all sorts of internal and external perturbations.

But as every practicing manager knows, problems occasionally arise that

are not amenable to the available and customary methods of analysis and solution. Although uncertain about which choice to make, a management may nevertheless have to make a decision. It is in situations of this kind that many of the popular traits attributed to leaders find their justification: quickness of decision, the courage to take risks, coolness under stress, intuition, and, even, luck. There is no doubt that quick, effective, and daring decisions are a highly prized commodity in a crisis, but just as precious a commodity is the art of planning and organizing so that such crises do not occur. The trend of management has been to remove as many of its decisions as possible from the area of hunch and intuition to that of rational calculation. More and more, organizations are choosing to depend less on the peculiar abilities of rare individuals and to depend instead on the orderly processes of research and analysis. The occasions and opportunities for personal leadership in the old sense still exist, but they are becoming increasingly rare and circumscribed.

This new emphasis has not eliminated the role of personal leadership, but it has significantly redefined it. Under normal conditions of operation, leadership in the modern organization consists not so much in the making of decisions personally as it does of maintaining the operational effectiveness of the decision-making systems which comprise the management of the organization. The picture of the leader who keeps his own counsel and in the nick of time pulls the rabbit out of the hat is out of date. The popular stereotype now is the thoughtful executive discussing in committee the information supplied by a staff of experts. In fact it may be that the brilliant innovator, in the role of manager, is rapidly becoming as much an organizational embarrassment as he is an asset.

This trend, reasonable though it may appear on the surface, conceals two serious dangers. First, we may be systematically giving up the opportunity of utilizing the highest expressions of personal leadership in favor of managerial arrangements which, although safer and more reliable, can yield at best only a high level of mediocrity. And second, having committed ourselves to a system that thrives on the ordinary, we may, in the interests of maintaining and improving its efficiency, tend to shun the extraordinary.

It is no accident that daring and innovation wane as an organization grows large and successful. On different levels this appears to have been the history of men, of industries, of nations, and even of societies and cultures. Success leads to "obligations"—not the least of which is the obligation to hold what has been won. Therefore, the energies of a man or administration may be absorbed in simply maintaining vested interests. Similarly, great size requires "system," and system, once established, may easily become an end in itself.

This is a gloomy picture, because it is a picture of decay. It has been claimed, usually with appeals to biological analogies, that this is an inevitable cycle, but this view is, very probably, incorrect. Human organizations are not biological organisms; they are social inventions.

51　Styles of leadership

FRED E. FIEDLER

Leadership is a personal relationship in which one person directs, coordinates, and supervises others in the performance of a common task. This is especially so in "interacting groups," where men must work together cooperatively in achieving organizational goals.

In oversimplified terms, it can be said that the leader manages the group in either of two ways. He can:

Tell people what to do and how to do it.

Or share his leadership responsibilities with his group members and involve them in the planning and execution of the task.

There are, of course, all shades of leadership styles in between these two polar positions, but the basic issue is this: the work of motivating and coordinating group members has to be done either by brandishing the proverbial stick or by dangling the equally proverbial carrot. The former is the more

Abridged from "Engineer the Job To Fit the Manager," **Harvard Business Review**, 43, 115–22 (©
1965 by the President and Fellows of Harvard College; all rights reserved), with permission of the
author and the publisher.

orthodox job-centered, autocratic style. The latter is the more nondirective, group-centered procedure.

Research evidence exists to support both approaches to leadership. Which, then, should be judged more appropriate? On the face of it, the first style of leadership is best under some conditions, while the second works better under others. Accepting this proposition immediately opens two avenues of approach. Management can:

Determine the specific situation in which the directive or the nondirective leadership style works best, and then select or train men so that their leadership style fits the particular job.

Or determine the type of leadership style which is most natural for the man in the executive position, and then change the job to fit the man.

The first alternative has been discussed many times before; the second has not. We have never seriously considered whether it would be easier to fit the executive's job to the man.

Needed style?

How might this be done? Some answers have been suggested by a research program on leadership effectiveness that I have directed under Office of Naval Research auspices since 1951. This program has dealt with a wide variety of different groups, including basketball teams, surveying parties, various military combat crews, and men in open-hearth steel shops, as well as members of management and boards of directors. When possible, performance was measured in terms of objective criteria—for instance, percentage of games won by high school basketball teams; tap-to-tap time of open-hearth shops (roughly equivalent to the tonnage of steel output per unit of time); and company net income over a three-year period. Our measure of leadership style was based on a simple scale indicating the degree to which a man described, favorably or unfavorably, his least-preferred co-worker (LPC). This co-worker did not need to be someone he actually worked with at the time, but could be someone the respondent had known in the past. Whenever possible, the score was obtained before the leader was assigned to his group.

The study indicates that a person who describes his least-preferred co-worker in a relatively favorable manner tends to be permissive, human relations-oriented, and considerate of the feelings of his men. But a person who describes his least-preferred co-worker in an unfavorable manner—who has what we have come to call a low LPC rating—tends to be managing, task-controlling, and less concerned with the human relations aspects of the job. It also appears that the directive, managing, and controlling leaders tend to perform best in basketball and surveying teams, in open-hearth shops, and (provided the leader is accepted by his group) in military combat crews and company managements. On the other hand, the nondirective, permissive, and human relations-oriented leaders tend to perform best in decision-making and policy-making teams and in groups that have a creative task—provided that the group likes the leader or the leader feels that the group is pleasant and free of tension.

Critical dimensions

But in order to tell which style fits which situation, we need to categorize groups. Our research has shown that "it all depends" on the situation. After reviewing the results of all our work and the findings of other investigators, we have been able to isolate three major dimensions that seem to determine, to a large part, the kind of leadership style called for by different situations.

It is obviously a mistake to think that groups and teams are all alike and that each requires the same kind of leadership. We need some way of categorizing the group-task situation, or the job environment within which the leader has to operate. If leadership is indeed a process of influencing other people to work together effectively in a common task, then it surely matters how easy or difficult it is for the leader to exert his influence in a particular situation.

Leader-member relations. The factor that would seem most important in determining a man's leadership influence is the degree to which his group members trust and like him, and are willing to follow his guidance. The trusted and well-liked leader obviously does not require special rank or power in order to get things done. We can measure the leader-member relationship by the so-called sociometric nomination techniques that ask group members to name in their group the most influential person, or the man they would most like to have as a leader. It can also be measured by a group-atmosphere scale indicating the degree to which the leader feels accepted and comfortable in the group.

The task structure. The second important factor is the "task structure." By this term I mean the degree to which the task (a) is spelled out step by step for the group and, if so, the extent to which it can be done "by the

numbers" or according to a detailed set of standard operating instructions, or (b) must be left nebulous and undefined. Vague and ambiguous or unstructured tasks make it difficult to exert leadership influence, because neither the leader nor his members know exactly what has to be done or how it is to be accomplished.

Why single out this aspect of the task rather than the innumerable other possible ways of describing it? Task groups are almost invariably components of a larger organization that assigns the task and has, therefore, a big stake in seeing it performed properly. However, the organization can control the quality of a group's performance only if the task is clearly spelled out and programmed or structured. When the task can be programmed or performed "by the numbers," the organization is able to back up the authority of the leader to the fullest; the man who fails to perform each step can be disciplined or fired. But in the case of ill-defined, vague, or unstructured tasks, the organization and the leader have very little control and direct power. By close supervision one can ensure, let us say, that a man will correctly operate a machine, but one cannot ensure that he will be creative.

It is therefore easier to be a leader in a structured task situation in which the work is spelled out than in an unstructured one which presents the leader and his group with a nebulous, poorly defined problem.

Position power. Thirdly, there is the power of the leadership position, as distinct from any personal power the leader might have. Can he hire or fire and promote or demote? Is his appointment for life, or will it terminate at the pleasure of his group? It is obviously easier to be a leader when the position power is strong than when it is weak.

Model for analysis

When we now classify groups on the basis of these three dimensions, we get a classification system that can be represented as a cube; see Exhibit 1. As each group is high or low in each of the three dimensions, it will fall into one of the eight cells.

From examination of the cube, it seems clear that exerting leadership influence will be easier in a group in which the members like a powerful leader with a clearly defined job and where the job to be done is clearly laid out (Cell 1); it will be difficult in a group where a leader is disliked, has little power, and has a highly ambiguous job (Cell 8).

In other words, it is easier to be the well-esteemed foreman of a construction crew working from a blueprint than it is to be the disliked chairman of a volunteer committee preparing a new policy.

I consider the leader-member relations the most important dimension,

Exhibit 1. A model for classifying group-task situations.

and the position-power dimension the least important, of the three. It is, for instance, quite possible for a man of low rank to lead a group of higher-ranking men in a structured task—as is done when enlisted men or junior officers conduct some standardized parts of the training programs for medical officers who enter the Army. But it is not so easy for a disrespected manager to lead a creative, policy-formulating session well, even if he is the senior executive present.

Varying requirements

By first sorting the eight cells according to leader-member relations, then task structure, and finally leader position power, we can now arrange them in order according to the favorableness of the environment for the leader. This sorting leads to an eight-step scale, as in Exhibit 2. This exhibit portrays the results of a series of studies of groups performing well but (a) in different situations and conditions, and (b) with leaders using different leadership styles. In explanation:

The *horizontal* axis shows the range of situations that the groups worked in, as described by the classification scheme used in Exhibit 1.

The *vertical* axis indicates the leadership style which was best in a certain

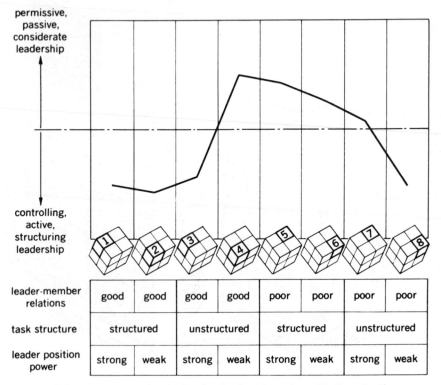

Exhibit 2. How the style of effective leadership varies with the situation.

situation, as shown by the correlation coefficient between the leader's LPC and his group's performance.

A positive correlation (falling above the midline) shows that the permissive, nondirective, and human relations-oriented leaders performed best; a negative correlation (below the midline) shows that the task-controlling, managing leader performed best. For instance, leaders of effective groups in situation categories 1 and 2 had LPC-group performance correlations of $-.40$ to $-.80$, with the average between $-.50$ and $-.60$; whereas leaders of effective groups in situation categories 4 and 5 had LPC-group performance correlations of .20 to .80, with the average between .40 and .50.

Exhibit 2 shows that both the directive, managing, task-oriented leaders and the non-directive, human relations-oriented leaders are successful under some conditions. Which leadership style is the best depends on the favorableness of the particular situation for the leader. In very favorable or in very unfavorable situations for getting a task accomplished by group effort, the autocratic, task-controlling, managing leadership works best. In situations intermediate in difficulty, the nondirective, permissive leader is more successful.

This corresponds well with our everyday experience. For instance:

Where the situation is very favorable, the group expects and wants the leader to give directions. We neither expect nor want the trusted airline pilot to turn to his crew and ask, "What do you think we ought to check before take-off?"

If the disliked chairman of a volunteer committee asks his group what to do, he may be told that everybody ought to go home.

The well-liked chairman of a planning group or research team must be nondirective and permissive in order to get full participation from his members. The directive, managing leader will tend to be more critical and to cut discussion short; hence he will not get the full benefit of the potential contributions by his group members.

The varying requirements of leadership styles are readily apparent in organizations experiencing dramatic changes in operating procedures. For example:

The manager or supervisor of a routinely operating organization is expected to provide direction and supervision that the subordinates should follow. However, in a crisis the routine is no longer adequate, and the task becomes ambiguous and unstructured. The typical manager tends to respond in such instances by calling his principal assistants together for a conference. In other words, the effective leader changes his behavior from a directive to a permissive, nondirective style until the operation again reverts to routine conditions.

In the case of a research planning group, the human relations-oriented and permissive leader provides a climate in which everybody is free to speak up, to suggest, and to criticize. Osborn's brainstorming method (1953) in fact institutionalizes these procedures. However, after the research plan has been completed, the situation becomes highly structured. The director now prescribes the task in detail, and he specifies the means of accomplishing it. Woe betide the assistant who decides to be creative by changing the research instructions!

Practical tests

Remember that the ideas I have been describing emanate from studies of real-life situations; accordingly, as might be expected, they can be validated by organizational experience. Take, for instance, the dimension of leader-member relations described earlier. We have made three studies of situations in which the leader's position power was strong and the task relatively structured with clear-cut goals and standard operating procedures. In such groups as these the situation will be very favorable for the leader if he is accepted; it will be progressively unfavorable in proportion to how much a leader is disliked. What leadership styles succeed in these varying conditions? The studies confirm what our theory would lead us to expect. In all three studies, the highly accepted and strongly rejected leaders perform best if they are controlling and managing, while the leaders in the intermediate acceptance range, who are neither rejected nor accepted, perform best if they are permissive and nondirective.

52   Contemporary trends in the analysis of leadership processes

EDWIN P. HOLLANDER and JAMES W. JULIAN

Within the present era, characterized by a greater sensitivity to the social processes of interaction and exchange, it becomes clearer that the two research emphases represented by the trait and situational approaches to leadership afforded a far too glib view of reality. Indeed, in a true sense, neither approach ever represented its own philosophical underpinning very well, and each resulted in a caricature. The purpose here is to attempt a rectification of the distortion that these traditions represented, and to point up the increasing signs of movement toward a fuller analysis of leadership as a social influence process, and not as a fixed state of being.

Slightly abridged from the **Psychological Bulletin**, 71, 387–97 (Copyright © 1969 by the American Psychological Association), with permission of the authors and the publisher.

An overview

By way of beginning, it seems useful to make a number of observations to serve as an overview. First, several general points which grow out of current research and thought on leadership are established. Thereafter, some of the directions in which these developments appear to be heading are indicated, as well as those areas which require further attention.

One overriding impression conveyed by surveying the literature of the 1960s, in contrast to the preceding two decades, is the redirection of interest in leadership toward processes such as power and authority relationships (e.g., Blau, 1964; Emerson, 1962; Janda, 1960; Raven, 1965). The tendency now is to attach far greater significance to the interrelationship between the leader, the followers, and the situation (see, e.g., Fielder, 1964, 1965, 1967; Hollander, 1964; Hollander & Julian, 1968; Steiner, 1964). In consequence, the problem of studying leadership and understanding these relationships is recognized as a more formidable one than was earlier supposed (cf. Cartwright & Zander, 1968). Several of the particulars which signalize this changing emphasis may be summarized under four points, as follows:

1. An early element of confusion in the study of *leadership* was the failure to distinguish it as a process from the *leader* as a person who occupies a central role in that process. Leadership constitutes an influence relationship between two, or usually more, persons who depend upon one another for the attainment of certain mutual goals within a group situation. This situation not only involves the task but also comprises the group's size, structure, resources, and history, among other variables.

2. This relationship between leader and led is built *over time*, and involves an exchange or *transaction* between leaders and followers in which the leader both gives something and gets something. The leader provides a *resource* in terms of adequate role behavior directed toward the group's goal attainment, and in return receives greater influence associated with status, recognition, and esteem. These contribute to his "legitimacy" in making influence assertions, and in having them accepted.

3. There are differential tasks or functions attached to being a leader. While the image of the leader frequently follows Hemphill's (1961) view of one who "initiates structure," the leader is expected to function too as a mediator within the group, as a group spokesman outside it, and very often also as the decision maker who sets goals and priorities. Personality characteristics which may fit a person to be a leader are determined by the perceptions held by followers, in the sense of the particular role expectancies and satisfactions, rather than by the traits measured via personality scale scores.

4. Despite the persisting view that leadership traits do not generalize across situations, leader effectiveness can and should be studied as it bears on the group's achievement of desired outputs (see Katz & Kahn, 1966). An approach to the study of leader effectiveness as a feature of the group's success, in system terms, offers a clear alternative to the older concern with what the leader did do or did not do.

A richer, more interactive conception of leadership processes would entertain these considerations as points of departure for further study. Some evidence for a trend toward this development is considered in what follows.

Whither the "situational approach"?

What was the essential thrust of the situational approach, after all? Mainly, it was to recognize that the qualities of the leader were variously elicited, valued, and reacted to as a function of differential group settings and their demands. Hemphill (1949a) capped the point in saying "there are no absolute leaders, since successful leadership must always take into account the specific requirements imposed by the nature of the group which is to be led, requirements as diverse in nature and degree as are the organizations in which persons band together [p. 225]."

Though leadership events were seen as outcomes of a relationship that implicates the leader, the led, and their shared situation, studies conducted within the situational approach, usually left the *process* of leadership unattended. Much of the time, leaders were viewed in positional terms, with an emphasis on the outcome of their influence assertions. Comparatively little attention was directed to followers, especially in terms of the phenomenon of emergent leadership (cf. Hollander, 1961). With a few exceptions, such as the work of McGregor (see 1966) and others (e.g., Slater & Bennis, 1964), the leader's maintenance of his position was emphasized at the expense of understanding the attainment of it through a process of influence.

But even more importantly, the situational view made it appear that the leader and the situation were quite separate. Though they may be separable for analytic purposes, they also impinge on one another in the perceptions of followers. Thus, the leader, from the follower's vantage point, is an element in the situation, and one who shapes it as well. As an active agent of influence he commu-nicates to other group members by his words and his actions, implying demands which are reacted to in turn. In exercising influence, therefore, the leader may set the stage and create expectations regarding what he should do and what he will do. Rather than standing apart from the leader, the situation perceived to exist may be his creation.

It is now possible to see that the trait and situational approaches merely emphasize parts of a process which are by no means separable. One kind of melding of the trait and situational approaches, for example, is found in the work of Fiedler. His essential point, sustained by an extensive program of research (see 1958, 1964, 1965, 1967), is that the leader's effectiveness in the group depends upon the structural properties of the group and the situation, including interpersonal perceptions of both leader and led. He finds, for example, that the willingness of group members to be influenced by the leader is conditioned by leader characteristics, but that the quality and direction of this influence is contingent on the group relations and task structure (1967). This work will be discussed further in due course.

Another kind of evidence about the importance to group performance of the leader's construction of the situation is seen in recent research on conflict. Using a role-playing test situation involving four-person groups, Maier and Hoffman (1965) found that conflict is turned to productive or nonproductive ends, depending on the attitude of the discussion leader. Where the leader perceived conflict in terms of "problem subordinates," the quality of the decision reached in these discussion groups was distinctly inferior to that reached under circumstances in which the discussion leader perceived disagreements as the source for ideas and innovation. In those circumstances, innovative solutions increased markedly.

A leader, therefore, sets the basis for relationships within the group, and thereby can affect outcomes. As Hemphill (1961) suggested, the leader initiates structure. But more than just structure in a concrete sense, he affects the process which occurs within that structure. Along with other neglected aspects of process in the study of leadership is the goal-setting activity of the leader. Its importance appears considerable, though few studies give it attention. In one of these, involving discussion groups, Burke (1966) found that the leader's failure to provide goal orientations within the group led to antagonism, tension, and absenteeism. This effect was most acute when there was clear agreement within the group regarding who was to act as the leader. Though such expectations about the leader undoubtedly are pervasive in groups studied in research on leadership, they are noted only infrequently.

Legitimacy and social exchange in leadership

Among the more substantial features of the leader's role is his perceived legitimacy—how he attains it and sustains it. One way to understand the process by which the leader's role is legitimated is to view it as an exchange of rewards operating to signalize the acceptance of his position and influence.

In social exchange terms, the person in the role of leader who fulfills expectations and achieves group goals provides rewards for others which are reciprocated in the form of status, esteem, and heightened influence. Because leadership embodies a two-way influence relationship, recipients of influence assertions may respond by asserting influence in return, that is, by making demands on the leader. The very sustenance of the relationship depends upon some yielding to influence on both sides. As Homans (1961) put it, "Influence over others is purchased at the price of allowing one's self to be influenced by others [p. 286]." To be influential, authority depends upon esteem, he said. By granting esteem itself, or symbolic manifestations of it, one may in turn activate leadership, in terms of a person taking on the leader role.

The elicitation of leader behavior is now a demonstrable phenomenon in various experimental settings. In one definitive study conducted by Pepinsky, Hemphill, and Shevitz (1958), subjects who were low on leader activity were led to behave far more actively in that role by the group's evident support for their assertions. Alternatively, other subjects known to be high on leader activity earlier were affected in precisely the opposite way by the group's evident disagreement with their statements. In simplest terms, an exchange occurs between the group and the target person. The group provides reinforcement which in turn elicits favored behaviors. In other terms, the reinforcement of a person's influence assertions substantiates his position of authority.

Other, more recent, work suggested that even the use of lights as reinforcers exerts a significant effect on the target person's proportion of talking time as well as his perceived leadership status (Bavelas, Hastorf, Gross, & Kite, 1965; Zdep & Oakes, 1967). Thus, the lights not only produced a heightening of leader acts, but also created the impression of greater influence with the implication of legitimacy as well.

In a similar vein, Rudraswamy (1964) conducted a study in which some subjects within a group were led to believe they had higher status. Not only did they attempt significantly more leadership acts than others in their group, but they even outdistanced those subjects who were given more relevant information about the task itself.

It is also clear that agreement about who should lead has the effect in groups of increasing the probability of leader acts (e.g., Banta & Nelson, 1964). Relatedly, in a study of five-man groups involving changed as against unchanged leadership, Pryer, Flint, and Bass (1962) found that group effectiveness was enhanced by early agreement on who should lead.

When a basis is provided for legitimately making influence assertions, it is usually found that individuals will tend to act as leaders. This, of course, does not deny the existence of individual differences in the propensity for acting, once these conditions prevail. In a recent study by Gordon and Medland (1965), they found that positive peer ratings on leadership in army squads was consistently related to a measure of "aspiration to lead." Similarly, research findings on discussion groups (e.g., Riecken, 1958) indicated that the more vocal members obtain greater reinforcement, and hence experience the extension of legitimacy.

The "idiosyncrasy credit" concept (Hollander, 1958) suggests that a person's potential to be influential arises out of the positive dispositions others hold toward him. In simplest terms, competence in helping the group achieve its goals, and early conformity to its normative expectations for members, provide the potential for acting as a leader and being perceived as such.

Then, assertions of influence which were not tolerated before are more likely to be acceptable. This concept applies in an especially important way to leadership succession, since it affords the basis for understanding how a new leader becomes legitimized in the perceptions of his peers. Further work on succession phenomena appears, in general, to be another area of fruitful study. There are many intriguing issues here, such as the question of the relative importance in legitimacy of factors such as "knowledge" and "office," in Max Weber's terms, which deserve further consideration (see, e.g., Evan & Zelditch, 1961).

The perception of leadership functions within group structure

A major deficiency in the older trait approach was its conception of "traits" within the framework of classic personality typologies. Personality measures were applied to leaders, often in profusion, without reference either to the varying nature of leadership roles or the functions they were to fulfill. As Mann's (1959) review revealed, such measures indeed do yield inconsistent relationships among leaders, variously defined. To take a common instance, dominance and extroversion are sometimes related positively to status as the leader, but mainly are neither related positively nor negatively to this status. On the other hand, Stogdill (1948) reported that such characteristics as "originality," "initiative," and "adaptability" have a low but positive relationship with leader status.

Granting that some essentially personality-type variables are more often found among those designated as leaders than among those designated as nonleaders, there can be no dismissing the widespread failure to treat the characteristics of the leader as they are perceived —and, what is more, as they are perceived as *relevant*—by other group members within a given setting. As Hunt (1965) and Secord and Backman (1961) pointed out, traits are viewed relative to the interpersonal context in which they occur. In short, followers hold expectations regarding what the leader ought to be doing here and now, and not absolutely.

One probable source for the disparate findings concerning qualities of the leader is the existence of differential expectations concerning the functions the leader is to perform. In simplest terms, there are various leadership roles. Without nearly exhausting the roster, it helps to realize that the leader in various time-space settings may be a task director, mediator, or spokesman, as well as a decision maker who, as Bavelas (1960) put it, "reduces uncertainty."

Whether in the laboratory or the field, studies of the perceptions of the leader's functions often have depended upon a sociometric approach (cf. Hollander, 1954). Thus, Clifford and Cohen (1964) used a sociometric device to study leadership roles in a summer camp, with 79 boys and girls, ranging in age from 8 to 13 years. Over a period of 4 weeks, they had nine elections by secret ballot asking the youngsters to indicate how the others would fit into various roles, including such things as planner, banquet chairman, swimming captain, and so forth. Their results indicated that the perceived attributes of campers were tied variously to their election for different leader roles. In line with the earlier point about the interpersonal context of leader traits, these researchers say, "the problem should be rephrased in terms of personality variables required in a leader role in a specific

situation, which is in turn a function of the follower's perceptions [p. 64]."

Apart from personality traits, one prevailing expectation which does yield consistent findings across situations is that the leader's competence in a major group activity should be high. Dubno (1965), for example, reported that groups are more satisfied when leaders are demonstrably competent in a central function and do most of the work associated with that function. This is seen, too, in an experiment with five-man discussion groups, from which Marak (1964) found that the rewards associated with the leader's ability on a task led to greater perceived as well as actual influence. In general, the greater influence of a leader perceived to be more competent was verified experimentally by Dittes and Kelley (1956) and by Hollander (1960), among others.

Another leader attribute which evidently determines the responsiveness of followers is his perceived motivation regarding the group and its task. This was seen in Rosen, Levinger, and Lippitt's (1961) finding that helpfulness was rated as the most important characteristic leading to high influence potential among adolescent boys. In a more recent study of the role dimensions of leader-follower relations, Julian and Hollander (1966) found that, aside from the significance of task competence, the leader's "interest in group members" and "interest in group activity" were significantly related to group members' willingness to have a leader continue in that position. This accords with the finding of a field study by Nelson (1964) among 72 men who spent 12 months together in the Antarctic. While those men most liked as leaders had characteristics highly similar to those who were most liked as followers, Nelson reported that perceived motivation was the major factor which distinguished the two. Hollander (1958) considered this as one critical factor determining the leader's ability to retain status, even though nonconforming. In Nelson's study, the highly liked leaders were seen significantly more to be motivated highly toward the group in line with his hypothesis that, "a critical expectation held of the leader, if he is to maintain esteem, is that he display strong motivation to belong to the group [p. 165]."

A study by Kirkhart (1963) investigated group leadership among Negro college students as a function of their identification with their minority group. In terms of follower expectations, he found that those selected most frequently by their peers for leadership roles, in both the "internal system" and the "external system" activities of the group, scored higher on a questionnaire expressing Negro identification. This quality of being an exemplar of salient group characteristics was noted long ago by Brown (1936) as a feature of leadership. Its relationship to processes of identification with the leader is discussed shortly.

Source and nature of leader authority

The structural properties of groups affect the processes which occur within them. In leadership, the source of the leader's authority constitutes a significant element of structure. Yet, experimentation on leadership has given little attention to this variable, apart from some promising earlier work by Carter et al. (1951) with appointed and emergent leaders, and the work by Lewin and his associates on the style of the leader and its consequences to the group's social climate (Lewin et al., 1939; see also

Preston & Heintz, 1949). More recently, Cohen and Bennis (1961) demonstrated that where groups could elect their leaders, the continuity of leadership was better maintained than where their leaders were appointed. In research on the productivity of groups, Goldman and Fraas (1965) found that differences occurred among four conditions of leader selection, including election and appointment.

With four-man discussion groups, Julian, Hollander, and Regula (1969) employed a multifactor design to study three variables: the source of a leader's authority, in either election or appointment; his competence, in terms of perceived capability on the task; and his subsequent task success. Their main dependent measure was the members' acceptance of the leader as a spokesman for the group. The findings of this experiment indicated that the latter two variables were significantly related to this acceptance, but that these relationships were differentially affected by whether the leader was appointed or elected. The shape of the three-way interaction suggested that election, rather than making the leader more secure, made him more vulnerable to censure if he were either initially perceived to be incompetent or subsequently failed to secure a successful outcome as spokesman for the group. While this finding alone does not sustain a generalization that the appointed leader necessarily is more firmly entrenched, it does support the conclusion that the leader's source of authority is perceived and reacted to as a relevant element in the leadership process.

Other work on a differentiation of the leader's role, through the social structure, was conducted by Anderson and Fiedler (1964). In their experiment with four-man discussion groups, half the groups had leaders who were told to serve as a "chairman" in a participatory way, and the other groups had leaders who were told to serve as an "officer in charge" in a supervisory way. They found that the nature of the leadership process was affected markedly by this distinction, thus paralleling the main findings of Preston and Heintz (1949). In general, the more participatory leaders were significantly more influential and made more of a contribution to the group's performance. But, more to the point, the relationship between leader attributes, such as intelligence and performance, was significant for certain tasks under the participatory condition, though not for any of the tasks under the supervisory condition. The conclusion that Anderson and Fiedler reached, therefore, is that the characteristics of a leader, including intelligence and other personality attributes, become more salient and more highly relevant to group achievement under conditions of participation by the leader, as against circumstances where a highly formal role structure prevails.

Effectiveness of the leader

By now it is clear that an entire interpersonal system is implicated in answering the question of the leader's effectiveness. The leader is not effective merely by being influential, without regard to the processes at work and the ends achieved. Stressing this point, Selznick (1957) said that, "far more than the capacity to mobilize personal support . . . (or) the maintenance of equilibrium through the routine solution of everyday problems," the leader's function is "to define the ends of group existence, to design an enterprise distinctively adapted to these ends, and to see that the design becomes a living reality [p. 37]."

As Katz and Kahn (1966) observed, any group operates with a set of resources to produce certain outputs. Within this system, an interchange of inputs for outputs occurs, and this is facilitated by leadership functions which, among other things, direct the enterprise. The leader's contribution and its consequences vary with system demands, in terms of what Selznick referred to as "distinctive competence." Taken by itself, therefore, the typical conception of leadership as one person directing others can be misleading, as already indicated. Though the leader provides a valued resource, the group's resources are not the leader's alone. Together, such resources provide the basis for functions fulfilled in the successful attainment of group goals, or, in other terms, group outputs.

Given the fact that a group must work within the set of available resources, its effectiveness is gauged in several ways. Stogdill (1959), for one, distinguished these in terms of the group's performance, integration, and member satisfaction as group outputs of a leadership process involving the use of the group's resources. Thus, the leader and his characteristics constitute a set of resources contributing to the effective utilization of other resources. A person who occupies the central role of leader has the task of contributing to this enterprise, within the circumstances broadly confronting the group.

One prominent exemplification of the system's demands and constraints on the leader's effectiveness is seen in Fiedler's "contingency model" (1964, 1965, 1967). He predicted varying levels of effectiveness for different *combinations* of leader and situational characteristics.

Thus, depending upon the leader's orientation toward his co-workers, in the context of three situational variables—the quality of leader-member liking, the degree of task structure, and the position power of the leader—he finds distinct variations in this effectiveness.

In a recent test of his model, Fiedler (1966) conducted an experiment to compare the performance of 96 three-man groups that were culturally and linguistically homogeneous or heterogeneous. Some operated under powerful and others under weak leadership positions on three types of tasks varying in structure and requirements for verbal interaction. Despite the communication difficulties and different backgrounds, heterogeneous groups performed about as well on the nonverbal task as did the homogeneous groups. Groups with petty officers as leaders (powerful) did about as well as the groups with recruits as leaders (weak). The main finding of the experiment was support for the hypothesis from the contingency model that the specific leadership orientation required for effectiveness is contingent on the favorableness of the group-task situation. Partial support for this hypothesis came also from a study by Shaw and Blum (1966) in which they manipulated some of the same variables with five-person groups, and with three tasks selected to vary along a dimension reflecting different levels of favorability for the leader. Their results indicated that the directive leader was more effective than the nondirective leader only when the group-task situation was highly favorable for the leader, but not otherwise.

Identification with the leader

For any leader, the factors of favorability and effectiveness depend upon the perceptions of followers. Their identification with him implicates significant psychological ties which may affect materially his ability to be influential. Yet the study of identification is passé in leadership research. Though there is a recurring theme in the literature of social science, harking back to Weber (see 1947), about the so-called "charismatic leader," this quality has a history of imprecise usage; furthermore, its tie with identification processes is by no means clear. Putting the study of the sources and consequences of identification with the leader on a stronger footing seems overdue and entirely feasible.

Several lines of work in social psychology appear to converge on identification processes. The distinction made by Kelman (1961) regarding identification, internalization, and compliance, for example, has obvious relevance to the relationship between the leader and his followers. This typology might be applied to the further investigation of leadership processes. The work of Sears (1960) and of Bandura and Walters (1963), concerning the identification of children with adult models, also has implications for such study.

One point which is clear, though the dynamics require far more attention, is that the followers' identification with their leader can provide them with social reality, in the sense of a shared outlook. An illustration of this is seen in work on the social psychology of political leadership by Hollander (see 1963). In two phases, separated by an interval of 8 years, he studied Republicans in 1954 who had voted for President Eisenhower in 1952 and who would or would not vote for him again in 1954; and then in 1962, he studied Democrats who had voted for President Kennedy in 1960 and who would or would not vote for him again in 1962. He found that continuing loyalty to the President of one's party, among these respondents, was significantly associated with their views on issues and conditions and with their votes for the party in a midterm congressional-senatorial election. The defectors showed a significant shift in the precise opposite direction, both in their attitudes and in their voting behavior. In both periods, the ideology of loyalists was highly consistent with the leader's position. In the economic realm, for example, even where actual well-being varied considerably among loyalists, this identification with the President yielded highly similar attitudes regarding the favorability of the economic picture facing the nation.

With appropriate concern for rectifying the balance, there may be virtue in reopening for study Freud's (1922) contention that the leader of a group represents a common "ego ideal" in whom members share an identification and an ideology. Laboratory experimentation on groups offers little basis for studying such identification in light of the ephemeral, ad hoc basis for the creation of such groups. In fact, a disproportionate amount of our current knowledge about leadership in social psychology comes from experiments which are methodologically sophisticated but bear only a pale resemblance to the leadership enterprise that engages people in persisting relationships.

There also is the problem of accommodating the notion of identification within prevailing conceptions of leader-follower transactions and social exchange. But that is not an insurmountable difficulty with an expansion of the reward concept to include, for instance, the value of social reality. In any case, as investigators move increasingly from the laboratory to studies in more naturalistic settings, one of the significant qualities that may make a difference in leadership functioning is precisely this prospect for identification.

Some conclusions and implications

The present selective review and discussion touches upon a range of potential issues for the further study of leadership. The discussion is by no means exhaustive in providing details beyond noting suggestive developments. It is evident, however, that a new set of conceptions about leadership is beginning to emerge after a period of relative quiescence.

In providing a bridge to future research here, these newer, general ideas are underscored in a suggestive way. The methodologies they demand represent a challenge to imaginative skill, especially toward greater refinements in the conduct of field experiments and field studies which provide a look at the broader system of leadership relationships. Then, too, there is a need to consider the two-way nature of the influence process, with greater attention paid to the expectations of followers within the system. As reiterated here, the key to an understanding of leadership rests in seeing it as an influence process, involving an implicit exchange relationship over time.

No less important as a general point is the need for a greater recognition of the system represented by the group and its enterprise. This recognition provides a vehicle by which to surmount the misleading dichotomy of the leader and the situation which so long has prevailed. By adopting a systems approach, the leader, the led, and the situation defined broadly, are seen as interdependent inputs variously engaged toward the production of desired outputs.

Some release is needed from the highly static, positional view of leadership if we are to analyze its processes. A focus on leadership maintenance has weighted the balance against a more thorough probe of emerging leadership and succession phenomena. Investigators should be more aware of their choice and the differential implications, as between emerging and ongoing leadership. In this regard, the significance of the legitimacy of leadership, its sources, and effects requires greater attention in future investigations.

In studying the effectiveness of the leader, more emphasis should be placed on the outcomes for the total system, including the fulfillment of expectations held by followers. The long-standing overconcern with outcome, often stated only in terms of the leader's ability to influence, should yield to a richer conception of relationships geared to mutual goals. Not irrelevantly, the perception of the leader held by followers, including their identification with him, needs closer scrutiny. In this way, one may approach a recognition of stylistic elements allowing given persons to be effective leaders.

Finally, it seems plain that research on task-oriented groups must attend more to the organizational frameworks within which these groups are imbedded. Whether these frameworks are industrial, educational, governmental, or whatever, they are implicated in such crucial matters as goal-setting, legitimacy of authority, and leader succession. Though not always explicit, it is the organizational context which recruits and engages members in particular kinds of tasks, role relationships, and the rewards of participation. This context deserves more explicitness in attempts at understanding leadership processes.

53   The bases of power

JOHN R. P. FRENCH, JR. and BERTRAM H. RAVEN

By the basis of power we mean the relationship between O and P which is the source of that power.[1] It is rare that we can say with certainty that a given empirical case of power is limited to one source. Normally, the relation between O and P will be characterized by several qualitatively different variables which are bases of power (Lippitt, et al., 1952, Ch. 11). Although there are undoubtedly many possible bases of power which may be distinguished, we shall here define five which seem especially common and important. These five bases of O's power are: (1) reward power, based on P's perception that O has the ability to mediate rewards for him; (2) coercive power, based on P's perception that O has the ability to mediate punishments for him; (3) legitimate power, based on the perception by P that O has a legitimate right to prescribe behavior for him; (4) referent power, based on P's identification with O; (5) expert power, based on the perception that O has some special knowledge or expertness.

Our first concern is to define the bases which give rise to a given type of power. Next, we describe each type of power according to its strength, range,

and the degree of dependence of the new state of the system which is most likely to occur with each type of power. We shall also examine the other effects which the exercise of a given type of power may have upon P and his relationship to O. Finally, we shall point out the interrelationships between different types of power, and the effects of use of one type of power by O upon other bases of power which he might have over P. Thus we shall both define a set of concepts and propose a series of hypotheses. Most of these hypotheses have not been systematically tested, although there is a good deal of evidence in favor of several. No attempt will be made to summarize that evidence here.

Reward power

Reward power is defined as power whose basis is the ability to reward. The strength of the reward power of O/P increases with the magnitude of the rewards which P perceives that O can mediate for him. Reward power depends on O's ability to administer positive valences and to remove or decrease negative valences. The strength of reward power also depends upon the probability that O can mediate the reward, as perceived by P. A common example of reward power is the addition of a piece-work rate in the factory

[1] "Our theory of social influence and power is limited to influence on the person, P, produced by an agent, O, where O can be either another person, a role, a norm, a group, or a part of a group" (French & Raven, 1959, p. 151).—Eds.

Excerpted from "The Bases of Social Power," Chapter 9 of D. Cartwright (Ed.) **Studies in Social Power**, Ann Arbor: University of Michigan, Institute for Social Research, 1959, pp. 150–67, with permission of the authors and the publisher.

as an incentive to increase production.

The new state of the system induced by a promise of reward (for example the factory worker's increased level of production) will be highly dependent on O. Since O mediates the reward, he controls the probability that P will receive it. Thus P's new rate of production will be dependent on his subjective probability that O will reward him for conformity minus his subjective probability that O will reward him even if he returns to his old level. Both probabilities will be greatly affected by the level of observability of P's behavior. Incidentally, a piece rate often seems to have more effect on production than a merit rating system because it yields a higher probability of reward for conformity and a much lower probability of reward for nonconformity.

The utilization of actual rewards (instead of promises) by O will tend over time to increase the attraction of P toward O and therefore the referent power of O over P. As we shall note later, such referent power will permit O to induce changes which are relatively independent. Neither rewards nor promises will arouse resistance in P, provided P considers it legitimate for O to offer rewards.

The range of reward power is specific to those regions within which O can reward P for conforming. The use of rewards to change systems within the range of reward power tends to increase reward power by increasing the probability attached to future promises. However, unsuccessful attempts to exert reward power outside the range of power would tend to decrease the power; for example if O offers to reward P for performing an impossible act, this will reduce for P the probability of receiving future rewards promised by O.

Coercive power

Coercive power is similar to reward power in that it also involves O's ability to manipulate the attainment of valences. Coercive power of O/P stems from the expectation on the part of P that he will be punished by O if he fails to conform to the influence attempt. Thus negative valences will exist in given regions of P's life space, corresponding to the threatened punishment by O. The strength of coercive power depends on the magnitude of the negative valence of the threatened punishment multiplied by the perceived probability that P can avoid the punishment by conformity, i.e., the probability of punishment for nonconformity minus the probability of punishment for conformity (French, et al., 1960). Just as an offer of a piece-rate bonus in a factory can serve as a basis for reward power, so the ability to fire a worker if he falls below a given level of production will result in coercive power.

Coercive power leads to dependent change also; and the degree of dependence varies with the level of observability of P's conformity. An excellent illustration of coercive power leading to dependent change is provided by a clothes presser in a factory observed by Coch and French (1948). As her efficiency rating climbed above average for the group the other workers began to "scapegoat" her. That the resulting plateau in her production was not independent of the group was evident once she was removed from the presence of the other workers. Her production immediately climbed to new heights.

At times, there is some difficulty in distinguishing between reward power and coercive power. Is the withholding of a reward really equivalent to a punishment? Is the withdrawal of punishment equivalent to a reward? The answer must be a psychological one—it depends upon the situation as it exists for P. But ordinarily we would answer these questions in the affirmative; for P, receiving a reward is a positive valence as is the relief of suffering. There is some evidence that conformity to group norms in order to gain acceptance (reward power) should be distinguished from conformity as a means of forestalling rejection (coercive power) (Dittes & Kelley, 1956).

The distinction between these two types of power is important because the dynamics are different. The concept of "sanctions" sometimes lumps the two together despite their opposite effects. While reward power may eventually result in an independent system, the effects of coercive power will continue to be dependent. Reward power will tend to increase the attraction of P toward O; coercive power will decrease this attraction (French, et al., 1960; Raven & French, 1958b). The valence of the region of behavior will become more negative, acquiring some negative valence from the threatened punishment. The negative valence of punishment would also spread to other regions of the life space. Lewin (1935, pp. 114–70) has pointed out this distinction between the effects of rewards and punishment. In the case of threatened punishment, there will be a resultant force on P to leave the field entirely. Thus, to achieve conformity, O must not only place a strong negative valence in certain regions through threat of punishment, but O must also introduce restraining forces, or other strong valences, so as to prevent P from withdrawing completely from O's range of coercive power. Otherwise the probability of receiving the punishment, if P does not conform, will be too low to be effective.

Legitimate power

Legitimate power is probably the most complex of those treated here, embodying notions from the structural sociologist, the group-norm and role oriented social psychologist, and the clinical psychologist.

There has been considerable investigation and speculation about socially prescribed behavior, particularly that which is specific to a given role or position. Linton (1945) distinguishes group norms according to whether they are universals for everyone in the culture, alternatives (the individual having a choice as to whether or not to accept them), or specialties (specific to given positions). Whether we speak of internalized norms, role prescriptions and expectations, or internalized pressures (Herbst, 1953), the fact remains that each individual sees certain regions toward which he should locomote, some regions toward which he should not locomote, and some regions toward which he may locomote if they are generally attractive for him. This applies to specific behaviors in which he may, should, or should not engage; it applies to certain attitudes or beliefs which he may, should, or should not hold. The feeling of "oughtness" may be an internalization from his parents, from his teachers, from his religion, or may have been logically developed from some idiosyncratic system of ethics. He will speak of such behaviors with expressions like "should," "ought to," or "has a right to." In many cases, the original source of the requirement is not recalled.

Though we have oversimplified such

evaluations of behavior with a positive-neutral-negative trichotomy, the evaluation of behaviors by the person is really more one of degree. This dimension of evaluation, we shall call "legitimacy." Conceptually, we may think of legitimacy as a valence in a region which is induced by some internalized norm or value. This value has the same conceptual property as power, namely an ability to induce force fields (Lewin, 1951, pp. 40–41). It may or may not be correct that values (or the super-ego) are internalized parents, but at least they can set up force fields which have a phenomenal "oughtness" similar to a parent's prescription. Like a value, a need can also induce valences (i.e., force fields) in P's psychological environment, but these valences have more the phenomenal character of nox-ious or attractive properties of the object or activity. When a need induces a valence in P, for example, when a need makes an object attractive to P, this attraction applies to P but not to other persons. When a value induces a valence, on the other hand, it not only sets up forces on P to engage in the activity, but P may feel that all others ought to behave in the same way. Among other things, this evaluation applies to the legitimate right of some other individual or group to prescribe behavior or beliefs for a person even though the other cannot apply sanctions.

Legitimate power of O/P is here defined as that power which stems from internalized values in P which dictate that O has a legitimate right to influence P and that P has an obligation to accept this influence. We note that legitimate power is very similar to the notion of legitimacy of authority which has long been explored by sociologists, particularly by Weber (1947), and more recently by Goldhammer and Shils (1939). However, legitimate power is not always a role relation: P may accept an induction from O simply because he had previously promised to help O and he values his word too much to break the promise. In all cases, the notion of legitimacy involves some sort of code or standard, accepted by the individual, by virtue of which the external agent can assert his power. We shall attempt to describe a few of these values here.

Bases for legitimate power. Cultural values constitute one common basis for the legitimate power of one individual over another. O has characteristics which are specified by the culture as giving him the right to prescribe behavior for P, who may not have these characteristics. These bases, which Weber (1947) has called the authority of the "eternal yesterday," include such things as age, intelligence, caste, and physical characteristics. In some cultures, the aged are granted the right to prescribe behavior for others in practically all behavior areas. In most cultures, there are certain areas of behavior in which a person of one sex is granted the right to prescribe behavior for the other sex.

Acceptance of the social structure is another basis for legitimate power. If P accepts as right the social structure of his group, organization, or society, especially the social structure involving a hierarchy of authority, P will accept the legitimate authority of O who occupies a superior office in the hierarchy. Thus legitimate power in a formal organization is largely a relationship between offices rather than between persons. And the acceptance of an office as *right* is a basis for legitimate power—a judge has a right to levy fines, a foreman should assign work, a priest is justified in prescribing religious beliefs, and it is the management's prerogative to make certain decisions (French, et al., 1957). However, legitimate power also involves the perceived right of the person to hold the office.

Designation by a legitimizing agent is a third basis for legitimate power. An influencer O may be seen as legitimate in prescribing behavior for P because he has been granted such power by a legitimizing agent whom P accepts. Thus a department head may accept the authority of his vice-president in a certain area because that authority has been specifically delegated by the president. An election is perhaps the most common example of a group's serving to legitimize the authority of one individual or office for other individuals in the group. The success of such legitimizing depends upon the acceptance of the legitimizing agent and procedure. In this case it depends ultimately on certain democratic values concerning election procedures. The election process is one of legitimizing a person's right to an office which already has a legitimate range of power associated with it.

Range of legitimate power of O/P. The areas in which legitimate power may be exercised are generally specified along with the designation of that power. A job description, for example, usually specifies supervisory activities and also designates the person to whom the job-holder is responsible for the duties described. Some bases for legitimate authority carry with them a very broad range. Culturally derived bases for legitimate power are often especially broad. It is not uncommon to find cultures in which a member of a given caste can legitimately prescribe behavior for all members of lower castes in practically all regions. More common, however, are instances of legitimate power where the range is specifically and narrowly prescribed. A sergeant in the army is given a specific set of regions within which he can legitimately prescribe behavior for his men.

The attempted use of legitimate power which is outside of the range of legitimate power will decrease the legitimate power of the authority figure. Such use of power which is not legitimate will also decrease the attractiveness of O (French, *et al.*, 1960; Raven & French, 1958a, 1958b).

Legitimate power and influence. The new state of the system which results from legitimate power usually has high dependence on O though it may become independent. Here, however, the degree of dependence is not related to the level of observability. Since legitimate power is based on P's values, the source of the forces induced by O include both these internal values and O. O's induction serves to activate the values and to relate them to the system which is influenced, but thereafter the new state of the system may become directly dependent on the values with no mediation by O. Accordingly this new state will be relatively stable and consistent across varying environmental situations since P's values are more stable than his psychological environment.

We have used the term legitimate not only as a basis for the power of an agent, but also to describe the general behaviors of a person. Thus, the individual P may also consider the legitimacy of the attempts to use other types of power by O. In certain cases, P will consider that O has a legitimate right to threaten punishment for nonconformity; in other cases, such use of coercion would not be seen as legitimate. P might change in response to coercive power of O, but it will make a considerable difference in his attitude and conformity if O is not seen as having a legitimate right to use such coercion. In such cases, the attraction of P for O will be particularly diminished, and the influence attempt will arouse more resistance (French, et al., 1960). Similarly the utilization of reward power may vary in legitimacy; the word "bribe," for example, denotes an illegitimate reward.

Referent power

The referent power of O/P has its basis in the identification of P with O. By identification, we mean a feeling of oneness of P with O, or a desire for such an identity. If O is a person toward whom P is highly attracted, P will have a desire to become closely associated with O. If O is an attractive group, P will have a feeling of membership or a desire to join. If P is already closely associated with O he will want to maintain this relationship. P's identification with O can be established or maintained if P behaves, believes, and perceives as O does. Accordingly O has the ability to influence P, even though P may be unaware of this referent power. A verbalization of such power by P might be, "I am like O, and therefore I shall behave or believe as O does," or "'I want to be like O, and I will be more like O if I behave or believe as O does." The stronger the identification of P with O the greater the referent power of O/P.

Similar types of power have already been investigated under a number of different formulations. Festinger (1950) points out that in an ambiguous situation, the individual seeks some sort of "social reality" and may adopt the cognitive structure of the individual or group with which he identifies. In such a case, the lack of clear structure may be threatening to the individual and the agreement of his beliefs with those of a reference group will both satisfy his need for structure and give him added security through increased identification with his group (Hochbaum, 1954; Jackson & Saltzstein, 1958).

We must try to distinguish between referent power and other types of power which might be operative at the same time. If a member is attracted to a group and he conforms to its norms only because he fears ridicule or expulsion from the group for nonconformity, we would call this coercive power. On the other hand if he conforms in order to obtain praise for conformity, it is a case of reward power. The basic criterion for distinguishing referent power from both coercive and reward power is the mediation of the punishment and the reward by O: to the extent that O mediates the sanctions (i.e., has means control over P) we are dealing with coercive and reward power; but to the extent that P avoids discomfort or gains satisfaction by conformity based on identification, regardless of O's responses, we are dealing with referent power. Conformity with majority opinion is sometimes based on a respect for the collective wisdom of the group, in which case it is expert power. It is important to distinguish these phenomena, all grouped together elsewhere as "pressures toward uniformity," since the type of change which occurs will be different for different bases of power.

The concepts of "reference group" (Kelley, 1952) and "'prestige suggestion" may be treated as instances of referent power. In this case, O, the prestigeful person or group, is valued by P; because P desires to be associated or identified with O, he will assume attitudes or beliefs held by O. Similarly a negative reference group which O dislikes and evaluates negatively may exert negative influence on P as a result of negative referent power.

It has been demonstrated that the power which we designate as referent power is especially great when P is attracted to O (Back, 1951; Festinger, 1950; Festinger, et al., 1952; Festinger, et al., 1953; Gerard, 1954; Kelman, 1961; Lippitt, et al., 1952). In our terms, this would mean that the greater the attraction, the greater the identification, and consequently the greater the referent power. In some cases, attraction or prestige may have a specific basis, and the range of referent power will be limited accordingly: a group of campers may have great referent power over a member regarding campcraft, but considerably less effect on other regions (Lippitt, et al., 1952). However, we hypothesize that the greater the attraction of P toward O, the broader the range of referent power of O/P.

The new state of a system produced by referent power may be dependent on or independent of O; but the degree of dependence is not affected by the level of observability to O (Festinger, 1953; Kelman, 1961). In fact, P is often not consciously aware of the referent power which O exerts over him. There is probably a tendency for some of these dependent changes to become independent of O quite rapidly.

Expert power

The strength of the expert power of O/P varies with the extent of the knowledge or perception which P attributes to O within a given area. Probably P evaluates O's expertness in relation to his own knowledge as well as against an absolute standard. In any case expert power results in primary social influence on P's cognitive structure and probably not on other types of systems. Of course changes in the cognitive structure can change the direction of forces and hence of locomotion, but such a change of behavior is secondary social influence. Expert power has been demonstrated experimentally (Festinger, et al., 1952; Moore, 1921). Accepting an attorney's advice in legal matters is a common example of expert influence; but there are many instances based on much less knowledge, such as the acceptance by a stranger of directions given by a native villager.

Expert power, where O need not be a member of P's group, is called "informational power" by Deutsch and Gerard (1955). This type of expert power must be distinguished from influence based on the content of communication as described by Hovland, et al. (Hovland, et al., 1949; Hovland & Weiss, 1951; Kelman, 1961; Kelman & Hovland, 1953). The influence of the content of a communication upon an opinion is presumably a secondary influence produced after the *primary* influence (i.e., the acceptance of the information). Since power is here defined in terms of the primary changes, the influence of the content on a related opinion is not a case of expert power as we have defined it, but the initial acceptance of the validity of the content does seem to be based on expert power or referent power. In other cases, however, so-called facts may be accepted as self-evident because they fit into P's cognitive structure; if this impersonal acceptance of the truth of the fact is independent of the more or less enduring relationship between O and P, then P's acceptance of the fact is not an actualization of expert power. Thus we distinguish between expert power based on the credibility of O and informational influence which is based on characteristics of the stimulus such as the logic of the argument or the "self-evident facts."

Wherever expert influence occurs it seems to be necessary both for P to think that O knows and for P to trust that O is telling the truth (rather than trying to deceive him).

Expert power will produce a new cognitive structure which is initially relatively dependent on O, but informational influence will produce a more independent structure. The former is likely to become more independent with the passage of time. In both cases the degree of dependence on O is not affected by the level of observability.

The "sleeper effect" (Hovland & Weiss, 1951; Kelman & Hovland, 1953) is an interesting case of a change in the degree of dependence of an opinion on O. An unreliable O (who probably had negative referent power but some positive expert power) presented "facts" which were accepted by the subjects and which would normally produce secondary influence on their opinions and beliefs. However, the negative referent power aroused resistance and resulted in negative social influence on their beliefs (i.e., set up a force in the direction opposite to the influence attempt), so that there was little change in the subjects' opinions. With the passage of time, however, the subjects tended to forget the identity of the negative communicator faster than they forgot the contents of his communication, so there was a weakening of the negative referent influence and a consequent delayed positive change in the subject's beliefs in the direction of the influence attempt ("sleeper effect"). Later, when the identity of the negative communicator was experimentally reinstated, these resisting forces were reinstated, and there was another negative change in belief in a direction opposite to the influence attempt (Kelman & Hovland, 1953).

The range of expert power, we assume, is more delimited than that of referent power. Not only is it restricted to cognitive systems but the expert is seen as having superior knowledge or ability in very specific areas, and his power will be limited to these areas, though some "halo effect" might occur. Recently, some of our renowned physical scientists have found quite painfully that their expert power in physical sciences does not extend to regions involving international politics. Indeed, there is some evidence that the attempted exertion of expert power outside of the range of expert power will reduce that expert power. An undermining of confidence seems to take place.

54 The process of social power

MARVIN E. OLSEN

An inevitable outcome of all social organization, whenever and wherever it occurs, is the creation of social power. By ordering their social interactions and infusing their relationships with common meanings, participants in social organizations collectively exercise power that none of them could exert individually. Whether these organizations be small groups, families, communities, formal associations, functional networks, or total societies, their actions and activities always involve the wielding of power in social life. Social power is generated through the process of social organization and is inseparable from it. As expressed by Amos Hawley (1963): "Every social act is an exercise of power, every social relationship is a power equation and every social group or system is an organization of power. Accordingly, it is possible to transpose any system of social relationships into terms of potential or active power. Perhaps such a transposition is nothing more than the substitution of one terminology for another."

Power is not only a direct consequence of social organization but also a causal factor contributing to the creation of additional organization. As power is generated through the process of social organization, it can then be used to impose further patterns of social order or cultural ideas upon either that particular area of social life or other areas. In other words, power can be employed to strengthen existing social organization or to create new organization. Although power will not directly increase the integration of an organization, it can be used to establish the social conditions and patterns of order that contribute to the process of social integration.

We shall focus our attention here on the fundamental nature of social power, the process of power exertion, various subtypes of power, two attempts to explain how power is created through social activities, and several uses of power in social life.

Nature of social power

For our purposes, *social power is the ability to affect social life (social actions, social order, or culture)*.[1] Whenever a social actor in any way affects the course

[1] The only other definition of social power that approaches this one in scope is by Talcott Parsons (1960): "Power . . . is the generalized capacity of a social system to get things done in the interest of collective goals." Many definitions of social power include the idea of overcoming resistance, including both direct opposition and indirect limitations and scarcities. This phrase is redundant, however, since the ability to affect social life logically implies overcoming resistance. That is, if an actor cannot overcome whatever resistance he encounters in a particular situation, he has no power to affect that sphere of social life. Nevertheless, he might be able to exercise power in other situations that offer less resistance to his actions.

of a social or cultural process or phenomenon, social power is being exercised.

Social power is a relational, not a psychological phenomenon. That is, *social power always exists within social relationships, never within individual persons.* Individuals may themselves possess a certain amount of physical strength, special knowledge or competence, strong personality qualities, or particular interaction abilities such as leadership skills, but none of these capabilities constitutes social power. One's personal characteristics can contribute to his power in a particular situation, but social power always resides within social relationships and patterns of social order. The chairman of a committee, for instance, might exercise power over the actions of the other members and over the activities of the committee as a whole, but this power lies in his relationships within the committee—in the roles he enacts and the position he occupies. Personal capabilities, such as skill in conducting meetings, can facilitate his acquiring and exercising of power, but they are not themselves social power. If he should be removed from office or leave the group, he will no longer wield the power created by the group, even though he retains his skill at conducting meetings.

The terms "influence" and "control" are frequently used as synonyms for social power, though they might more properly be thought of as special cases of power. *Social influence is an instance of power in which outcomes are not predetermined.* Influence can only be attempted, not enforced, and its results are always problematic. It follows, then, that the object of an attempt at influence can either accept or reject the influence. In contrast, *social control is an instance of power in which outcomes are largely or totally predetermined.* Control can be exercised regardless of the wishes of the recipient, with little or no doubt concerning its results. To mention one example, a railroad company might be able to exert only moderate influence over a large metropolis but be able to control the economic fate of a small business that relies on rail shipment of its products. Both influence and control are relative phenomena, depending on the amounts of power wielded by each actor in a given situation, and might perhaps be thought of as constituting the opposite ends of a continuum.

Although power always exists within social relationships, the actors who exercise it can be either individuals or organizations. To distinguish between these two kinds of power phenomena we use the concepts of interpersonal and organizational power situations. *A social power relationship is interpersonal if the actors exercising power are individuals, and organizational if they are social organizations.* Real social life contains endless diverse combinations of interpersonal and organizational power. A husband who determines how much money his wife spends on household expenses each week is wielding interpersonal power; as a social unit his family exerts organizational power in relation to other social organizations with which it interacts, including local businesses, perhaps a church or school, and to some extent the entire community. The president of a corporation might personally influence the other executives (and secretaries) with whom he comes into daily contact, but the business as a whole rather than the president himself controls the work schedule (and hence influences the family routines) of its employees, and buys and sells goods with other organizations.

Similarly, one member of a national legislature may wield interpersonal power over another member, while the legislature as a whole exercises organizational power over its component parts (such as committees) and over many other organizations within the society, as well as the entire nation.

The theoretical distinction between interpersonal and organizational power situations is fairly clear. In practice, however, it is often very difficult to separate these two phenomena. This problem arises because organizational power must be exerted by individuals acting as representatives of that organization, yet individuals often use their organizational roles and positions as resources for interpersonal power. In other words, how do we tell whether a person is acting as an involved part of some larger social entity and thus merely administering organizational power, or acting as an autonomous element and thus exercising interpersonal power? It is true that we frequently label our power acts as either personal ("do this for me") or organizational ("this church opposes . . ."), but our actions do not always substantiate our words. The conceptions of interpersonal and organizational power, therefore, remain only heuristic analytical tools rather than empirical variables.

The exercise of social power can also be classified along several other analytical dimensions, including the following four:

(1) Purposeful versus nonpurposeful power. If a social actor intentionally affects other actors, patterns of social order, or cultural ideas, his exertion of social power is clearly purposeful. In other cases, though, his actions might have the same social effects even though he had no intention of wielding power.

Often an action has both intended and unintended power consequences, as when a newspaper union calls a strike to gain higher wages for its members, and the strike has extensive side effects on stores, theatres, voluntary associations, and other community organizations.

(2) Positive versus negative power. Positive power is the ability to accomplish something that otherwise would not occur, while negative power is the ability to prevent something that otherwise would occur.[2] Any given exercise of social power can operate positively or negatively or both ways simultaneously.

(3) Internal versus external power. Internal power is exerted by an organization over its own members or subunits. External power is wielded by an individual or an organization over some other actor in the social environment. By definition, internal power can be exerted only by organizations, since only they contain partially autonomous subunits. External power, though, might be exercised by individuals or organizations.

(4) Direct versus indirect power. The exercise of social power is direct when it flows from the power wielder straight to the power recipient. It becomes indirect when it passes through one or more intermediate stages before reaching its ultimate destination. Indirect social power frequently takes the form of ordering social situations in particular ways, which in turn produce certain specific actions or activities. Much of any organization's power, for instance, lies in its ability to shape the social context in which its members act and the

2 The only major discussion of social power that treats it solely as a negative phenomenon (in the form of either blocking actions or withdrawing benefits) is Blau (1964), Chap. 5.

social environment in which other organizations exist.

Exercise of social power

To exert power in a social relationship, an actor must have resources upon which he can draw. *A resource is anything that an actor can use to produce social power.* The most obvious resources for social power are possessions, such as goods, money, or knowledge. Resources can also take the form of occupancy of vital organizational roles and positions, grants of legitimacy to the actor by others, communicative and persuasive skills, and special qualities of the actor that others find attractive. In addition, if the actor is an organization, its available resources might include the size and quality of its population, the strength of its integration, the degree of its stability and flexibility, its overall operational effectiveness, and various customs and traditions contained in its culture. Whatever the specific resources employed in a given situation, it is by using them (or threatening to use them) that an actor gains social power. The main distinction between resources and power is that resources are possessed by an actor himself, whereas power is only exercised by an actor in a social relationship.

Resources provide a person or organization with a basis for generating social power. However, if the use of these resources is prevented or if they are inadequate to overcome whatever resistance exists, the actor cannot realistically be said to exert any power in this situation. Resistance can take many forms, including direct opposition by a counterpower, indirect limitations or scarcities inherent in the situation, avoidance of the relationship through alternative courses of action, or indifference to the effects of the power. In general, the amount of power one actor exercises over others in a given relationship is a resultant of the extent and adequacy of the resources actually used (sometimes called inducements) minus the degree of resistance encountered.

Given a relationship in which social power is actively being exercised, the next concern is to describe and analyze this situation. Two main approaches are commonly used: distributive and developmental analysis. These approaches are in no way incompatible, but they do involve different questions and perspectives. *Distributive analysis examines the way in which the total amount of power being exerted at any one time within a given situation is divided among the participating actors.* Is power shared relatively equally by all actors, is it wielded almost exclusively by a single actor, or does some intermediate condition prevail? The usual result of distributive analysis is a structural description of the distribution of power among the actors at one particular time. In contrast, *developmental analysis investigates increases and decreases through time in the total amount of power being exercised within a given relationship or organization.* To what extent has the creation of social organization and the accumulation of resources over time augmented the total amount of power being employed by all participants? Or, conversely, has the disintegration of social organization or the depletion of available resources reduced the amount of power they can exert? The usual outcome of developmental analysis is an explanation of changes that have occurred through time in dynamic power processes. For example, a study showing that businessmen presently have more influence on community decisions than do politicians would be distributive in nature, while a study of growth in the effectiveness of community decision-making during the past twenty years would be developmental in nature.

Both of these approaches to power analysis are equally valid and productive of scientific knowledge, but serious problems arise if one's conception of social power is not appropriate for the kind of analysis being performed. For distributive analysis we must temporarily assume a *zero-sum conception* of social power, which sees the total amount of power being exercised at any specific time as fixed or finite. Developmental analysis, on the other hand, requires the temporary assumption of a *positive-sum conception* of social power, which sees the total amount of power being exerted through time as varying or infinite. These are simply heuristic conceptions of the nature of power which the analyst temporarily accepts as a basis for performing either distributive or developmental analysis. They are in no way contradictory, as long as one keeps the time factor clearly in mind. Unfortunately, not all writers have done so. For instance, if we demonstrate that large businesses, the executive branch of the federal government, and the military have all grown in power in the United States during the past thirty years (Mills, 1956), this is clearly developmental analysis. On the basis of this information alone, however, we cannot simply assume that other parts of the society—such as Congress, state and community governments, schools, churches, labor unions, political parties, and voluntary associations—have necessarily all lost power. If such a conclusion were reached without additional information concerning these other realms of society,

we would be assuming a zero-sum conception of social power when our developmental analysis requires a positive-sum conception. The total amount of social power being exerted in the United States might have increased considerably during this period, so that these other unexamined parts of the society could have grown in power at equal or even faster rates than businesses, government, and the military.

Types of social power

As a fundamental social process, the exercise of social power occurs whenever a social actor affects social life. This process can take many different forms. We shall now attempt to clarify and interrelate what appear to be the four major types of social power: force, dominance, attraction, and authority (cf. Bierstedt, 1950; French & Raven, 1959; Lipset, 1960, Ch. 3; Park, 1952; Weber, 1947, pp. 324–363). These four types are analytically distinct, although any particular power phenomenon might include several or all of them.

In its broadest meaning, *force is the application of pressures as a means of gaining results*. These pressures range from subtle hints to monetary payments to physical punishments. Although we commonly equate the idea of force with overt coercion or violence, the sociological meaning of this concept is considerably more inclusive, covering all forms of social pressures. The resource base for the exercise of force thus consists of all actual or threatened pressures that one actor can bring to bear upon others.

More specifically, three identifiable subtypes of force are (a) compensation, or providing desired objects or conditions in return for compliance, (b) deprivation, or administering punishments or withholding expected benefits as a consequence of noncompliance, and (c) persuasion, or the manipulation of information, emotions, special knowledge, or social values. The use of force can thus be seen in the payment of wages for work, in the expulsion of a member from a professional association, and in newspaper editorials.

The exercise of force commonly occurs within exchange relationships, and in a very general sense the two phenomena of force and exchange are synonymous. That is, the exertion of force can be seen as the exchange of pressures for compliance, while exchange involves a commitment of resources to elicit desired responses from other participants. In both everyday and sociological usage, however, the ideas of exchange and force are at least partially distinct. We generally think of exchange relationships as being relatively balanced, with all participants possessing roughly equal resources. Force relationships, on the other hand, are predominantly one-sided or unbalanced, with the power wielder employing (or at least possessing) superior resources. This is a useful analytical distinction, but it leaves unanswered the basic question of how unbalanced a relationship must become before it shifts from a process of exchange to one of force. The apparent resolution is to conceive of exchange and force as the end points on a continuum, ranging from perfect balance among all actors to total control by one actor. Most actual situations then fall somewhere between these two extremes (cf. Blau, 1964, Chap. 5).

Force can be an easily exercised and very powerful means of achieving desired ends, provided one can employ adequate resources. Nevertheless, because the exertion of force is especially likely to arouse opposition, it often remains a relatively unstable and unreliable type of social power.

Dominance is the ability to affect social processes because of an actor's roles or activities within a social organization. Functional specialization and interdependence among the members and subunits of an organization tend to make each part vulnerable to the actions of all the other parts with which it is functionally interrelated. Through the routine performance of its normal roles or activities, therefore, a given subpart often influences or controls the functioning of many other interdependent parts. Whatever it does has either direct or indirect effects on these other parts, and also on the entire organization. To the extent that a subpart of an organization wields this kind of functional influence or control, it exercises dominance over social processes within the organization. Hence the greater its functional effectiveness the stronger will be its dominance. The resource base for the exertion of dominance as a type of social power is therefore the roles or social functions that an actor performs within a larger organization.

Dominance is perhaps most commonly observed in such realms as (a) economics, as when an industry, a university, a military installation, or some other large organization provides the primary economic foundation for an entire community, (b) information, as when a few radio, television, and newspaper chains supply most of the news reaching the population of a society, and (c) decision-making, as when the major policy decisions for a whole society are made by a single centralized government.

A social actor can use a position of dominance within an organizational structure as a basis for exerting force, by threatening to withhold services until certain demands are met. In practice, therefore, force and dominance are often very difficult to disentangle, but theoretically they remain distinct. Whereas force always requires the actual or threatened exertion of additional pressures, dominance flows from the routine performance of a subpart's activities within an organization. To the extent that an organization is unified and its subunits are institutionalized, dominance can obviously become an extremely stable and predictable type of social power.

Attraction is power based on the appeal that one social actor has for others. If people are for some reason attracted to an individual or an organization, he or it will be able to wield a certain amount of influence or even control over them. These persons will tend to shape their actions in accord with the ideas or activities of the actor to whom they are attracted, regardless of whether or not this actor exerts any pressures upon them or is functionally related to them. The resource base for the exercise of this type of social power therefore lies in psychological bonds among actors.

Three common sources of attraction are (a) cognitive identification by one person with another, or by individuals (either members or non-members) with an organization, (b) feelings of affectivity or "liking" toward an individual or an organization, and (c) charisma, or the attributing of "superhuman" or "divine" qualities to a person or an organization. Thus individuals might submit to the dictates of a political party because they identified with its policies, because it had always been their family's party, or because they believed that the party or its leaders were carrying out some "ultimate" mission.

In these ways attraction provides a basis for social power, but the recipient of this attraction is never directly assured that his lead will be followed by others. The strength of his power is determined by the amount of attraction others feel toward him, not strictly by his own actions. Consequently, power based on attraction tends to be unstable and unreliable, though at times it can become extremely strong. In practice, attractive power often shades into force, as the recipient of attraction seeks to manipulate or utilize these feelings as a means of exerting pressures upon the attracted individuals.

Very briefly, *authority can be described as the exercise of legitimacy within a social organization.* If a social actor is granted the legitimate right to make decisions, direct activities, or otherwise exert influence and control, we say that this individual or organization exercises authoritative power. Authoritative dictates are voluntarily complied with because they are seen as legitimate. To understand authority, we must therefore clarify the idea of legitimacy. *Legitimacy is the right to exercise power within and for an organization,* as voluntarily granted to an actor by other members of that organization. To the extent that legitimacy is granted, a government has authority to wield power over all other parts of a society, the personnel office of a company has authority to hire and fire workers, and a committee chairman has authority to conduct meetings. The other subparts and members of these organizations recognize the right of their leaders to exercise power over them as agents of the total organization. Grants of legitimacy thus provide the resource base for the wielding of authoritative power.

Legitimacy is sometimes granted through formal procedures, such as elections or vows of obedience, but more commonly it is informally expressed through a decision to remain a member of an organization or by failure to oppose the demands of leaders who claim legitimacy. Although the leaders of many organizations commonly employ force, dominance, and attraction to supplement and support their formal authority, in a theoretical sense the exercise of authority is always based on voluntary grants of legitimacy.

Three significant grounds on which legitimacy and authority often rest are (a) traditional values, as well as related beliefs, norms, and customs, (b) legal prerogatives established through agreements among many or most members of the organization, and (c) rational expertise or technical knowledge relevant to organizational activities that is possessed by particular actors. Legitimacy is especially strong when these are combined, as when a government supports traditional societal values, is legally selected through popular elections, and operates on the basis of rational knowledge. In addition, exercise of any of the other three types of social power—force, dominance, or attraction—can also lead to the granting of legitimacy. If a social actor wields extensive force long enough, effectively performs vital functions for an encompassing social organization, or is attractive to others, any or all of these factors can serve as further grounds for legitimacy.

Because authority is by far the most stable and reliable type of social power, leaders of organizations almost invariably seek at least a minimum amount of legitimacy, regardless of how they first acquired power. Even if a government comes to power through violent revolution and controls its society with rigid totalitarian practices, it will still seek to create an image of legitimacy among its subjects through such devices as plebiscites and mass communications. Indeed,

it can hardly afford to do otherwise, since until it gains the use of authority it must rely largely on force to maintain its own position, as well as order throughout society.

If we now stop to compare these four major types of social power, we note that two separate analytical dimensions cut through them. First, both force and dominance rely ultimately on the performance of overt social activities, and hence in a broad sense may be described as operational or "functional power." Attraction and authority, meanwhile, both rely fundamentally on the acceptance of normative ideas, and hence might loosely be described as "normative power." Second, when individuals or organizations exercise either force or attraction in social interaction, they are at least temporarily acting as relatively independent elements, since their power does not depend on their being parts of any larger social entities. To exert either dominance or authority, though, a social actor must be a relatively integral part of some encompassing organization, since these types of power are derived solely from the larger organization.

When these two analytical dimensions—functional versus normative power, and power wielding by independent elements versus organizational parts—are cross-classified, they produce a chart into which the four types of social power can be fitted. This chart (Figure 1) provides an analytical scheme for comparing and relating force, dominance, attraction, and authority as distinct but interrelated types of social power.

Theories of power creation

The *dependency theory of social power* begins with the assumption that power is always a property of social relation-

power-wielder acts as an

	independent element	organizational part
functional power	**force** (compensation, deprivation, and persuasion)	**dominance** (over the economy, information, or decision-making)
normative power	**attraction** (identification, affectivity, and charisma)	**authority** (traditional, rational, and legal)

Figure 1. Cross-classification of four types of social power.

ships among two or more actors. Most social relationships entail at least some ties of mutual interdependence among the participants, and this interdependency provides a basis for social power. One actor (A) exercises power over another actor (B) to the extent that B depends upon A for some goal he seeks, and vice versa. This power becomes manifest as A uses B's dependency to make demands upon B that result in changes in B's actions despite his resistance. More formally, the theory states that the dependency of B on A is directly proportional to B's motivational investment in goals mediated by A, and inversely proportional to the availability of those goals to B outside of this relationship. In turn, the power of A over B is determined by the degree of B's dependency on A and by the amount of resistance by B that A can overcome. In short, "the power of A over B is equal to, and based upon, the dependence of B upon A: $P_{AB} = D_{AB}$ (cf. Emerson, 1962; Blau, 1964).

The *trust theory* also begins with the assumption that the basis of social power is interdependence. From this theoretical perspective, however, the essence of interdependence is men's investment of trust in others and in social organizations. This investment of trust occurs when an individual believes that the other persons or the organization will act in ways that are beneficial for him. In relatively small and intimate organizations, the existence of shared common values is enough to assure the individual that an investment of trust will benefit him. In more complex and formal organizations, though, the individual often requires some kind of guaranteed protection—such as a legal contract or established control procedures—before he will render himself vulnerable by investing trust in the organization. In either case, this investment of trust in an organization by its members gives the organization power and enables it to obtain goals. As individuals commit themselves to an organization and act as responsible parts of it, both the organization as a whole and they as agents of the organization gain increased social power (cf. Parsons, 1963; Coleman, 1957).

Quite clearly, neither of these theories offers a complete explanation of all the ways in which social power is created, but they do offer numerous promising ideas for further work. In particular, the theme of social interdependence which they share appears to be a fundamental starting point from which to explore the creation of social power. Given the existence of interdependence, the next question is: how do the participating actors use this interdependence? Are they acting as relatively independent elements in pursuit of their own goals, or are they acting as relatively committed parts in a collective effort to obtain organizational goals? In the former case, we will tend to see an actor's exercise of influence and control as "power over others," and we may find Emerson's dependency theory particularly useful. In the latter case, we will see an actor's exercise of influence and control as "power to accomplish something with others," and we will probably find Parsons' trust theory more fruitful. In the first case we are also more likely to take a zero-sum perspective on social power and to perform distributive analysis, while in the second case we will probably assume a positive-sum perspective and perform developmental analysis. Once again, our theoretical viewpoint hinges on whether we consider the actors in a given social situation to be acting primarily as independent elements or as involved organizational parts.

Uses of social power

Once social power has been created in a social relationship, what consequences does its exercise have for organizations? How do organizations use social power? The major consequences of power exertion can be divided into four general categories: internal ordering, internal coordination, external procurement, and external attainment. The first two processes occur among the subunits comprising the power-wielding organization; the last two involve its relationships with the natural and social environments.

The primary necessity of any social organization is survival. No organization will survive long if the stresses and strains that continually disrupt it are not dealt with. If an organization has achieved relatively high degrees of functional and normative integration and has also developed effective conflict-management techniques, it may be able to tolerate and even benefit from a considerable amount of social conflict. Lacking these characteristics, however, an organization must rely upon the use of power—especially force—as a means of maintaining social order. And even strongly integrated organizations frequently employ power to cope with disruptions that cannot be handled by other means. Thus *the most basic use of social power by organizations is for the protection and perpetuation of boundaries and patterns of social relationships —or the ensuring of internal order.*

Beyond mere survival, most organizations normally strive to increase the efficiency of their internal functioning, so as to satisfy more effectively their operational requirements. As the size and internal complexity of an organization increases, so does the functional specialization, or division of labor, among its subunits. This in turn requires a certain amount of centralized coordination, communication, regulation, and planning. It also requires overall direction of the internal allocation process, by which the benefits of collective action are distributed to the members of the organization. To establish and operate such centralized coordination and administration among its subparts, an organization must utilize power. Any (or all) of the four major types of power can be used, although authority is particularly advantageous because of its predictability and stability. In general, *the second way in which all organizations use power is for the promotion of overall operational efficiency through standardized administration—or the ensuring of internal coordination.*

Turning outward, all social organizations depend upon their natural and social environments for the procurement of resources necessary for their operation. Whether they be goods, people, services, or information, these vital resources are frequently acquired by using some type of power. Although organizations sometimes gain necessary resources solely through balanced exchange relationships, most of the time they must also seek to influence or control portions of the external world. This generalization holds whether the organization relies on forceful pressures, functional dominance, authority, or voluntary attraction to obtain its resources. We may say, therefore, that *the third way in which all organizations use social power is to procure necessary resources from its environment.*

Finally, to obtain whatever goals they seek, social organizations must further influence or control other organizations, individuals, or natural phenomena. De-

pending on the nature of the organization, goal attainment may involve selling goods and services (as in the case of business concerns), disseminating information (in the case of communication media), providing personal services (in the case of hospitals), educating and training individuals (in the case of schools), gaining acceptance of values and beliefs (in the case of churches), providing public services (in the case of communities), or dealing with other societies (in the case of national governments). As in the process of resource procurement, organizations may employ force, exploit functional dominance, exercise authority, or make normative appeals in order to gain the goals it seeks, but all such activities involve the exertion of power. Thus *the fourth use of social power by all organizations is to attain goals through activities in its environment.*

All four of these uses of social power have been described from the point of view of the organization exercising power —and hence appear to be beneficial for it. From the viewpoint of other organizations, however, this wielding of power can be quite detrimental. These other organizations may be forced to provide resources or benefits to the power-wielding organization against their "wishes" or best interests, they may be restrained from influencing the powerful organization but may themselves be severely controlled by it, or they may even be totally destroyed by other organizations with superior power. In other words, "power serves him who holds it," but not necessarily others.

55 Influence, social control, and change

WILLIAM A. GAMSON

I

If the concept of influence is to remain useful, it should not be asked to do too much. Many things happen without influence being the cause. Influence, as used here, is not equivalent to anything that affects decisions but is reserved for the intended effects of actors upon the decisions of other actors. This leaves a great deal of explaining for such things as the demands of the physical environment, values, norms, social institutions, internal predispositions and the like. If we say that a voter is "influenced" in his voting choice by the beliefs of his deceased parents or by his religion and social class, we are not using the term influence in the narrower sense. Rather, we are talking about certain social forces which operate upon his choice and create a context in which influence may or may not occur. These forces may be so great that there is little another actor can do to influence his vote and influence adds nothing to an explanation of why he votes as he does.

Bachrach and Baratz point out that influence is also "exercised when A devotes his energies to creating or reinforcing social and political values and institutional practices that limit the scope of the political process to public consideration of only those issues which are comparatively innocuous to A" (1962, p. 948). Cartwright (1965, pp. 19–20) covers such influence under the more general concept of "ecological control." "When O influences P by ecological control, he takes some action which modifies P's social or physical environment on the assumption that the new environment will subsequently bring about the desired change in P." Such ecological control is covered by the concept of influence when the actions of partisan groups alter the probability of preferred outcomes. But the environmental forces which affect the decisions are not included. Only actors influence.

One can both overemphasize and underemphasize influence as a determinant of the actions of authorities. The overemphasis treats all decisions as if they were completely "free" and unconstrained by role requirements or by other limits on the freedom of authorities. This is a very easy trap for partisans to fall into. The limits may not be very visible to outsiders and the efforts of authorities to make partisans aware of such limits are often treated as rationalizations. A typical case is the authority who will not pursue a course of action because he says it "will not work." The partisan does not see this as reason for not trying it and, indeed, it is difficult for the authority to make a convincing case without demonstrating the limits of his freedom by violating them. He is reluctant to do this because it is costly and wasteful to him. It is this type of interaction that leads au-

Slightly abridged from Chapter 9 of **Power and Discontent**, pp. 188–194, Homewood, Illinois: The Dorsey Press, 1968, with permission of the author and the publisher.

thorities to regard criticism from those without authority as "irresponsible." They mean that, not having to face the costs and personal consequences of proposed actions, the critics are able to treat choices as free and unconstrained by the social environment.

When influence is overemphasized as a cause of behavior, the failure to get a preferred outcome appears to be due to some rival who has exerted greater influence. If no such rival is visible, then it must be postulated as a hidden influence. An overemphasis on influence can easily lead to conspiratorial theories of events. By taking as a *premise* the fact that some group of actors are influencing the choices of authorities, one is necessarily left with covert influence as an explanation whenever noninfluence factors are really determining the actions.

The conspiratorial fallacy is the result of an overemphasis on influence but the underemphasis has an analogous fallacy [1] This view plays down or ignores the impact of the decisions of authorities. Their choices are viewed as pseudo choices at worst and as trivial choices at best. Authorities have the illusion of exercising some personal discretion in decision, the argument runs, when in fact any person in their position would be led into the same choice. It is not uncommon for authorities to take this view of themselves. "If Barry Goldwater were President," a high-ranking Defense Department official once remarked during the Kennedy administration, "by the end of a few weeks he would find himself acting exactly as President Kennedy is acting." A Presidential candidate can hardly offer a choice when the hard realities of the situation make all incumbents echoes of each other.

[1] Cf. Mills's (1956, pp. 15–18) discussion of the "omnipotent" and the "impotent" elite.

Those who emphasize the technical nature of decisions sometimes adopt this illusory choice fallacy. By emphasizing the collective aspects of decisions and their complexity, any problem may be treated as involving a technical matter of the effectiveness of different alternatives in producing public goods. If a decision to plan a deliberate budget deficit is really only a matter of a sophisticated understanding of the economics involved, then opposition and charges of "fiscal irresponsibility" are simply matters of misunderstanding or superstition. Thus, many acts of influence on authorities are regarded as misguided and based on a lack of proper communication; the partisans fail to appreciate, in this view, the very limited maneuverability left after the range of choice has been greatly narrowed by the environment.

Underemphasis on influence is undoubtedly the more likely occupational hazard for sociologists. After all, a great deal of behavior can be explained by the social environment without invoking the intended influence of actors. If one were interested, for example, in the relative amount spent on education by a series of communities, it might be possible to explain all or almost all of the variance between communities without invoking political decisions. Differences in resources available to communities may leave those who wish to upgrade the quality of their schools with little real opportunity to do so. It might be argued that a reasonable strategy of explanation is to first see how much one can explain without invoking decisions. Only when the impact of structural limits has been thoroughly explored should one analyze the process of influence upon decisions of other actors in the system.

Nevertheless, it is easily possible to underrate the significance of decisions. First, they may singly or in aggregate have far-reaching effects on the social structure and thus may change the kinds of limits that will operate on future decisions. And even small differences in choice can have very large consequences. No one could deny, for example, that the President of the United States has some choice about whom he appoints as an ambassador. At the point of making this choice, the President may be less concerned with competence than with the repayment of a political debt. Yet this ambassador's actions and advice may be critical in later decisions—as, for example, Ambassador W. Tapley Bennett's advice was in President Johnson's decision to send American Marines into a civil struggle in the Dominican Republic. Small differences in trajectory may produce very large differences when projected over time. Thus, there is danger in treating the choices of actors as irrelevant.

II

Social change can come through a process of influence, but it can also come as a developmental outgrowth of societal processes. In the normal functioning of any complex social system, certain strains and tensions are generated. In addition, there is a problem of adaptation to an environment which is rarely fixed. Changes from these sources do not necessarily involve influence although most specific changes probably are the result of a combination of conscious decision and developmental forces.

Take, for example, the issue of the concentration of power in the hands of a small number of people. If we assume, for the sake of argument, that such a change has occurred in American so-ciety, there are explanations that invoke influence and those that do not. Without invoking influence, one can argue as Parsons (1960) does, that the demands of governing a mature, industrialized society and of meeting a changed U.S. role in the world create this concentration. The flow of personnel between the top echelons of the military, industry, and government may simply be taken as evidence of the interchangeability of the technical and managerial skills involved in different sectors. Power is concentrated, in this argument, not because any individual or group sets out to get it but because it is necessary for effective government, i.e., it works better. "Structural differentiation" is a prime example of a developmental change which does not stem primarily from the influence of partisans on authorities.

Social change may also occur through conscious, explicit decisions which alter the social structure. Laws are an example of such decisions. One might well argue that the major thrust of social change in the United States has been to subject more and more forces to the manipulation of conscious decision. Many forces which were taken as "given," as the uncontrollable set of limiting conditions for decisions, are now regarded as in part manipulable. This is nowhere clearer than in the economic realm where such things as fluctuations in the business cycle, growth rate, price stability, unemployment, and many other economic factors used to be regarded as the inexorable facts of life within which a government must work. Now, these forces have become the subject of conscious economic policy. The control is not complete, of course, but these forces are regulated and harnessed for certain ends.

An area of decision for one body or at one point in time may become an environmental constraint for another body or for the same body at a different time. Yesterday's decisions represent commitments which serve as limits on today's decisions. Decisions at the national level may set conditions for lower levels. Thus, a state governor may simply have to accept a given rate of unemployment in his state as an inexorable fact even as the federal government attempts to deal with it through conscious economic policy. The essential point here is that change may occur through influence on a series of decisions which alter the social structure even though freedom of action is limited on *each one* by conditions which are, momentarily, taken as given.

Influence which leads to a rapid and major reorganization of society is most likely to come from an alienated group or collection of groups which constitute a social movement. The success of such a movement in bringing about social change must be regarded, from the standpoint of the authorities, as a failure of social control. If successful social control had been operating, then influence would have been contained and, at the least, change would have occurred more slowly. "Effective conflict regulation," Dahrendorf suggests (1959, p. 234), "serves to reduce the suddenness of change. Well-regulated conflict is likely to lead to very gradual change. . . ."

Major changes through the influence of social movements can occur for two reasons: bad decisions or social control errors. Authorities may make decisions which adversely affect such a large and influential group that even the most skillful efforts at social control are insufficient to contain influence. Or, the techniques of social control used may be so clumsy and ineffective that they stimulate rather than contain influence.

Partisan groups may try to increase their resources by deliberately trying to create an "error" in social control (that is, the use of an inappropriate control device which increases potential influence). Such errors may be quite important in accelerating the pace of change: it may lead a social movement to new allies and stronger commitment of its supporters, it may lead to the withdrawal of legitimacy and trust from existing authorities and thus weaken their ability to enforce decisions and make new commitments, and it may create such serious instability that many who were not convinced of the need for change will now find the status quo intolerable. In this situation, the natural advantage which accrues to those supporting the status quo switches to those who support change. A sense of this reversal has on occasion led revolutionaries to welcome a worsening of social conditions. They reason that the resultant crisis will weaken existing arrangements and thereby enhance the possibilities of social change. Unfortunately, many different kinds of changes may follow and the relative probability of changes that are deplored may be enhanced even more than the probability of desired changes.

While social control errors may accelerate the pace of change, a group which deliberately tries to create them is playing with fire. Political professionals, as Dahl (1961, p. 320) points out, "have access to extensive political resources which they employ at a high rate with superior efficiency. Consequently, a challenge to the existing norms is bound to be costly to the challenger, for legitimist professionals can quickly shift their skills and resources into the urgent task of doing in the dissenter."

Still, the application of social control is a delicate business, requiring great self-control and intelligence on the part of authorities if it is to dampen influence more than stimulate it. The shattered remains of many administrations and regimes testify to the fact that errors are made. It is worth examining some of these more specifically. Removal of partisan leaders by exile, imprisonment, or execution can backfire. It offers a movement with strong secondary leadership an opportunity to mobilize its supporters to the fullest and to draw in sympathetic bystanders, particularly if the pretext for repression is a weak one. But repression may be successful if the solidary group is sufficiently weak and the regime is sufficiently strong, making repression an extremely dangerous control device for a solidary group to invite.

A complementary and less risky error is the admission of a partisan group to access through an exaggerated estimate of their strength. In general, an error of repression is most likely when the authorities underestimate the strength and support of a solidary group; an error in granting access is most likely when the authorities overestimate the strength and support. It also follows that the less accurate the estimate of a solidary group's strength, the more likely it is to benefit by an access error. Or, put in other words, the more accurate the authorities are in their perception of a solidary group's strength, the less likely they are to make a social control error of this sort.

Similar considerations apply to social control errors in the use of constraints. Attempts to degrade and slander partisans can arouse sympathy and support for them among a wider group. If there is latent support, constraints may bring it into the open and thus strengthen the group. It may also succeed in scaring off some supporters, perhaps at the same time it helps the group grow. Attacks can do both simultaneously by polarizing the attitudes of potential followers.

A good illustration of the interplay between social control errors and the ebb and flow in the strength of a social movement is provided by an incident in the protest movement against American military actions in Vietnam. In October, 1965, a group of students staged a sit-in at a local Selective Service Board in Ann Arbor, Michigan, as part of a national protest against the war in Vietnam. This action and the generally strident tone of the protest helped to lend sustenance to administration charges that the protesters were an isolated fringe group without substantial wider sympathy in the community and nation. This impact was offset, however, by an error on the part of Selective Service officials. Several of the students were reclassified and this action rallied widespread support for the students on civil liberty grounds and brought the Selective Service System under a barrage of criticism. While the Selective Service System was only a subsidiary target for the protest movement, it was viewed as an instrument of the Vietnam policy and its self-created vulnerability proved a convenience to the protesters.

It is even possible to create increased pressure for change by persuasion errors involving what might be called a Frankenstein mechanism. Authorities may, in order to mobilize support for a policy, make strenuous efforts at persuading potential partisans through the mass media and in other ways. If such efforts are successful, the same officials may find themselves under fire from the very people most persuaded. For example, having made strenuous efforts to convince potential partisans of the righteousness of a war, the convinced partisans may use the administration's own arguments to press for dramatic military action which the administration is reluctant to undertake. "Overpersuasion" may generate pressure for more extreme action.

A Frankenstein mechanism may also work in the form of stimulating expectations which go unfulfilled. Broken promises fail to stimulate influence when they were regarded with cynicism in the first place. But making such promises more credible without fulfilling them makes them more likely to mobilize pressure for influence.

III

Control has a pejorative ring, even when it is benevolently motivated, and authorities surely appear in a better light when we examine how they solve problems. The emphasis on control comes from the focus on decisions involving conflicts of interests and values. The other kinds of decisions, those involving collective interests and shared values, exist and are certainly worthy of discussion. If authorities are treated primarily as "controllers" here, they are certainly given their due as "leaders" elsewhere.

Sometimes authorities refuse to act as controllers and unobligingly contradict the central argument in this book. Nothing in the preceding pages would lead us to expect federal officials to push actively for "maximum participation of the poor" in the poverty program. If the analysis here is correct, it makes no sense that an alienated group which is not actively engaged in influence should be mobilized by a major target of its potential influence. It was not hard to anticipate that such alienated groups would begin to put pressure on urban political machines and that the influential leaders of such machines would, in turn, direct pressure at Washington. For poverty officials to urge the participation of the poor in their program can only be regarded as asking for trouble and, yet, such trouble was sought in this case.

Such anomalies exist and they put a different slant on the sources of social change. Some men in positions of authority have their own concerns about injustice and the adequacy of social institutions. When authorities begin identifying with alienated groups and their causes, presumably changes can come without influence "from below." Until that day, a little influence helps.

IX ORGANIZATIONAL PROCESSES

By all accounts, much of the life of Western Man has increasingly come under the domination of large, formal organizations. Bureaucratic structures and organizations of all sorts—business, governmental, educational, social—have proliferated in our modern era to the point where much of our daily life, one way or another, is spent in organizational activity. So complete has this organizational immersion become that social commentators like William H. Whyte (1956), and such scholars as Miller and Swanson (1958), discern a fundamental shift of American values from traditional entrepreneurial outlooks toward a more managerial-administrative orientation. Whyte considers this a shift from the traditional "Protestant ethic" to a newer "social ethic." It has led, he contends, to a conversion of Western character and the appearance of the "organization man." According to social critics like Whyte, the values of the organization in essence have become the values of society. With special reference to relations between business, government, society, and individual welfare, the writings of McGuire (1963) and Galbraith (1967) are also pertinent here.

Whatever may be the specific merits of arguments such as Whyte's, the same concerns have also motivated others toward searching appraisals of relations between the individual and the group, epitomized perhaps by Gardner's discussion in Section II. Moreover, there has emerged a new and increasingly vociferous interest in close scrutiny of institutions and organizational values to measure the degree to which these values contribute to the "good life," as well as to organizational efficiency. Max Weber's warning of the social alienation of modern man caught in the remote, impersonal toils of giant and fractionated organizations has taken on a renewed and vigorous meaning in the America of computers and automated factories (see, e.g., Etzioni, 1964, and especially, 1968). In one way or another, the papers in this section reflect the efforts of contemporary organization theorists to understand organizations as abstract social systems and to come to grips with normative managerial issues so that organizations may be fit places for people to live.

Actually "organization" is probably a poor choice of terms, for it mixes a label for a social phenomenon with a term referring to a social process. By definition, organization is a basic property of groups. All groups, large or small, are organized in some fashion; hence, in a manner of speaking, all groups are organizations. However, the noun organization is rarely used so broadly. More usually, the term is used to specify special cases of groups which are often, although not always, large in size, and in which the *fact* of organization is somehow especially striking or salient. In the study of organizations, description of their particular structure is therefore generally of more immediate interest than it is in analyses of other social aggregations.

Specifically, the phenomenon of the organization has been variously defined in the literature; the reader interested in more extended and technical discussion of definitional matters can find exemplary treatments in March's *Handbook of Organizations* (1964), in W. R. Scott's chapter in the *Handbook of Modern Sociology* (1964), in Katz and Kahn's textbook (1966), and in other useful textbooks by Sayles & Straus (1966), W. G. Scott (1967), and W. F. Whyte (1969). In general, however, an organization may be characterized as a generally orderly arrangement of particular social means geared to the accomplishment of certain more or less specific goals or ends. Put differently, organizations are "species of social systems in which an attempt has been made to formulate rationally a position-role pattern productive of some predetermined end" (R. G. Hunt, 1965, p. 37). Etzioni (1964), too, has emphasized the "deliberate" or self-conscious quality of organizations, but the inference must not therefore be drawn that *all* organizational events are either rational or planned (see Hunt in this Section). Indeed, more than a little organizational analysis has been concerned to show the operation of nonrational, unplanned, and even capricious happenings in organizations (see, e.g., March & Simon, 1958, especially Ch. 6). Furthermore, the fact is familiar that organizations tend to have a life of their own that makes them as much the masters as the servants of men.

Organizations may be populated with and worked by people, but their structures tend to be elaborated independently of any particular individuals or groups of individuals. They reflect primarily the demands imposed by impersonal goals as these may be defined at some point in time. When we speak of formal organizations, then, it is these abstract, impersonal features we have in mind.

Co-extensive with the formal organization, however, is an *informal* one consisting of a unique system of particular interpersonal relations. Informal organizations necessarily arise as soon as the formal structure is fleshed-out with persons some of whose needs differ from those of the organization, yet who operate within it.

Groups or organizations differ in the comparative degree to which formal and informal processes predominate and, really, formality-informality is best thought of as a continuous organizational dimension rather than as a typology. Organizations might range from highly formal bureaucracies to very informal temporary social aggregations, but none would be regarded either as purely formal or informal.

The significance of informal interpersonal aspects of organization was first clearly recognized in the wake of the now famous studies at the Hawthorne plant of the Western Electric Company. They provided the impetus for a drastic change in the perspectives of organizational analysis from a preoccupation with work as such to an interest in human relations.

Leading off this section, Scott, in the course of his comprehensive review of the major schools of thought about organizations, takes note of that development. After some comments on the functions of organization, he presents a delineation of, in his terminology, classical theory, neo-classical theory, and modern theory. The first of these is intimately tied to Taylor's so-called scientific management and has been aptly called "physiological organization theory" by March and Simon because of its preoccupation with relations between components of work routines and the physical capacities of workers. As Scott makes evident, machine-oriented classical theory devoted the major share of its attention to the *forms* of organization. Time and methods study is its major tool and the legendary "efficiency expert" its symbol. And both Bell (1954) and Neff (1968), for example, have made this symbol the focal point for stinging attacks on the "cult of efficiency."

Neo-classical theory, or the human relations approach, most clearly associated initially with the name of Elton Mayo and the work during the late 'twenties and early 'thirties at the Hawthorne plant, signaled a shift of emphasis from the formal to the informal organization—from the forms to the functions of organization. Although the human relations approach has had its vocal critics (and Carey, 1967, has scorned the methodology of the Hawthorne studies), Scott indicates that its broad conceptual contributions are beyond basic dispute. He points out, furthermore, that the neo-classical emphasis on organizations as "social systems" forms a direct bridge to modern system theories of organization.

The burden of modern theory has been to reintegrate the formal and informal organization, via the concept of the system, so as to portray the mutual structural-functional patterns of influence that lie at its core. In addition to the works of March and Simon and of Haire, mentioned by Scott as representative of this outlook, a most provocative discussion of organizational models can be found in Gouldner's chapter in *Sociology Today* (1959); useful excursions into the difficult system concept are to be found in Katz and Kahn (1966), and in Allport in Section III, and, closer at hand, Miller and Rice in this Section.

What modern system theorists have in mind is the idea that the distinction between formal and informal organization is much more conceptual than actual. In reality a functional organization is a complex, synthesized resultant of dynamic structural and interpersonal processes rather than an uncertain marriage of expedient convenience between separate, and competing, formal and informal systems. This idea is made explicit in the concept of the sociotechnical system developed by the Tavistock group in Britain and is basic to the view of organization as a patterning of activities expressed here by E. J. Miller and the late A. K. Rice. Their discussion of the organization as an open system, linked with its environment by various "import-conversion-export" cycles, speaks to the basic nature of organization and to that fundamental but elusive concept, structure (see Katz and Kahn, 1966; Whyte, 1969; and, in this section, Hunt, for further airings of this matter).

Miller and Rice describe organization in relation to several indispensable kinds of activities—operating, maintenance, and regulatory—which come to be integrated into distinctive task systems that include the requisite human and material resources for performing the organization's tasks. In the book from which the present selection was taken, Miller and Rice reformulate the old formal-informal distinction, developing the idea that, along with task systems, "sentient" (or, loosely speaking, friendship) systems grow in working organizations. Reconciling task and sentient systems they nominate as a central managerial responsibility that grows out of the more general need to regulate organizational system boundaries.

The ways subsystems are nested in larger systems within complex organizations is nicely shown by Miller and Rice, as is the dynamic or relative nature of real organizations. The concepts of the "primary task" and the "dominant process" help to show how concepts and models of the organization may vary over time, shift with circumstances, or depend upon points of view conditioned sometimes by one's position in the organization and sometimes by external influences. How this can make for conflict and either facilitate or inhibit change are further topics of interest to Miller and Rice.

Some of the same concerns with structure and its dependence on task properties may be found in the next paper here in which Hunt provides an analysis of relations between organization and technology. Hunt focuses attention on the wide variety of existing organizations, underscoring the significance to theory of comparative studies. In this connection he reviews newer developments in making technological variables more readily measurable and traces the linkages between technology and organization structure. In doing so he draws out some implications for the purposive planning of operating systems.

Hunt's paper deals directly with essential determinants of organizational structure or, to relate it to Miller and Rice's formulations, the bases for the patterning of activities. Dealing with this issue, Hunt gives special prominence to technological complexity and the role of uncertainty as constraints upon system design. From a basically "cognitive" standpoint two fundamentally different organizational models are differentiated: one oriented toward problem-solving and the other toward performance or operation. Hunt maintains that most management theories are sharply limited in scope and applicability, pertaining to the latter, but not to the former. And he reiterates the need for more comparative organizational analysis as a means of remedying that unsatisfactory condition.

Hunt and Miller and Rice exemplify the resurgent interest in structure fostered by modern system viewpoints; but it remains true that people and their properties populate organizational structures—indeed, their activities define them. They affect them (the structures) as well as being affected by them. These human facts about organizations are delineated well in Katz's examination here of the vital motivational processes by which persons become attached to organizations and, once they are attached, are prompted to perform in them. In essential harmony with the preceding ideas, Katz identifies three behavioral requirements fundamental to organizational functioning: recruitment and retention of personnel; dependable performance of assigned roles; nonroutine innovative problem-solving. He then proceeds to show that different inducements and organizational circumstances are relevant to each of these requirements and to present a systematic analysis of the conditions conducive to motivating their fulfillment (see Katz and Kahn, 1966, Ch. 12).

Katz's references to innovative requirements, of course, redirect attention to problems of leadership as reviewed in Section VIII. The papers there by Bavelas and by Fiedler are of special relevance to organizational interests. In that regard, Fiedler's emphasis upon relations between leader styles and properties of the situation as determinants of leadership outcomes is most pertinent to the kinds of questions raised by Katz. Moreover, Fiedler's view, and Bavelas's as well, fits neatly into the system ethos.

There is also an obvious connection between leadership and power in organizational functioning. In addition to ways of dividing and relating work, organizations include control systems with rules for allocating and using power (see Whyte, 1969). However, the topics discussed in Sections V and VII are no less vital to an understanding of organizational processes; questions of normative behavior, conformity, roles, and other group processes are fully cogent to them as social systems—all of which illustrates the fact that, whatever they are in particular, organizations in general are groups and no social process is wholly irrelevant to them.

We have already taken notice of a contemporary concern with relations between the individual and the organization. Such concerns were central to the neo-classical preoccupation with the informal organization and are implicit in Katz's interest in motivation and Miller and Rice's concern with integrating task and sentient systems. At the forefront of those students of organization who have fastened their interests on person-organization relations is Chris Argyris, whose books *Personality and Organization* (1957) and *Integrating the Individual and the Organization* (1964) are basic references in this area. His paper in this Section relates nicely to Katz's comments on the relations between individual needs and organizational participation and, from a sharply evaluative stance, it highlights some important difficulties besetting attempts to achieve satisfactory integration of the individual with the traditional organization. Argyris demonstrates the essential incompatibility of human needs with the requirements of such organizations, but his is not a bleakly fatalistic view; as he says, the problem is one of redesigning organizations to improve their human fit. The fact that such reformation can be seen to be in the organization's and society's interests, supports an optimistic appraisal of eventual prospects, despite Hunt's earlier cautionary note here.

In any event, whether from "humanistic" (e.g., Bennis, 1965) or from "technical" (e.g., Miller & Rice, 1967) perspectives, belaboring the iniquities of bureaucratic designs has emerged as a popular pastime; it seems apparent that there are times when such formats make sense (see Thompson, 1967; and Hunt in this Section), but many management philosophers and theorists have dedicated themselves to a search for alternatives to bureaucracy.

Bennis, in particular, has been vocal about the inflexibility of bureaucratic structures, charging that they obstruct organizational adaptation to changing environments. He and Slater (1968) have offered forecasts of futuristic organization designs in which special purpose, nonhierarchic structures figure prominently. He has recently modified his views in some important ways (see Bennis, 1970), but in common with his late mentor, Douglas McGregor, who was a principal protagonist of participative management (see 1960), Bennis still places confidence in group methods for organizational administration rather than in authority per se (see also Gross, 1965). He views organizational response to changing needs and issues in terms of special-purpose "task-forces," group decision-making, and administrators as "coordinators" of problem-solving activities throughout the organization. The manager thus becomes a kind of "linking-pin" tying together into a coherent system the individual functional units that are the organization's elements.

The idea of the linking-pin is the key concept in Rensis Likert's group-based view of organizational conduct. The selection we have included here from his influential book, *New Patterns of Management* (1961) provides an excellent summary of his basic thought. Likert not only clarifies the essential meaning of participative management, he provides an empirically based structure, albeit not a universally accepted one, for its implementation. More recently (1967) he has enunciated a comprehensive method, called "System 4," for applying his ideas.

In his books, he presents detailed summaries of the research, much of it conducted under his direction at the University of Michigan's Institute for Social Research, justifying his assertions that, in practice, the most productive managers are employee-centered rather than work-centered in their orientations toward their jobs. In effect, Likert reasons that if it is even a part of one's purpose effectively to redesign organizational formats, one might sensibly take as guidelines the kinds of things already happening in the most successful organizations. It is reasonable, after all, to assume that these organizations will have developed generally suitable means for the satisfaction of the organizational requirements identified by Katz and Argyris—which would presumably be the reason for their success. Moreover, comparative analyses of different kinds of organizations (see, e.g., Etzioni, 1961, 1964; Udy, 1965), and of "good" and "bad" ones, can serve as a means for directly testing the validity of the general premises undergirding modern theories of organization.

Looked at as a whole, this Section affords a quite comprehensive view of contemporary thinking about organizations. It is, however, a view more of the forest than of the trees. But if we bear in mind that organizations are social systems, it will be realized that much of the material in this book provides the means for understanding the inner workings of organizational processes.

56   Organization theory: an overview and an appraisal

WILLIAM G. SCOTT

Man is intent on drawing himself into a web of collectivized patterns. "Modern man has learned to accommodate himself to a world increasingly organized. The trend toward ever more explicit and consciously drawn relationships is profound and sweeping; it is marked by depth no less than by extension" (Seidenberg, 1951, p. 1). This comment by Seidenberg nicely summarizes the pervasive influence of organization in many forms of human activity.

Some of the reasons for intense organizational activity are found in the fundamental transitions which revolutionized our society, changing it from a rural culture, to a culture based on technology, industry, and the city. From these changes, a way of life emerged characterized by the *proximity* and *dependency* of people on each other. Proximity and dependency, as conditions of social life, harbor the threats of human conflict, capricious antisocial behavior, instability of human relationships, and uncertainty about the nature of the social structure with its concomitant roles.

Traditionally, organization is viewed as a vehicle for accomplishing goals and objectives. While this approach is useful, it tends to obscure the inner workings and internal purposes of organization itself. Another fruitful way of treating organization is as a mechanism having the ultimate purpose of offsetting those forces which undermine human collaboration. In this sense, organization tends to minimize conflict, and to lessen the significance of individual behavior which deviates from values that the organization has established as worthwhile. Further, organization increases stability in human relationships by reducing uncertainty regarding the nature of the system's structure and the human roles which are inherent to it. Corollary to this point, organization enhances the predictability of human action, because it limits the number of behavioral alternatives available to an individual.

In addition to all of this, organization has built-in safeguards. Besides prescribing acceptable forms of behavior for those who elect to submit to it, organization is also able to counterbalance the influence of human action which transcends its established patterns.[1]

[1] Regulation and predictability of human behavior are matters of degree varying with different organizations on something of a continuum. At one extreme are bureaucratic type organizations with tight bonds of regulation. At the other extreme are voluntary associations, and informal organizations with relatively loose bonds of regulation.
This point has an interesting sidelight. A bureaucracy with tight controls and a high degree of predictability of human action appears to be unable to distinguish between destructive and creative deviations from established values. Thus the only thing which is safeguarded is the status quo.

Abridged from the **Journal of the Academy of Management**, 1961, 4, 7–27, with permission of the author and the publisher.

Organization theory, however, is not a homogeneous science based on generally accepted principles. Various theories of organization have been, and are being evolved. For example, something called "modern organization theory" has recently emerged, raising the wrath of some traditionalists, but also capturing the imagination of a rather elite *avant-garde*.

In any event, three theories of organization are having considerable influence on management thought and practice. They are arbitrarily labeled in this paper as the classical, the neo-classical, and the modern. Each of these is fairly distinct; but they are not unrelated. Also, these theories are on-going, being actively supported by several schools of management thought.

The classical doctrine

For lack of a better method of identification, it will be said that the classical doctrine deals almost exclusively with the *anatomy of formal organization*. This doctrine can be traced back to Frederick W. Taylor's interest in functional foremanship and planning staffs. But most students of management thought would agree that in the United States, the first systematic approach to organization, and the first comprehensive attempt to find organizational universals, is dated 1931 when Mooney and Reiley published *Onward Industry* (1931). Subsequently, numerous books, following the classical vein, have appeared. Two of the more recent are Brech's, *Organization* (1957) and Allen's, *Management and Organization* (1958).

Classical organization theory is built around four key pillars. They are the division of labor, the scalar and functional processes, structure, and span of control. Given these major elements just about all of classical organization theory can be derived.

(1) *The division of labor* is without doubt the cornerstone among the four elements (e.g., Koontz & O'Donnell, 1959, Ch. 7). From it the other elements flow as corollaries. For example, *scalar* and *functional* growth requires specialization and departmentalization of functions. Organization *structure* is naturally dependent upon the direction which specialization of activities travels in company development. Finally, *span of control* problems result from the number of specialized functions under the jurisdiction of a manager.

(2) *The scalar and functional processes* deal with the vertical and horizontal growth of the organization, respectively (see Davis, 1951, Ch. 7). The scalar process refers to the growth of the chain of command, the delegation of authority and responsibility, unity of command, and the obligation to report.

The division of the organization into specialized parts and the regrouping of the parts into compatible units are matters pertaining to the functional process. This process focuses on the horizontal evolution of the line and staff in a formal organization.

(3) *Structure* is the logical relationships of functions in an organization, arranged to accomplish the objectives of the company efficiently. Structure implies system and pattern. Classical organization theory usually works with two basic structures, the line and the staff. However, such activities as committee and liaison functions fall quite readily into the purview of structural considerations. Again, structure is the vehicle for introducing logical and con-

sistent relationships among the diverse functions which comprise the organization (see Newman, 1951, Ch. 16).

(4) *The span of control* concept relates to the number of subordinates a manager can effectively supervise. Graicunas (1937) has been credited with first elaborating the point that there are numerical limitations to the subordinates one man can control. In a recent statement on the subject, Brech points out, "span" refers to ". . . the number of persons, themselves carrying managerial and supervisory responsibilities, for whom the senior manager retains his over-embracing responsibility of direction and planning, co-ordination, motivation, and control" (1957, p. 78). Regardless of interpretation, span of control has significance, in part, for the shape of the organization which evolves through growth. Wide span yields a flat structure; short span results in a tall structure. Further, the span concept directs attention to the complexity of human and functional interrelationships in an organization.

It would not be fair to say that the classical school is unaware of the day-to-day administrative problems of the organization. Paramount among these problems are those stemming from human interactions. But the interplay of individual personality, informal groups, intraorganizational conflict, and the decision-making processes in the formal structure appears largely to be neglected by classical organization theory. Additionally, the classical theory overlooks the contributions of the behavioral sciences by failing to incorporate them in its doctrine in any systematic way. In summary, classical organization theory has relevant insights into the nature of organization, but the value of this theory is limited by its narrow concentration on the formal anatomy of organization.

Neoclassical theory of organization

The neoclassical theory of organization embarked on the task of compensating for some of the deficiencies in classical doctrine. The neoclassical school is commonly identified with the human relations movement. Generally, the neoclassical approach takes the postulates of the classical school, regarding the pillars of organization as givens. But these postulates are regarded as modified by people, acting independently or within the context of the informal organization.

One of the main contributions of the neoclassical school is the introduction of behavioral sciences in an integrated fashion into the theory of organization. Through the use of these sciences, the human relationists demonstrate how the pillars of the classical doctrine are affected by the impact of human actions. Further, the neoclassical approach includes a systematic treatment of the informal organization, showing its influence on the formal structure.

Thus, the neoclassical approach to organization theory gives evidence of accepting classical doctrine, but superimposing on it modifications resulting from individual behavior, and the influence of the informal group. The inspiration of the neoclassical school were the Hawthorne studies (see Roethlisberger & Dickson, 1939). Current examples of the neoclassical approach are found in human relations books like Gardner and Moore, *Human Relations in Industry* (1955), and Davis, *Human Relations in Business* (1957). To a more limited extent, work in industrial sociology also reflects a neoclassical point of view (see, e.g., Miller & Form, 1951).

It would be useful to look briefly at some of the contributions made to organization theory by the neoclassicists. First to be considered are modifications of the pillars of classical doctrine; second is the informal organization.

EXAMPLES OF THE NEOCLASSICAL
APPROACH TO THE PILLARS OF
FORMAL ORGANIZATION THEORY

(1) The *division of labor* has been a long standing subject of comment in the field of human relations. Very early in the history of industrial psychology study was made of industrial fatigue and monotony caused by the specialization of the work (see Munsterberg, 1913). Later, attention shifted to the isolation of the worker, and his feeling of anonymity resulting from insignificant jobs which contributed negligibly to the final product.[2]

Also, specialization influences the work of management. As an organization expands, the need concomitantly arises for managerial motivation and coordination of the activities of others. Both motivation and coordination in turn relate to executive leadership. Thus, in part, stemming from the growth of industrial specialization, the neoclassical school has developed a large body of theory relating to motivation, coordination, and leadership. Much of this theory is derived from the social sciences.

(2) Two aspects of the *scalar and functional* processes which have been treated with some degree of intensity by the neoclassical school are the delegation of authority and responsibility, and gaps in or overlapping of functional

jurisdictions. The classical theory assumes something of perfection in the delegation and functionalization processes. The neoclassical school points out that human problems are caused by imperfections in the way these processes are handled.

For example, too much or insufficient delegation may render an executive incapable of action. The failure to delegate authority and responsibility equally may result in frustration for the delegatee. Overlapping of authorities often causes clashes in personality. Gaps in authority cause failures in getting jobs done, with one party blaming the other for shortcomings in performance (see Davis, 1957, pp. 60–66).

The neoclassical school says that the scalar and functional processes are theoretically valid, but tend to deteriorate in practice. The ways in which they break down are described, and some of the human causes are pointed out. In addition the neoclassicists make recommendations, suggesting various "human tools" which will facilitate the operation of these processes.

(3) *Structure* provides endless avenues of analysis for the neoclassical theory of organization. The theme is that human behavior disrupts the best laid organizational plans, and thwarts the cleanness of the logical relationships founded in the structure. The neoclassical critique of structure centers on frictions which appear internally among people performing different functions.

Line and staff relations is a problem area, much discussed, in this respect. Many companies seem to have difficulty keeping the line and staff working together harmoniously. Both Dalton (1950) and Juran (1956) have engaged in research to discover the causes of friction, and to suggest remedies.

[2] Probably the classic work is: Elton Mayo, **The Human Problems of an Industrial Civilization** (1946), first printed in 1933.

Of course, line-staff relations represent only one of the many problems of structural frictions described by the neoclassicists. As often as not, the neoclassicists will offer prescriptions for the elimination of conflict in structure. Among the more important harmony-rendering formulae are participation, junior boards, bottom-up management, joint committees, recognition of human dignity, and "better" communication.

(4) An executive's *span of control* is a function of human determinants, and the reduction of span to a precise, universally applicable ratio is silly, according to the neoclassicists. Some of the determinants of span are individual differences in managerial abilities, the type of people and functions supervised, and the extent of communication effectiveness.

Coupled with the span of control question are the human implications of the type of structure which emerges. That is, is a tall structure with a short span or a flat structure with a wide span more conducive to good human relations and high morale? The answer is situational. Short span results in tight supervision; wide span requires a good deal of delegation with looser controls. Because of individual and organizational differences, sometimes one is better than the other. There is a tendency to favor the looser form of organization, however, for the reason that tall structures breed autocratic leadership, which is often pointed out as a cause of low morale (Gardner & Moore, 1955).

THE NEOCLASSICAL VIEW OF THE INFORMAL ORGANIZATION
Nothing more than the barest mention of the informal organization is given even in the most recent classical treatises on organization theory (see, e.g.,

Brech, 1957; Allen, 1958). Systematic discussion of this form of organization has been left to the neoclassicists. The informal organization refers to people in group associations at work, but these associations are not specified in the "blueprint" of the formal organization. The informal organization means natural groupings of people in the work situation.

In a general way, the informal organization appears in response to the social need—the need of people to associate with others. However, for analytical purposes, this explanation is not particularly satisfying. Research has produced the following, more specific determinants underlying the appearance of informal organizations.

(1) The *location* determinant simply states that in order to form into groups of any lasting nature, people have to have frequent face-to-face contact. Thus, the geography of physical location in a plant or office is an important factor in predicting who will be in what group (see Festinger, *et al.*, 1950).

(2) *Occupation* is a key factor determining the rise and composition of informal groups. There is a tendency for people performing similar jobs to group together (see, e.g., Cottrell, 1940, Ch. 3).

(3) *Interests* are another determinant for informal group formation. Even though people might be in the same location, performing similar jobs, differences of interest among them explain why several small, instead of one large, informal organizations emerge.

(4) *Special issues* often result in the formation of informal groups, but this determinant is set apart from the three previously mentioned. In this case, people who do not necessarily have similar

interests, occupations, or locations may join together for a common cause. Once the issue is resolved, then the tendency is to revert to the more "natural" group forms.[3] Thus, special issues give rise to a rather impermanent informal association; groups based on the other three determinants tend to be more lasting.

When informal organizations come into being they assume certain characteristics. Since understanding these characteristics is important for management practice, they are noted below:

(1) Informal organizations act as agencies of *social control*. They generate a culture based on certain norms of conduct which, in turn, demands conformity from group members. These standards may be at odds with the values set by the formal organization. So an individual may very well find himself in a situation of conflicting demands.

(2) The form of human interrelationships in the informal organization requires *techniques of analysis* different from those used to plot the relationships of people in a formal organization. The method used for determining the structure of the informal group is called sociometric analysis. Sociometry reveals the complex structure of interpersonal relations which is based on premises fundamentally unlike the logic of the formal organization.

(3) Informal organizations have *status and communication* systems peculiar to themselves, not necessarily derived from the formal systems. For example, the grapevine is the subject of much neoclassical study.

(4) Survival of the informal organization requires stable continuing relationships among the people in them. Thus, it has been observed that the informal organization *resists change* (see e.g., Coch & French, 1948). Considerable attention is given by the neoclassicists to overcoming informal resistance to change.

(5) The last aspect of analysis which appears to be central to the neoclassical view of the informal organization is the study of the *informal leader*. Discussion revolves around who the informal leader is, how he assumes this role, what characteristics are peculiar to him, and how he can help the manager accomplish his objectives in the formal organization (see e.g., Saltonstall, 1959; Davis, 1957).

This brief sketch of some of the major facets of informal organization theory has neglected, so far, one important topic treated by the neoclassical school. It is the way in which the formal and informal organizations interact.

Some neoclassical writing in organization theory, especially that coming from the management-oriented segment of this school, gives the impression that the formal and informal organizations are distinct, and at times, quite irreconcilable factors in a company. The interaction which takes place between the two is something akin to the interaction between the company and a labor union, or a government agency, or another company.

The concept of the social system is another approach to the interactional climate. While this concept can be properly classified as neoclassical, it borders on the modern theories of organization. The phrase "social system" means that an organization is a complex of mutually interdependent, but variable, factors.

---

[3] Except in cases where the existence of an organization is necessary for the continued maintenance of employee interest. Under these conditions the previously informal association may emerge as a formal group, such as a union.

These factors include individuals and their attitudes and motives, jobs, the physical work setting, the formal organization, and the informal organizations. These factors, and many others, are woven into an overall pattern of interdependency. From this point of view, the formal and informal organizations lose their distinctiveness, but find real meaning, in terms of human behavior, in the operation of the system as a whole. Thus, the study of organization turns away from descriptions of its component parts, and is refocused on the system of interrelationships among the parts.

The neoclassical school of organization theory has been called bankrupt. Criticisms range from, "human relations is a tool for cynical puppeteering of people," to "human relations is nothing more than a trifling body of empirical and descriptive information." There is a good deal of truth in both criticisms, but another appraisal of the neoclassical school of organization theory is offered here. The neoclassical approach has provided valuable contributions to lore of organization. But, like the classical theory, the neoclassical doctrine suffers from incompleteness, a shortsighted perspective, and lack of integration among the many facets of human behavior studied by it. Modern organization theory has made a move to cover the shortcomings of the current body of theoretical knowledge.

Modern organization theory

The distinctive qualities of modern organization theory are its conceptual-analytical base, its reliance on empirical research data and, above all, its integrating nature. These qualities are framed in a philosophy which accepts the prem-ise that the only meaningful way to study organization is to study it as a system. As Henderson put it, the study of a system must rely on a method of analysis, ". . . involving the simultaneous variations of mutually dependent variables" (1935, p. 13). Human systems, of course, contain a huge number of dependent variables which defy the most complex simultaneous equations to solve.

Nevertheless, system analysis has its own peculiar point of view which aims to study organization in the way Henderson suggests. It treats organization as a system of mutually dependent variables. As a result, modern organization theory, which accepts system analysis, shifts the conceptual level of organization study above the classical and neoclassical theories. Modern organization theory asks a range of interrelated questions which are not seriously considered by the two other theories.

Key among these questions are: (1) What are the strategic parts of the system? (2) What is the nature of their mutual dependency? (3) What are the main processes in the system which link the parts together, and facilitate their adjustment to each other? (4) What are the goals sought by systems?

Modern organization theory is in no way a unified body of thought. Each writer and researcher has his special emphasis when he considers the system. Perhaps the most evident unifying thread in the study of systems is the effort to look at the organization in its totality. Representative books in this field are March and Simon, *Organizations* (1958), and Haire's anthology, *Modern Organization Theory* (1959a).

Instead of attempting a review of different writers' contributions to modern organization theory, it will be more useful to discuss the various ingredients involved in system analysis. They are the parts, the interactions, the processes, and the goals of systems.

THE PARTS OF THE SYSTEM AND THEIR INTERDEPENDENCY

The first basic part of the system is the *individual*, and the personality structure he brings to the organization. Elementary to an individual's personality are motives and attitudes which condition the range of expectancies he hopes to satisfy by participating in the system.

The second part of the system is the formal arrangement of functions, usually called the *formal organization*. The formal organization is the interrelated pattern of jobs which make up the structure of a system. Certain writers, like Argyris (see 1957, esp. Chs. 2, 3, 7), see a fundamental conflict resulting from the demands made by the system, and the structure of the mature, normal personality. In any event, the individual has expectancies regarding the job he is to perform; and, conversely, the job makes demands on, or has expectancies relating to, the performance of the individual. Considerable attention has been given by writers in modern organization theory to incongruencies resulting from the interaction of organizational and individual demands.

The third part in the organization system is the *informal organization*. Enough has been said already about the nature of this organization. But it must be noted that an interactional pattern exists between the individual and the informal group. This interactional arrangement can be conveniently discussed as the mutual modification of expectancies. The informal organization has demands which it makes on members in terms of anticipated forms of behavior, and the individual has expectancies of satisfaction he hopes to derive from association with people on the job. Both these sets of expectancies interact, resulting in the individual modifying his behavior to accord with the demands of the group, and the group, perhaps, modifying what it expects from an individual because of the impact of his personality on group norms (see Homans, 1950, Ch. 5).

Much of what has been said about the various expectancy systems in an organization can also be treated using status and role concepts. Part of modern organization theory rests on research findings in social psychology relative to reciprocal patterns of behavior stemming from role demands generated by both the formal and informal organizations, and role perceptions peculiar to the individual. Bakke's *fusion process* (1959) is largely concerned with the modification of role expectancies. The fusion process is a force, according to Bakke, which acts to weld divergent elements together for the preservation of organizational integrity.

The fifth part of system analysis is the *physical setting* in which the job is performed. Although this element of the system may be implicit in what has been said already about the formal organization and its functions, it is well to separate it. In the physical surroundings of work, interactions are present in complex man-machine systems. The human "engineer" cannot approach the problems posed by such interrelationships in a purely technical, engineering fashion. As Haire says, these problems lie in the domain of the social theorist (1959b). Attention must be centered on responses demanded from a logically ordered production function, often with the view of minimizing the error in the system. From this standpoint, work cannot be effectively organized unless the psychological, social, and physiological characteristics of people participating in the work environment are considered. Machines and processes should be designed to fit certain generally observed psychological and physiological properties of men, rather than hiring men to fit machines.

In summary, the parts of the system which appear to be of strategic importance are the individual, the formal structure, the informal organization, status and role patterns, and the physical environment of work. Again, these parts are woven into a configuration called the organizational system. The processes which link the parts are taken up next.

THE LINKING PROCESSES

One can say, with a good deal of glibness, that all the parts mentioned above are interrelated. Although this observation is quite correct, it does not mean too much in terms of system theory unless some attempt is made to analyze the processes by which the interaction is achieved. Role theory is devoted to certain types of interactional processes. In addition, modern organization theorists point to three other linking activities which appear to be universal to human systems of organized behavior. These processes are communication, balance, and decision making.

(1) Communication is mentioned often in neoclassical theory, but the emphasis is on description of forms of communication activity, i.e., formal-informal, vertical-horizontal, line-staff. Communication, as a mechanism which links the segments of the system together, is overlooked by way of much considered analysis.

One aspect of modern organization theory is study of the communication network in the system. Communication is viewed as the method by which action is evoked from the parts of the system. Communication acts not only as stimuli resulting in action, but also as a control and coordination mechanism linking the decision centers in the system into a synchronized pattern. Deutsch points out that organizations are composed of parts which communicate with each other, receive messages from the outside world, and store information. Taken together, these communication functions of the parts comprise a configuration representing the total system (Deutsch, 1952). More is to be said about communication later in the discussion of the cybernetic model.

(2) The concept of *balance* as a linking process involves a series of some rather complex ideas. Balance refers to an equilibrating mechanism whereby the various parts of the system are maintained in a harmoniously structured relationship to each other.

The necessity for the balance concept logically flows from the nature of systems themselves. It is impossible to conceive of an ordered relationship among the parts of a system without also introducing the idea of a stabilizing or an adapting mechanism.

Balance appears in two varieties— quasi-automatic and innovative. Both forms of balance act to insure system integrity in face of changing conditions, either internal or external to the system. The first form of balance, quasi-automatic, refers to what some think are "homeostatic" properties of systems. That is, systems seem to exhibit built-in propensities to maintain steady states.

If human organizations are open,

self-maintaining systems, then control and regulatory processes are necessary. The issue hinges on the degree to which stabilizing processes in systems, when adapting to change, are automatic. March and Simon (1958) have an interesting answer to this problem, which in part is based on the type of change and the adjustment necessary to adapt to the change. Systems have programs of action which are put into effect when a change is perceived. If the change is relatively minor, and if the change comes within the purview of established programs of action, then it might be fairly confidently predicted that the adaptation made by the system will be quasi-automatic.

The role of innovative, creative balancing efforts now needs to be examined. The need for innovation arises when adaptation to a change is outside the scope of existing programs designed for the purpose of keeping the system in balance. New programs have to be evolved in order for the system to maintain internal harmony.

New programs are created by trial and error search for feasible action alternatives to cope with a given change. But innovation is subject to the limitations and possibilities inherent in the quantity and variety of information present in a system at a particular time. New combinations of alternatives for innovative purposes depend on:

(a) the possible range of output of the system, or the capacity of the system to supply information.

(b) the range of available information in the memory of the system.

(c) the operating rules (program) governing the analysis and flow of information within the system.

(d) the ability of the system to "forget" previously learned solutions to

change problems (Cadwallader, 1959, p. 156). A system with too good a memory might narrow its behavioral choices to such an extent as to stifle innovation. In simpler language, old learned programs might be used to adapt to change, when newly innovated programs are necessary.

Much of what has been said about communication and balance brings to mind a cybernetic model in which both these processes have vital roles. Cybernetics has to do with feedback and control in all kinds of systems. Its purpose is to maintain system stability in the face of change. Cybernetics cannot be studied without considering communication networks, information flow, and some kind of balancing process aimed at preserving the integrity of the system.

Cybernetics directs attention to key questions regarding the system. These questions are: How are communication centers connected, and how are they maintained? Corollary to this question: what is the structure of the feedback system? Next, what information is stored in the organization, and at what points? And as a corollary: how accessible is this information to decision-making centers? Third, how conscious is the organization of the operation of its own parts? That is, to what extent do the policy centers receive control information with sufficient frequency and relevancy to create a real awareness of the operation of the segments of the system? Finally, what are the learning (innovating) capabilities of the system? (These are questions adapted from Deutsch, 1952.)

Answers to the questions posed by cybernetics are crucial to understanding both the balancing and communication processes in systems (see Beer, 1959).

Although cybernetics has been applied largely to technical-engineering problems of automation, the model of feedback, control, and regulation in all systems has a good deal of generality. Cybernetics is a fruitful area which can be used to synthesize the processes of communication and balance.

(3) A wide spectrum of topics dealing with types of decisions in human systems makes up the core of analysis of another important process in organizations. Decision analysis is one of the major contributions of March and Simon in their book *Organizations* (1958, Chs. 3 & 4). The two major classes of decisions they discuss are decisions to produce and decisions to participate in the system.

Decisions to produce are largely a result of an interaction between individual attitudes and the demands of organization. Motivation analysis becomes central to studying the nature and results of the interaction. Individual decisions to participate in the organization reflect on such issues as the relationship between organizational rewards versus the demands made by the organization. Participation decisions also focus attention on the reasons why individuals remain in or leave organizations.

March and Simon treat decisions as internal variables in an organization which depend on jobs, individual expectations and motivations, and organizational structure. Marschak (1959) looks on the decision process as an independent variable upon which the survival of the organization is based. In this case, the organization is viewed as having, inherent to its structure, the ability to maximize survival requisites through its established decision processes.

THE GOALS OF ORGANIZATION

Organization has three goals which may be either intermeshed or independent ends in themselves. They are growth, stability, and interaction. The last goal refers to organizations which exist primarily to provide a medium for association of its members with others. Interestingly enough these goals seem to apply to different forms of organization at varying levels of complexity, ranging from simple clockwork mechanisms to social systems.

These similarities in organizational purposes have been observed by a number of people, and a field of thought and research called general system theory has developed, dedicated to the task of discovering organizational universals. The dream of general system theory is to create a science of organizational universals, or if you will, a universal science using common organizational elements found in all systems as a starting point.

Modern organization theory is on the periphery of general system theory. Both general system theory and modern organization theory studies:

(1) the parts (individuals) in aggregates, and the movement of individuals into and out of the system.

(2) the interaction of individuals with the environment found in the system.

(3) the interactions among individuals in the system.

(4) general growth and stability problems of systems (see Boulding, 1956).

Modern organization theory and general system theory are similar in that they look at organization as an integrated whole. They differ, however, in terms of their generality. General system theory is concerned with every level of system, whereas modern organizational theory focuses primarily on human organization.

Modern organization theory leads, as it has been shown, almost inevitably into a discussion of general system theory. A science of organization universals has some strong advocates, particularly among biologists (see, e.g., von Bertalanffy, 1952). Organization theorists in administrative science cannot afford to overlook the contributions of general system theory. Indeed, modern organization concepts could offer a great deal to those working with general system theory. But the ideas dealt with in the general theory are exceedingly elusive.

Speaking of the concept of equilibrium as a unifying element in all systems, Easton says, "It [equilibrium] leaves the impression that we have a useful general theory when in fact, lacking measurability, it is a mere pretence for knowledge" (1953, p. 39). The inability to quantify and measure universal organization elements undermines the success of pragmatic tests to which general system theory might be put.

57   The motivational basis of organizational behavior

DANIEL KATZ

The basic problem to which I shall address myself is how people are tied into social and organizational structures so that they become effective functioning units of social systems. What is the nature of their involvement in a system or their commitment to it?

The major input into social organizations consists of people. The economist or the culturologist may concentrate on inputs of resources, raw materials, technology. To the extent that human factors are recognized, they are assumed to be constants in the total equation and are neglected. At the practical level, however, as well as for a more precise theoretical accounting, we need to cope with such organizational realities as the attracting of people into organizations, holding them within the system, insuring reliable role performance, and in addition stimulating actions which are generally facilitative of organizational accomplishment. The material and psychic returns to organizational members thus constitute major determinants, not only of the level of effectiveness of organizational functioning, but of the very existence of the organization.

The complexities of motivational

Reprinted with slight abridgment from **Behavioral Science**, 1964, 9, 131–46, with permission of the author and the publisher.

problems in organizations can be understood if we develop an analytic framework which will be comprehensive enough to identify the major sources of variance and detailed enough to contain sufficient specification for predictive purposes. The framework we propose calls for three steps in an analysis process, namely, the formulation of answers to these types of questions: (1) What are the types of behavior required for effective organizational functioning? Any organization will require not one, but several patterns of behavior from most of its members. And the motivational bases of these various behavioral requirements may differ. (2) What are the motivational patterns which are used and which can be used in organizational settings? How do they differ in their logic and psycho-logic? What are the differential consequences of the various types of motivational patterns for the behavioral requirements essential for organizational functioning? One motivational pattern may be very effective in bringing about one type of necessary behavior and completely ineffective in leading to another. (3) What are the conditions for eliciting a given motivational pattern in an organizational setting? We may be able to identify the type of motivation we think most appropriate for producing a given behavioral outcome but we still need to know how this motive can be aroused or produced in the organization (Katz, 1962).

Behavioral requirements

Our major dependent variables are the behavioral requirements of the organization. Three basic types of behavior are essential for a functioning organization: (1) People must be induced to enter and remain within the system. (2) They must carry out their role assignments in a dependable fashion. (3) There must be innovative and spontaneous activity in achieving organizational objectives which go beyond the role specifications.

ATTRACTING AND HOLDING PEOPLE IN A SYSTEM

First of all, sufficient personnel must be kept within the system to man its essential functions. People thus must be induced to enter the system at a sufficiently rapid rate to counteract the amount of defection. High turnover is costly. Moreover, there is some optimum period for their staying within the system. And while they are members of the system they must validate their membership by constant attendance. Turnover and absenteeism are both measures of organizational effectiveness and productivity, though they are partial measures. People may, of course, be within the system physically but may be psychological absentees. The child may be regular and punctual in his school attendance and yet daydream in his classes. It is not enough, then, to hold people within a system.

DEPENDABLE ROLE PERFORMANCE

The great range of variable human behavior must be reduced to a limited number of predictable patterns. In other words, the assigned roles must be carried out and must meet some minimal level of quantity and quality of performance. A common measure of productivity is the amount of work turned out by the individual or by the group carrying out their assigned tasks. Quality of performance is not as easily measured and the problem is met by quality controls which set minimal standards for the pieces of work sampled. In general, the major role of the member is clearly set forth by organizational protocol and leadership. The man on the assembly line, the nurse in the hospital, the teacher in the elementary school all know what their major job is. To do a lot of it and to do it well are, then, the most conspicuous behavioral requirements of the organization. It may be, of course, that given role requirements are not functionally related to organizational accomplishment. This is a different type of problem and we are recognizing here only the fact that some major role requirements are necessary.

INNOVATIVE AND SPONTANEOUS BEHAVIOR

A neglected set of requirements consists of those actions not specified by role prescriptions which nevertheless facilitate the accomplishment of organizational goals. The great paradox of a social organization is that it must not only reduce human variability to insure reliable role performance but that it must also allow room for some variability and in fact encourage it.

There must always be a supportive number of actions of an innovative or relatively spontaneous sort. No organizational planning can foresee all contingencies within its operations, or can anticipate with perfect accuracy all environmental changes, or can control perfectly all human variability. The resources of people in innovation, in spontaneous co-operation, in protective and creative behavior are thus vital to organizational survival and effectiveness. An organization which depends solely upon its blueprints of prescribed behavior is a very fragile social system.

CO-OPERATION

The patterned activity which makes up an organization is so intrinsically a co-operative set of interrelationships, that we are not aware of the co-operative nexus any more than we are of any habitual behavior like walking. Within every work group in a factory, within any division in a government bureau, or within any department of a university are countless acts of co-operation without which the system would break down. We take these everyday acts for granted, and few, if any, of them form the role prescriptions for any job. One man will call the attention of his companion on the next machine to some indication that his machine is getting jammed, or will pass along some tool that his companion needs, or will borrow some bit of material he is short of. Or men will come to the aid of a fellow who is behind on his quota. In a study of clerical workers in an insurance company one of the two factors differentiating high-producing from low-producing sections was the greater co-operative activity of the girls in the high-producing sections coming to one another's help in meeting production quotas (Katz, Maccoby, & Morse, 1950). In most factories specialization develops around informal types of help. One man will be expert in first aid, another will be expert in machine diagnosis, etc. We recognize the need for co-operative relationships by raising this specific question when a man is considered for a job. How well does he relate to his fellows, is he a good team man, will he fit in?

PROTECTION

Another subcategory of behavior facilitative of organizational functioning is the action which protects the organization against disaster. There is nothing in the role prescriptions of the worker which specifies that he be on the alert to save life and property in the organization. Yet the worker who goes out of his way to remove the boulder accidentally lodged in the path of a freight car on the railway spur, or to secure a rampant piece of machinery, or even to disobey orders when they obviously are wrong and dangerous, is an invaluable man for the organization.

CONSTRUCTIVE IDEAS

Another subcategory of acts beyond the line of duty consists of creative suggestions for the improvement of methods of production or of maintenance. Some organizations encourage their members to feed constructive suggestions into the system, but coming up with good ideas for the organization and formulating them to management is not the typical role of the worker. An organization that can stimulate its members to contribute ideas for organizational improvement is a more effective organization in that people who are close to operating problems can often furnish informative suggestions about such operations. The system which does not have this stream of contributions from its members is not utilizing its potential resources effectively.

SELF-TRAINING

Still another subcategory under the heading of behavior beyond the call of duty concerns the self-training of members for doing their own jobs better and self-education for assuming more responsible positions in the organization. There may be no requirement that men prepare themselves for better positions. But the organization which has men spending their own time to master knowledge and skills for more responsible jobs in the system has an additional resource for effective functioning.

FAVORABLE ATTITUDE

Finally, members of a group can contribute to its operations by helping to create a favorable climate for it in the community, or communities, which surround the organization. Employees may talk to friends, relatives, and acquaintances about the excellent or the poor qualities of the company for which they work. A favorable climate may help in problems of recruitment, and sometimes product disposal.

In short, for effective organizational functioning many members must be willing on occasion to do more than their job prescriptions specify. If the system were to follow the letter of the law according to job descriptions and protocol, it would soon grind to a halt. There have to be many actions of mutual co-operation and many anticipations of organizational objectives to make the system viable.

Now these three major types of behavior, and even the subcategories, though related, are not necessarily motivated by the same drives and needs. The motivational pattern that will attract and hold people to an organization is not necessarily the same as that which will lead to higher productivity. Nor are the motives which make for higher productivity invariably the same as those which sustain co-operative interrelationships in the interests of organizational accomplishment. Hence, when we speak about organizational practices and procedures which will further the attainment of its mission, we need to specify the type of behavioral requirement involved.

Types of motivational patterns

It is profitable to consider the possible motivational patterns in organizations under six major headings. Before considering their specific modes of operation and their effects, let me briefly describe the six motivational patterns which seem most relevant. These patterns are: (1) conformity to legal norms or rule compliance; (2) instrumental system rewards; (3) instrumental individual rewards; (4) intrinsic satisfaction from role performance; (5) internalization of organizational goals and values; and (6) involvement in primary-group relationships.

Rule compliance or conformity to system norms. Conformity constitutes a significant motivational basis for certain types of organizational behavior. Though people may conform for different reasons I am concerned here with one common type of reason, namely a generalized acceptance of the rules of the game. Once people enter a system they accept the fact that membership in the system means complying with its legitimate rules. In our culture we build up during the course of the socialization process a generalized expectation of conforming to the recognized rules of the game if we want to remain in the game. We develop a role readiness, i.e., a readiness to play almost any given role according to the established norms in those systems in which we become involved.

Instrumental system rewards. These are the benefits which accrue to individuals by virtue of their membership in the system. They are the across-the-board rewards which apply to all people in a given classification in an organization. Examples would be the fringe benefits, the recreational facilities, and the working conditions which are available to all members of the system or subsystem. These rewards are instrumental in that they provide incentives for entering and remaining in the system and thus are instrumental for the need satisfaction of people.

Instrumental reward geared to individual effort or performance. System rewards apply in blanket fashion to all members of a subsystem. Individual rewards of an instrumental character are attained by differential performance. For example, the piece rate in industry or the singling out of individuals for honors for their specific contributions would fall into this category of instrumental individual rewards.

Intrinsic satisfactions accruing from specific role performance. Here the gratification comes not because the activity leads to or is instrumental to other satisfactions such as earning more money but because the activity is gratifying in itself. The individual may find his work so interesting or so much the type of thing he really wants to do that it would take a heavy financial inducement to shift to a job less congenial to his interests. It is difficult to get professors in many universities to take administrative posts such as departmental chairmanships or deanships because so many of them prefer teaching and research. This motivational pattern has to do with the opportunities which the organizational role provides for the expressions of the skills and talents of the individual.

Internalized values of the individual which embrace the goals of the organization. Here the individual again finds his organizational behavior rewarding in itself, not so much because his job gives him a chance to express his skill, but because he has taken over the goals of the organization as his own. The person who derives his gratifications from being a good teacher could be equally happy in teaching in many institutions but unhappy as an administrator in any one. The person who has identified himself with the goals of his own particular university and its specific problems, potentialities, and progress wants to stay on at his university and, moreover, is willing to accept other assignments than a teaching assignment.

Social satisfactions derived from primary-group relationships. This is an important source of gratification for organizational members. One of the things people miss most when they have to withdraw from organizations is the sharing of experiences with like-minded colleagues, the belonging to a group with which they have become identified. Whether or not these social satisfactions become channelled for organizational objectives leads us to a consideration of the two basic questions with which we started: (1) What are the consequences of these motivational patterns for the various organizational requirements of holding people in the system, maximizing their role performances, and stimulating innovative behavior? and (2) What are the conditions under which these patterns will lead to a given organizational outcome?

Motivational patterns: consequences and conditions

COMPLIANCE WITH LEGITIMIZED RULES

In discussing bureaucratic functioning Max Weber pointed out that the acceptance of legal rules was the basis for much of organizational behavior (Weber, 1947). Compliance is to some extent a function of sanctions but to a greater extent a function of generalized habits and attitudes toward symbols of authority. In other words, for the citizen of modern society the observance of legitimized rules has become a generalized value. A great deal of behavior can be predicted once we know what the rules of the game are. It is not necessary to take representative samplings of the behavior of many people to know how people will conduct themselves in structured situations. All we need is a single informant who can tell us the legitimate norms and appropriate symbols of authority for given types of behavioral settings. Individuals often assume that they can control their participation with respect to organizational requirements when they enter an organization. Before they are aware of it, however, they are acting like other organizational members and complying with the rules and the authorized decisions.

The major impact of compliance with the legitimate rules of the organization primarily concerns only one type of organizational requirement, namely reliable role performance. The way in which any given role occupant is to perform in carrying out his job can be determined by the rules of the organization. But individuals cannot be held in the system by rule enforcement save for exceptions like the armed services. Nor can innovative behavior and actions beyond the call of duty be prescribed.

Though compliance with legitimate rules is effective for insuring reliable role performance it operates to insure minimal observance of role requirements. In other words, the minimal standards for quantity and quality of work soon become the maximum standards. The logic of meeting legal norms is to avoid infractions of the rules and not to go beyond their requirements, for as Allport has pointed out (1934), it is difficult, if not impossible, to be more proper than proper. Why, however, cannot the legal norms be set to require high standards with respect to both quantity and quality of production? Why cannot higher production be legislated? It can, but there is an important force working against such raising of standards by changing rules. The rule which sets a performance standard in a large organization is also setting a uniform standard for large numbers of people. Hence it must be geared to what the great majority are prepared to do. If not, there will be so many defections that the rule itself will break down. Timing of jobs in industry illustrates this principle. Management does not want a loose standard, but if the standards are set so that many workers can meet them only with difficulty, management is in for trouble.

In the third area of behavior necessary for effective organizational functioning, namely innovative and spontaneous acts which go beyond the call of duty, rule compliance is useless by definition. There can be exceptions, in that rules can be devised to reward unusual behavior under specified conditions. The army, for example, will move the man who has pulled off a brilliant military exploit from a court martial to a court of honors. Though such exceptions may occur, organizations cannot stimulate innovative actions by decreeing them. In general the greater the emphasis upon compliance with rules the less the motivation will be for individuals to do more than is specified by their role prescriptions. The great weakness of a system run according to rules is the lack of the corrective factor of human enterprise and spontaneity

when something goes wrong. Two years ago in a hospital in New York State several infants died because salt rather than sugar was put into the formula. The large container for sugar had been erroneously filled with salt. The tragic fact was that day after day for about a week the nurses fed the babies milk saturated with salt in spite of the fact that the infants reacted violently to the food, crying and vomiting after each feeding session. But the hospital continued poisoning the children until many of them died. Not a single nurse, attendant, supervisor, or person connected with the nursery tasted the milk to see what was wrong. The error was discovered only when a hospital employee broke a rule and used some of the substance in the sugar container in her own coffee.

CONDITIONS CONDUCIVE TO THE
ACTIVATION OF RULE ACCEPTANCE
Though compliance with rules can bring about reliable role performance, the use of rules must take account of the following three conditions for maximum effectiveness: (1) the appropriateness of the symbols of authority and the relevance of rules to the social system involved; (2) the clarity of the legal norms and rule structure; and (3) the reinforcing character of sanctions.

Appropriateness and relevance. The acceptance of communications and directives on the basis of legitimacy requires the use of symbols and procedures recognized as the proper and appropriate sources of authority in the system under consideration. The worker may grumble at the foreman's order but he recognizes the right of the foreman to give such an order. The particular directives which are accepted as legitimate will depend upon their matching the type of authority structure of the system. The civilian in the army with officer status, uniform, and unassimilated rank is not accepted by the enlisted man as the proper giver of orders. In a representative democracy a policy decision of an administrator may be rejected since it lacks the legal stamp of the accepted procedures of the system. An industrial company may have a contract with a union that changes in the speed of the assembly line have to be agreed to by both organizations. The workers accordingly will accept a speedup in the line if it is sanctioned by the union-management agreement, but not if it is the work of a foreman attempting to impress his superiors.

The acceptance of legal rules is also restricted to the relevant sphere of activity. Union policy as formulated in its authority structure is binding upon its members only as it relates to relations with the company. The edicts of union officials on matters of desegregation or of support of political parties are not necessarily seen as legal compulsions by union members. In similar fashion, employees do not regard the jurisdiction of the company as applying to their private lives outside the plant. And areas of private behavior and personal taste are regarded in our democratic society as outside the realm of coercive laws. The most spectacular instance of the violation of a national law occurred in the case of the Volstead Act. While people were willing to accept laws about the social consequences resulting from drinking, such as reckless driving, many of them were not willing to accept the notion that their private lives were subject to federal regulation.

Another prerequisite to the use of rules as the appropriate norms of the system is their impersonal character.

They are the rules of the system and are not the arbitrary, capricious decisions of a superior aimed at particular individuals. The equivalents of bills of attainder in an organization undermine rule compliance. We speak of the officiousness of given individuals in positions of authority when they use their rank in an arbitrary and personal fashion.

Clarity. A related condition for the acceptance of legal norms is the clarity of authority symbols, of proper procedures, and the content of the legitimized decisions. Lack of clarity can be due to the vagueness of the stimulus situation or to the conflict between opposed stimulus cues. In some organizations, symbols of authority are sharply enough defined, but the relationship between competing symbols may lack such clarity of definition. One difficulty of using group decision in limited areas in an otherwise authoritarian structure is that group members may not perceive the democratic procedure as legitimized by the structure. They will question the compelling effect of any decisions they reach. And often they may be right. Moreover, the procedure for the exercise of power may not be consistent with the type of authority structure. The classic case is that *of ordering* a people to be democratic.

Specific laws can be ambiguous in their substance. They can be so complex, so technical, or so obscure that people will not know what the law is. The multiplication of technical rulings and the patchwork of legislation with respect to tax structure means that while people may feel some internal compulsion to pay taxes, they also feel they should pay as little as they can without risking legal prosecution. A counter dynamic will arise to the tendency to comply with legal requirements, namely, the use of legal loopholes to defy the spirit of the law. Any complex maze of rules in an organization will be utilized by the guardhouse lawyers in the system to their own advantage.

Though our argument has been that legal compliance makes for role performance rather than for holding people in a system, the clarity of a situation with well-defined rules is often urged as a condition making for system attractiveness. People know what is expected of them and what they should expect in turn from others, and they much prefer this clarity to a state of uncertainty and ambiguity. There is merit in this contention, but it does not take into account all the relevant variables. The armed services were not able to hold personnel after World War II, and recruitment into systems characterized by rules and regulations is traditionally difficult in the United States. The mere multiplication of rules does not produce clarity. Even when certainty and clarity prevail they are not relished if it means that individuals are certain only of non-advancement and restrictions on their behavior.

In brief, the essence of legal compliance rests upon the psychological belief that there are specific imperatives or laws which all good citizens obey. If there is doubt about what the imperative is, if there are many varying interpretations, then the law is not seen as having a character of its own but as the means for obtaining individual advantage. To this extent, the legitimacy basis of compliance is undermined.

Reinforcement. To maintain the internalized acceptance of legitimate authority there has to be some reinforcement in the form of penalties for violation of the rules. If there is no policing of laws governing speeding, speed limits will lose their force over time for many people. Sometimes the penalties can come from the social disapproval of the group as well as from legal penalties. But the very concept of law as an imperative binding upon everyone in the system requires penalties for violation either from above or below. Where there is no enforcement by authorities and no sanctions for infractions from the group itself, the rule in question becomes a dead letter.

INSTRUMENTAL SYSTEM REWARDS

It is important to distinguish between rewards which are administered in relation to individual effort and performance and the system rewards which accrue to people by virtue of their membership in the system. In the former category would belong piece-rate incentives, promotion for outstanding performance, or any special recognition bestowed in acknowledgment of differential contributions to organizational functioning. In the category of system rewards would go fringe benefits, recreational facilities, cost of living raises, across-the-board upgrading, job security save for those guilty of moral turpitude, pleasant working conditions. System rewards differ, then, from individual rewards in that they are not allocated on the basis of differential effort and performance but on the basis of membership in the system. The major differentiation for system rewards is seniority in the system—a higher pension for thirty years of service than for twenty years of service. Management will often overlook the distinction between individual and system rewards and will operate as if rewards administered across the board were the same in their effects as individual rewards.

System rewards are more effective for holding members within the organization than for maximizing other organizational behaviors. Since the rewards are distributed on the basis of length of tenure in the system, people will want to stay with an attractive setup which becomes increasingly attractive over time. Again the limiting factor is the competition with the relative attraction of other systems. As the system increases its attractions, other things being equal, it should reduce its problems of turnover. In fact, it may sometimes have the problem of too low turnover with too many poorly motivated people staying on until retirement.

System rewards will not, however, lead to higher quality of work or greater quantity than the minimum required to stay in the organization. Since rewards are given across-the-board to all members or differentially to them in terms of their seniority, they are not motivated to do more than meet the standards for remaining in the system. It is sometimes assumed that the liking for the organization created by system rewards will generalize to greater productive effort within the system. Such generalization of motivation may occur to a very limited extent, but it is not a reliable basis for the expectation of higher productivity. Management may expect gratitude from workers because it has added some special fringe benefit or some new recreational facility. The more likely outcome is that employees will feel more desirous of staying in an enterprise with such advantages than of working harder for the company for the next twelve months.

System rewards will do little, moreover, to motivate performance beyond the line of duty, with two possible exceptions. Since people may develop a liking for the attractions of the organization they may be in a more favorable mood to reciprocate in co-operative relations with their fellows toward organizational goals, provided that the initiation of task-oriented co-operation comes from some other source. Otherwise, they may just be co-operative with respect to taking advantage of the system's attractions, such as the new bowling alley. Another possible consequence of system rewards for activity supportive of organizational goals is the favorable climate of opinion for the system in the external environment to which the members contribute. It may be easier for a company to recruit personnel in a community in which their employees have talked about what a good place it is to work.

Though the effects of system rewards are to maintain the level of productivity not much above the minimum required to stay in the system, there still may be large differences between systems with respect to the quantity and quality of production as a function of system rewards. An organization with substantially better wage rates and fringe benefits than its competitors may be able to set a higher level of performance as a minimal requirement for its workers than the other firms and still hold its employees. In other words, system rewards can be related to the differential productivity of organizations as a whole, though they are not effective in maximizing the potential contributions of the majority of individuals within the organization. They may account for differences in motivation between systems rather than for differences in motivation between individuals in the same system. They operate through their effects upon the minimal standards for all people in the system. They act indirectly in that their effect is to make people want to stay in the organization; to do so people must be willing to accept the legitimately derived standards of role performance in that system. Hence, the direct mechanism for insuring performance is compliance with legitimacy, but the legal requirements of the organization will not hold members if their demands are too great with respect to the demands of other organizations. The mediating variable in accounting for organizational differences based upon system rewards is the relative attractiveness of the system for the individual compared to other available systems in relation to the effort requirements of the system. If the individual has the choice of a job with another company in the same community which requires a little more effort but offers much greater system rewards in the way of wages and other benefits, he will in all probability take it. If, however, the higher requirements of the competing system are accompanied by very modest increases in system rewards, he will probably stay where he is.

CONDITIONS CONDUCIVE TO EFFECTIVE
SYSTEM REWARDS

We have just described one of the essential conditions for making system rewards effective in calling attention to the need to make the system as attractive as competing systems which are realistic alternatives for the individual. In this context seniority becomes an important organizational principle in that the member can acquire more of the rewards of the system the longer he stays in it. The present trends to permit the transfer of fringe benefits of all types across systems undercuts the advantages to any one system of length of membership in it, though of course there are other advantages to permitting people to retain their investment in seniority when they move across systems.

Another condition which is important for the effective use of system rewards is their uniform application for all members of the system or for major groupings within the system. People will perceive as inequitable distinctions in amounts of rewards which go to members by virtue of their membership in the system where such differences favor some groups over other groups. Management is frequently surprised by resentment of differential system rewards when there has been no corresponding resentment of differential individual rewards. One public utility, for example, inaugurated an attractive retirement system for its employees before fringe benefits were the acceptable pattern. Its employees were objectively much better off because of the new benefits and yet the most hated feature about the whole company was the retirement system. Employee complaints centered on two issues: years of employment in the company before the age of thirty did not count toward retirement pensions, and company officials could retire on livable incomes because of their higher salaries. The employees felt intensely that if they were being rewarded for service to the company it was unfair to rule out years of service before age thirty. This provision gave no recognition for the man who started for the company at age twenty compared to the one who started at age thirty. Moreover, the workers felt a lifetime of service to the company should enable them to retire on a livable income just as it made this possible for company officials. The company house organ directed considerable space over a few years to showing how much the worker actually benefited from the plan, as in fact was the case. On the occasion of a company-wide survey, this campaign was found to have had little effect. The most common complaint still focused about the patent unfairness of the retirement system.

The critical point, then, is that system rewards have a logic of their own. Since they accrue to people by virtue of their membership or length of service in an organization, they will be perceived as inequitable if they are not uniformly administered. The perception of the organization member is that all members are equal in their access to organizational benefits. Office employees will not be upset by differences in individual reward for differences in responsibility. If, however, their organization gives them free meals in a cafeteria and sets aside a special dining room for their bosses, many of them will be upset. In our culture we accept individual differences in income but we do not accept differences in classes of citizenship. To be a member of an organization is to be a citizen in that community, and all citizens are equal in their membership rights. A university which does not extend the same tenure rights and the same fringe benefits accorded its teaching staff to its research workers may have a morale problem on its hands.

INSTRUMENTAL INDIVIDUAL REWARDS

The traditional philosophy of the free-enterprise system gives priority to an individual reward system based upon the quality and quantity of the individual effort and contribution. This type of motivation may operate effectively for the entrepreneur or even for the small organization with considerable independence of its supporting environment. It encounters great difficulties, however, in its application to large organizations which are in nature highly interdependent co-operative structures. We shall examine these difficulties in analyzing the conditions under which individual rewards of an instrumental character are effective.

Basically the monetary and recognition rewards to the individual for his organizational performance are directed at a high level of quality and quantity of work. In other words, they can be applied most readily to obtain optimal role performance rather than to innovative and nonspecific organizational needs. They may also help to hold the individual in the organization, if he feels that his differential efforts are properly recognized. Nonetheless there is less generalization, or rubbing off, of an instrumental individual reward to love for the organization than might be anticipated. If another organization offers higher individual rewards to a person, his own institution may have to match the offer to hold him.

Individual rewards are difficult to apply to contributions to organizational functioning which are not part of the role requirements. Spectacular instances of innovative behavior can be singled out for recognition and awards. In the armed services, heroism beyond the call of duty is the basis for medals and decorations, but the everyday co-operative activities which keep an organization from falling apart are more difficult to recognize and reward. Creative suggestions for organizational improvement are sometimes encouraged through substantial financial rewards for employees' suggestions. The experience with suggestion systems of this sort has not been uniformly positive though under special conditions they have proved of value.

CONDITIONS CONDUCIVE TO EFFECTIVE INDIVIDUAL INSTRUMENTAL REWARDS

If rewards such as pay incentives are to work as they are intended they must meet three primary conditions. (1) They must be clearly perceived as large enough in amount to justify the additional effort required to obtain them. (2) They must be perceived as directly related to the required performance and follow directly on its accomplishment. (3) They must be perceived as equitable by the majority of system members many of whom will not receive them. These conditions suggest some of the reasons why individual rewards can work so well in some situations and yet be so difficult of application in large organizations. The facts are that most enterprises have not been able to use incentive pay, or piece rates, as reliable methods for raising the quality and quantity of production (McGregor, 1960).

In terms of the first criterion many companies have attempted incentive pay without making the differential between increased effort and increased reward proportional from the point of view of the worker. If he can double his pay by working at a considerably increased tempo, that is one thing. But if such increased expenditure means a possible 10 per cent increase, that is another. Moreover, there is the tradition among workers, and it is not without some factual basis, that management cannot be relied upon to maintain a high rate of pay for those making considerably more than the standard and that their increased efforts will only result in their "being sweated." There is, then, the temporal dimension of whether the piece rates which seem attractive today will be maintained tomorrow.

More significant, however, is the fact that a large-scale organization consists of many people engaging in similar and interdependent tasks. The work of any one man is highly dependent upon what his colleagues are doing. Hence individual piece rates are difficult to apply on any equitable basis. Group incentives are more logical, but as the size of the interdependent group grows, we move toward system rather than toward individual rewards. Moreover, in large-scale production enterprises the role performance is controlled by the tempo of the machines and their co-ordination. The speed of the worker on the assembly line is not determined by his decision but by the speed of the assembly line. An individual piece rate just does not accord with the systemic nature of the co-ordinated collectivity. Motivational factors about the amount of effort to be expended on the job enter the picture not on the floor of the factory but during the negotiations of the union and management about the manning of a particular assembly line. Heads of corporations may believe in the philosophy of individual enterprise, but when they deal with reward systems in their own organizations they become realists and accept the pragmatic notion of collective rewards.

Since there is such a high degree of collective interdependence among rank-and-file workers the attempts to use individual rewards are often perceived as inequitable. Informal norms develop to protect the group against efforts which are seen as divisive or exploitive. Differential rates for subsystems within the organization will be accepted much more than invidious distinctions within the same subgrouping. Hence promotion or upgrading may be the most potent type of individual reward. The employee is rewarded by being moved to a different category of workers on a better pay schedule. Some of the same problems apply, of course, to this type of reward. Since differential performance is difficult to assess in assembly-type operations, promotion is often based upon such criteria as conformity to company requirements with respect to attendance and absenteeism, observance of rules, and seniority. None of these criteria are related to individual performance on the job. Moreover, promotion is greatly limited by the technical and professional education of the worker.

It is true, of course, that many organizations are not assembly-line operations, and even for those which are, the conditions described here do not apply to the upper echelons. Thus General Motors can follow a policy of high individual rewards to division managers based upon the profits achieved by a given division. A university can increase the amount of research productivity of its staff by making publication the essential criterion for promotion. In general, where assessment of individual performance is feasible and where the basis of the reward system is clear, instrumental individual rewards can play an important part in raising productivity.

INTRINSIC JOB SATISFACTION

The motivational pathway to high productivity and to high-quality production can be reached through the development of intrinsic job satisfaction. The man who finds the type of work he delights in doing is the man who will not worry about the fact that the role requires a given amount of production of a certain quality. His gratifications accrue from accomplishment, from the expression of his own abilities, from the exercise of his own decisions. Craftsmanship was the old term to refer to the skilled performer who was high in intrinsic job satisfaction. This type of performer is not the clock watcher, nor the shoddy performer. On the other hand, such a person is not necessarily tied to a given organization. As a good carpenter or a good mechanic, it may matter little to him where he does work, provided that he is given ample opportunity to do the kind of job he is interested in doing. He may, moreover, contribute little to organizational goals beyond his specific role.

CONDITIONS CONDUCIVE TO AROUSAL OF INTRINSIC JOB SATISFACTION

If intrinsic job satisfaction or identification with the work is to be aroused and maximized, then the job itself must provide sufficient variety, sufficient complexity, sufficient challenge, and sufficient skill to engage the abilities of the worker. If there is one confirmed finding in all the studies of worker morale and satisfaction, it is the correlation between the variety and challenge of the job and the gratifications which accrue to workers (Morse, 1953). There are, of course, people who do not want more responsibility and people who become demoralized by being placed in jobs which are too difficult for them. These are, however, the exceptions. By and large people seek more responsibility, more skill-demanding jobs than they hold, and as they are able to attain these more demanding jobs, they become happier and better adjusted. Obviously, the condition for securing higher motivation to produce, and to produce quality work, necessitates changes in organizational structure—specifically job enlargement rather than job fractionation. And yet the tendency in large-scale organizations is toward increasing specialization and routinization of jobs. Workers would be better motivated toward higher individual production and toward better quality work if we discarded the assembly line and moved toward the craftsmanlike operations of the old Rolls Royce type of production. Industry has demonstrated, however, that it is more efficient to produce via assembly-line methods with lowered motivation and job satisfaction than with highly motivated craftsmen with a large area of responsibility in turning out their part of the total product. The preferred path to the attainment of production goals in turning out cars or other mass physical products is, then, the path of organizational controls and not the path of internalized motivation. The quality of production may suffer somewhat, but it is still cheaper to buy several mass-produced cars, allowing for programming for obsolescence, than it is to buy a single quality product like the Rolls Royce.

In the production of physical objects intended for mass consumption, the assembly line may furnish the best model. This may also apply to service operations in which the process can be sufficiently simplified to provide service to masses of consumers. When, however, we move to organizations which have the modifications of human beings as their product, as in educational institutions, or when we deal with treating basic problems of human beings, as in hospital, clinics, and remedial institutions, we do not want to rely solely upon an organizational control to guarantee minimum effort of employees. We want employees with high motivation and high identification with their jobs. Jobs cannot profitably be fractionated very far and standardized and co-ordinated to a rigorous time schedule in a research laboratory, in a medical clinic, in an educational institution, or in a hospital.

In addition to the recognition of the inapplicability of organizational devices of the factory and the army to all organizations, it is also true that not all factory operations can be left to institutional controls without regard to the motivations of employees. It frequently happens that job fractionation can be pushed to the point of diminishing returns even in industry. The success of the Tavistock workers in raising productivity in the British coal mines through job enlargement was due to the fact that the specialization of American long-wall methods of coal mining did not yield adequate returns when applied to the difficult and variable conditions under which British miners had to operate (Trist & Bamforth, 1951). The question of whether to move toward greater specialization and standardization in an industrial operation or whether to move in the opposite direction is generally an empirical one to be answered by research. One rule of thumb can be applied, however. If the job can be so simplified and standardized that it is readily convertible to automated machines, then the direction to take is that of further institutionalization until automation is possible. If, however, the over-all performance requires complex judgment, the differential weighing of factors which are not markedly identifiable, or creativity, then the human mind is a far superior instrument to the computer.

The paradox is that where automation is feasible, it can actually increase the motivational potential among the employees who are left on the job after the change-over. Mann and Hoffman (1960) conclude from their study of automation in an electric power plant that the remaining jobs for workers can be more interesting, that there can be freer association among colleagues, and that the elimination of supervisory levels brings the top and bottom of the organization closer together.

INTERNALIZATION OF ORGANIZATIONAL
GOALS AND VALUES

The pattern of motivation associated with value expression and self-identification has great potentialities for the internalization of the goals of subsystems and of the total system, and thus for the activation of behavior not prescribed by specific roles. Where this pattern prevails individuals take over organizational objectives as part of their own personal goals. They identify not with the organization as a safe and secure haven but with its major purposes. The internalization of organizational objectives is generally confined to the upper echelons or to the officer personnel. In voluntary organizations it extends into some of the rank-and-file, and in fact most voluntary organizations need a core of dedicated people—who are generally referred to as the dedicated damn fools.

Now the internalization of organizational goals is not as common as two types of more partial internalization. The first has to do with some general organizational purposes which are not unique to the organization. A scientist may have internalized some of the research values of his profession but not necessarily of the specific institution to which he is attached. As long as he stays in that institution, he may be a well-motivated worker. But he may find

it just as easy to work for the things he believes in in another institution. There is not the same set of alternative organizations open to liberals who are political activists and who are part of the core of dedicated damn fools in the Democratic party. They have no other place to go, so they find some way of rationalizing the party's deviation from their liberal ideals.

A second type of partial internalization concerns the values and goals of a subsystem of the organization. It is often easier for the person to take over the values of his own unit. We may be attached to our own department in a university more than to the goals of the university as a whole.

CONDITIONS CONDUCIVE TO
INTERNALIZATION OF SYSTEM GOALS

Internalization of organization objectives can come about through the utilization of the socialization process in childhood or through the adult socialization which takes place in the organization itself. In the first instance, the selective process, either by the person or the organization, matches the personality with the system. A youngster growing up in the tradition of one of the military services may have always thought of himself as an Air Force officer. Similarly, the crusader for civil liberties and the American Civil Liberties Union find one another.

The adult socialization process in the organization can build upon the personal values of its members and integrate them about an attractive model of its ideals. People can thus identify with the organizational mission. If the task of an organization has emotional significance, the organization enjoys an advantage in the creation of an attractive image. If the task is attended by hazard, as in the tracking down of criminals by the FBI, or of high adventure, as in the early days of flying, or of high service to humanity, as in a cancer research unit, it is not difficult to develop a convincing model of the organization's mission.

The imaginative leader can also help in the development of an attractive picture of the organization by some new conceptualization of its mission. The police force entrusted with the routine and dirty business of law enforcement carried out by dumb cops and "flatfeet" can be energized by seeing themselves as a corps of professional officers devoted to the highest form of public service. Reality factors limit the innovative use of symbols for the glorification of organizations. Occupational groups, however, constantly strive to achieve a more attractive picture of themselves, as in the instances of press agents who have become public relations specialists or undertakers who have become morticians.

Internalization of subgroup norms can come about through identification with fellow group members who share the same common fate. People take over the values of their group because they identify with their own kind and see themselves as good group members, and as good group members they model their actions and aspirations in terms of group norms. This subgroup identification can work for organizational objectives only if there is agreement between the group norms and the organizational objectives. Often in industry the norms of the work group are much closer to union objectives than to company objectives.

This suggests three additional factors which contribute to internalization of group objectives: (1) participating in important decisions about group objectives; (2) contributing to group performance in a significant way: and (3) sharing in the rewards of group accomplishment. When these three conditions are met, the individual can regard the group as his, for he in fact has helped to make it.

SOCIAL SATISFACTIONS FROM
PRIMARY-GROUP RELATIONSHIPS

Human beings are social animals and cannot exist in physical or psychological isolation. The stimulation, the approval, and the support they derive from interacting with one another comprise one of the most potent forms of motivation. Strictly speaking, such affiliative motivation is another form of instrumental-reward-seeking, but some of its qualitative aspects are sufficiently different from the instrumental system and individual rewards previously described to warrant separate discussion.

The desire to be part of a group in itself will do no more than hold people in the system. The studies of Elton Mayo and his colleagues during World War II showed that work groups which provided their members social satisfactions had less absenteeism than less cohesive work groups (Mayo & Lombard, 1944). Mann and Baumgartel (1953) corroborated these findings in a study of the Detroit Edison Company. With respect to role performance, moreover, Seashore (1954) has demonstrated that identification with one's work group can make for either above-average or below-average productivity depending upon the norms of the particular group. In the Seashore study the highly-cohesive groups, compared to the low-cohesive groups, moved to either extreme in being above or below the production standards for the company.

Other studies have demonstrated that though the group can provide important socioemotional satisfactions for the members it can also detract from task orientation (Bass, 1960). Members can have such a pleasant time interacting with one another that they neglect their work. Again the critical mediating variable is the character of the values and norms of the group. The affiliative motive can lead to innovative and co-operative behavior, but often this assumes the form of protecting the group rather than maximizing organizational objectives. So the major question in dealing with the affiliative motive is how this motive can be harnessed to organizational goals.

58   Systems of organization

ERIC J. MILLER and A. KENNETH RICE

Any enterprise may be seen as an open system which has characteristics in common with a biological organism. An open system exists, and can only exist, by exchanging materials with its environment. It imports materials, transforms them by means of conversion processes, consumes some of the products of conversion for internal maintenance, and exports the rest. Directly or indirectly, it exchanges its outputs for further intakes, including further resources to maintain itself. These import-conversion-export processes are the work the enterprise has to do if it is to live.

One intake of a biological organism is food; the corresponding conversion process is the transformation of food into energy and waste matter. Some of the energy is used up in procuring further supplies of food, some in fighting, or in securing shelter from hostile forces in the environment, some in the functioning and growth of the system itself, and some in reproductive activities. In the same way, a joint stock company imports capital through the sale of shares or the raising of loans, converts the capital into income by investment in commercial and industrial enterprises, uses some of the results to maintain itself and to grow, and exports the remainder in the form of dividends and taxes. A manufacturing enterprise imports raw materials, converts them into products, and sells the products. From its returns on the sale it acquires more raw materials, maintains and develops the enterprise, and satisfies the investors who provided the resources to set it up.

Other kinds of enterprise have differ-

Excerpted from **Systems of Organisation,** London: Tavistock Publications, 1967, with permission of E. J. Miller and the publisher.

ent intakes and different conversion processes, and the returns they obtain from the environment in exchange for their outputs take different forms. An educational enterprise, for example, imports students, teaches them and provides them with opportunities to learn; it exports ex-students who have either acquired some qualification or failed. The proportion that qualifies and the standard the individuals are perceived to have attained determine the extent to which the environment provides students and resources to maintain the enterprise. In a learned society the primary pay-off may not be expressible in monetary terms or in terms of securing further material or human intakes but rather in prestige and self-esteem. Such pay-offs, however, are important for educational enterprises and may not be unimportant for profit-making enterprises as well.

THE PROCESSES AND ACTIVITIES OF AN ENTERPRISE

An enterprise relates to its environment through a variety of import-conversion-export processes, which require a corresponding variety of activities. A manufacturing company, as we have said, imports raw materials, converts them into products, and acquires a pay-off from selling the products. But it also recruits employees, trains them, assigns them to jobs, and sooner or later exports them by resignation, retirement, or dismissal. It imports and consumes stores and power. It also collects intelligence about its market and its competitors, analyzes this information, makes decisions about design, quantity, quality, and price of products, and issues communications of different kinds as a result of the decisions taken.

In the analysis of an enterprise, or of a unit within an enterprise, we reserve the term *operating activities* for those activities that directly contribute to the import, conversion, and export processes which define the nature of the enterprise or unit and differentiate it from other enterprises or units. Thus in a shoe-manufacturing company the operating activities are those that procure the leather and other raw materials, convert these materials into shoes, and sell and dispatch the shoes to customers. Similarly, in an airline the operating activities are those that directly contribute to the process of transforming potential travellers into ticketed passengers and of transporting these passengers from a departure point to a destination. If the unit of analysis is an accounts department, then the operating activities will be those through which the relevant data are acquired, processed, and exported in the form of invoices, cheques, cost reports, payrolls, and accounts of various kinds.

Besides operating activities, two other types of activity may be identified: maintenance and regulation.

Maintenance activities procure and replenish the resources that produce operating activities. Thus not only the purchase, maintenance, and overhaul of machinery, but also the recruitment, induction, training, and motivation of employees come under this heading.

Regulatory activities relate operating activities to each other, maintenance activities to operating activities, and all internal activities of the enterprise (or unit) to its environment.

Maintenance and regulatory activities can themselves be analysed in import-conversion-export terms. In regulatory activities, for example, the intake is information about the process being regulated, the conversion process is the comparison of the data against objectives or standards of performance, and the output the decision to stop or to modify (or not to stop or modify) the process, or the decision to accept or to reject the product. Similarly, to take the selection procedure for new employees as an example of a maintenance process, import activities procure an applicant, conversion activities apply the procedure through which comes the decision to select or to reject, and export activities place the new employee or dispose of the rejected applicant.

SYSTEMS OF ACTIVITY

A system of activities *is that complex of activities which is required to complete the process of transforming an intake into an output.*

A task system *is a system of activities plus the human and physical resources required to perform the activities.*

The term "system," as we use it here, implies that each component activity of the system is interdependent in respect of at least some of the other activities of the same system, and that the system as a whole is identifiable as being in certain, if limited, respects independent of related systems.

Thus a system has a boundary which separates it from its environment. Intakes cross this boundary and are subjected to conversion processes within it. The work done by the system is therefore, at least potentially, measurable by the difference between its intakes and its outputs.

But a measurable difference between output and intake does not of itself imply that the boundary so identified is the boundary of a system of activities. For example, in an automatic transfer line a component passes through a suc-

cession of machines, each of which performs a distinct operation, the output/input ratio of which can be measured; yet the machines are so interconnected that all either operate together or stop together. Even if variable-feed devices are introduced between the machines, the output/input ratio that is significant is that of the whole line. A system boundary implies a discontinuity. We make the hypothesis that the discontinuity at the boundary constitutes a differentiation of technology, territory, or time, or of some combination of these (Miller, 1959).

In a simple system there are no internal system boundaries either between one operating activity and another or between operating activities on the one hand and maintenance and regulatory activities on the other. A complex system contains such internal boundaries. In a large complex system there may be several orders of differentiation: major operating systems themselves being differentiated into bounded sub-systems, which in their turn may also be differentiated, and so on until simple undifferentiated systems are reached.

Most enterprises have the characteristics of complex systems: they include a number of identifiable sub-systems of activities through which the various processes of the enterprise are carried out. These constituent systems, like the enterprise as a whole, are open systems which acquire intakes form the environment, transform them, and export the results. Thus one department in a manufacturing process may have as its intakes part-processed products which are the outputs of departments preceding it in the process. In its turn, it exports to succeeding departments the same products at a later stage in manufacture. The total enterprise is therefore a significant part of the environment for its component systems of activity.

When maintenance activities are carried out in differentiated component systems of an enterprise they too can be treated as systems of activity with their own operating activities and related maintenance and regulatory activities.

MONITORING AND BOUNDARY
CONTROL ACTIVITIES

What distinguishes a system from an aggregate of activities and preserves its boundary is the existence of regulation. Regulation relates activities to throughput, ordering them in such a way as to ensure that the process is accomplished and that the different import-conversion-export processes of the system as a whole are related to the environment.

Most processes are in some measure "self-regulating" in the sense that the nature or structure of the process imposes disciplines and constraints on the associated system of activities. Thus a given operation that is part of a series of operations is "regulated" by preceding and succeeding operations. Similarly, in parts of the chemical industry, once chemicals have been mixed, and heating, flow, and other processes started, technology takes over and for the most part determines quantity, quality, and speed of output. Important though these inherent constraints and disciplines are, they are not regulatory *activities* as such.

In the analysis of systems of activities two types of regulatory activity can be identified: monitoring and boundary control.

Whenever an operating activity is stopped, for however short a time, to check that it is achieving its purpose, a regulatory activity is introduced: operating activity/check/resumption of operating activity. Thus when a carpenter,

sawing a piece of wood, pauses to make sure that his cut is in the right direction, he is changing his activity from operation to regulation. An example of a less perceptible change of activity occurs in the task of a salesman. In his transactions with a potential customer the salesman is carrying out a regulatory activity whenever he monitors what he has said already, assesses what effect this has had on the customer, and on this basis decides whether to continue the same approach or to adopt a different mode of attack. We use the term *monitoring* to refer to such intra-system regulatory activities, which are different in kind from, and not directly related to, the controls activated at the boundaries of the system.

Regulatory activities that relate a system of activities to its environment occur at the boundary of the system and the environment and control the import and export transactions across it. Boundary regulation is therefore external to the operating activities of the system. The important implication is that the boundary round a system of activities is not simply a line but a region with two boundaries, one between the internal activities of the system and the region of regulation, and a second between the region of regulation and the environment. For this form of regulation we use the term *boundary control function*.[1]

Task priorities and constraints

We have said that any enterprise may be considered as an open system, that exists, and only can exist, by exchanging

[1] At this point in the text the authors discuss in detail boundary control functions and monitoring activities, relating these to analyses of individuals, groups and inter-group transactions.—Eds.

materials with its environment. It imports materials, converts them, and exports some of the results. Its outputs enable it to acquire more intakes, and the import-conversion-export process is the work the enterprise has to do to live. The task of any enterprise can be defined in the most general way, therefore, as to secure a pay-off by converting intakes into outputs—the minimum pay-off being the postponement of death.

But even simple enterprises, as we have shown, have multiple intakes and outputs and hence perform multiple tasks. They correspond to the operating, maintenance, and regulatory activities we have identified. We postulate that at any given time an enterprise has a *primary task—the task that it must perform if it is to survive.*

THE CONCEPT OF THE PRIMARY TASK

The primary task is essentially a heuristic concept, which allows us to explore the ordering of multiple activities (and of constituent systems of activity where these exist). It makes it possible to construct and compare different organizational models of an enterprise based on different definitions of its primary task; and to compare the organizations of different enterprises with the same or different primary tasks. The definition of the primary task determines the dominant import-conversion-export system, and the operating, as distinct from the maintenance and regulatory, activities. It specifies the resources required and hence determines the priorities of constituent systems.

One implication of this is that there may be conflict between the way in which a constituent system defines its primary task and the way in which the superordinate system defines it. For ex-

ample, the internally defined primary task of a factory department might be to maximize the output of a particular product; from the perspective of the enterprise, however, a greater pay-off might be secured by limiting the output of this department and increasing that of another, or even by requiring from it a different kind of output and modifying its resources accordingly. On a larger scale, the definition of the primary task of medical services as to save life can, in developing and overcrowded countries, lead to tragic consequences when what is required to sustain the inevitably increased population—food, housing, and other resources—is not also made available.

Similarly, environmental definitions of the primary task of an enterprise may differ from and impose constraints on its own definition. A community, for example, may define the primary task of the largest company in the district as that of providing essential employment for the local population. Such a definition may contradict the policy of the company, which, to improve performance of the primary task as defined by its own management—to carry out a profitable manufacturing operation—may require a more mechanized production process and a correspondingly reduced labour force.

In most industries, however, the general "public" definition of the identity and purpose of an institution assigns long-term priority to a particular task and hence to a particular import-conversion-export system. Thus an educational enterprise must export some trained students and a manufacturing enterprise must produce some goods; and unless they secure such a return from their outputs that they are able to procure fresh intakes—of students and of raw materials, respectively—they cannot survive.

But tasks that are in the long-term ancillary to the primary task may temporarily become primary. For example, in a factory, the production system that converts raw materials into finished products has long-term priority, and the primary task is the conversion of raw materials into products. But if the machinery breaks down the primary task of the conversion system shifts from producing goods to repairing machines. The maintenance system of activities (which "imports" malfunctioning machinery and spare parts and "exports" repaired machinery) has priority. Similarly, an educational institution's primary task is jeopardized if it cannot procure staff, so that at certain times the primary task may shift from education to recruitment.

In the analysis of organization, the primary task often has to be inferred from the behaviour of the various systems of activity, and from the criteria by which their performance is regulated. One may then be able to make such statements as: "This enterprise is behaving as if its primary task were . . ."; or: "This part of the enterprise is behaving as if the primary task of the whole were . . ." Such formulations may be compared with explicit statements by the leaders of the enterprise and of its parts about their definitions of the primary task.

The primary task is not a normative concept. We do not say that every enterprise *must* have a primary task or even that it must define its primary task; we put forward the proposition that every enterprise, or part of it, *has*, at any given moment, one task which is primary. What we also say, however, is that, if, through inadequate appraisal of

internal resources and external forces, the leaders of an enterprise define the primary task in an inappropriate way, or the members—leaders and followers alike—do not agree on their definition, then the survival of the enterprise will be jeopardized. Moreover, if organization is regarded primarily as an instrument for task performance, we can add that, without adequate task definition, disorganization must occur.[2]

Organizational model-building

Organization is the patterning of activities through which the primary task of the enterprise is performed. Thus the optimum form of organization is that which best fits the requirements of primary task performance. But the organizational form must also take account of the human and physical, scientific and technical resources available for task performance, and of the human, political, economic, and social constraints on both definition and performance.

Our starting-point, then, is a definition of the primary task for the performance of which the organization is required. To build an appropriate organizational model this definition should be precise. However, we have to recognize that the gradual course of enterprise growth may lead to imprecision. Thus in a textile company that has diversified and now produces chemicals as well, one definition of the primary task could be, "to make a profit from producing and selling textiles and chemicals." But an alternative definition could be, "to make a profit from investing in a variety of manufacturing and selling opera-

[2] Omitted here are discussions of some aspects of temporary shifts in the primary task, the ordering of task priorities, and the constraining effects upon task performance of various organizational resources.—Eds.

tions." In the second definition, textile and chemical operations would be current examples.

DISCONTINUITIES IN THE
DOMINANT PROCESS
The primary task identifies the dominant import-conversion-export process. In the first example just quoted, the first definition implies a dual throughput of textiles and chemicals in first-order constituent systems. The second, on the other hand, defines the overall enterprise as a holding company with a throughput of money, and the textile and chemical operations become the tasks of second-order constituent "sub-enterprises."

The dominant process in turn identifies the nature of intakes, the activities required to convert these into, and dispose of, outputs, and the human and physical resources needed to provide or facilitate these activities.

The next step is to discover the discontinuities in the process which mark the boundaries of systems of activity. Several orders of differentiation may be entailed in a large enterprise. To take again the example of a textile-cum-chemical manufacturing company, *prima facie*

six constituent operating systems of activity can be identified. They are shown in *Figure 1*.

This framework offers the possibility of two technological differentiations: one between chemicals and textiles (with a second-order differentiation between purchasing, manufacturing, and marketing), as shown in *Figure 2*; the other between purchasing, manufacturing, and marketing (with a second-order differentiation between chemicals and textiles), as shown in *Figure 3*. Again, it would be possible to conceive of a first-order differentiation into a combined purchasing system (with a second-order differentiation between chemicals and textiles), two separate manufacturing systems, and a combined marketing system, as shown in *Figure 4*. Factors such as the overlap between the two markets, the size of the investment in raw materials, similarities between these materials, the care with which they have to be stored, and the location of the factories will usually point towards one or another kind of differentiation.

The types of control that are required provide a means of judging the efficiency of the solution. A system boundary, as we have seen, implies a boundary

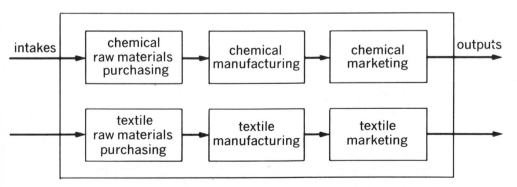

Figure 1. Six constituent systems of a textile and chemical enterprise.

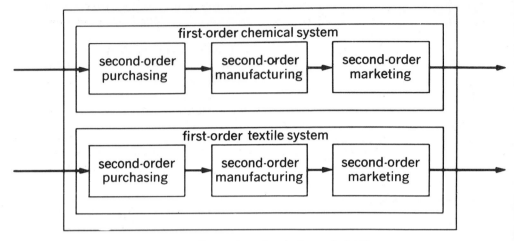

Figure 2. First-order chemicals and textiles.

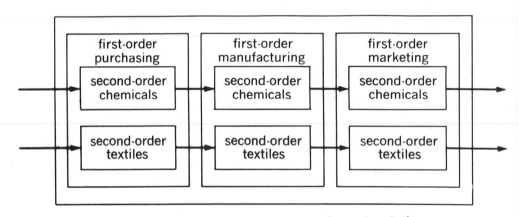

Figure 3. First-order purchasing, manufacturing, and marketing.

control function. If a boundary is imposed at a point of substantial discontinuity in the process, intra-system and inter-system regulation will be simpler and, because there will be a "pause" to check previous performance, more efficient. (The interacting development of operational research techniques and of computer technology has improved the tools available for logical systems analysis and for the determination of criteria of efficiency for task systems.) If the discontinuity is slight, a more elaborate apparatus of regulation will be required, first, to preserve the differentiation between the two systems, and, second, to secure co-ordination between them. If there is no discontinuity there can be no control region, and hence no boundary control function. And, without boundary controls, there can be no realistic way of determining what is inside and

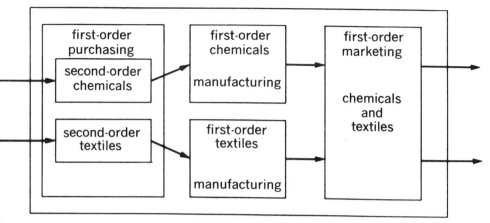

Figure 4. Mixed dimensions of differentiation.

what outside. In practice, however, an organizational boundary may have to be drawn at a point where there is no discontinuity because existing regulatory mechanisms cannot span the system (the "span of control" of classical theories of organization); but it is important to recognize that such a boundary is determined by constraints, and not by task requirements. It is the result of compromise, not of activity system differentiation.

With the delineation of the boundaries of activity systems and of the nature of the regulatory and maintenance activities required, we can now set up a model organization for task performance.

MANAGING SYSTEMS

When a complex enterprise is differentiated into constituent systems we have used the term *operating systems* for those systems of activity through which the dominant import-conversion-export process is accomplished. With such differentiation, regulation of the relationships between the constituent systems,

and between the whole enterprise and its environment, cannot be contained in any one constituent system, and a system external to the operating systems is required. This we have called the *managing system* (Rice & Trist, 1952; Rice, 1958, 1963). It is this system that provides the regulatory and maintenance activities to keep the operating systems going. Where regulation and maintenance are differentiated as discrete activity systems, they will thus be contained in the managing system. If a first-order operating system is differentiated into second-order systems, then they too will need regulation and maintenance, and a second-order managing system will be required which, in its turn, may contain differentiated systems for regulation and maintenance.[3]

ACTIVITIES, ROLES, AND ORGANIZATION

Most systems of activity include some human activities; some systems depend entirely on human resources. When an

[3] More detailed consideration of the ordering of systems will be found in the original source.— Eds.

enterprise imports human resources, it is inevitably taking on more than the specific activities it requires of them. Without human creativity enterprises could not exist. One of the strengths of a human group is its capacity to turn itself into many different kinds of activity system in pursuit of different tasks. At one moment its task may be to design a strategy; at another, to execute it. It may then monitor its performance, remuster, procure reinforcements, and execute a fresh strategy. But this very adaptability can, as we have shown, be a major constraint in an enterprise in which the contribution required by an activity system from individual or group is limited and specific.

We have used the term *role* to refer to the activities that the individual contributes to a particular activity system and to the interrelations involved in carrying out those activities. Thus the role of a machine operator may require him to receive material from a preceding operator, to monitor the performance of the machine (a regulatory activity), to pass material to a succeeding operator, and also to accept instructions from a foreman affecting the rate and quality of output.

Through its organization an enterprise assigns activities to roles and roles to individuals and groups; but the enterprise cannot always predetermine the consequential role-sets. These are nevertheless highly relevant to its effectiveness.

Management of an enterprise requires, therefore, four kinds of boundary control:

i. regulation of task-system boundaries (i.e. regulation of the enterprise as a whole as an import-conversion-export system, and regulation of constituent systems of activity);

ii. regulation of sentient-group boundaries (i.e. the boundaries of the groupings to which people belong either directly through their roles in systems of activity, or indirectly through their role-sets);

iii. regulation of organizational boundaries;

iv. regulation of the relation between task, sentient, and organizational boundaries.

Task, organizational, and sentient boundaries may coincide. Indeed, they must coincide to some extent at the boundary of the enterprise if it is to continue to exist. The enterprise may also be differentiated into parts, which are similarly defined by coinciding boundaries. But there are dangers in such coincidence.

One danger is that the members of a group may so invest in their identity as a group that they will defend an obsolescent task system from which they derive membership. We can now add the possibility that the identification of change in task-system boundaries, and even the identification of the boundaries themselves, can be made difficult by the existence of group boundaries that are strongly defended. The representative who identifies more with his customer than with his own company, the politician who identifies more with his party than with his constituents, are not unfamiliar figures.

In general, we can say that, without adequate boundary definitions for activity systems and groups, organizational boundaries are difficult to define and frontier skirmishing is inevitable. It is perhaps a major paradox of modern complex enterprises that the more certainly boundaries can be located, the more easily formal communication systems can be established. Unless a boundary is adequately located, different people will draw it in different places and hence there will be confusion between inside and outside. In the individual this confusion leads to breakdown; in enterprises, to inefficiency and failure.

59   Technology and organization

RAYMOND G. HUNT

Beginning at least with Veblen and Marx, material technology has been regularly proposed as a major influence on organizational phenomena. Indications of its broad significance can be found in Toynbee's (1956) demonstration of changing forms of English social organization as new industrial technologies emerged during the eighteenth and nineteenth centuries, and Margaret Mead's (1955) vivid portrayals of interrelations between technological advances and social patterns. More recently, Dubin (1958) has nominated technology as the single most important determinant of work behavior, and Mouzelis (1967) has spoken at length of the determining effect of technological structures and processes on organizational interaction. Stinchcombe (1965), too, in context with his discussion of "motives for organizing," mentions technology among the basic variables affecting organizing capacity, while Olsen (1968) lists material technology as one of four primary factors underlying forms of social organization—the other three being the natural environment, population, and the human being. Finally, in his excellent review of comparative studies, Udy (1965) points out two basic "causal mechanisms" that shape organizations: One operating via *people* to affect structures, the other being *ecological* and having to do with how activity is limited and channeled. Together with the "social setting," which we are disregarding here, technology can be construed as imposing ecological limits on organizational properties.

Adapted from the **Academy of Management Journal,** 1970, 13, 235–252, with permission of the author and the publisher.

Organizational structure

By technology or process we mean the various things done, with or without tools and machines, to transform inputs into outputs (cf. Hickson *et al.*, 1969, for a useful discussion of definitional issues). Our definition encompasses the three facets of technology (i.e., operations, materials, and knowledge) differentiated by Hickson *et al.* (1969) and includes the sequencing of activities involved in the conversion process, thereby including what Whyte (1967, Ch. 3), among others, refers to as "work flow."

The properties of organization with which we are concerned are chiefly those signified by the terms "structure" or "design." However, we favor a rather broad conception of structure that identifies it with the varied patterns of interaction, intended or otherwise, that characterize an organization. To the degree these patterns are codified or standardized, we can speak of the organization as being formal, defining "formal organizational structure" in terms of organizational prescriptions regarding lines of authority, divisions of labor and allocations of resources (cf. Pugh *et al.*, 1968; Whyte, 1969). These patterns and prescriptions are, of course, often found memorialized in organization charts, job descriptions, budgetary formulas, and the like, which travel under various aggregative banners, such as bureaucracy, project organization, and line-staff formats.

A significant empirical literature has now emerged relating technology to various organizational matters. Among the most prominent examples are Joan Woodward's (1965) seminal studies. Her work and other relevant investiga-

tions have been amply reviewed by Perrow (1967a), J. D. Thompson (1967), and by Hickson *et al.* (1969), so that there is no need for repetition here. It is sufficient to observe that the main point of her findings is to show that technology affects structure, shapes interaction, and influences the personal characteristics of organizational members (cf. Blauner, 1964), although the precise nature, degree, and conditions of its effects remain controversial (cf. Hickson *et al.*, 1969).

Moreover, there are indications that organizational success depends on a meshing of structure with technology. For example, Woodward found that successful firms tended to have little in common organizationally, *except* within technological groups. As a generality she found successful firms to be those that exhibited organizational patterns *typical* of their technological kind. Yet, as late as 1964, W. R. Scott felt constrained to mark the infrequency with which technological variables had been built into theory. The reasons for this seem to reside partly in a preoccupation of organizational scholars with nonstructural human relations or "informal" processes (cf. Mouzelis, 1967) and partly from the fact that, although technological phenomena were widely recognized and sometimes even categorized, until recently there literally were no technological *variables* to build into theory (cf. Whyte, 1969, Ch. 3). What perhaps is most important in the technology-organization literature of the past few years, therefore, aside from empirical explication, is that it has begun to give form to conceptualizations of manageable technological variables or dimensions. Prominent in this connection have been the works of Bell (1967), Perrow (1967a, 1967b), Harvey (1968),

Whyte (1969), and Pugh & Hickson (cf. Hickson *et al.*, 1969).

The technology variable

Productive as it was empirically, the technology variable is ambiguous in Woodward's classification scheme. She regards her entire scheme as a direct index of technology, even as a scale of technological complexity ranging from unit to mass to process modes of production.[1] Harvey (1968), however, has quite reasonably pointed out that the complexity scale could equally well be the reverse. Woodward's own finding, that unit production and continuous process organizations tended to exhibit many common characteristics which contrasted sharply with other kinds of organizations, could imply a "circular" interpretation of the technological dimension underlying her classification.

The precise mechanisms linking technologies with organizational forms are still problematical; but, as a generality, the critical technological element to which organizational structure must respond seems best conceptualized as *complexity*. This is something unit production organizations, for instance, may have at least as much as their continuous process counterparts—a moment's reflection on the many esoteric one-of-a-kind products produced under the American space program vindicates that assertion. To state it simply, what this signifies is that it is *less* the concrete manifestations of technology that matter, and *more* the essential complex-

ity underlying them. Having said that, however, it is necessary to acknowledge immediately that complexity is an elusive concept that takes many forms.

Bell (1967), for instance, has dealt explicitly with the matter of complexity and structure in his study of spans of control (ratios of personnel to supervisors) in a large hospital. He defined complexity as: (a) the degree of predictability of work demands; (b) the discretion provided for in a position; (c) the responsibility of the job holder (construed as the time lapse between decision and its supervisory review or assessment); and (d) the number of tasks performed by the job holder. Bell then showed that as complexity increased, with regard to either subordinates' or supervisors' roles, the span of control decreased.

Harvey (1968) has used Woodward's work as a point of departure, in speaking of a complexity dimension ranging from technical diffuseness to specificity. He argues that one needs to take account not only of the *form* of technology, as Woodward tried to do, but also the amount of "changefulness" *within* a form. To paraphrase Harvey, a unit production firm might produce the same thing most of the time and so be "specific," or, it might vary its outputs and so be "diffuse." In his research, Harvey postulated that the diffuseness or specificity of the organization's task will have differential implications for its structural characteristics. He conceived three "sociotechnical types," i.e., marriages of technology and internal organizational structure, defined in terms of frequency of product change: Diffuse, Intermediate, and Specific. He showed that when compared with Specific types, Diffuse types had fewer specialized subunits, fewer levels of authority, a lower

---

[1] Unit production systems (e.g., custom tailors, research labs) yield unique outputs, one-at-a-time. Mass production systems (e.g., automotive assembly plants) produce, step-wise, large quantities of standardized items; continuous process systems are exemplified by fully automated oil refineries.

ratio of managers and supervisors to total personnel, and a lesser degree of performance program specification.

Cognitive interpretations of technology

Probably the most generalized attempt at conceptualizing technology and relating it to organizational processes can be found in Perrow's work with his "contingent two-dimensional model" (1967a) which elaborates a distinction between routine and nonroutine technologies. Perrow's emphasis is on classifying technologies as to the frequency with which exceptional cases are encountered and with reference to the nature of the search process (for solutions) that ensues when exceptions do occur. Using this general model he relates task-structure to analogous control-coordination processes, involving variations in individual or group discretion, and the nature of the feedback mechanisms controlling performance (i.e., their degree of "programming"). In a later paper Perrow (1967b) has refined his basic model and extended it to connect with the psychological processes of its human operatives. He stresses a "cognitive" conception of technology which works as a system of cues that signal the initiation of performance routines, but with provision for handling exceptions.

The notable feature of Perrow's construction is that, regardless of how complicated or elaborate, a system may be viewed as technologically "routine" to the extent that: (1) the signals that initiate its processes are unambiguous; (2) the performance processes so cued are themselves programmed; and (3) when faced with exceptions not covered by regular performance routines, search processes and problem-solving methods

are programmed. The properties of technology emphasized by other writers can probably be treated in Perrow's formulation as either sources of cognitive complexity (exceptions) or as proxies for it.

Perrow's cognitive constructions rather closely parallel the much more general cybernetic model of human problem-solving of Miller, Galanter, and Pribram (1960). These authors construe individual performance in relation to a cognitive TOTE (Test-Operate-Test-Exit) unit, basic to which is the notion of "plan," which they define as any hierarchical process controlling the *sequence* in which a set of operations is performed. They discuss a variety of ways plans may differ (communicability, source, detail, flexibility, etc.), and also discuss plans for searching and solving, distinguishing between systematic and heuristic varieties.

Very briefly, the Miller, Galanter, and Pribram idea is that people have images of reality and an array of plans for dealing with it. As information, in the form of environmental signals, flows into a human performance system, it is "tested" for fit with existing plans which then may be put into operation. Results of action are appraised via feedback from the performance and the system moves on either to another performance segment or, if a problem has arisen, to a more or less standardized search routine. Of course, the system could cycle into a search routine immediately if the initial "test" yielded no suitable performance program. From their presentation it is evident that, when a search plan exists, one may not even be aware of it, although it is necessary to perceive the exception—indeed, it is the function of the TOTE unit to guarantee that. Thus, regardless of how complicated it may be materially, at the behavioral level, technology can be defined in terms of an ordered set of skills or habits that differ mainly in their degree of routinization, integration, or mechanization. Complicated material technologies may be more difficult to program and they may place greater demands on human resources, but operationally what really counts is behavioral routinization.

It may be concluded from the foregoing that it is not material technology per se that presents organizational challenges, but the nature of the problem-solving tasks confronting those operating the system at all levels. The extent to which the organization's task systems can be programmed, and uncertainty eliminated, seem to be the critical circumstances. However, no performance program can anticipate every contingency. Exceptions will occur. Even if it can be reduced, uncertainty cannot be totally eliminated. Consequently, as Perrow has maintained, the decisive structural determinants are apt to be associated with the handling of exceptions to task programs. The frequency of such exceptions will, of course, be related to the complexity of material technology. However, even very complicated material technologies may be highly programmed. The essential point is how important exceptions are to the viability of the organization, and how they can be handled by it.

In this connection, it seems reasonable to assume that the more a system depends upon its performance programs to control its outputs, the more seriously it must view exceptions to their application or breakdowns in their operation and, hence, the more it must be geared to deal with them. If problem-solving processes are routinized along with task performance, one could expect a dif-

ferent kind of organization from the one that would obtain when they are not.

Performance vs problem-solving systems

If all this is sensible, a potential basis for the similarity found by Woodward between unit production and process organizations is discoverable via the simple expedient of conceiving, somewhat after the fashion of Burns and Stalker (1961), of two quite different kinds of organization: One geared chiefly to *performance*, as in a mass production factory or a modern bank, and the other to *problem-solving*, as in a hospital, or a design and development enterprise. In a unit production firm, the system deals almost entirely with exceptions and its problem-solving modes are likely to be unroutinized, especially if it is technologically diffuse (cf. Harvey, 1968). In automated continuous process organizations, whether exceptions are frequent or not, they will be critical when they occur so that such systems, too, are likely to be structured as problem-solving or trouble-shooting affairs. Thus, unit production organizations, especially diffuse ones with complicated material technologies, *and* continuous process organizations are both likely to be similarly structured as organic problem-solving systems. Other operations facing fewer exceptions and less vitally affected by ones that occur are likely to be differently structured as mechanistic performance systems. While we shall not now go into the matter further, it does seem likely that over the long run firms may tend to organize more and more as performance systems, whether or not it is good for them to do so (cf. discussions of processes of bureaucratization in

Mouzelis, 1967, and Olsen, 1968, Ch. 17).

Organization-level analysis of technology and structure

So far, we have talked of relations between technology and structure mostly at the so-called "level" of the organization, treating the system as a unitary entity. Yet, we have mentioned the frequent internal technological diversity of organizations—a fact that confronts organization-level analyses with thorny problems. In addition to complicating life, it prompts serious questions about suitable units of system analysis, for there is no inherent reason to expect technologically diverse organizations to be any less diverse structurally. Therefore assessments of technology-structure correlations might profit from being based on homogeneous organizational sub-systems instead of "forcing" aggregated total systems into statistically defined "types." Or, a system-level alternative might be to devise suitable indexes of technological diversity for use either as independent variables or as "test factors."

To illustrate the force of this point: It is possible that one reason Hickson et al. (1969) found stronger relations between organizational size and structure, than between technology and structure, leaving aside their definition of technology, is that size may well be correlated with diversity. Small unit-production firms, which were missing from the study by Hickson et al., are likely to be technologically more homogeneous, in the cognitive sense described above, than are very large firms, which were heavily represented in their study. This issue of size deserves further attention in future research.

Designing organizational structures

The design of an organization refers to the composition of its structure; moreover, "design" implies a purposive formulation legitimized by an organization's formal authority (cf. Haberstroh, 1965). Certainly, there is a presumption of organizational rationality implicit in the idea of design. It connotes a sense of organizational construction neatly adapted by managerial plan to the objectives and circumstances, technological or other, of a particular organization; and these adaptations are presumably optimized by careful analyses and the systematic application of "principles" of organization and management theory. Yet, curiously enough, in her extensive studies, Woodward found firms, successful and unsuccessful alike, to vary markedly in "organization consciousness." Even among firms "in which production systems were basically the same," considerable difference could be found in the extent to which they tried "to rationalize their production, in their awareness of technical developments, and in their use of techniques such as work study, methods engineering, and operations research" (1967, p. 42).

Woodward was led to the view that conscious organizational planning rarely is based on technical considerations, that it amounts mostly to implicit recognition of technologically constrained situational demands and represents the institutionalization of prevailing organizational realities. In Woodward' studies, so "unconscious" was organizational designing that most managers were not even aware of how their organizations compared structurally with others.

Findings like Woodward's suggest that planning is often absent, or that it is more apparent than real, coming to little more than formalization of what already exists. Undoubtedly much ostensible organizational analysis and design does represent a sort of managerial doodling instigated by external affiliations (cf. Woodward, 1967, p. 21), or motivated by managers' desires to display virtuosity, or to "keep up with the Joneses." It may also depend heavily upon having time to think about such things—on organizational "slack," as Perrow puts it (1967b). Furthermore, Blau and Scott (1962) and V. A. Thompson (1961) have suggested that organizational elaboration often arises from various desires on the part of those in power to evade unpleasant tasks, to bolster the prevailing status structure, or from other considerations extraneous to the technical requirements of organizational tasks.

Another of Woodward's findings, however, was that "organic" firms tended as a group to be low in organization-consciousness, thus implying that these things may not depend altogether on managerial caprice. And, while organization-consciousness was not always a mark of "mechanistic" orientations, consciousness did not seem to be altogether random as regards technology. In short, some technologies seem to prompt more concern with design than do others.

These issues have been well covered by J. D. Thompson (1967), who offers an array of propositions relating technology to organizational operations and thence to rational organizational design. His book nicely illustrates how operations depend on technology, and how various principles of organizational design implicitly assume sustaining technologies. This last matter is of overarching significance, highlighted by Woodward's finding that success was associated with "textbook" management

applications only in one technological setting, i.e., large batch concerns. This suggests the conclusion that prevailing management theory has been largely based on this technological model without that fact having been understood. If that is true, application of standard managerial precepts in other technological contexts is likely to yield less than salutary consequences. Miller and Rice (1967) have made just this point, commenting that classical theories of organization drew mainly on experience in industries representative of only a narrow technological range. They add that their own experiences support Woodward's implication that the models and principles thus derived do not fit either process or unit-production industries. Hickson et al. (1969) have also argued the relativity of design precepts to technological environments.

There probably can be no "one best" organizational structure or managerial orientation—not participative management, not bureaucracy, not any single fashionable methodology. In this regard one might call to mind Fielder's (1967) persuasive arguments that effective leadership entails an adaptation of "style" to organizational context.[2] In just the same way, organizational success depends fundamentally upon meshing design, social technology (cf. Olsen, 1968), with the material technology from which the organization's tasks emerge. It may be, as Woodward's work suggests, that organizations tend as a "natural" process to shape themselves into at least a loose match of technologies, but that does not mean that management design activity is irrelevant or that management ought to become passive and desist from efforts to plan

[2] See his paper in Section VIII here.—Eds.

and enhance operational effectiveness; what follows is only that it must acknowledge the "technological imperative" (cf. Hickson et al., 1969). Social and material technology must be mutually adapted in system designs. Admittedly, until more adequately differentiated social-technological models become available from comparative studies this will be hard to do. But, who ever said management was easy?

Concluding observations

We have distinguished between two fundamentally different models for organization—performance and problem-solving. Analogous in conception to Burns and Stalker's (1961) mechanistic and organic management models, this distinction has the virtue of making management methods means to ends —e.g., problem-solving—rather than things good or bad in themselves. In any event we have also suggested that most management theories pertain to performance models not to problem-solving models of organization, but that, for various reasons, organizations tend to evolve toward performance models, that is, they endeavor to increase routinization. It may be, as Olsen (1968, pp. 300–301) says, that such tendencies arise from the organization's continual efforts to rationalize its functioning in order to achieve its goals more effectively, but nevertheless there are many times when such movement is premature

and disfunctional. Consequently it will sometimes require deliberate managerial effort to resist such evolution when it would compromise the flexibility and creativity of the system and defeat effective goal achievement.

Probably nowhere is this principle more applicable than in research and development environments, whether in industry, universities, or wherever. Decentralized, organically operated project organizations have been effective vehicles for accomplishing goals in such contexts, but the moral of our story, paradoxically perhaps, is that centralized authority may be necessary to preserve their adaptive integrity in the face of "natural" forces toward bureaucratization. Udy (1965), for instance, has hypothesized that technological "complexity" stimulates concerns for coordination that tend to lead toward elaboration and formalization of administration. Furthermore, the generation of inflexibility occasioned by predilections toward "empire building" within projects, and by dispositions to assimilate project organizations to functional or administrative divisions, are familiar experiences in research and development environments (cf. Haberstroh, 1965, pp. 1208–9, for a brief discussion). One unfortunate, or fortunate, depending on your view, consequence of this policy is that it leaves the organization in a condition of heavy dependence on the commitment and competence of the people who run it—or at least those who manage it.

60   Being human and being organized

CHRIS ARGYRIS

It is hard to imagine being "civilized" without being "organized." Yet too much organization, or the wrong kind, can injure the individuals involved and through them can spoil an organization or a civilization. How can we design or "grow" organizations that maintain the right balance between individual needs on the one hand, and organizational requirements on the other?

The classical design for a formal organization has some very serious flaws. The nature of these flaws appears when we set side by side two pictures: first, a view of how human beings need to behave in our society in order to be healthy, productive, growing individuals; and second, how a formal organization (a factory, business, or hospital) requires them to behave. Comparing these pictures, we see that the organization's requirements, as presented by "classical" descriptions, are sharply opposed to the individual's needs. We can, however, suggest some lines along which action and study might improve the "fit" between the human being and the non-human organization.

Picture of health

There are certain lines along which the child becoming a man develops, in our culture. We can discuss, as being most important, seven of these "developmental dimensions":

From being passive as infants, humans grow toward activeness as adults.

From being dependent on others, an individual grows toward being relatively independent of others. He develops the ability to "stand on his own two feet" while at the same time acknowledging a healthy dependency. He does not react to others (his boss, for instance) in terms of patterns learned during childhood; thus, such independence is partly a matter of accurate perception of himself and those around him.

From only a few types of reaction or behavior, he develops many.

He moves from the shallow, brief, and erratic interests of his infancy to the intense, long-term, and coherent commitments of adulthood. He requires increasingly varied challenges; he wants his tasks to be not easy but hard, not simple but complex, not a collection of separate things but a variety of parts he can put together.

He begins to want long-term challenges that link his past and future, in place of the old brief and unconnected jobs which typically were engaged in by him as a child.

He begins wanting to go up the totem pole, instead of staying in the low place a child has.

He develops from being not very self-aware and impulsive to being both self-aware and self-controlled, and this lets him develop a sense of integrity and self-worth.

No one, of course, finishes his development along these seven lines. For one thing, if everyone became totally inde-

Reprinted from **Trans-action**, 1964, 1, 3–6, with permission of the author and the publisher.

pendent, incessantly active, and completely equal if not superior, society would be in a pretty difficult situation —sort of all fleas and no dog. One function of culture is to hold back, by our manners and morals, the self-expression of some individualists, so that others may also have a chance at self-development. Then too, people simply differ in needs and skills; not everybody wants to go into orbit, and some are too frail, too fat, or too stupid to be given the chance.

Admitting, then, that no one is ever through developing along these dimensions, we can still say that his self-actualization is the overall "profile" of how far he has developed along them. At this point we must add that in drawing this profile, not the surface appearance but the underlying meanings of a man's behavior are what have to be considered. For instance, an employee might seem to be always going against what management wants, so that people call him "independent," yet his contrariness may be due to his great need to be dependent on management, a need he dislikes to admit. The truly independent person is the one whose behavior is not mainly a reaction against the influence others have over him (though, of course, no person is totally independent). The best test of such independence is how fully the person will let other people be independent and active. Autocratic leaders may claim to like independent underlings, yet many studies have shown that autocratic leadership only makes both boss and underlings more dependence-ridden.

The formal organization

We now turn from the picture of a developing self to the organization. What are its properties, and what impact can we expect these to make on the human personality we have just viewed? What reactions can we expect from this impact?

To begin, the most basic feature of a formal organization is that it is "rational"—that is, it has been "designed," and its parts are purposefully related within this design; it has pattern and is shaped by human minds to accomplish particular rational objectives. For instance, jobs within it must be clearly defined (in terms of rank, salary, and duties) so that the organization can have logical training, promotion, and resignation or retirement policies.

But most experts on such organizations are not content to point to, as Herbert Simon (1957) does, this "rational design"—they go on to say that this rationality, though an ideal that may have to be modified now and then, requires people in an organization to be very loyal to its formal structure if it is to work effectively. They have to "go by the rules." And the experts claim such design is "more human" in the long run than creating an organization haphazardly. It is senseless, cruel, wasteful, and inefficient, they argue, not to have a logical design. It is senseless to pay a man highly without clearly defining his position and its relation to the whole. It is cruel, because eventually people suffer when no structure exists. It is wasteful because without clearly pre-defined jobs it is impossible to plan a logical training or promotion or resignation or retirement policy. And it is inefficient because it allows the "personal touch" to dominate and this, in turn, is "playing politics."

In contrast to such experts, some human-relations researchers have unfortunately given the impression that formal structures are bad, and that individual needs should come first in creating and running an organization. These latter men, however, are swinging (as recent analysis of their research has shown) to recognize that an extreme emphasis on the individual's needs is not a very tenable position either, and that organizational rules can be well worth keeping.

Principles of design

What are the principles by which an organization is "rationally designed"? The traditionalists among experts in this field have singled out certain key assumptions about the best design for a formal organization. In our comments here these will be dealt with not as beyond question but only as the most useful and accurate so far offered. By accepting them to this extent, we can go on to look at the probable impact on human beings of an organization based on them.

As Gillespie (1948) suggests, these principles may be traced back to certain "principles of industrial economics," the most important of which is that "the concentration of effort on a limited field of endeavor increases quality and quantity of output." This principle leads to another: that the more similar the things that need doing, the more specialization will help to do them.

Specializing

The design-principle just mentioned carries three implications about human beings within organizations. First, that the human personality will behave more efficiently as the job gets more specialized. Second, that there can be found a one best way to define the job so it will be done faster. Third, that differences between human personalities may be ignored by transferring more skill and thought to machines.

But all these assumptions conflict sharply with the developmental needs or tendencies of human personality as a growing thing; a human being is always putting himself together, pushing himself into the future. How can we assume that this process can be choked off, or that the differences between individuals which result from the process can be ignored?

Besides, specialization requires a person to use only a few of his abilities, and the more specialized the task the simpler the ability involved. This goes directly counter to the human tendency to want more complex, more interesting jobs as he develops. Singing the same tune over and over is boring enough, but repeating the same note is absolutely maddening.

The chain of command

Mere efficiency of parts is not enough; an organization needs to have a pattern of parts, a chain of command. Thus, planners create "leadership," to control and coordinate. They assume that efficiency is increased by a fixed hierarchy of authority. The man at the top is given formal power to hire and fire, reward and penalize, so that employees will work for the organization's objectives.

The impact of this design-feature on human personality is clearly to make the individuals dependent on, passive and subordinate to, the leader. The results are obviously to lessen their self-control and shorten their time-perspective. It would seem, then, that the design-feature of hierarchic structure works against four of the growth-lines, pushing individuals back from active toward passive, from equal toward subordinate, from self-controlled toward dependent, from being aware of long time-perspectives toward having only a short time-perspective. In all these four ways, the result is to move employees back from adulthood toward immaturity.

Planners have tried to cushion this impact in several ways. First, they see to it that those who perform well in the hierarchy are rewarded. But the trouble with this is that the reward ought to be psychological as well as material—and yet, because of the job-specialization which simplifies and does not satisfy a worker, few psychological rewards are possible. So the material reward has to seem more important, and has to be increased. To do this, however, means that one does nothing about the on-the-job situation that is causing the trouble, but instead pays the employee for the dissatisfaction he experiences. Obviously, management in doing this leaves an employee to feel that basic causes of dissatisfaction are built into industrial life, that the rewards received are wages for dissatisfaction, and that any satisfaction to be gained must be looked for outside the organization.

Other things are wrong with raising wages to make up for dissatisfaction. For it assumes that the worker can so split himself up that he can be quite satisfied with the anomalous situation we have just described him as being in. Second, it assumes he is mainly interested in what money can get. And third, it assumes he is best rewarded as an individual producer, without regard to the work group in which he belongs. This may well mean that a worker

whose group informally sanctions holding production down will therefore have to choose between pleasing the boss and getting paid more, or pleasing his fellows and getting paid less.

Keeping personalities out

A second "solution" has been suggested by planners: to have very good bosses. The leaders, that is, should be objective, rational, and personify the reasonableness of the organizational structure. To do this means they keep from getting emotionally involved; as one executive states, "We must try to keep our personalities out of the job." Evaluating others, he sets aside his own feelings. And, of course, he must be loyal to the organization.

But this solution too violates some of the basic properties of personality. To split what one does from what one is, or to ask others to do it, is to violate one's self-integrity, and the same goes for the effort to keep personality out of the job. (As for impartiality, as May (1953) has pointed out, the best way to be impartial is to be as partial as one's needs require but stay aware of this partiality so as to "correct" for it at the moment of decision.)

One other solution has been offered: to encourage competition among employees, so as to get them to show initiative and creativity. Competing for promotions, this "rabble hypothesis" suggests, will increase the efficiency of the competitors.

Williams (1956), however, conducting some controlled experiments, shows that this assumption is not necessarily valid for people placed in competitive situations. Deutsch (1949) supports Williams's results with extensive controlled research, and goes much further, suggesting that competitive situations make for so much tension that they lessen efficiency. Levy and Freedman (1956) confirm Deutsch's work and go on to relate competition to psychoneurosis.

Unity of direction

We have looked at the design-features of job-specialization and hierarchic structure. A final principle of design is *unity of direction*: efficiency is supposed to increase if each administrative unit has a single activity planned and directed by a single leader. The implication is that this leader sets the goal, the conditions for meeting the goal, and the path toward it, for all his employees. If, because of job-specialization, the workers are not personally interested in the work-goal, then unity of direction creates the ideal conditions for psychological failure. For each individual basically (as we have said) aims at psychological success, which comes only when he defines his own goals, in relation to his personal needs and to the difficulties of reaching the goals.

Human needs vs. organizational requirements

What we have seen is that if we use the principles of formal organization as ideally defined, employees will be working in an environment where (1) they have little or no control over their workaday world; (2) they are expected to be passive, dependent, and subordinate; (3) they are expected to have a short time-perspective; (4) job-specialization asks them to perfect and value only a few of their simplest abilities; and (5) they are asked to produce under conditions (imposed by the principle of unity of direction) ideal for psychological failure.

Since behavior in these ways is more childish than adult, it appears that formal organizations are willing to pay high wages and provide adequate seniority if mature adults will, for eight hours a day, behave like children. It is obvious that such behavior is incompatible with the human need to develop and "grow up." And it appears that the incongruency increases as (1) the employee is of greater maturity; (2) the formal structure is tightened in search of efficiency; (3) one goes down the line of command; (4) jobs become more mechanized.

That such incongruency will result in frustration, failure, short time-perspective and conflict hardly needs demonstration. How, in the face of all this, will the employee be able to maintain a sense of his own integrity? He will react in part like a turtle and in part like a porcupine: by leaving, by "ladder-climbing" within the organization, by such defense reactions as daydreaming, aggression, ambivalence, regression, projection, and so on; or by becoming apathetic toward the organization's makeup and goals. If this occurs, he will be apt to start "goldbricking" or even cheating. He may create informal groups who agree that it is right to be apathetic and uninvolved, and these informal groups may become formalized —instead of just gathering to gripe they will hold meetings and pass resolutions. Or he may take the view that money and "what's in it for me" have become the really important things about his work, and the "psychological rewards" are just malarkey. And he will end up by indoctrinating the new employees so that they will see the organization through the same mud-colored glasses as he does.

What to do?

There is only one real way to improve the sad picture described above: by *decreasing* the dependency, decreasing the subordination, and decreasing the submissiveness expected of employees. It can be shown that making a job "bigger"—not more specialized and small—will help do these things; and that employee-centered (or democratic or participative) leadership also will improve the situation.

Yet, these remedies are limited, for they require employees who are already highly interested in the organization. And the situation which makes them needed is one in which employees are anything but interested. In such a situation, strongly directive leadership is almost necessary to get the apathetic employee to move at all. This, in its own turn, helps to create the very problem it is trying to solve!

An unresolved dilemma

The dilemma, then, is basic and is a continuing challenge to the social scientist and the leader in an organization. They may well begin their efforts to work for a solution—one in which the organization will be as efficient as possible, while the people in it will be as free and strongly developing as possible —by considering two facts. The first is that no organization can be maximally efficient that stunts its own vital parts. And the second is that our culture and each of its institutions, from family through nations and beyond, are one vast interlocking set of organizations.

61 An overview of new patterns of management

RENSIS LIKERT

Based upon the principles and practices of the managers who are achieving the best results, a newer theory of organization and management can be stated. An attempt will be made here to present briefly some of the over-all characterics of such a theory and to formulate a general integrating principle which can be useful in attempts to apply it.

Research findings indicate that the general pattern of operations of the highest-producing managers tends to differ from that of the managers of mediocre and low-producing units by more often showing the following characteristics:

A preponderance of favorable attitudes on the part of each member of the organization toward all the other members, toward superiors, toward the work, toward the organization—toward all aspects of the job. These favorable attitudes toward others reflect a high level of mutual confidence and trust throughout the organization. The favorable attitudes toward the organization and the work are not those of easy complacency, but are the attitudes of identification with the organization and its objectives and a high sense of involvement in achieving them. As a consequence, the performance goals are high and dissatisfaction may occur whenever

achievement falls short of the goals set.

This highly motivated, cooperative orientation toward the organization and its objectives is achieved by harnessing effectively all the major motivational forces which can exercise significant influence in an organizational setting and which, potentially, can be accompanied by cooperative and favorable attitudes. Reliance is not placed solely or fundamentally on the economic motive of buying a man's time and using control and authority as the organizing and coordinating principle of the organization. On the contrary, the following motives are all used fully and in such a way that they function in a cumulative and reinforcing manner and yield favorable attitudes:

The ego motives. These are referred to throughout this volume as the desire to achieve and maintain a sense of personal worth and importance. This desire manifests itself in many forms, depending upon the norms and values of the persons and groups involved. Thus, it is responsible for such motivational forces as the desire for growth and significant achievement in terms of one's own values and goals, i.e., self-fulfillment, as well as the desire for status, recognition, approval, acceptance, and power and the desire to undertake significant and important tasks.

The security motives.

Curiosity, creativity, and the desire for new experiences.

The economic motives.

By tapping all the motives which yield favorable and cooperative attitudes, maximum motivation oriented toward realizing the organization's goals as well as the needs of each member of the organization is achieved. The substantial decrements in motivational forces which occur when powerful motives are pulling in opposite directions are thereby avoided. These conflicting forces exist, of course, when hostile and resentful attitudes are present.

The organization consists of a tightly knit, effectively functioning social system. This social system is made up of interlocking work groups with a high degree of group loyalty among the members and favorable attitudes and trust between superiors and subordinates. Sensitivity to others and relatively high levels of skill in personal interaction and the functioning of groups are also present. These skills permit effective participation in decisions on common problems. Participation is used, for example, to establish organizational objectives which are a satisfactory integration of the needs and desires of all members of the organization and of persons functionally related to it. High levels of reciprocal influence occur, and high levels of total coordinated influence are achieved in the organization. Communication is efficient and effective. There is a flow from

one part of the organization to another of all the relevant information important for each decision and action. The leadership in the organization has developed what might well be called a highly effective social system for interaction and mutual influence.

Measurements of organizational performance are used primarily for self-guidance rather than for superimposed control. To tap the motives which bring cooperative and favorable rather than hostile attitudes, participation and involvement in decisions is a habitual part of the leadership processes. This kind of decision-making, of course, calls for the full sharing of available measurements and information. Moreover, as it becomes evident in the decision-making process that additional information or measurements are needed, steps are taken to obtain them.

In achieving operations which are more often characterized by the above pattern of highly cooperative, well-coordinated activity, the highest producing managers use all the technical resources of the classical theories of management, such as time-and-motion study, budgeting, and financial controls. They use these resources at least as completely as do the low-producing managers, but in quite different ways. This difference in use arises from the differences in the motives which the high-producing, in contrast to the low-producing, managers believe are important in influencing human behavior.

The low-producing managers, in keeping with traditional practice, feel that the way to motivate and direct behavior is to exercise control through authority. Jobs are organized, methods are prescribed, standards are set, performance goals and budgets are established. Compliance with them is sought through the use of hierarchical and economic pressures.

Widespread use of participation is one of the more important approaches employed by the high-producing managers in their efforts to get full benefit from the technical resources of the classical theories of management coupled with high levels of reinforcing motivation. This use of participation applies to all aspects of the job and work, as, for example, in setting work goals and budgets, controlling costs, organizing the work, etc. The high-producing managers have developed their organizations into highly coordinated, highly motivated, cooperative social systems. Under their leadership, the different motivational forces in each member of the organization have coalesced into a strong force aimed at accomplishing the mutually established objectives of the organization. This general pattern of highly motivated, cooperative members seems to be a central characteristic of the newer management system being developed by the highest-producing managers.

How do these high-producing managers build organizations which display this central characteristic? The research findings show, for example, that those supervisors and managers whose pattern of leadership yields consistently favorable attitudes more often think of employees as "human beings rather than just as persons to get the work done." Consistently, in study after study, the data show that treating people as "human beings" rather than as "cogs in a machine" is a variable highly related to the attitudes and motivation of the subordinate at every level in the organization.

The superiors who have the most favorable and cooperative attitudes in their work groups display the following characteristics:

The attitude and behavior of the superior toward the subordinate as a person, *as perceived by the subordinate*, is as follows:

He is supportive, friendly, and helpful rather than hostile. He is kind but firm, never threatening, genuinely interested in the well-being of subordinates and endeavors to treat people in a sensitive, considerate way. He is just, if not generous. He endeavors to serve the best interests of his employees as well as of the company.

He shows confidence in the integrity, ability, and motivations of subordinates rather than suspicion and distrust.

His confidence in subordinates leads him to have high expectations as to their level of performance. With confidence that he will not be disappointed, he expects much, not little. (This, again, is fundamentally a supportive rather than a critical or hostile relationship.)

He sees that each subordinate is well trained for his particular job. He endeavors also to help subordinates be promoted by training them for jobs at the next level. This involves giving them relevant experience and coaching whenever the opportunity offers.

He coaches and assists employees whose performance is below standard. In the case of a subordinate who is clearly misplaced and unable to do his job satisfactorily, he endeavors to find a position well suited to that employee's abilities and arranges to have the employee transferred to it.

The behavior of the superior in directing the work is characterized by such activity as:

Planning and scheduling the work to be done, training subordinates, supplying them with material and tools, initiating work activity, etc. Providing adequate technical competence, particularly in those situations where the work has not been highly standardized.

The leader develops his subordinates into a working team with high group loyalty by using participation and other kinds of group-leadership practices.

The integrating principle

These results and similar data from other studies (Argyris, 1957; March & Simon, 1958; Viteles, 1953) show that subordinates react favorably to experiences which they feel are supportive and contribute to their sense of importance and personal worth. Similarly, persons react unfavorably to experiences which are threatening and decrease or minimize their sense of dignity and personal worth. These findings are supported also by substantial research on personality development (Argyris, 1957; Rogers, 1942; Rogers, 1951) and group behavior (Cartwright & Zander, 1960). Each of us wants appreciation, recognition, influence, a feeling of accomplishment, and a feeling that people who are important to us believe in us and respect us. We want to feel that we have a place in the world.

This provides the basis for stating the general principle which the high-pro-ducing managers seem to be using and which will be referred to as the *principle of supportive relationships*. This principle, which provides an invaluable guide in any attempt to apply the newer theory of management in a specific plant or organization, can be briefly stated: *The leadership and other processes of the organization must be such as to ensure a maximum probability that in all interactions and all relationships with the organization each member will, in the light of his background, values, and expectations, view the experience as supportive and one which builds and maintains his sense of personal worth and importance.*

The central role of the work group

An important theoretical derivation can be made from the principle of supportive relationships. This derivation is based directly on the desire to achieve and maintain a sense of personal worth, which is a central concept of the principle. The most important source of satisfaction for this desire is the response we get from the people we are close to, in whom we are interested, and whose approval and support we are eager to have. The face-to-face groups with whom we spend the bulk of our time are, consequently, the most important to us. Our work group is one in which we spend much of our time and one in which we are particularly eager to achieve and maintain a sense of personal worth. As a consequence, most persons are highly motivated to behave in ways consistent with the goals and values of their work group in order to obtain recognition, support, security, and favorable reactions from this group. It can be concluded, therefore, that *management will make full use of the potential capacities of its human resources only when each person in an organization is a member of one or more effectively functioning work groups that have a high degree of group loyalty, effective skills of interaction, and high performance goals.*

The full significance of this derivation becomes more evident when we examine the research findings that show how groups function when they are well knit and have effective interaction skills. Research shows, for example, that the greater the attraction and loyalty to the group, the more the individual is motivated (1) to accept the goals and decisions of the group; (2) to seek to influence the goals and decisions of the group so that they are consistent with his own experience and his own goals; (3) to communicate fully to the members of the group; (4) to welcome communication and influence attempts from the other members; (5) to behave so as to help implement the goals and decisions that are seen as most important to the group; and (6) to behave in ways calculated to receive support and favorable recognition from members of the group and especially from those who the individual feels are the more powerful and higher-status members (Cartwright & Zander, 1960).

As our theoretical derivation has indicated, an organization will function best when its personnel function not as individuals but as members of highly effective work groups with high performance goals. Consequently, management should deliberately endeavor to build these effective groups, linking them into an over-all organization by means of people who hold overlapping group membership. The superior in one group is a subordinate in the next group, and so on through the organiza-

tion. If the work groups at each hierarchical level are well knit and effective, the linking process will be accomplished well.

An effectively functioning group pressing for solutions in the best interest of *all* the members and refusing to accept solutions which unduly favor a particular member or segment of the group is an important characteristic of the group pattern of organization. It also provides the president, or the superior at any level in an organization, with a powerful managerial tool for dealing with special requests or favors from subordinates. Often the subordinate may feel that the request is legitimate even though it may not be in the best interest of the organization. In the man-to-man operation the chief sometimes finds it difficult to turn down such requests. With the group pattern of operation, however, the superior can suggest that the subordinate submit his proposal to the group at their next staff meeting. If the request is legitimate and in the best interest of the organization, the group will grant the request. If the request is unreasonable, an effectively functioning group can skillfully turn it down by analyzing it in relation to what is best for the entire organization. Subordinates in this situation soon find they cannot get special favors or preferred treatment from the chief. This leads to a tradition that one does not ask for any treatment or decision which is recognized as unfair to one's colleagues.

Group decision-making

With the group model of organization, persons reporting to the president, such as vice presidents for sales, research, and manufacturing, contribute their technical knowledge in the decision-making process. They also make other contributions. One member of the group, for example, may be an imaginative person who comes up rapidly with many stimulating and original ideas. Others, such as the general counsel or the head of research, may make the group do a rigorous job of sifting ideas. In this way, the different contributions required for a competent job of thinking and decision-making are introduced.

In addition, these people become experienced in effective group functioning. They know what leadership involves. If the president grows absorbed in some detail and fails to keep the group focused on the topic for discussion, the members will help by performing appropriate leadership functions, such as asking, "Where are we? What have we decided so far? Why don't we summarize?"

There are other advantages to this sort of group action. The motivation is high to communicate accurately all relevant and important information. If any one of these men holds back important facts affecting the company so that he can take it to the president later, the president is likely to ask him why he withheld the information and request him to report it to the group at the next session. The group also is apt to be hard on any member who withholds important information from them. Moreover, the group can get ideas across to the boss that no subordinate dares tell him. As a consequence, there is better communication, which brings a better awareness of problems, and better decision-making than with the man-to-man system.

Another important advantage of effective group action is the high degree of motivation on the part of each member to do his best to implement decisions and to achieve the group goals. Since the goals of the group are arrived at through group decisions, each individual group member tends to have a high level of ego identification with the goals because of his involvement in the decisions.

Finally, there are indications that an organization operating in this way can be staffed for less than peak loads at each point. When one man is overburdened, some of his colleagues can pick up part of the load temporarily. This is possible with group methods of supervision because the struggle for power and status is less. Everybody recognizes his broad area of responsibility and is not alarmed by occasional shifts in one direction or the other. Moreover, he knows that his chances for promotion depend not upon the width of his responsibility, but upon his total performance, of which his work in the group is an important part. The group, including the president, comes to know the strengths and weaknesses of each member well as a result of working closely with him.

The "linking pin" function

The preceding discussion has been concerned with the group pattern of organization at the very top of a company. Our theoretical derivation indicates, however, that this pattern is equally applicable at all levels of an organization. If an organization is to apply this system effectively at all organizational levels, an important linking function must be performed.

The concept of the "linking pin" is shown by the arrows in Figure 1.

The linking pin function requires effective group processes and points to the following:

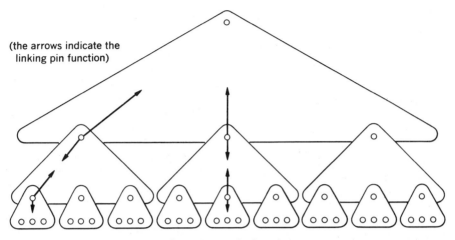

(the arrows indicate the linking pin function)

Figure 1. The linking pin.

An organization will not derive the full benefit from its highly effective groups unless they are linked to the total organization by means of equally effective overlapping groups. The use of highly effective groups in only one part or in scattered portions of an organization will fail, therefore, to achieve the full potential value of such groups.

The potential power of the overlapping group form of organization will not be approached until all the groups in the organization are functioning reasonably well. The failure of any group will adversely affect the performance of the total organization. The higher an ineffective group is in the hierarchy, the greater is the adverse effect of its failure on the performance of the organization. The linking process is more important at high levels in an organization than at low because the policies and problems dealt with are more important to the total organization and affect more people.

To help maintain an effective organi-

zation, it is desirable for superiors not only to hold group meetings of their own subordinates, but also to have occasional meetings over two hierarchical levels. This enables the superior to observe any breakdown in the linking pin process as performed by the subordinates reporting to him. If in such meetings the subordinates under one of his subordinates are reluctant to talk, never question any procedure or policy, or give other evidence of fear, the superior can conclude that he has a coaching job to do with his own subordinate, who is failing both as a leader and in his performance of the linking pin function. This subordinate needs help in learning how to build his own subordinates into a work group with high group loyalty and with confidence and trust in their supervisor.

An organization takes a serious risk when it relies on a single linking pin or single linking process to tie the organization together. An organization is strengthened by having staff groups and *ad hoc* committees provide multiple overlapping groups through which linking functions are performed and the organization bound together.

Organizational objectives and goals of units

The ability of a superior to behave in a supportive manner is circumscribed by the degree of compatibility between the objectives of the organization and the needs of the individuals comprising it. If the objectives of the organization are in basic conflict with the needs and desires of the individual members, it is virtually impossible for the superior to be supportive to subordinates and at the same time serve the objectives of the organization. The principle of supportive relationships, consequently, points to the necessity for an adequate degree of harmony between organizational objectives and the needs and desires of its individual members.

Neither the needs and desires of individuals nor the objectives of organizations are stable and unchanging. The desires of individuals grow and change as people interact with other people. Similarly, the objectives of organizations must change continuously to meet the requirements of changed technologies, changed conditions, and the changes in needs and desires of those involved in the organization or served by it. The interaction process of the organization must be capable of dealing effectively with these requirements for continuous change.

In every healthy organization there is, consequently, an unending process of examining and modifying individual goals and organizational objectives as well as consideration of the methods for achieving them. The newer theory specifies that:

The objectives of the entire organization and of its component parts must be in satisfactory harmony with the relevant needs and desires of the great majority, if not all, of the members of the organization and of the persons served by it.

The goals and assignments of each member of the organization must be established in such a way that he is highly motivated to achieve them.

The methods and procedures used by the organization and its subunits to achieve the agreed-upon objectives must be developed and adopted in such a way that the members are highly motivated to use these methods to their maximum potentiality.

The members of the organization and the persons related to it must feel that the reward system of the organization—salaries, wages, bonuses, dividends, interest payments—yields them equitable compensation for their efforts and contributions.

The overlapping group form of organization offers a structure which, in conjunction with a high level of group interactional skills, is particularly effective in performing the processes necessary to meet these requirements.

Constructive use of conflict

An organization operating under the newer theory is not free from conflict. Conflict and differences of opinion always exist in a healthy, virile organization, for it is usually from such differences that new and better objectives and methods emerge. Differences are essential to progress, but bitter, unresolved differences can immobilize an organization. The central problem, consequently, becomes not how to reduce or eliminate conflict, but how to deal constructively with it. Effective organizations have extraordinary capacity to handle conflict. Their success is due to three very important characteristics:

1. They possess the machinery to deal constructively with conflict. They have an organizational structure which facilitates constructive interaction between individuals and between work groups.

2. The personnel of the organization is skilled in the processes of effective interaction and mutual influence.

3. There is high confidence and trust among the members of the organization in each other, high loyalty to the work group and to the organization, and high motivation to achieve the organization's objectives. Confidence, loyalty, and cooperative motivation produce earnest, sincere, and determined efforts to find solutions to conflict. There is greater motivation to find a constructive solution than to maintain an irreconcilable conflict. The solutions reached are often highly creative and represent a far better solution than any initially proposed by the conflicting interests (Metcalf & Urwick, 1940).

The discussion in this chapter has deliberately focused on and emphasized the group aspects of organization and management. This has been done to make clear some of the major differences between the classical and the newer theories of management. It should also sharpen the awareness of the kind of changes needed to start applying the newer theory.

Any organization which bases its operation on this theory will necessarily make use of individual counseling and coaching by superiors of subordinates. There is need in every situation for a balanced use of both procedures, individual and group. Here, as with other aspects of supervision, the balance which will be most appropriate and work best will depend upon the experience, expectations, and skills of the people involved.

X INTERGROUP RELATIONS

Of the several areas of social psychology that we have touched on, inter-group relations constitute one of especially pressing concern in present-day life. Whether distinctions are made in terms of the many different groups which comprise a society, or in terms of international relations, problems of hostility and conflict are much in evidence. Social tensions, which may underlie intergroup conflict as well as be increased by it, are thus perpetuated. In this section, we are mainly interested in intergroup relations, but we interpret it broadly enough to include sources of social tension such as poverty and urban life, without in any sense exhausting what is a massive field of study in its own right.

Fundamentally, intergroup conflict stems from the identification of individuals with groups in terms of an "in-group" versus "out-group" distinction. The perceptual discrimination of group differences is common-place, but the imposition of value judgments of the "we" versus "they" variety holds the potentiality for socially disruptive consequences. Through the oversimplified mechanism of "stereotypes," it is all too easy to see all virtue residing in one's own group and all evil residing in others.

Sharp demarcations of this kind, especially where they are heavily over-laden with this evaluative quality, impede effective communication and lead to a breakdown of understanding and cooperation. Furthermore, they are unrealistic in terms of their single-mindedness. As Allport indicates here, loyalties can be concentric, with the larger ones containing the smaller, and no exclusions implied. Thus, whatever distinctions are made in segmenting the populace in various ways, all people share certain common interests as residents of a neighborhood, or a city, or a nation, or the planet. Growing interest in air and water pollution, the conservation of natural resources, and the battle against disease, reflect human concerns which go beyond the various group distinctions which we make in our everyday thinking and actions. Yet, intergroup conflict poses a constant hazard to the preservation of society and indeed to the world, as a scanning of the daily paper reveals.

Social psychologists have long been concerned with understanding the processes underlying such conflicts, especially in terms of prejudice. Among those who have done significant work in this area, Gordon Allport and his colleagues have been in the forefront. His book *The Nature of Prejudice* (1958), from which the selection here is drawn, is a landmark in understanding the processes and effects of prejudice.

Essentially, prejudice is an intergroup phenomenon that involves a negative attitude, a prejudgment, regarding other individuals in terms of their perceived group affiliations. Distinctions between in-group and out-group, often in the form of negative stereotypes, sustain prejudice. The difficulty in overcoming prejudice stems from the combination of psychological and social factors which serve to bolster it. Features of the social structure, such as class distinctions, employment and residential patterns, are structural elements sustaining prejudice. Allport indicates that there is an equally potent psychological structure which may breed and maintain prejudice. The basis for prejudice often resides in individual attitudes which are related to the ego needs discussed by Katz in Section VI. As Allport aptly notes, both perspectives on prejudice tell us that the problem ". . . is stitched into the fabric of social living." Yet, he advises caution lest we be falsely pessimistic about the prospects for change. Environmental supports for prejudice can be and are altered. Concern that people will not *accept* such change usually proves misplaced, especially where change is backed by law. Thus, studies of integration in the military services and in public housing demonstrate the effectiveness of legal supports in smoothing such change (e.g., Stouffer *et al.*, 1949, Vol. I, Ch. 10; Deutsch & Collins, 1951).

Allport's positive principles for dealing with prejudice are a useful summary of what is known about coping with intergroup relationships of this kind. Among his more noteworthy points, he argues against any single approach, and especially one which fails to accept cultural pluralism (see Gordon, Section II). While Allport favors open communication and the publishing of scientifically sound information, he stresses that educational programs are not a panacea since they have only limited utility by themselves. Because so much of prejudice is rationalized, campaigns of this kind can be equally well rationalized, as Bauer's paper in Section VI indicates, at least by implication.

In overcoming prejudice, Allport mainly urges active involvement through action programs that do something, apart from preaching and exhortation. On the other hand, Allport is encouraging about the long-range effectiveness of teaching children about prejudice and its nature as part of intercultural education.

The judgmental feature of prejudice is captured in the idea of stereotypes. As Campbell observes in his paper here, these can both reflect the character of the group being described and of the group doing the describing. Thus, the shared social reality of a group imposes a view of other groups as well as of itself. This phenomenon implicates processes of conformity, as discussed in Section VII. Pressures for adherence to the group's perspective, as evidence of loyalty, become especially demanding under conditions of intergroup conflict (see Sherif, 1961, 1966).

Adopting the adaptation level concept as a basis for analysis, Campbell indicates that the differences between groups are the aspects most likely to appear in the stereotyped imagery they have of each other. But there are still other variables at work in producing stereotypes, including the degree of actual contact between the groups. Even when groups are quite similar, however, they may generate reciprocal stereotypes which have a universal character. Thus, a highly prized characteristic, such as loyalty to one's own group, is seen as clannishness and exclusivity in the other group.

Campbell then considers the venerable issue of the validity or falseness of stereotypes and points out that a "grain of truth" may exist in a stereotype which in fact grew out of the very process of prejudice itself; thus, an undesirable consequence of segregation may be turned into an argument for its maintenance. After reviewing some of the more significant studies on stereotypes conducted over several decades, Campbell indi-

623

cates that while there is merit in emphasizing the "overall errorfulness" of stereotypes, this does not mean that group differences should be denied. In a trenchant argument, he contends that we can easily be taken in by the simplistic view that it is the different characteristics of the outgroup which *cause* hostility. He says that educational programs would benefit by less emphasis on denying or disproving stereotypes and more emphasis on the sequence by which hostility toward the out-group—whether generated by real threat, ethnocentrism, displacement, or whatever—*creates* the circumstances in which all possible differences are opportunistically interpreted as bad.

Bound into the problem of prejudice is the distinctive quality of the various subcultures within a society. In Section II, Pettigrew presents a picture of the effect of prejudice in producing a quality of life for the Negro which is at variance with the modal cultural pattern of American Society. This differential is made more acute by the inordinate number of Negroes who are represented among America's poor (see Harrington, 1963). In his paper here, Lewis briefly reviews the qualities he discerns in the "culture of poverty." His books, *The Children of Sanchez* (1961), a poignant account of a typical family in a poorer stratum of Mexican society, and *La Vida* (1965), about Puerto Rican migrants to New York, are significant additions to the documentation of life among the poor.

What Lewis has to say here about poverty, however, takes on a significance that transcends any given country or skin color. The marginality and alienation from organized society that he reports constitute a worldwide intergroup problem. A fair share of the world's population lives in the culture of poverty and this stands as a potent fact of life, with strong ideological overtones, which is not likely to diminish even with a broad program of social assistance for the satisfaction of physical survival needs. Indeed, the central idea that Lewis conveys is that poverty is as much a psychological state, with reference group features, as a state of want. In proposing and implementing programs to aid those who are poor, his point is that we recognize that cultural change is what is at stake. The potentialities for unrest inherent in a miscarriage of this social process are considerable, as Turner's paper here indicates.

Turner's main focus is on the way in which protest movements can be effective without increasing intergroup conflict. A pivotal point in his

624

analysis is the delicate balance represented in maintaining the legitimacy of a grievance, an image of injustice, while at the same time indulging in public displays of pressure, including disruption, that may lead to a sense of threat and immoderate fear. There are, Turner says, a number of elements of overriding significance to maintaining credibility in the eyes of the relevant public, prominent among them being that ". . . a disturbance must follow an extended period in which both the powerlessness and the grievances have been repeatedly and emphatically advertised." He also contends that a credible protest ideally displays some indication of restraint.

How various segments of the public perceive protest movements is itself an intriguing question. Turner finds that the groups who are in about the same position or even more disadvantaged than the protesters are *least* willing to grant a protest interpretation to disturbances. Furthermore, groups who live the greatest distance from the site of unrest are more inclined to accept the protest interpretation and to feel less threatened than those close to it. All in all, the maintenance of an optimal mixture of appeal and threat is difficult to achieve over a period of time. Turner sees the need for conciliation, not only to limit the intergroup character of the conflict but to symbolize the willingness to grant the injustice which has been done. Pushing beyond this point, he asserts, has potentially disastrous consequences in terms of the persisting relationships necessary in the society. Though bargaining is often indicated as a concomitant of conciliation, Turner raises the important caution that, as disturbances recur and become routinized, the cause of the protest may be undermined. The danger, he says, arises from the calculating nature of bargaining which, after a while, renders social protest as nothing more than moves in a competitive game. For this, and related considerations, Turner is not optimistic about what may be gained by the technique of disorderly protest when it is used repetitively.

When groups are in conflict, the problem of prejudice acquires a dimension that can produce violent results. One's own group is seen as noble in its aspirations and entirely justified in the actions it takes. The adversary is painted in precisely opposite terms. In open conflicts, such as warfare, each side asserts its determination not to compromise but to fight harder in the face of a setback. Where ideologies—in the sense of strongly held beliefs—are involved, force often produces the opposite effect from that intended. Group ties are intensified and willing sacrifice becomes increasingly normative.

Muzafer Sherif has conducted extensive studies in the area of intergroup conflict (see Sherif, 1958; Sherif & Sherif, 1953). He finds that a major device that appears to have a significant positive effect is the invocation of superordinate goals that have an appeal to both groups in the conflict. The analogue in the sphere of international relations is seen when two countries enter into an agreement, exemplified by many international treaties, because of the mutual advantage of a higher level goal to both parties.

One of the most striking findings in Sherif's work is the degree to which leadership is constrained by the group members' attitudes of hostility toward the competitive group (1962). It thus becomes more difficult for a leader to reach an accommodation with the other group lest he be seen as violating his group's position. The implications for this in terms of bargaining and negotiation are readily observed in such a crisis as a strike, where entrenched positions are held at least partly because of the heavy weight of prior attitudinal commitments within the contending groups. In line with Turner's observations, it can do little good to open discussions in such an atmosphere. If contact between leaders takes place in a context of hostility, and *without* the perception of superordinate goals to be achieved, then communication may only serve as a medium for further accusations and recriminations.

On the international scene, parallel patterns may be found though in more intensified form. Nations are political-geographical entities, but they also carry considerable psychological commitment for their citizenry. Manifestations of international conflict take on a particularly acute intensity with regard to shared attitudes of hostility or fear. In this context, Deutsch is concerned here with the broader policy questions surrounding the development of "mutual trust" to replace "mutual terror." His research on conflict dates back to his early work on interpersonal cooperation and competition (Deutsch 1949a, b). More recently, he has devoted attention to trust and threat, among other variables affecting bargaining and negotiation (see Deutsch, 1969).

The nub of the matter, from Deutsch's viewpoint, is that several kinds of psychological processes encourage trust, including a positive orientation to mutual welfare and signs of trustworthiness. He raises doubts about whether national policies aimed at military superiority and stable deterrence can, in and of themselves, induce a reduction of hostility and a movement toward trust. Thus, he notes among other points the endlessly regressive arms race quality of the former, and the built-in hazards of the latter. In particular, he points to the irrational elements that pervade these approaches and which make them fragile structures on which to rely. The alternatives he offers, from a social psychological perspective, emphasize rationality with a concomitant lessening of conditions leading to disorder and a strengthening of those conditions which are likely to maintain order.

Various proposals from social psychologists and other social scientists have been put forth along the same line recently. The growth of this interest is attested to in such books as Osgood (1962), Wright, Evan & Deutsch (1962), Kelman (1965), McNeil (1965), Sherif (1966), deRivera (1968), and Pruitt & Snyder (1969). Research on international systems, through "internation simulation" techniques, have also been pursued with promising results for the understanding of social psychological factors in international relations (see Guetzkow *et al.*, 1963).

The concluding paper here deals with the effects of life in the city. Given the character of our increasingly urban society, problems of intergroup relations are thrown into bold relief in cities, which have become their major arena. Various kinds of ethnic, religious, and social class distinctions are nudged up against one another, and the potentiality for conflict is rife. In his probing analysis, Milgram speaks to a number of the critical elements which go together to define the psychological qualities of city life.

Drawing from Louis Wirth's (1938) sociological analysis of the city, Milgram observes that the factors that he had distinguished in city life, i.e., large numbers of people, high density, and heterogeneity of population, are all linked to the modern concept of "overload." Accordingly, Milgram contends that the experience of city life must be understood as constituting ". . . a continuous set of encounters with adaptations to overload." And this, he says, shapes daily life in many ways, including role performance, social norms, and cognitive functioning. Most importantly, he discusses the implications of these effects for the individual's sense of social responsibility, involvement, and trust, and provides data from a number of unusual and imaginative experiments demonstrating differences in response from city dwellers and town dwellers, for example, in offering aid to a stranger. He concludes that it is not so much that the people are different but that they are responding to different contexts demanding adaptations which move the city dweller toward anonymity and uninvolvement, in a self-protective way.

On a grand scale, Milgram is dealing with the same kinds of elements and dynamics which propel the work of others with an ecological orientation represented here, i.e., Barker (Section I), Jackson (Section II), and Sommer (Section V). The city is the setting par excellence for a more intense mode of life, with the enhancement of pleasurable as well as painful experiences. At the same time that the new city dweller finds greater freedom and greater choices, as Gardner (1963) has pointed out, he may also encounter a detachment and fractionation of life. Milgram's analysis and studies lend more substance to the implications of this in terms of social psychological dimensions.

When the question of "relevance" is raised, it is evident that social psychology has made and offers the potential for making distinctive contributions to both the theoretical and practical side of intergroup and international relations. While it has no monopoly on answers to these extraordinarily complex and insistent problems, it provides an approach which stands as a constructive alternative or complement to others which have been tried. There are, for instance, historical, economic, political, and legal factors at work in intergroup relations, but those have long been foci of attention, often at the expense of the distinctly "human element" represented in social psychology's interest in the individual's construction of his world as it is influenced by his social milieu, especially cultural and group-based attachments. There is, therefore, more than a little hope that the further extension of social psychological concepts and research in this vital area may yield understanding aimed at social progress.

62   On reducing prejudice

GORDON W. ALLPORT

Special obstacles

Anyone who works in the field of intercultural relations knows how often in his community he hears the remark, "There is no problem." Parents, teachers, public officials, police, community leaders seem unaware of the undercurrents of friction and hostility. Until or unless violence breaks out "there is no problem" (see G. Watson, 1947).

We spoke earlier of the "mechanism of denial," of the tendency for the ego to defend itself when conflict threatens to upset its equilibrium. The strategy of denial is a quick reflex against disturbing thoughts.

Sometimes the denial is not so deeply bedded, but rests upon sheer habituation to the status quo. People are so accustomed to the prevailing system of caste and discrimination that they think it eternally fixed and entirely satisfactory to all concerned. We have mentioned the finding that most American whites believe that American Negroes are on the whole well satisfied with conditions as they are, an assumption woefully contrary to fact. But even conceding that honest ignorance and sheer habituation account for some of the denial, we must also grant that the deeper mechanism is often at work. We have previously seen that those who are deeply prejudiced are inclined to deny that they are prejudiced. Lacking personal insight, they are unable to take an objective view of conditions in their community. Even a citizen without prejudices of his own is likely to blind himself to injustices and tensions which, if acknowledged, could only upset the even tenor of his life.

One encounters this obstacle widely in school systems, where principals, teachers, and parents often oppose the introduction of intercultural education. Even in communities seething with prejudice we hear, "There is no problem; aren't we all Americans?" "Why put ideas into children's heads?" The attitude reminds us of the resistance shown by many parents, schools, and churches to sex education on the grounds that children might think taboo thoughts (that are surely already in their minds in a muddled fashion).

Some people have the tendency, through ignorance or through maliciousness, to identify all advocates of civil rights and all workers in behalf of ethnic relations as "subversive" elements. McCarthyism is a specter that haunts every worker in the field. While the victim himself sees through the irrationality of the name-calling, most citizens do not. They are led to perceive the worker and his program as vaguely allied to communism. How to combat this irrational overcategorization is a baffling problem. The realistic conflict between east-west ideologies spreads out to include total irrelevancies.

Excerpted from Chapter 31 of **The Nature of Prejudice**, Garden City: Doubleday-Anchor, 1958, pp. 463–75, with permission of the author and the copyright owners, Addison-Wesley Publishing Company, Incorporated.

All of these obstacles are profoundly serious, representing as they do the most firmly entrenched aspects of irrationalism in people and in social systems. But no one has thought that the task of improving group relations is an easy one.

The social system

The sociologist correctly points out that all of us are confined within one or more social systems. While these systems have some variability, they are not infinitely plastic. Within each system there will be inevitable tensions between groups, due to economic rivalry, crowded housing or transportation facilities, or to traditions of conflict. To meet the strain, the society accords certain groups a superior, and other groups an inferior, position. Custom regulates the distribution of limited privileges, goods, and prestige. Vested interests are pivots within the system, and these in particular resist any attempts at basic change. Further, tradition earmarks certain groups as legitimate scapegoats within the system. Hostility is taken for granted. For example, minor ethnic riots may be tolerated as by-products of the existing strain. Chiefs of police may wink at ethnic gang fights, declaring them normal and natural "kid stuff." To be sure, if the disruption goes too far, the riot squad is called for, or reformers press for legislative relief of the excess tension. But this relief is only sufficient to restore the uneasy equilibrium. If relief went too far it also would destroy the system.

The point of view of the economic determinist is similar. He argues that all theories of individual causation are eyewash. A basic structure exists wherein people with higher socioeconomic status cannot, and will not, tolerate equality between laborers, immigrants, Negroes, and other needed peons, and themselves. Prejudice is merely an invention to justify economic self-interest. Until some drastic reform brings true industrial democracy, there can be no effective alteration in the basic social foundations upon which all prejudice rests.

You and I are not normally aware of the extent to which our behavior is constrained and regulated by such features of the social system. We ought not to expect a few detached hours of intercultural education to offset the total press of the environment. People who see a pro-tolerance film will view it as a specific episode and not allow it to threaten the foundations of the system they live in.

The theory holds further that one cannot change segregation, employment customs, or immigration without letting off a chain of effects that would cumulate to produce threatening fractures in the total structure. Each folkway is an ally of every other. If too strong an initial push is allowed it might lead to an acceleration of forces that would destroy the whole system, and therewith our sense of security. Such is the structural view of the sociologist.

The psychologist, too, it will be recalled, has a structural argument. A prejudiced attitude is not like a cinder in the eye that can be extracted without disturbing the integrity of the organism as a whole. On the contrary, prejudice is often so deeply embedded in character-structure that it cannot be changed unless the entire inner economy of the life is overhauled. Such embeddedness occurs whenever attitudes have "functional significance" for the organism. You cannot expect to change the part without changing the whole.

And it is never easy to remake the whole of a personality.

Some authors stress the interlocking dependence of both the personal and the social system. They say that one must attack an attitude with due regard to both kinds of systems, which, in combination, hold the attitude embedded in a structural matrix (cf. Vallance, 1951). Newcomb states the case as follows: "Attitudes tend to be persistent (relatively unchanged) when the individual continues to perceive objects in a more or less stable frame of reference" (1950, p. 233). A stable frame of reference may be anchored in the social environment. (All immigrants live on one side of the tracks, all native Americans on the other.) Or it may be an *inner* frame of reference (I am threatened by any alien). Or it may be both. This combined structural view would insist that a shift in the relevant frames of reference must precede change in attitude.

Critique. Whether sociological, psychological, or both, the structural point of view has great merit. It explains why piecemeal efforts are not more effective than they are. It tells us that our problem is stitched into the fabric of social living. It convinces us that the cinder-in-the-eye theory is too simple.

Yet, if we are not careful, the structural view may lead both to false psychology and to false pessimism. It really is not sensible to say that before we change personal attitudes we must change total structure; for in part, at least, the structure is the product of the attitudes of many single people. Change must begin somewhere. Indeed, according to the structural theory, it may start *anywhere*, for every system is to some extent altered by the change in any of its parts. A social or a psycho-logical system is an equilibrium of forces, but it is an unstable equilibrium. The "American dilemma," for example, as Myrdal (1962) shows, is a case of such instability. All our official definitions of the social system call for equality, while many (not all) of the informal features of this system call for inequality. There is thus a state of "unstructuredness" in even our most structured systems. And while your personality or mine is certainly a system, can we say that it is impervious to change, or that alteration in the whole must *precede* alteration of parts? Such a view would be absurd.

Granted that America possesses a fairly stable class system wherein ethnic groups have an ascribed status, with prejudice as an accompaniment, still there are also in the American system factors that make for constant change. Americans, for example, seem to have great faith in the changeability of attitudes. The goliath of advertising in this country is erected on this faith; and we are equally confident in the power of education. Our system itself rejects the belief that "you can't change human nature." While this faith may not be entirely justified, the point is that the faith itself is a factor of prime importance. If everyone expects attitudes to change through education, publicity, therapy, then of course they are *more likely* to do so than if no one expects them to change. Our very gusto for change may bring it about, if anything can. A social system does not necessarily retard change; sometimes it encourages it.

Positive principles

We are not rejecting the structural argument, but rather pointing out that it cannot be used to justify total pessimism. It calls attention forcefully to limitations that exist, but does not deny that new horizons in human relationships are opening.

It is, for example, a perfectly sensible question to ask where, in order to alter social structure or personality structure, change may best begin. The following principles seem particularly germane.

1. Since the problem is many-sided, there can be no sovereign formula. The wisest thing to do is to attack all fronts simultaneously. If no single attack has large effect, yet many small attacks from many directions can have large cumulative results. They may even give the total system a push that will lead to accelerated change until a new and more agreeable equilibrium is attained.

2. Meliorism should be our guide. People who talk in terms of the ultimate assimilation of all minority groups into one ethnic stock are speaking of a distant Utopia. To be sure, there would be no minority-group problems in a homogeneous society, but it seems probable that in the United States our loss would be greater than our gain. In any case, it is certain that artificial attempts to hasten assimilation will not succeed. We shall improve human relations only by learning to live with racial and cultural pluralism for a long time to come.

3. It is reasonable to expect that our efforts will have some unsettling effects. The attack on a system always has. Thus a person who has been exposed to the intercultural education, to tolerance propaganda, to role-playing, may show greater inconsistency of behavior than before. But from the point of view of attitude change, this state of "unstructuredness" is a necessary stage. A wedge has been driven. While the individual may be more uncomfortable than before, he has at least a chance of recentering his outlook in a more tolerant manner. Investigation shows that people who are aware of, and ashamed of, their prejudices are well on the road to eliminating them (cf. G. W. Allport & Kramer, 1946).

4. Occasionally there may be a "boomerang effect." Efforts may serve only to stiffen opposition in defense of existing attitudes, or offer people unintended support for their hostile opinions (Hovland, et al., 1949, pp. 46–50). Such evidence as we have indicates that this effect is relatively slight. It also is a question whether the effect may not be temporary, for any strategy sufficiently effective to arouse defensiveness may at the same time plant seeds of misgiving.

5. From what we know of mass media, it seems wise not to expect marked results from this method alone. Relatively few people are in the precise stage of "unstructuredness," and in precisely the right frame of mind, to admit the message. Further, it seems well, on the basis of existing evidence, to focus mass propaganda on specific issues rather than upon vague appeals that may not be understood.

6. The teaching and publishing of scientifically sound information concerning the history and characteristics of groups, and about the nature of prejudice, certainly does no harm. Yet it is not the panacea that many educators like to believe. The outpouring of information probably has three benign effects: (a) It sustains the confidence of minorities to see an effort being made to blanket prejudice with truth. (b) It encourages and reinforces tolerant people by integrating their attitudes with knowledge. (c) It tends to undermine

the rationalization of bigots. Belief in the biological inferiority of the Negro, for example, is wavering under the impact of scientific fact; racist doctrines today are on the defensive. Erroneous ideas, Spinoza observed, lead to passion —for they are so confused that no one can use them as a basis for realistic adjustment. Correct and adequate ideas, by contrast, pave the way for a true assessment of life's problems. While not everyone will admit correct ideas when they are offered, it is well to make them available.

7. Action is ordinarily better than mere information. Programs do well therefore to involve the individual in some project, perhaps a community self-survey or a neighborhood festival. When he *does* something, he *becomes* something. The deeper the acquaintance and the more realistic the contacts, the better the results.

By working in the community, for example, the individual may learn that neither his self-esteem nor his attachments are actually threatened by Negro neighbors. He may learn that his own security as a citizen is strengthened when social conditions improve. While preaching and exhortation may play a part in the process, the lesson will not be learned at the verbal level alone. It will be learned in muscle, nerve, and gland best through participation.

8. None of our commonly used methods is likely to work with bigots whose character structure is so inaccessible that it demands the exclusion of out-groups as a condition of life. Yet even for the rigid person there is left the possibility of individual therapy— an expensive method and one that is sure to be resisted; but in principle at least, we need not yet despair completely of the extreme case, especially if tackled young, perhaps in clinics of child guidance, or by wise teachers.

9. While there is no relevant research on the point, it seems likely that ridicule and humor help to prick the pomposity and irrational appeal of rabble-rousers. Laughter is a weapon against bigotry. It too often lies rusty while reformers grow unnecessarily solemn and heavy-handed.

10. Turning now to social programs (the social system), there is first of all considerable agreement that it is wiser to attack segregation and discrimination than to attack prejudice directly. For even if one dents the attitudes of the individual in isolation, he is still confronted by social norms that he cannot surmount. And until segregation is weakened, conditions will not exist that permit equal-status contacts in pursuit of common objectives.

11. It would seem intelligent to take advantage of the vulnerable points where social change is most likely to occur. As Saenger says, "Concentrate on the areas of least resistance." Gains in housing and economic opportunities are, on the whole, the easiest to achieve. Fortunately, it is these very gains that minorities most urgently desire.

12. Generally speaking, a *fait accompli* that fits in with our democratic creed is accepted with little more than an initial flurry of protest. Cities that introduce Negroes into public jobs find that the change soon ceases to attract attention. Sound legislation is similarly accepted. Official policies once established are hard to revoke. They set models that, once accepted, create habits and conditions favorable to their maintenance.

Administrators, more than they realize, have the power to establish desirable changes by executive order in industry, government, and schools. In 1848 a Negro applied for admission to Harvard College. There were loud protests. Edward Everett, then President, replied, "If this boy passes the examinations he will be admitted and, if the white students choose to withdraw, all the income of the college will be devoted to his education" (Frothingham, 1925, p. 299). Needless to say, no one withdrew, and the opposition quickly subsided. The College lost neither income nor prestige, though both at first seemed threatened. Clean-cut administrative decisions that brook no further argument are accepted when such decisions are in keeping with the voice of conscience.

13. The role of the militant reformer must not be forgotten. It is the noisy demands of crusading liberals that have been a decisive factor in many of the gains thus far made.

These conclusions represent some of the positive principles that derive from research and theory. They are not intended as a complete blueprint—such would be pretentious. The points represent rather certain wedges which if driven with skill might be expected to crack the crust of prejudice and discrimination.

Imperatives of intercultural education

Without prolonging our discussion of programs unduly, we wish to call attention once more to the role of the school. We do so partly because of the characteristic faith that Americans have in education, and partly because it is easier to install remedial programs in the school than in the home. School children comprise a vast captive audience; they study what is set before them.

While school boards, principals, and teachers may resist the introduction of intercultural education, yet it is increasingly included in the curriculum.

Learning prejudice and learning tolerance are subtle and complex processes. The home is undoubtedly more important than the school. And the *atmosphere* of the home is as important, perhaps more important, than the parents' specific teaching concerning minority groups.

It is probably too much to expect teachers to offset the home environment, and yet, as the evaluative studies cited [see G. W. Allport, 1958. Ch. 30] show, a good deal can be accomplished. The school, like the church and the laws of the land, can set before the child a higher code than is learned at home, and may create a conscience and a healthful conflict even if the prejudiced teachings of the home are not entirely overcome.

As in the home, the atmosphere that surrounds the child at school is exceedingly important. If segregation of the sexes or races prevails, if authoritarianism and hierarchy dominate the system, the child cannot help but learn that power and status are the dominant factors in human relationships. If, on the other hand, the school system is democratic, if the teacher and child are each respected units, the lesson of respect for the person will easily register. As in society at large the *structure* of the pedagogical system will blanket, and may negate, the specific intercultural lessons taught (Brameld, 1946).

We have seen that instruction of the sort that involves the whole child in intercultural activities is probably more effective than merely verbal learning or exhortation. While information is likewise essential, facts stick best when embedded in the soil of interested activity.

Granted these points, the question remains as to what concrete lessons the child or adolescent should learn in the course of his school training. What should be the *content* of intercultural education? Here, as before, we cannot claim that all evidence is in. But we may suggest a few of the imperatives for intergroup education.

The age at which these lessons should be taught need not worry us. If taught in a simple fashion all the points can be made intelligible to younger children and, in a more fully developed way, they can be presented to older students in high school or college. In fact, at different levels of advancement, through "graded lessons," the same content can, and should, be offered year after year.

(1) *Meaning of race.* Various films, filmstrips, and pamphlets are available for school use; these present anthropological facts in as much detail as the child can absorb. The child should certainly learn the confusion that occurs between genetic and social definitions of race. For example, he should understand that many "colored" people are racially as much Caucasian as Negro, but that a caste definition obscures this biological fact. The misconceptions of racism in its various forms, and the psychology underlying racist myths, can be made clear to older children.

(2) *Customs and their significance in various ethnic groups.* Schools have traditionally taught this lesson, but in a dubious way. Modern exhibits and festivals give a more adequate impression, as do reports in the classroom from children who come from diverse ethnic backgrounds. Especially needed are sympathetic accounts of linguistic and religious backgrounds, with particular reference to the significance of religious holy days. Visits to places of worship in the community help anchor the lesson.

(3) *Nature of group differences.* Less easy to teach, but needed for the purpose of generalizing the two preceding lessons, is a sound understanding of the ways in which human groups differ and do not differ. It is here that fallacious stereotypes can be combatted, likewise "belief in essence." The fact that some differences are merely imaginary, some fall on overlapping normal curves, and some follow a *J*-curve distribution, can be taught in a simplified way. A child who understands the precise nature of group differences is less likely to form overbroad categories. The lesson should likewise include a restatement of the role of biological and social factors in producing these differences.

(4) *Nature of tabloid thinking.* Fairly early, children can be made critical of their own too simple categories. They can learn that Foreigner 1 is not the same as Foreigner 2. They can be shown how the law of linguistic precedence in learning creates dangers for them, particularly in the form of derogatory epithets such as "nigger" and "wop." Simple lessons in semantics and in elementary psychology are neither dull nor incomprehensible to children.

(5) *The scapegoating mechanism.* Even a seven-year-old can understand the displacement of guilt and aggression. As children grow older they can see the relevance of this principle to the persecution of minority groups throughout the ages.

(6) *Traits sometimes resulting from victimization.* The way in which ego defenses develop as a result of persecution is not hard to understand—though it is a delicate lesson to teach. The danger lies in creating a stereotype to the effect that *all* Jews are ambitious and aggressive in order to compensate for their handicaps; or that all Negroes are inclined to sullen hate or petty thieving.

The lesson can, however, be taught without primary reference to minority groups. It is essentially a lesson in mental hygiene. Through fiction, to start with, a youngster may learn of the compensations a handicapped (perhaps crippled) child develops. He may go from that point to a discussion of hypothetical cases in class. Through role-playing he may gain insight into the operation of ego defenses. By the age of fourteen the adolescent may be led to see that his own insecurity is due to his lack of firm ground: he is sometimes expected to act like a child, sometimes like an adult. He wants to be an adult, but the conduct of others makes him unsure of whether he belongs to the world of childhood or of adulthood. The teacher may point out that the predicament of the adolescent resembles the permanent uncertainty under which many minority groups have to live. Like adolescents, they sometimes show restlessness, tension, ego defensiveness, which occasionally lead to objectionable behavior. It is far better for the young person to learn the grounds for ego-defensive behavior than for him to be left with the idea that objectionable traits are inherent in certain groups of mankind.

(7) *Facts concerning discrimination and prejudice.* Pupils should not be kept ignorant of the blemishes of the society in which they live. They should know that the American Creed demands more equality than has been achieved. Children should know about the inequalities of housing and educational and job opportunities. They should know how Negroes and other minorities feel about their situation; what it is they especially resent; what hurts their feelings; and what elementary courtesies are in order. Films may be used in this connection, so too the "literature of protest," especially biographical accounts of young American Negroes, such as Richard Wright's *Black Boy.*

(8) *Multiple loyalties are possible.* Schools have always inculcated patriotism, but the terms of allegiance are often narrowly conceived The fact that loyalty to the nation requires loyalty to all subgroups within the nation is seldom pointed out. The institutional patriot, the superpatriotic nationalist, is more often than not a thoroughgoing bigot. The teaching of exclusive loyalty —whether to nation, school, fraternity, or family—is a method of instilling prejudice. The child may be brought up to see that loyalties are concentric, the larger may contain the smaller, with no exclusion implied.

63 Stereotypes and the perception of group differences

DONALD T. CAMPBELL

Perception and group stereotypes of other groups

If we take the stereotypes or images which persons or groups have of each other, we see that such stereotypes can at one and the same time reflect both the character of the group being described, and projectively, the character of the group doing the describing or holding the stereotypes (as Allport, 1954, emphasizes). This frees us from the either-or analysis of stereotypes in which, when interpreting stereotypes to be symptoms of the preoccupations of the stereotype holder, one implicitly regards the outgroup as a "living ink-blot" (e.g., Ackerman & Jahoda, 1950) whose characteristics, if any, are independent of the content of the stereotype. In the terms of Zawadski's (1942) analysis, the "well-deserved reputation" theory of prejudiced stereotypes and the "scape-goating" theory can both be appropriate in the same setting.

In many instances, the relative strength of various stimuli is obvious—in general, the more physical energy in a physical stimulus such as sound wave or light beam, the stronger the stimulus strength. However, closer analysis shows that a still more appropriate statement of stimulus strength is in terms of *relative* physical energy in contrast to previous stimulations or stimuli from other parts of the stimulus field, i.e., relative to *adaptation level* (Campbell & Kral, 1958; Helson, 1964; Krantz & Campbell, 1961). A stimulus intensity below the adaptation level can be as stimulating as one above. Thus, turning the light off in a room can be as striking a stimulus as turning the light on. Thus, rats can be conditioned to jump to the turn-off of an otherwise continuous sound as well as to the turn-on of a sound interrupting an otherwise continuous silence. Thus, the same saline solution can taste salty on one occasion and sweet on another, depending on what saturation the mouth has previously been adapted to.

The upshot of this principle is that the greatest contrasts provide the strongest stimuli. When we consider the perceptions which groups will have of each other, this prediction results: *The greater the real differences between groups on any particular custom, detail of physical appearance, or item of material culture, the more likely it is that that feature will appear in the stereotyped imagery each group has of the other.*

Note that this prediction implies that attributes of a group which in some intergroup contexts would go totally unnoticed, may become the object of vivid disparaging imagery by other groups in a cultural context in which this stands out.

Other features than group differences per se also contribute to stimulus strength: The more opportunities for observation and the longer the exposure to the outgroup, the larger the role of real differences in the stereotypes. This implies that the nearer outgroups will be more accurately stereotyped, and that outgroups with which most interchange of persons and interaction occurs will be most accurately stereotyped. To state it in opposite terms: The more remote and less well known the outgroup, the more purely projective the content of the stereotype and the less accurate it will be. An analogous principle recognizes that the content of intergroup interaction provides greatest stimulus strength for those traits invoked in the interaction: Those trait differences involved in intergroup interaction will be most strongly and accurately represented in mutual stereotypes. Another important principle is that among trait differences of approximately equal contrast, those which are drive and incentive relevant, and which are familiar, are most apt to be noticed and represented

in stereotyped imagery. We assume from other analyses such as frustration-aggression-displacement theory that there is a positive incentive for disparaging the outgroup; thus, those stimuli most offering opportunity for this response will be most represented in stereotypes. The subset chosen is thus symptomatic of the intrapsychic determinants of the ingroup.

For a given individual, this implies that the more familiar he is with making prejudiced statements, the easier such a statement will appear on any given occasion—or the more readily the stereotyped difference will be perceived. This does not provide a very useful prediction at the group level—except some sort of perseveration or inertia to stereotypes: Once a stereotype or perception of differences is established, less real difference is required to maintain or revoke it.

The above analysis deals with traits on which groups differ. Similar effects can occur for certain traits on which groups are similar, but for which the conditions of observation are such that the behavior on one's own part is per-

SELF-DESCRIPTION	STEREOTYPE OF OUTGROUP
1. We have pride, self-respect and revere the traditions of our ancestors.	They are egotistical and self-centered. They love themselves more than they love us.
2. We are loyal.	They are clannish, exclude others.
3. We are honest and trustworthy among ourselves, but we're not suckers when foreigners try their tricks.	They will cheat us if they can. They have no honesty or moral restraint when dealing with us.
4. We are brave and progressive. We stand up for our own rights, defend what is ours, and can't be pushed around or bullied.	They are aggressive and expansionistic. They want to get ahead at our expense.
5. We are peaceful, loving people, hating only our vile enemies.	They are a hostile people who hate us.
6. We are moral and clean.	They are immoral and unclean.

ceived in a different context than is comparable behavior on the part of an outgrouper. This will be particularly true of behavior directed toward the outgroup. Such "mote-beam" or "pot-calling-the-kettle-black" sets of reciprocal stereotypes have been noted by a number of observers (e.g., Bronfenbrenner, 1961; Ichheiser, 1947; Merton, 1957). If most or all groups are in fact ethnocentric, then it becomes an "accurate" stereotype to accuse an outgroup of some aspects of ethnocentrism. This generates a set of "universal" stereotypes, of which each ingroup might accuse each outgroup, or some outgroup, or the average outgroup (Campbell & LeVine, 1961).

This last point is, of course, based upon differences in particular customs, but becomes a universal stereotype if the particular ingredients of immorality and uncleanliness are not specified.

Social psychology's emphasis on the falseness of stereotypes

The prediction that the greater a difference between groups, the more likely that difference will appear in the stereotypes they hold of each other, seems obvious when one starts from the anthropological position that groups, cultures, etc., do in fact differ, and asks then the question as to how these differences will be treated in mutual imagery. Sociology also provides an expectation of a "grain of truth" in stereotypes, in descriptions of social class differences and the tendency for ethnic groups to become concentrated in one social class. Thus across-class ethnic stereotypes might be expected to involve a group of one class accusing groups of another class of having class-related

traits. (For example, popular American stereotypes of Negroes and Mexicans predominately attribute to them lower-class attributes.) Role specialization within class, as by trade or profession, provide further sociological basis for a "grain of truth" in stereotypes. Still more relevant is the extensive sociological analysis of the effects on personality, aspirations, achievement effort, and moral behavior caused by oppressed minority status, segregation, lack of access to upward social mobility, and exclusion from the larger moral community. As Allport (1954) has emphasized, minority status has effects, producing "traits due to victimization." Such differences might be expected to appear in majority group stereotypes of minority groups. Such stereotypes would have the great unfairness of justifying segregation by "validly" accusing minority group members of having the very traits which segregation had produced. Nonetheless, taken as descriptions (rather than as justifications or causal explanations, as will be discussed below), they would have a "grain of truth."

In contrast to such anthropological and sociological bases for expecting real group differences to provide in some sense "accurate" components for stereotypes, there has grown up in social and educational psychology a literature and teaching practice which says that all stereotypes of group differences are false, and, implicitly, that all groups are on the average identical.

This social-psychological literature was perhaps started by the excellent and classic study of Katz and Braly (1933) which showed that college students had stable and elaborate stereotypes of a wide variety of minority and nationality groups. They found no relation between the elaborateness and uniformity of these stereotypes and the amount of contact with the groups in question. For groups actually quite unknown, such as the Turks and the Japanese, there were as vivid stereotypes of as high consensus as there was for more familiar groups such as American Negroes. Other research of the 1930s showed that whites with no personal acquaintance with Negroes held, if anything, more elaborate and disparaging stereotypes of them than did whites who had Negro acquaintances (Horowitz, 1936; Minard, 1931; Smith, 1943). A classic study by LaPiere (1936) showed that when checked, the stereotype held in Fresno, California, about the local Armenian minority was point-by-point in error. Levinson and Sanford (1944) showed that anti-Semites accused Jews of such contrary traits as both sticking to themselves and trying to force themselves into gentile society (Harding, Kutner, Proshansky, & Chein, 1954, provide an extensive review of the many similar studies).

Certainly this literature did demonstrate that stereotypes can be completely false and can be held in absence of validating contact with the group in question. But aside from the one La-Piere study, there was little or no comparison of the content of stereotypes with the corresponding social statistics and anthropological data. Neglected were comparisons of the group data on intelligence test performance (e.g., Klineberg, 1944, pp. 82–96) and the stereotypes about stupidity and shrewdness (relevant even though functional intelligence be recognized as poor evidence of innate intelligence). There was little or no recognition of the fact that predominantly lower-class minority groups were being accused of the lower-class morality and the lack of achieve-ment orientation also demonstrated in the sociologist's statistics. This summary is perhaps overdrawn, and certainly Gordon Allport (1954) and Krech and Crutchfield (1948, pp. 171–172) must be exempted, but it is probably an accurate description of most teachings about prejudice and stereotypes in social psychology courses offered in psychology and education departments even today.

While stereotypes may often have a grain of descriptive truth, social psychologists have been, of course, right in emphasizing their overall errorfulness. The problem is how to state the errors, without claiming that all groups are identical.

The first wrongness is in the phenomenal absolutism of the normal ingroup member's imagery of the outgrouper or minority group member. Naïvely, one assumes without question that the outgroup is as one perceives it, or as the ingroup informs one about it. Awareness that one's own preoccupations have projectively contributed to the content, that fallible communication and knowledge processes are involved, that the image could be totally wrong, or even where correct, can be selectively distorted and emphasized—all such awareness is lacking. For many a social psychologist, his own overcoming such an ethnocentric enculturation is a deeply experienced revelation, and one he wants to communicate. In so doing, the message that stereotypes contain a large portion of error and projection becomes overcompensated into an implicit denial of group differences. The message that stereotypes of groups or images of specific others contain a projective contribution from one's own (or one's ingroup's) personality, either in fabricated content or in selective attention to pejorative content, is an unsuspected lesson which every normal undergraduate needs to learn. But it must be taught without denying group differences.

A second wrongness is in the degree of difference perceived, the exaggeration of the homogeneity with which either ingroup or outgroup members have the trait in question, and the underestimation of the amount of overlap between the groups as Allport (1954) has emphasized. If test results in a given community (e.g., Klineberg, 1944) were to provide an average IQ of 95 for Negroes and 103 for Jews to be compared with 100 for the general population, the corresponding stereotypes would be that all Negroes are dumb, all Jews are smart. If an average person were asked what percent of all Negroes are brighter than he is, he probably would give a reply nearer to none or 5%, rather than the 38% figure to which the 95 IQ figure would more nearly correspond. Such effects correspond to pervasive cognitive processes, noted in perception research as the enhancement of contrast through homogenization of differences within gestalt boundaries and the exaggeration of differences across boundaries. The effect for a group learning situation follows directly (if tediously) from elementary considerations of stimulus generalization in learning theory. In a classroom in which there is some average race difference in examination performance, in intermediate stages when students know something of the performance levels of their individual classmates, and in which skin color leads to greater generalization (or confusion) within racial groupings than between, the generalization effect predictably leads to the underestimation of the overlap between the two groups (Campbell, 1956; Clarke & Campbell, 1955). Thus another contribution of learning and perception theory is the law that differ-

ences between ingroup and outgroup, if sufficient to be noted, will be exaggerated in the mutual stereotypes each holds of the other. Awareness of any such bias is, of course, absent phenomenally.

A third wrongness in the naïve ingrouper's stereotypes of outgroups is an erroneous causal perception (e.g., Heider, 1944; Michotte, 1946, 1962). This is the tendency to perceive racial rather than environmental causes for group differences. Perception of causality occurs most readily between stimuli that are spatially and temporally contiguous. It centers around those stimuli which are strongest, most vivid, and striking. Again, contrast provides this stimulus strength. To take a domestic American example, the white person in contact with uneducated Negroes might conceivably perceive the lack of education as caused by the environmental background. But stimuli representing the environmental factors are not present or visible in the immediate situation. In addition, they are multiple, diffuse, and complex. On the other hand, the stimuli of race such as skin color, physiognomy, accent, and name, are visible and vivid. They are also spatially and temporally contiguous to the patent signs of uneducatedness. Thus the established principles of causal perception strongly favor the perception of race as the cause of the ignorance. A parallel conditioned-response analysis is also possible, coming to the same predictions (Campbell, 1963, pp. 122–123).

A fourth error is also one of causal misperception and is the most important although the most difficult to explicate. It has to do with the relationship between the content of the stereotype and the hostility felt toward the outgroup. The naïve ingrouper perceives the different characteristics of the outgroup as causing his hostility (Ichheiser, 1949). He feels that were it not for these despicable traits, the outgroup would be loved. The outgroup's opprobrious characteristics seem to him to fully justify the hostility and rejection he shows toward it. The social scientist sees the opposite causal direction: Causally, first is the hostility toward the outgrouper, generated perhaps by real threat, perhaps by ethnocentrism, perhaps by displacement. In the service of this hostility, all possible differences are opportunistically interpreted as despicable, and the most plausibly despicable traits are given most attention.

So flexible is our emotional language that a difference in almost any direction can be anathematized. An outgroup can be hated as too lazy or as too industrious, as too dumb or as too shrewd, as too forward or too reclusive, as too emotional or as too cold, as too generous or too thrifty (Merton, 1949). In southern legislatures in the last 100 years, the alleged intellectual inferiority of Negroes has played an important role. Removing the belief that Negroes are inferior would not, however, remove the hostility, although it would change the content of stereotype. Had the World War I test results showing northern Negroes to be more intelligent than southern whites been effectively publicized in the South, opportunistic hostility could certainly have created an image of the northern Negro carpetbagger whose opprobrious traits included shrewdness, trickiness, and egg-headed intellectuality. Remedial education in race relations focused on denying or disproving stereotypes implicitly accepts the prejudiced ingrouper's causal conception rather than the social scientists', and is undermined where actual group differences are found.

64   The culture of poverty

OSCAR LEWIS

I want to take this opportunity to clear up some possible misunderstanding concerning the idea of a "culture of poverty." I would distinguish sharply between impoverishment and the culture of poverty. Not all people who are poor necessarily live in or develop a culture of poverty. For example, middle class people who become impoverished do not automatically become members of the culture of poverty, even though they may have to live in the slums for a while. Similarly, the Jews who lived in poverty in eastern Europe did not develop a culture of poverty because their tradition of literacy and their religion gave them a sense of identification with Jews all over the world. It gave them a sense of belonging to a community which was united by a common heritage and common religious beliefs.

In the introduction to *The Children of Sanchez* (Lewis, 1961), I listed approximately fifty traits which constitute what I call the culture of poverty. Although poverty is only one of the many traits which, in my judgment, go together, I have used it to name the total system because I consider it terribly important. However, the other traits, and especially the psychological and ideological ones, are also important and I should like to elaborate on this a bit.

The helpless and the homeless

The people in the culture of poverty have a strong feeling of marginality, of helplessness, of dependency, of not belonging. They are like aliens in their own country, convinced that the existing institutions do not serve their interests and needs. Along with this feeling of powerlessness is a widespread feeling of inferiority, of personal unworthiness. This is true of the slum dwellers of Mexico City, who do not constitute a distinct ethnic or racial group and do not suffer from racial discrimination. In the United States the culture of poverty of the Negroes has the additional disadvantage of racial discrimination.

People with a culture of poverty have very little sense of history. They are a marginal people who know only their own troubles, their own local conditions, their own neighborhood, their own way of life. Usually, they have neither the knowledge, the vision nor the ideology to see the similarities between their problems and those of others like themselves elsewhere in the world. In other words, they are not class conscious, although they are very sensitive indeed to status distinctions. When the poor become class conscious or members of trade union organizations, or when they adopt an internationalist outlook on the world they are, in my view, no longer part of the culture of poverty although they may still be desperately poor.

Is it all bad?

The idea of a culture of poverty that cuts across different societies enables us

Reprinted from **Trans-action**, 1963, 1, 17–19, with permission of the author and the publisher.

to see that many of the problems we think of as distinctively our own or distinctively Negro problems (or that of any other special racial or ethnic group), also exist in countries where there are no ethnic groups involved. It also suggests that the elimination of physical poverty as such may not be enough to eliminate the culture of poverty which is a whole way of life. One can speak readily about wiping out poverty; but to wipe out a culture or sub-culture is quite a different matter, for it raises the basic question of our respect for cultural differences.

Middle class people, and this certainly includes most social scientists, tend to concentrate on the negative aspects of the culture of poverty; they tend to have negative feelings about traits such as an emphasis on the present and a neglect of the future, or on concrete as against abstract orientations. I do not intend to idealize or romanticize the culture of poverty. As someone has said, "It is easier to praise poverty than to live it." However, we must not overlook some of the positive aspects that may flow from these traits. Living immersed in the present may develop a capacity for spontaneity, for the enjoyment of the sensual, the indulgence of impulse, which is too often blunted in our middle class future-oriented man. Perhaps it is this reality of the moment that middle class existentialist writers are so desperately trying to recapture, but which the culture of poverty experiences as a natural, everyday phenomenon. The frequent use of violence certainly provides a ready outlet for hostility, so that people in the culture of poverty suffer less from repression than does the middle class.

In this connection, I should also like to take exception to the trend in some studies to identify the lower class almost exclusively with vice, crime and juvenile delinquency, as if most poor people were thieves, beggars, ruffians, murderers or prostitutes. Certainly, in my own experience in Mexico, I found most of the poor decent, upright, courageous and lovable human beings. I believe it was the novelist Fielding who wrote, "The sufferings of the poor are indeed less observed than their misdeeds."

It is interesting that much the same ambivalence in the evaluation of the poor is reflected in proverbs and in literature. Some see the poor as virtuous, upright, serene, independent, honest, secure, kind, simple and happy, while others see them as evil, mean, violent, sordid and criminal.

Most people in the United States find it difficult to think of poverty as a stable, persistent, ever present phenomenon, because our expanding economy and the specially favorable circumstances of our history have led to an optimism which makes us think that poverty is transitory. As a matter of fact, the culture of poverty in the United States is indeed of *relatively* limited scope; but as Michael Harrington (1963) and others show, it is probably more widespread than has been generally recognized.

Poverty here and abroad

In considering what can be done about the culture of poverty, we must make a sharp distinction between those countries in which it involves a relatively small segment of the population, and those in which it constitutes a very large section. Obviously, the solutions will have to differ in these two areas.

In the United States, the major solution proposed by planners and social workers for dealing with what are called "multiple problem families," the "undeserving poor," and the "hard core of poverty," is slowly to raise their level of living and eventually incorporate them into the middle class. And, wherever possible, there is some reliance upon psychiatric treatment in an effort to imbue these "shiftless, lazy, unambitious people" with the higher middle class aspirations.

In the undeveloped countries, where great masses of people share in the culture of poverty, I doubt that social work solutions are feasible. Nor can psychiatrists begin to cope with the magnitude of the problem. They have all they can do to deal with the growing middle class.

In the United States, delinquency, vice and violence represent the major threats to the middle class from the culture of poverty. In our country there is no threat of revolution. In the less developed countries of the world, however, the people who live in the culture of poverty may one day become organized into political movements that seek fundamental revolutionary changes and that is one reason why their existence poses terribly urgent problems.

If my brief outline of the basic psychological aspects of the culture of poverty is essentially sound, then it may be more important to offer the poor of the world's countries a genuinely revolutionary ideology rather than the promise of material goods or a quick rise in the standards of living.

It is conceivable that some countries can eliminate the culture of poverty (at least in the early stages of their industrial revolution) without at first eliminating impoverishment, by changing the value systems and attitudes of the people so they no longer feel helpless and homeless—so they begin to feel that they are living in their own country, with their institutions, their government and their leadership.

65   The public perception of protest

RALPH H. TURNER

The year 1965 marked a dramatic turning point in American reactions to racial
disorder. Starting with Watts, dominant
community sentiment and the verdicts
of politically sensitive commissions have
identified mass violence by blacks primarily as acts of social protest. In
spite of its well advertized failings,
the McCone Commission (Governor's
Commission on the Los Angeles Riots,
1965) devoted most of its attention to
reporting the justified complaints of
Negroes and proposing their amelioration. The Kerner Report (National Advisory Commission on Civil Disorders,
1968) went further in predicating
recommendations for action on the assumption that disorders must be understood as acts of social protest, and not
merely as crime, anti-social violence, or
revolutionary threats to law and order.
A few earlier bodies had seen minority
protest as a component in racial disorders (Silver, 1968), but in most cases
these commissions were far removed
from the political process. Even when
whites had perpetrated most of the
violence, public officials before 1965
typically vented their most intense anger
against Negroes, Negro leaders, and
their white allies (Lee and Humphrey,
1943; Rudwick, 1964). If comparable
data were available from earlier racial
disturbances, it is unlikely they would
match Morris and Jeffries' (1967, p. 5)
finding that 54% in a sample of white

Los Angeles residents viewed the disturbance as Negro protest.

The aim of this paper is to suggest
several theoretical vantage points from
which to predict when a public will and
will not view a major disturbance as an
act of social protest. Historically, labor
strife has sometimes been understood as
protest and sometimes not. Apparently
the protest meaning in the activities of
Caesar Chavez and his farm laborers is
discounted by most Americans today.
A gang *rumble* is seldom viewed as
protest, even when Puerto Ricans and
other minorities are prominently involved. Three-fourths of an unspecified
sample of Los Angeles residents in May,
1969, are reported to have seen disorders
in secondary schools as the work of agitators and not as social protest (Los
Angeles Times, May 19, 1969), even
though Mexican-Americans and blacks
have played the leading roles. Events of
early 1969 hint at a rising movement to
redefine all racial and youthful disturbances in other terms than social protest.

The meaning of protest. Protest has
been defined as "an expression or declaration of objection, disapproval, or dissent, often in opposition to something
a person is powerless to prevent or
avoid" (Random House Dictionary,
1967). An act of protest includes the
following elements: the action expresses
a grievance, a conviction of wrong or
injustice; the protestors are unable to

Abridged from the **American Sociological Review**, 1969, 34, 815–31, with permission of the author
and the publisher.

correct the condition directly by their own efforts; the action is intended to draw attention to the grievances; the action is further meant to provoke ameliorative steps by some target group; and the protestors depend upon some combination of sympathy and fear to move the target group in their behalf. Protest ranges from relatively persuasive to relatively coercive combinations (Bayley, 1962), but always includes both. Many forms of protest involve no violence or disruption, but these will not concern us further in this paper.

When violence and disorder are identified as social protest, they constitute a mode of communication more than a form of direct action. Looting is not primarily a means of acquiring property, as it is normally viewed in disaster situations (Dynes and Quarantelli, 1968); breaking store windows and burning buildings is not merely a perverted form of amusement or immoral vengeance like the usual vandalism and arson; threats of violence and injury to persons are not simply criminal actions. All are expressions of outrage against injustice of sufficient magnitude and duration to render the resort to such exceptional means of communication understandable to the observer.

In deciding that individuals view a disturbance as social protest, it is helpful but not conclusive to note whether they apply the term protest. Defining a disturbance as protest does not preclude disapproving the violence or disorder by which the protest is expressed, nor does it preclude advocating immediate measures to control and suppress the disturbance.

Definitions by publics. We assume that individuals and groups of individuals assign simplifying meanings to

events, and then adjust their perceptions of detail to these comprehensive interpretations. Lemert's (1951) pioneering examination of deviance as a label applied by society's agents serves as a valuable prototype for the analysis of responses to public disturbances. We scrupulously avoid assuming that there are objectifiable phenomena that must be classified as deviance, as protest, or as rebellion. We further assume that participant motivations are complex and diverse, so that a given disturbance is not simply protest, or not protest, according to participant motives. Just as Negroes and whites used different labels for the Watts disturbance (Tomlinson and Sears, 1967), we also assume that publics will often interpret the events quite differently from the participants.

The question of labelling disturbances has been examined by other investigators from somewhat different points of view. Lang and Lang (1968) have observed that the label "riot" is used to identify quite different kinds of events that are similar only in the kind of official response they evoke. Grimshaw (1968) pointed out the different labels attached to recent disturbances according to whether they are seen as racial clashes, class conflict, or civil disturbances in which the theme of intergroup conflict is de-emphasized.

The nature of the public definition undoubtedly has consequences for the course and recurrence of the disturbance, and for short- and long-term suppression or facilitation of reform. One of the most important consequences is probably that a protest definition spurs efforts to make legitimate and nonviolent methods for promoting reform more available than they had been previously, while other definitions are followed by even more restricted access to legitimate means for promoting change (Turner and Killian, 1957, pp. 327–329).

The rest of this paper will be devoted to suggesting five theoretical vantage points from which it is possible to formulate hypotheses regarding the conditions under which one group of people will define as disturbances and some other group as social protest. First, publics test events for *credibility* in relation to folk–conceptions of social protest and justice. Second, disturbances communicate some combination of *appeal and threat*, and the balance is important in determining whether the disturbances are regarded as social protest. Third, disturbances instigate conflict with a target group, who may define them as social protest in the course of attempted *conciliation* to avoid full scale conflict. Fourth, defining disturbances as protest is an invitation from a third party for the troublemaking group to form a *coalition*. And fifth, acting as if the disturbances were social protest can be a step by public officials in establishing a *bargaining* relationship.

The paper offers theoretical proposals and not tested findings. The proposals are not a complete catalogue of causes for protest interpretation; notably omitted are such variables as understanding, empathy, and kindness. The proposals generally assume that there is no well-established tradition of disruptive or violent protest (Silver, 1968), that the society is not sharply polarized, and that the disturbances emanate from a clearly subordinated segment of the society.

Credibility and communication

If a disturbance is to be viewed as social protest, it must somehow look and sound like social protest to the people witnessing it. If they see that the events are widely at variance from their conception of social protest, they are unlikely to identify the disturbance as social protest in spite of any intergroup process in which they are involved. On the other hand, if events are clearly seen to correspond precisely with people's idea of social protest, intergroup processes will have to operate with exceptional force to bring about a different definition. It is within the limits imposed by these two extreme conditions that the intergroup process variables may assume paramount importance. Hence it is appropriate to begin our analysis by examining these limiting considerations.

Credibility: the folk concept. The main outlines of a *folk concept* (Turner, 1957) of social protest appear to be identifiable in contemporary American culture. The folk concept is only partially explicit, and is best identified by examining the arguments people make for viewing events and treating troublemakers in one way or another. Letters to newspapers and editorial and feature columns supply abundant material in which to conduct such a search. More explicit statements are to be found in essays that present reasoned arguments for viewing disturbances as protest (Boskin, 1968). The folk concept supplies the criteria against which people judge whether what they see looks like social protest or not. Often the process works in reverse: people who are predisposed to interpret a disturbance as protest, or as criminal rioting, perceive events selectively so as to correspond with the respective folk concept.

Several components of the folk concept of social protest emerge from examination of relevant materials. To be credible as protestors, troublemakers must seem to constitute a major part of a group whose grievances are already well documented, who are believed to be individually or collectively powerless to correct their grievances, and who show some signs of moral virtue that render them "deserving." Any indication that only few participated or felt sympathy with the disturbances predisposes observers to see the activities as deviance or as revolutionary activity by a small cadre of agitators. The claim that a group's conditions explain their resort to unusual means for gaining public attention to their plight is undermined when it appears that many persons in identical situations will not join or support the protest.

Common arguments against protest interpretation take the following form: "Unemployed? Let him go out, walk the streets, and find a job the way I did!" "They have one vote each the same as we do!" Powerlessness and grievance probably cannot be effectively communicated for the first time in a large-scale disturbance. To be credible as protest, a disturbance must follow an extended period in which both the powerlessness and the grievances have already been repeatedly and emphatically advertized.

Any weak individual or group who comes with a plea to more powerful personages is normally required to be more circumspect and more virtuous than those to whom he appeals. The normative principle would not be endorsed in this explicit form by majority groups. But the *de facto* principle operates because the sincerity and justifiability of the pleader's claim is subject to investigation and test while there is no investigation of the other's legitimacy. Since violence and disruption immediately call virtue into question, there must be offsetting indications of goodness in the group's past or current behavior. The group in question must be customarily law-abiding and must have used acceptable means and exercised restraint on other occasions. Nonviolent movements that precede violent disruptions help to establish the credibility of protest. Widespread support and sympathy for the objectives of protest coupled with the group's principled rejection of the violent means employed by a few of their members help to establish the deserving nature of the group without undermining the pervasive character of their grievances.

To be credible as protest, the disturbance itself must be seen either as a spontaneous, unplanned, and naive outburst, or as an openly organized protest of more limited nature that got tragically out of hand. Any evidence of covert planning, conspiracy, or seriously intended threats of violence before the event would weaken the credibility of the protest interpretation. On the other hand, naive expressions of rage, released under the stimulus of rumor and crowd excitement, are consistent with a folk-image of protest. In this connection the protest interpretation is supported by demonstrating that what triggered the disturbances was some incident or act of provocation, and that a succession of recent provocations had prepared the ground for an eruption.

To be credible as protest, indications of the use of riots for self-aggrandisement, the settlement of private feuds, or enjoyment of violence and destruction must be subordinated to naive anger and desperation. Looting for personal gain and the attitude that rioting is "having a ball" are two features of the racial disturbances since 1965 that have repeatedly detracted from the image of social protest. In a widely read article typical of many such statements,

Eric Severeid (1967) challenged the protest definition by describing the carnival atmosphere at certain stages in many of the disturbances.

Finally, some indications of restraint are important cues to interpretation as protest. A belief that only property and not personal injury was the object of attack, that deaths and severe injuries to persons resulted only under special circumstances of confusion and provocation, and that rioters went to exceptional lengths in a few dramatic instances to protect a white person or guarantee a college administrator safe passage is often salient in the imagery of persons defining the activity as protest.

Credibility: the admission of injustice. Interpretations of disruptive activity as protest invoke conceptions of justice and injustice. Homans (1961) and Blau (1964a and 1964b) are among those who interpret the sense of injustice as a feeling of inadequate reciprocation in social exchange. Runciman (1966), applying Merton and Kitt's (1950) conception of relative deprivation, proposes that the selection of reference groups determines whether there is a sense of injustice with respect to the rewards of position. But these theories do not answer the question: when is it possible and probable that one group will see another group's position as unjust to the point of accepting violence and disruption as the natural expression of that injustice?

If we assume that each group tends to employ its own situation as the point of reference in assessing another group's claims of injustice, we are led to the conclusion that groups who are clearly *advantaged* by comparison with the "protestors" can find the claim of injustice more credible than groups less advantaged. Crucial here is the assumption that objective and detached comparison between the situations of the troublemakers and the target groups is less powerful in shaping the assessment of injustice than the observing group's position vis-a-vis the troublemakers. Consequently, the great middle segment of American population finds it easier to identify black ghetto disturbances as social protest than to interpret college student demonstrations in the same sense. Similarly, black student demonstrations are less amenable to interpretation as protest than ghetto demonstrations.

According to this view, groups who see themselves as even more disadvantaged than the protestors are least likely to grant their claim. Viewed from below, disturbances are most easily comprehended as power plays or as deviance. Groups who see their situation as about the same as that of the protestors likewise do not find it easy to accord the protest interpretation.

Appeal and threat messages

It is a reasonable assumption that most observers could, under appropriate circumstances, see both an *appeal* and a *threat* in a violent disturbance. If this combination of messages is present, reading the disturbance as protest means that the appeal component is more salient to the observer than the threat component. For we can safely assume that when the preoccupation with threat to self and to those objects identified with self is foremost, appeals are no longer heard. Threat so often monopolizes attention to the exclusion of appeals, and acknowledging justice in the appeals weakens the foundation for defensive efforts required to meet the threat. Thus we are led to the proposition that disruptions are interpreted as protest only when the experience of threat is not excessive.

The foregoing observation however is incomplete. Somehow the appeal message must command attention, the resistance to acknowledging the protest message must be overcome. The *credibility* requirements we have just outlined are so restrictive that a positive incentive is required to overlook some of the criteria. An appeal by itself is normally a weak attention-getter; threat is much stronger in this respect. A combination of threat and appeal serves to gain attention and to create the sense of urgency necessary to overcome the resistance to acknowledging protest. When threat is insufficient, the events can be disregarded or written off as deviance, to be contained by the established systems of social control. An optimal combination of threat and appeal is necessary for the probability of seeing disturbance as protest. When the threat component falls below the optimal range, the most likely interpretation is deviance; above the optimal range, preoccupation with threat makes rebellion the probable interpretation.

Differential perception of threat by population segments is affected by a combination of personal involvement and proximity to the events and of ability to perceive the limits and patterns of disorder realistically. On this basis it is easiest for groups who live a safe distance from black neighborhoods and who have no stake in ghetto businesses to turn their attention toward the appeal component of the disturbance message. But we must also take note of the principle suggested by Diggory's (1956) findings regarding a rabid fox scare in Pennsylvania. While fear was greater among persons near to the rumored center of rabid fox sightings, the tendency to exaggerate the extent of the menace was less. Persons closest to the events were able to form a more realistic picture. Similarly, whites closest to the disturbances may be better able to discount inflated reports of violence against the persons of whites, and to see a pattern in the properties attacked and protected. Thus persons close enough to fear any spread of disorders but not close enough to correct exaggerated reports from personal experience may find it most difficult to see the activities as protest.

After the 1964 riots, Harper's (1968) Rochester *suburban* subjects were most likely to acknowledge that Negroes had a right to complain; city residents living more than one block from a Negro family were least likely to grant Negroes this right; and subjects living within one block of a Negro family were intermediate in their responses. After the 1965 Watts disorder, Morris and Jeffries (1967) found upper-middle-class Pacific Palisades residents most likely to identify the events as Negro protest and all-white low socioeconomic status Bell residents least likely, among the six white areas of Los Angeles County sampled.

The experience of threat is not entirely an individual matter. The self-conception is made up of group memberships, and the individual is threatened whenever an important membership group seems to be the object of threat. Consequently, we should expect members of such groups as small merchants, police, and firemen, even though they were personally unaffected by the disturbances, to experience much threat because of their identification with these same groups immediately involved in the confrontation. Police and merchants within the ghettos were not generally disposed to view racial disorder as social protest (Rossi *et al.*, 1968). It would be surprising to discover many people among these groups in the larger community who see the events primarily as protest.

Finally, according to the assumption of an optimal mixture of threat and appeal, it may be difficult to keep the awareness of protest dominant for an extended period of time. We have noted that escalation of violence is likely to preclude protest definition because of preoccupation with the threat. But repeated threat that is not followed by tangible injury to the threatened loses its impact. The diminishing force of repeated destructive activity confined to ghettos lessens the concern that originally directed attention toward the appeal component. Hence, repeated unescalated disturbances are likely to be accompanied by decreasing degrees of interpretation as protest, replaced by increasing tendencies to see the events as deviance.

Conciliation of conflict

A more complex basis for predicting the assignment of meaning to disorders is supplied by viewing the protestors and the interpreters as engaged in a real or potential process of conflict. The aggressive initiative of the moment lies with the protestors. Interpreting the disturbances as protest can then usefully be seen as a *gesture of conciliation,* an action to forestall the incipient conflict or to reduce or conclude the conflict without victory or surrender. We can justify this assertion and use it to suggest conditions leading to protest interpretation only after briefly reviewing the nature of the conflict process.

We shall use the term "conflict," not in the broad sense that includes all disagreements and all efforts by people or groups to pursue incompatible goals, but in the tradition of Simmel (1955), Von Wiese (1932, p. 246) and Park and Burgess (1921). In Coser's (1968, p. 232) definition of conflict as "a struggle over values or claims to status, power, and scarce resources, in which the claims of the conflicting parties are not only to gain the desired values but also to neutralize, injure, or eliminate their rivals," we underline the latter portion. Conflict has properties that distinguish it from other processes revolving about disagreement because there is an autonomous goal of injuring the antagonist—autonomous in the sense that efforts to injure the antagonist are not fully subjected to the test of effectiveness in promoting the other ostensible goals of the conflicting party. Conflict exists when the relationship between groups is based on the premise that whatever enhances the well-being of one group lessens the well-being of the other, and that impairing the well-being of the antagonist is a favored means for enhancing the well-being of one's own group.

The strategy of conflict centers about injuring the other without simultaneously injuring the self, while inhibiting and defending against retaliatory injury from the opponent. Consequently, conflict tends particularly as it persists and intensifies, to be volatile and comprehensive with respect to the issues that divide the combatants. Combatants must be able to shift grounds and issues as necessary to fight on terrains that are strategically favorable for them. There has probably never been a war or violent revolution in which the question of what either side was fighting for did not become unclear, nor in which the issue at the close of fighting was defined in the same way as at the start of combat.

When conflict occurs between groups regarded as members of some common social order, the process is circumscribed by a somewhat distinctive set of conflict norms. In certain respects the conflict normative system grants license not available to other relationships. In other respects it imposes stricter obligations, such as those requiring demonstrations of ingroup loyalty. Two consequences of assimilation of conflict to a normative order have bearing on our subsequent discussion of conciliation.

First, because conflict involves inflicting injury on persons who are part of a common social order, a course of action that is not normatively sanctioned except within a recognized conflict relationship, the preoccupation with normative considerations is heightened. There is special attention to painting the antagonist as villainous and to establishing the virtuousness of the protagonist group. An important aspect of conflict strategy is to manipulate the normative aspects of the exchange so as to justify the claim to a reserve of moral credit upon which the combatant can draw when he engages in what might otherwise be considered shocking or reprehensible behavior.

Second, a great deal of conflict is fought symbolically with symbolic injuries in the form of insults and threats and symbolic defenses against such injuries. Much of the symbolic conflict consists of testing the other and jockeying for position. But because the combatants are members of a social order, the effective use of symbols so as to place the other in an unfavorable light is a way of inflicting injury upon him. Thus, what Waller and Hill (1951) called "manipulation of morality" in family

conflict is an important part of the repertoire of symbolic tactics available for use in any conflict.

There is frequently confusion between the steps from disagreement toward agreement and the process of conflict resolution. Conflict resolution is more complicated because the combatants must cope with both disagreement and the pattern of reciprocal injury. The past and projected mutual injury is the more fundamental problem since it is possible to resolve conflict without agreement on substantive issues, but agreement on these issues does not erase the injury that each has done to the other in the course of the conflict. The latter supplies independent momentum for the continuation of conflict. Hence the key to all conflict resolution is the repair of previous injury and protection against future injury. When conflict resolution is by surrender, the victor disarms the vanquished and extracts reparations. The vanquished party cannot usually exact compensation in repairing the injury to himself, but he normally surrenders under the assumption that once he no longer offers any threat of injury to the victor, he will be immune from further injury by the victor. When conflict resolution occurs without surrender, both parties must give assurances against doing harm in the future and both must take steps to ameliorate the injury that each has already done to the other. Since surrender is an unlikely response to current disorders, our interest is in conflict resolutions characterized by some degree of mutuality.

We shall refer to any act whose aim is to avert or discontinue conflict without either asking or offering surrender as conciliation. To be effective, a conciliatory act must incorporate both an offer to discontinue attacks and a tender of help to correct the harm already done. To the extent to which the conflict is being fought at the symbolic level, the remedies are partially symbolic. With respect to the exchange of threats and insults (i.e., symbolic conflict), conciliation is an offer to discontinue such attacks and to discount the meaning of prior threats and insults. In order to participate in conciliatory exchange, the combatant must be prepared to believe that the other did not fully mean what he said, that his threats were not really meant to be carried out, and that his insults did not express his more enduring feelings and views. Hence an act of conciliation must provide the other with a basis on which such beliefs are credible.

If we omit the possibility of surrender, the remaining alternative is to extend an offer of conciliation. The prospect of conflict is accepted as real, but the aim is to interrupt the reciprocation of attack that locks the combatants into full-scale conflict. The conciliator offers public acknowledgment that he has done injury to the protestor, promising repentence and corrective actions. By making this acknowledgment he grants that there is some justification for the other's hostility toward him, and he also supplies the basis for believing that the other's antagonism is not unalterable and is not personal to himself or his group. The white man can say that the black's antagonism is not really directed against the white man, but merely against those people who happen to be doing the black an injustice at a particular time. Conciliation is thereby rendered a viable posture, because there is no reason to expect the other to continue his attacks once he is assured of compensation and security from further injury.

Interpreting violent and disruptive action as protest is following exactly this pattern. It means assuming that the intent to do injury is secondary in importance to the effort to secure redress, and it means acknowledging that there is some basis in the behavior of one's own group for the antagonism displayed by the protestor.

Because of the tendency for moralistic perspectives to be an inseparable part of conflict, an offer of conciliation is typically viewed by the conciliator as an act of generosity, going beyond what could be expected or required of him. Under the reciprocity principle (Gouldner, 1960) the act of placing a more generous than necessary interpretation on the other's actions obligates the latter to make generous response. Because the normative system of conflict permits a combatant to place a less favorable interpretation on the other's actions, the sense of self-righteous virtue attached to protest interpretation can be great. Furthermore, the protest interpretation with its clearly implied admission of fault places the conciliator in a precarious position, for his admission of prejudice, militarism, or insensitivity to student needs, for instance, can be used against him later if the other does not respond in kind. The risk he knows he is taking enhances the conciliator's self-righteousness. Hence, there is a strong tendency for conciliatory gestures to be withdrawn and replaced by active promotion of conflict when there is no discontinuance of insults and threats and no retraction of earlier attacks.

Third party point of view

From both the appeal-threat and conflict-conciliation approaches comes the hint that a *third party* may under some circumstances find it easier to interpret disturbance as protest than does the group against whom the disturbance is directed. For the target group, the merit of conciliation rather than accepting the challenge of conflict declines as the prospective costs of conciliation increase. Furthermore, whenever group membership is a salient aspect of personal identity, it is difficult to accept group fault without offsetting the admission by assessing equal or greater fault to the protestors. But a third party is not so directly threatened and does not pay most of the costs of conciliation and, consequently, is able to sustain a protest view of the disturbances after such an interpretation ceases to be tenable for the target group.

To account for third party protest interpretation, we must first ask why the third party should be sufficiently concerned about a conflict, in which they are bystanders, to acknowledge grievances and take a sympathetic stand. The question implies the answer: that protest interpretations by third parties are only likely to occur when there is some threat of third party involvement in the conflict or a strong basis for identification with one of the two parties. American people seldom concerned themselves sufficiently to make *any* interpretation of student riots abroad until student disorders became an immediate concern at home. Labor-management strife in the United States today attracts sufficient attention only when it threatens the supply of goods and services to the community.

Third party protest interpretations indicate either the defense of neutrality against the threat of partisan involvement in conflict or the active acceptance of partisanship on the side of the protestors. The bystander who is endangered by conflict is not inclined toward a sympathetic interpretation of either side, but rather toward wishing "a plague on both your houses!" Only when identities or interests pull him in one direction or the other can the threat of involvement press him to see the disturbance as protest.

Partisan protest interpretation is likely under two conditions: shared membership group identities and circumstances that facilitate coalition formation. We have already observed that objectively similar plights are not usually enough to lead to partisan support. The poor white man is often the last to view black activism as social protest, and the large Mexican-American vote in Los Angeles was a liability rather than an asset for the black candidate for mayor in 1969. Identification through a common membership group that is a salient component of the self-conception is required for partisanship.

Coalitions with disruptive groups are more likely to be favorable for groups of higher standing whose own position is strengthened by adding the threat of disorder from the protesting group to their own established power. Groups and agencies who are in a position to serve as the intermediate link in distributing benefits to protestors may invite the protestors into a coalition by announcing acknowledgment of the latter's grievances. In return for support of the protestors, they offer the power of their own position in helping to legitimate the grievance claims and in applying pressure on the target group.

We have spoken as if the target group were precisely designated and the line between the target group and third parties were precise. But the protest message is usually vague and with varying targets, leaving considerable latitude for identifying the boundaries. Existing cleavages within the more broadly defined target group then mark off as third parties those segments to whom coalitions with the protestors would enhance their position in internecine strife. Thus "anti-establishment" whites may ally themselves symbolically with blacks in identifying "whitey" as referring only to "establishment" whites. Interpreting ghetto disorder as protest can then serve as an invitation to blacks to join them in a coalition.

Official actions

We have spoken of the predisposition by various groups to identify disturbances under varying circumstances as social protest. But we have neglected thus far to assign enough importance to the actions of officials and formal leaders who must react conspicuously. On the basis of well established principles in the study of public opinion, opinion leadership and keynoting by officials should be a substantial determinant of public definitions (Katz and Lazarsfeld, 1955).

The problem of officials in the face of disturbance differs from the problem of others as action differs from attitude. The adoption of an attitude by itself has no consequences, and for most people its public enunciation has very little effect. But official action has consequences with respect to effectiveness, reactions provoked, and public commitments made.

The effect of these official responses is initially to keynote and legitimate the protest interpretation by various community segments. When these responses coincide with substantial prestigious community definitions of the events, the effect is further to establish a situational

norm identifying the proper or publicly acceptable interpretation. Views that the disturbances are simply crime on a larger scale demanding strengthened law enforcement, or that they are sinister rebellions to be handled as internal wars, tend to be suppressed, even though many individuals and groups incline toward such views. The result is an unstable situation in which temporarily the socially sanctioned view sees disturbance as protest, while dissident views subsist as an audible rumbling in the background.

A strong government with assured community support is unlikely to tolerate massive disruption to the extent of viewing it as social protest. But when the grievance is not so limited and specific that it can be easily and quickly righted, when complete confidence in official capability to suppress massive crime or rebellion is lacking, or when community support is uncertain, the standard official approach is to explore the possibilities of resolving the confrontation through bargaining. Accounts of the 1967 racial disorders indicate repeated efforts to identify black representatives who could bargain for the protestors, and numerous instances of tentative bargains that failed because agents on one side or the other could not command the support of the group they were supposed to represent. Official entry into a bargaining relationship serves initially to validate a public definition of the disturbances as social protest, acknowledging the merit of some grievances. But the impersonal and calculating nature of bargaining, especially as it recurs and is routinized, works against seeing the trouble as social protest. The disturbance soon becomes a move in a competitive game, to be met by minimal and calculated concessions. And as the masters of urban political machines have long understood, "buying off" protest leaders, directly, tends to be a less costly and more immediately effective tactic of bargaining than offering programs for amelioration of underlying grievances.

Our final observation is that interpreting public disorders as social protest is an unstable and precarious condition. It requires an optimally balanced set of conditions, and is difficult to maintain over an extended period of time. Insofar as such interpretations are favorable to social reform, it appears that they must be capitalized quickly, while conditions are favorable, through programs that can be implemented on a continuing basis by a more routinized and impersonal bargaining. Perhaps a residue of understanding that can be favorable to future reforms may remain in spite of community redefinition. Perhaps, also, reformers should not overestimate what can be gained by disorderly protest in relation to the many other means for effecting change.

66   Some considerations relevant to national policy

MORTON DEUTSCH

Peace is currently maintained by a delicate balance of terror. The delicacy of the balance has justifiably alarmed many of those who are aware of the awesome destructive power of nuclear weapons. A common response of intellectuals, military strategists, and statesmen alike to this alarm has been to focus their attention upon the problem of making the balance steadier and more durable. The interest in "arms control" and in the concept of "stable deterrence" reflects this focus. Although efforts to reduce the military insecurities of East and West are obviously laudable, I believe that the current emphasis on methods of stabilizing the mutual terror should be viewed as, at best, dealing with stopgap measures. The "hostile peace" of stabilized mutual terror and of institutionalized mutual suspicion is intrinsically vulnerable to the social and psychological maladies that breed in an atmosphere of tension and suspicion. We must begin to find roads to a peace rooted in mutual interests and mutual respect.

Thus, the basic theme of my paper centers on the question: How do we move from a peace of mutual terror to a peace of mutual trust? This question proliferates into many other, related questions, e.g.: What should our military policy be; what steps can we take to

Reprinted from the **Journal of Social Issues**, 1961, 17, 57–68, with permission of the author and the Society for the Psychological Study of Social Issues.

strengthen existing elements of international order; how can mutual suspicions be reduced; how can we learn to communicate with one another more effectively; what non-violent techniques for resolving international conflicts can be developed; how can the problems of a disarmed world be coped with? These are some of the difficult questions to which the social sciences must address themselves if civilization is to survive. Here, I cannot hope to do more than deal with some limited aspects of our military and international policy. For a fuller discussion of these matters see Wright, Evan, and Deutsch (1962).

Let me indicate in a brief, summary fashion some of the basic psychological assumptions underlying my discussion of national policy in this paper: assumptions which come from theoretical and experimental research that I have been doing on interpersonal trust and suspicion and interpersonal bargaining (Deutsch, 1949; 1958; 1960a; 1960b; 1961; Deutsch and Krauss, 1960).

1. There are social situations which do not allow the possibility of "rational" behavior so long as the conditions for mutual trust do not exist. I believe our current international situation is a situation of this kind. A characteristic symptom of such "nonrational situations" is that any attempt on the part of any individual or nation to increase its own welfare or security (without regard to the security or welfare of others) is self-defeating. Thus, for example, if the Soviet Union attempts to increase its security by taking over Berlin, it will decrease its real security by increasing the likelihood of nuclear war. In such situations the only way that an individual or nation can avoid being trapped in a mutually reinforcing, self-defeating cycle is to attempt to change the situation so that a basis of mutual trust can develop.

2. Mutual trust is most likely to occur when people are positively oriented to each other's welfare—i.e., when each has a stake in the other's doing well rather than poorly. Unfortunately, the East and West, at present, appear to have a stake in each other's defects and difficulties rather than in each other's welfare. Thus the Communists gloat over our racial problems and our unemployment and we do likewise over their agricultural failures and their lack of civil liberties.

3. To induce a mutual welfare orientation in another, you have to demonstrate toward the other that your own behavior is based upon such a premise and that he cannot improve his welfare by violation of it.

4. Another person is likely to be convinced that your behavior is guided by a mutual welfare orientation (i.e., is more likely to be *trusting*) as a function of such factors as: the amount and frequency of the benefits he receives from your behavior; the confidence he has that your behavior has no other purpose than to provide mutual benefit. The other is most likely to perceive that your behavior is not guided by ulterior purpose if it does not result in disproportionate gain or loss for yourself and if your behavior is not seen to be determined by weakness, insanity, or inanity.

5. Another person is less likely to violate a mutual welfare orientation (i.e., is more likely to be *trustworthy*) if he can trust you; if he knows what you consider to be a violation; and if he knows that you will neither condone a violation nor use an apparent one as an excuse for destructive retaliation but will, instead, attempt to restore coopera-

tion without allowing yourself to be, or remain disadvantaged, by it.

6. Mutual trust can occur even under circumstances where the parties involved are unconcerned with each other's welfare. The presence of third parties who are "neutral" or who are valued in the same way (either favorably or unfavorably) may enable the development of limited forms of mutual trust. Thus, neutral nations, if they were sufficiently united and uncommitted, might facilitate communication or mediate conflicts between the East and West.

Military policy

I shall discuss briefly two concepts: military superiority and stable deterrence.

MILITARY SUPERIORITY

A public opinion poll would, undoubtedly, show that most Americans accept the traditional view that the security of the United States would be enhanced if we had a clear-cut military superiority over the Soviet Union. However, in the age of hydrogen bombs and missiles, the quest for military superiority is dangerous, provocative, and enhances the possibility of war. The basic axiom of military doctrine for *both* the United States and the Soviet Union in the missile age must be the recognition that *military actions should only be taken which increase the military security of both sides; military actions which give a military superiority to one side or the other should be avoided.* We should recognize that we have a positive interest in the other side's military security as well as in our own. The military forces of both sides should be viewed as having the common primary aim of preventing *either* side (one's own or the other side) from starting a deliberate or accidental war. Possibly, periodic meeting of military leaders from East and West might foster the mutual awareness of common concerns.

The assumption here, as I see it, is very simple: neither the United States nor the Soviet Union will allow itself to be intimidated by the other on a vital matter. If one side envisages that the other may achieve a temporary military superiority, it may be frightened into rash actions to prevent this from occurring. If one side feels it has achieved a temporary military superiority it may be emboldened to attempt to intimidate the other before the seesaw shifts its balance. We must recognize that just as military inferiority is dangerous, so is military "superiority"; we neither want to *tempt* nor *frighten* a potential enemy into military action.

STABLE DETERRENCE

The recognition that none of the participants in a nuclear war are likely to be victorious has led to the concept of *stable deterrence* through a balance of mutual terror. The essential idea is that if each side has a nuclear retaliatory capacity which has a high degree of invulnerability (i.e., a capacity to inflict "unacceptable damage" on the other side which is unlikely to be destroyed by a surprise attack), neither side would dare to initiate a nuclear war against the other.

The proponents of the theory of stable deterrence have made a very valuable analysis of the delicacy of the present balance of terror and have presented important suggestions for making the balance steadier. However, some of the sources of instability are inherent even in "stable deterrents," others inhere in the atmosphere of tension and suspicion of the present "hostile peace." These latter sources of instability lead even some proponents of the doctrine of stable deterrence to neglect the *mutuality* of interest of both sides (i.e., that the weapon systems of the Soviet Union as well as those of the United States be equally invulnerable to surprise attack) which is implicit in the doctrine; it leads others who are not fully aware of the implications of the theory of stable deterrence to support such unstabilizing viewpoints as the doctrine of "massive retaliation" and the doctrine of "instantaneous, automatic retaliation."

Below, we examine some of the assumptions involved in the concept of "stable deterrence" and indicate some of the instabilities which plague it. A stable balance of terror implies (at the minimum): (1) the *mutual invulnerability* of nuclear weapon systems; (2) the *mutual vulnerability* of civilian populations; (3) *rational, responsible control* over the use of the weapon systems including the ability to prevent accident, misunderstanding, insanity, or local decision as the basis for use of the weapons; (4) an *unnervous* self-confidence in the face of potential attack or of an undeliberate attack. Moreover, for the "balance of terror" to serve as a deterrent to an attack, it is implied that: (5) the threat of retaliation is *credible* to the potential attacker; (6) the threat is *unprovocative* (i.e., does not stimulate what it is attempting to deter) and is appropriate rather than unjust; (7) the potential attacker is neither masochistic (i.e., is not self-destructive) nor irrational (e.g., has grandiose delusions of invulnerability); (8) the attacker can be correctly identified. In addition, any doctrine which

is concerned with stability should provide some compensating mechanism to restore stability when it is threatened or disrupted, e.g., to prevent a vicious spiral of mutual misunderstandings about whether a deliberate attack is taking place.

Let us now consider the implicit assumptions we have listed above to see how likely they are to be realized and to see if some assumptions don't inherently conflict with others.

1. *Mutual invulnerability of weapon systems.* As Herman Kahn (1960) has pointed out, if the present level of expenditure on research relating to military weapons continues, one can be reasonably certain that new, surprising weapons will be developed. Weapons which are now considered to be relatively invulnerable will become relatively vulnerable. Recognition of this possibility has led military theorists to the view that it would be dangerous to "place all their eggs in one basket"— i.e., to rely on one weapons system (e.g., the Polaris submarine) rather than upon a mixture of different weapons systems. However, without an effective agreement to limit and control weapons development, one may expect that, sooner or later, unpredictable research developments will make the balance of mutual terror teeter to one side or the other. Pessimistically, one may even say that an agreement which limits and controls weapons and their development, even if "fully-inspected," might not prevent an imbalance from developing unless the agreement expresses or produces the intention not to violate it. This is possible because the technology of inspection *evasion* could, under some circumstances, develop more rapidly than the technology of detecting incipient evasions.

2. *Mutual vulnerability of popula-*

tions. The "balance of terror" doctrine not only assumes that the nuclear weapons are mutually invulnerable but also that they are mutually effective. Anything which *one-sidedly* limits the destructiveness of the other side's weapons disturbs the balance. Thus, if one side begins to develop a large-scale civil defense program, the other side may feel that it will lose its ability to deter an attack since its retaliation will not be so fearsome. Yet it is evident that there are strong pressures for a *unilateral* development of civil defense. Some of these pressures, oddly enough, originate in strong proponents of the doctrine of stable deterrence: they warn of the dangerous implications for world peace were the Soviet Union to initiate unilaterally a civil defense program against nuclear attack, but advocate that we do so unilaterally (Rand Corporation Study, 1958). Perhaps their recommendations are based upon the assumption that the Soviet Union has already initiated such a program; if so, this basis for our action should be clearly stated. My criticism here is not of defensive measures (whether they be anti-missile or civil defense) *per se* but rather of measures which are not *mutual* in orientation.

3. *Rational, responsible control of the decision to use the weapons.* One of the greatest sources of instability arises from the possibility that one side or the other will use nuclear weapons without having made a responsible decision to use them or will use them because of misinformation or misunderstanding concerning the other side. The fact is that the facilities for gathering and processing information, the communication network, the governmental decision-making apparatus, and the military command and control techniques required to make a quick de-

cision to use nuclear weapons are extremely complex. It is very unlikely that any nation has the capabilities necessary to make such a decision, which would not, in all likelihood, be regretted after the fact. Moreover, there is always the possibility that the decision to use the bomb would be made by an irresponsible local unit—by a "mischievous" missile squad, a "grandiose" bomber crew, a "paranoid" submarine crew—which could carry out its own decision. As a social psychologist, I do not minimize the possibility of something which may be described as "collective madness" in times of acute international crisis. For reports of some studies of social behavior in situations of stress see Maccoby, Newcomb, and Hartley (1958).

4. *Nervousness, the need to respond quickly because of the fear that one will lose either the desire or ability to respond, enhances the likelihood that a response will be triggered off by an insufficient stimulus and, thus, makes for instability.* The proponents of "stable deterrence," of course, strongly oppose reliance on retaliatory forces which would be destroyed if not used quickly. Some of the "nervousness" in military circles arises, however, from the fear of loss of a desire to retaliate if deterrence has failed.

5. *For a military threat of retaliation to deter, it must, at the minimum, have some credibility.* The doctrine of massive nuclear retaliation in relation to non-nuclear aggressions lost much of its credibility after the Soviet Union acquired nuclear weapons systems. Of course, both the Soviet Union and the United States in contemplating the use of conventional military weapons also have to contemplate the dangerous possibility that a conventional war, out of its own dynamism, will mushroom into

a nuclear war. However, neither we nor our Allies now believe that we would initiate an all-out nuclear war unless the facts showed we were in danger of all-out devastation ourselves. (See Kahn, 1960a.)

The implication of the foregoing is that, in the present situation, the threat of massive retaliation is itself largely deterred by the counter-threat of massive retaliation: deterrence is deterred. In a similar manner, one can argue that if one side has launched a surprise attack but has failed to wipe out the other side's nuclear striking force and has not done intolerable damage to its civilian population, the attacked nation would be deterred from a massive retaliation directed at their opponent's civilian population because of fear of counter-retaliation directed at its own population. Possibly thoughts such as those advanced in the preceding sentence have led to the doctrine of instant, automatic massive retaliation in relation to any nuclear attack: a doctrine seriously advanced by high ranking military leaders to insure the "credibility" of the threat. It is not necessary to dwell upon the great moral and physical dangers of being "nervous" and over-ready to kill 100 million or more people. Apart from the dangerous provocation and lack of control implicit in the concept of immediate and automatic retaliation, if attack and counter-attack by missiles are not separated in time, how could the survivors know who started the war?

If we take the theory of stable deterrence seriously, the doctrine of retaliatory response to a nuclear attack should be a doctrine calling for an unanxious, deliberate, delayed response which permits the nuclear aggressor to be identified unambiguously before the world and before its own people. Such a doctrine might encompass the threat of limited retaliation (of *no more* than an eye for an eye) to induce the people of the aggressor nation to overthrow their government and to surrender to the U.N. The threat of limited retaliation in relation to limited aggression, in addition to being more justifiable (i.e., less provocative) and less likely to result in unlimited catastrophe, is also probably more credible than the threat of massive retaliation in relation to limited destruction.

6. *An effective threat does not provoke the events which it is trying to deter.* Psychologists, sociologists, and psychiatrists, who have long been concerned with the prevention and control of antisocial behavior, would undoubtedly agree that one of the great dangers in the threat of force (in a "get tough" policy) is that it often incites the behavior it is attempting to prevent. There are several common reasons why threats provoke rather than deter: (a) the threat of using force is perceived to be an expression of an underlying intent to injure, rather than of self-defense (e.g., if a military leader boasts of his nation's ability to destroy an attacker, the statement is more likely to be seen as aggressive "rocket rattling" than as peaceful in purpose); (b) the threat of force is perceived to be an attempt unjustly to restrain actions which the threatened party feels entitled to engage in; (c) the threatened party has desire to be a "martyr" or to be punished; (d) the threatener is perceived to be bluffing; and (e) the threatener is perceived to be so irresponsible or incompetent that he can not control the use or non-use of his threatened force and, hence, the only way to control him is to destroy his capacity to threaten.

If we examine our recent and current policies to see whether they provoke or deter, we must conclude that some of our policies are not unprovocative. The placement of vulnerable nuclear weapons and missiles in Europe and the use of vulnerable overseas bases by bombers carrying nuclear weapons are highly provocative, because the weapons and bases would not survive a nuclear attack and, hence, could not be used as a retaliatory force: their only feasible use is to initiate attack. Brinkmanship, the reliance on the perceived possibility that limited conflicts (e.g., over Berlin and over Quemoy) might escalate to all-out nuclear war as a means of deterring limited war, and the search for information which would make the other side's retaliatory force vulnerable to surprise attack are two examples of provocative policy. To be sure, military provocativeness is not limited to one side.

7. *The theory of stable deterrence assumes that the potential attacker is rational in the economic sense that he will not attack if the expected gain resulting from the attack is smaller than the expected loss and if the expected loss from not attacking is less than that from attacking.* Moreover, it assumes that the potential retaliator has a reasonably accurate conception of the nature of the potential attacker's complex system of values and disvalues. Both assumptions seem to be rather dubious. Behavior, particularly in a time of high tension and crisis, is more likely to be determined by anxiety, stereotypes, self-esteem defensive maneuvers, and social conformity pressures than by simple rational estimates of "economic" gain and loss. Further, there is little evidence to suggest that the Russians really understand us (or themselves) or that we understand them (or ourselves); certainly the Voice of America's conception of the Soviets is rejected by the Soviet citizens as is *Pravda's* conception of America rejected by us.

8. *The theory of stable deterrence is a two-country theory.* No one appears to have been able to think through what happens when nuclear weapons become an "N-country" problem. That is, the diffusion of nuclear weapons creates extremely complex problems for such concepts as stability and deterrence, problems which have not been solved. What would represent a stable distribution of nuclear weapons? Whom to deter?

The point of my discussion of the theory of stable deterrence is: the notion that invulnerable nuclear weapons, in themselves, produce *stability* is a dangerously misleading notion. They do not. Stability depends also on many considerations. Do not misunderstand me, however; my view is that if nuclear weapons are to be maintained, it is better that these weapons be invulnerable to surprise attack.

Let me summarize my discussion of military policy by stating that: the central point which we must grasp is that *there is no rational solution possible to our problems of security in a nonrational world except to make the world more rational.* We are in a type of international situation which is similar to that of a panicky crowd in a theatre when there is a fire. By attempting to achieve individual safety without regard for the safety of others, a person enhances the danger for all. In such a situation, the only reasonable course of action that will avert catastrophe is to take the initiative in *creating order* by persuasively suggesting rules and procedures which will permit an organized exit from the situation before the fire rages out of control.

Some suggestions for international policy

But how does one create order out of potential chaos? How does one take the initiative in such an attempt? What rules and procedures should be developed? How can one be confident that the rules will be followed? These are difficult questions, but I venture to sketch an answer in the following paragraphs. It is self-evident that to facilitate the development of order and justice in international relations we must weaken the conditions which promote disorder and injustice and strengthen the conditions which promote the opposite state of affairs.

WEAKENING THE CONDITIONS LEADING TO DISORDER

The major conditions leading to disorder in the present international scene are:

1. *The revolution in military technology and the arms race.* To overcome the dangers inherent in this situation we need to: (a) develop a counter-revolution in disarmament technology; (b) negotiate agreements and take steps unilaterally which will decrease military instability by preventing the diffusion of nuclear weapons, by reducing fear of surprise attacks, and by reducing the likelihood of devastating incidents through accident, misunderstanding, or insanity; and (c) move toward disarmament theory and technology which permits a reliable disarmament. It seems to me unlikely that substantial disarmament will be feasible before a marked change has occurred in the international atmosphere.

Consider only the unrealism of disarmament negotiations without the participation of Communist China.

2. *The widening gap in standards of living between the rich countries of Europe and North America and the poor countries of Asia, Africa, and Latin America, coupled with the increasing awareness of this difference and a rising "revolution of expectations."* It is obvious that the rich countries have to spend much more organized, research-tutored effort in the attempt to assist the people in the "underdeveloped" countries to acquire the educational, economic, and political skills and resources to become *independent*, thriving nations. I stress "independent" to emphasize the importance of not involving these underdeveloped nations in the cold war, the importance of allowing them to develop in ways which do not pressure them to be committed to one "bloc" or the other.

3. *The existence of two organized crusading ideologies, one centered in the U.S. and the other in the Soviet Union, which emphasize their antagonistic interests while neglecting their mutually cooperative interests.* I think it is the special duty of the social scientists in each "bloc" to expose the mythologies of each system, to accurately describe and analyze the complexities of each society, and to point out the similarities as well as the differences. Our analysis can not be content with such ideologically determined categories as "free enterprise system," "Communism," "Democratic," "totalitarian." This is not to deny that there are real and important differences between the United States and the Soviet Union, but we should attempt to understand these differences by objective analysis and description rather than by using political slogans as

labels for very complex social systems. An objective analysis would see each society in an appropriate historical perspective in terms of the conditions which have given rise to and which maintain its particular institutions. In addition, such an analysis would point to the future by understanding the implications of the revolutionary changes in education, communications, industrial technology, and standards of living occurring in each society (see, for example, Rostow, 1960). Moreover, such an analysis would avoid the mythological tendencies which lead to the identification of oneself with the "angels" and the others with the "devils." It is interesting to note that in the mythology of each nation, the other nation is essentially characterized as a social system in which "the many are involuntarily exploited by the few," "the mass of the people are not really sympathetic to the regime," "the government is dominated by groups who will attempt to impose their views upon the rest of the world, by force if necessary" (Bronfenbrenner, 1961).

STRENGTHENING THE ELEMENTS OF ORDER

International order presupposes rules which effectively regulate the interaction among nations. Until there is a world government with sufficient power to coerce compliance with international rules, it is evident that powerful governments will comply with rules, whether they are formalized in treaties or not, only so long as they perceive that compliance is more beneficial than detrimental to their enlightened over-all self-interests. Any system of rules which is supported primarily through voluntary compliance is likely to be initiated and maintained only if sufficient communication among the potential participants in the system of rules is also maintained so that: (a) they can recognize that they hold certain values in common; (b) rules can be articulated which fairly represent the shared values, without systematically disadvantaging a given participant; (c) they can be reasonably certain that compliance is mutual; and (d) they can agree on procedures to resolve the misunderstanding and disputes about compliance which will inevitably occur. The ability of a system of rules to weather disputes and short-run disadvantages to a given participant is a function of the strength of the internal commitment to the system of rules and of the strength of the cooperative bonds that exist among the participants.

I shall employ this rather condensed presentation of "the conditions of normative order" to make some proposals for our international policy.

1. *We must be unremitting in our attempt to communicate with members of the Communist bloc in such a way that the mutual recognition of our sharing many values in common (e.g., peace, technological advance, prosperity, science, health, education, cultural progress) is fostered.* We should neither *initiate nor reciprocate* barriers to communication. Clearly our policy of non-communication with Communist China makes no sense if we ever expect them to participate in arms control or disarmament agreements.

2. *To develop a system of rules, our course of conduct in international affairs should exemplify supra-nationalistic or universalistic values; it should constantly indicate our willingness to live up to the values that we expect other to adhere to.* We must give up the doctrine

of "special privilege" and the "double standard" in judging our own conduct and that of the Communist nations. In my view, only a double standard would suggest that Communist China is aggressive toward us, but that we have not been so toward them; that the use of military force to maintain the status-quo is peace-preserving while the use of force to change it is aggressive; that Communist bases near the United States are menacing while United States bases adjacent to the Soviet Union are peaceful, etc.

3. *To cut through the atmosphere of basic mistrust which exists, the United States should engage in a sustained policy of attempting to establish cooperative bonds with the Communist block.* I emphasize "sustained" to indicate that the policy should not be withdrawn in the face of initial rebuffs, which may be expected. Our policy should be to avoid the reciprocation of hostility and to always leave open the possibility of mutual cooperation despite prior rebuff. This means that we should have a positive interest in helping people in the Communist nations toward a higher standard of living and our trade policies should reflect this. It means that we should have an active interest in reducing their fears that they may be the victims of military aggression. It means, basically, that we should attempt to relate to them as though they were human. Relating to them as though they are devils, or some inhuman horde, will only help to confirm our nightmares.

The thesis of this paper has been that an orientation to the other's welfare, *as well as to one's own,* is a basic prerequisite to a peace sustained by mutual confidence rather than by mutual terror. "As well as to one's own welfare" is underlined here to emphasize that loss of self-identity is a poor foundation for cooperation in international as well as in interpersonal relations. Thriving societies that are coping successfully with their own internal problems have less ground for the fears and less need for the hostilities that interfere with the international cooperation necessary to construct a civilized world for the genus man.

67   The experience of living in cities

STANLEY MILGRAM

Obviously cities have great appeal because of their variety, eventfulness, possibility of choice, and the stimulation of an intense atmosphere that many individuals find a desirable background to their lives. Where face-to-face contacts are important, the city offers unparalleled possibilities. It has been calculated by the Regional Plan Association (1969) that in Nassau County, a suburb of New York City, an individual can meet 11,000 others within a 10-minute radius of his office by foot or car. In Newark, a moderate-sized city, he can meet more than 20,000 persons within this radius. But in midtown Manhattan he can meet fully 220,000. So there is an order-of-magnitude increment in the communication possibilities offered by a great city. That is one of the bases of its appeal and, indeed, of its functional necessity. The city provides options that no other social arrangement permits. But there is a negative side also, as we shall see.

Granted that cities are indispensable in complex society, we may still ask what contribution psychology can make to understanding the experience of living in them. What theories are relevant? How can we extend our knowledge of the psychological aspects of life in cities through empirical inquiry? If empirical inquiry is possible, along what lines should it proceed? In short, where do we start in constructing urban theory and in laying out lines of research?

Observation is the indispensable starting point. Any observer in the streets of midtown Manhattan will see (i) large numbers of people, (ii) a high population density, and (iii) heterogeneity of population. These three factors need to be at the root of any sociopsychological theory of city life, for they condition all aspects of our experience in the metropolis. Louis Wirth (1938), if not the first to point to these factors, is nonetheless the sociologist who relied most heavily on them in his analysis of the city. Yet, for a psychologist, there is something unsatisfactory about Wirth's theoretical variables. Numbers, density, and heterogeneity are demographic facts but they are not yet psychological facts. They are external to the individual. Psychology needs an idea that links the individual's *experience* to the demographic circumstances of urban life.

One link is provided by the concept of overload. This term, drawn from systems analysis, refers to a system's inability to process inputs from the environment because there are too many inputs for the system to cope with, or because successive inputs come so fast that input A cannot be processed when input B is presented. When overload is present, adaptations occur. The system must set priorities and make choices. A may be processed first while B is kept in abeyance, or one input may be sacrificed altogether. City life, as we experience it, constitutes a continuous set of encounters with overload, and of resultant adaptations. Overload characteristically deforms daily life on several levels, impinging on role performance, the evolution of social norms, cognitive functioning, and the use of facilities.

The concept has been implicit in several theories of urban experience. In 1903 George Simmel (see 1950) pointed out that, since urban dwellers come into contact with vast numbers of people each day, they conserve psychic energy by becoming acquainted with a far smaller proportion of people than their rural counterparts do, and by maintaining more superficial relationships even with these acquaintances. Wirth (1938) points specifically to "the superficiality, the anonymity, and the transistory character of urban social relations."

One adaptive response to overload, therefore, is the allocation of less time to each input. A second adaptive mechanism is disregard of low-priority inputs. Principles of selectivity are formulated such that investment of time and enegry are reserved for carefully defined inputs (the urbanite disregards the drunk sick on the street as he purposefully navigates through the crowd). Third, boundaries are redrawn in certain social transactions so that the overloaded system can shift the burden to the other party in the exchange; thus, harried New York bus drivers once made change for customers, but now this responsibility has been shifted to the client, who must have the exact fare ready. Fourth, reception is blocked off prior to entrance into a system; city dwellers increasingly use unlisted telephone numbers to prevent individuals from calling them, and a small but growing number resort to keeping the telephone off the hook to prevent incoming calls. More subtly, a

city dweller blocks inputs by assuming an unfriendly countenance, which discourages others from initiating contact. Additionally, social screening devices are interposed between the individual and environmental inputs (in a town of 5000 anyone can drop in to chat with the mayor, but in the metropolis organizational screening devices deflect inputs to other destinations). Fifth, the intensity of inputs is diminished by filtering devices, so that only weak and relatively superficial forms of involvement with others are allowed. Sixth, specialized institutions are created to absorb inputs that would otherwise swamp the individual (welfare departments handle the financial needs of a million individuals in New York City, who would otherwise create an army of mendicants continuously importuning the pedestrian). The interposition of institutions between the individual and the social world, a characteristic of all modern society, and most notably of the large metropolis, has its negative side. It deprives the individual of a sense of direct contact and spontaneous integration in the life around him. It simultaneously protects and estranges the individual from his social environment.

Many of these adaptive mechanisms apply not only to individuals but to institutional systems as well, as Meier (1962) has so brilliantly shown in connection with the library and the stock exchange.

In sum, the observed behavior of the urbanite in a wide range of situations appears to be determined largely by a variety of adaptations to overload. I now deal with several specific consequences of responses to overload, which make for differences in the tone of city and town.

Social responsibility

The principal point of interest for a social psychology of the city is that moral and social involvement with individuals is necessarily restricted. This is a direct and necessary function of excess of input over capacity to process. Such restriction of involvement runs a broad spectrum from refusal to become involved in the needs of another person, even when the person desperately needs assistance, through refusal to do favors, to the simple withdrawal of courtesies (such as offering a lady a seat, or saying "sorry" when a pedestrian collision occurs). In any transaction more and more details need to be dropped as the total number of units to be processed increases and assaults an instrument of limited processing capacity.

The ultimate adaptation to an overloaded social environment is to totally disregard the needs, interests, and demands of those whom one does not define as relevant to the satisfaction of personal needs, and to develop highly efficient perceptual means of determining whether an individual falls into the category of friend or stranger. The disparity in the treatment of friends and strangers ought to be greater in cities than in towns; the time allotment and willingness to become involved with those who have no personal claim on one's time is likely to be less in cities than in towns.

Bystander intervention in crises. The most striking deficiencies in social responsibility in cities occur in crisis situations, such as the Genovese murder in Queens. In 1964, Catherine Genovese, coming home from a night job in the early hours of an April morning, was stabbed repeatedly, over an extended period of time. Thirty-eight residents of a respectable New York City neighborhood admit to having witnessed at least a part of the attack, but none went to her aid or called the police until after she was dead. Milgram and Hollander, writing in *The Nation* (1964), analyzed the event in these terms:

Urban friendships and associations are not primarily formed on the basis of physical proximity. A person with numerous close friends in different parts of the city may not know the occupant of an adjacent apartment. This does not mean that a city dweller has fewer friends than does a villager, or knows fewer persons who will come to his aid; however, it does mean that his allies are not constantly at hand. Miss Genovese required immediate aid from those physically present. There is no evidence that the city had deprived Miss Genovese of human associations, but the friends who might have rushed to her side were miles from the scene of her tragedy.

Further, it is known that her cries for help were not directed to a specific person; they were general. But only individuals can act, and as the cries were not specifically directed, no particular person felt a special responsibility. The crime and the failure of community response seem absurd to us. At the time, it may well have seemed equally absurd to the Kew Gardens residents that not one of the neighbors would have called the police. A collective paralysis may have developed from the belief of each of the witnesses that someone else must surely have taken that obvious step.

Latané and Darley (1969)[1] have reported laboratory approaches to the study of bystander intervention and have established experimentally the following principle: the larger the number of bystanders, the less the likelihood that any one of them will intervene in an emergency. Gaertner and Bickman (1968) of The City University of New York have extended the bystander studies to an examination of help across ethnic lines. Blacks and whites, with clearly identifi-

[1] This research is reported in Section VII here. —Eds.

able accents, called strangers (through what the caller represented as an error in telephone dialing), gave them a plausible story of being stranded on an outlying highway without more dimes, and asked the stranger to call a garage. The experimenters found that the white callers had a significantly better chance of obtaining assistance than the black callers. This suggests that ethnic allegiance may well be another means of coping with overload: the city dweller can reduce excessive demands and screen out urban heterogeneity by responding along ethnic lines; overload is made more manageable by limiting the "span of sympathy."

In any quantitative characterization of the social texture of city life, a necessary first step is the application of such experimental methods as these to field situations in large cities and small towns. Theorists argue that the indifference shown in the Genovese case would not be found in a small town, but in the absence of solid experimental evidence the question remains an open one.

More than just callousness prevents bystanders from participating in altercations between people. A rule of urban life is respect for other people's emotional and social privacy, perhaps because physical privacy is so hard to achieve. And in situations for which the standards are heterogeneous, it is much harder to know whether taking an active role is unwarranted meddling or an appropriate response to a critical situation. If a husband and wife are quarreling in public, at what point should a bystander step in? On the one hand, the heterogeneity of the city produces substantially greater tolerance about behavior, dress, and codes of ethics than is generally found in the small town, but this diversity also encourages people to withhold aid for fear of antagonizing the partici-

pants or crossing an inappropriate and difficult-to-define line.

Moreover, the frequency of demands present in the city gives rise to norms of noninvolvement. There are practical limitations to the Samaritan impulse in a major city. If a citizen attended to

TABLE 1

PERCENTAGE OF ENTRIES ACHIEVED BY INVESTIGATORS FOR CITY AND TOWN DWELLINGS (SEE TEXT).

Experimenter	Entries achieved (%)	
	City*	Small town†
Male		
No. 1	16	40
No. 2	12	60
Female		
No. 3	40	87
No. 4	40	100

* Number of requests for entry, 100.
† Number of requests for entry, 60.

every needy person, if he were sensitive to and acted on every altruistic impulse that was evoked in the city, he could scarcely keep his own affairs in order.

Willingness to trust and assist strangers. We now move away from crisis situations to less urgent examples of social responsibility. For it is not only in situations of dramatic need but in the ordinary, everyday willingness to lend a land that the city dweller is said to be deficient relative to his small-town cousin. The comparative method must be used in any empirical examination of this question. A commonplace social situation is staged in an urban setting and in a small town—a situation to which a subject can respond by either extending help or withholding it. The responses in town and city are compared.

One factor in the purported unwillingness of urbanites to be helpful to strangers may well be their heightened sense of physical (and emotional) vulnerability—a feeling that is supported by urban crime statistics. A key test for distinguishing between city and town behavior, therefore, is determining how city dwellers compare with town dwellers in offering aid that increases their personal vulnerability and requires some trust of strangers. Altman, Levine, Nadien, and Villena (1969) of The City University of New York devised a study to compare the behaviors of city and town dwellers in this respect. The criterion used in this study was the willingness of householders to allow strangers to enter their home to use the telephone. The student investigators individually rang doorbells, explained that they had misplaced the address of a friend nearby, and asked to use the phone. The investigators (two males and two females) made 100 requests for entry into homes in the city and 60 requests in the small towns. The results for middle-income housing developments in Manhattan were compared with data for several small towns (Stony Point, Spring Valley, Ramapo, Nyack, New City, and West Clarkstown) in Rockland County, outside of New York City. As Table 1 shows, in all cases there was a sharp increase in the proportion of entries achieved by an experimenter when he moved from the city to a small town. In the most extreme case the experimenter was five times as likely to gain admission to homes in a small town as to homes in Manhattan. Although the female experimenters had notably greater success both in cities and in towns than the male experimenters had, each of the four students did at least twice as well in towns as in cities. This suggests that the city-town distinction overrides even the predictably greater fear of male strangers than of female ones.

The lower level of helpfulness by city dwellers seems due in part to recognition of the dangers of living in Manhattan, rather than to mere indifference or coldness. It is significant that 75 percent of all the city respondents received and answered messages by shouting through closed doors and by peering out through peepholes; in the towns, by contrast, about 75 percent of the respondents opened the door.

Supporting the experimenters' quantitative results was their general observation that the town dwellers were noticeably more friendly and less suspicious than the city dwellers. In seeking to explain the reasons for the greater sense of psychological vulnerability city dwellers feel, above and beyond the differences in crime statistics, Villena (Altman, et al., 1969) points out that, if a crime is committed in a village, a resident of a neighboring village may not perceive the crime as personally relevant, though the geographic distance may be small, whereas a criminal act committed anywhere in the city, though miles from the city-dweller's home is still verbally located within the city; thus, Villena says, "the inhabitant of the city possesses a larger vulnerable space."

Civilities. Even at the most superficial level of involvement—the exercise of everyday civilities—urbanites are reputedly deficient. People bump into each other and often do not apologize. They knock over another person's packages and, as often as not, proceed on their way with a grumpy exclamation instead of an offer of assistance. Such behavior, which many visitors to great cities find distasteful, is less common, we are told, in smaller communities, where traditional courtesies are more likely to be observed.

In some instances it is not simply that, in the city, traditional courtesies are violated; rather, the cities develop new norms of noninvolvement. These are so well defined and so deeply a part of city life that *they* constitute the norms people are reluctant to violate. Men are actually embarrassed to give up a seat on the subway to an old woman; they mumble "I was getting off anyway," instead of making the gesture in a straightforward and gracious way. These norms develop because everyone realizes that, in situations of high population density, people cannot implicate themselves in each others' affairs, for to do so would create conditions of continual distraction which would frustrate purposeful action.

In discussing the effects of overload I do not imply that at every instant the city dweller is bombarded with an unmanageable number of inputs, and that his responses are determined by the excess of input at any given instant. Rather, adaptation occurs in the form of gradual evolution of norms of behavior. Norms are evolved in response to frequent discrete experiences of overload; they persist and become generalized modes of responding.

Overload on cognitive capacities: anonymity. That we respond differently toward those whom we know and those who are strangers to us is a truism. An eager patron aggressively cuts in front of someone in a long movie line to save time only to confront a friend; he then behaves sheepishly. A man is involved in an automobile accident caused by another driver, emerges from his car shouting in rage, then moderates his behavior on discovering a friend driving the other car. The city dweller, when walking through the midtown streets, is in a state of continual anonymity vis-à-vis the other pedestrians.

Anonymity is part of a continuous spectrum ranging from total anonymity to full acquaintance, and it may well be

that measurement of the precise degrees of anonymity in cities and towns would help to explain important distinctions between the quality of life in each. Conditions of full acquaintance, for example, offer security and familiarity, but they may also be stifling, because the individual is caught in a web of established relationships. Conditions of complete anonymity, by contrast, provide freedom from routinized social ties, but they may also create feelings of alienation and detachment.

Empirically one could investigate the proportion of activities in which the city dweller or the town dweller is known by others at given times in his daily life, and the proportion of activities in the course of which he interacts with individuals who know him. At his job, for instance, the city dweller may be known to as many people as his rural counterpart. However, when he is not fulfilling his occupational role—say, when merely traveling about the city— the urbanite is doubtless more anonymous than his rural counterpart.

Limited empirical work on anonymity has begun. Zimbardo (1969) has tested whether the social anonymity and impersonality of the big city encourage greater vandalism than do small towns. Zimbardo arranged for one automobile to be left for 64 hours near the Bronx campus of New York University and for a counterpart to be left for the same number of hours near Stanford University in Palo Alto. The license plates on the two cars were removed and the hoods were opened, to provide "releaser cues" for potential vandals. The New York car was stripped of all movable parts within the first 24 hours, and by the end of 3 days was only a hunk of metal rubble. Unexpectedly, however, most of the destruction occurred during daylight hours, usually under the scrutiny of observers, and the leaders in the vandalism were well-dressed, white adults. The Palo Alto car was left untouched.

Zimbardo attributes the difference in the treatment accorded the two cars to the "acquired feelings of social anonymity provided by life in a city like New York," and he supports his conclusions with several other anecdotes illustrating casual, wanton vandalism in the city. In any comparative study of the effects of anonymity in city and town, however, there must be satisfactory control for other confounding factors: the large number of drug addicts in a city like New York; the higher proportion of slum-dwellers in the city; and so on.

Another direction for empirical study is investigation of the beneficial effects of anonymity. The impersonality of city life breeds its own tolerance for the private lives of the inhabitants. Individuality and even eccentricity, we may assume, can flourish more readily in the metropolis than in the small town. Stigmatized persons may find it easier to lead comfortable lives in the city, free of the constant scrutiny of neighbors. To what degree can this assumed difference between city and town be shown empirically? Judith Waters (1969), at The City University of New York, hypothesized that avowed homosexuals would be more likely to be accepted as tenants in a large city than in small towns, and she dispatched letters from homosexuals and from normal individuals to real estate agents in cities and towns across the country. The results of her study were inconclusive. But the general idea of examining the protective benefits of city life to the stigmatized ought to be pursued.

Role behavior in cities and towns.

Another product of urban overload is the adjustment in roles made by urbanites in daily interactions. As Wirth (1938) has said: "Urbanites meet one another in highly segmental roles. . . . They are less dependent upon particular persons, and their dependence upon others is confined to a highly fractionalized aspect of the other's round of activity." This tendency is particularly noticeable in transactions between customers and individuals offering professional or sales services. The owner of a country store has time to become well acquainted with his dozen-or-so daily customers, but the girl at the checkout counter of a busy A & P, serving hundreds of customers a day, barely has time to toss the green stamps into one customer's shopping bag before the next customer confronts her with his pile of groceries.

Meier, in his stimulating analysis of the city (1962), discusses several adaptations a system may make when confronted by inputs that exceed its capacity to process them. Meier argues that, according to the principle of competition for scarce resources, the scope and time of the transaction shrink as customer volume and daily turnover rise. This, in fact, is what is meant by the "brusque" quality of city life. New standards have developed in cities concerning what levels of services are appropriate in business transactions.

McKenna and Morgenthau (1969), in a seminar at The City University of New York, devised a study (i) to compare the willingness of city dwellers and small-town dwellers to do favors for strangers that entailed expenditure of a small amount of time and slight inconvenience but no personal vulnerability, and (ii) to determine whether the more compartmentalized, transitory relationships of the city would make urban salesgirls less likely than small-town salesgirls to carry out, for strangers, tasks not related to their customary roles.

To test for differences between city dwellers and small-town dwellers, a simple experiment was devised in which persons from both settings were asked (by telephone) to perform increasingly onerous favors for anonymous strangers.

Within the cities (Chicago, New York, and Philadelphia), half the calls were to housewives and the other half to salesgirls in women's apparel shops; the division was the same for the 37 small towns of the study, which were in the same states as the cities. Each experimenter represented herself as a long-distance caller who had, through error, been connected with the respondent by the operator. The experimenter began by asking for simple information about the weather for purposes of travel. Next the experimenter excused herself on some pretext (asking the respondent to "please hold on"), put the phone down for almost a full minute, and then picked it up again and asked the respondent to provide the phone number of a hotel or motel in her vicinity at which the experimenter might stay during a forthcoming visit. Scores were assigned the subjects on the basis of how helpful they had been. McKenna summarizes her results in this manner:

People in the city, whether they are engaged in a specific job or not, are less helpful and informative than people in small towns; . . . People at home, regardless of where they live, are less helpful and informative than people working in shops.

However, the absolute level of cooperativeness for urban subjects was found to be quite high, and does not accord with the stereotype of the urbanite as aloof, self-centered, and unwilling to help strangers. The quantitative differences obtained by McKenna and Morgenthau are less great than one might have expected. This again points up the need for extensive empirical research in rural-urban differences, provided in the few illustrative pilot studies presented here. At this point we have very limited objective evidence on differences in the quality of social encounters in city and small town.

But the research needs to be guided by unifying theoretical concepts. As I have tried to demonstrate, the concept of overload helps to explain a wide variety of contrasts between city behavior and town behavior: (i) the differences in role enactment (the tendency of urban dwellers to deal with one another in highly segmented, functional terms, and of urban sales personnel to devote limited time and attention to their customers); (ii) the evolution of urban norms quite different from traditional town values (such as the acceptance of noninvolvement, impersonality, and aloofness in urban life); (iii) the adaptation of the urban dweller's cognitive processes (his inability to identify most of the people he sees daily, his screening of sensory stimuli, his development of blasé attitudes toward deviant or bizarre behavior, and his selectivity in responding to human demands); and (iv) the competition for scarce facilities in the city (the subway rush; the fight for taxis; traffic jams; standing in line to await services). I suggest that contrasts between city and rural behavior probably reflect the responses of similar people to very different situations, rather than intrinsic differences in the personalities of rural and city dwellers. The city is a situation to which individuals respond adaptively.

BIBLIOGRAPHY

Abelson, R. P. Computers, polls, and public opinion. Some puzzles and paradoxes *Trans-action*, 1968, 5, 20–28.

Abelson, R. P., Aronson, E., McGuire, W. J., Newcomb, T. M., Rosenberg, M. J., & Tannenbaum, P. H. (Eds.), *Theories of cognitive consistency: a source book.* Chicago: Rand McNally, 1968.

Aberle, D. F. Culture and socialization. In F. L. K. Hsu (Ed.), *Psychological anthropology.* Homewood, Ill.: Dorsey, 1961. Pp. 381–400.

Ackerman, N. W., & Jahoda, M. *Anti-Semitism and emotional disorder.* New York: Harper, 1950.

Adams, J. S. Inequity in social exchange. In L. Berkowitz (Ed.), *Advances in experimental social psychology.* Vol. 2. New York: Academic Press, 1965. Pp. 267–299.

Adler, F. A unit concept for sociology. *Amer. J. Sociol.,* 1960, 66, 356–364.

Adorno, T. W., Frenkel-Brunswik, Else, Levinson, D., & Sanford, N. *The authoritarian personality.* New York: Harper & Brothers, 1950.

Allen, L. A. *Management and organization.* New York: McGraw-Hill, 1958.

Allen, V. L. Situational factors in conformity. In L. Berkowitz (Ed.), *Advances in experimental social psychology.* Vol. 2. New York: Academic Press, 1965. Pp. 133–175.

Allport, F. H. The influence of the group upon association and thought. *J. exp. Psychol.,* 1920, 3, 159–182.

Allport, F. H. The J-curve hypothesis of conforming behavior. *J. soc. Psychol.,* 1934, 5, 141–183.

Allport, F. H. *Theories of perception & the concept of structure.* New York: Wiley, 1955.

Allport, G. W. Attitudes. In C. Murchison (Ed.), *A handbook of social psychology.* Worcester: Clark Univer. Press, 1935. Pp. 798–844.

Allport, G. W. *Personality: a psychological interpretation.* New York: Holt, 1937.

Allport, G. W. Effect. A secondary principle of learning. *Psychol. Rev.,* 1946, 53, 335–347.

Allport, G. W. *Becoming.* New Haven: Yale Univer. Press, 1955.

Allport, G. W. *The nature of prejudice.* Cambridge, Mass.: Addison-Wesley, 1954. (Paperback edition by Doubleday Anchor, 1958).

Allport, G. W. The open system in personality theory. *J. abnorm. soc. Psychol.* 1960, 61, 301–311.

Allport, G. W. *Pattern and growth in personality.* New York: Holt, Rinehart, & Winston, 1961.

Allport, G. W. Traits revisited. *Amer. Psychologist,* 1966, 21, 1–10.

Allport, G. W. The historical background of modern social psychology. In G. Lindzey & E. Aronson (Eds.), *The handbook of social psychology.* 2nd ed. Vol. 1. Reading, Mass.: Addison-Wesley, 1968. Pp. 1–80.

Altman, D., Levine, M., Nadien, M., & Villena, J. Trust of the stranger in the city and the small town. Unpublished research, New York: Graduate Center, The City Univer. of New York, 1969.

Angelini, A. L. Um novo método para avaliar a motivacão humana. Doctoral dissertation, São Paulo, Brazil: Universidade de São Paulo, 1955.

Angyal, A. *Foundations for a science of personality.* New York: Commonwealth Fund, 1941.

Argyle, M. Social pressure in public and private situations. *J. abnorm. soc. Psychol.,* 1957, 54, 172–175.

Argyris, C. Being human and being organized. *Trans-action,* 1964, 1, 3–6.

Argyris, C. *Personality and organization.* New York: Harper, 1957.

Argyris, C. *Integrating the individual and the organization.* New York: Wiley, 1964.

Aronson, E. The effect of effort on the attractiveness of rewarded and unrewarded stimuli. *J. abnorm. soc. Psychol.*, 1961, 63, 375–380.

Aronson, E. Problem: To find evidence of discomfort as a function of "dissonant" success. In *Methodological problems of social psychology* for the XVIII International Congress of Psychology, 34th Symposium, Moscow, August, 1966.

Aronson, E. Dissonance theory: progress and problems. In R. P. Abelson *et al.*, *Theories of cognitive consistency: a sourcebook.* Chicago: Rand McNally, 1968. Pp. 5–27.

Aronson, E., & Carlsmith, J. M. Performance expectancy as a determinant of actual performance. *J. abnorm. soc. Psychol.*, 1962, 65, 178–182.

Aronson, E. & Carlsmith, J. M. Effect of the severity of threat on the valuation of forbidden behavior. *J. abnorm. soc. Psychol.*, 1963, 66, 584–588.

Aronson, E. & Mills, J. The effect of severity of initiation on liking for a group. *J. abnorm. soc. Psychol.*, 1959, 59, 177–181.

Asch, S. E. Effects of group pressure upon the modification and distortion of judgments. In H. Guetzkow (Ed.), *Groups, leadership, and men.* Pittsburgh: Carnegie Press, 1951.

Asch, S. E. *Social psychology.* New York: Prentice-Hall, 1952.

Asch, S. E. Studies of independence and conformity: a minority of one against a unanimous majority. *Psychol. Monogr.*, 1956, 70 (9, Whole No. 416).

Asch, S. E. A perspective on social psychology. In S. Koch (Ed.), *Psychology: a study of a science.* Vol. 3. New York: McGraw-Hill, 1959. Pp. 363–384.

Ashton, Margaret. An ecological study of the stream of behavior. Unpublished master's thesis, Univer. of Kansas, 1964.

Astin, A. W. *Document No. 7262, ADI auxiliary publications project,* Photoduplication Service. Washington: Library of Congress, 1962.

Atkinson, J. W. (Ed.). *Motives in fantasy, action, and society.* Princeton, N.J.: Van Nostrand, 1958.

Atkinson, J. W., & Reitman, W. R. Performance as a function of motive strength and expectancy of goal-attainment. *J. abnorm. soc. Psychol.*, 1956, 53, 361–366.

Aurthur, R. A. Review of *The western hero. The Nation,* January 24, 1966, p. 107.

Bachrach, P. & Baratz, M. S. Two faces of power. *Amer. Polit. Sci. Rev.*, Dec. 1962, 56, 947–952.

Back, K. Personal communication, 1959.

Back, K. W. Influence through social communication. *J. abnorm. soc. Psychol.*, 1951, 46, 9–23.

Bakke, E. W. Concept of the social organization. In M. Haire (Ed.), *Modern organization theory.* New York: Wiley, 1959. Pp. 60–61.

Baldwin, J. *Notes of a native son.* Boston: Beacon Press, 1955.

Bales, R. F. *Interaction process analysis: a method for the study of small groups.* Reading, Mass.: Addison-Wesley, 1950.

Bales, R. F. The equilibrium problem in small groups. In T. Parsons, R. F. Bales, & E. A. Shils, *Working papers in the theory of action.* Glencoe, Ill.: Free Press, 1953. Pp. 111–161.

Bales, R. F., Task roles and social roles in problem-solving groups. In Eleanor E. Maccoby, M. Newcomb, & E. L. Hartley (Eds.), *Readings in social psychology.* 3d ed. New York: Holt, 1958. Pp. 437–447.

Bales, R. F., *Personality and interpersonal behavior,* New York: Holt, Rinehart & Winston, 1970.

Bales, R. F. Interaction Process Analysis. In D. S. Sills (Ed.), *International encyclopedia of the social sciences.* Vol. 8. New York: Crowell Collier and Macmillan, 1968. Pp. 465–471.

Bales, R. F., & Borgatta, E. F. Size of group as a factor in the interaction profile. In R. F. Bales & E. F. Borgatta (Eds.), *Small groups: studies in social interaction.* Rev. ed. New York: Knopf, 1965.

Bales, R. F., & Hare, A. P. Diagnostic use of the interaction profile. *J. of soc. Psychol.*, 1965, 67, 239–258.

Bales, R. F., & Strodtbeck, F. L. Phases in problem-solving. *J. abnorm. soc. Psychol.*, 1951, 46, 485–495.

Ball, W. W. Calculating prodigies. In J. R. Newman (Ed.), *The world of mathematics.* New York: Simon & Schuster, 1956.

Bandura, A., & Walters, R. H. *Adolescent aggression.* New York: Ronald, 1959.

Bandura, A., & Walters, R. H. *Social learning and personality development*. New York: Holt, Rinehart, & Winston, 1963.

Banta, T. J., & Nelson, C. Experimental analysis of resource location in problem-solving groups. *Sociometry*, 1964, 27, 488–501.

Banton, M. *Roles: an introduction to the study of social relations*. New York: Basic Books, 1965.

Barker, R. G. Ecology and motivation. In M. R. Jones (Ed.), *Nebraska symposium on motivation*. Lincoln: Univer. of Nebraska Press, 1960. Pp. 1–49.

Barker, R. G. *Ecological psychology: concepts and methods for studying the environment of human behavior*. Stanford, Cal.: Stanford Univer. Press, 1968.

Barker, R. G., & Gump, P. V. *Big school, small school*. Stanford, Calif.: Stanford Univer. Press, 1964.

Barker, R. G. & Wright H. F. *Midwest and its children*. New York: Harper & Row, 1955.

Barker, R. G., Wright, H. F., Barker, L. S., & Schoggen, M. *Specimen records of American and English children*. Lawrence: Univer. of Kansas Press, 1961.

Barnard, C. I. *The functions of the executive*. Cambridge, Mass.: Harvard Univer. Press, 1938.

Barron, F. An ego-strength scale which predicts response to psychotherapy. *J. consult. Psychol.*, 1953, 17, 327–333.

Barth, F. Models of social organization. Royal Anthropological Institute of Gr. Britain and Ireland, Occasional paper No. 23, 1966.

Barton, A. H. The concept of property space in social research. In P. F. Lazarsfeld and M. Rosenberg (Eds.), *The language of social research*. Glencoe, Ill.: Free Press, 1955. Pp. 40–54.

Bass, B. M. *Leadership, psychology, and organizational behavior*. New York: Harper, 1960.

Bastide, R. *Sociologie et psychanalyse*. Paris: Presses Univer. de France, 1950.

Bauer, R. A. Risk handling in drug adoption: the role of company preference. *Publ. Opin. Quart.*, 1961, 25, 546–559.

Bauer, R. A. The initiative of the audience. Paper read at New England Psychological Association, Boston, November, 1962.

Bauer, R. A. The obstinate audience: the influence process from the point of view of social communication. *Amer. Psychologist*, 1964, 19, 319–328.

Bauer, R. A., Pool, I. de Sola., & Dexter, L. A. *American business and public policy*. New York: Atherton Press, 1963.

Bavelas, A. Leadership: man and function. *Admin. Sci. Quart.*, 1960, 4, 491–498.

Bavelas, A., Hastorf, A. H., Gross, A. E., & Kite, W. R. Experiments on the alteration of group structure. *J. exp. soc. Psychol.*, 1965, 1, 55–70.

Bayer, E. Beiträge zur Zweikomponententheorie des Hungers. *Zeitschrift für Psychol.*, 1929, 112, 1–54.

Bayley, D. H. The pedagogy of democracy: coercive public protest in India. *Amer. Polit. Sci. Rev.*, 1962, 56, 663–672.

Beach, F. A. Current concepts of play in animals. *Amer. Natur.*, 1945, 79, 523–541.

Beck, R. Coalitions in a three-person matrix game under conditions of negotiation and non-negotiation. Unpublished honor's thesis, State Univer. of New York at Buffalo, 1968.

Becker, H. S. *Outsiders*. New York: Free Press, 1963.

Becker, H. S. Personal change in adult life. *Sociometry*, 1964, 27, 1, 40–53.

Becker, H. S., Geer, B., Hughes, E. C. & Strauss, A. *Boys in white: student culture in medical school*. Chicago, Ill.: Univer. of Chicago Press, 1961.

Beer, S. *Cybernetics and management*. New York: Wiley, 1959.

Bell, G. B., & Hall, H. E. The relationship between leadership and socioempathy. *J. abnorm. soc. Psychol.*, 1954, 49, 156–157.

Bell, G. D. Determinants of span control. *Amer. J. Sociol.*, 1967, 73, 90–101.

Beloff, H. Two forms of social conformity: acquiescence and conventionality. *J. abnorm. soc. Psychol.*, 1958, 56, 99–104.

Benedict, R. Continuities and discontinuities in cultural conditioning. In P. Mullahy (Ed.), *A study of interpersonal relations*. New York: Heritage Press, 1949, pp. 297–308.

Bennis, W. Organic populism. *Psychology Today*, 1970, 3, 48–71.

Bennis, W. G. Beyond bureaucracy. *Transaction*, 1965, 2, 31–35.

Bennis, W. G., Benne, K. D., & Chin, R. *The planning of change*. 2nd ed. New York: Holt, Rinehart & Winston, 1969.

Bennis, W. G., Berkowitz, N., Affinito, M., & Malone, M. Group influence in marketing and public relations. Ann Arbor: Foundation for Research on Human Behavior, 1956.

Bennis, W. G., Berkowitz, N., Affinito, M., & Malone, M. Reference groups and loyalties in the out-patient department. Admin. Sci. Quart., 1958, 2, 481–500.

Bennis, W., & Slater, P. E. The temporary society. New York: Harper & Row, 1968.

Berelson, B. What missing the newspaper means. In P. F. Lazarsfeld & F. N. Stanton (Eds.), Communications research, 1948–1949. New York: Harper, 1949. Pp. 111–129.

Berelson, B., & Salter, Patricia J. Majority and minority Americans: an analysis of magazine fiction. Publ. Opin. Quart., 1946, 10, 168–190.

Berg, I. A., & Bass, B. M. (Eds.), Conformity and deviation. New York: Harper, 1961.

Berkowitz, L. Liking for the group and the perceived merit of the group's behavior. J. abnorm. soc. Psychol., 1957, 54, 353–357.

Berkowitz, L., & Macaulay, J. R. Some effects of differences in status level and status stability. Hum. Relat., 1961, 14, 135–148.

Berlyne, D. E. Conflict, arousal, and curiosity. New York: McGraw-Hill, 1960.

Bexton, W. H., Heron, W., & Scott, T. H. Effects of decreased variation in the sensory environment. Canad. J. Psychol., 1954, 8, 70–76.

Biddle, B. J., & Thomas, E. J. (Eds.). Role theory: concepts and research. New York: Wiley, 1966.

Bierstedt, R. An analysis of social power. Amer. sociol. Rev., 1950, 15, 730–738.

Birdwhistell, R. L. Introduction to kinesics. Washington: Foreign Service Institute, 1952.

Blake, R. R., Helson, H., & Mouton, J. S. The generality of conformity behavior as a function of factual anchorage, difficulty of task, and amount of social pressure. J. Personal., 1956, 25, 294–305.

Blake, R. R., & Mouton, J. S. Conformity, resistance and conversion. In I. A. Berg & B. M. Bass (Eds.), Conformity and deviation. New York: Harper, 1961. Pp. 1–37.

Blalock, H. M., & Blalock, A. B. Methodology in social research. New York: McGraw-Hill, 1968.

Blau, P. The dynamics of bureaucracy. Chicago: Univer. Chicago Press, 1955.

Blau, P. M. Justice in social exchange. Sociol. Inquiry, 1964a, 34, 193–206.

Blau, P. M. Exchange and power in social life. New York: Wiley, 1964b.

Blau, P. M., & Scott, W. R. Formal organizations. San Francisco: Chandler, 1962.

Blauner, R. Alienation and freedom. Chicago: Univ. of Chicago Press, 1964.

Bliss, E. L., Sandberg, A. A., Nelson, D. H., & Eik-Nes, K. The normal levels of 17-hydrocorticosteroids in the peripheral blood of man. J. clin. Invest., 1953, 32, 9.

Block, B., & Trager, G. L. Outline of linguistic analysis. Baltimore: Waverly Press, 1942.

Bloomfield, L. Language. New York: Henry Holt, 1933.

Board, F., Persky, H., & Hamburg, D. A. Psychological stress and endocrine functions. Psychosom. Med., 1956, 18, 324–333.

Bogardus, E. S. Contemporary sociology. Los Angeles: Univer. of Southern Calif. Press, 1931.

Bogart, L. Adult talk about newspaper comics. Amer. J. Sociol., 1955, 61, 26–30.

Borgatta, E. F. The stability of interpersonal judgments in independent situations. J. abnorm. soc. Psychol., 1960, 60, 188–194.

Borgatta, E. F., Cottrell, L. S., & Meyer, H. J. On the dimensions of group behavior. Sociometry, 1956, 19, 223–240.

Borgatta, E. F., & Lambert, W. W. (Eds.). Handbook of personality theory and research. Chicago: Rand McNally, 1968.

Boskin, J. Violence in the ghettoes: a consensus of attitudes. New Mexico Quart., 1968, 37, 317–334.

Boulding, K. E. General system theory— the skeleton of a science. Mgmt. Sci., 1956, 2, 197–208.

Bovard, E. W. The effects of social stimuli on the response to stress. Psychol. Rev., 1959, 66, 267–277.

Brech, E. F. L. Organization. London: Longmans, Green & Co., 1957.

Bredemeier, H. C., & Stephenson, R. M. The analysis of social systems. New York: Holt, Rinehart, & Winston, 1962.

Brehm, J. W. Post-decision changes in the desirability of alternatives. J. abnorm. soc. Psychol., 1956, 52, 384–389.

Brehm, J. W. A *theory of psychological reactance*. New York: Academic Press, 1966.

Brehm, J. W. & Cohen, A. R. *Explorations in cognitive dissonance*. New York: Wiley, 1962.

Brehm, M. L., Back, K. W., & Bogdonoff, M.D. A physiological effect of cognitive dissonance under stress and deprivation. *J. abnorm. soc. Psychol.*, 1964, 69, 303–310.

Bridgman, P. W. *The nature of physical theory*. Princeton, N.J.: Princeton Univer. Press, 1936.

Brim, O. G. Jr., *Education for child rearing*. New York: Russell Sage Foundation, 1959.

Brim, O. J., & Wheeler, S. *Socialization after childhood*. New York: Wiley, 1966.

Bronfenbrenner, U. Socialization and social class through time and space. In E. E. Maccoby, T. M. Newcomb, & E. L. Hartley (Eds.), *Readings in social psychology*. 3rd ed. New York: Holt, Rinehart, & Winston, 1958. Pp. 400–425.

Bronfenbrenner, U. Some familial antecedents of responsibility and leadership in adolescents. In L. Petrullo & B. M. Bass (Eds.), *Leadership and interpersonal behavior*. New York: Holt, Rinehart, and Winston, 1961a.

Bronfenbrenner, U. The changing American child—a speculative analysis. *J. soc. Issues*, 1961b, 17, 6–18.

Bronfenbrenner, U. The mirror image in Soviet-American relations. *J. soc. Issues*, 1961c, 17, 45–56.

Brown, J. F. *Psychology and the social order*. New York: McGraw-Hill, 1936.

Brown, R. How shall a thing be called? *Psychol. Rev.*, 1958a, 65, 14–22.

Brown, R. *Words and things*. Glencoe, Ill.: Free Press, 1958b.

Brown, R. W. Mass phenomena. In G. Lindzey (Ed.), *Handbook of social psychology*, Vol. 2, Cambridge: Addison-Wesley, 1954.

Brown, R. W. *Social psychology*. New York: Free Press, 1965.

Bruce, D. Effects of context upon the intelligibility of heard speech. In C. Cherry (Ed.), *Information theory*. London: Butterworths, 1956. Pp. 245–252.

Bruner, J. S. On perceptual readiness. *Psychol. Rev.*, 1957, 64, 123–152.

Bruner, J. S., Matter, J., & Papanek, M. L.

Breadth of learning as a function of drive level and mechanization. *Psychol. Rev.*, 1955, 62, 1–10.

Brunswik, E. *Wahrnehmung und Gegenstandswelt*. Leipzig and Vienna: Deuticke, 1934.

Brunswik, E. The conceptual framework of psychology. In *International encyclopedia of unified science*. Vol. I. Chicago: Univer. of Chicago Press, 1952.

Bühler, K. Displeasure and pleasure in relation to activity. In M. L. Reymert (Ed.), *Feelings and emotions: The Wittenberg symposium*. Worcester, Mass.: Clark Univer. Press, 1928. Ch. 14, pp. 195–199.

Bühler, K. *Die Krise der Psychologie*. Jena: G. Fischer, 1929.

Burke, P. J. Authority relations and descriptive behavior in small discussion groups. *Sociometry*, 1966, 29, 237–250.

Burns, T., & Stalker, G. M. *The management of innovation*. London: Tavistock Publications, 1961.

Burton, R. V., & Whiting, J. W. M. The absent father and cross-sex identity. *Merrill-Palmer Quart.*, 1961, 7, 85–95.

Butler, R. A. Discrimination learning by rhesus monkeys to visual exploration motivation. *J. comp. physiol. Psychol.*, 1953, 46, 95–98.

Cadwallader, M. L. The cybernetic analysis of change in complex social organizations. *Amer. J. Sociol.*, 1959, 60, 156–157.

Cain, L. D., Jr. Life course and social structure. In R. E. L. Faris (Ed.), *Handbook of modern sociology*. Chicago: Rand McNally, 1964. Pp. 272–310.

Caldwell, B. M. The usefulness of the critical period hypothesis in the study of filiative behavior. *Merrill-Palmer Quarterly*, 1962, 8, 4.

Campbell, A., Converse, P. E., Miller, W. E., & Stokes, D., *The American voter*, New York: Wiley, 1960.

Campbell, A., Gurin, G., & Miller, W. E. *The voter decides*. Evanston, Ill.: Row, Peterson & Co., 1954.

Campbell, D. T. Enhancement of contrast as a composite habit. *J. abnorm. soc. Psychol.*, 1956, 53, 350–355.

Campbell, D. T. Social attitudes and other acquired behavioral dispositions. In S. Koch (Ed.), *Psychology: A study of a science*. Vol. 6. New York: McGraw-Hill, 1963. Pp. 94–172.

Campbell, D. T. Stereotypes and the perception of group differences. *Amer. Psychologist*, 1967, 22, 817–829.

Campbell, D. T., & Kral, T. P. Transposition away from a rewarded stimulus card to a nonrewarded one as a function of a shift in background. *J. comp. Physiol. Psychol.*, 1958, 51, 592–595.

Campbell, D. T., & LeVine, R. A. A proposal for cooperative cross-cultural research on ethnocentrism. *J. Conflict Resolution*, 1961, 5(1), 82–108.

Cannon, W. B. *The wisdom of the body*. New York: Norton, 1932.

Cantril, H. Perception and interpersonal relations. *Amer. J. Psychiat.*, 1957, 114, 119–127.

Cantril, H. The human design. *J. ind. Psychol.*, 1964, 20, 129–136.

Cantril, H. *The pattern of human concerns*. New Brunswick, N.J.: Rutgers Univer. Press, 1965.

Cantril, H., & Livingston, W. K. The concept of transaction in psychology and neurology. *J. indiv. Psychol.*, 1963, 19, 3–16.

Caplow, T. A theory of coalitions in the triad. *Amer. sociol. Rev.*, 1956, 21, 489–493.

Carey, A. The Hawthorne studies: a radical criticism. *Amer. sociol. Rev.*, 1967, 32, 403–417.

Carlsmith, J. M. & Freedman, J. L. Personal communication, 1968.

Carlsmith, J. M., Collins, B. E., & Helmreich, R. L. Studies in forced compliance: 1. the effect of pressure for compliance on attitude change produced by face-to-face role playing and anonymous essay writing. *J. of Personal. and soc. Psychol.*, 1966, 4, 1–13.

Carlson, R. O. The influence of community and the primary group on the reactions of southern Negroes to syphilis. Unpublished Ph.D. dissertation, Columbia Univer., 1952.

Carroll, J. B. *The study of language*. Cambridge, Mass.: Harvard Univer. Press, 1955.

Carson, R. C. *Interaction concepts of personality*. Chicago: Aldine, 1969.

Carter, L. F. Evaluating the performance of individuals as members of small groups.

Personnel Psychol., 1954, 7, 477–484.

Carter, L. F., Haythorn, W., Meirowitz, B., & Lanzetta, J. The relation of categorizations and ratings in the observation of group behavior. *Hum. Relat.*, 1951, 4, 239–253.

Cartwright, D. Some principles of mass persuasion: selected findings of research on the sale of United States War Bonds. *Hum. Relat.*, 1949, 2, 253–267.

Cartwright, D. Achieving change in people: Some applications of group dynamics theory. *Hum. Relat.*, 1951, 4, 381–393.

Cartwright, D. (Ed.). *Field theory in social science*. (Kurt Lewin) New York: Harper & Row, 1951.

Cartwright, D. Power: a neglected variable in social psychology. In D. Cartwright (Ed.), *Studies in social power*. Ann Arbor: Institute for Social Research, Univer. of Michigan, 1959. Pp. 1–14.

Cartwright, D. Influence, leadership, control. In J. March (Ed.), *Handbook of organizations*. Chicago: Rand McNally, 1965.

Cartwright, D., & Zander, A. (Eds.). *Group dynamics*. New York: Harper & Row, 1953 (2nd ed., 1960; 3rd ed., 1968).

Cattell, R. B. *Personality and motivation structure and measurement*. New York: World Book, 1957.

Cayton, H. R. The psychology of the Negro under discrimination. In A. Rose (Ed.), *Race prejudice and discrimination*. New York: Knopf, 1951. Pp. 276–290.

Chapanis, N. P. & Chapanis, A. Cognitive dissonance: Five years later. *Psychol. Bull.*, 1964, 61, 1–22.

Charters, W. W. & Newcomb, T. M. Some attitudinal effects of experimentally increased salience of a membership group. In E. E. Maccoby, T. M. Newcomb, & E. L. Hartley (Eds.), *Readings in social psychology*. 3rd ed. New York: Holt, Rinehart, & Winston, 1958. Pp. 276–281.

Chen, S. C. Social modification of the activity of ants in nest-building. *Physiol. Zool.*, 1937, 10, 420–436.

Child, I. Socialization. In G. Lindzey (Ed.), *Handbook of social psychology*. Vol. 2. Cambridge, Mass.: Addison-Wesley, 1954. Pp. 655–692.

Child, J. L. Problems of personality and some relations to anthropology and sociology. In S. Koch (Ed.), *Psychology:*

a study of a science. Vol. 3. New York: McGraw-Hill, 1963. Pp. 593–639.

Chomsky, N. *Syntactic structures.* The Hague: Mouton, 1957.

Chomsky, N. Review of *Verbal Behavior* (B. F. Skinner). *Language,* 1959, 35, 26–58.

Chomsky, N. Explanatory models in linguistics. In E. Wagel, P. Suppes, & A. Tarski (Eds.), *Logic, methodology, and philosophy of science.* Stanford, Calif.: Stanford Univer. Press, 1962. Pp. 528–550.

Chomsky, N. *Cartesian linguistics.* New York: Harper & Row, 1966.

Chomsky, N. *Language and mind.* New York: Harcourt, Brace & World, 1968.

Chomsky, N. Language and the Mind, I & II. *Columbia University Forum,* 1968, XI, 1, 5–10; 3, 23–24.

Chowdhry, K., & Newcomb, T. M. The relative abilities of leaders and non-leaders to estimate opinions of their own groups. *J. abnorm. soc. Psychol.,* 1952, 47, 51–57.

Christie, R., & Geis, Florence. Some consequences of taking Machiavelli seriously. In E. F. Borgatta & W. W. Lambert (Eds.), *Handbook of personality theory and research.* Chicago: Rand McNally, 1968. Pp. 959–973.

Christie, R., & Geis, Florence. *Studies in Machiavellianism.* New York: Academic Press, 1970.

Christie, R., Havel, Joan, & Seidenberg, B. Is the F scale irreversible? *J. abnorm. soc. Psychol.,* 1958, 56, 143–159.

Clark, K. B. *Prejudice and your child.* (2nd ed.) Boston, Mass.: Beacon Press, 1963.

Clark, K. B., & Clark, Mamie P. Racial identification and preference in Negro children. In T. M. Newcomb & E. L. Hartley (Eds.), *Readings in social psychology.* 1st ed. New York: Holt, 1947. Pp. 169–178.

Clark, R. B., & Campbell, D. T. A demonstration of bias in estimates of Negro ability. *J. abnorm. soc. Psychol.,* 1955, 51, 585–588.

Clausen, J. A. (Ed.), *Socialization and society.* Boston: Little, Brown and Co., 1968.

Clifford, C., & Cohen, T. S. The relationship between leadership and personality attributes perceived by followers. *J. soc. Psychol.,* 1964, 64, 57–64.

Coch, L., & French, J. R. P., Jr. Overcoming resistance to change. *Hum. Relat.,* 1948, 1, 512–532.

Cofer, C. N., & Apley, M. H. *Motivation: theory and research.* New York: Wiley, 1964.

Cohen, A. K. & Short, J. F. Jr. Juvenile delinquency. In R. K. Merton & R. A. Nisbet (Eds.), *Contemporary social problems.* New York: Harcourt, Brace and World, Inc., 1961. P. 87.

Cohen, A. M., & Bennis, W. G. Continuity of leadership in communication networks. *Hum. Relat.,* 1961, 14, 351–367.

Cohen, A. R. Some implications of self-esteem for social influence. In C. I. Hovland & I. L. Janis (Eds.), *Personality and persuasibility.* New Haven: Yale Univer. Press, 1959. Pp. 102–120.

Cohen, A. R. An experiment on small rewards for discrepant compliance and attitude change. In J. W. Brehm & A. R. Cohen, *Explorations in cognitive dissonance.* New York: Wiley, 1962. Pp. 73–78.

Coleman, J. *Community conflict.* New York: Free Press, 1957.

Coleman, J., Menzel, H., & Katz, E. Social processes in physicians' adoption of a new drug. *J. chron. Diseases,* 1959, 9, 1–19.

Cooley, C. H. *Human nature and the social order.* New York: Scribner's, 1902 (Rev. ed., 1922); reprinted by Free Press, 1956.

Coser, L. Conflict: social aspects. *Int. Encyclopedia soc. Sciences,* 1968, 3, 232–236.

Cottrell, W. F. *The railroader.* Palo Alto, Calif.: Stanford Univer. Press, 1940.

Couch, A. S. Psychological Determinants of Interpersonal Behavior. Unpublished doctoral dissertation, Harvard Univer., 1960.

Cox, D. F. Information and uncertainty: their effects on consumers' product evaluations. Unpublished doctoral dissertation, Harvard Univer., Graduate School of Bus. Admin., 1962.

Croner, M. D., & Willis, R. H. Perceived differences in task competence and asymmetry of dyadic influence. *J. abnorm. soc. Psychol.,* 1961, 62, 705–708.

Crutchfield, R. S. Conformity and character. *Amer. Psychologist,* 1955, 10, 191–198.

Crutchfield, R. S. Conformity and creative thinking. In H. E. Gruber, G. Terrell, & M. Wertheimer (Eds.), *Contemporary approaches to creative thinking.* New

York: Atherton, 1962. Pp. 120–140.

Crutchfield, R. S. Independent thought in a conformist world. In S. M. Farber & R. H. L. Wilson (Eds.), Conformity and conflict: control of the mind. Part 2. New York: McGraw-Hill, 1963. Pp. 208–228.

Cyert, R. M., & March, J. G. Organizational design. In W. W. Cooper, H. J. Leavitt, & M. W. Shelly (Eds.), New perspectives in organization research. New York: Wiley, 1964. Pp. 557–567.

Dahl, R. A. Who governs? New Haven, Conn.: Yale Univer. Press, 1961.

Dahrendorf, R. Class and class conflict in industrial society. Stanford, Calif.: Stanford Univer. Press, 1959.

Dalton, M. Conflicts between staff and line managerial officers. Amer. sociol. Rev., 1950, 15, 342–351.

Dashiell, J. F. An experimental analysis of some group effects. J. abnorm. soc. Psychol., 1930, 25, 190–199.

Davidson, J. R. & Kiesler, S. Cognitive behavior before and after decisions. In L. Festinger, Conflict, decision, and dissonance. Stanford: Stanford Univer. Press, 1964. Pp. 10–21.

Davie, M. Negroes in American society. New York: McGraw-Hill, 1949.

Davis, J. A. A formal interpretation of the theory of relative deprivation. Sociometry, 1959, 22, 280–296.

Davis, K. Human society. New York: Macmillan, 1949.

Davis, K. Human relations in business. New York: McGraw-Hill, 1957.

Davis, R. C. The fundamentals of top management. New York: Harper, 1951.

Davison, W. P. On the effects of communication. Publ. Opin. Quart., 1959, 23, 343–360.

Davitz, J. R., & Mason, D. J. Socially facilitated reduction of a fear response in rats. J. comp. physiol. Psychol., 1955, 48, 149–151.

DeLaguna, Grace. Speech: its functions and development. New Haven: Yale Univer. Press, 1927.

Dennenberg, V. H. The effects of early experience. In E. S. E. Hafez (Ed.), The behavior of domestic animals. London: Balliere, Tindall, & Cox, 1962. Ch. 6.

Dennis, W. Causes of retardation among institutional children: Iran. J. genet. Psychol., 1960, 96, 47–59.

deRivera, J. The psychological dimension of foreign policy. Columbus, Ohio: Bobbs-Merrill, 1968.

DeSoto, C. B. The predilection for single orderings. J. abnorm. soc. Psychol., 1961, 62, 16–23.

Deutsch, K. W. On communication models in the social sciences. Publ. Opin. Quart., 1952, 16, 356–380.

Deutsch, M. An experimental study of the effects of cooperation and competition upon group processes. Hum. Relat., 1949a, 2, 199–232.

Deutsch, M. A theory of cooperation and competition. Hum. Relat., 1949b, 2, 129–152.

Deutsch, M. Trust and suspicion. J. Conflict Resolution, 1958, 2, 265–279.

Deutsch, M. The effect of motivational orientation upon trust and suspicion. Hum. Relat., 1960a, 13, 123–140.

Deutsch, M. Trust, trustworthiness, and the F scale. J. abnorm. soc. Psychol., 1960b, 61, 138–140.

Deutsch, M. Some considerations relevant to national policy. J. soc. Issues, 1961, 17, 57–68.

Deutsch, Morton. Socially relevant science: Reflections on some studies of interpersonal conflict. Amer. Psychol., 1969, 24, 1076–1092.

Deutsch, M. Socially relevant science: Reflections on some studies of interpersonal conflict. Amer. Psychol., 1969, 24, 1076–1092.

Deutsch, M., & Gerard, H. B. A study of normative and informational influences upon individual judgment. J. abnorm. soc. Psychol., 1955, 51, 629–636.

Deutsch, M., & Krauss, R. M. The effect of threat upon interpersonal bargaining. J. abnorm. soc. Psychol., 1960, 61, 181–189.

Deutsch, M., & Krauss, R. M. Theories in social psychology. New York: Basic Books, 1965.

Deutsch, M., & Solomon, L. Reactions to evaluations by others as influenced by self-evaluations. Sociometry, 1959, 22, 93–112.

Dewey, J. How we think. New York: Macmillan, 1910.

Diamond, S. A neglected aspect of motivation. Sociometry, 1939, 2, 77–85.

Diggory, J. C. Some consequences of proximity to a disease threat. *Sociometry*, 1956, 19, 47–53.

Dittes, J. E., & Kelley, H. H. Effects of different conditions of acceptance upon conformity to group norms. *J. abnorm. soc. Psychol.*, 1956, 53, 100–107.

Dodds, E. R. *The Greeks and the irrational.* Boston: Beacon Press, 1957.

Dollard, J., Doob, L. W., Miller, N. E., Mowrer, O. H., & Sears, R. R. *Frustration and aggression.* New Haven, Conn.: Yale Univer. Press, 1939.

Dubin, R. *The world of work.* Englewood Cliffs, N.J.: Prentice Hall, 1958.

Dubno, P. Leadership, group effectiveness, and speed of decision. *J. soc. Psychol.*, 1965, 65, 351–360.

Duesenberg, J. S. *Income, saving, and the theory of consumer behavior.* Cambridge: Harvard Univer. Press, 1949.

Duffy, E. *Activation and behavior.* New York: Wiley, 1962.

Durkheim, E. *The division of labor in society.* (Trans. by George Simpson.) Glencoe, Ill.: Free Press, 1950.

Dynes, R. & Quarantelli, E. L. What looting in civil disturbances really means. *Trans-action*, 1968, 5, 9–14.

Easton, D. Limits of the equilibrium model in social research. In *Profits and problems of homeostatic models in the behavioral sciences.* Publication I, Chicago Behavioral Sciences, 1953. P. 39.

Edwards, A. L. *Techniques of attitude scale construction.* New York: Appleton-Century-Crofts, 1957.

Eisenstadt, S. N. Studies in reference group behavior. *Hum. Relat.*, 1954, 7, 191–206, 212–213.

Elkin, L. The behavioural use of space by children. Unpublished manuscript, 1964.

Elkins, S. *Slavery.* Chicago: Univer. of Chicago Press, 1959.

Elms, A. C. & Janis, I. L. Counter-norm attitudes induced by consonant versus dissonant conditions of role-playing. *Journal of Experimental Research in Personality*, 1965, 1, 50–60.

Emerson, R. M. Power-dependence relations. *Amer. sociol. Rev.*, 1962, 27, 31–41.

Emery, F. E., & Katz, F. M. Social theory and minority group behavior. *Austral. J. Psychol.*, 1951, 3, 22–35.

Endler, N. S., & Hunt, J. McV. Sources of variance in reported anxiousness as measured by the S-R Inventory. (Mimeographed publication, Psychology Dept., Univer. of Illinois, 1964.)

Endler, N. S., Hunt, J. McV., & Rosenstein, A. J. An S-R Inventory of anxiousness. *Psychol. Monogr.*, 1962, 76, No. 17, 1–33.

Epstein, W. The influence of syntactical structure on learning. *Amer. J. Psychol.*, 1961, 74, 80–85.

Erikson, E. H. The problem of ego identity. *J. Amer. psychoanal. Assn.*, 1956, 4, 56.

Erikson, E. H. *Childhood and society*, 2nd ed. New York: Norton, 1963.

Erikson, E. H. *Identity: youth and crisis.* New York: Norton, 1968.

Eskola, A. *Social influence and power in two-person groups.* Copenhagen: Munksgaard, 1961. (Doctoral dissertation, Univer. of Helsinki; Vol. 6 of the *Transactions of the Westermarck Society.*)

Etzioni, A. *A comparative analysis of complex organizations.* New York: Free Press, 1961.

Etzioni, A. *Modern organizations.* Englewood Cliffs, N.J.: Prentice-Hall, 1964.

Etzioni, A. *The active society.* New York: Free Press, 1968.

Evan, W. M., & Zelditch, M. A laboratory experiment on bureaucratic authority. *American Sociological Review*, 1961, 26, 883–893.

Eysenck, H. J. *The structure of human personality.* New York: Wiley, 1953.

Eysenck, H. J. The science of personality: Nomothetic! *Psychol. Rev.*, 1954, 61, 339–343.

Farber, I. E. Response fixation under anxiety and non-anxiety conditions. *J. exp. Psychol.*, 1948, 38, 111–131.

Faris, R. E. L. (Ed.). *Handbook of modern sociology.* Chicago: Rand McNally, 1964.

Feshback, S. & Feshback, N. Influence of the stimulus object upon the complementary and supplementary projections of fear. *J. abnorm. soc. Psychol.*, 1963, 66, 498–502.

Festinger, L. The role of group-belongingness in a voting situation. *Hum. Relat.*, 1947, 1, 154–180.

Festinger, L. Informal social communication. *Psychol. Rev.*, 1950, 57, 271–282.

Festinger, L. An analysis of compliant behavior. In M. Sherif & M. O. Wilson (Eds.), *Group relations at the crossroads*. New York: Harper, 1953. Pp. 232–256.

Festinger, L. A theory of social comparison processes. *Hum. Relat.*, 1954, 7, 117–140.

Festinger, L. *A theory of cognitive dissonance*. Evanston, Ill.: Row, Peterson, 1957.

Festinger, L. Behavioral support for opinion change. *Public Opinion Quarterly*, 1964a, 28, 404–417.

Festinger, L. *Conflict, decision and dissonance*. Stanford: Stanford Univer. Press, 1964b.

Festinger, L. & Aronson, E. The arousal and reduction of dissonance in social contexts. In D. Cartwright & A. Zander (Eds.), *Group dynamics* 2nd ed. Evanston, Ill.: Row-Peterson, 1960. Pp. 214–231.

Festinger, L., Back, K., Schachter, S., Kelley, H. H., & Thibaut, J. *Theory and experiment in social communication*. Ann Arbor: Institute for Social Research, Univer. of Michigan, 1950.

Festinger, L. & Bramel, D. The reactions of humans to cognitive dissonance. In A. Bachrach (Ed.), *The experimental foundations of clinical psychology*. New York: Basic Books, 1962. Pp. 254–279.

Festinger, L. & Carlsmith, J. M. Cognitive consequences of forced compliance. *J. abnorm. soc. Psychol.*, 1959, 58, 203–210.

Festinger, L. & Freedman, J. L. Dissonance reduction and moral values. In P. Worchel & D. Byrne (Eds.), *Personality change*. New York: Wiley, 1964. Pp. 220–243.

Festinger, L., Gerard, H. B., Hymovitch, B., Kelley, H. H., & Raven, B. The influence process in the presence of extreme deviates. *Hum. Relat.* 1952, 5, 327–346.

Festinger, L., & Katz, D. (Eds.). *Research methods in the behavioral sciences*. New York: Holt, 1953.

Festinger, L., Riecken, H., & Schachter, S. *When prophecy fails*. Minneapolis: University of Minnesota Press, 1956.

Festinger, L., Schachter, S., & Back, K. *Social pressures in informal groups: A study of a housing project*. New York: Harper, 1950.

Festinger, L., Schachter, S., & Back, K. The operation of group standards. In D. Cartwright & A. Zander, *Group dynamics: research and theory*. Evanston, Ill.: Row, Peterson, 1953. Pp. 204–223.

Fiedler, F. E. *Leader attitudes and group effectiveness*. Urbana: Univer. of Illinois Press, 1958.

Fiedler, F. E. A contingency model of leadership effectiveness. In L. Berkowitz (Ed.), *Advances in experimental social psychology*. Vol. 1. New York: Academic Press, 1964.

Fiedler, F. E. Engineer the job to fit the manager. *Harvard Bus. Rev.*, 1965, 43, 115–122.

Fiedler, F. E. The effect of leadership and cultural heterogeneity on group performance: a test of a contingency model. *J. exp. soc. Psychol.*, 1966, 2, 237–264.

Fiedler, F. E. *A theory of leadership effectiveness*. New York: McGraw-Hill, 1967.

Fishman, J. A. Childhood indoctrination for minority-group membership. *Daedalus: the Journal of the American Academy of Arts and Sciences*, 1961, 90, 329–349.

Fitts, P. M., & Posner, M. I. *Human performance*. Belmont, Cal.: Brooks/Cole (Wadsworth), 1967.

Forgays, D. G., & Forgays, Janet W. The nature of the effect of free environmental experience in the rat. *J. comp. physiol. Psychol.*, 1952, 45, 322–328.

Forgus, R. H. The effect of early perceptual learning on the behavioral organization of adult rats. *J. comp. physiol. Psychol.*, 1954, 47, 331–336.

Foundation for Research on Human Behavior. *Group influence in marketing and public relations*. Ann Arbor, Michigan, 1956.

Frank, J. D. Experimental studies of personal pressure and resistance: II. Methods of overcoming resistance. *J. gen. Psychol.*, 1944, 30, 43–46.

Frazier, E. F. *The Negro in the United States*. Rev. ed. New York: Macmillan, 1957.

Freedman, J. L. Attitudinal effects of inadequate justification. *J. Pers.*, 1963, 31, 371–385.

Freedman, J. L. Confidence, utility, and selective exposure: a partial replication. *J. Pers. and soc. Psychol.*, 1965, 2, 778–780.

French, Elizabeth G. Some characteristics

of achievement motivation. *J. exp. Psychol.*, 1955, *50*, 232–236.

French, J. R. P., Jr. A formal theory of social power. *Psychol. Rev.*, 1956, *63*, 181–194.

French, J. R. P., Jr. The social environment and mental health. *J. soc. Issues*, 1963, *19*, 39–56.

French, J. R. P., Jr., Israel, Joachim, & Äs, Dagfinn. Arbeidernes medvirkning i industribedriften. En eksperimentell undersøkelse. Oslo: Institute for Social Research, 1957.

French, J. R. P., Jr., Morrison, H. W., & Levinger, G. Coercive power and forces affecting conformity. *J. abnorm. soc. Psychol.*, 1960, *61*, 93–101.

French, J. R. P., Jr., & Raven, B. The bases of social power. In D. Cartwright (Ed.), *Studies in social power.* Ann Arbor: Institute for Social Research, Univer. of Michigan, 1959. Ch. 9.

Freud, S. *Group psychology and the analysis of the ego.* London & Vienna: International Psychoanalytic Press, 1922.

Freud, S. *New introductory lectures.* New York: Norton, 1933.

Fries, C. C. *The structure of English.* New York: Harcourt Brace, 1952.

Fromm, E. *Escape from freedom.* New York: Rinehart, 1941.

Fromm, E. *Man for himself.* New York: Rinehart, 1947.

Gaertner, S., & Bickman, L. The ethnic bystander. Unpublished research, New York: Graduate Center, The City Univer. of New York, 1968.

Galbraith, J. K. *The new industrial state.* Boston: Houghton Mifflin, 1967.

Gamson, W. A. A theory of coalition formation. *Amer. sociol. Rev.*, 1961, *26*, 373–382.

Gamson, W. A. *Power and discontent.* Homewood, Ill.: Dorsey Press, 1968.

Gardner, B. B., & Moore, D. G. *Human relations in industry.* Homewood, Ill.: Irwin, 1955.

Gardner, J. W. *Self-renewal: the individual and the innovative society.* New York: Harper, 1963.

Garfinkel, H. Research notes on inter- and intra-racial homicides. *Social Forces*, 1949, *27*, 369–381.

Gerard, H. B. The anchorage of opinions in face-to-face groups. *Hum. Relat.*, 1954,

7, 313–325.

Gerard, H. B. & Mathewson, G. C. The effects of severity of initiation on liking for a group: a replication. *J. exp. soc. Psychol.*, 1966, *2*, 278–287.

Gibson, J. J. *The perception of the visual world.* Boston: Houghton Mifflin, 1950.

Gibson, J. J., & Gibson, Eleanor J. Perceptual learning: differentiation or enrichment? *Psychol. Rev.*, 1955, *62*, 32–41.

Gillespie, J. J. *Free expression in industry.* London: Pilot Press, 1948.

Glaser, B. G., & Strauss, A. L. *Awareness of dying.* Chicago: Aldine, 1965.

Gleason, H. A. *An introduction to descriptive linguistics.* New York: Holt, 1961.

Gleser, Goldine C., Cronbach, L. J., & Rajaratnam, N. Generalizability of scores influenced by multiple sources of variance. Mimeographed Tech. Rep., Bureau of Educat. Res., Univer. of Ill., 1961.

Glick, P. C. *American families.* New York: John Wiley, 1957.

Goffman, E. *The presentation of self in everyday life.* Garden City, New York: Doubleday Anchor, 1959.

Goffman, E. *Asylums.* Garden City, N.Y.: Doubleday Anchor, 1961.

Goffman, E. *Encounters.* Indianapolis, Ind.: Bobbs-Merrill, 1961.

Goffman, E. The insanity of place. *Psychiatry*, 1969, *31*, 357–388.

Goldberg, S. C. Three situational determinants of conformity to social norms. *J. abnorm. soc. Psychol.*, 1954, *49*, 325–329.

Goldfarb, W. Emotional and intellectual consequences of psychological deprivation in infancy: a re-evaluation. In P. H. Hoch & J. Zubin (Eds.), *Psychopathology of childhood.* New York: Grune & Stratton, 1955. Pp. 105–119.

Goldhammer, H., & Shils, E. A. Types of power and status. *Amer. J. Sociol.*, 1939, *45*, 171–178.

Goldman, Jacquelin R. The effects of handling and shocking in infancy upon adult behavior in the albino rat. *J. genet. Psychol.*, 1964, *104*, 301–310.

Goldman, M., & Fraas, L. A. The effects of leader selection on group-performance. *Sociometry*, 1965, *28*, 82–88.

Goldstein, K. *Human nature in the light of psychotherapy.* Cambridge, Mass.: Harvard Univer. Press, 1940.

Gooddy, W. Two directions of memory. *J. indiv. Psychol.*, 1959, *15*, 83–88.

Goodman, Mary E. *Race awareness in young children.* Cambridge, Mass.: Addison-Wesley, 1952.

Gorden, R. L. Interaction between attitude and the definition of the situation in the expression of opinion. *Amer. sociol. Rev.*, 1952, 17, 50–58.

Gordon, L. V. & Medland, F. F. Leadership aspiration and leadership ability. *Psychol. rep.*, 1965, 17, 388–390.

Gordon, M. M. *Assimilation in American life: the role of race, religion, and national origins.* New York: Oxford Univer. Press, 1964.

Goskin, W. F., & John, Vera P. The study of spontaneous talk. In R. G. Barker (Ed.), *The stream of behavior.* New York: Appleton-Century-Crofts, 1963. Pp. 228–281.

Goslin, D. A. (Ed.). *Handbook of socialization theory and research.* Chicago: Rand McNally, 1969.

Gouldner, A. W. Situations and groups: The situationist critique. In A. W. Gouldner (Ed.), *Studies in leadership.* New York: Harper, 1950. Pp. 25–33.

Gouldner, A. W. Some observations on systematic theory, 1945–55. In H. L. Zetterberg (Ed.), *Sociology in the United States of America.* Paris: UNESCO, 1956.

Gouldner, A. W. Organizational analysis. In R. K. Merton, L. Broom, & L. S. Cottrell (Eds.), *Sociology today.* New York: Basic Books, 1959a. Pp. 400–429.

Gouldner, A. W. Reciprocity and autonomy in functional theory. In L. Gross (Ed.), *Symposium on sociological theory.* Evanston, Ill.: Row, Peterson, 1959b.

Gouldner, A. W. The norm of reciprocity: a preliminary statement. *Amer. sociol. Rev.*, 1960, 25, 161–179.

Governor's Commission on the Los Angeles Riots. *Violence in the city—an end or a beginning?* Los Angeles, 1965.

Graham, D. Experimental studies of social influence in simple judgment situations. *J. soc. Psychol.*, 1962, 56, 245–269.

Graicunas, V. A. Relationships in organization. *Papers on the science of administration.* New York: Columbia Univer. Press, 1937.

Green, A. W. *Sociology: an analysis of life in a modern society.* New York: McGraw-Hill, 1956.

Greenberg, J. (Ed.). *Universals of language.* Cambridge, Mass.: MIT Press, 1963.

Greenwald, A. G., Brock, T. C., & Ostrom, T. M. (Eds.). *Psychological foundations of attitudes.* New York: Academic Press, 1968.

Griffiths, W. J., Jr. Effects of isolation and stress on escape thresholds of albino rats. *Psychol. Rep.*, 1960, 6, 623–629.

Grimshaw, A. D. Three views of urban violence: civil disturbance, racial revolt, class assault. In L. H. Masotti & D. R. Bowen (Eds.), *Riots and rebellion.* Beverly Hills, Cal.: Sage Publications, 1968. Pp. 103–119.

Gross, L. Hierarchical authority in educational institutions. In H. J. Hartley & G. E. Holloway (Eds.), *Focus on change and the school administrator.* Buffalo, N.Y.: School of Education, State Univer. of New York, 1965, Pp. 23–37.

Gross, N., Mason, W. S., & McEachern, A. W. *Explorations in role analysis.* New York: Wiley, 1958.

Guetzkow, H., Alger, C. F., Brody, R. A., Noel, R. C., & Snyder, R. C. *Simulation in international relations: Developments for research and teaching.* Englewood Cliffs, N.J.: Prentice-Hall, 1963.

Gump, P., Schoggen, P., & Redl, F. The camp milieu and its immediate effects. *J. soc. Issues*, 1957, 13, 40–46.

Gump, P., Schoggen, P., & Redl, F. The behavior of the same child in different milieus. In R. G. Barker (Ed.), *The stream of behavior.* New York: Appleton-Century-Crofts, 1963. Pp. 169–202.

Gump, P., & Sutton-Smith, B. Activity-setting and social interaction. *Amer. J. Orthopsychiat.*, 1955, 25, 755–760.

Gurnee, H. Effect of . collective learning upon the individual participants. *J. abnorm. soc. Psychol.*, 1939, 34, 529–532.

Haberstroh, C. J. Organization design and systems analysis. In J. G. March (Ed.), *Handbook of organizations.* Chicago: Rand McNally, 1965. Pp. 142–194.

Haire, M. (Ed.). *Modern organization theory.* New York: Wiley, 1959a.

Haire, M. Psychology and the study of business: joint behavioral sciences. In *Social science research on business: product and potential.* New York: Columbia Univer. Press, 1959b. Pp. 53–59.

Hall, C. S. Emotional behavior in the rat. I. Defecation and urination as measures of individual differences in emotionality. *J. comp. Psychol.*, 1934, 18, 385–403.

Hall, C. S., & Lindzey, G. *Theories of personality.* New York: Wiley, 1957 (2nd ed., 1970).

Hall, E. T. *The silent language.* Garden City, N.Y.: Doubleday, 1959.

Hall, E. T. *The hidden dimension.* Garden City, N.Y.: Doubleday, 1966.

Halle, M., & Stevens, K. N. Speech recognition: a model and a program for research. *IRE Transactions on Information Theory,* 1962, 8, 155–159.

Hand, Learned. *The spirit of liberty.* New York: Knopf, 1952.

Handlin, O., & Handlin, Mary F. The United States. In *The positive contribution by immigrants.* Paris: UNESCO, 1955. Ch. 1.

Hanfmann, E. Social perception in Russian displaced persons and an American comparison group. *Psychiatry,* 1957, 20, 131–149.

Harding, J., Kutner, B., Proshansky, H., & Chein, I. Prejudice and ethnic relations. In G. Lindzey (Ed.), *Handbook of social psychology* Vol. 2. Cambridge: Addison-Wesley, 1954. Pp. 1021–1061.

Hare, A. P. Situational differences in leader behavior. *J. abnorm. soc. Psychol.* 1957, 55, 132–135.

Hare, A. P. *Handbook of small group research.* New York: Free Press, 1962.

Hare, A. P., Borgatta, E. F., & Bales, R. F. *Small groups.* New York: Knopf, 1955 (2nd edition, 1965).

Harlow, H. F. Social facilitation of feeding in the albino rat. *J. genet. Psychol.,* 1932, 43, 211–221.

Harlow, H. F. Learning and satiation of response in intrinsically motivated complex puzzle performance by monkeys. *J. comp. physiol. Psychol.,* 1950, 43, 289–294.

Harlow, H. F. The nature of love. *Amer. Psychologist,* 1958, 13, 673–685.

Harlow, H. F., Harlow, M. K., & Meyer, D. R. Learning motivated by a manipulation drive. *J. exp. Psychol.,* 1950, 40, 228–234.

Harper, D. White reactions to a riot. In L. H. Masotti & D. R. Bowen (Eds.), *Riots and rebellion.* Beverly Hills, Cal.: Sage Publications, 1968. Pp. 307–314.

Harrington, M. *The other America.* Baltimore, Md.: Penguin Books, 1963.

Hartley, E. L., & Hartley, R. *Fundamentals of social psychology.* New York: Knopf, 1952.

Hartley, R. Relationships between perceived values and acceptance of a new reference group. *J. soc. Psychol.,* 1960a, 51, 181–190.

Hartley, R. Personal needs and the acceptance of a new group as a reference group. *J. soc. Psychol.,* 1960b, 51, 349–358.

Harvey, E. Technology and the structure of organizations. *Amer. sociol. Rev.,* 1968, 33, 247–259.

Haskell, M. R. Toward a reference group theory of juvenile delinquency. *Soc. Prob.,* 1961, 8, 220–230.

Hawley, A. H. Community power and urban renewal success. *Amer. J. Sociol.,* 1963, 68, 422–431.

Hayakawa, S. I. *Language in thought and action.* New York: Harcourt Brace, 1951 (2nd ed., 1964).

Hayek, F. A. *The sensory order.* Chicago: Univer. of Chicago Press, 1952.

Hearn, G. Leadership and the spatial factor in small groups. *J. abnorm. soc. Psychol.,* 1957, 54, 269–272.

Hebb, D. O. On the nature of fear. *Psychol. Rev.,* 1946, 53, 259–276.

Hebb, D. O. The effects of early experience on problem-solving at maturity. *Amer. Psychologist,* 1947, 2, 306–307. (Abstract)

Hebb, D. O. *The organization of behavior.* New York: Wiley, 1949.

Hebb, D. O. *A textbook of psychology.* Philadelphia: Saunders, 1966.

Hebb, D. O. & Williams, K. A method of rating animal intelligence. *J. genet. Psychol.,* 1946, 34, 59–65.

Heider, F. Social perception and phenomenal causality. *Psychol. Rev.,* 1944, 51, 358–374.

Heider, F. *The psychology of interpersonal relations.* New York: Wiley, 1958.

Heider, F., & Simmel, Marianne. An experimental study of apparent behavior. *Amer. J. Psychol.,* 1944, 57, 243–259.

Heinicke, C., & Bales, R. F. Developmental trends in the structure of small groups. *Sociometry,* 1953, 16, 7–38.

Heinroth, O. Beiträge zur Biologie, namentlich Ethnologie und Physiologie der Anatiden. *Verhl. Internat. Ornith. Congr.,* 1910, 5, 589–702.

Helmreich, R. & Collins, B. Studies in forced compliance: Commitment and magnitude of inducement to comply as determinants of opinion change. *J. Pers. soc. Psychol.*, 1968, 10(1), 75–81.

Helson, H. Adaptation-level as a basis for a quantitative theory of frames of reference. *Psychol. Rev.*, 1948, 55, 297–313.

Helson, H. Adaptation level theory. In S. Koch (Ed.), *Psychology: a study of a science. Vol. I. Sensory, perceptual, and physiological formulations.* New York: McGraw-Hill, 1959. Pp. 565–621.

Helson, H. *Adaptation-level theory.* New York: Harper & Row, 1964.

Hemphill, J. K. The leader and his group. *Education Research Bulletin*, 1949, 28, 225–229, 245–246.

Hemphill, J. K. Administration as problem-solving. In A. W. Halpin (Ed.), *Administrative theory in education.* Chicago: Midwest Administration Center, 1958.

Hemphill, J. K. Why people attempt to lead. In L. Petrullo & B. M. Bass (Eds.), *Leadership and interpersonal behavior.* New York: Holt, Rinehart, & Winston, 1961.

Henderson, L. J. *Pareto's general sociology.* Cambridge, Mass.: Harvard Univer. Press, 1935.

Hendrick, I. The discussion of the "instinct to master." *Psychoanal. Quart.*, 1943, 12, 561–565.

Henry, J. Attitude organization in elementary classrooms. *Amer. J. Orthopsychiat.*, 1957, 27, 117–133.

Herberg, W. *Protestant-Catholic-Jew.* New York: Doubleday, 1955.

Herbst, P. G. Analysis and measurement of a situation. *Hum. Relat.*, 1953, 2, 113–140.

Herzog, Herta. What do we really know about daytime serial listeners? In P. F. Lazarsfeld & F. N. Stanton (Eds.), *Radio research, 1942–1943.* New York: Duell, Sloan & Pearce, 1944. Pp. 3–33.

Hickson, D. J., Pugh, D. S., & Pheysey, D. C. Operations technology and organization structure: an empirical reappraisal. *Admin. Sci. Quart.*, 1969, 14, 378–397.

Hilgard, E. R. Human motives and the concept of the self. *Amer. Psychologist*, 1949, 4, 374–382.

Hilgard, E. R. *Introduction to psychology.* New York: Harcourt, Brace & World, 1953.

Hiller, E. T. *Social relations and structure.* New York: Harper, 1947.

Himmelstrand, U. Verbal attitudes and behavior. *Public opin. Quart.*, 1960, 24, 224–250.

Hitt, W. D. Two models of man. *Amer. Psychologist*, 1969, 24, 651–658.

Hochbaum, G. M. Self-confidence and reactions to group pressures. *Amer. soc. Rev.*, 1954, 19, 678–687.

Hoffer, E. *The true believer.* New York: Harper, 1951.

Hollander, E. P. Authoritarianism and leadership choice in a military setting. *J. abnorm. soc. Psychol.*, 1954, 49, 365–370.

Hollander, E. P. Conformity, status, and idiosyncrasy credit. *Psychol. Rev.*, 1958, 65, 117–127.

Hollander, E. P. Some points of reinterpretation regarding social conformity. *Sociol. Rev.*, 1959, 7, 159–168.

Hollander, E. P. Competence and conformity in the acceptance of influence. *J. abnorm. soc. Psychol.*, 1960a, 61, 361–365.

Hollander, E. P. Reconsidering the issue of conformity in personality. Chapter XI in H. P. David and J. C. Brengelmann (Eds.), *Perspectives in personality research.* New York: Springer, 1960b. Pp. 210–225.

Hollander, E. P. Some effects of perceived status on responses to innovative behavior. *J. abnorm. soc. Psychol.*, 1961, 63, 247–250.

Hollander, E. P. The "pull" of international issues in the 1962 election. In S. B. Withey (Chm.), Voter attitudes and the war-peace issue. Symposium presented at the American Psychological Association, Philadelphia, August 1963.

Hollander, E. P. *Leaders, groups, and influence.* New York: Oxford Univer. Press, 1964.

Hollander, E. P., & Julian, J. W. Contemporary trends in the analysis of leadership processes. *Psychol. Bull.*, 1969, 76, 387–397.

Hollander, E. P., & Julian, J. W. Leadership. In E. F. Borgatta & W. W. Lambert (Eds.), *Handbook of personality theory and research.* Chicago: Rand McNally, 1968.

Hollander, E. P., Julian, J. W., & Haaland, G. A. Conformity process and prior group support. *J. Personal. soc. Psychol.*, 1965, 2, 852–858.

Hollander, E. P., & Willis, R. H. Conformity, independence, and anticonformity as determiners of perceived influence and attraction. In E. P. Hollander, *Leaders, groups, and influence.* New York: Oxford Univer. Press, 1964. Pp. 213–224.

Hollander, E. P., & Willis, R. H. Some current issues in the psychology of conformity and nonconformity. *Psychol. Bull.*, 1967, 68, 62–76.

Hollingshead, A. B. Trends in social stratification: a case study. *Amer. sociol. Rev.*, 1952, 17, 685.

Hollingshead, A. B., & Redlich, F. C. *Social class and mental illness.* New York: Wiley, 1958.

Holmes, Frances B. An experimental study of children's fears. In A. T. Jersild & Frances B. Holmes (Eds.), *Children's fears.* New York: Teachers College, Columbia Univer., 1935. (*Child Develpm. Monogr.*, 20.)

Holsti, O. R. *Content analysis for the social sciences and humanities.* Reading, Mass.: Addison-Wesley, 1969.

Homans, G. C. Fundamental social processes. In N. Smelser (Ed.), *Sociology.* New York: Wiley, 1967. Pp. 27–78.

Homans, G. C. *The human group.* New York: Harcourt Brace, 1950.

Homans, G. C. Social behavior as exchange. *Amer. J. Sociol.*, 1958, 63, 597–606.

Homans, G. C. *Social behavior: its elementary forms.* New York: Harcourt, Brace & World, 1961.

Homans, G. C. *Sentiments and activities.* New York: The Free Press, 1962.

Homans, G. C. *The nature of social science.* New York: Harcourt, Brace & World, 1967.

Horowitz, E. L. The development of attitudes toward the Negro. *Archives of Psychology*, 1936, 28, (194).

Horwitz, M. The veridicality of liking and disliking. In R. Tagiuri & L. Petrullo (Eds.), *Person perception and interpersonal behavior.* Stanford: Stanford Univer. Press, 1958.

Hovland, C. I., Mandell, W., Campbell, Enid H., Brock, T., Luchins, A. S., Cohen, A. R., McGuire, W. J., Janis, I. L., Feierabend, Rosalind L., & Anderson, N. H. *The order of presentation in persuasion.* New Haven: Yale Univer. Press, 1957.

Hovland, C. I. Reconciling conflicting results derived from experimental and survey studies of attitude change. *Amer. Psychologist*, 1959, 14, 8–17.

Hovland, C. I., & Janis, I. L. (Eds.). *Personality and persuasibility.* New Haven: Yale Univer. Press, 1959.

Hovland, C. I., Janis, I. L., & Kelley, H. H. *Communication and persuasion.* New Haven: Yale Univer. Press, 1953.

Hovland, C. I., Lumsdaine, A. A., & Sheffield, F. D. *Experiments on mass communication.* Princeton: Princeton Univer. Press, 1949.

Hovland, C. I., & Weiss, W. The influence of source credibility on communication effectiveness. *Publ. Opin. Quart.*, 1951, 15, 635–650.

Hsu, F. L. K. (Ed.) *Psychological anthropology: approaches to culture and personality.* Homewood, Ill.: Dorsey, 1961.

Hull, C. L. *Principles of behavior: an introduction to behavior theory.* New York: Appleton-Century, 1943.

Hunt, J. McV. The effects of infantile feeding-frustration upon adult hoarding in the albino rat. *J. abnorm. soc. Psychol.*, 1941, 36, 338–360.

Hunt, J. McV. Experimental psychoanalysis. In P. L. Harriman (Ed.), *Encyclopedia of psychology.* New York: Philosophical Library, 1946.

Hunt, J. McV. Experience and the development of motivation: some reinterpretations. *Child Develpm.*, 1960, 31, 489–504.

Hunt, J. McV. Motivation inherent in information processing and action. In O. J. Harvey (Ed.), *Motivation and social interaction: the cognitive determinants.* New York: Ronald Press, 1963a. Ch. 3.

Hunt, J. McV. Piaget's observations as a source of hypotheses concerning motivation. *Merrill-Palmer Quart.*, 1963b, 9, 263–275.

Hunt, J. McV. Traditional personality theory in the light of recent evidence. *Amer. Scientist*, 1965, 53, 80–96.

Hunt, J. McV., Schlosberg. H., Solomon, R. L., & Stellar, E. Studies of the effects of infantile experience on adult behavior in rats. I. Effects of infantile feeding-frustration on adult hoarding. *J. comp. physiol. Psychol.*, 1947, 40, 291–304.

Hunt, J. McV. *Intelligence and experience*. New York: Ronald, 1961.

Hunt, J. McV., & Uzgiris, Ina C. Cathexis from recognitive familiarity: an exploratory study. In P. R. Merrifield (Ed.), *Personality and intelligence: papers honoring J. P. Guilford*. Ohio: Kent State Univer. Press, 1966.

Hunt, R. G. Role and role conflict. In H. J. Hartley & G. E. Holloway (Eds.), *Focus on change and the school administrator*. Buffalo, N.Y.: State Univer. of New York, School of Education, 1965. Pp. 37–46.

Hunt, R. G. Review of *Systems of organization* (E. J. Miller & A. K. Rice). *Admin. Sci. Quart.*, 1968, 13, 360–362.

Hunt, R. G. Technology and Organization. *Acad. Mgmt J.*, 1970, 13, 235–252.

Husband, R. W. Analysis of methods in human maze learning. *J. genet. Psychol.*, 1931, 39, 258–278.

Hyman, H. H. The psychology of status. *Arch. Psychol.* No. 269, 1942.

Hyman, H. H. Reflections on reference groups. *Pub. Opin. Quart.*, 1960, 24, 383–396.

Hyman, H. H., & Sheatsley, P. B. Some reasons why information campaigns fail. *Publ. Opin. Quart.*, 1947, 11, 412–423.

Hyman, H. H., & Sheatsley, P. B. The authoritarian personality: a methodological critique. In R. Christie & M. Jahoda (Eds.), *Studies in the scope and method of the authoritarian personality*. Glencoe, Ill.: Free Press, 1954.

Hyman, H. H. *Survey design and analysis*. Glencoe, Ill.: Free Press, 1955.

Hyman, H. H., & Singer, E. Introduction. *Readings in reference group theory and research*. New York: Free Press, 1968. Pp. 3–21.

Hyman, H. H., & Singer, E. (Eds.). *Readings in reference group theory and research*. New York: Free Press, 1968.

Hyman, H. H., Wright, C. R., & Hopkins, T. K. *Applications of methods of evaluation*. Berkeley: Univer. of California, 1962.

Hymovitch, B. The effects of experimental variations in early experience on problem-solving in the rat. *J. comp. physiol. Psychol.*, 1952, 45, 313–321.

Ichheiser, G. Misunderstandings in human relations. *Amer. J. Sociol.*, 1949, 55, 2, Part 2.

Ihrig, H. Literalism and animism in schizophrenia. Unpublished doctoral dissertation, Univer. of Kansas, 1953.

Imms, A. D. *Recent advances in entymology*. Philadelphia: Blakiston's Sons, 1931.

Inkeles, A., & Bauer, R. A. *The Soviet citizen*. Cambridge, Mass.: Harvard Univer. Press, 1959.

Insko, C. A. *Theories of attitude change*. New York: Appleton-Century-Crofts, 1967.

International Kindergarten Union. *A study of the vocabulary of children before entering the first grade*. Baltimore: Williams & Wilkins, 1928.

Jackson, J. M., & Saltzstein, H. D. The effect of person-group relationships on conformity processes. *J. abnorm. soc. Psychol.*, 1958, 57, 17–24.

Jackson, P. W. *Life in classrooms*. New York: Holt, Rinehart & Winston, 1968.

Jacobs, R. C., & Campbell, D. T. The perpetuation of an arbitrary tradition through several generations of a laboratory microculture. *J. abnorm. soc. Psychol.*, 1961, 62, 649–658.

Jahoda, Marie. Conformity and independence: a psychological analysis. *Hum. Relat.*, 1959, 12, 99–120.

Jahoda, Marie, Deutsch, M., & Cook, S. W. *Research methods in social relations*. 2 vols. New York: Dryden, 1951.

Jakobovits, L. A., & Miron, M. S. *Readings in the psychology of language*. Englewood Cliffs, N.J.: Prentice-Hall, 1967.

James, W. *Principles of psychology*. New York: Holt, 1890.

James, W. *Psychology: Briefer course*. New York: Henry Holt, 1892.

James, W. T. Social facilitation of eating behavior in puppies after satiation. *J. comp. physiol. Psychol.*, 1953, 46, 427–428.

James, W. T. The development of social facilitation of·eating in puppies. *J. genet. Psychol.*, 1960, 96, 123–127.

James, W. T., & Cannon, D. J. Variation in social facilitation of eating behavior in puppies. *J. genet. Psychol.*, 1956, 87, 225–228.

Janda, K. F. Towards the explication of the concept of leadership in terms of the concept of power. *Human Relations*, 1960, 13, 345–363.

Janis, I. L. Personality correlates of susceptibility to persuasion. *J. Pers.*, 1954, 22, 504–518.

Janis, I. L., & Field, P. B. A behavioral assessment of persuasibility: consistency of individual differences. *Sociometry*, 1956, 19, 241–259.

Janis, I. L. & Gilmore, J. B. The influence of incentive conditions on the success of role playing in modifying attitudes. *J. Pers. soc. Psychol.*, 1965, 1, 17–27.

Jecker, J. D. The cognitive effects of conflict and dissonance. In L. Festinger, *Conflict, decision and dissonance*. Stanford: Stanford University Press, 1964a. Pp. 21–32.

Jecker, J. D. Selective exposure to new information. In L. Festinger, *Conflict, decision and dissonance*. Stanford: Stanford University Press, 1964b. Pp. 65–82.

Jecker, J. D. Conflict and dissonance: a time of decision. In R. P. Abelson, *et al.* (Eds.), *Theories of cognitive consistency: a source-book*. Chicago, Ill.: Rand McNally, 1968. Pp. 571–576.

Jenkins, W. O., & Stanley, J. C. Partial reinforcement: a review and critique. *Psychol. Bull.*, 1950, 47, 193–234.

Jenness, A. Social influences in the change of opinion. *J. abnorm. soc. Psychol.*, 1932a, 27, 29–34.

Jenness, A. The role of discussion in changing opinions regarding a matter of fact. *J. abnorm. soc. Psychol.*, 1932b, 27, 279–296.

Jespersen, O. *The philosophy of grammar.* London: Allen & Unwin, 1924.

Johnson, C. S. *Growing up in the black belt.* Washington, D.C.: American Council on Education, 1941.

Johnson, E. E. The role of motivational strength in latent learning. *J. comp. physiol. Psychol.*, 1953, 45, 526–530.

de Jonge, D. Applied hodology. *Landscape*, XVII, Winter 1967–68, 10–11.

Jones, E. E. *Ingratiation.* New York: Appleton-Century-Crofts, 1964.

Jones, E. E. Conformity as a tactic of ingratiation. *Science*, 1965, 149, 144–150.

Jones, E. E., Gergen, K. J., & Jones, R. G. Tactics of ingratiation among leaders and subordinates in a status hierarchy. *Psychol. Monogr.*, 1963, 77 (Whole No. 566).

Jones, F. N., & Arrington, M. G. The explanations of physical phenomena given by white and Negro children. *Comp. Psychology Monogr.*, 1945, 18 (5), 1–43.

Jordan, N. Some formal characteristics of the behavior of two disturbed boys. In R. G. Barker (Ed.), *The stream of behavior.* New York: Appleton-Century-Crofts, 1963. Pp. 203–218.

Julian, J. W., & Hollander, E. P. A study of some role dimensions of leader-follower relations. Technical Report No. 3, April 1966, State University of New York at Buffalo.

Julian, J. W., Hollander, E. P., & Regula, C. R. Endorsement of the group spokesman as a function of his source of authority, competence, and success. *Journal of Personality and Social Psychology*, 1969, 11, 42–49.

Julian, J. W., & Steiner, I. D. Perceived acceptance as a determinant of conformity behavior. *J. soc. Psychol.*, 1961, 55, 191–198.

Juran, J. M. Improving the relationship between staff and line: an assist from the anthropologists. *Personnel*, 1956, 32, 515–524.

Kahn, H. The arms race and some of its hazards. *Daedalus*, 1960, 89, 744–781.

Kahn, R. L., Wolfe, D. M., Quinn, R. P., Snock, J. D., & Rosenthal, R. A. *Organizational stress.* New York: Wiley, 1964.

Kardiner, A. *The individual and his society.* New York: Columbia Univer. Press, 1939.

Katz, D. The functional approach to the study of attitudes. *Publ. Opin. Quart.*, 1960, 24, 163–204.

Katz, D. Human interrelationships and organizational behavior. In S. Mailick & E. H. Van Ness (Eds.), *Concepts and issues in administrative behavior.* New York: Prentice-Hall, 1962. Pp. 166–186.

Katz, D. The motivational basis of organizational behavior. *Behav. Sci.*, 1964, 9, 131–146.

Katz, D., & Braly, K. Racial stereotypes of one hundred college students. *J. abnorm. soc. Psychol.*, 1933, 28, 280–290.

Katz, D., & Eldersveld, S. J. The impact of local party activity upon the electorate. *Publ. Opin. Quart.*, 1961, 25, 1–24.

Katz, D., & Kahn, R. *The social psychology of organizations.* New York: Wiley, 1966.

Katz, D., Maccoby, N., & Morse, Nancy. *Productivity, supervision and morale in an office situation.* Ann Arbor: Institute for Social Research, Univer. of Michigan, 1950.

Katz, D., Sarnoff, I., & McClintock, C. Ego-defense and attitude change. *Hum. Relat.*, 1956, 9, 27–45.

Katz, D., & Stotland, E. A preliminary statement to a theory of attitude structure and change. In S. Koch (Ed.), *Psychology: a study of a science.* Vol. 3. New York: McGraw-Hill, 1959. Pp. 423–475.

Katz, E., & Lazarsfeld, P. F. *Personal influence.* Glencoe, Ill.: Free Press, 1955.

Katz, I., & Benjamin, L. Effects of white authoritarianism in biracial work groups. *J. abnorm. soc. Psychol.*, 1960, 61, 448–456.

Katz, J. J., & Fodor, J. A. The structure of semantic theory. *Language*, 1963, 34, 170–210.

Kelly, G. A. *A theory of personality: The psychology of personal constructs* (Norton Library Edition). New York: Norton, 1963.

Kelley, H. H. Two functions of reference groups. In G. E. Swanson, T. M. Newcomb, & E. L. Hartley, *Readings in social psychology.* New York: Holt, 1952. Pp. 410–414.

Kelley, H. H. Salience of membership and resistance to change of group-anchored attitudes. *Hum. Relat.*, 1955, 3, 275–289.

Kelly, G. A. *The psychology of personal constructs.* New York: Norton, 1955. 2 vols.

Kelman, H. C. Effects of success and failure on "suggestibility" in the autokinetic situation. *J. abnorm. soc. Psychol.*, 1950, 45, 267–285.

Kelman, H. C. Attitude change as a function of response restriction. *Hum. Relat.*, 1953, 6, 185–214.

Kelman, H. C. Compliance, identification, and internalization: three processes of attitude change. *J. Conflict Resol.*, 1958, 2, 51–60.

Kelman, H. C. Processes of opinion change. *Publ. Opin. Quart.*, 1961, 25, 57–78.

Kelman, H. C. Deception in social research. *Transaction*, 1966, 3, 20–24.

Kelman, H. C., & Hovland, C. I. "Reinstatement" of the communicator in delayed measurement of opinion change. *J. abnorm. soc. Psychol.*, 1953, 48, 327–335.

Kemper, T. D. Reference groups, socialization and achievement. *Amer. sociol. Rev.*, 1968, 33, 31–46.

Kidd, J. S., & Campbell, D. T. Conformity to groups as a function of group success. *J. abnorm. soc. Psychol.*, 1955, 51, 390–393.

Kierkegaard, S. "That individual": two "notes" concerning my work as an author, 1859. In S. Kierkegaard, *The point of view.* (Translated by W. Lowrie.) New York: Oxford Univer. Press, 1939.

Kiesler, C. A. Group pressures and conformity. In J. Mills (Ed.), *Experimental social psychology.* New York: Macmillan, 1969. Pp. 233–306.

Kiesler, C. A., Collins, B. E., & Miller, N. *Attitude change.* New York: Wiley, 1969.

Kiesler, C. A., & Kiesler, S. B. Role of forewarning in persuasive communications. *J. abnorm. soc. Psychol.*, 1964, 68, 547–549.

Kimball, P. People without papers. *Publ. Opin. Quart.*, 1959, 23, 389–398.

Kirkhart, R. O. Minority group identification and group leadership. *J. soc. Psychol.*, 1963, 59, 111–117.

Kish, L. *Survey sampling.* New York: Wiley, 1965.

Kitsuse, J. Societal reaction to deviance: problems of theory and method. *Social Problems*, Winter, 1962, 9, 247–256.

Klapper, J. *The effects of mass communication.* Glencoe, Ill.: Free Press, 1960.

Kleck, R. Physical stigma and nonverbal cues emitted in face-to-face interaction. *Hum. Relations*, 1968, 21, 19–28.

Kleck, R., Buck, P. L., Goller, W. L., London, R. S., Pfeiffer, J. R. & Vukcevic, D. P. Effect of stigmatizing conditions on the use of personal space. *Psychol. rep.*, 1968, 23, 111–118.

Klein, G. The personal world through perception. In R. R. Blake & G. V. Ramsey (Eds.), *Perception: an approach to personality.* New York: Ronald, 1951.

Klineberg, O. *Characteristics of the American Negro.* New York: Harper, 1944.

Klineberg, O. *Social psychology.* Rev. ed. New York: Holt, 1954.

Kluckhohn, C. *Mirror for man.* New York: McGraw-Hill, 1949.

Kluckhohn, C. Culture and behavior. In G. Lindzey (Ed.), *Handbook of social psychology.* Vol. I. Cambridge, Mass.: Addison-Wesley, 1954.

Kluckhohn, C., & Mowrer, O. H. Culture and personality: a conceptual scheme. *Amer. Anthropologist*, 1944, 46, 4.

Kluckhohn, C., Murray, H. A., & Schneider, D. *Personality in nature, society, and culture.* 2nd ed. New York: Knopf, 1953.

Kluckhohn, F. Dominant and variant value orientation. In. C. Kluckhohn & H. A. Murray (Eds.), *Personality in nature, society and culture.* Revised and enlarged edition. New York: Knopf, 1953. Pp. 342–357.

Koch, Helen L. The social distance between certain racial, nationality, and skin pigmentation groups in selected populations of American school children. *J. genet. Psychol.*, 1946, 68, 63–95.

Koch, S. Clark L. Hull. In W. K. Estes, et al. (Eds.), *Modern learning theory: a critical analysis of five examples.* New York: Appleton-Century-Crofts, 1954. Pp. 1–76.

Köhler, W. *Gestalt psychology.* New York: Liveright, 1929.

Koontz, H., & O'Donnell, C. *Principles of management.* New York: McGraw-Hill, 1959.

Korzybski, A. *Science and sanity: an introduction to non-Aristotelian systems and general semantics.* Rev. ed. Lancaster, Pa.: Science Press, 1941.

Krantz, D. L., & Campbell, D. T. Separating perceptual and linguistic effects of context shifts on absolute judgments. *J. exp. Psychol.*, 1961, 62, 35–42.

Krech, D., & Crutchfield, R. S. *Theory and problems of social psychology.* New York: McGraw-Hill, 1948.

Krech, D., Crutchfield, R. S., & Ballachey, E. *Individual in society.* New York: McGraw-Hill, 1962.

Kroeber, A. L. (Ed.) *Anthropology today.* Chicago: Univer. Chicago Press, 1953.

Kuhn, A. *The study of society: a unified approach.* Homewood, Ill.: Dorsey Press, 1963.

Kuhn, M. H. Self-attitudes by age, sex and professional training. *Sociol. Quart.*, 1960, 2, 39–56.

Kuhn, M. H. The Reference Group Reconsidered. *Sociol. Quart.*, 1964, 5, 5–21.

Kuhn, M. H., & McPartland, T. S. An empirical investigation of self-attitudes. *Amer. sociol. Rev.*, 1954, 19, 68–76.

Lana, R. E. *Assumptions of social psychology.* New York: Appleton-Century-Crofts, 1969.

Landreth, Catherine, & Johnson, Barbara C. Young children's responses to a picture and inset test designed to reveal reactions to persons of different skin color. *Child Develpm.*, 1953, 24, 63–80.

Lang, K. & Lang, G. E. Racial disturbances as collective protest. In L. H. Masotti & Bowen, D. R. (Eds.), *Riots and rebellion.* Beverly Hills, Cal.: Sage Publications, 1968. Pp. 121–130.

LaPiere, R. T. Type-rationalizations of group antipathy. *Social Forces*, 1936, 15, 232–237.

Lasagna, L., & McCann, W. P. Effect of "tranquilizing" drugs on amphetamine toxicity in aggregated mice. *Science*, 1957, 125, 1241–1242.

Lashley, K. S. The problem of cerebral organization in vision. In H. Klüver, *Visual mechanisms.* Lancaster, Pa.: Jacques Cattell, 1942. Pp. 301–322.

Lashley, K. S., & Wade, Marjorie. The Pavlovian theory of generalization. *Psychol. Rev.*, 1946, 53, 72–87.

Latané, B. Studies in social comparison-introduction. *J. exper. soc. Psychol.*, 1966. Supplement 1, 2, 1–5.

Latané, B. & Darley, J. M. Group inhibition of bystander intervention in emergencies. *J. Pers. soc. Psychol.*, 1968, 10, 215–221.

Latané, B., & Darley, J. Bystander apathy. *Amer. Scientist*, 1969, 57, 244–268.

Latané, B. & Glass, D. C. Social and nonsocial attraction in rats. *J. Pers. soc. Psychol.*, 1968, 9, 142–146.

Latané, B. & Rodin, J. A lady in distress: inhibiting effects of friends and strangers on bystander intervention. *J. exp. soc. Psychol.*, 1969, 5, 189–202.

Lawrence, D. H. & Festinger, L. *Deterrents and reinforcement.* Stanford: Stanford University Press, 1962.

Lazarsfeld, P. F., Berelson, B., & Gaudet, Hazel. *The people's choice.* New York: Duell, Sloan, and Pearce, 1944. 2nd ed. New York: Columbia Univer. Press, 1948.

Lazarsfeld, P. F., & Rosenberg, M. (Eds.) *The language of social research.* Glencoe, Ill.: Free Press, 1955.

Leary, T. *Interpersonal diagnosis of personality: a functional theory and methodology for personality evaluation.* New York: Ronald Press, 1957.

Leavitt, H. J. *Managerial psychology.* Rev.

ed. Chicago: Univer. of Chicago Press, 1964.

Leavitt, H. J. Unhuman organizations. In *Readings in managerial psychology*. Chicago: Univer. of Chicago Press, 1964. Pp. 542–556.

LeBon, G. *The crowd*. London: Ernest Benn (1896), 1952.

Lee, A. M. & Humphrey, N. D. *Race riot*. New York: Dryden, 1943.

Leipold, W. E. Psychological distance in a dyadic interview. Doctoral thesis, Univer. of North Dakota, 1963.

Lemert, E. M. *Social pathology*. New York: McGraw-Hill Book Co. Inc., 1951.

Lenneberg, E. Language, evolution and purposive behavior. In *Culture in history: Essays in honor of Paul Radin*. New York: Columbia Univer. Press, 1960.

Lenneberg, E. Understanding language without ability to speak: A case report. *J. abnorm. soc. Psychol.*, 1962, 65, 419–425.

Lenneberg, E. A biological perspective of language. In E. Lenneberg (Ed.), *New directions in the study of language*. Cambridge, Mass.: MIT Press, 1964. Pp. 65–88.

Lependorf, S. The effects of incentive value and expectancy on dissonance resulting from attitude-discrepant behavior and disconfirmation of expectancy. Unpublished doctoral dissertation, State University of New York at Buffalo, 1964.

Lerner, D. *The passing of traditional society*. Glencoe, Ill.: Free Press, 1958.

LeVine, R. Political socialization and culture change. In C. Geetz (Ed.), *Old societies and new states*. Glencoe, Ill.: The Free Press, 1963. Pp. 280–303.

Levine, S. The effects of differential infantile stimulation on emotionality at weaning. *Canad. J. Psychol.*, 1959, 13, 243–247.

Levine, S. Psychophysiological effects of early stimulation. In E. Bliss (Ed.), *Roots of behavior*. New York: Hoeber, 1961.

Levinson, D. J., & Sanford, R. N. A scale for the measurement of anti-Semitism. *J. Psych.*, 1944, 17, 339–370.

Levy, S., & Freedman, L. Z. Psychoneurosis and economic life. *Soc. Problems*, 1956, 4, 55–67.

Lewin, K. *A dynamic theory of personality*. New York: McGraw-Hill, 1935.

Lewin, K. *Principles of topological psychology*. New York: McGraw-Hill, 1936.

Lewin, K. *Resolving social conflicts*. New York: Harper, 1948.

Lewin, K. *Field theory in social science*. New York: Harper, 1951.

Lewin, K., Lippitt, R., & White, R. K. Patterns of aggressive behavior in experimentally created "social climates." *J. soc. Psychol.*, 1939, 10, 271–299.

Lewis, M. Some nondecremental effects of effort. *J. Comp. Physiol. Psychol.*, 1964, 57, 367–372.

Lewis, O. *The children of Sanchez*. New York: Random House, 1961.

Lewis, O. The culture of poverty. *Transaction*, 1963, 1, 17–19.

Lewis, O. *La Vida*. New York: Random House, 1965.

Lichtman, C. M., & Hunt, R. G. Personality and organization theory. *Psychol. Bull.*, in press.

Lieberman, B. Human behavior in a strictly determined 3 x 3 matrix game. *Beh. Sci.*, 1960, 5, 317–322.

Lieberman, B. Experimental studies of conflict in some two-person and three-person games. In J. H. Criswell, H. Solomon, & P. Suppes (Eds.), *Mathematical methods in small group processes*. Stanford: Stanford Univer. Press. 1962.

Lifton, R. J. "Thought reform" of Western civilians in Chinese Communist prisons. *Psychiatry*, 1956, 19, 173–195.

Likert, R. *New patterns of management*. New York: McGraw-Hill, 1961.

Likert, R. *The human organization*. New York: McGraw-Hill, 1967.

Linder, D. E., Cooper, J., & Jones, E. E. Decision freedom as a determinant of the role of incentive magnitude in attitude change. *J. Pers. soc. Psychol.*, 1967, 6, 245–254.

Lindesmith, A., & Strauss, A. *Social psychology*. Rev. ed. New York: Holt, Rinehart & Winston, 1956.

Lindzey, G. (Ed.) *Handbook of social psychology*. 2 vols. Cambridge, Mass.: Addison-Wesley, 1954.

Lindzey, G., & Aronson, E. (Eds.), *The handbook of social psychology*. 2nd ed. Reading, Mass.: Addison-Wesley, 1968. 5 vols.

Lindzey, G., & Hall, G. S. *Theories of personality: Primary sources and research*. New York: Wiley, 1965.

Lindzey G., Lykken, D. T., & Winston, H. C. Infantile trauma, genetic factors, and adult temperament. *J. abnorm. soc. Psychol.*, 1960, 61, 7–14.

Linton, R. *The cultural background of personality.* New York: Appleton-Century-Crofts, 1945.

Lippitt, R., Polansky, N., Redl, F., & Rosen, S. The dynamics of power. *Hum. Relat.*, 1952, 5, 37–64.

Lippitt, R., Watson, J., & Westley, B. *The dynamics of planned change.* New York: Harcourt Brace, 1958.

Lippmann, W. *Public opinion.* New York: Macmillan, 1922. (Pelican edition, 1946)

Lipset, S. M. *Political Man.* New York: Doubleday, 1960.

Litwak, E., Reference group theory, bureaucratic career, and neighborhood primary group cohesion. *Sociometry*, 1960, 23, 72–73.

Logan, R. *The Negro in American life and thought: the Nadir, 1877–1901.* New York: Dial, 1954.

Lorenz, K. Der Kumpan in der Umwelt des Vögels. *J. Ornith.*, 1935, 83, 137–214, 289–413. (Cited by W. H. Thorpe, Jr. in *Learning and instinct in animals.* London: Methuen, 1956.)

Luce, R. D., Bush, R. R., & Galanter, E. *Handbook of mathematical psychology.* New York: Wiley, 1963.

Luchins, A. S., & Luchins, E. H. On conformity with judgments of a majority or an authority. *J. soc. Psychol.*, 1961, 53, 303–316.

MacBeath, A. *Experiments in living.* London: Macmillan, 1952.

MacLeod, R. B. The place of phenomenological analysis in social psychological theory. In J. Rohrer & M. Sherif (Eds.), *Social psychology at the crossroads.* New York: Harper-Row, 1951. Pp. 215–241.

McCarthy, Dorothea. Language development in children. In L. Carmichael (Ed.), *Manual of child psychology.* New York: Wiley, 1946. Pp. 477–581.

McClelland, D. C. The psychology of mental content reconsidered. *Psychol. Rev.*, 1955, 62, 297–302.

McClelland, D. C. *The achieving society.* Princeton, N.J.: Van Nostrand, 1961.

McClelland, D. C., Atkinson, J. W., Clark, R. A., & Lowell, E. L. *The achievement motive.* New York: Appleton-Century-Crofts, 1953.

McClelland, D. C., & Winter, D. G. *Motivating economic achievement.* New York: Free Press, 1969.

McDougall, W. *An introduction to social psychology.* London: Methuen, 1908.

McDougall, W. *An introduction to social psychology.* Boston: John W. Luce & Co., 1921. Pp. 200–201.

McDougall, W. *Outline of psychology.* New York: Scribner's, 1923.

McDougall, W. Tendencies as indispensable postulates of all psychology. *Proc. XIth Int. Congr. Psychol.*, Paris, 1937. Pp. 157–170.

McGrath, J. E., & Altman, I. *Small group research: A synthesis and critique of the field.* New York: Holt, Rinehart, Winston, 1966.

McGregor, D. *The human side of enterprise.* New York: McGraw-Hill, 1960.

McGregor, D. *Leadership and motivation.* (Essays edited by W. G. Bennis & E. H. Schein) Cambridge, Mass.: M.I.T. Press, 1966.

McGuire, J. W. *Business and society.* New York: McGraw-Hill, 1963.

McGuire, W. J. Inducing resistance to persuasion. In L. Berkowitz (Ed.), *Advances in experimental social psychology.* Vol. I. New York: Academic Press, 1964. Pp. 191–229.

McGuire, W. J. Attitudes and opinions. *Annual Review of Psychology*, 1966, 17, 475–514.

McGuire, W. J. *Immunization against persuasion.* New Haven: Yale Univer. Press, 1968.

McGuire, W. J., & Millman, S. Anticipatory belief lowering following forewarning of a persuasive attack. *J. Personal. soc. Psychol.*, 1965, 2, 471–479.

MacIver, R. M. *The more perfect union.* New York: Macmillan, 1948.

MacIver, R. M., & Page, C. H. *Society: an introductory analysis.* New York: Rinehart, 1949.

McKelvey, R. K., & Marx, M. H. Effects of infantile food and water deprivation on adult hoarding in the rat. *J. comp. physiol. Psychol.*, 1951, 44, 423–430.

McKenna, W., & Morgenthau, S. Urban-rural differences in social interaction: a study of helping behavior. Unpublished research, New York: Graduate Center, The City Univer. of New York, May, 1969.

McNeil, E. B. (Ed.) *The nature of human conflict*. Englewood Cliffs, N.J.: Prentice-Hall, 1965.

Macmurray, J. *The self as agent*. New York: Harper, 1957.

Macmurray, J. *Persons in relation*. London: Faber & Faber, 1961.

McQuown, N. A. Analysis of the cultural content of language materials. In H. Hoijer (Ed.), *Language in culture*. Chicago: Univer. of Chicago Press, 1954.

McQuown, N. A. Linguistic transcription and specification of psychiatric interview materials. *Psychiatry*, 1957, 20, 79–86.

Maccoby, Eleanor E. Why do children watch TV? *Publ. Opin. Quart.*, 1954, 18, 239–244.

Maccoby, Eleanor E., Newcomb, T., & Hartley, E. (Eds.), *Readings in social psychology*. New York: Holt, 1958.

Maccoby, N., & Maccoby, Eleanor E. Homeostatic theory in attitude change. *Publ. Opin. Quart.*, 1961, 25, 535–545.

Maier, N. R., & Hoffman, L. R. Acceptance and quality of solutions as related to leader's attitudes toward disagreement in group problem solving. *J. Appl. Beh. Sci.*, 1965, 1, 373–386.

Malinowski, B. *Crime and custom in savage society*. London: Paul, Trench, Trubner, 1932.

Mann, F. C., & Baumgartel, H. J. *Absences and employee attitudes in an electric power company*. Ann Arbor: Institute for Social Research, Univer. of Michigan, 1953.

Mann, F. C., & Hoffman, R. L. *Automation and the worker*. New York: Holt, Rinehart, & Winston, 1960.

Mann, R. D. A review of the relationship between personality and performance in small groups. *Psychol. Bull.*, 1959, 56, 241–270.

Marak, G. E. The evolution of leadership structure. *Sociometry*, 1964, 27, 174–182.

March, J. G. Group norms and the active minority. *Amer. sociol. Rev.*, 1954, 19, 733–741.

March, J. G., & Simon, H. *Organizations*. New York: Wiley, 1958.

March, J. G. (Ed.) *Handbook of organizations*. Chicago, Ill.: Rand-McNally, 1964.

Marrow, A. J. *The practical theorist: The life and work of Kurt Lewin*. New York: Basic Books, 1969.

Marschak, J. Efficient and viable organizational forms. In M. Haire (Ed.), *Modern organization theory*. New York: Wiley, 1959. Pp. 307–320.

Marwell, G., & Schmitt, D. R. Are "trivial" games the most interesting psychologically? *Beh. Sci.*, 1968, 13, 125–128.

Marx, M. H. Infantile deprivation and adult behavior in the rat: retention of increased rate of eating. *J. comp. physiol. Psychol.*, 1952, 45, 43–49.

Maslow, A. H. *Motivation and personality*. Rev. ed. New York: Harper, 1970.

Mason, J. W., & Brady, J. V. The sensitivity of psychoendocrine systems to social and physical environment. In P. H. Leiderman & D. Shapiro (Eds.), *Psychobiological approaches to social behavior*. Stanford, Calif.: Stanford Univer. Press, 1964. Pp. 4–23.

Mausner, B. Studies in social interaction: III. Effect of variation in one partner's prestige on the interaction of observer pairs. *J. appl. Psychol.*, 1953, 37, 391–393.

Mausner, B. The effect of prior reinforcement on the interaction of observer pairs. *J. abnorm. soc. Psychol.*, 1954a, 49, 65–68.

Mausner, B. The effect of one partner's success in a relevant task on the interaction of observer pairs. *J. abnorm. soc. Psychol.*, 1954b, 49, 557–560.

Mausner, B., & Block, B. L. A study of the additivity of variables affecting social interaction. *J. abnorm. soc. Psychol.*, 1957, 54, 250–256.

May, R. Historical and philosophical presuppositions for understanding therapy. In O. H. Mowrer (Ed.), *Psychotherapy: theory and research*. New York: Ronald Press, 1953. Pp. 9–43.

Mayo, E. *The human problems of an industrial civilization*. Cambridge, Mass.: Harvard Univer. Press, 1946.

Mayo, E., & Lombard, G. *Teamwork and labor turnover in the aircraft industry of Southern California. Business Res. Studies No. 32*. Cambridge, Mass.: Harvard Univer., 1944.

Mead, G. H. *Mind, self, and society*. Chicago: Univer. Chicago Press, 1934.

Mead, M. (Ed.). *Cultural patterns and technical change*. New York: New American Library, 1955.

Mehrabian, A. *An analysis of personality theories.* New York: Prentice Hall, 1968.

Meier, R. L. *A communications theory of urban growth.* Cambridge: MIT Press, 1962.

Menzel, H., & Katz, E. Social relations and innovations in the medical profession: The epidemiology of a new drug. *Publ. Opin. Quart.*, 1955, 19, 337–352.

Merei, F. Group leadership and institutionalization. *Hum. Relat.*, 1949, 2, 23–39.

Merton, R. K. Discrimination and the American creed. In R. M. MacIver (Ed.), *Discrimination and national welfare.* New York: Harper, 1949.

Merton, R. K. *Social theory and social structure.* Glencoe, Ill.: Free Press, 1957. (Rev. ed., 1968).

Merton, R. K. Continuities in the theory of reference groups and social structure. In Robert K. Merton, *Social theory and social structure.* New York: Free Press, 1957. Pp. 281–368.

Merton, R. K. & Kitt, Alice S. Contributions to the theory of reference group behavior. In R. K. Merton & P. F. Lazarsfeld (Eds.), *Studies in the scope and method of "The American Soldier."* Glencoe, Ill.: Free Press, 1950. Pp. 40–105.

Merton, R. K. & Rossi, Alice K. Contributions to the theory of reference group behavior. In R. K. Merton, *Social theory and social structure,* New York: Free Press, 1957; Rev. ed., 1968. Pp. 225–275.

Metcalf, H. C., & Urwick, L. (Eds.). *Dynamic administration: the collected works of Mary Parker Follett.* New York: Harper, 1940.

Michotte, A. *La perception de la causalite.* Louvain: l'Institut superieur de Philosophie, 1946.

Michotte, A. *Causalite, Permanence, et Realite Phenomenales.* Louvain: Publications Universitaires de Louvain, 1962.

Mierke, K. Über die Objectionfähigkeit und ihre Bedeutung für die Typenlehre. *Arch. gest. Psychol.*, 1933, 89, 1–108.

Milbrath, L. W. Personal communication, 1958.

Milgram, S. Nationality and conformity. *Scientific American,* 1961, 205(6), 45–51.

Milgram, S. Liberating effects of group pressure. *J. Personal. soc. Psychol.*, 1965, 1, 127–134.

Milgram, S., & Hollander, P. Paralyzed witnesses: the murder they heard. *The Nation,* 1964, 25, 602–604.

Miller, D. C., & Form, W. H. *Industrial sociology.* New York: Harper, 1951.

Miller, D. R. The study of social relationships: Situation, identity, and social interaction. In S. Koch (Ed.), *Psychology: a study of a science.* Vol. 5. New York: McGraw-Hill, 1963. Pp. 639–738.

Miller, D. R., & Swanson, G. E. *The changing American parent.* New York: Wiley, 1958.

Miller, D. R., & Swanson, G. E. *Inner conflict and defense.* New York: Henry Holt, 1960.

Miller, E. J. Technology, territory and time: the internal differentiation of complex production systems. *Hum. Relat.*, 1959, 12, 243–272.

Miller, E. J., & Rice, A. K. *Systems of organization.* London: Tavistock Publications, 1967.

Miller, G. A. What is information measurement? *Amer. Psychologist,* 1953, 8, 3–12.

Miller, G. A. The psycholinguists. *Encounter,* 1964, 23, 29–37.

Miller, G. A. Some preliminaries to psycholinguistics. *Amer. Psychologist,* 1965, 20, 15–20.

Miller, G. A., Galanter, E., & Pribram, K. H. *Plans and the structure of behavior.* New York: Holt, Rinehart & Winston, 1960.

Miller, G. A., & Isard, S. Some perceptual consequences of linguistic rules. *J. verbal Learn. verbal Behav.*, 1963, 2, 217–228.

Miller, N. E., & Dollard, J. *Social learning and imitation.* New Haven: Yale Univer. Press, 1941.

Mills, C. W. *The power elite.* New York: Oxford Univ. Press, 1956.

Milner, Esther. Some hypotheses concerning the influence of segregation on Negro personality development. *Psychiatry,* 1953, 16, 291–297.

Minard, R. D. Race attitudes of Iowa children. *University of Iowa Studies of Character,* 1931, 4 (2).

Mischel, W. Preference for delayed reinforcement and social responsibility. *J. abnorm. soc. Psychol.*, 1961a, 62, 1–7.

Mischel, W. Delay of gratification, need for achievement, and acquiescence in another culture. *J. abnorm. soc. Psychol.*, 1961b, 62, 543–552.

Mischel, W. Father-absence and delay of

gratification: cross-cultural comparisons. *J. abnorm. soc. Psychol.*, 1961c, 63, 116–124.

Montgomery, K. C. Exploratory behavior as a function of "similarity" of stimulus situations. *J. comp. physiol. Psychol.*, 1953, 46, 129–133.

Montgomery, K. C. The relation between fear induced by novel stimulation and exploratory behavior. *J. comp. physiol. Psychol.*, 1955, 48, 254–260.

Mooney, J. D., & Reiley, A. C. *Onward industry.* New York: Harper & Bros., 1931.

Moore, H. T. The comparative influence of majority and expert opinion. *Amer. J. Psychol.*, 1921, 32, 16–20.

Morland, J. K. Racial recognition by nursery school children in Lynchburg, Virginia. *Soc. Forces*, 1958, 37, 132–137.

Morris, R. T. & Jeffries, V. *Los Angeles riot study: the White reaction.* Los Angeles: U.C.L.A. Institute of Government and Public Affairs, 1967.

Morse, Nancy. *Satisfactions in the white collar job.* Ann Arbor: Institute for Social Research, Univer. of Michigan, 1953.

Mouton, J. S., Blake, R. R., & Olmstead, J. A. The relationship between frequency of yielding and the disclosure of personal identity. *J. Personal.*, 1956, 24, 339–347.

Mouzelis, N. P. *Organization and bureaucracy.* Chicago: Aldine, 1967.

Mowrer, O. H. *Learning theory and behavior.* New York: Wiley, 1960.

Mowrer, O. H., & Ullman, A. D. Time as a determinant in integrative learning. *Psychol. Rev.*, 1945, 52, 61–90.

Muller, H. J. *The uses of the past.* New York: Mentor, 1954.

Münsterberg, H. *Psychology and industrial efficiency.* Boston: Houghton Mifflin, 1913.

Murdock, G. P. How culture changes. In H. L. Shapiro (Ed.), *Man, culture, and society.* New York: Oxford Univer. Press, 1956, Pp. 247–260.

Murphy, G. *Personality: a biosocial approach to origins and structures.* New York: Harper & Row, 1947.

Murray, H. A. *Explorations in personality.* New York: Oxford Univer. Press, 1938.

Mussen, P. H. (Ed.) *Handbook of research methods in child development.* New York: Wiley, 1960.

Mussen, P. H. (Ed.) *Carmichael's Manual of Child Psychology.* Rev. ed. New York: Wiley, 1970.

Mussen, P. H., & Conger, J. J. *Child development and personality.* New York: Harper, 1956.

Mussen, P. H., & Distler, L. Masculinity, identification, and father-son relationships. *J. abnorm. soc. Psychol.*, 1959, 59, 350–356.

Myrdal, G. *An American dilemma.* New York: Harper, 1944 (Rev. ed., 1962).

National Advisory Commission on Civil Disorders. *Report of the National Advisory Committee on Civil Disorders (the Kerner report).* Washington: U.S. Government Printing Office, 1968.

Nealey, S. M., & Fiedler, F. E. Leadership functions of middle managers. *Psychol. Bull.*, 1968, 70, 313–329.

Neff, W. S. *Work and human behavior.* New York: Atherton, 1968.

Nelson, D. H., & Samuels, L. T. A method for the determination of 17-hydroxy-corticosteroids in blood: 17-hydroxycorticosterone in the peripheral circulation. *J. clin. Endocrin.*, 1952, 12, 519–526.

Nelson, P. D. Similarities and differences among leaders and followers. *J. Soc. Psychol.*, 1964, 63, 161–167.

Neugarten, B. L. Personality changes during the adult years. In R. G. Kuhlen (Ed.), *Psychological background of adult education.* Chicago, Ill.: Center for the study of Liberal Education for Adults, 1963. Pp. 43–76.

Newcomb, T. M. *Personality and social change.* New York: Dryden, 1943.

Newcomb, T. M. The influence of attitude climate upon some determinants of information. *J. abnorm. soc. Psychol.*, 1946, 41, 291–302.

Newcomb, T. M. *Social psychology.* New York: Holt, Rinehart & Winston, 1950.

Newcomb, T. M. An approach to the study of communicative acts. *Psychol. Rev.*, 1953, 60, 393–404.

Newcomb, T. M. The prediction of interpersonal attraction. *Amer. Psychologist*, 1956, 11, 575–586.

Newcomb, T. M. Individual systems of orientation. In S. Koch (Ed.), *Psychology: a study of a science.* Vol. 3. New York: McGraw-Hill, 1959.

Newcomb, T. M. *The acquaintance process.*

New York: Holt, Rinehart, and Winston, 1961.

Newcomb, T. M. Persistence and regression of changed attitudes: long-range studies. *J. soc. Issues*, 1963, 19, 3–14.

Newman, W. H. *Administrative action.* Englewood Cliffs, N.J.: Prentice-Hall, 1951.

Newsweek editors. How whites feel about Negroes: a painful American dilemma. *Newsweek*, October 21, 1963, 62, 44–57.

Nida, E. A. *Morphology.* Ann Arbor: Univer. of Michigan Press, 1943.

Nissen, H. W. A study of exploratory behavior in the white rat by means of the obstruction method. *J. genet. Psychol.*, 1930, 37, 361–376.

Norum, G., Russo, N. & Sommer, R. Seating patterns and group task. *Psychology in the schools*, 1967, 4, 276–280.

Nowlis, H. H. The influence of success and failure on the resumption of an interrupted task. *J. exp. Psychol.*, 1941, 28, 304–325.

Nuttin, J. M., Jr. Dissonant evidence about dissonance theory. Paper presented at the Second Conference of Experimental Social Psychologists in Europe, Frascati, Italy, 1964.

Olds, J., & Milner, P. Positive reinforcement produced by electrical stimulation of septal area and other regions of rat brain. *J. comp. physiol. Psychol.*, 1954, 47, 419–427.

Oldfield, R. C., & Marshall, J. C. *Language.* New York: Penguin Books, 1968.

Olesen, V. L., & Whittaker, E. W. *The silent dialogue: a study in the social psychology of professional socialization.* San Francisco: Jossey-Bass, 1968.

Olsen, M. E. *The process of social organization.* New York: Holt, Rinehart & Winston, 1968.

Orlansky, H. Infant care and personality. *Psychol. Bull.*, 1949, 46, 1–48.

Orne, M. T. On the social psychology of the psychological experiment: with particular reference to demand characteristics and their implications. *Amer. Psychologist*, 1962, 17, 776–783.

Ortgier, D., & Hunt, R. G. Staff-patient attitudes and the selection of patients for psychotherapy. *Int. J. soc. Psychiat.*, 1965, 11, 46–53.

Osborn, A. F. *Applied imagination.* New York: Charles Scribner's Sons, 1953.

Osgood, C. E. The nature and measurement of meaning. *Psychol. Bull.*, 1952, 49, 197–237.

Osgood, C. E. Cognitive dynamics in human affairs. *Publ. Opin. Quart.*, 1960, 24, 341–365.

Osgood, C. E. *An alternative to war or surrender.* Urbana: Univer. Ill. Press, 1962.

Osgood, C. E. *Method and theory in experimental psychology.* New York: Oxford Univer. Press, 1953.

Osgood, C. E. Psycholinguistics. In S. Koch (Ed.), *Psychology: a study of a science.* Vol. 6. New York: McGraw-Hill, 1963. Pp. 244–317.

Osgood, C. E., Saporta, S., & Nunnally, J. C. Evaluative assertion analysis. *Litera.*, 1956, 3, 47–102.

Osgood C. E., & Sebeok, T. *Psycholinguistics.* Supplement to the *J. abnorm. soc. Psychol.*, 1954, 49, No. 4, Part 2.

Osgood, C. E., Suci, G. J., & Tannenbaum, P. H. *The measurement of meaning.* Urbana: Univer. of Illinois Press, 1957.

Osgood, C. E., & Tannenbaum, P. H. The principle of congruity in the prediction of attitude change. *Psychol. Rev.*, 1955, 62, 42–55.

Paget, R. *Human Speech.* New York: Harcourt Brace, 1930.

Park, R. E. *Human communities.* New York: Free Press, 1952.

Park, R. E. & Burgess, E. W. *Introduction to the science of sociology.* Chicago: Univer. Chicago Press, 1921.

Parsons, T. An approach to psychological theory in terms of the theory of action. In S. Koch (Ed.), *Psychology: A study of a science.* Vol. 3. New York: McGraw-Hill, 1959.

Parsons, T. On the concept of influence. *Publ. Opin. Quart.*, 1963, 27, 37–62.

Parsons, T. *The social system.* Glencoe, Ill.: Free Press, 1951.

Parsons, T. *Structure and process in modern societies.* New York: Free Press, 1960.

Parsons, T., & Shils, E. A. (Eds.). *Toward a general theory of action.* Cambridge, Mass.: Harvard Univer. Press, 1951.

Patchen, M. The effect of reference group standards on job satisfaction. *Hum. Relat.*, 1958, 11, 303–314.

Pepinsky, P. N. Social exceptions that prove the rule. In I. A. Berg & B. M. Bass (Eds.), *Conformity and deviation*. New York: Harper, 1961. Pp. 424–434.

Pepinsky, Pauline, Hemphill, J. K., & Shevitz, R. N. Attempts to lead, group productivity, and morale under conditions of acceptance and rejection. *J. abnorm. soc. Psychol.*, 1958, 57, 47–54.

Perrow, C. A. A framework for the comparative analysis of organizations. *Amer. sociol. Rev.*, 1967a, 32, 195–208.

Perrow, C. A. Technology and structural changes in business firms. Paper presented at First World Congress, International Industrial Relations Assn., Geneva, September, 1967b.

Perrow, C. A. Working paper on technology and structure. Univer. of Wisconsin, mimeo, 1970.

Pessin, J. The comparative effects of social and mechanical stimulation on memorizing. *Amer. J. Psychol.*, 1933, 45, 263–270.

Pessin, J., & Husband, R. W. Effects of social stimulation on human maze learning. *J. abnorm. soc. Psychol.*, 1933, 28, 148–154.

Petegorsky, D. W. On combating racism. In A. Rose (Ed.), *Race prejudice and discrimination*. New York: Knopf, 1951.

Pettigrew, T. F. A *profile of the Negro American*. Princeton, N.J.: Van Nostrand, 1964.

Piaget, J. *The origins of intelligence in children*. (Trans. by M. Cook.) New York: International Univer. Press, 1952.

Pike, K. L. *Phonetics*. Ann Arbor: Univer. of Michigan Press, 1943.

Pittenger, R. E., & Smith, H. L. A basis for some contributions of linguistics to psychiatry. *Psychiatry*, 1957, 20, 61–78.

Pool, I. deSola, & Shulman, J. Newsmen's fantasies, audiences, and newswritings. *Pub. Opin. Quart.*, 1959, 23, 145–158.

Preston, M. G., & Heintz, R. K. Effects of participatory vs. supervisory leadership on group judgment. *J. abnorm. soc. Psychol.*, 1949, 44, 345–355.

Pruitt, D. G., & Snyder, R. (Eds.). *Theory and research on the causes of war*. Englewood Cliffs, N.J.: Prentice-Hall, 1969.

Pryer, M. W., Flint, A. W., & Bass, B. M. Group effectiveness and consistency of leadership. *Sociometry*, 1962, 25, 391–397.

Pugh, D. S., Hickson, D. J., Hinings, C. R., & Turner, C. Dimensions of organization structure. *Admin. Sci. Quart.*, 1968, 13, 65–105.

Pumpian-Mindlin, E. Propositions concerning energetic-economic aspects of libido theory. *Ann. N. Y. Acad. Sci.*, 1959, 76, 1038–1052.

RAND Corporation Study, Report on a study of non-military defenses. July 1, 1958. *Hearings before the Subcommittee on National Policy Machinery of the Committee on Governmental Operations United States Senate, Eighty-sixth Congress, Second Session, February 23, 24, and 25, 1960. Part 120*. Washington, D.C.: U. S. Government Printing Office, 1960.

Random House. *Random House dictionary of the English language*. New York: Random House 1967.

Rapoport, A. *Two-person game theory*. Ann Arbor: Univer. of Michigan Press, 1966.

Rausch, H. L., Dittman, A. T., & Taylor, T. J. Person, setting, and change in social interaction. *Hum. Relat.*, 1959, 12, 361–378.

Rausch, H. L., Dittman, A. T., & Taylor, T. J. Person. Setting, and change in social interaction: II. A normal control study. *Hum. Relat.*, 1960, 13, 305–332.

Raven, B. H. Social influence and power. In I. D. Steiner & M. Fishbein (Eds.), *Current studies in social psychology*. New York: Holt, Rinehart & Winston, 1965. Pp. 371–382.

Raven, B. H., & French, J. R. P., Jr. Group support, legitimate power, and social influence. *J. Pers.*, 1958a, 26, 400–409.

Raven, B. H., & French, J. R. P., Jr. Legitimate power, coercive power, and observability in social influence. *Sociometry*, 1958b, 21, 83–97.

Razran, G. H. S. Conditioning away social bias by the luncheon technique. *Psychol. Bull.*, 1938a, 35, 693.

Razran, G. H. S. Music, art, and the conditioned response. Paper read at Eastern Psychol. Assoc., April, 1938b.

Reeder, L., Donohue, G. A., & Biblarz, A. Conceptions of self and others. *Amer. J. Sociol.*, 1960, 66, 153–159.

Regional Plan Association (1969). The

second regional plan. *The New York Times*, Sec. 12, June 15, 1969.

Rice, A. K. *Productivity and social organization: the Ahmedabad experiment*. London: Tavistock Publications, 1958.

Rice, A. K. *The enterprise and its environment*. London: Tavistock Publications, 1963.

Rice, A. K., & Trist, E. L. Institutional and sub-institutional determinants of change in labour turnover. *Hum. Relat.*, 1952, 5, 347–371.

Richardson, S. A., Dohrenwend, B. S., & Klein, D. *Interviewing: its forms and functions*. New York: Basic Books, 1965.

Riecken, H. W. The effect of talkativeness on ability to influence group solutions to problems. *Sociometry*, 1958, 21, 309–321.

Rieff, P. *Freud: the mind of the moralist*. New York: Viking, 1959.

Riesman, D., Glazer, N., & Denney, R. *The lonely crowd: a study of the changing American character*. New Haven: Yale Univer. Press, 1950.

Roby, T. B. An opinion on the construction of behavior theory. *Amer. Psychologist*, 1959, 14, 127–134.

Roche, J. P., & Gordon, M. M. Can morality be legislated? In M. L. Barron (Ed.), *American minorities*. New York: Knopf, 1957.

Roethlisberger, F. J., & Dickson, W. J. *Management and the worker*. Cambridge, Mass.: Harvard Univer. Press, 1939.

Rogers, C. R. *Counseling and psychotherapy*. Boston: Houghton Mifflin, 1942.

Rogers, C. R. *Client-centered therapy: Its current practice, implications, and theory*. Boston: Houghton Mifflin, 1951.

Rogers, C. R. A theory of therapy, personality, and interpersonal relationships, as developed in the client-centered framework. In S. Koch (Ed.), *Psychology: a study of a science*, Vol. 3. New York: McGraw-Hill, 1959. Pp. 184–256.

Rogers, E. M. Reference group influences on student drinking behavior. *Quart. J. stud. Alcohol.*, 1958, 19, 244–254.

Rogers, E. M., & Beal, G. M. *Reference groups' influence in the adoption of agricultural technology*. Iowa Agricultural and Home Economies Experiment Station Project No. 1236, 1958.

Rokeach, M. *The open and closed mind*. New York: Basic Books, 1960.

Rokeach, M. *Beliefs, attitudes, and values*. San Francisco: Jossey-Bass, 1968.

Rokeach, M. The organization and modification of beliefs. *Centennial Rev.*, 1963, 7, 375–395.

Rommetveit, R. *Social norms and roles*. Minneapolis: Univer. of Minnesota Press, 1954.

Rose, A. The influence of legislation on prejudice. In A. Rose (Ed.), *Race prejudice and discrimination*. New York: Knopf, 1951.

Rose, A. (Ed.) *Human behavior and social processes*. Boston: Houghton Mifflin, 1962.

Rose, A. M. & Prell, A. E. Does the punishment fit the crime?—A study in social valuation. *Amer. J. Soc.*, 1955, 61, 247–259.

Rosen, S., Levinger, G., & Lippitt, R. Perceived sources of social power. *J. abnorm. social Psychol.*, 1961, 62, 439–441.

Rosenberg, M. J. When dissonance fails: on eliminating evaluation apprehension from attitude measurement. *J. Pers. soc. Psychol.*, 1965, 1, 28–42.

Rosenberg, M. J. Some limits of dissonance: toward a differentiated view of counterattitudinal performance. In S. Feldman (Ed.), *Cognitive consistency: motivational antecedents and behavioral consequent*. New York: Academic Press, 1966. Pp. 135–170.

Rosenfeld, H. M. Effect of an approval-seeking induction on interpersonal proximity. *Psychol. rep.*, 1965, 17, 120–122.

Rosenzweig, S. Preferences in the repetition of successful and unsuccessful activities as a function of age and personality. *J. genet. Psychol.*, 1933, 42, 423–441.

Rosenzweig, S. The place of the individual and of idiodynamics in psychology: A dialogue. *J. indiv. Psychol.*, 1958, 14, 3–21.

Rossi, P. H., Berk, R. A., Boesel, D. P., Eidson, B. K. & Groves, W. E. Between white and black: the faces of American institutions in the ghetto. In *Supplemental studies for the National Advisory Commission on Civil Disorders*. Washington: U.S. Government Printing Office, 1968.

Rostow, W. W. *The stages of economic growth*. New York: Cambridge Univer. Press, 1960.

Rubin, I., & Hunt, R. G. Some aspects of managerial control in interpenetrating systems: the case of government-industry relations. Technical Report #7, NASA Grant NGR 33–015–061, State Univ. of New York at Buffalo, July, 1969.

Rudraswamy, V. An investigation of the relationship between perceptions of status and leadership attempts. *Journal of the Indian Academy of Applied Psychology*, 1964, *1*, 12–19.

Rudwich, E. M. *Race riot in East St. Louis, July 2, 1917*. Carbondale, Ill.: Southern Illinois Univer. Press, 1964.

Runciman, W. G. *Relative deprivation and social justice*. Berkeley, Cal.: Univ. California Press, 1966.

Russo, N. Connotation of seating arrangements. *Cornell Journal of Social Relations*, 1967, *2*, 37–44.

Sabath, G. The effect of disruption and individual status on person perception and group attraction. *J. soc. Psychol.*, 1964, *64*, 119–130.

Salama, A. A. Fixation in the rat as a function of infantile shocking, handling, and gentling. Unpublished doctoral dissertation, Univer. of Ill., 1962.

Salama, A. A., & Hunt, J. McV. Fixation in the rat as a function of infantile shocking, handling, and gentling. *J. genet. Psychol.*, 1964, *105*, 131–262.

Saltonstall, R. *Human relations in administration*. New York: McGraw-Hill, 1959.

Sanford, N. Personality: its place in psychology. In S. Koch (Ed.), *Psychology: a study of a science*. Vol. 5. New York: McGraw-Hill, 1963. Pp. 488–593.

Sanford, N. *Self and society*. New York: Atherton, 1966.

Sarbin, T. R., & Allen, V. L. Role theory. In G. Lindzey & E. Aronson (Eds.), op. cit. Vol. 1, pp. 488–568.

Sarnoff, I. Psychoanalytic theory and social attitudes. *Publ. Opin. Quart.*, 1960, *24*, 251–279.

Sarnoff, I., & Katz, D. The motivational bases of attitude change. *J. abnorm. soc. Psychol.*, 1954, *49*, 115–124.

Sayles, L. R., & Strauss, G. *Human behavior in organizations*. Englewood Cliffs, N.J.: Prentice Hall, 1966.

Schachtel, E. G. The development of focal attention and the emergence of reality. *Psychiatry*, 1954, *17*, 309–324.

Schachter, S. *The psychology of affiliation*. Palo Alto: Stanford Univer. Press. 1959.

Schelling, T. C. An essay on bargaining. *Amer. Econ. Rev.*, 1956, *46*, 281–306.

Schoggen, P. A study in psychological ecology: a description of the behavior objects which entered the psychological habitat of an eight-year-old girl during the course of one day. Unpublished master's thesis, Univer. of Kansas, 1951.

Schonbar, R. A. The interaction of observer-pairs in judging visual extent and movement: the formation of social norms in "structured" situations. *Arch. Psychol.*, 1945, *41*, No. 299.

Scott, W. A. Attitude change through reward of verbal behavior. *J. Abnorm. soc. Psychol.*, 1957, *55*, 72–75.

Scott, W. A. Rationality and non-rationality of international attitudes. *J. Conflict Resolution*, 1958, *2*, 9–16.

Scott, W. A. Attitude change by response reinforcement: Replication and extension. *Sociometry*, 1959, *22*, 328–335.

Scott, W. A. Attitude measurement. In G. Lindzey & E. Aronson (Eds.), op. cit., Vol. II, pp. 204–273.

Scott, W. G. Organization theory: an overview and an appraisal. *J. Acad. Management*, 1961, *4*, 7–27.

Scott, W. G. *Organization theory: a behavioral analysis for management*. Homewood, Ill.: Irwin, 1967.

Scott, W. R. Theory of organizations. In R. E. L. Faris (Ed.), *Handbook of modern sociology*. Chicago: Rand McNally, 1964. Pp. 485–530.

Sears, D. O. Political behavior. In G. Lindzey & E. Aronson (Eds.), op. cit., Vol. V, pp. 315–349.

Sears, R. R. A theoretical framework for personality and social behavior. *Amer. Psychologist*, 1951a, *6*, 476–483.

Sears, R. R. Effects of frustration and anxiety on fantasy aggression. *Amer. J. Orthopsychiat.*, 1951b, *21*, 498–505.

Sears, R. R. The 1958 summer research project on identification. *Journal of Nursery Education*, 1960, *16*, (2).

Sears, R. R., Maccoby, E., & Levin, H. *Patterns of child-rearing*. Evanston, Ill.: Row, Peterson, 1957.

Seashore, S. *Group cohesiveness in the industrial work group*. Ann Arbor: Institute for Social Research, Univer. of Michigan, 1954.

Secord, P. F., & Backman, C. W. Personality theory and the problem of stability and change in individual behavior: an interpersonal approach. *Psychol. Rev.*, 1961, 68, 21–23.

Seeman, M. A situational approach to intragroup Negro attitudes. *Sociometry*, 1946, 9, 199–206.

Seidenburg, R. *Post historic man.* Boston: Beacon Press, 1951.

Seidenfeld, M. A. Consumer psychology in public service and government. In R. W. Seaton (Chm.), *Consumer psychology: the growth of a movement.* Symposium presented at Amer. Psychol. Assn., New York, Sept., 1961.

Selltiz, Claire, Jahoda, Marie, Deutsch, M., & Cook, S. W. *Research methods in social relations.* Rev. ed. New York: Henry Holt, 1959.

Selye, H. The general adaptation syndrome and the diseases of adaptation. *J. clin. Endocrin.*, 1946, 6, 117–230.

Selye, H. *Stress.* Montreal: Acta, 1950.

Selznick, P. *Leadership in administration.* Evanston: Row, Peterson, 1957.

Sevareid, E. Dissent or destruction. *Look*, 1967, 31 (Sept. 5), pp. 21ff.

Sewell, W. H. Some recent developments in socialization theory and research. *Ann. Amer. Acad. Pol. Soc. Sci.*, 1963, 349, 163–181.

Shaw, M. E., & Blum, J. M. Effects of leadership style upon group performance as a function of task structure. *J. Pers. social Psychology*, 1966, 3, 238–242.

Shaw, M. E. & Costanzo, P. R. *Theories of social psychology.* New York: McGraw-Hill, 1970.

Shaw, M. E., & Wright, J. M. *Scales for the measurement of attitudes.* New York: McGraw-Hill, 1967.

Shears, L. M. Patterns of coalition formation in two games played by male tetrads. *Beh. Sci.*, 1967, 12, 130–137.

Sherif, Carolyn W., Sherif, M., & Nebergall, R. E. *Attitude and attitude change: the social judgment-involvement approach.* Philadelphia: W. B. Saunders Co., 1965.

Sherif, M. A study of some social factors in perception. *Arch. Psychol.*, 1935, 27, No. 187.

Sherif, M. *The psychology of social norms.* New York: Harper, 1936.

Sherif, M. *An outline of social psychology.* New York: Harper & Row, 1948.

Sherif, M., & Sherif, Carolyn W. *Groups crossroads.* New York: Harper & Brothers, 1953.

Sherif, M. Superordinate goals in the reduction of intergroup conflict. *Amer. J. Sociol.*, 1958, 63, 349–358.

Sherif, M. Conformity-deviation, norms, and group relations. In I. A. Berg & B. M. Bass (Eds.), *Conformity and deviation.* New York: Harper, 1961. Pp. 159–198.

Sherif, M. (Ed.). *Intergroup relations and leadership.* New York: Wiley, 1962.

Sherif, M. The self and reference groups: meeting ground of individual and group approaches. *Annals N. Y. Acad. Sci.*, 1962, 96(3), 797–813.

Sherif, M. *In common predicament: social psychology of intergroup conflict and cooperation.* Boston: Houghton Mifflin, 1966.

Sherif, M., & Hovland C. *Social judgment.* New Haven: Yale University Press, 1961.

Sherif, M. The concept of reference groups in human relations. In M. Sherif & M. O. Wilson (Eds.), *Group relations at the in harmony and tension.* New York: Harper & Row, 1953.

Sherwood, J. Self-identity and referent others. *Sociometry*, 1965, 28, 66–81.

Shibutani, T. Reference groups as perspectives. *Amer. J. Soc.*, 1955, 60, 562–570.

Shibutani, T. *Society and personality.* New York: Prentice-Hall, 1961.

Shibutani, T. Reference groups and social control. In A. M. Rose (Ed.), *Human behavior and social processes.* Boston: Houghton Mifflin, 1962. Pp. 128–147.

Shonbar, R. A. The interaction of observer-pairs in judging visual extent and movement: the formation of social norms in "structured" situations. *Arch. Psychol.*, 1945, 41 (299).

Shontz, F. C. *Research methods in personality.* New York: Appleton-Century-Crofts, 1965.

Shuey, Audrey, King, Nancy, & Griffith, Barbara. Stereotyping of Negroes and whites: an analysis of magazine pictures. *Publ. Opin. Quart.*, 1953, 17, 281–287.

Silver, A. A. Official interpretations of racial riots. In R. H. Connery (Ed.), *Urban riots: violence and social change.* New York: Academy of Political Science, 1968.

Silverstein, A. B. Personal communication, 1959.

Simmel, G. The number of members as determining the sociological form of the group. *Amer. J. Sociol.*, 1902–03, 8, 19n.

Simmel, G. Die Grosstadte und das Geistesleben Die Grosstadt (Dresden, 1903). Reprinted as The metropolis and mental life. In Kurt H. Wolff (Ed.), *The sociology of George Simmel*. New York: The Free Press, 1950.

Simmel, G. *Conflict and the web of group-affiliations* (Trans. K. Wolff & R. Bendix). New York: Free Press of Glencoe, 1955.

Simmel, G. The significance of numbers for social life. In A. P. Hare, E. F. Borgatta, & R. F. Bales (Eds.), *Small groups: studies in social interaction*. Rev. ed. New York: Knopf, 1965.

Simon, H. *Administrative behavior*. 2nd ed. New York: Macmillan, 1957.

Singer, J. E. The use of manipulative strategies: Machiavellianism and attractiveness. *Sociometry*, 1964, 27, 128–150.

Skedgell, R. A. How computers pick an election winner. *Transaction*, 1966, 4 (1), 42–46.

Skinner, B. F. *Science and human behavior*. New York: Macmillan, 1953.

Skinner, B. F. *Verbal behavior*. New York: Appleton-Century-Crofts, 1957.

Slater, P. E., & Bennis, W. G. Democracy is inevitable. *Harvard Business Review*, 1964, 42 (2), 51–59.

Smelser, N. J., & Smelser, W. T. *Personality and social systems*. New York: Wiley, 1963.

Smith, B. L., Lasswell, H. D., & Casey, R. D. *Propaganda, communication and public opinion*. Princeton: Princeton Univer. Press, 1946.

Smith, F., & Miller, G. A. *The genesis of language*. Cambridge, Mass.: MIT Press, 1966.

Smith, K. H. Ego strength and perceived competence as conformity variables. *J. abnorm. soc. Psychol.*, 1961, 62, 169–171.

Smith, M. B. The personal setting of public opinions: a study of attitudes toward Russia. *Publ. Opin. Quart.*, 1947, 11, 507–523.

Smith, M. B., Bruner, J. S., & White, R. W. *Opinions and personality*. New York: Wiley, 1956.

Smith, M. E. An investigation of the development of the sentence and the extent of vocabulary in young children. *Univer.*

Iowa Stud. Child Welfare, 1926, 3, No. 5.

Smith, T. *An experiment in modifying attitudes toward the Negro*. New York: Teachers College, Columbia University, 1943.

Sommer, R. Studies in personal space. *Sociometry*, 1959, 22, 247–260.

Sommer, R. Small group ecology. *Psychol. Bull.*, 1967, 67, 145–152.

Sommer, R. *Personal space: the behavioral basis of design*. Englewood Cliffs, N.J.: Prentice-Hall, 1969.

Soskin, W. F. & John, Vera P. The study of spontaneous talk. In R. G. Barker (Ed.), *The stream of behavior*. New York: Appleton-Century-Crofts, 1963. Pp. 228–281.

Spence, K. W. *Behavior theory and conditioning*. New Haven, Conn.: Yale Univer. Press, 1956.

Spier, Leslie. Inventions and human society. In H. L. Shapiro (Ed.), *Man, culture and society*. New York: Oxford Univer. Press, 1956. Pp. 224–246.

Spitz, R. A. The smiling response: a contribution to the ontogenesis of social relations. *Genet. Psychol. Monogr.*, 1946, 34, 67–125.

Staats, A. W. & Staats, C. K. *Complex human behavior*. New York: Holt, Rinehart and Winston, 1963.

Stagner, R. Homeostasis as a unifying concept in personality theory. *Psychol. Rev.*, 1951, 58, 5–18.

Steiner, I. D. Interpersonal behavior as influenced by accuracy of social perception. *Psychol. Rev.*, 1955, 62, 268–274.

Steiner, I. Group dynamics. *Annual review of psychology*, 1964, 15, 421–446.

Steinzor, B. The spatial factor in face-to-face discussion groups. *J. abnorm. soc. Psychol.*, 1950, 45, 552–555.

Stern, Clara, & Stern, W. *Die Kindersprache*. Leipzig: Barth, 1920.

Stevenson, H. W., & Stewart, E. C. A developmental study of racial awareness in young children. *Child Develpm.*, 1958, 29, 399–409.

Stewart, G. R. *American ways of life*. New York: Doubleday, 1954.

Stinchcombe, A. L. Social structure and organization. In J. G. March (Ed.), *Handbook of organizations*. Chicago: Rand McNally, 1965. Pp. 142–194.

Stogdill, R. M. Personal factors associated

with leadership: a survey of the literature. *J. Psychol.*, 1948, 25, 35–71.

Stogdill, R. M. *Individual behavior and group achievement.* New York: Oxford Univer. Press, 1959.

Stouffer, S. A., *et al. The American Soldier.* Princeton: Princeton Univer. Press, 1949.

Strauss, A. L. (Ed.). *The social psychology of George Herbert Mead.* Chicago: Univer. of Chicago Press, 1956.

Strauss, A. L. *George Herbert Mead on social psychology.* Chicago: Univer. of Chicago Press, 1964.

Strodtbeck, F. L. Husband-wife interaction over revealed differences. *Amer. sociol. Rev.*, 1951, 16, 468–473.

Strodtbeck, F. L., & Mann, R. D. Sex role differentiation in jury deliberations. *Sociometry*, 1956, 19, 3–11.

Sullivan, H. S. *The interpersonal theory of psychiatry.* New York: Norton, 1953.

Sutherland, E. H. White collar criminality. *American Soc. Rev.*, Feb. 1940, 5, 1–12.

Taft, R. Minority group behavior and reference group theory. *Austral. J. Psychol.*, 1952, 4, 10–23.

Tagiuri, R. Person perception. In G. Lindzey & E. Aronson (Eds.), op. cit., Vol. 3, pp. 395–450.

Tagiuri, R. Perceptual sociometry: Introduction. In J. L. Moreno, *et al.* (Eds.), *The sociometry reader.* Glencoe, Ill.: Free Press, 1960.

Tagiuri, R., & Petrullo, L. (Eds.) *Person perception and interpersonal behavior.* Stanford: Stanford Univer. Press, 1958.

Tannenbaum, F. *Slave and citizen: the Negro in the Americas.* New York: Knopf, 1947.

Tannenbaum, F. *Crime and the community.* New York: McGraw-Hill Book Co. Inc., 1951.

Taylor, R. G. Experimental design: A cloak for intellectual sterility. *Brit. J. Psychol.*, 1958, 49, 106–116.

Thibaut, J. W., & Kelley, H. H. *The social psychology of groups.* New York: Wiley, 1959.

Thibaut, J. W., & Riecken, H. W. Some determinants and consequences of the perception of social causality. *J. Personal.* 1955, 24, 113–133.

Thibaut, J. W., & Strickland, L. H. Psychological set and social conformity. *J. Pers.*, 1956, 25, 115–129.

Thiessen, D. D. Population density, mouse genotype, and endocrine function in behavior. *J. comp. physiol. Psychol.*, 1964, 57, 412–416.

Thompson, J. D. *Organizations in action.* New York: McGraw-Hill, 1967.

Thompson, J. D., & Bates, F. L. Technology, organization and administration. *Admin. Sci. Quart.*, 1957, 2, 325–342.

Thompson, V. A. *Modern organization.* New York: Knopf, 1961.

Thompson, W. R., & Heron, W. The effects of restricting early experience on the problem-solving capacity of dogs. *Canad. J. Psychol.*, 1954, 8, 17–31.

Thorndike, E. L., & Lorge, I. *The teacher's word book of 30,000 words.* New York: Teachers Coll., Columbia Univer., 1944.

Thorpe, W. H., Jr. Some problems of animal learning. *Proc. Linn. Soc. Lond.* 1944, 156, 70–83.

Thurnwald, R. *Economics in primitive communities.* London: Oxford Univer. Press, 1932.

Tillich, P. *The courage to be.* New Haven, Conn.: Yale Univer. Press, 1952.

Tinbergen, N. *The study of instinct.* London: Oxford Univer. Press, 1951.

Titchener, E. B. *A beginner's psychology.* New York: Macmillan, 1916.

Toch, H. H., & Hastorf, A. H. Homeostasis in psychology. *Psychiatry*, 1955, 18, 81–91.

Titus, H. E., & Hollander, E. P. The California F scale in psychological research: 1950–1955. *Psychol. Bull.*, 1957, 54, 47–65.

Toda, M. Information-receiving behavior of man. *Psychol. Rev.*, 1956, 63, 204–213.

Tolman, C. W., & Wilson, G. F. Social feeding in domestic chicks. *Animal Behaviour*, 1965, 13, 134–142.

Tolman, E. C. Cognitive maps of rats and men. *Psychol. Rev.*, 1948, 55, 189–208.

Tomlinson, T. M. & Sears, D. O. *Los Angeles riot study: Negro attitudes toward the riot.* Los Angeles: U.C.L.A. Institute of Government and Public Affairs, 1967.

Toynbee, A. *The industrial revolution.* Boston: Beacon, 1956.

Trager, G. L. Paralanguage: a first approximation. *Studies in Linguistics*, 1958, 13, 1–12.

Trager, G. L., & Smith, H. L. *An outline of English structure.* Washington, D.C.: American Council of Learned Societies, 1951.

Trager, Helen G., & Yarrow, Marian R. *They live what they learn.* New York: Harper, 1952.

Travis, L. E. The effect of a small audience upon eye-hand coordination. *J. abnorm. soc. Psychol.,* 1925, 20, 142–146.

Triplett, N. The dynamogenic factors in pacemaking and competition. *Amer. J. Psychol.,* 1897, 9, 507–533.

Trist, E., & Bamforth, K. W. Some social and psychological consequences of the long wall method of coal-getting. *Hum. Relat.,* 1951, 4, 3–38.

Tuddenham, R. D. Correlates of yielding to a distorted group norm. *J. Personal.,* 1959, 27, 272–284.

Turner, E. A. & Wright, J. Effects of severity of threat and perceived availability on the attractiveness of objects. *J. Pers. soc. Psychol.,* 1965, 2, 128–132.

Turner, R. H. Reference groups of future-oriented men. *Soc. Forces,* 1955, 34, 130–136.

Turner, R. H. The normative coherence of folk concepts. *Res. stud. State College Wash.,* 1957, 25, 127–136.

Turner, R. H. The public perception of protest. *Amer. sociol. Rev.,* 1969, 34, 815–831.

Turner, R. H. & Killian, L. M. *Collective behavior.* Englewood Cliffs, N.J.: Prentice-Hall, 1957.

Udy, S. H. The comparative analysis of organizations. In J. G. March (Ed.), *Handbook of organizations.* Chicago: Rand McNally, 1965. Pp. 678–710.

United States Bureau of the Census, *U.S. Census of population. General social and economic characteristics, United States summary.* Final Report PC (1)—1C Washington, D.C.: U.S. Gov. Printing Office, 1962.

Vallance, T. R. Methodology in propaganda research. *Psychol. Bull.,* 1951, 48, 32–61.

Varma, B. N. Community studies and the concept of caste. *Indian J. soc. Res.,* 1965, 6, 251–262.

Vaughan, G. M. The trans-situational aspect of conformity behavior. *J. Personal.,* 1964, 32, 335–354.

Vaughan, G. M., & Mangan, G. L. Conformity to group pressure in relation to the value of the task material. *J. abnorm. soc. Psychol.,* 1963, 66, 179–183.

Vickery, W. E., & Cole, S. G. *Intercultural education in American schools.* New York: Harper, 1943.

Vinacke, W. E. Motivation as a complex problem. *Nebraska symposium on motivation,* 1962, 10, 1–46.

Vinacke, W. E. Negotiations and decisions in a politics game. Technical Report No. 13, 1968, State Univer. of New York at Buffalo, Contract Nonr 4374(00).

Vinacke, W. E. Variables in experimental games: toward a field theory. *Psychol. Bull.,* 1969, 71, 293–318.

Vinacke, W. E., Cherulnik, P. D., & Lichtman, C. M. Strategy in intratriad and intertriad interaction. *J. soc. Psychol.,* 1970, 81, 183–198.

Vincent, C. *Unmarried mothers.* New York: The Free Press of Glencoe, 1961.

Vincent, C. E. Socialization data in research on young marriers. *Acta Sociologica,* 8, Aug. 1964.

Viteles, M. S. *Motivation and morale in industry.* New York: Norton, 1953.

Volkart, E. H. *Social behavior and personality: the contributions of W. I. Thomas to theory and social research.* New York: Social Science Research Council, 1951.

von Bertalanffy, L. *Problems of life.* (Trans. of *Das biologische Weltbild,* 1949.) New York: Wiley, 1952.

von Frisch, K. *Bees, their vision, chemical senses, and language.* Ithaca, N.Y.: Cornell Univer. Press, 1950.

Walker, E. L., & Heyns, R. W. *An Anatomy for conformity.* Englewood Cliffs, N.J.: Prentice-Hall, 1962.

Waller, W., and Hill, R. *The family: a dynamic interpretation.* New York: Dryden, 1951.

Warner, W. L., & Henry, W. E. The radio daytime serial: a symbolic analysis. *Genet. Psychol. Monogr.,* 1948, 37, 3–71.

Waters, J. *The relative acceptance accorded a discreditable person in rural and metropolitan areas.* Unpublished research, New

York: Graduate Center, The City University. of New York, 1969.

Watson, G. *Action for unity.* New York: Harper, 1947.

Webb, E. J., Campbell, D. T., Schwartz, R. D., & Sechrest, L. *Unobtrusive measures: nonreactive research in the social sciences.* Chicago: Rand-McNally, 1966.

Weber, M. *Essays in sociology.* (Edited by H. H. Gerth & C. W. Mills.). New York: Oxford Univer. Press, 1946.

Weber, M. *Theory of social and economic organization.* (Trans. by A. M. Henderson & T. Parsons.) New York: Oxford Univer. Press, 1947.

Weick, K. E. Social psychology in an era of social change. *Amer. Psychologist,* 1969, *24,* 990–998.

Weiner, H., & McGinnies, E. Authoritarianism, conformity, and confidence in a perceptual judgment situation. *J. soc. Psychol.,* 1961, *55,* 77–84.

Welty, J. C. Experiments in group behavior of fishes. *Physiol. Zool.,* 1934, *7,* 85–128.

Werner, H. *Comparative psychology of mental development.* Rev. ed. Chicago: Follett, 1948.

Westermarck, E. *The origin and development of the moral ideas.* Vol. 2. London: Macmillan, 1908.

White, L. A. *The science of culture.* New York: Grove, 1949.

White, L. A. The concept of culture. *Amer. Anthropologist,* 1959, *61,* 227–252.

White, R. W. Motivation reconsidered: the concept of competence. *Psychol. Rev.,* 1959, *66,* 297–333.

Whitehead, A. N. *Process and reality.* New York: Macmillan, 1929.

Whitehead, A. N. *Modes of thought.* New York: Macmillan, 1938.

Whiting, J. Sorcery, sin, and the superego. In M. R. Jones (Ed.), *Nebraska symposium on motivation.* Lincoln, Nebr.: Univer. of Nebraska Press, 1959.

Whiting, J. Socialization process and personality. In F. L. K. Hsu (Ed.), *Psychological anthropology.* Homewood, Ill.: Dorsey, 1961. Pp. 355–381.

Whiting J., & Child, I. *Child training and personality.* New Haven: Yale Univer. Press, 1953.

Whorf, B. L. *Language, thought, and reality.* New York: Wiley, 1956.

Whyte, W. F. When workers and customers meet. In W. F. Whyte (Ed.), *Industry and society.* New York: McGraw-Hill, 1946. Pp. 132–133.

Whyte, W. F. *Organizational behavior: theory and application.* Homewood, Ill.: Irwin-Dorsey, 1969.

Whyte, W. H., Jr. *The organization man.* New York: Simon & Schuster, 1956.

Wicker, A. W. Students experiences in behavior settings of large & small high schools: an examination of behavior setting theory. Unpublished doctoral dissertation, Univer. of Kansas, 1967.

von Wiese, L. *Systematic sociology* (Adapted and amplified by H. Becker). New York: Wiley, 1932.

Wiggins, J. A., Dill, F., & Schwartz, R. D. On "status-liability." *Sociometry,* 1965, *28,* 197–209.

Wilensky, H. L. The moonlighter: a product of relative deprivation. *Indust. Relat.,* 1963, *3,* 105–124.

Williams, D. Effects of competition between groups in a training situation. *Occupational Psychology,* 1956, *30,* 85–93.

Williams, J. L. Personal space and its relation to extraversion-introversion. Master's thesis, Univer. of Alberta, 1963.

Williams, K. A. The reward value of a conditioned stimulus. *Univer. Calif. Publ. Psychol.,* 1929, *4,* 31–55.

Williams, S. B., & Williams, E. Barrier-frustration and extinction in instrumental learning. *Amer. J. Psychol.,* 1943, *56,* 247–261.

Willis, R. H. Social influence and conformity—some research perspectives. *Acta Sociologica,* 1961, *5,* 100–114.

Willis, R. H. Coalitions in the tetrad. *Sociometry,* 1962, *25,* 358–376.

Willis, R. H. Two dimensions of conformity—non-conformity. *Sociometry,* 1963, *26,* 499–513.

Willis, R. H. Descriptive models of social response. Technical Report, November 1964, Washington Univer. Nonr 816(12), Office of Naval Research.

Willis, R. H. Conformity, independence and anti-conformity. *Hum. Relat.,* 1965a, *18,* 373–388.

Willis, R. H. The phenomenology of shifting agreement and disagreement in dyads. *J. Personal.,* 1965b, *33,* 188–199.

Willis, R. H. Social influence, information processing, and net conformity in dyads. *Psychol. Rep.,* 1965c, *17,* 147–156.

Willis, R. H. Shifting agreement and disagreement in dyads under conditions of perceived differences in task competence. Technical Report, August 1966, Washington Univer., Nonr 816(12), Office of Naval Research.

Willis, R. H., & Hollander, E. P. An experimental study of three response modes in social influence situations. *J. abnorm. soc. Psychol.*, 1964a, 69, 150–156.

Willis, R. H., & Hollander, E. P. Supplementary note: modes of responding in social influence situations. *J. abnorm. soc. Psychol.*, 1964b, 69, 157.

Wilson, R. S. Personality patterns, source attractiveness, and conformity. *J. Personal.*, 1960, 28, 186–199.

Winick, C. Teenagers, satire and *Mad*. *Merrill-Palmer Quart.*, 1962, 8, 183–203.

Winter, E. H., *Bwamba economy*. Kampala, Uganda: East African Institute of Social Research, East African Studies, No. 5, 1955.

Wirth, L. Urbanism as a way of life. *Amer. J. Sociol.* July, 1938, 44, 1–24. Reprinted in A. J. Reiss (Ed.), *Louis Wirth on cities and social life*. Chicago: Univer. of Chicago Press, 1964. Pp. 68–83.

Wispe, L. G., & Lloyd, K. E. Some situational and psychological determinants of the desire for structural interpersonal relations. *J. abnorm. soc. Psychol.*, 1955, 51, 57–60.

Wolf, I. S. Social influence: self-confidence and prestige determinants. *Psychol. Rec.*, 1959, 9, 71–79.

Woodward, J. *Industrial organization: theory and practice*. London: Oxford Univer. Press, 1965.

Wright, Q., Evan, W. M., & Deutsch, M. (Eds.) *Preventing World War III: some proposals*. New York: Simon & Schuster, 1962.

Writers' War Board. *How writers perpetuate stereotypes*. New York: Writers' War Board, 1945.

Wrong, D. H. The oversocialized conception of man in modern sociology. *Amer. sociol. Rev.*, 1961, 26, 183–193.

Yarrow, Marian R. (Ed.). Interpersonal dynamics in a desegregation process. *J. soc. Issues*, 1958, 14, 3–63.

Yerkes, R. M., & Dodson, J. D. The relation of strength of stimulus to rapidity of habit-formation. *J. comp. Neurol.*, 1908, 18, 459–482.

Yinger, J. M. *Toward a field theory of behavior*. New York: McGraw-Hill, 1965.

Young, K. *Social psychology*. 3rd ed. New York: Appleton-Century-Crofts, 1956.

Zajonc, R. B. Social facilitation. *Science*, 1965, 149, 269–274.

Zajonc, R. B. (Ed.). *Animal social psychology: a reader of experimental studies*. N.Y.: Wiley, 1969.

Zajonc, R. B., & Nieuwenhuyse, B. Relationship between word frequency and recognition: perceptual process or response bias? *J. exp. Psychol.*, 1964, 67, 276–285.

Zawadski, B. Limitations of the scapegoat theory of prejudice. *J. abnorm. soc. Psychol.*, 1942, 43, 127–141.

Zdep, S. M., & Oakes, W. I. Reinforcement of leadership behavior in group discussion. *J. exp. soc. Psychol.*, 1967, 3, 310–320.

Zetterberg, H. L. Compliant actions. *Acta Sociologica*, 1957, 8, 179–190.

Zimbardo, P. G. The effect of effort and improvisation on self-persuasion produced by role-playing. *J. exp. soc. Psychol.*, 1965, 1, 103–120.

Zimbardo, P. G. The human choice: individuation, reason and order as deindividuation, impulse and chaos. *Nebraska symposium on motivation*. Lincoln, Neb.: Univ. Nebraska Press, 1969.

Zimmerman, Claire, & Bauer, R. A. The effects of an audience on what is remembered. *Publ. Opin. Quart.*, 1956, 20, 238–248.

Zipf, G. K. *The psycho-biology of language*. Boston: Houghton Mifflin, 1935.

Name Index

709

Subject Index